Worlds Apart Trading Together

The organisation of long-distance trade between Rome and India in Antiquity

Kasper Grønlund Evers

Archaeopress Roman Archaeology 32

ARCHAEOPRESS PUBLISHING LTD
Gordon House
276 Banbury Road
Oxford OX2 7ED

www.archaeopress.com

ISBN 978 1 78491 742 5
ISBN 978 1 78491 743 2 (e-Pdf)

Printed in England by Oxuniprint, Oxford
This book is available direct from Archaeopress or from our website www.archaeopress.com

Contents

List of Figures and Maps

Preface

This book is a revised and enlarged version of my PhD thesis in History (*Worlds Apart Trading Together—the organisation of long-distance trade between the Mediterranean and the Indian Ocean, 1st-6th cen. CE*; successfully defended on May 30th, 2016), conducted at Copenhagen University's Saxo Department in 2012–16 under the guidance of Prof. Vincent Gabrielsen.

In the following chapters, an attempt is made to bridge disciplines and distances in time and space, and although not able to be anywhere near exhaustive or expert on many of the issues, a *glo-cal* approach (global perspective backed by local case-studies) strives to put the analysis on a sound empirical footing. Thus, the hope is that experts within specific fields or regions will not find this study too exasperating in its lack of depth within their particular area of expertise, but, rather, appreciate it for what it is: a modest attempt to provide a common context for a number of issues traditionally studied in separation. One consequence of the choice of narrative framework selected for this monograph, though, is a slight tendency towards repetitiousness, as some issues are referred to and some evidence employed in more than one chapter, but hopefully the reader will bear with this.

The numerous maps are quite simple and only show the most important places and routes explicitly mentioned in the main text. On this note, copyright permissions for a number of photographs were, unfortunately, not possible to obtain, so although the plates included illustrate the most important objects and monuments dealt with in this book, the relevant footnotes refer the reader to publications with better images in them. Translations are pulled from the Loeb Classical Library, if nothing else is noted.

Before proceeding, however, I would like to thank the Saxo Institute at Copenhagen University for having granted me a free PhD scholarship, making the kind of research conducted for this book possible. Second, I need to extend my gratitude to the Royal Danish Library which has acquired immense amounts of books and articles for me from abroad. Third, it has been a privilege to be part of the *Copenhagen Associations Project* and enjoy the company of such excellent scholars as Stella Skaltsa, Annelies Cazemier, Mario C. D. Paganini, Jan-Mathieu Carbon and Christian Ammitzbøll Thomsen. Moreover, special thanks for advice, encouragement and invitations are due to Rolf M. Schneider, Eivind H. Seland, Jane Fejfer, Roberta Tomber, Berit Hildebrandt and Matthew Cobb, as well as to my PhD assessment committee consisting of Grant Parker, Sunil Gupta and Peter F. Bang, but I must emphasise that I am likewise grateful to a number of other inspiring colleagues and academics from near and far who have been kind to me throughout the last six years. Fourth, I can hardly begin to express the joy I feel at having had the occasion to study and conduct my doctoral research under the aegis of my long-term supervisor, Vincent Gabrielsen. His support and feedback has been crucial, his company always a pleasure.

And, as always, I must thank Marianne S. Winther who has shown me the world and made this study possible. This time around, she has not only been patient with me and tried to improve my work with clever anthropological insights, but has also joined me in excursions to far-away Indian villages, scaling steep cliffs and avoiding the snakes, in order to explore rock temples and photograph inscriptions. She and little Sigurd are owed a deep debt of gratitude for putting up with me (or, rather, making do without me for much of the time) during the making of this manuscript.

The remaining errors and mistakes are entirely my own.

Abbreviations

Greek inscriptions are abbreviated according to *PHI Greek Inscriptions—The Packard Humanities Institute*, 'Bibliography,' available at http://epigraphy.packhum.org/biblio

Latin inscriptions are abbreviated according to *Epigraphische Datenbank Clauss-Slaby*, 'Abkürzungen,' available at: http://db.edcs.eu/epigr/hinweise/abkuerz.html

Papyri and ostraca are abbreviated according to the *Duke Checklist of Editions*, available at: http://library.duke.edu/rubenstein/scriptorium/papyrus/texts/clist.html

Finally, Roman literary sources are to the greatest extent possible abbreviated according to the conventions of the *Oxford Classical Dictionary*.

Other abbreviations

Arthas	R. Kangle (edr) 1965–72. *The Kautilya Arthashastra*. 3 vols. Bombay.
Chr.Top.	W. Wolska-Conus (edr) 1968–73. *Cosmas Indicopleustès. Topographie Chrétienne*. 3 vols. Paris.
CKI	*Corpus of Kharoshthi Inscriptions*, available online at: https://gandhari.org/a_inscriptions.php
Expositio	J. Rouge (edr) 1966. *Expositio totius mundi et gentium. Introduction, texte critique, traduction et commentaire*. Paris.
Inv.	*Inventaire des inscriptions de Palmyre*, 1930–75. Beirut and Damascus.
IRPEXP	Cherian (edr) 2007–12. *Interim Reports of the Pattanam Excavations/Explorations*. Trivandrum.
LC	G. Marrone and E. Pettenò 2009–10. *Supellex ex plumbo. Laminae Concordiensis*. Le laminette commerciali da Iulia Concordia. *Atti dell'istituto Veneto di scienze, lettere ed Arti* 168: 43–110.
LTUR	E. Steinby (edr) 1993–99. *Lexicon Topographicum Urbis Romae*. 6 vols. Rome.
PAT	D. Hillers and E. Cussini (eds) 1996. *Palmyrene Aramaic Texts*. Baltimore.
Periplus	L. Casson (edr) 1989. *The Periplus Maris Erythraei. Text with introduction, translation, and commentary*. Princeton, NJ.
Tab.Vindol.	A. Bowman and J. Thomas (eds) 1983–2003. *Tabulae Vindolandenses I-III*. London.

Introduction

Important discoveries made within the last few decades provide vital new information about the trade between the Roman Mediterranean and the Indian Ocean in Antiquity. Accordingly, it is becoming ever more clear that the long-distance trade between Rome and the states of the Indian Ocean littoral was conducted on a hitherto unprecedented scale, altering patterns of consumption and modes of production in both India, South Arabia and the Roman Empire. Moreover, whereas this commerce between East and West, traditionally termed 'Indo-Roman trade,' has previously been described primarily in terms of Roman interests and carriers, new source material, as well as more comprehensive use of the existing Indian evidence, now makes it possible to accord Indian producers, shippers and merchants their due importance. Fittingly, a new narrative like this mirrors present developments, these years witnessing India's transformation into an economic and political world power in its own right.

Indeed, present debates on globalisation even seem to have spilled over into an artistic appropriation of trade between the Roman Mediterranean and the Indian Ocean in Antiquity. Thus, that most avant-garde of conceptual artists, Damien Hirst, has recently staged an exhibition pretending to be pieces from an exotic Roman art collection, including many Indian pieces (and even some Indian-Roman hybrids, as well as pre-Hispanic artefacts!), raised from an early second century AD wreck purportedly 'discovered' off ancient Azania in South East Africa.[1] In light of the real finds of Indian artefacts and goods in the Roman Empire and Roman ditto in Early Historic India, as well as the discovery of Roman-era shipwrecks at several sites in the Indian Ocean, art now seems to be closely imitating actual archaeological findings, whilst, fortunately, still upstaging itself enough to be distinguishable from real historical artefacts by its more absurd elements.

On this note, and as a traditional academic study of the topic, the focus of this book will not be on what has traditionally been called 'Indo-Roman trade' generally, but on the particular organisations making the exchange possible in the first place, namely, networks, diasporas and associations. In practice, these categories were rarely clear-cut and very often overlapping, so any empirical example must rather be placed on a spectrum of mercantile organisation ranging from the individual trader acting more or less on his own to those who were part of larger private networks, such as family or friends, patronage or professional networks, via diasporas based on shared ethnicity and religion to associations defined by formal membership, set internal rules, and communal funds and property.

In consequence, the overarching research question to be pursued here is how best to comprehend the organisation of long-distance trade between the Roman Empire and Early Historic India. This entails conducting case-studies to shed light on the organisation of trade in its entirety, that is, not merely the distribution of products, but also their production, transport and consumption by different groups along the trade routes. Thus, only select strands of the ancient long-distance commerce will be examined, abstaining from attempting to provide an exhaustive history of trade between the Mediterranean and the Indian Ocean, generally, encompassing all of its political and cultural aspects, as well, throughout the centuries in question.

In order to conduct such a study, a very wide framework must, necessarily, be employed. Whereas previous authors have chosen to deal with geographically limited segments of the trade routes, this study opts not only to follow the goods traded from Indian ports to Rome, but even from their inland centres of production to their furthest places of consumption in the Roman provinces. In short, the geographical scope extends from Hadrian's Wall in *Britannia* to the Bay of Bengal and beyond. As regards the temporal span, the point of departure has been chosen as Augustus' incorporation of Egypt as a Roman province in 30 BC, giving Roman and Indian traders direct access to one another via ports of the

[1] *Treasures from the Wreck of the Unbelievable*, April–December 2017, at Palazzo Grassi and Punta della Dogana, Venice. On the role of Azania in ancient Indian Ocean trade of the 1st–2nd century AD, see *Periplus* 16–18 and Ptol. *Geog.*, I.9.

Red Sea. Correspondingly, the end of the study has been set to the final years of the sixth century AD, when the formerly important Red Sea harbour of Berenike in Egypt had been abandoned (around AD 550) and shortly before the loss of that province—and with it the remaining ports on the Red Sea—to the Muslim Arabs in the 640s AD. However, due to the uneven distribution of Roman and Indian evidence for the organisation of long-distance trade throughout this period, no attempt will be made to provide a balanced and continuous historical narrative for the 1st–6th century AD—the analysis will simply wax and wane as conditioned by the available source material, more detailed information being available generally for the first half of the period.

Concerning the layout of this book, it begins with two brief introductory chapters on historiography and theory, respectively, followed by six analytical chapters dealing with different segments of the long-distance trade routes, the narrative proceeding from Rome and its provinces in the West to the Early Historic kingdoms of India in the East. Such a 'West to East'-narrative entails an inherent 'Romano-centrism,' simply because the narrative might as well have proceeded from East to West or had a non-directional focus, such as the Indian Ocean itself. However, while an 'East to West'-narrative was always beyond the skills of this author, an Indian Ocean framework in isolation would also have precluded a number of informative case-studies in the West, consequently introducing a bias favouring the Eastern segment of the routes over Western ones.

Moving on to a short description of the individual chapters, the first one addresses the historiography of the subject and argues the need for a wider synchronic perspective encompassing economic activities in both the Roman West and India to the East, as well as in the areas in-between, because the long-distance trade cannot be properly studied from an isolated Roman or Indian perspective. Chapter two provides the theoretical and methodological underpinnings for the ensuing analysis, establishing a perspective focusing on concrete demand from the ground up, in consequence also shedding substantial light on the role of the institution of the market as it relates to long-distance exchange. In the process, key theoretical concepts like 'network,' 'diaspora,' 'association' and 'relational contracts' are discussed and practical definitions developed for subsequent application.

Chapter three, being the first analytical chapter, is, on the one hand, an innovative case-study of a well-known Indian ivory figurine from Pompeii, of its proper context and interpretation, while, at the same time, it also serves as a more fully developed model for comparable cases in the following chapters. Thus, the characteristic aspects of the organisation of trade between Rome and India foregrounded here anticipate the central arguments of the book, to be corroborated in subsequent analyses of both Roman, Near Eastern and Indian source material. Chapter four broadens the analysis to engage with the available evidence for organised retail trade by *collegia* in Rome of goods imported from the Indian Ocean, being twinned with chapter five, which argues that prices for some of these goods could be comparatively modest and that supply was even plentiful enough to reach provincial markets. Both of these chapters in unison act as the Western counterparts to chapter eight on the organisation of production in India of these very commodities and their subsequent export.

Chapter six on specifically Greco-Roman networks participating in the long-distance trade with Indian Ocean ports via Egypt is the Roman counterpart to the ensuing chapter seven on Indian Ocean-based networks. Significantly, we find not only Roman families operating out of Southern *Italia* and Alexandria active in Egypt's Red Sea ports, but also Arabs, Axumites and Indians, all three of the latter groups sailing out of their own ports and cities around the shores of the Indian Ocean. What is more, the available evidence reveals that very large and extremely valuable cargoes could travel from East to West in the possession of even a single merchant acting on his own, and that the mercantile networks of some of the involved city-based financiers could double as contracting agents of the relevant states, too, when these needed specialist services for fiscal purposes.

Finally, chapter eight investigates the Indian organisations creating the necessary supply to meet demand at Rome and in the Western provinces at the hands of *collegia* and commercial networks. Production in India was organised by urban associations of merchants (the *nigama*) and craftsmen (the *shreni*), seeing to the supply of commodities very much in demand in the Roman West. Export was handled by merchants and shippers inhabiting well-regulated trading villages, market towns and ports, these groups constituting formal professional communities headed by their own leaders. Thus, demand and supply was channelled through organisations which interacted economically from the extreme opposite ends of trade routes operated by the multiple economic actors to be outlined in chapters six and seven, the demand represented by the *collegia* at Rome in chapter four, and by provincial trade in these goods in chapter five, being met by organisations harnessing supply in India in chapter eight.

Thus, in unison, the following chapters provide an outline, grounded in a string of empirical studies, of the organisation of long-distance trade between Rome and India in Antiquity.

Chapter 1

What's in a name?
A brief historiography of Indo-Roman trade

Traditionally, the Mediterranean has been perceived of as a meaningful geographical unit, the political, economic, religious and other cultural phenomena of which can be dealt with in unison for purposes of large-scale analysis.[2] Arguably, the single most famous proponent of *longue durée* history and the active agency of the Mediterranean as a region, Fernand Braudel, himself tried his hand at an interpretation of the region's historical development from the dawn of time until the High Roman Empire, in 1968–69, although only published posthumously many years later.[3] However, more famous, informed and successful in its purpose has been Peregrine Horden's and Nicholas Purcell's *The Corrupting Sea* from 2000, which once and for all did for Mediterranean Antiquity what Braudel had achieved for later times, now supplemented by Cyprian Broodbank's *The Making of the Middle Sea* from 2013, which extends the scope backwards from Classical Antiquity to well before the last ice age.[4]

However, what if the Mediterranean is better perceived of, at least for the purposes of some studies, not as a unit, but as only one part of a greater whole, such as the Eurasian landmass, or, in this study, the periphery of the Indian Ocean? In this case, we need to think about the historiographical consequences of shifting Rome from being *the* centre, to being *a* centre in the peripheral west of Eurasia, which is really just a late and overdue consequence of old and new discussions about the implications of postcolonialism and globalisation for our interpretation of the Roman Empire.[5] At the very least, then, it becomes necessary to begin considering the historical development and *longue durée* of the Indian Ocean, as well, vis-à-vis that of the Mediterranean. As regards the present study, this entails a merging of the timeframes and historical units known in Western academia as the Roman Mediterranean and to Eastern academics as Early Historic India, respectively. Fortunately, Indian scholars have been more appreciative of this long-distance large-scale interaction 2000 years ago, so some scholarly attempts at joining together 'Roman' and 'Indian' historical narratives otherwise considered in isolation have already been made, Western studies now beginning to follow suit.[6] While the reader is referred to the just mentioned accounts for a fuller historiographical overview, the main works on trade between Rome and India in the early centuries of the Common Era will briefly be listed in the following.

The first dedicated historical monographs were published in quick succession by H. G. Rawlinson in 1916, M. P. Charlesworth in 1924, and E. H. Warmington in 1928.[7] While Rawlinson's study was very ambitious in its temporal scope ('from the earliest times') and field of study (sustaining a broad focus on philosophy, religion, literature, art, etc.), the narrative space left over for economic interaction was really rather limited, as was the treatment in Charlesworth's book, which, although focusing on trade routes alone, dealt with the one to India as only one among a dozen. Warmington's study, however, was much more monumental, and has mainly become outdated due to its strong colonial insistence on Roman agents and dominance, as well as preponderant use of more widely available Western source material. The latter bias was arguably unavoidable until M. Wheeler's publication of the excavations at Arikamedu in the later 1940s and early 1950s, from which point in time Indian archaeological data has become ever more plentiful. Wheeler, nonetheless, remained stuck in the old colonial academic rut, so what was in fact a

[2] Going back to at least the 19th century AD: Ben-Artzi 2004.
[3] Braudel 2002.
[4] Horden and Purcell 2000; Broodbank 2013.
[5] Generally, Goody 2012: 26–67; more specifically, Fitzpatrick 2011. Groundbreaking study of Roman interaction with the Near East in particular, but also more peripherally with Central Asia and India, in Ball 2000.
[6] E.g. Ray 2003, Gupta 2005. See now also Seland 2014a.
[7] Rawlinson 1916, Charlesworth 1926 (with a brief resurvey in1969), Warmington 1974.

thoroughly Tamil port site was interpreted as an 'Indo-Roman' trading station, meaning not so much an 'Indian' but rather a 'Roman' mercantile colony.[8]

A more postcolonially informed appreciation of the roles played by numerous peoples and polities in the Eastern trade and a strong, but much needed, counter dose of informed ('primitivist') scepticism about the size and nature of ancient long-distance commerce, was subsequently introduced in a gargantuan study by M. G. Raschke in 1978.[9] This remains one of the main works on the subject, and is only hampered by never having been updated, thus, not including important new evidence discovered since. A subsequent development has been the discussion over whether the Roman authorities took a 'proactive' or 'reactive' stance towards Indian Ocean trade, S. E. Sidebotham arguing the former and G. K. Young the latter, both conducting meticulous studies focused on the Roman Red Sea ports, their supporting infrastructure and the evidence for the organisation and, particularly, taxation of trade.[10] Meanwhile, F. de Romanis published a study thoroughly integrating a prosopographical approach to the Roman agents of the trade, drawing extensively on graffiti from Egypt's Eastern Desert, with an overall analysis of the Roman trade with the Indian Ocean.[11]

Recent years have seen the publication of G. Parker's theoretically well-developed discursive analysis of 'Roman India,' one chapter being specifically devoted to a study of the commodities imported from India, providing an important cultural contextualisation of Indian objects as items of Roman consumption.[12] Moreover, R. Tomber has now provided a fundamental study of the archaeology of Indian Ocean trade in Antiquity, providing a lucid overview over a huge corpus of archaeological data, not least the actual items of trade themselves.[13] Approaching Indian Ocean trade from more or less the opposite perspective, the macro-level, E. H. Seland has constructed a model in which the different polities of the Arabian Sea reacted similarly to the evolving long-distance trade, conducting 'proactive' policies of centralisation to maximise their fiscal revenues, thus, following the lead of Sidebotham as argued for the Roman ports.[14] Another new publication, by R. McLaughlin, although impressive in its scope and inclusion of source material from far apart in Eurasia, sadly fails to move beyond the outdated viewpoints of both 'Indo-Roman trade' and a grossly inflated ('modernist') idea of an almost globalised commerce between Rome and the East in Antiquity.[15] Finally, numerous smaller studies have been published in edited volumes from the early 1990s until the present, many of which are included here in subsequent chapters,[16] and new important monographs and edited volumes are still being published, as academic interest in the topic continues to flourish.[17]

In summary, the problems with the older, and even some of the more recent, literature on trade between the Mediterranean and the Indian Ocean in the early centuries of the Common Era, are mainly twofold: first, the old ways of writing about 'Indo-Roman' trade die hard, infusing studies with a 'Romano-centric' bias as regards the sources singled out for analysis, in turn emphasising Roman carriers of the trade and a Roman chronology for trade in the Indian Ocean (meaning a sharp decline in the 3rd century AD).[18] Second, and inevitably, the important discoveries made within the last few decades, such as the so-called Muziris Papyrus, graffiti in the Hoq Cave on Socotra, excavations at Pattanam (likely ancient Muziris), and the new (in some cases renewed) archaeological work carried out at Berenike, Myos Hormos, Qana,

[8] Wheeler 1946, 1954. Crucial further work at Arikamedu being done by Begley 1996, 2004.
[9] Raschke 1978. Published alongside were Dihle 1978 and Ferguson 1978.
[10] Sidebotham 1986, Young 2001.
[11] Romanis 1996a.
[12] Parker 2008: 147–202. See also his earlier articles on the subject: 2002, 2004.
[13] Tomber 2008. A similar archaeological synthesis, but mainly restricted to Egypt, is Sidebotham 2011. For a study of Roman objects in India, Suresh 2004.
[14] Seland 2010.
[15] McLaughlin 2010, now followed by the even more extreme 2014.
[16] Especially: Begley and de Puma 1991; Boussac and Salles 1995; Ray and Salles 1996; Reade 1996; Romanis and Tchernia 1997; Gupta 2002; Seland 2007a; Boussac, Salles and Yon 2012; Mathew 2015; Romanis and Maiuro 2015; Boussac, Salles and Yon 2016. In addition, a great number of relevant papers are to be found in the published *Proceedings of Red Sea Project I–V* (2004–10), and presumably in the forthcoming publications of presentations from the ensuing *Red Sea Conference VI* (2013) and *VII* (2015).
[17] E.g. the eagerly awaited monograph by Cobb: forthcoming.
[18] Rawlinson 1916: 151–2; Charlesworth 1926: 72; Warmington 1974: 136; Wheeler 1954: 135, 176; Raschke 1978: 678; McLaughlin 2010: 59–60, 172–74; while Young 2001 is ordered around an AD 300 divide, but mentions subsequent revival: 82–86.

Sumhuram, Arikamedu, etc., must profoundly alter our perception of trade and traders in the Ancient Indian Ocean.[19]

Adopting a perspective endeavouring to encompass both Rome and India, we may, to anticipate the conclusion of chapter three, finally turn the tables on Indo-Roman trade for good, so that the role of Early Historic India in the trade between East and West is duly recognised,[20] as well as the parts played by people from other areas of the ancient Indian Ocean. Moreover, a thorough analysis of the entire corpus of diverse source material now available for closer study makes it possible to provide a picture not of separate Mediterranean 'connectivity,' on the one hand, and Indian Ocean interaction, on the other, but of *longue durée* reciprocal exchanges between these two regions in the form of trade. Indeed, as chapters three to eight show, particular nodes in this commercial network came to exhibit very long-distance connectivity, a sort of 'longectivity,'[21] creating strong economic ties between places as far apart as, *inter alia*, Rome, Alexandria, Koptos, Berenike (and Myos Hormos), Adulis, Qana, Barygaza and Muziris. Finally, as will become clear in chapters three, four and eight, and chapters five to seven, respectively, we can even provide a rather detailed description of the organisation of such long-distance trade, consisting of corresponding urban associations organising demand and supply at either end of the trade routes, as well as the organised merchants moving commodities between them across incredible distances and difficult terrain.

[19] All to be dealt with in detail in the following chapters.
[20] Indeed, interpretations favouring Roman agency in the long-distance trade still flourish, e.g. Gurukkal 2013.
[21] Augmenting the conclusions of Horden and Purcell 2000: 123–72.

Chapter 2

Ancient history 'from below' Theoretical perspectives

While the relatively sparse source material surviving from Antiquity to the present day makes the writing of ancient history 'from below,' as envisaged by E. Hobsbawm in 1985 for much later periods of history, exceedingly difficult, we may nonetheless still strive to write historical narratives which 'uncover the lives and thoughts of common people.'[22] In so far as this may be possible for ancient economic history, this study will attempt to do so in providing a study of consumers and the demand they exerted, the products and their producers, travelling traders and organised merchants and craftsmen, primarily in the words of their own inscriptions, papyri and graffiti, as well as based on what archaeological traces they may have left behind in the conduct of their daily lives and business.

Indeed, this is a basic methodological approach which has recently been strongly advertised in economic studies of the Classical Greek and Hellenistic periods. Specifically, the overarching idea is to 'look at economic relationships "from the ground up",'[23] that is, to avoid overly generalising models positing that the ancient economy was either small or large (the 'primitivist' versus 'modernist' debate), or that the institution of the market was either ineffectual or strong enough to underpin an ancient market economy (the 'substantivist' versus 'formalist' views).[24] Instead, our point of departure should be human needs and 'the effective demand for those needs to be satisfied, to trace the flows of goods and services generated by that pattern and level of demand,' which in turn means looking at commodities and finding out where they were produced, where they ended up, who transported them in what quantities at what cost and what profit, and paying how much in taxes for state services or intervention.[25]

Furthermore, by selecting cases for study which represent demand for commodities originating very far away, we may grow significantly wiser about the workings of ancient long-distance trade,[26] that is, the efficacy of the market in coupling demand with supply across seemingly insurmountable distances. Accordingly, the traditional order of 'supply and demand' needs to be inverted, so that we take our cue from specific consumer demand and investigate to what extent this was satisfied.[27] In this light, unlike the supply-driven growth during and after the Industrial Revolution,[28] demand becomes the 'great mover' and engine of economic growth,[29] making possible, as we shall see, long-distance trade not only in high-end products for elite consumption, like Chinese silks in Rome, but also the supply of spices and aromatics, like pepper, incense and myrrh- and nard-based perfumes, for consumers in the provinces.

By now, it should already be apparent, too, that in addition to demand the institution of the market will also play a prominent role in the following analysis. Oddly enough, it is at present a characteristic choice in itself to offer the market a leading role in an account of the Roman economy.[30] This is not so much in keeping with Karl Polanyi's original theoretical concept of 'substantivism,' arguing that ancient economic activities were embedded in non-economic institutions (political, social, religious),[31] but rather due to the lingering influence of Moses Finley's idiosyncratic 1973-vision of not only an embedded ancient economy, but also one that was characteristically primitive. That is, an ancient world which was

[22] Hobsbawm 1997: 266–86, quote from p. 285.
[23] Archibald 2005: 2; Archibald and Davies 2011: 2.
[24] This is a grossly simplified version, for more detailed summaries of these parallel discussions, see, e.g. Morris 1999; Morley 2007: 2–12; Bang 2011: 17–60; Bresson 2016: 1–15.
[25] Davies 2001: 22.
[26] Davies 2015.
[27] Gabrielsen 2011: 441–43.
[28] Mokyr 1985.
[29] See Flohr 2016: 24, on demand as the driver of innovation in Mediterranean material culture in the 1st–2nd century AD.
[30] See discussion in Harris and Lewis 2015: 3–9
[31] Polanyi, Arensberg and Pearson 1965[1957].

not organised for the satisfaction of its material wants by a conglomeration of interdependent markets, and in relation to which a market-centred analysis is inapplicable.[32]

Consequently, a major recent work like *The Cambridge Economic History of the Greco-Roman World* (2007) has as its stated purpose to employ the *New Institutional Economics* (*NIE*) of Nobel prize-winner Douglass North[33] to sidestep the issue of the market in preference for allegedly more tangible economic phenomena such as 'performance' and 'structure.' To some extent, this might not seem such a bad idea. However, when the consequence is that the role of the market in the ancient economy is deconstructed by separate treatment of the economic spheres of production, distribution and the role of the state, we ought to seriously consider the ramifications of such an agenda. Especially when the framing editorial view at the outset of the volume is explicitly stated as being that 'states remained major economic actors; markets were fragmented and shallow, with high transaction costs; investment opportunities were limited; money and markets generated intense ideological conflicts; and the economy remained minuscule by modern standards.'[34] This is not transcending the old debates by employing new tools from *NIE*,[35] rather, this is simply the old Finley model in an updated *NIE* version.

Although *NIE* must, in all fairness, be credited with the potential of informing the historiographical debates over the ancient economy in some ways, by providing new ways of thinking about some of the old problems, this does not mean that *NIE* holds a monopoly on the right to model and interpret the ancient economy—'Not by one avenue only can we arrive at so tremendous a secret,' to quote the words of the pagan senator Symmachus against the Christians in AD 384.[36] Indeed, while institutional analysis is central to the case-studies conducted in this book, and while many of *NIE*'s main concepts have helped shape this author's understanding of a number of aspects to do with institutional economics,[37] the tradition of institutional analysis in itself goes at least as far back as Adam Smith,[38] having a worth of its own beyond that of its most recent flowering in the guise of *NIE*. Moreover, it is highly significant that modern scholars employing *NIE* on the same historical phenomenon, in this specific context ancient Greco-Roman associations or similar organisations, base their analyses on different assumptions and therefore reach differing conclusions.[39] While this is not exactly surprising, it certainly cautions against assuming that *NIE* on its own is the only modern alternative for research on the ancient economy or even a superior theoretical paradigm.[40]

Whether using *NIE* or not, we should instead be trying to nuance the picture and accord the institution of the market its due role in ancient society as one very important means of exchange among others,[41] such as Polanyi's categories of redistribution and reciprocity,[42] or, as has recently been suggested, the subsistence and command modes.[43] Accordingly, the market will have been more or less prominent in different economic contexts of ancient society, being embedded to varying degrees (from unrestrained to suppressed) in social, political or religious institutions, depending upon the specific sphere of activity.[44] In fact, such a more complex and context-specific understanding of the dynamic aspects of the ancient economy, which cannot adhere to the tenets of any one single model,[45] also better explains the widely differing interpretations of the Roman economy as a whole by the most prominent modern scholars of the field.[46]

---

[32] Finley 1999: 22, 26.
[33] The seminal work is North 1990.
[34] Morris, Saller, and Scheidel 2007, quote from p. 10; discussed in Harris and Lewis 2015: 8.
[35] As claimed by some, e.g. Bang 2009a: 197.
[36] Symm. *Relat.* 3.10: *Uno itinere non potest perveniri ad tam grande secretum.* Transl. Barrow 1973.
[37] For useful summaries of the practical use of *NIE* for analysis of ancient economic activity, see especially (but, significantly, also highly normatively, being based on cases from the Roman legal *corpora*) Frier and Kehoe 2007, Kehoe, Ratzan and Yiftach 2015: 1–27.
[38] Smith 1761[1759], cf. Woolcock 1998: 160. More generally, Nye 2008: 68.
[39] E.g. Bang 2011: 239–89, Broekaert 2011, Hawkins 2012; 2016: 66–129, Terpstra 2013.
[40] For a more thorough, and ultimately positive, evaluation of the use of *NIE* in ancient history, see Verboven 2015.
[41] Harris and Lewis 2015: 9–31.
[42] Polanyi 1965: 250–6. An example of such an attempted study is Evers 2011.
[43] Archibald and Davies 2011: 3.
[44] Compare Feinman 2017a: 139–41, 145–46.
[45] Feinman 2017b, especially p. 412.
[46] Compare e.g. Bang 2011, arguing for a Roman 'bazaar,' that is, characterised by fragmentary market integration, with Temin 2013, arguing for

As regards conceptual clarification of the term 'market' to be used in the subsequent chapters, this is taken to signify a price-setting mechanism assigning value to goods or services in response to the perceived demand for and supply of the good or service in question.[47] Thus, market trade constitutes transactions conducted mainly in relation to the market price, not transactions effected by power of command or primarily with an eye to social obligations, although, and this is important, both of these types of redistributive and reciprocal exchanges could, and often did, affect market transactions.[48] From a theoretical perspective, moreover, markets are 'integrated' if they are fully responsive to changes in demand and supply vis-à-vis one another, and correspondingly they can be characterised as 'fragmentary' if fluctuations in one market does not affect price-setting in another market.[49] Consequently, it should be apparent that the relay of *information* about demand and supply from market to market assumes vital importance for the workings of the price-setting market mechanisms:[50] lack of communication about variations in demand and supply result in fragmentation, and misleading or obsolete information results in market failures (setting prices too high or too low until the receipt of valid information entails a market correction), whereas anything from sparse to abundant information can support some degree of integration, whether more or less being dependant on the amount and strength of this information.[51]

Crucially, though, ancient markets rarely offer clear-cut cases of integration or fragmentation, often merely being distinguished by appearing more or less integrated or fragmentary relative to other markets.[52] Accordingly, other telltale factors causing integration or fragmentation include transport distance (short and easy versus long and hazardous), redistributive processes (heavy subsidies of import or export versus heavy taxation on import or export), social or political attitudes towards exchange of specific items (*de facto* inelastic conspicuous consumption versus political restrictions on private purchase of specific items, e.g. silk), and deliberate market manipulation (such as successful attempts to corner the market or obtain partial or complete monopolies, legal or otherwise)—we shall encounter examples like these, or *transaction costs* in *NIE* terminology,[53] in concrete empirical cases in the following chapters.[54]

Remarkably, just such an experience of an actual ancient market, that of Rome itself, is reflected in a passage by Pliny the Elder, thus datable to the 70s AD:

> We are not unaware that the prices of articles (*pretia rerum*) which we have stated at various points differ in different places and alter nearly every year, according to the shipping costs or the terms on which a particular merchant has bought them, or as some dealer dominating the market may whip up the selling price...[55]

This description encapsulates a learned observer's understanding of the workings of price-setting markets in different goods, prices soaring, diving or evening out as a function of the demand for and supply of a particular commodity. Now, if geographically distant markets were fully integrated, we should not expect to see such fluctuations, but, at the same time, if these same markets were operating in complete

an integrated Roman market economy. A computational evaluation of the main hypotheses of these two authors is now available in Brughmans and Poblome 2016, tentatively emphasising the importance of market integration for generating results fitting the archaeological record of ancient tableware. See also the divergent views on the Roman economy expressed in the handy collection of Wilson *et al.* 2012a. Note, furthermore, that economists are likewise divided about the role and efficiency of markets in modern economies, thus, *The Sveriges Riksbank Prize in Economic Sciences in Memory of Alfred Nobel* 2013 was ironically split between a proponent of markets consistently producing correct prices (E. Fama) and another who argued that they are more often wide off the mark (R. Shiller).

[47] For an exhaustive and technical definition, see Temin 2013: 9–24.

[48] Polanyi 1965: 253.

[49] Compare Temin 2013: 18–22.

[50] On information as the key transaction cost, see North 1990: 27.

[51] Traders acted on the available information they had, interpreting it as best they could, an important circumstance termed 'bounded rationality;' Williamson 1985: 30, North 1990: 96, Ricketts 2002: 35.

[52] Regarding ancient traders' perception of the relation between market prices and information about supply and demand, see e.g. (in reverse chronological order) Cic. *Off.* 3.50, Dem. 56.8, Xen. *Oec.* 20.27–28, Lys. 22.14. On communications and long-distance trade more generally, see now Terpstra 2017.

[53] 'Transaction costs are the economic equivalent of friction in physical systems,' Williamson 1985: 19. North 1990: 5–6, Frier and Kehoe 2007: 117–18.

[54] On transactions costs causing fragmentary market integration, see especially Bang 2011: 131–201.

[55] Plin. *HN*, XXXIII.57.

isolation, suffering absolute fragmentation, we would not see any regular prices either, in fact, not any sustained trade in the commodity at all. So, the task at hand is to examine the degree to which, if any, ancient organisations managed to cope with the challenges of long-distance trade between the Roman Mediterranean and the Indian Ocean, connecting Western demand and Eastern supply.[56]

Accordingly, this book will employ a consistent 'bottom-up' focus on the demand for particular imports, mainly from India to Rome, to investigate the role of the market in long-distance trade. Thus, instead of positing high or low transaction costs (based on academic assumption *in lieu* of sufficient ancient evidence) for either production or the multiple aspects of distribution (causing markets to appear integrated or fragmentary depending on historiographical stance), this study will attempt to abstain from deductions grounded in *NIE*-theory alone, but will instead strive to base conclusions as much as possible on concrete evidence for production, transport, transactions, etc. Conversely, a transaction costs analysis might well have assumed that transport costs, taxes and expenses incurred to avoid a range of risks (natural as well as human) would prohibit any large-scale long-distance trade between Rome, or at least its western provinces, and the Indian Ocean. However, if the available evidence shows pepper and nard being traded on what appears to be ordinary market terms in the provinces, that is, not moved about due to state redistribution or elite gift giving, and that very large quantities of Indian Ocean goods were imported overall, keeping prices comparatively low, then these specific historical conditions should take precedence over assumptions about transaction costs.

Admittedly, this theoretical viewpoint renders generalisations, sweeping conclusions and grand models pretty nigh impossible to make, but the restrained conclusions arrived at are much more valuable, each contributing in its own small way to a more nuanced picture of the puzzle that is the ancient economy—a puzzle which we do not, and never will, hold all the pieces to. Accordingly, this is not an attempt at writing history without theory (which would be impossible and self-deluding), nor a choice of historical pragmatism over theory (which seems a futile exercise), but simply the deliberate choice of a theory exhibiting a strong degree of methodological caution, namely, the 'bottom up-' or 'history from below'-approach. In practice, this entails identifying and tracing the involvement of particular organisations involved in the long-distance trade, specifically the overlapping categories of networks, diasporas and associations, which really represent a spectrum of group formalisation rather than distinct types.

Starting out with the basic idea of a 'network,' these come into being when people interact on a regular basis, or have done so previously and have the potential to do so again in the future, such connections often being grounded in one or more shared values or similar attributes. In so far as a network is instrumental to its members in accomplishing desired outcomes, it will represent a lesser or greater resource to them,[57] its concrete worth being measurable in terms of the 'social capital' which constitutes the actual relations between members,[58] and upon which both individuals as well as the group as a whole can draw for different purposes.[59] According to the sociologist J. Coleman, we can distinguish between three different categories of social capital, namely: obligations and expectations, information channels, and norms and effective sanctions. Besides, the more members of a network are united by factors such as kinship, ethnicity, religion, occupation, etc. (all of which we shall encounter among ancient networks), the more 'closure' this network will exhibit, generating not only stronger norms and sanctions but even 'trustworthiness' itself as an additional form of social capital.[60]

Significantly, two other sociological studies have emphasised, respectively, how, on the one hand, 'weak ties' between members in a network (such as local members of a given occupation) nonetheless yield

[56] Indeed, large-scale and long-distance trade has recently been emphasised by Morley as the defining hallmarks of the Roman economy, *inter alia* in foreign and exotic objects crucial for consumption and display among the urban elites; 2007: 16, 102.
[57] Following Field 2008: 1, 23.
[58] Coleman 1988: 98, 100–1.
[59] Coleman 1988: 108–9.
[60] Coleman 1988: 102–8. Compare the theoretical frameworks of Ogilvie 2005: 5–6 and Ricketts 2002: 20–5, as well as the comparable application to Roman *collegia* of a similar theoretical approach by Hawkins 2016: 115.

relatively greater economic advantages for its members,[61] and, on the other hand, how social capital can be used to not only construct strong ties with some network members ('bonding,' e.g. family ties) and weaker ties with others ('bridging,' for instance, shared occupation), but also be used for connecting with and obtaining leverage over individuals outside the network ('linking,' such as a lower-status group obtaining the patronage of a powerful individual).[62] In consequence, not only Coleman's more well-defined and closure-prone networks but also looser networks based on weak ties are able to reap organisational benefits for their members, in the guise of social capital providing economic advantages based on cooperation.

Building on these theoretical insights, networks can help their members minimise the problems of 'opportunism,' pertaining to anybody who cheats in a casual one-off exchange, and 'moral hazard,' being a technical term signifying the ever-present risk of a partner to a permanent contract knowingly acting to the detriment of his counterpart.[63] The costliness of contracting in a pure market situation, due to the expenses incurred in safeguarding against all plausible kinds of opportunism and moral hazard, renders the parties to a long-term commercial relationship less likely to re-negotiate by forging formal contracts every time—it is simply not economically efficient.[64] Thus, continued dealings cause economic relationships to become embedded within '"relational contracts" in which cooperation is enforced by reputation and trust rather than courts.'[65] Specifically, public courts are expensive and slow compared to any kind of 'private ordering,' that is, settlement by arbitration, and courts are therefore, in practice, relegated to being bodies of ultimate appeal.[66]

In consequence, 'relational contracts' are forged which allow parties to 'save on negotiations and enforcement' and instead to 'rely on formal and informal institutional frameworks (in particular social networks) since these provide them with rules and resources to coordinate'--relational contracts are, in other words, embedded in relevant institutions.[67] Moreover, as concerns the specific problem that an agent often has greater knowledge about a business situation than his principal, called 'the problem of agency,'[68] relational contracts can be used to forge links with trustworthy agents or more active partners who are invested with an 'open-ended' mandate: as neither of the two sides to the transaction(s) can account for future developments, it is in the interests of both that contracts are not too specific, but allow enough freedom to make the right, profitable, choices.[69] Consequently, as will be shown in the following chapters, established networks with developed social capital constitute prime recruitment pools for partners or agents to a relational contract, in which the contract is simply embedded in already existing relations, being the ties of the network.

Moving on from the theoretical aspects of networks generally, this study will also engage at length with two special kinds of networks which created institutional frameworks fostering the creation of relational contracts, namely: diasporas and associations.[70] Briefly put, the members of a diaspora shared common ethnic origin, religion and, very often at least, mercantile occupation, being settled abroad but retaining a culturally distinct group cohesion in relation to the host society and maintaining trade and communication channels with their country of origin.[71] An association, on the other hand, was defined by a proper name identifying it as an organisation, by formal membership, entailing adherence to the group's elected rules, and by an internal organisation distributing duties, powers and privileges, thus, making the group manageable.[72] As a result, associations constitute a highly formalised and concrete

[61] Granovetter 1973.
[62] Woolcock 2001: 13; elaborated upon by Field 2008: 46, 73.
[63] Ricketts 2002: 35.
[64] González-Díaz and Vázquez 2008: 263.
[65] Pénard 2008: 172.
[66] Williamson 1985: 18, 32, 75, 164.
[67] Brousseau 2008: 47.
[68] Frier and Kehoe 2007: 122–26.
[69] Frier and Kehoe 2007: 130.
[70] Hawkins 2016: 103, 108, attempts to argue for relational contracting within *collegia* in particular.
[71] Curtin 1984 and Stein 1999: 166–73, generally. On diasporas of the Roman Mediterranean, see Terpstra 2013, while on Indian Ocean diasporas of the early centuries AD, see Seland 2016a. Compare also Gabrielsen 2016a: 141–7 on 'ethno-congregational associations.'
[72] Gabrielsen and Thomsen 2015: 9–12.

example of ancient networks,[73] and, as we shall see, were a vital feature of economic life in both the Greco-Roman Mediterranean as well as contemporary South Asia and the Near East.

In rounding off (or getting started, as it is), we shall briefly return to Finley, who, ironically, belittled both the role of Roman associations in the economy[74] as well as that of Roman long-distance trade, stating the following about the latter:

> The mere presence of trade over long distances is of course a necessary condition for interdependence but it is not a sufficient condition. After all, long-distance trade has existed ever since the Stone Age. That trade of itself does not warrant such jargon as 'a large unified economic space' unless it can be demonstrated, or at least suggested with some measure of reasonableness, that the kind of reciprocal relationship that existed between Polish grain production and Dutch grain imports was present [referred to by Finley previously in the same paragraph], for instance in the case of glass from Cologne exported to Egypt. Otherwise, 'a large unified economic space' is no more than a fancy way of saying that goods were exchanged within that area, and then I see no reason for not including China, Ceylon and Malaysia in the same economic space as Rome because the latter received its silks and much of its spices from eastern Asia.[75]

Well, Finley was never shy of demanding a lot from those who would disagree with his views on the impossibility of long-distance trade and degree of market integration in Antiquity.[76] In the following, although it is not possible to produce series of corresponding Roman and Indian market prices, it will nonetheless be 'suggested with some measure of reasonableness, that a kind of reciprocal relationship existed,' to paraphrase Finley, between production centres in India and South Arabia, on the one hand, and market demand in the Roman Empire, on the other—and even that ancient associations played an important role in this long-distance trade.

[73] Gabrielsen 2007; Vlassopoulos 2007: 12–15; Rathbone 2007a: 314.

[74] Finley 1999[1973]: 81, 137–8, 195–6; 1981: 17–8, 186. His main critique of their economic role is that they were unlike later Medieval European guilds with their monopolies and active member protectionism, but this is beside the point—Greco-Roman associations may, as we shall see, have had other important economic functions.

[75] Finley 1999: 177–8, similar remark on p. 34. See comments on these passages by Millar 1998: 121–22; and Fitzpatrick 2011: 27–8.

[76] Unsurprisingly, the foremost moderniser of his day, M. Rostovtzeff, had no qualms interpreting the trade between Rome and India as 'commerce' proper: 'The development of commerce also gradually assumed new and unexpected aspects, especially in the East. We have seen how the trade with Arabia and India, which had dealt almost exclusively in luxuries, began to play a certain part in the commercial relations of the Roman Empire in the time of Augustus...;' cf. 1957, I: 94–97 incl. nn17–18, quote from p. 94. On Rostovtzeff and the Eastern trade, see also Fitzpatrick 2011: 29.

Chapter 3

Turning the tables on Indo-Roman trade

Setting out with a case-study that moves back and forth between Rome and India, the immediate aim will be to lay the foundations for a comparative analysis of the organisation of long-distance trade in the early centuries of the Common Era. Accordingly, the following chapter will enquire into how and by whom one specific strand of the trade was conducted. By implication, this necessitates the formulation of answers to questions about the purpose and organisation of certain groups in Rome and Western India, as well as about the origin and different Indian and Roman uses of a well-defined category of objects with which they dealt. Finally, the findings made will be used in a preliminary manner to question the nature and scale of the entire maritime exchange circuit between the Mediterranean and the Indian Ocean.

Speaking more concretely, this means taking a closer look at some particularly fashionable Roman furniture in order to provide an outline of a chain of purpose-made mercantile organisations bridging 8000 kilometres of sea and desert in the later 1st–early 2nd century AD to market Indian craftsmanship in Rome. In the process, the involved parties managed to effect a change of fashion among the Roman aristocracy, as well as to spur development of a local production of what had originally been long-distance imports. Consequently, this should force us to reconsider any preconceived notions we might harbour about the debilitating logistical barriers to trade caused by long distances. The more so in light of the fact that we often lack this kind of detailed evidence for other categories of products exchanged between Rome and India, for which this case-study ought to be considered diagnostic.

In order to understand the nature of some of the most prominent Roman and Indian organisations involved in this long-distance trade, though, a superficial survey of the genesis of professional associations is necessary. Starting out here with an introduction to Mediterranean associations generally and Roman *collegia* in particular, we shall briefly touch upon the existence of similar and contemporary South Asian associations further below in this chapter, before duly engaging in a proper introduction to Indian associations in chapter eight.

Regarding the earliest origins of a Mediterranean tradition for forming associations, often called 'clubs' or 'societies' in the older literature on the subject,[77] these can be traced as far back as Classical and Hellenistic Greece, blooming in the Eastern Mediterranean from the later 4th century BC onwards.[78] During the Hellenistic period in particular, the habit of establishing associations for an ever-widening range of purposes (social, religious, economic, political, etc., often in combination) spread from the Levant to Sicily and southern Italy,[79] coming into contact with Romans not only on their own Italian soil,[80] but also in the busy ports of the Eastern Mediterranean.[81] Regarding associations based exclusively on profession, the Romans themselves ascribed the early organisation of about half a dozen important

[77] E.g. Tod 1932: 71–93.

[78] The seminal work is Poland 1909; for the Classical period, see Jones 1999, for the Hellenistic, Arnaoutoglou 2003. The new monumental inventory of all recorded Greek associations of the Eastern Mediterranean by the *Copenhagen Associations Project* (*CAP*) (http://copenhagenassociations.saxo.ku.dk/capinventory/) will soon supersede previous publications, though; for a preliminary introduction to the work of the *CAP*-project, see now Gabrielsen and Thomsen 2015. Note, moreover, that Gabrielsen 2016a shows that the birth of the Greek association phenomenon cannot be narrowed down to early Hellenistic times, as the historiography of the subject tends to assume, rather, the development leading up to this 'take-off' is attested epigraphically from no later than the beginning of the 4th century BC.

[79] See especially Gabrielsen 2007 on the far-reaching 'industrious revolution' that the Greek association phenomenon constituted in a wider Mediterranean context.

[80] An early example of organisational influence from Greek religious associations on their Roman counterparts is *CIL* I², 581 (a *senatus consultum* against Bacchanalic groups; 186 BC), cf. the historical account in Livy *Epit.*, XXXIX.8–18; while an example of a 'Hellenised' professional association in Rome is *CIL* I², 2519 (a *syn{h}odos societas cantorum Graecorum*, mid-1st century BC; *synodos* being one of the most common traditional Greek terms for an association, cf. Poland 1909: 158–63).

[81] E.g. Hatzfeld 1912; 1919. An empirical example being that of the Roman banker, Marcus Minatius, on 2nd century BC Delos, who became an honorary member of the 'Berytian worshippers of Poseidon, being merchants, shippers and warehouse-owners;' *ID* 1520, cf. Tod 1934 and Rauh 1993. More on this in chapter six.

occupations into *collegia* to their earliest history, allegedly being the work of king Numa of the late 8th-early 7th century BC,[82] although this historical tradition is unlikely to have any factual roots.[83]

In due course, however, Roman associations, mainly in the guise of *collegia* and *corpora*,[84] appear in inscriptions from as early as the 2nd century BC and in the literary sources from the 60s BC.[85] Nonetheless, the earliest surviving inscriptions containing the rules, that is, *leges*, of Roman associations do not appear until the later 1st–2nd century AD, and only one of these few specimens, furthermore, belongs to a *collegium* defined by occupation.[86] Significantly, the Roman government was highly anxious about the potential of associations as *foci* of social and political unrest, both in Republican times and during the early Empire, but there was never any general or permanent prohibition on the establishment of associations, instead there were temporary clampdowns in connection with political crises at Rome, as well as local bans in provinces where cities might be prone to civil disturbances. As a result, most of those who would wish to establish an association had to apply to the emperor or Senate for permission to be recognised as a lawful *collegium* by their local authorities.[87]

Indeed, although we term a distinct sub-group of Roman associations 'professional' or 'occupational *collegia*,' it is important to make it absolutely clear that these were not merely united for purely 'economic' reasons to do with their shared professions, but just like in other Roman associations (and in their Hellenistic predecessors before them) additional reasons for joining together included social, religious, funerary and political activities, very often in a mix of different measures depending on the specific association in question.[88] Thus, feasts and banquets, private cult and worship, communal staging of fitting burials and political endorsements, loom large in the epigraphic record. In addition, groups organised in a *collegium* could obtain the grace and favours of a local patron in return for their public support, occupied a recognised niche in the civic world of their host municipality, and were granted certain legal privileges as lawful associations.[89]

Among these latter prerogatives are two which we need to be acquainted with before proceeding, because we shall encounter their practical consequences repeatedly, namely, those of corporate economic status and eligibility for the receipt of endowments. Starting out with the former, a Roman law from the 2nd century AD states that persons permitted to constitute a corporation, such as a *collegium*, could transact as a municipal body with common property, common funds and a representative authorised to act on the general behalf of the entire membership.[90] In fact, this appears to be a necessary precondition for a law dating back to Marcus Aurelius, 161–80 AD, which stipulated that endowments could be made to lawful *collegia* as organisations, not merely to members as individuals,[91] being for the ornament of cities, honour of certain groups (especially commemoration of patrons) or charity for the poor.[92]

[82] Pliny *NH*, XXXIV.1, XXXV.46; Plut. *Vit. Num.*, XVII.2.

[83] Gabba 1984.

[84] The historiographically most influential works on Roman associations being Waltzing 1895–1900, de Robertis 1973, Ausbüttel 1982 and Tran 2006. On the historiography of Roman *collegia*, see especially Perry 2006.

[85] For the earliest origins, see Waltzing 1895–1900, I: 61–90; III: 1–2; Tran 2006: 1–21; Diosono 2007: 24–33; Liu 2013: 352–3. One of the earliest epigraphically attested *collegia* is that of the Faliscan cooks, see chapter four, while religious, or cultic, associations are the target of the *senatus consultum* of 186 BC mentioned above, n80; for an early literary reference to *collegia*, see Cicero *Comment. pet.*, VIII.29–30 (*c.* 65–4 BC).

[86] *Lex familiae Silvani*, *c.* 60 AD (*AE* 1929, 161; Buonocore and Diliberto 2003); *lex* of the *collegium salutare* of Diana and Antinous, AD 136 (*CIL* XIV, 2112; Bendlin 2011; to be compared with the highly fragmentary *CIL* XIV, 4548, elucidated in Laubry and Zevi 2010, which may also be the remnant of a charter); and the *lex* of the *collegium* of Aesculapius and Hygia, AD 153 (*CIL* VI, 10234; Ascough *et al.* 2012: 207–10). The *lex* of the *negotiatores eborarii et citriarii* will be dealt with in detail below.

[87] On the highly complicated issue of the Roman government's attitude to *collegia*, see De Ligt 2000, Arnaoutoglou 2002, 2005, and Liu 2005, 2013: 353–7. A good example of the ambiguous attitude of the emperors towards the establishment of associations is Plin. *Ep.*, X.33–4, 92–3, in light of e.g. *Dig.* III.4.1 (Gaius, second century AD), XLVII.22.3.1 (Marcianus, early third century AD)

[88] Cf. Gabrielsen 2016b: 88–91; and conversely, associations which did not flag profession in their formal group name could nonetheless have economic funtions.

[89] For a recent overview of the ambiguous characteristics of Roman *collegia*, see Verboven 2011a acting as introduction to the ensuing articles of Arnaoutoglou 2011, Broekaert 2011, Gibbs 2011 and Tran 2011; also the concise survey in Liu 2013. More detailed studies of professional *collegia* are available in van Nijf 1997, Dittmann-Schöne 2001, Zimmerman 2002, Liu 2009, Rohde 2012, Flohr 2013: 308–9, 334–7, Hawkins 2016: 66–129, and Venticinque 2016.

[90] *Dig.* III.4.1.1 (Gaius)

[91] *Dig.* XXXIV.5.20 (Paul)

[92] *Dig.* XXX.122 (Paul), on legacies generally XXX.116 (Florentinus).

Basically, such endowments were money intended to create more money by generating annual revenue through being lent out at interest, and are therefore indicative of the rules and rates of ancient credit markets.[93] Moreover, endowments as such were different in nature from ancient financial foundations generally, for while the latter served the private—and often specifically economic—interests of their instigators, the former were also strictly tied to the fulfilment of beneficial religious or social aspirations. While the earliest organisations accepting endowments were religious and political institutions (temples, sanctuaries and cities), a new development from Hellenistic times onwards was the eligibility of private associations, i.e. groups of co-religionists or fellow-professionals (or both) meeting voluntarily, as recipients and trustees of endowments.[94] Significantly, such associations constituted an organisational setup combining the religious and civic spheres of ancient society by virtue of the religious beliefs and citizenships of their members.[95] This made associations ideal wardens of institutions like endowments, in the service of which their members would manage the entrusted money against the vicissitudes of the market, generate religious merit for the founder through annual activities such as charity or commemorative religious rituals, and, ultimately, perpetuate his memory for as long as they themselves would retain corporate existence as a group.

In consequence, a number of Greco-Roman associations of the empire were closely connected by strict regulations to the running of endowments. A collation of data from the Roman West reveals that more than 80 perpetual endowments nested with *collegia* of various kinds are known, most dating from the 2nd-3rd century AD, although two have survived from both the 1st and the 4th century AD, as well. Concretely, the majority of the endowments were in the guise of cash foundations with interest rates ranging from 5–12 per cent per year, while a few were rent-producing properties.[96] Summing up, endowments represent a highly interesting junction between the continuous need to raise money on market terms and the act of making this operation subservient to wider philanthropic and religious concerns of society, thus, harnessing the power of the institution of the market by embedding it in communal institutions, being associations in this study, imbued with values strong enough to keep a check on the potentially corrupting effects of profit-making.[97]

The collegium of ivory- and citrus wood traders

Having thus been briefly introduced to the history and workings of Roman *collegia*, we shall now proceed to a case-study of the fragmentarily preserved *lex* of the *collegium negotiatorum eborariorum et citriariorum*, which shall serve as a concrete historical example of this important institution of Roman society. Attested in greater Rome itself at the time of Hadrian, AD 117–38, this *collegium* is known from an inscription found in Trastevere, across the Tiber [**Figure 1**]. The text is the preserved right-hand half of an introductory preamble written above two columns of which only the second has survived, belonging to a charter, *lex collegii*, setting out the rules and annual banquets of an association of *negotiatores eborarii et citriarii*, that is, of 'ivory- and citrus wood traders.'[98] The specific coupling of these two otherwise different mercantile specialisations in one *collegium* calls for an explanation, though: what was the connection between trade in citrus wood and ivory? The more so, seeing as members were recruited exclusively from these two vocations, which, as we shall return to below, was quite an uncommon practice.

Fortunately, we happen to know that the most fashionable kind of Roman furniture from the mid-1st century AD onwards was made from exactly these two materials: citrus wood and ivory.[99] The foremost category of such consisted of round tables made with tabletops of citrus wood and supported by three

[93] On Greek and Roman endowments generally, see the seminal work of Laum 1914, and on Roman endowments specifically, Duncan-Jones 1974, Andreau 1977, Mrozek 2000 and Pickert 2005.
[94] Gabrielsen 2005.
[95] Gabrielsen 2007: 196.
[96] Liu 2008a: 233–4, 247.
[97] See Sosin 2000 on the economic and financial capability and efficiency of ancient endowments from Hellenistic times onwards.
[98] *CIL* VI, 33885 = *ILS* 7214. Cf. Borsari 1887; Waltzing 1895–1900, III: 316, no. 1347. Translations are available in Bäumler 2014 (German), Erno 2015 (Hungarian) and further below in this chapter (English).
[99] For a brief overview, see Weeber 2003: 111–14; Lapatin 2015: 180–81.

Figure 1
Inscription of the *collegium* of *negotiatores eborarii et citriarii*; *CIL* VI, 33,885. Source: Borsari 1887: pl. 1.

legs, in traditional fashion, or possibly by a single solid pedestal, both versions being carved from ivory.[100] Related kinds of furniture included citrus wood and ivory bookcases, citrus wood doors, and citrus wood and ivory ornamented ceilings, such extravagant home furnishings being the prerogative of the super-rich. Ostentatious writing-tablets were also made from these materials.[101] Accordingly, it was the combined interests of traders dealing in either citrus wood or ivory in the even greater profits to be obtained from composite products manufactured from their respective wares, which led them to enter into formal association with one another no later than the early 2nd century AD. In the following, we shall start out by taking a look at each commodity in turn.

The citrus tree, *Thuja articulata*,[102] originally grew from Mauretania on the Atlantic via Numidia all the way east to Cyrenaica, but already in Hellenistic times it disappeared from Cyrenaica due to over-cutting, and by Pliny's time the supply had become exhausted even as far westward as Nearer Mauretania. Citrus wood (Gr.: *thyon*; Lat.: *citrum*) had been known since Homer for its aromatic properties, was described

[100] Richter 1966: 70–1 (type 4), 111–2 (type 3), 122; Croom 2007: 20–21, 68–70; Ulrich 2007: 225–7, 247–8. Cass. Dio LXI.10.3, explicitly states that Seneca had three-legged ivory tables (*tripodes*) and Luc. *Pharsalia*, X, l. 144f, refers to tusks in the plural as supports of citrus tabletops, while Juv. XI, l. 122f, speaks of a table supported by one large piece of ivory, and Mart. *Epigr.*, XIV.3, refers to a supporting ivory tusk in the singular. However, both Juvenal and Martial might simply in these instances have been substituting a singular for the plural for poetic reasons, cf. Karttunen 1997: 560.

[101] Sen. *Tranq.*, IX.9.6; Stat. *Silv.*, I.3.35; Hor. *Carm.*, IV.1.20; Apul. *Met.*, V.1; Mart. *Epigr.*, XIV.3, XIV.5.

[102] A useful summary of its botanical and English names can be found in Ulrich 2007: 247.

on a more scientific basis by Theophrastus, and became a luxurious adornment of Hellenistic monarchs for monumental doors and statues. Among the Romans, the beautiful gleam and wavy veins of polished citrus wood made it all the rage with the rich at Rome during the Late Republic, although first Cato and subsequently Varro had denounced its use as a symptom of lavishness.[103] Pliny later described this development as the start of the 'table madness' (*mensarum insania*): while Cicero on the one hand castigated the former governor of Sicily, Verres, for *inter alia* appropriating a splendid citrus wood table while administering the island,[104] Cicero himself in spite of his limited means paid half a million *sesterces* for a citrus wood table that survived up to Pliny's day. This was only the beginning, however, and under the successive reigns of Augustus and Tiberius such citrus wood tables continued to fetch record-high prices, eventually topping at 1.3 million *sesterces* for an antique.[105] As Seneca remarked, these prices in excess of a million for one table actually exceeded the property qualification for a senator, but this was only moral posturing on his behalf, though, for he himself mentions possessing citrus wood and ivory bookcases, while later sources attribute a huge collection of citrus wood tables with ivory legs to none other than him.[106]

Suffering the same fate as Seneca—death—in the years AD 65–66 under Nero, the contemporaries Petronius Arbiter and Annaeus Lucan also made explicit references to citrus wood tables, Lucan being the earliest attested source to mention that these could be fitted with ivory legs.[107] As regards the later part of the 1st century AD, in addition to Pliny who speaks of both citrus wood tables and ivory table legs, Statius explicitly mentions citrus wood tables supported by legs of Indian ivory twice, while Martial refers repeatedly to citrus wood tables generally, and twice each to citrus wood tables with legs of, respectively, Indian and Libyan ivory.[108] Finally, the entire span of the 2nd century AD is scattered with jumbled references to citrus wood, round tables and ivory feet, made by Juvenal (round tabletop on ivory pedestal, ivory obtained from Mauretanians and Indians), Lucian (ivory-legged tables), Apuleius (tables of citrus wood and ivory), Clement of Alexandria (ivory-legged table) and Athenaeus of Naucratis (ivory-legged maple tables).[109]

Significantly, Juvenal adds the valuable detail in his description of a table that it was supported by a solid piece of ivory carved to resemble a rampant (that is, upright standing) panther, *pardus*, with a gaping jaw. However, it is more than likely that all ivory table legs were to some extent carved, ivory being most eminently suited for decorations, and the legs of round, three-legged tables were, in fact, traditionally finely carved in wood,[110] wrought in bronze (tripod tables, a related design being braziers),[111] or chiselled in marble (heavy ornamental tables),[112] as were the supports of other kinds of furniture,[113] often ending in feline (or, specifically, lion) paws. Indeed, there is plenty of both archaeological and literary evidence that first the Greeks and later on the Romans were highly active in carving ivory (and bone[114]) for use with furniture from no later than the 6th century BC, and probably considerably earlier, through Hellenistic

[103] Meiggs 1982: 286–91.
[104] Cic. *Verr.*, IV.37.
[105] Pliny *NH*, XIII.29–30.
[106] Sen. *Ben.*, VII.9.2; *Tranq.*, IX.9.6. Cass. Dio LXI.10.3, reports the surely exaggerated piece of information that Seneca possessed 500 three-legged citrus tables with feet made of ivory.
[107] Petron. *Sat.*, CXIX. Luc. *Pharsalia*, IX, ll. 426ff (citrus wood table), X, ll. 144f (citrus wood table with ivory legs): Lucan's subject here is a banquet given by Cleopatra in honour of Julius Caesar, and although the latter was certainly also fond of citrus wood (Vell. Pat. II.56.2), Lucan is obviously extrapolating luxury objects of his own day back into a different historical setting.
[108] Pliny *NH*, V.1.12, XII.2.5; Stat. *Silv.*, III.3.94ff, IV.2.38ff; Mart. *Epigr.*, IX.59, XII.66, XIV.89, XIV.91 generally, IX.22 and XIV.3 on Libyan ivory legs, and II.43 and X.98 on Indian ivory legs.
[109] Juv. I, l. 122f; Lucian, *Gallus*, XIV; Apul. *Met.*, II.19, 5.1; Clement of Alexandria, *Paedagogus*, II.3.37.3; Athenaeus of Naucratis, *Deipnosophists*, II.49a. To these later authors can be added, moreover, Cassius Dio writing about Seneca, cf. n106. Most of the literary references in the immediately preceding footnotes are conveniently listed in and quoted by Karttunen 1997.
[110] The most illuminating collection of wooden tables is the six preserved from Herculaneum, Mols 1999: 44–52, nos. 14–22. The few other surviving examples are listed in the standard literature, cf. n100.
[111] Harl-Schaller 1976–7: cat. A); Vermeule 1981: cat. II), bronze specimens.
[112] Moss 1988: cat. C1–118.
[113] Ulrich 2007: 216 (throne-like chairs with animal legs), 220 (benches with supporting slabs carved like stylized animal legs), 222 (folding stools with animal decorations), 228 (elaborate s-shaped legs for cupboards). Mols 1999: 35 (beds with lathe-turned legs), 53 (benches with supporting slabs carved like stylized animal legs). Cohon 1984: types II–VII (slab-sided marble supports for tables with elaborately carved decorations at each end, griffins being most numerous by far).
[114] A great and developed industry in Hellenistic and Roman Egypt, see Marangou 1976.

and Imperial times up to and beyond Late Antiquity.[115] A telling early example is constituted by the two workshops in Athens, with more than 50 slaves employed, inherited by the famous 4th century BC orator, Demosthenes, which produced couches and swords inlaid with ivory, each workshop consuming at least two *minae* of ivory per month.[116]

However, just as the Maurusian forests had been depleted of citrus trees by the third quarter of the 1st century AD, so Pliny records that the North African provinces had by his time ceased to yield large tusks, these being now available only from India, developing into an alternative supply of Roman ivory.[117] Indeed, this question of a shift in supply would explain why Statius and Martial writing in the later 1st century AD, as well as Juvenal in the early 2nd century AD, all refer to Indian ivory.

Moreover, although there is a tendency in the writings of the later ancient authors, from the 4th century AD onwards, to confuse Africa beyond Egypt with India,[118] the literary references of the High Empire are corroborated by the mid-1st century AD *Periplus Maris Erythraei* (abbreviated *Periplus*),[119] being a seagoing merchant's guide to ports of trade in the Indian Ocean, which informs us that good quality tusks could be obtained not only from the ivory-rich areas south of Roman Egypt or beyond, in Axum and Azania (present-day Tanzania), but also from India.[120] In fact, the ivory trade with India is, by a rare stroke of luck, attested in detail on a papyrus of the mid-second century AD, which records how the ship *Hermapollon* carried, merely as one small part of its cargo, nearly four tonnes of ivory (uncarved, divided into whole tusks and fragments) back from Muziris in Kerala, South India, to Egypt.[121] Thus, even though the ancient authors were often confused as to the origins of ivory in general, the important point here is that we know it was obtained in great quantities via both the old channels from Africa *and* via new channels from India, no later than the mid-1st century AD. Indeed, tortoiseshell widely used alongside citrus wood and ivory for the embellishment of furniture was also obtained via ports in the Indian Ocean.[122]

Significantly, there is a story in the contentious *Historia Augusta*, variously dated late 3rd–late 4th century AD,[123] about emperor Aurelian obtaining two ten-foot tusks of Indian ivory in AD 273 (from Firmus, the Egyptian pretender), of which he intended to make a throne for a temple image of Jupiter, but which ended up being used for a couch.[124] Obviously, thrones and couches are other kinds of furniture that ivory could be used for as ornamental legs, armrests, structural supports, or for plating with veneer, in addition to tables.

Accordingly, citrus wood tables with nondescript supports had been in great demand among the Romans from no later than the 2nd quarter of the 1st century BC, while the literary evidence (and a find from Pompeii, as we shall see below) suggests that a new development more than a 125 years later, under Nero (AD 54–68), was that the already excessively expensive tabletops now became fitted with ivory legs. In consequence, it was exorbitantly priced composite products such as these tables which must have prompted the establishment of the *collegium* of *negotiatores eborarii et citriarii* no later than the rule of Hadrian. These were neither the first nor the only group of people involved in trade in these commodities to organise themselves, though.

[115] Rodziewicz 1968; 1971; Barnett 1982: 56–72; Lapatin 2001: 46–7, 120, 128; 2015: 171–9, pls. 146–66; St. Clair 2003: 7–37.
[116] Dem. XXVII.30–33.
[117] Pliny *NH*, VIII.4.
[118] Mayerson 1993.
[119] For a recent overview of research on this key source, see Seland 2010: 13–15 for a brief overview, Marcotte 2012 for the most plausible hypothesis on the provenance of the extant manuscript, and Romanis 2016 on its origin in an ancient 'travelogue tradition,' the latter summarising that the text 'was written for (and read by) an audience of Alexandrian merchants, financiers and prospective Indian Ocean sailors' by one of their own number (p. 106). On *periploi* in Antiquity more generally, Olshausen 2013.
[120] *Periplus* 3, 6, 7, 10, 17, 49, 56. A trade in, and, hence, taxing of, ivory being attested at what is most likely to have been Alexandria: *Dig.* XXXIX.4.16.7, *ebur*; this so-called 'Alexandrian tariff' to be treated more thoroughly in chapter six.
[121] *P. Vindob. G.* 40,822 (= *SB* XVIII, 13,167), *verso ii*, l. 5ff. See chapter six for an extensive treatment. This document henceforth referred to as the 'Muziris Papyrus.'
[122] For the furniture, e.g., Mart. *Epigr.*, IX.59, XII.66; for the sources of tortoise shell: *Periplus* 3, 6, 7, 10, 13, 17, 30, 56, 63. Richter 1966: 126; Croom 2007: 27–8.
[123] Useful summaries of the scholarship on the *Historia Augusta* and the vexed questions of its dating and single or multiple authors can be found in Gurney and Gurney 1998 and den Hengst 2010.
[124] *SHA*, 'Firmus,' 3–5.

An inscription dated to the mid-2nd century AD, from outside the city walls of Rome on the Via Appia, reveals the existence of a communal burial ground owned by the *citr<i>arii Neapolitani*. On this piece of land owned collectively by the association, which might well have constituted a formal *collegium*, one member donated part of his own plot to two of his freedmen, presumably skilled labourers of his.[125] Most likely, the *citriarii* were implicitly *fabri*, that is, specialised cabinetmakers working with the chic citrus wood. Evidently, these craftsmen felt the need to differentiate themselves from other groups of *citriarii* in the capital, thus styling themselves 'the ones with ties to Neapolis' in the vicinity of Rome's old deep-sea port and commercial hub, Puteoli.

The ownership of communal property by these *citriarii Neapolitani* in Rome must have been necessitated by permanent business activities of theirs in this most important of markets. This could have been either in the simple form of a warehouse outlet or in the more elaborate guise of a showroom and sales office, a *statio* or *officina*,[126] with accompanying burial facilities on the Via Appia for those of their members who came to reside permanently in the capital. In a similar movement, Tyrian émigré merchants and shippers decided to establish a *statio* in Rome around AD 170, successfully competing against an older *statio* of their fellow countrymen in Puteoli.[127]

Moreover, an early clustering of *fabri* and *politores eborarii* is attested by epigraphy, revealing that six of the ten ivory craftsmen for which there is evidence in ancient Rome were clustered to the north, in the very same neighbourhood near the later *Porta Salaria* of the Aurelian Wall,[128] all except one dated to the 1st century BC and the last to the end of that century.[129] Interestingly, Pliny adds to this list a famous female painter and engraver of ivory from the early years of the 1st century BC, as well.[130] At least two of these late Republican *eborarii* appear to have been clients of senatorial and equestrian families doing business in the African provinces, and, thus, providing these families with the means to both import ivory to Rome as well as process it, and, plausibly but sadly unattested, sell it.[131] The one undated epitaph of a *negotiator eborarius* that we do have, though, was set up in Capena, Etruria, some 30 km from Rome,[132] attesting the widespread networks of traders in ivory, reaching considerably beyond the confines of the capital itself. Moreover, archaeological evidence from the northeast slope of the Palatine Hill has revealed the existence of an ivory and bone workshop somewhere nearby, operating continuously throughout the 1st–5th century AD.[133]

Consequently, the contemporary evidence for craftsmen and traders working and dealing in the same materials, but, significantly, only one *or* the other, serves to emphasise the highly specialised *raison d'être* of the association of ivory *and* citrus wood traders, which we shall now subject to a more thorough study:[134]

Lex of the *collegium of negotiatores eborarii et citriarii (CIL VI, 33,885)*[135]

(*ll. 1-3, preamble*) Julius] Aelianus has granted right of use of the four-columned clubhouse (*schola tetrastylus*) [...] where there assembles from the traders [...] to the citrus wood and ivory (traders).

125 *CIL* VI, 9258; elucidated in Rodriguez Adrados 1989.
126 Holleran 2012: 150–1; Terpstra 2013: 130–47.
127 *CIG* 5853, see chapter six.
128 Vergantini 1987: 93–94. Cf. Gatti 1905 for the layout of the area. The epitaphs excavated in the area are: *CIL* VI, 7885, 33,423, 37,374, 37,793; while *CIL* VI, 30,907 identifies this as the site of the *eborarii ab Hercule Primigenio*: *CIL* VI, 7655; *AE* 1990: 76. For the shrine, cf. Richardson 1992: 188, *s.v.* 'Hercules Primigenius.'
129 The four attested from other parts of the city are: *CIL* VI, 9375, 9397; *AE* 1968: 37; and *ICUR* X, 26,558.
130 Pliny *NH*, XXXV.40.
131 Tassini 1994: 690, regarding *CIL* VI, 9397, 33,423.
132 *CIL* XI, 3948.
133 St. Clair 2003: 38–55. Some of the products of the *eborarii* of Rome would have been ivory dolls, miniature chests, combs and handles, such as those unearthed in later 2nd century AD graves in and around Rome, cf. Bedini 1995: nos. 42–3, 47, 57–8, 67.
134 A more formalistic analysis of this association's rules and reguluations is available in Evers: forthcoming.
135 Based on Erno's Latin edition (2015: 304–8) and mainly in agreement with Bäumler's highly useful German translation (2014: 64–66). The above version represents this author's own feeble attempt at a much-needed English translation, but hopefully a more qualified scholar will soon take up the challenge.

(*ll. 4-6, from the top of the second column onwards*) Likewise], it is decided that if anyone but an ivory or citrus wood trader is admitted into this association (*collegium*) by deceit of the officers (*curatores*), the officers should for this [rea]son be struck from the membership list (*album*) by the member assembly (*ordo*).
(*ll. 6-7*) In any case, the officers shall be under obligation to report beforehand to the president(s) (*quinquennalis/-es*) about the one [wh]o is to be admitted.
(*ll. 8-9*) Likewise [it is decided] that on the first of January, a New Year's gift of five *denarii* (should be provided) out of our coffers (*arca*) by the officers, four by number, in their [year], and must-cake, date, Carian fig and pe[ar should be provided.
(*ll. 9-11*) Likewise] on the 24th of January, [on the birthday of] Hadrian Augustus, cash-gifts of five *denarii* should be provided and it is decided that [bread and] wine [and] hot water is to be presented by the officers to all those, who shall have come to dine at the clubhouse.
(*ll. 12-14*) Likewise ... on the birthday of] Julius Aelianus, cash-gifts of three *denarii* should be provided out of the coffers and it is decided that [bread and wine and hot water] is to be presented by the officers to all those, who shall have come to dine at the clubhouse.
(*ll. 14-15*) Likewise ... on the birthday of] Julius Flaccus, the son (of Julius Aelianus), cash-gifts of three *denarii* should be provided out of the coffers and it is decided that [bread and wine and hot water] is to be presented by the officers to [all] those, who shall have come to dine at the clubhouse.
(*ll. 16-17*) Likewise ...] cash-gifts of three *denarii* should be provided out of the coffers and bread and wine and hot water (is to be presented by the officers) to all those, [who] shall have [come to dine at the clubhouse]
(*ll. 17-18*) Likewise it is decided that a proper dinner, on the 11th of August, the day of [Hadrian Augustus'] accession [...] five [...] cash-gifts should be provided by the officers, four by number, in their year.
(*l. 19*) Likewise it is decided...] *denarii* [...] should be distributed every year.
(*ll. 19-20*) Likewise there should be [four officers every] year according to the order of the membership list.
(*ll. 20-21*) Likewise it is decided that [...] they should receive all privileges in their year (of office).
(*ll. 22-24*) Every year] the officers should divide into equal [parts that which remains] in the coffers of the association (*corpus*) [or, if] they repay [anything too late], one per cent is to be paid by the officers every [month.]
(*ll. 24-25*) Likewise it is decided that those admitted [...] should not stand (for office) in the same year, [and in the same manner the expenses] for both should be paid [...
(*ll. 25-26, fragmentary end of the second column*) Likewise it is decided [that whoever should be admitted] pays into the coffers ? *denarii* [...

Taking a closer look at this charter, one clause in particular stands out because it is unique: the *lex* states at the top of its preserved second column that 'if anyone but an ivory or citrus wood trader is admitted into this association (*collegium*) by deceit of the officers (*curatores*), the officers should for this [rea]son be struck from the membership list (*album*) by the member assembly (*ordo*).'[136] In addition, although new members were only accepted at the personal responsibility of these four annually elected *curatores*, candidates still had to be approved by one or more president(s), *quinquennalis/-es*.[137]

In light of the use of the term *ordo* in this specific context, as well as among similar and contemporary *collegia* more generally, we may infer that this association was organised around a formal member assembly, an *ordo*, with power of majority vote and decision-making over members, officers and president(s) alike. What the lost first column of the inscription must have stated about other activities and prerogatives of the assembly and officers we will probably never know, but the extant half on its own speaks of strong institutions for private ordering within the *collegium* itself.[138]

[136] *CIL* VI, 33,885, ll. 4–7: *si alius quam negotiator eborarius aut citriarius* [*p*]*er* / [*fr*]*audem curatorum in hoc collegium adlectus esset uti curatores eius* / [*cau*]*sa ex albo raderentur ab ordine debebunt utique curatores de eo* / [*que*]*m adlecturi fuerint ante ad quinq(uennales) re*[*fe*]*rre*. Demoted officials generally, though, are also known from other *collegia*, cf. Tran 2007a: 124f.
[137] Although their official title was 'five-year presidents,' Royden 1989 has shown that their time in office could also be shorter, for instance, a tenure of three years.
[138] Regarding associative *ordines* in general: Tran 2006: 335–46; on this specific *ordo*, Tran 2007a: 124. Unfortunately, we cannot tell how many members this *collegium* had.

This is, in fact, the only extant case of such explicit regulations of exclusivity ensuring strict control of members' occupations from anywhere in the ancient Mediterranean. In other words, the membership was a very select group, indeed, most other associations exhibiting a rather more relaxed attitude to members of other backgrounds, allowing entry by those whom they would consider beneficial for the common good.[139] At the same time, enrolment must have been attractive enough to draw in applicants ready to pay a price for entering the association, seeing as newly admitted members had to pay an entrance-fee, could not stand for offices in their first year, and might have had to pay for their own costs during this initial year on top of that.[140] Furthermore, members were in due course elected *curatores* according to rotation based on the order of the membership list, *album*,[141] and in their year of office they seem to have been obliged to provide food and drinks for at least five celebrations[142] at the 'four-columned club house' (*schola tetrastylus*) provided for gatherings (*convenire*) by their patron, Julius Aelianus, who retained ownership of the building, though, merely giving the association 'right of use,' *ius*.[143]

The six stipulated annual celebrations are significant, moreover, for in addition to the standard patron's and patron's son's birthdays, as well as a New Year's Day party on January 1st, the *collegium* was also required to commemorate both the birthday of the emperor Hadrian and his accession to the purple.[144] Not only do the inclusion of the latter days in the calendar of the association reveal aspirations to wider civic recognition, the stipulated expenditures at each banquet also reveal a subtle understanding of hierarchy in imperial Rome. Thus, whereas the two dates associated with the patron's family entailed cash distributions of three *denarii* to each member from the association treasury (called both *arca nostra* and *arca corporis*), the dates related to the emperor were to be marked by hand-outs of five *denarii*, and unlike all the other banquets consisting of bread, wine, and hot water, the day of Hadrian's accession was to be celebrated with a proper dinner, *cena recta*.[145]

Finally, at the end of every year, the *curatores* were to distribute the remaining common funds in the treasury equally among all members, possibly providing the pretext for a seventh celebration, or face a monthly fine of one per cent of the amount until they did so.[146] Significantly, and unlike some other well-documented contemporary *collegia*, the association of citrus wood and ivory traders was a remarkably egalitarian institution. Not only were all members to receive equal portions of money back from the club coffers, they also received the same cash hand-outs at celebrations, and all who attended were to be treated to the same food and drink—thus, neither *curatores* nor *quinquennales*, more well-to-do traders or well-connected members, were to receive any kind of benefits marking them out as of superior rank in the eyes of the *ordo*.[147] In consequence, both individual members and the two different lines of trade generally were fused together by this egalitarian principle during a number of annual events, particularly the six fixed celebrations, suitable for affirming and strengthening the social and professional ties between the entire membership.[148]

In short, the *collegium* of *negotiatores eborarii et citriarii* appears to have been a select club with strict restrictions on membership, an up-to-date list of members (*album*), a club house (*schola*), four annual *curatores* with financial obligations, one or more president(s), an autonomous assembly (*ordo*), at least six fixed annual celebrations, and money being paid into the club coffers (*arca*) every year and being spent again on special hand-outs and final dividends. All in all, this would have served to formalise and fuse into one two otherwise distinct occupational networks of traders in Rome by employing the institution

[139] Tran 2007a: 122–3. Also Ausbüttel 1982: 37–8 and Liu 2013: 360–61. Obviously, however, other assocations also strove to exclude outsiders from their internal activities, such as those who were not proper members or, in some cases, slaves.
[140] *CIL* VI, 33,885, ll. 24–26.
[141] *CIL* VI, 33,885, l. 20.
[142] *CIL* VI, 33,885, ll. 8–9, 10–11, 12–14, 14–15, 16–17; the standard formula, repeated with slight variations, being: *a curatoribus praestari placuit panem et vinum et caldam*. Office might have entailed other expenses, too, but due to the fragmentary nature of the inscription this is uncertain.
[143] *CIL* VI, 33,885, ll. 1–3.
[144] *CIL* VI, 33,885, ll. 8–18.
[145] Bäumler 2014: 75, 78–9.
[146] *CIL* VI, 33,885, ll. 19, 22–24.
[147] Bäumler 2014: 72–3, 75.
[148] Bäumler 2014: 77–9, inspired by Luhmann 1969.

of a Roman *collegium* to 'bridge' access to one another's networks, increasing the number of weak ties which might potentially be of help to any individual member.[149] Furthermore, uniting in a formal *collegium* with rules enforced by penalties (being internal 'norms and effective sanctions') and regular meetings of the member assembly as well as convivial gatherings (constituting 'information channels' in making both official dissemination of information and gossiping possible) would only have increased the potential for regular business and collaboration between members (creating external 'obligations and expectations') by generating 'trustworthiness.'[150] Thus, it promoted circumstances highly conducive to the forging of 'relational contracts' between the traders, which would have been economically beneficial to the members, but it did not, most emphatically, regulate or intervene in their economic activities, which were considered external to the association itself.[151] Moreover, we can tell that they also managed as joint networks to exercise 'linking' with a more wealthy individual, Julius Aelianus, whose patronage of their *collegium* entailed lending them a house and economic support (albeit apparently not in the guise of a perpetual endowment to finance their activities, as some patrons did, as we shall see below), and possibly other things which we cannot know.[152]

On the whole, though, the benefits to be had from cooperation and trustworthy dealings, both within the two trades and between them, made the upgrade of simpler occupational networks into the trust-generating institution of a highly regulated *collegium* a prudent development. Otherwise, due to the costly nature of the raw materials required, expensive expert craftsmanship needed to work the citrus wood, carve the ivory, and fit it together into composite pieces of furniture, as well as the necessary commercial ties to elite buyers, losses could mount very quickly in case of fraud or freewheeling among the traders. Specifically, we know that by Pliny's time bone often acted as an easily available substitute for ivory, making it a vital concern for *negotiatores eborarii* to secure a steady supply to sell on and perhaps to avoid skilful bone carvings being passed off as ivory to affluent but inexpert buyers.[153] Even more so, the issues of supply and forgery were a concern for the *negotiatores citriarii*, for not only did the scarcity of citrus wood tempt people to veneer an inconspicuous wooden core with a thin, expensive outer layer, but starting under Nero cheap horn and tortoise-shell first began being processed and painted to resemble the dear citrus, making it possible to construct fake citrus couches which had nothing to do with the real thing, not even sporting the 'borrowed feathers' of veneering.[154]

In summary, this particular *collegium* is a prime example of an organisation shaped by the nature of the products its members dealt in, that is, of a vocational dependency and associational bonding made necessary and opportune exactly because of the existence of a strong demand for citrus tables with ivory legs and similar kinds of composite furniture.

Beyond the mirror: the cultural biography of an ivory statuette

Traditionally, this is more or less what it has been possible to say on the subject of the *negotiatores eborarii et citriarii*, their *collegium* and its trade in expensive Roman furniture. However, as it happens, an archaeological find from Pompeii—traditionally misinterpreted and therefore for decades treated in isolation as a unique category of evidence—adds an entirely new dimension to the knowledge we have so far acquired from the literary and epigraphic sources about this trade.

[149] Such a set of weak ties organising a large group of artisans was probably employed by a high-ranking magistrate of the *collegium* of builders and carpenters in Rome, who contracted for public works, making it easier for him to sub-contract within the framework of the *collegium*; cf. Liu 2013: 357–8 on *CIL* VI, 9034. Indeed, such an argument is central to Hawkins 2016: 68–129.

[150] Compare on this specific association Hawkins 2012: 192; Hawkins 2016: 116–17, 120–21.

[151] In theory, of course, such stipulations might have been contained in the lost first column of the charter, but no other unambiguous evidence of a Roman *collegium* with such rules exist. For the alleged 'association' of Tebtynis in Roman Egypt with such rules, see chapter six.

[152] Patrons could defend the interests of their *collegium* of choice in various ways: e.g. Tran 2014 (on *CIL* XIV, 4144, and his nn63–4 on *CIL* VI, 29,814–15) and Liu 2013: 364 (on *CIL* VI, 1872).

[153] Pliny *NH*, VIII.4.

[154] Pliny *NH*, XVI.84.

In sketching the 'cultural biography' of this artefact by enquiring about its origins, makers, original purpose, later adaptations and changing cultural markers,[155] it will be demonstrated in the following that: 1) contemporary South Asia also had a significant production of furniture adorned with carved ivory, likewise organised to a considerable extent by comparable Indian associations; 2) Indian ivory furniture decorations travelled along the trade routes, reaching Pompeii and Rome no later than the time of Nero; and 3) carved Indian ivories became integrated into the different context of Roman furniture, inspiring new fashions which bloomed in the late 1st–early 2nd century AD. In the process, what follows will expand the scope of the analysis to engage with source material from Early Historic India, Gandhara and Afghanistan, to put the trade and its organisation in the proper perspective.

The item in question is a small statuette of a woman in the nude, flanked by two small attending maids, partly covered by her jewellery and braided hair in characteristically Indian style, being carved out of ivory, 24.5 centimetres tall, and almost entirely intact after restoration [**Figures 2–3**].[156] The eruption of Mount Vesuvius both preserved the artefact remarkably well[157] and provides a handy *ante quem* for its arrival in Pompeii of AD 79. The statuette was discovered in October 1938, in what is today labelled as *Regio* I, *Insula* 8, *Casa* 5 (i.e. I.8.5), between the *Casa dei Qattro Stili* and the *Via dell'Abbondanza*. Note that although the find-spot of the statuette is often erroneously reported as being the more famous adjacent 'House of the Four Styles,' this does most emphatically not fit with the description originally penned by its excavator, Amadeo Maiuri. Shortly afterwards, in 1939, it was published as a handle of some sort, based on a hole penetrating the figure from the crown of the head to the waist for holding a tang [**Figure 4**], either to support a decorative or sacred symbol, or, as it was suggested, for later adapted use of the figurine as a handle for something practical 'which could be a mirror.'[158] Moreover, Maiuri considered it probable that its archaeological context, the *domus* it was found in, was to be interpreted as Neronian, providing a tentative *post quem* of AD 54.[159]

While the exact identification and artistic style of the female figure was the subject of some debate in ensuing years, nobody thought of seriously questioning what had merely been a hypothetical assumption in Maiuri's original article, namely that its *post-Indian* function *could* have been that of a mirror handle. Thus, a note in the *Annual Bibliography of Indian Archaeology* for the year 1938 stated that the 'suggestion that [Maiuri's] find may have been the handle of a metal mirror seems to us extremely plausible,'[160] a view since perpetuated in the standard works on Indian archaeology and ivories which put this object down simply as 'probably a mirror handle.' Two remarkably similar ivory finds from Ter[161] and contemporary 1st century AD Bhokardan,[162] in Maharashtra, India, were subsequently also interpreted as 'probably mirror handles' with reference to the function of the Pompeian specimen.[163]

However, while it is true that an ivory handle in the shape of an anthropomorphic figure would be reminiscent of somewhat similar mirror handles from the Ancient Near East,[164] Pharaonic Egypt,[165]

155 Kopytoff 1986: 66.

156 On display at *Museo archeologico Nazionale di Napoli*, in the 'Gabinetto Segreto,' inv.no. 149425.

157 Nonetheless, the entire archaeological context had been disturbed, and the objects partly damaged, by agricultural work in the overlying fields which used to cover the ancient remains; cf. Maiuri 1938–39: 111.

158 Maiuri 1938–39: 111f, 'quale poteva essere uno specchio.'

159 Maiuri 1938–39: 115.

160 Vogel 1940: 4. Likewise the stylistic study of the figurine by D'Ancona 1950 neither touches upon the actual function of the object nor questions it.

161 Barrett 1960: 8–9, pls. 10–11; Dehejia 1972: pl. 85; Chandra 1960; Deshpande 1961; more thoroughly described by During Caspers 1981: 349ff. On stylistic grounds, Barret is inclined to date it to the later 1st century AD, while Chandra and Deshpande opts for early- to mid-2nd century AD. In addition, the site has yielded earlier as well as later ivory, bone and stone figurines, although much less skilfully carved: Dwivedi 1976: 63, pl. 38 (bone, 1st century BC, 16 cm); 99, pl. 70 (ivory, 5th century AD); and Chandra 1960: 8–9, fig. 2, augmented by the identification of the correct material in Deshpande 1961: 56 (white soft stone, mid-1st century AD).

162 Deo 1974: 188–90, dated to *c.* 1st century AD based on stratigraphy. Dwivedi 1976: 67, pls. 43–44. Mehendale 1993: 530ff.

163 Cf. especially Ghosh 1990, I, 348, 18:5; and II, 74f, *s.v.* 'Bhokardan' and, 436, 'Ter;' as well as Dwivedi 1976: 65 (Pompeii), 81 (Ter), while no comment is made on the function of the Bhokardan piece, 67, although it is compared stylistically to the Pompeii figurine, but its excavator, Deo 1974: 188, also suggests that its original use was as a mirror handle.

164 Albenda 1985.

165 Bianchi 1985.

Figure 2
Ivory statuette from Pompeii, front; height 24.5 cm. Museo archeologico Nazionale di Napoli, in the 'Gabinetto Segreto,' inv. no. 149425. Photograph by the author.

Figure 3
Same as Figure 2, back. Photograph by the author.

Figure 4
Same as Figure 2, detail of hole penetrating the crown of the head down to the waist. Photograph by the author.

Archaic and Classical Greece,[166] and, thus, by extension also the Hellenistic Mediterranean,[167] Etruscan[168] and Roman Italy,[169] this can only be relevant for the later, post-Indian use of the statuette in its new Roman context. Accordingly, Maiuri's hypothesis about a subsequent Roman adapted use of the ivory figurine as a mirror handle tells us nothing about the object's original purpose, which must be found within the context of Indian art history.

On that note, we do in fact have a pretty good idea about what Indian ivory and bone handles looked like around the turn of the Common Era: at Nevasa, lying close in-between Ter and Bhokardan, have

[166] Congdon 1985.
[167] See the ivory (142β) and bone handles (142γ), assumed to be for mirrors, from Hellenistic Amorgos, but most likely of Alexandrian workmanship, in Marangou 2002: 139–41. I thank Christian A. Thomsen for this reference.
[168] de Grummond 1985.
[169] Graeven 1903: no. 50, especially cat. nos. 39–40.

been found three simple conventional handles;[170] from Anuradhapura on Sri Lanka one ivory handle mirror stand;[171] from Taxila in Gandhara, one ivory and thirteen bone handles, all with traditional grips and simple decorations;[172] and from Tillya Tepe in Bactria can be adduced three actual mirrors with intact grips, two with squat handles and one with a stand handle.[173] While none of these handles[174] look anything like the Pompeii, Ter, and Bhokardan pieces, they do, however, closely resemble the mirror handles displayed in the Indian influenced decorations on the 1st century AD bone and ivory plaques from Begram, Afghanistan—the ambiguous archaeological context of which will be explained below.[175]

Accordingly, the immensely more intricately carved, three-dimensional ivory figurines from Pompeii, Ter, and Bhokardan, were not originally mirror handles in their Indian context. In fact, this was pointed out with reference to the piece from Pompeii as early as 1979 by During Caspers, comparing it with the mirror handles represented in the Begram Ivories.[176] Further, she went on to point out that the Pompeian figurine has a slanted and sickle-shaped base which would invariably make it topple over if unsupported, unlike a mirror stand, and that its qualities as a handheld handle are very much lacking, seeing as the highly detailed carving's protuberances and hollows ruin any chance of a proper grip. In short, the figurine would make for an exceedingly unwieldy and impractical mirror stand or handle, and, crucially, it neither looks like a contemporary South Asian ivory or bone handle, nor does it show any signs of wear, as one would otherwise expect from a handle in daily use.[177]

On closer inspection, moreover, the statuette displays some odd features: a wedge-shaped opening is cut through the garment of one of the attendants on the lower back, coming through on the front left next to the statuette's crossed legs; a spike of hair projects from the left side of her head extending horizontally, but broken off;[178] and, finally, the bottom of the base is carved with a small symbol resembling a trident [**Figure 5**], likely the auspicious symbol of the *trishula* used as some kind of craftsman's mark.[179]

Comparing these three 1st century AD carved Indian statuettes, a number of observations come to mind. The figurines from Pompeii and Bhokardan both have a central female depicted wearing a waist girdle and shin bracelets, standing with legs crossed and being flanked by two smaller attendants. While the Pompeii piece is 24.5 centimetres tall, the extant plinth-to-waist half of the Bhokardan piece is 12.5 centimetres, thus making for the same original height of about 25 centimetres.[180] Both had a central hole drilled from the crown of the head to the waist, the mark still being visible in the fracture of the Bhokardan piece.[181] However, whereas it is clear that the Pompeii statuette was pierced a couple of centimetres above the plinth, it is impossible to tell with certainty whether anything (a clamp or fastening) went into the open, carved-out spaces between the legs and attendants of the Bhokardan piece,[182] although a small hollowed out gap between the lower left leg of the central figure and the attendant on its right actually makes up a similar but artistically integrated wedge-shaped hollow. Neither is it, for obvious reasons, possible to

170 Sankalia 1960: 469, ivory handles, nos. 9–10, fig. 197; 458, bone handle, no. 19, fig. 194; 2nd BC–2nd AD.
171 Coningham 2006, II: 568–9, 601, pl. 10.1, 611, fig. 10.1; 2nd BC–2nd AD.
172 Marshall 1951: 658, nos. 43–47 (bone), pl. 203; 659, nos. 48–55 (bone), no. 56 (ivory), pl. 199. Dated 1st century BC–1st century AD. Bone handle no. 55 was even found together with a tanged bronze mirror (no. 208, p. 584f), rendering it more than likely that this short and simple piece, only decorated with incised bands, was the relevant mirror handle.
173 Sarianidi 1985: no. 3.71 (ivory), no. 5.12 (bone or ivory), no. 6.30 (ivory); 1st century AD.
174 As regards tanged bronze mirrors themselves excavated throughout South Asia, a handy list is provided in de Puma 1991: 100.
175 Hackin 1954, no. 34 a.5, fig. 9; and Hackin 1939, no. 329a-b [183] figs. 175–6.
176 Paper given in 1979, published in 1981; During Caspers 1981: 346.
177 During Caspers 1981: 348–49.
178 Following, in the main, During Caspers 1981: 351.
179 Maiuri 1938–39: 112, thought that this symbol looks like the Kharoshthi letter 'śi,' and this view has been unanimously accepted in later studies. However, although this is strictly speaking possible, 'śi' resembles '∩' with a smaller single-stroke vowel mark '/' through the apex, but the mark in question has corners curving inward at the top like an 'm', not merely rounded or angular shoulders, and the middle is bisected by two strokes, not one. On formal grounds, then, it looks more like a carved *trishula*. While the Kharoshthi marks of the Begram Ivories are no surprise (see below, but note that these letters were made with ink, whereas geometrical symbols were incised), being so close to Gandhara (and the Brahmi marks being explained by their diffusion way beyond the Northwest), the use of the Kharoshthi script in Satavahana workshops would be somewhat surprising (Kharoshthi inscriptions having been found no closer to Satavahana territory than Mathura, more than 400 kilometres to the north; e.g., Konow 1929: no. 15).
180 Deo 1974: 190.
181 Deo 1974: 188.
182 Mehendale 1993: 536.

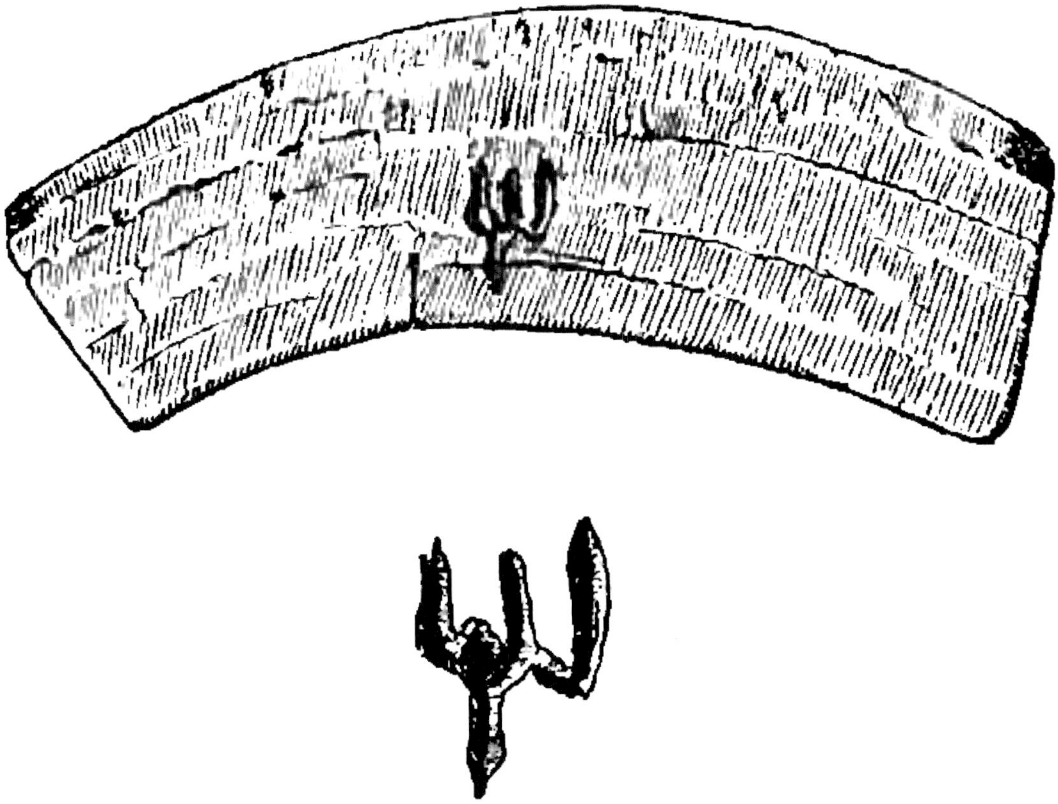

Figure 5
Drawing of Pompeii figurine's base. Source: Maiuri 1938–9: 112, fig. 1.

tell whether the missing upper part also displayed a horizontal projection (hair spike) from the side of the head.

As regards comparison with the Ter statuette, the latter appears, superficially at least, to differ somewhat from the other two: its pose is more frontal due to the legs not being crossed, its jewellery and hair is similar but more simple, it has no attendants, and, significantly, its height from the fracture below the knees to the top of the head is only a little more than 16 cm, thus, taking account of missing shins, feet, and plinth, putting its original height at some 20 cm, somewhat less than its counterparts.[183] However, like the other two it is pierced from the crown of the head to the waist, and like the Pompeian statuette it has a projection from the left side of its head.[184] The Ter specimen also has perforations slightly above what would have been the plinth, in this case two holes penetrating the upper calves, and a third hole on the flank penetrating the garment covering the left thigh; the left of the calf-holes as well as the thigh-hole both containing corroded fragments of iron pins. Seeing as the figure is carved with equal care on all sides for all-round display, these metals fastenings were previously a bit of a puzzle, and one way to explain them has been to argue that although originally a mirror handle, the statuette without mirror was later attached to the side of a toiletry box or similar.[185]

What were these three masterfully carved ivory figurines, then, found as far West as Pompeii, but manufactured in the 1st century AD kingdom of the Satavahanas (modern Maharashtra and Andra Pradesh), to judge from the finds at Ter and Bhokardan,[186] when, as should hopefully be apparent by now,

[183] During Caspers 1981: 349, and Mehendale 1993: 534, both follow Barret 1960: 9, in giving the extant height as 5 inches, i.e., *c.* 13 cm. However, Deshpande 1961: 55, studied the figurine in person and corrects Barret's measurement to 16.4 cm.
[184] During Caspers 1981: 349.
[185] Dwivedi 1976: 81, repeating Deshpande 1961: 55.
[186] The Satavahana kingdom will be described in more detail below.In the 1st century AD, Ter and Bhokardan were key cities in the core area of the western part of the Satavahana realm. Add to this our knowledge of expert and organised ivory carvers in the employ of the Satavahana king

they were certainly not mirror handles? Based on the two figurines known to her in 1979, the Pompeii and Ter specimens, During Caspers' ingenious solution was based on the carved fittings extraneous to the depictions in themselves, and is also applicable to the later inclusion of the Bhokardan piece in the group:[187] what is supposed to provide vertical support (the holes drilled vertically through the core of all three), while requiring a backwards fastening (the lower back apertures in the Ter and Pompeii figurines, and the possibility of attaching a clamp in the hollows of the Bhokardan piece), while the object itself is to be visible from all sides? Her simple answer was: 'a part of a piece of furniture, such as the leg of a small table, or as a support of a standing tray or dish.'[188]

Elisabeth During Caspers herself preferred to interpret the ivory figurines as 'caryatides,' four of which would have supported a low table or similar upper structure as legs positioned at each corner. Accordingly, the ivory statuettes would have been part of groups (with their exact place in the overall composition indicated by a fitter's mark underneath, like the *trishula* underneath the base of the Pompeii figurine, as known from the Begram ivories treated below)[189] supporting a tabletop, seat, or other superstructure with their heads, being kept in place by backward stretchers, preventing them from sliding outwards under pressure of weight and potentially collapsing the entire construction.[190] Later studies have conformed to her conclusions, now referring to the function of the statuettes not as mirror handles but as the legs of some kind of furniture, most often tables or footstools.[191]

The Indian statuette found in 1938 at Pompeii was no 'mirror handle,' then, and neither were the two ivory figurines found at Ter and Bhokardan. They are, instead, rare surviving remnants of ancient South Indian furniture. However, their identification as Indian table- or, more generally, furniture legs, is slightly problematic, for a survey of ancient Indian furniture as depicted in reliefs from Bharhut, Sanchi, Amaravati, Nagarjunakonda, Gandhara, and Mathura, as well as in the murals of Ajanta, reveals that throughout the entire area encompassed by these sites, and the timespan of the 2nd century BC–5th century AD, no such anthropomorphic furniture *legs* of any kind are to be found.[192] Consequently, this hypothesis does not quite seem to fit the available evidence, and therefore we shall have to examine what other function they might have served within the context of Indian furniture.

Fortunately, though, excavations at Begram in Afghanistan, mentioned above for its ivory and bone plaques, can shed further light on the subject. Begram is situated at a strategic and commercial crossroads, lying on a verdant plain just south of the most accessible routes over the otherwise daunting Hindu Kush range (either West via Bamiyan or East via the Khawak Pass) to Bactria, and being connected southwards to the route via Kabul and Ghazni to Arachosia, as well as towards the southeast by way of the Khyber Pass to Gandhara and India beyond. Excavations conducted in the late 1930s discovered not only a major urban settlement, but also a compound with two sealed-off rooms stacked with select items hailing from as far away as the Roman Empire and China.[193]

Arguably most famous of the lot is the ivory and bone plaques which had originally been attached to wooden frames to produce lavishly decorated furniture in a heavily Indian-influenced style.[194] In addition, it is significant that Roman bronze sculptures, fine glassware, alabaster vessels, porphyry pieces and plaster moulds (most likely associated with metalworking, see below), were found together

in the later 1st century BC, and there can be little doubt that these ivory figurines must be ascribed to the Satavahanas.

[187] The latter piece having afterwards been included in a comparative study by Mehendale 1993.

[188] During Caspers 1981: 351.

[189] This is the most reasonable role of marks in Kharoshthi and Brahmi known from the complex ivory ensembles of Begram, each consisting of numerous individually fitted pieces, cf. Mehendale 2001: 486f; and Simpson 2014: 16–7, who lists six Kharoshthi and two Brahmi letters in black ink, as well as six geometrical incised symbols (however, more marks appear to have been discovered during the original excavations but not properly recorded).

[190] During Caspers 1981: 351–53.

[191] Mehendale 1993: 535; 1997: 4.2.1; 2001: 497; Karttunen 1997; Gupta 2007a: 95; Parker 2008: 163–4; Basu 2010: 63.

[192] Cf. the handy survey in Murthy 1982.

[193] Hackin 1939; 1954. The difficult history of the excavations is admirably summarised by Simpson 2014: 1–9, whereas the subsequent fate of the steadily diminishing collection of artefacts after the outbreak of war in Afghanistan from 1979 onwards is vividly described on pp. 34–38.

[194] Most recently discussed in a comprehensive manner by Mehendale 1997.

so far away from the Mediterranean,[195] in rooms where pieces of Han lacquerware from China were also unearthed.[196] Studies of the Roman glass (1st–early 2nd century AD),[197] Indian ivories (1st century AD)[198] and Han lacquers (2nd quarter of 1st century BC–1st quarter of 1st century AD),[199] although not entirely in agreement, all converge on the 1st century AD, with a recent overview of studies attempting to date the diverse archaeological finds arguing for *c.* 100–25 AD as the years in which the storerooms were sealed.[200]

The nature of this group of objects continues to be a matter of debate, though, because the exact context of the finds is so poorly understood. The traditional hypothesis holds that the rooms represent the royal treasury of the Kushan summer palace in Kapisha, but a more recent interpretation stresses that the link between Begram and Kapisha of the Kushan kings is merely inferred, that the assemblage is unlikely to constitute a royal collection because it can be dated to a relatively short time span in the 1st century AD, and that some of the items, like plaster moulds and uncarved pieces of ivory, were of little intrinsic value in themselves. According to the latter view, then, the rooms would better fit the description of a commercial depot or warehouse, where goods purchased from near and far, or from passing merchants, were stored, together with moulds providing popular Hellenistic motifs for the production of local craftsmen,[201] for instance, ivory and bone carvers. Yet another theory is that the rooms contained the revenue collected from passing caravans by a local customs station.[202] Although the old royal treasury hypothesis can reasonably well be discarded, it is impossible to tell whether the objects were grouped by merchants or tax-collectors, but in either case the striking implication is that numerous specimens of Greco-Roman craftsmanship, none of them exceptional by Mediterranean standards, were being traded at the borders of Central and South Asia, mingling with products from Chinese and Indian workshops.[203]

In addition to the items of the assemblage already mentioned, Begram also yielded a group of ivory objects highly relevant to the matter at hand. Namely, three ivory figurines in almost exactly the same poses and guises as the Satavahana ivory statuettes, only larger (45–56 centimetres)[204] and belonging to a related but still distinguishably different Bactro-Gandharan school of ivory carving.[205] All three of them stand poised on the heads of *makaras* (mythical aquatic monsters of Hinduism[206]) which serve as bases, while one of them carries a turban and vase on her head suitable for an upper attachment, mortise-style; one seems to have the stump of a tenon protruding from her head **[Figure 6]**;[207] and the third has a pronounced sickle-shaped base like the Pompeii and Bhokardan pieces **[Figure 7]**.[208] Moreover, one of the statuettes was found fitted within a frame, being enclosed on the sides by double boards of ivory, the *makara* base resting on a 54 cm iron rod penetrating these walls and projecting beyond them on either

[195] The best recent treatment, well illustrated, being Hiebert and Cambon 2008.

[196] Elisseeff 1954.

[197] Whitehouse 1989. The glass can be traced back to Egypt, Alexandria in particular, based on stylistic analysis. See now also Cambon 2010 and Mairs 2012a.

[198] Mehendale 2001.

[199] Zhang 2011 superseding the dating of Elisseeff 1954.

[200] Simpson 2014: 28.

[201] On the purpose of these moulds, see Richter 1958.

[202] For a historiographical overview and discussion, see the contrasting articles by Mehendale 2008, who argues the former, and Cambon 2008, who argues the latter.

[203] Simpson 2014: 28–9 emphasises the seaborne 'Indo-Roman' trade as the underlying cause for this assembly of diverse artefacts, having arrived up from ports on the Arabian Sea via the Indus River (compare Seland 2010: 50 and Mairs 2012a).

[204] Hackin 1939: nos. 319, 320a, 320b. Best illustrated in Hiebert and Cambon 2008: 162, nos. 147–9. Hackin no. 320a differs slightly from the two other statuettes, though, in that it does not wear a *dhoti* around its waist but rather a tight-clinging gown falling from its shoulders; nor does it wear any elaborate jewellery, only two simple wrist bracelets—arguably this statuette is more 'Greek' in a philhellenic Gandharan style. The most thorough description of the three Begram statuettes is to be found in Mehendale 1997: 4.2.1.

[205] Mehendale 1997: 4.3.4–5; 2001: 486–7, 496. Significantly, Rosen Stone 2008 connects some of the other ivories to something as remote as a South Indian tradition of style and carving. Regarding the debate over styles, however, see now overview in Simpson 2014: 27.

[206] Johnson 2009: *s.v.* 'makara.'

[207] Respectively, Hackin 1939: nos. 319 and 320a. The latter, being best visible in the excellent photograph in Hiebert and Cambon 2008: 162, no. 147.

[208] Hackin 1939: 320b. Mehendale 1997: 4.2.1, pl. 201. Note that the head of this statuette was so damaged that its headdress and possible upper fitting is impossible to reconstruct, see original photos in Hackin 1939: fig. 81; Hackin 1954: fig. 235. Sickle-shaped base best visible in the photograph in Hiebert and Cambon 2008: 162, no. 148.

Figure 6
Begram ivory statuette, height 45 cm; Hackin 1939: no. 320a. Source: Hackin 1954: fig. 234.

Figure 7
Begram ivory statuette, height 45.6 cm; Hackin 1939: no. 320b. Source: Hackin 1954: fig. 235.

Figure 8
Ivory statuette encased in ivory frame at Begram. Source: Hackin 1939: fig. 75 (no. 320a in situ).

side through symmetrically positioned ivory rings and cylinders, ending in round three-tiered stopper-pieces [**Figure 8**].[209]

Now, in light of the fact that the three Begram statuettes compare well with the Pompeii, Ter, and Bhokardan specimens,[210] that the two rooms in which the Begram trove was found yielded numerous other pieces of carved ivory and bone which were part of furniture (most likely chairs in one room, footstools in the other),[211] and that one of the statuettes was actually found incorporated into a larger ivory structure, there can be little doubt that these Begram pieces must also have been intended as some kind of element for ancient South Asian furniture.[212]

Fortunately, other objects from Begram can help us shed a light on the role of the statuettes from Maharashtra and Begram by illuminating the relationship between archaeological finds and preserved ancient depictions of Indian furniture. First of all, there was found next to the statuettes two ivory pieces shaped as elephants, 26–7 centimetres high, wrapping their trunks around a bulbous leg extending below their heads, an iron rod penetrating through them and proceeding below [**Figure 9**], revealing that they were part of longer composite furniture legs, as is also revealed by the original photographs of the objects *in situ*. A similar piece shaped as a winged lion, 27 cm, appears to have had the same function.[213] Legs shaped as lions for elaborate chairs, or thrones, are widely attested from Gandhara via Mathura, Sanchi and Ajanta to Nagarjunakonda and Amaravati,[214] while elephant-headed legs remarkably like those uncovered at Begram can be found as bedstead supports in 1st–3rd century AD Gandharan reliefs [**Figure 10**].[215]

[209] Hackin 1939: 66 (no. 320a), figs. 75–78.
[210] Thorough comparison conducted by Mehendale 1997: 4.2.1.
[211] Mehendale 1997: 2.2.4; Simpson 2014: 25–6.
[212] Cf. Mehendale 1997: 2.2.3, 4.2.1; 2001: 498.
[213] Hackin 1939: nos. 342–43 [196–98], figs. 228–29, 230–1, 233; Hackin 1954: figs. 237–9; Hiebert and Cambon 2008: 165, no. 152.
[214] Murthy 1982: 15 c) (Sanchi); 16 c) (Amaravati); 18 e–f), figs. II.8–9 (Nagarjunakonda); 19 d), figs. III.15–16 (Gandhara); 20f, figs. III.17–20 (Mathura); 24 f), figs. V.32–33 (Ajanta).
[215] Marshall 1960: figs. 68, 127. Moreover, carved elephant heads as integrated supports of the back are known from thrones (with lion legs):

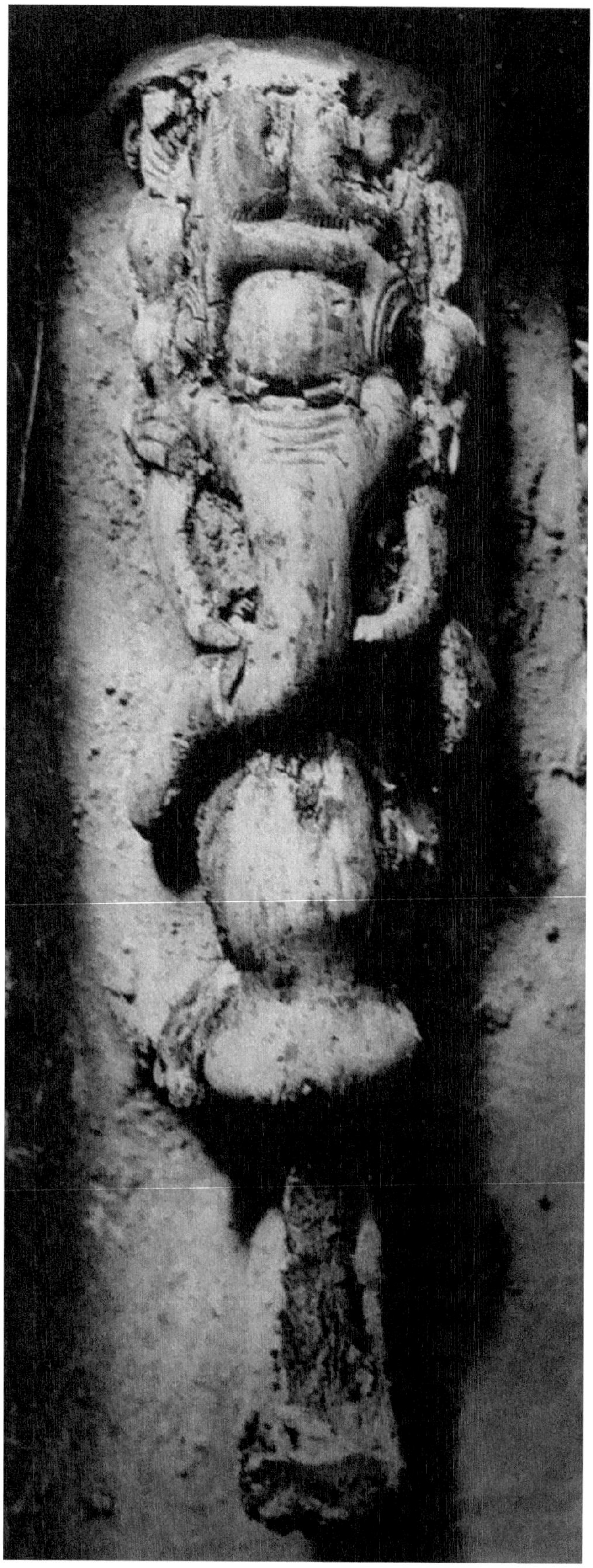

Figure 9
Elephant-headed ivory leg from Begram, height 26 cm; Hackin 1939: no. 342. Source: Hackin 1939: fig. 229.

In addition, two struts of solid ivory, 23 and 30 cm long, carved into griffins carrying riders and leaping out of the mouths of *makaras*, were evidently supposed to act as structural supports of armrests or elaborate chair backs, being originally fitted with tenons at both ends.[216] Such leaping or rearing animals, acting as structural supports for ornate chairs, couches and cane-seats, are depicted numerous times in reliefs and murals at Southern sites such as Ajanta, Nagarjunakonda and Amaravati.[217] Furthermore, *makaras* generally like those from the bases of the Begram statuettes and the lower end of the two struts, were, as it happens, quite a commonplace decoration as the terminals for top bars of chair backs as well as couches, even the finials of armrests.[218]

Now, considering the accumulated evidence for the use of the Indian ivory statuettes as pieces of furniture (the vertical holes drilled down all three Satavahana pieces, the horizontal attachments of the Pompeii and Ter statuettes, the possible top fittings of two of the Begram figurines, the *makaras* of all three, and the use of one of them in a larger ivory ensemble)[219] in conjunction with the proven correspondence between other Begram ivory artefacts and depictions of ancient Indian furniture generally, it would be of great interest if any matches could be found between the actual statuettes themselves and any sculpted or painted pieces of furniture.

Murthy 1982: 24 f), figs. V.32–33 (Ajanta).

[216] Hackin 1954: 216, no. 192a, 232, no. 201a, figs. 152–6; Hiebert and Cambon 2008: 196, no. 209. An additional example of a similar 'carved furniture element' is a curved bone support (12.6 cm height) with a head at the top, legs at the bottom, and a large dowel hole for fitting at the back, analysed in great detail in Ambers *et al.* 2014, cat. no. 20, pp. 314–26.

[217] Murthy 1982: 16 b–c) (Amaravati); 17 c), 18 e–f), figs. II.8–9 (Nagarjunakonda); 24 f), figs. V.32–34 (Ajanta); 29 a), fig. VIII.6 (Nagarjunakonda); 49 ii), fig. XI.18 (Amaravati); 51 iii), fig. XIII.27.

[218] Murthy 1982: 16 b–c) (Amaravati); 17 c) (Nagarjunakonda); 22 b), figs. V.26–7, VI.28, 23 e), fig. VI.31, 24f, figs. V.32, VI.34 (Ajanta); 28 a), fig. VII.1 (Amaravati); 30 c) (Nagarjunakonda). Yet another specimen is attested in Sivaramamurti 1956: 136, pl. XII.3. One might wonder whether the Hellenistic and Roman (particularly Late Antique) fashion for dolphin and fish armrests on chairs was in some way related to this equally long-running Indian tradition of decorating thrones and chairs similarly with *makaras*; on the Greco-Roman tradition, see Stern and Thimme 2007: 232–3.

[219] Indeed, the various bone and ivory objects and plaques from Begram were generally attached to wooden superstructures or fitted together with other pieces by use of not only integral tenons but also, significantly for this case-study, rivets, nails or long clamps, cf. Simpson 2014: 23–5.

Figure 10
Elephant-headed bed legs, stone relief from Gandhara. Source: Marshall 1960: pl. 91, fig. 127.
Copyright: Cambridge University Press.

In fact, such a match does exist. From Ajanta, in the old Satavahana heartland of Maharashtra, to the north of Ter and Bhokardan (only 30 km from the latter), murals datable to the 470s AD[220] from two of the more grand *viharas*, that is, monastic caves with both cells for accommodation and a central room for worship, show elaborate chairs or thrones which incorporate anthropomorphic statuettes as structural supports and parts of their decoration. The painting from Cave 1 shows two small human figures of indeterminate gender, on either side of the chair back, both tilted outwards a little to make room for prancing deer which rise up over them and run the full length of the chair back, the top bar of which is fittingly decorated with twin terminal *makaras* [**Figure 11**].[221] The two figures in question must be estimated at some 20–25 cm, like the three Satavahana pieces, and they seem to have had slanted bases forcing them to lean slightly outwards, like the Pompeii statuette whose slanted base the fitter's mark

[220] Spink 2008: 70–2.
[221] Takata 1971: pl. 89 (also pl. 84). Murthy 1982: 24 f), fig. VI.34

Figure 11
Drawing of detail from mural in Ajanta Cave 1, cf. Takata 1971: pl. 89.

assures us beyond doubt is the original surface. Although the depicted specimens from Cave 1 cannot have had any use of a hole drilled down through their upper parts, this might merely be down to the way the throne was represented by the artists working at Ajanta. On a final note, the seat, legs and decorations of the throne are all coloured creamy white, perhaps to represent ivory.

Similarly, the other painting from Ajanta's Cave 17 shows a seated Buddha in a throne-like chair, where the edges of the chair back are decorated with human figures, these running the entire height of the back, and for a viewer at the front being only halfway or sideways visible [**Figure 12**]. Once again, the top bar of the chair back is adorned with twin *makaras*.[222] The figurines portrayed here would have been comparably taller, perhaps more like the Begram statuettes with their 45–56 cm, and could very well have had holes drilled down through their heads, both for supporting the upper bar of the back and for keeping them fixed in position.

Although the paintings from Ajanta are some four centuries later than the extant ivory figurines from Maharashtra, they might well reflect a continuity within furniture fashion and decoration like that attested for the popular lion-shaped throne legs, which first appear in 1st century BC reliefs at Sanchi and continue to be in use up until their depiction at Ajanta in the later 5th century AD.[223] On that note, a pair of ivory throne legs carved as lions from Eastern India, as revealed by short auspicious inscriptions in proto-Bengali, are dated to the late 12th century AD, and sport bases for vertical support mounted on their heads.[224] Also from Eastern India (Odisha), and dated to the very same century, come two 35 cm tall ivory legs shaped as rearing elephants standing on their hind legs, both carrying a base for vertical support on their heads, at least one of them still retaining a square mortise-hole for attachment.[225] Likewise, ivory furniture struts carved as lions, similar to the Begram struts with griffins, were still produced by the 17th–18th century AD in South India.[226]

Finally, there is an earlier fit with the Begram statuettes, this being in the form of a 1st–3rd century AD stone relief from neighbouring Gandhara which portrays a throne with lion-shaped legs as well as pillars at the corners supporting a baldachin. Attached to the upper parts of the pillars, however, are yet another set of two small human figures.[227] One might have interpreted these as some kind of Gandharan-style Erotes, *putti*, and active participants in the narrative message of the relief, not passive furnishings of the throne. However, the similarly attested humanoid statuette decorations from Ajanta, as well as the throne's

[222] Takata 1971: pl. 36. Murthy 1982: 23 b), fig. VI.28
[223] Cf. n214.
[224] Dwivedi 1976: 114, pl. 97.
[225] Dwivedi 1976: 113–4, pl. 93–6.
[226] Jaffer 2002: 67, no. 26.
[227] Marshall 1960: fig. 102. Murthy 1982: 19 d), fig. III.15.

lion-shaped legs which, along with comparable elephant-headed legs, have direct counterparts among the Begram artefacts treated above, should alert us to the fact that these longish human figures might be representations of ivory statuettes, like the taller ones from Begram.

Figure 12
Drawing of detail from mural in Ajanta Cave 17, cf. Takata 1971: pl. 36.

As regards the choice of materials for thrones, we already know from the finds of lavish ivory and bone chairs and footstools at Begram, as well as the leg and strut furnishings of ivory, that thrones and chairs could be at least partially made from ivory (which the creamy colour of the throne in Ajanta Cave 1 might also be an indicator of), like the six statuettes whose functional role we are trying to pinpoint. In addition, though, literary evidence datable to the 4th–5th century AD from the Gupta Empire of North India, that is, in between Gandhara and Ajanta, reveals that expensive, richly decorated chairs (*pallankas*) could, indeed, be made from ivory.[228]

In summary, then, there is a strong case for arguing that the Indian ivory statuette found at Pompeii, along with its counterparts from Bhokardan and Ter, as well as the three similar statuettes from Begram, were neither mirror handles nor furniture legs in their original Indian context, as has been argued by previous scholars. Rather, they are more likely to have served as decorations, with or without supporting effect, integrated into larger pieces of furniture only preserved in ancient depictions as thrones or lavish chairs, but which would likely also have included other kinds of furniture. In fact, a 1st century AD incense burner from Gandhara—immediately east of Begram and its figurines—is held up by four winged bronze figurines, *c.* 17 cm tall, attached by their backs to the burner's raised base-plate, providing a neat contemporary parallel in bronze to the potential use of a set of ivory figurines of the same height as the Ter statuette.[229]

Interestingly, excavations at the royal city of Anuradhapura on Sri Lanka have also yielded an ivory figurine, dated 2nd century AD, which, although more crudely executed, is decorated in the same manner as the Indian statuettes: elaborate hair style, practically nude, and wearing a large necklace across the breast, a girdle around the waist, and what appears to be ankle bracelets. However, at a mere 7.5 cm from top to toe, this piece, which was found in the foundation casket of a *stupa*, is more likely to have been intended as a votive gift from the outset, not as part of any furniture. Yet, it further underlines the widespread production and use of this easily distinguishable category of carved ivory objects in ancient South Asia.[230]

From the Indian South, moreover, excavations at Arikamedu outside Pondicherry in Tamil Nadu, *Podukê* of the *Periplus*,[231] which received Roman imports as we shall see in chapter eight, have brought to light a largish piece of carved ivory some 13 cm in length, being plane and undecorated on one side, but decorated with bands and rosettes on the other (convex) side, and even sporting two mortise-holes

[228] Kalidasa, *Raghuvamsa*, XVII.21: 'Then, he occupied a pure ivory seat, supplied with a woollen carpet, placed in the court of another palace...'. For the dating, cf. Johnson 2009: *s.v.* 'Kalidasa.' On *pallankas*, see Sivaramamurti 1956: 136.
[229] Rosen Stone 2004: 70, fig. 1. A comparable construction with four *ureai* supports connecting base with top is known from small bronze altars of Greco-Roman Egypt, see Edgar 1904: nos. 27813–4.
[230] Ray 1959: 266f, pl. XIII.
[231] Wheeler 1946: 124. *Periplus* 60.

cut into the edge for fitting with a twinned part equipped with projecting tenons. Although put down as 'ivory handle (?),' by Mortimer Wheeler, its excavator, this object is also much more likely to have adorned some kind of furniture.[232] From Taxila at the eastern extremity of Gandhara, a piece of ivory has been found in the early 1st century AD layer, carved into a plain furniture leg some 18 cm long, decorated with a bulbous protrusion above the base, and with a projecting tenon at the upper end for mounting an extension.[233] Thus, there are other comparable examples of Early Historical production of ivory fittings for furniture from far and wide in South Asia.

Fitting Indian ivory with Roman furniture

Moving the focus back to Rome, it represented an important historiographical development in the tale of the Pompeian statuette when K. Karttunen in 1995 suggested a connection between this figurine's presence in the posh Campanian town and Pliny's account of the ongoing *mensarum insania* among the rich at Rome.[234] Thus, Karttunen seized on the quote by Juvenal, cited at the beginning of this chapter, about a table supported by a solid piece of ivory carved in the guise of a snarling panther, to argue that such supports would then have been basically similar to those found at Pompeii, Ter, and Bhokardan.

Although unknown to Karttunen, this similarity extends not only to the three Begram statuettes, but even more so to the animal-headed ivory legs found next to them, a lion and elephants. All of these carved ivories are dated to around the 1st century AD, with the Pompeii figurine's *ante quem* of AD 79 and tentative *post quem* of AD 54 being the most precise. In other words, the arrival in *Italia* of the carved Indian statuette found in Pompeii and the Roman fashion of ivory-legged citrus wood tables, developing from the 60s AD, as set forth above, coincide neatly—we even know that some, or most, of the ivory used was explicitly of Indian origin, larger pieces of ivory being available only from India. We might even wonder how some table legs of ivory came to be described as specifically 'Indian,' while others were 'African,' or nondescript. Obviously, if some legs consisted of ivory not only imported from India but carved with Indian motifs, this would certainly serve as an explanation.

Moreover, it is worth noting that Juvenal describes the ivory support as *ebur grande*, that is, of 'solid,' 'massive,' or 'heavy' ivory, while Statius once describes ivory legs as *columnae Indae*, hence, 'pillars' or 'columns,' both implying legs of pure and sound ivory,[235] which seems the more likely to suggest whole tusks in light of numerous references to table legs as simply *dentes*, 'teeth.'[236] This is remarkable, in so far as attested Roman ivory legs seem to have been manufactured either by stacking a number of disk-shaped, cylindrical or columnar ivory components, with a hole through the middle for mounting on an iron rod making up the core of the leg, or by elaborate ivory veneering of a fittingly shaped wooden core pierced by an upright iron rod—both kinds having been taken over from Greek prototypes during the Hellenistic period.[237] Indeed, recent excavations at Herculaneum have uncovered fragments of wooden legs for different pieces of furniture (tripods and tables), veneered with exquisitely carved Dionysiac-themed ivory panels on the upper parts, the two remaining lower parts terminating in lion's paws which are the only elements to be of solid ivory.[238] Consequently, legs of sound ivory were evidently not the norm among the Romans, whereas the Satavahana and Begram ivory furniture fittings comprise exactly that: solid, decorative pieces of ivory for use as integrated parts of furniture. Of much later date, the survival of the two rampant elephant ivory legs and the two ivory lion legs, mentioned above, both sets from 12th century Medieval India, further supplement our knowledge about how early Common Era legs could have looked.

[232] Wheeler 1946: 108, no. 3, plate XXXVI; undated surface find.
[233] Marshall 1951: 666, no. 124, pl. 204. Note also the more ornately decorated miniature ivory legs of a 'chest or toy table,' p. 664, nos. 100, 102.
[234] Paper of 1995: Karttunen 1997.
[235] Juv. XI, l. 123; Stat. *Silv.*, IV.2.38.
[236] Luc. *Pharsalia*, X, l. 144; Stat. *Silv.*, III.3.95; Mart. *Epigr.*, II.43, IX.22, X.98, XIV.3, XIV.91.
[237] St. Clair 2003: 18, 25–34, 42–6. Interestingly, fragments of a Hellenistic ivory leg of the cylindrical mounts type have survived as far east as Aï Khanoum in Bactria, thus, datable to its destruction in the mid-2nd century BC; Hiebert and Cambon 2008: 118, nos. 21–22.
[238] Guidobaldi 2010; Guidobaldi and Esposito 2010: 51–5; Lapatin 2015: 267, pl. 164. In addition, Stern and Thimme 2007 provide an exhaustive treatment of the find of elaborately ivory-veneered furniture (crossed-leg chairs and the cabriole legs of a cabinet) from the later 4th century AD port of Roman Corinth.

Figure 13
Wooden, three-legged Roman table form Herculaneum, animal legs and griffins' heads with ivory eyes (= Mols 1999: cat.no. 18). Copyright: S. Mols.

However, Karttunen's hypothesis requires some modifications to fit with Roman fashion. Ordinary, wooden three-legged Roman tables of the so-called *mensa delphica* type from Herculaneum [e.g. **Figure 13**], buried along with Pompeii in AD 79, varied in height between 59–68 cm, tabletops ranging between 42–57 cm, although one with a diameter as large as 61 cm was found but has not been preserved.[239] According to Pliny's description of record-price fetching citrus wood tables, though, these had even larger tabletops, the two specifically attested being one of 1.4 m, made up from two pieces, and another made from a single piece being 1.2 m.[240] Thus, at least the most expensive citrus tables were more than twice as large as ordinary three-legged tables, and therefore these oversize tables are not likely to have had legs shorter than the average 60-odd cm.

In consequence, an ivory leg of the size displayed by the Satavahana ivory statuettes, some 20–25 cm, would be far too short on its own, while longer specimens, like those from Begram being 45–56 cm, could perhaps have made up short legs in their own right of what would in that case have been particularly low tables.[241] Alternatively, either only the shorter Satavahana pieces or both these and the longer, but still sub-length, Begram specimens could have been incorporated into composite ivory legs, where the

239 Mols 1999: 49.

240 Croom 2007: 20–21.

241 Rather than traditional table height, a length of 45 cm puts two of the Begram figurines in the range of recorded stool (*sella*) height: a preserved four-legged specimen from Herculaneum has plain legs 42 cm long; Mols 1999: 54, cat. no. 23. Expensive Roman stools could, interestingly, also be adorned with ivory, cf. the *sella eburnea* of Livy *Epit.*, XLI.20.

figurines constituted the anthropomorphic decoration of the upper (more rarely lower) half, as is known from surviving legs made in one piece from bronze, marble and wood, of the traditional Roman style.[242] More abundant bronze and marble examples can be added to the rare wooden specimens preserved, seeing as the latter evidently served as templates for the former which retained as bronze or marble decorative details functional elements copied from wooden tables.[243]

Among the few surviving examples made from wood, unearthed at Herculaneum, is the head of a young male (Dionysus/Bacchus) rising from the top of a curved table leg, the eyes being inlaid with ivory, as are the eyes of a griffin's head belonging to another table, the latter even sporting preserved stretchers emanating from the creatures' backs [**Figure 13**]. Significantly, a third specimen carved with geometric adornments has legs of hard box wood (*Buxus*) and a tabletop of decorative walnut (*Juglans*), attesting to the construction of composite pieces of furniture, making optimal use of the material of each structural element.[244] In addition, the tripod legs from Herculaneum, mentioned above, attest the use of hardwood (whole legs of European ash, *Fraxinus excelsior*[245]), ivory veneer (carved relief panels on the upper legs, geometrical groove patterns on the lower), and pieces of solid ivory (the lions' feet), in one composite table-like structure.[246] The incorporation of an ivory figurine support as one element in a table or tripod configuration consisting of decorative feet, lower legs, upper legs and tabletop, is therefore quite feasible.

One especially evocative example of such a hypothetical construction is a bronze table which was later converted into a tripod brazier,[247] likely from Herculaneum,[248] where the lower legs are in the conventional guise of an animal's paws, terminating abruptly two-thirds up the length to serve as the seats of appended and independently fashioned sphinxes [**Figure 14**]. These support the superstructure above by means of a connecting rod emanating from their upper backs, while stretchers project backwards from the lower legs to join up at the centre-point between the three legs, providing sideways stability to the entire composition.[249] A similar set of legs sport the traditional animal feet with independently fashioned and freestanding anthropomorphic figures (nude Bacchus) on top of fluted columns, tendrils locking as stretchers behind, the Bacchi being 18 cm tall, with heads ending in square capitals to support a tabletop, legs in total reaching a height of 76 cm.[250]

In other words, the technical configuration of the Satavahana pieces, constituting decorative elements providing vertical support and with perforations towards the base allowing either attachment of backward stretchers or fastening to a leg below, is, *mutatis mutandis*, the same as that of the upper elements of legs of the ubiquitous Roman three-legged table. Even a little detail like the fitter's mark underneath the Pompeii figurine, also attested for the Begram Ivories, is likewise to be found among Roman furniture makers, where the practice is known from ornamental marble tables, which were marked to tell which upper and lower parts went together.[251]

Furthermore, it is possible, based on the original photographs of the objects *in situ*, to calculate that the two elephant-headed leg components from Begram were part of legs at least 90 cm tall, making for longer composite ivory legs which could be shortened down to the ordinary height of a three-legged table, or serve in their full length as legs for a particularly large citrus wood table, as we know that the most

[242] See especially the collection in Harl-Schaller 1976–7: cat. A.1–51 (bronze), B.1–24 (marble), the majority (median) of anthropomorphic elements listed herein being around 16 cm tall, while the average height is 30 cm. Moss 1988: Cat. C23, 45, 88–9, 97–9 (marble). For wooden legs see further below, likewise three more bronze specimens are to be treated individually in the following.

[243] Vermeule 1981: 182f; Cohon 1984: 20; Mols 1999: 51.

[244] Mols 1999: cat. no. 16 (human), figs. 102–5, no. 18 (griffin), figs. 111–4, both of them wood with ivory inlay; cat. no. 15, figs. 97–99, *Buxus* and *Juglans* combined; for their use in Roman carpentry, see Ulrich 2007: 245, 253.

[245] On the use of which in Roman carpentry, see Ulrich 2007: 251.

[246] Cf. n238 above.

[247] Pernice 1908: 110–1.

[248] See discussion in Mols 1999: 51, n246, who argues against the Isis temple of Pompeii being the find-spot.

[249] Museo Napoli 1999: 120, inv.no. 72995.

[250] Vermeule 1981: cat. II.19A: one leg in a private collection in New York, the other two in California; for the latter, see Del Chiaro 1973: #46 bis, illustrated p. 84 (stretcher-tendrils not visible on this photograph). Such tendrils are clearly visible on photographs of the 'Satyr tripod' (Museo Napoli, inv.no. 27874), though, where the stretchers emanate from the creatures' lower backs, e.g. illustration in Museo Napoli 1999: 84.

[251] Cohon 1984: 15f. Moss 1988: 197–8. Some of the marks are Greek and Latin letters, some are numbers, while some are arbitrary marks or non-alphabetical glyphs or symbols.

Figure 14
Roman bronze table converted into brazier. Source: Pernice 1908: 108, fig. 1.

expensive of them were. Indeed, a unique surviving table from Hellenistic Egypt (Luxor), with wooden legs in the guise of animal feet topped by swans' heads, has a height of 85 cm,[252] while similar bronze and marble legs within that range are also known.[253]

Significantly, a distinct category of marble table legs provides an interesting comparandum to the suggested use of Indian carved ivories as supports for Roman tables. Specifically, two Italian marble legs are fashioned in the guise of Eastern barbarians, recognisable by their tell-tale Phrygian caps, probably

[252] Richter 1966: 71, figs. 372, 377. The *mensa delphica* was introduced to Egypt by the Ptolemies and flourished there in various forms until Late Antiquity, cf. Vermeule 1981: 184.
[253] E.g., Harl-Schaller 1976–7: cat. A12, 24, B13, 16, 20, 21, 24.

more specifically depicting Ganymede, the divine cup-bearer. These legs reach a height of at least 77 cm, and while one was found in Pompeii, another has been dated stylistically to the 3rd–4th century AD. In consequence, such 'Eastern Other' caryatides were in vogue from at least the time when one of the legs was buried along with the Indian figurine in Pompeii and until the Later Empire. This fashion symbolises Rome's claim to sovereignty over the East, having its inhabitants support the Roman world order on their heads like a tabletop, as did imported Eastern slaves with their labours in a very concrete and unsymbolic way.[254] As it happens, then, Indian ivory figurines employed as legs supporting Roman tabletops mirror this long-running custom in marble remarkably well.[255]

However, other Roman uses of imported ivory fittings than table legs are certainly also plausible. For instance, one might imagine that the Satavahana pieces of 20–25 cm could have served as decorative armrest supports on a chair. As it happens, two wooden examples with mythological heads at the top (a Hellenistic sphinx [**Figure 15**] and a 'Persepolitan beast') and ending in animals' feet, from as far away as Loulan in the Tarim kingdom of Shanshan,[256] deserted in AD 376, bridges the gap between Roman and Indian furniture. Shanshan had experienced an inflow of Gandharan immigrants in the preceding two centuries, bringing their culture in the guise of the Kharoshthi script as well as Greco-Roman architectural and artistic motifs with them,[257] and the dry sands of the Taklamakan desert thus preserve a hybrid Gandharan fashion imported across the Karakorum from their native homeland.

Indeed, that imported Indian ivory figurines could have served various Roman furniture uses receives further support from a unique Campanian ivory exhibited at the *Museo archeologico Nazionale di Napoli*: a skilfully sculpted ivory statuette of a faun in the Hellenistic tradition, of roughly the same size as the Indian statuette found in Pompeii, interpreted as having acted as a decorative support integrated into a larger piece of furniture [**Figure 16**].[258] Other examples consist of decorative

Figure 15
Wooden armrest support from Loulan, Xinjiang. Source: Stein 1921, IV: pl. XXXIV.

[254] Schneider 1992; respectively Moss 1988: cat. A29, A59.

[255] A comparable group of evidence alerting us to an 'Indianising' influence on Roman ornamental furniture and artwork is constituted by some ten marble heads of 2nd century AD date, conspicuous for wearing their hair gathered in a topknot. Significantly, the topknot (Sanskrit: *ushnisha*) is a well-known iconographic mark of the Buddha as well as future Buddhahood of monks, cf., e.g., Zin 2003: 115–6. Remarkably, moreover, two of these portraits are sculpted from dark marble, thus, emphasising a non-Roman ethnic stereotype. Accordingly, although these marble heads are evidently the works of Western sculptors, they might be portraying Indian or 'Indianised' Buddhists in a Roman sculptural context; Schneider 1986: 156, 177–8, 218; Cimino 1994a:126–8; Parker 2008: 128.

[256] Stein 1921, IV: pl. XXXIV, cat.nos. L.B.IV.v.0023 and L.B.IV.v.0013.

[257] Hansen 2012: 26, 32, 37–8, 42, 44–8, 55.

[258] *Museo archeologico Nazionale di Napoli*, 1st floor, room LXXXVIII, 'La collezione degli oggetti in avorio ed osso,' in the middle of the upper shelf of the display-case holding ivories. The sign next to it reads: 'Statuetta di avorio rappresentante un fauno in funzione di sostegno, verosimilmente decorazione di un mobile. Opera di gusto ellenistico, probabilmente di importazione.' However, the Museum replied to a request by this author for more information that the object neither has an inventory number nor a documented archaeological provenance, although the archives of the

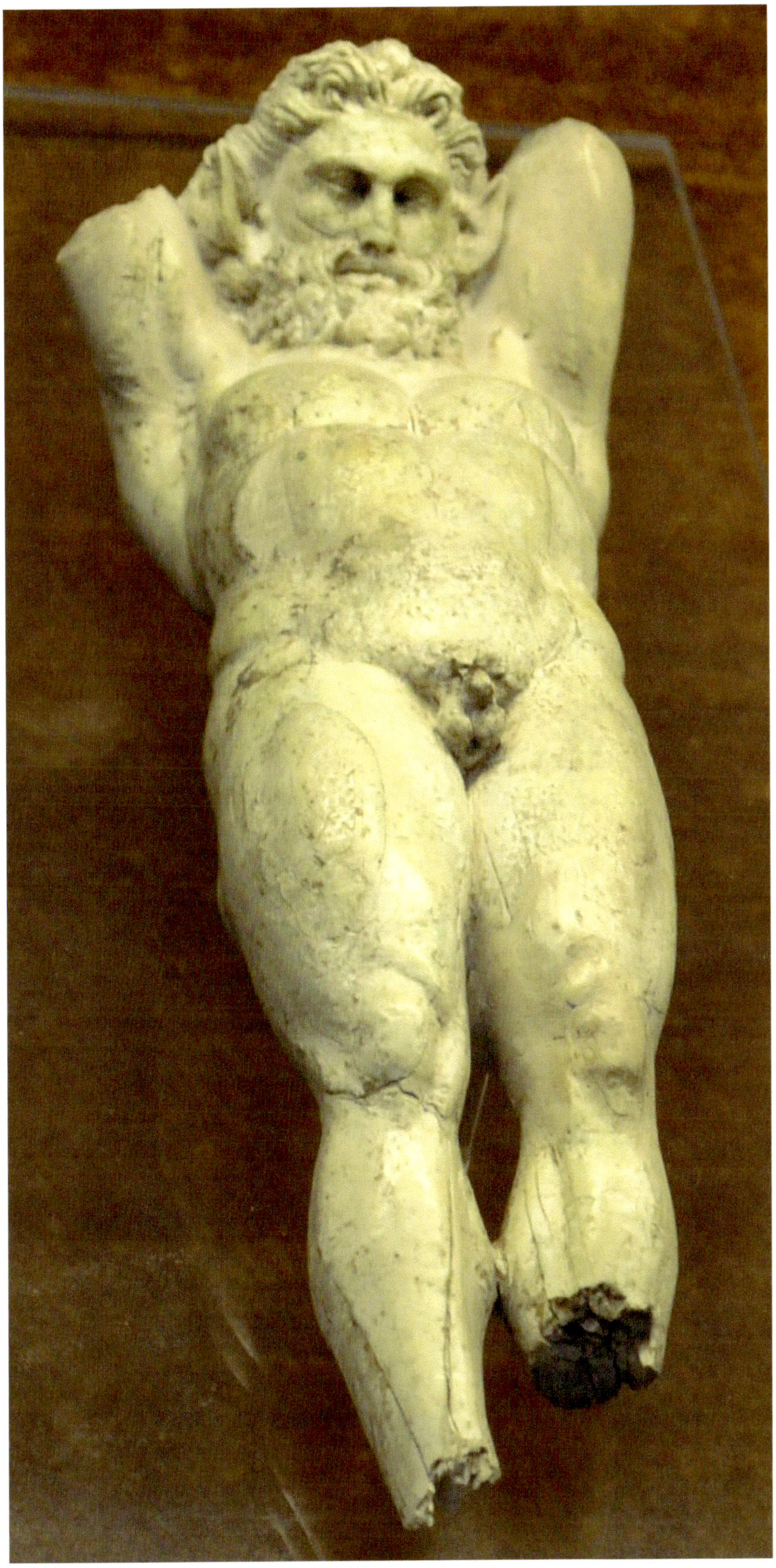

Figure 16
Ivory faun from the Naples area, approximate height 20–5 cm. In Museo archeologico Nazionale di Napoli, 1st floor, room LXXXVIII, 'La collezione degli oggetti in avorio ed osso.' Photograph by the author.

ivory plaques and small heads from Pompeii for adorning furniture (especially couches), an ivory toiletry box from nearby Cumae with carved panels on the sides and resting on four small square ivory feet carved in the guise of sirens,[259] as well as the finds of ivory legs for some kind of furniture at both Pompeii,[260] neighbouring Stabiae[261] and Herculaneum,[262] all adding up to emphasise the widespread local use of carved ivory objects for contemporary domestic fittings, *inter alia* legs.[263] In fact, even the presence of thuya tree samples, that is, the citrus wood of the Ancients, has now also been scientifically documented at Pompeii,[264] putting in one place at the time of the eruption of Mount Vesuvius both citrus wood and carved Indian ivory originally intended for use as part of furniture, providing an almost tangible link between the two in the shape of the luxurious citrus wood table with elaborate legs of Indian ivory, as attested in the ancient literature.

By now, it should hopefully be apparent that the main argument propounded here is that the existence of a category of expertly manufactured ivory furniture decorations in 1st century AD South Asia, coupled with the diagnostic find of an Indian ivory furniture decoration in contemporary Pompeii, and concurrent Roman references to ornate table legs of ivory, some of it Indian, must force us to consider whether carved Indian ivories were incorporated into Roman furniture fashion. A similar use of ivory fittings is plainly attested by the faun, mentioned above, of the same size and putative use, also housed at the Museum of Naples, as well as by the lions' feet of ivory for tripod legs from Herculaneum. Nonetheless, the specific context of the Pompeii statuette might imply that this particular specimen had found a slightly alternative use.

As briefly mentioned above, the statuette was found in a state of partial disintegration in the unpretentious brick peristyle of a large but simple Roman *domus* (I.8.5), where the wall paintings are of mediocre quality, the only characteristic decoration being graffiti of ships and navigation instruments, creating the impression that its owner might well have been engaged in maritime business.[265] Now, if it is not merely down to the poor survival rate of ivory in archaeological contexts[266] that only one Indian ivory statuette, not three, was found *in situ*, and that we would not expect to find a hugely expensive citrus wood table with Indian ivory legs in a rather plain Pompeian *domus*, we have to come up with an alternative hypothesis.

However, a relevant note of caution against modern assumptions about a fitting archaeological context for finds of ivory table legs arises from the fact that the ivory veneered tripod legs from at least four pieces of furniture from nearby Herculaneum were also found in a 'messy context.' That is to say, the tripods had perhaps been disassembled prior to the catastrophe (which would account for missing parts), and were found to one side in a monumental room opening on to a sea-facing terrace, where they might have been dumped intentionally or dragged from further inside the building by one of the violent surges of earthquake waves accompanying the eruption (also likely to have made bits disappear).[267] The superheated and several hundred kilometres per hour strong pyroclastic flows which hit Pompeii and smashed up buildings in their path would likewise have disturbed original contexts and have to be taken into account.

In addition, and more specifically, the slanted base of the Pompeii figurine entails that this specific statuette would have made for a particularly wobbly piece of furniture, no matter what kind of awkward leg it had

Museum may hold more information.

[259] Museo Napoli 1989a: 230–3, nos. 5, 11–15, 17–19.

[260] Dubois-Pelerin 2008: 227; according to the description, though, these four fragments belong to the conventional type of disk-shaped, pierced ivory mounts stacked on an iron rod to make up a leg.

[261] Camardo 2001: 94; too sparse available description to identify in any way.

[262] Cf. n238.

[263] A local tradition for carving ivory preserved from the Hellenistic period of Magna Graecia, cf. Rodziewicz 1971: 83–88.

[264] Fioravanti and Caramiello 1999: 85.

[265] Dubois-Pelerin 2008: 227 with n354. The Pompeian family of the *Munatii*, who were sea-going traders, might be attested on the route between Koptos and the Red Sea port of Berenike in Egypt, providing a good example of the statuette's potential owners, cf. Romanis 1996a: 214, no. 12, and pp. 254–7; Cuvigny *et al.* 1999: no. 10.

[266] Cf. St. Clair 2003: 5, 32.

[267] Guidobaldi and Esposito 2010: 51–2, also p. 49 on the consequences of violent surges for the interior decoration of the house.

to serve as, unless a special fitting for the base was added to compensate for the slant. Significantly, this only applies to the Pompeian specimen, for the Bhokardan and Begram figurines both have level bases (as did the one from Ter in all likelihood, but missing its lower legs we cannot tell). Obviously, this would not have hindered the statuette's original Indian appliance as throne-, or other furniture, decoration, especially not if it was to lean outward as in the mural of Ajanta Cave 1.

Consequently, if the Indian ivory statuette from Pompeii is diagnostic of a long-distance trade in carved ivories for furniture in which the concrete purpose of the figurines was changed, ending up as Roman table legs and other furniture decorations not explicitly mentioned in the ancient literature, but was itself less readily convertible into a composite 'upper and lower half'-table leg or other furnishing due to its natural tilt, what other use might it have served in light of its specific archaeological context? As it happens, the corner of the peristyle where the figurine was found also revealed imprints of a chest and a cupboard, typical of Herculaneum and Pompeii, as well as many different furnishings in bronze, glass and terracotta, which could provide an important clue.[268] Accordingly, this particular figurine might simply have been stored in the cupboard or the chest as an exotic object of artistic value, just like miniature votive figurines in ivory of Venus and Hercules having been unearthed elsewhere around town.[269]

This hypothesis is arguably the best available, especially seeing as the owner of the house was likely involved in maritime trade and could thus have acquired the object before it was sold on to become part of expensive luxury furniture. However, even though the specific context of the Indian statuette from Pompeii might not imply that it itself was ever fitted as support for a citrus table, this circumstance alone should not be allowed to diminish the important implications which its physical presence in Early Imperial Italy has for the trade in similar objects of carved ivory from South Asia.

Although only one carved Indian ivory furniture fitting has been found in the Roman Empire, we know from the literary sources that Indian ivory table legs—of a kind which could be carved as rampant animals—came into use in the later 1st century AD, and the find of the contemporary Begram statuettes alongside Roman merchandise further attests such a long-distance trade (while the Muziris Papyrus documents large-scale trade in unprocessed tusks and fragments). Upon arrival by ship from the Eastern Mediterranean to nearby Puteoli, or Portus at the mouth of the Tiber, imported Indian ivory furniture decorations became part of the commercial world of the *negotiatores eborarii et citriarii* in Rome. At some point in the process, moreover, they would have been passed on for fitting with citrus wood tabletops to both the *fabri* and *politores eborarii* of Rome, as well as such organised groups of craftsmen as the *citriarii Neapolitani*, who due to their geographical expansion would have been able to supply customers both in Rome and Campanian towns like Pompeii.

The shreni of ivory carvers

The question is, though, in what form this trade in carved ivory between India and Rome was conducted: were entire pieces of Indian furniture, that is, throne-like chairs and similar structures, shipped westwards, or was it only the carved Indian ivory components themselves?[270] We know from the contemporary *Periplus* that the major port of Western India, Barygaza, was an exporter of three precious hardwoods in the mid-1st century AD: teak, ebony, and sissoo.[271] Presumably, the furniture produced and used in this part of India would have been made of these three or similar kinds of expensive hardwood, but ivory fittings destined for the long-distance trade might not have been attached prior to export, as this would have made for a rather unwieldy and fragile type of long-distance trade commodity. Instead, bundles of carved ivory pieces could more feasibly have been packed in protective coverings by themselves, making for a very compact high-value, low-weight cargo. In fact, we know from one of Cicero's letters that he and a friend were collecting ornamental marble table legs from Greece as part of buying up pieces of art for

[268] Maiuri 1938–39: 111.
[269] Museo Napoli 1989a: 230, nos. 2–3.
[270] Modification of Karttunen 1997: 560.
[271] *Periplus* 36; the export is only mentioned with reference to Ommana in Parthian Carmania.

their homes in Italy, so a century later Roman aristocrats could equally well have been avid collectors of Indian ivory legs.[272]

More importantly, though, this question must also be viewed in light of the ancient Roman authors who consistently speak of citrus wood tables throughout the 1st century AD,[273] while the case is not entirely clear for the 2nd century AD, seeing references both to citrus wood and unspecified ivory-legged tables, whereas the latest source on the topic even mentions maple-topped tables with ivory feet.[274] In short, Pliny's *mensarum insania* of the 1st century AD was all about the citrus wood, to the exclusion of any other hardwood types, and we must therefore infer that the carved Indian ivories, for reasons of both ease of transport as well as patterns of consumption at Rome, were shipped separately for later fitting.

Indeed, Barygaza and, by inclusion, the ports of the Konkan Coast south of it are listed in the *Periplus* as exporters of ivory, with no mention of exports of furniture as such.[275] At this time, Scythians (Greek sources) or Shakas (Indian sources) slowly migrating south from Central Asia had become established as rulers of an area comparable to modern-day Gujarat, that is, centred on the Gulf of Khambhat, where lay Barygaza. Here they were to be known as the Western Kshatrapas.[276] The neighbouring kingdom towards the south-east was the indigenous Satavahana dynasty, which had risen to ascendancy over the fertile inland area of the upper Godavari Valley in the first century BC (in modern Maharashtra). The Satavahanas and the Western Kshatrapas were in continuous conflict from the 1st century AD over possession of the coastal plain which stretches south from Barygaza, containing port outlets at the end of the trade routes originating on the fertile inland plateau, the coast and the plateau being divided by the Sahyadri Range. Throughout the first and most of the second century AD, control over ports and mountain passes was continually shifting hands, but in the last quarter of the second century AD, the Satavahanas won a decisive victory, ending the struggle for good. Meanwhile, they had been expanding eastward along inland river valleys, acquiring a huge territory stretching as far as the River Krishna estuary on the east coast (in modern Andra Pradesh).[277]

However, the historical context aside, it is important to emphasise that Barygaza was not itself the primary producer or consumer of the wares mentioned as imports and exports in the *Periplus*, for that role fell to the ancient inland metropolis of Ujjain, later capital of the Western Kshatrapas.[278] Accordingly, one of the commodities arriving in the port town of Barygaza from Ujjain would have been ivory, and in addition to the actual 1st century AD ivory figurine finds from the Satavahana cities of Bhokardan and Ter, the Buddhist site of Sanchi, 200 kilometres further inland from Ujjain along the main overland trade route to North India,[279] provides earlier testimony of Satavahana ivory production.

Buddhist Sanchi dates back to around 250 BC, but in the later 1st century BC its great *stupa* was augmented with beautifully sculpted, high-arch stone gateways leading to the enclosure around the *stupa* itself.[280] On the southern gate, one ornately sculpted panel bears an inscription in Prakrit stating that the 'carving was done by the ivory carvers of Vidisha,'[281] the latter being the closest nearby city, an equally ancient commercial, religious and political centre.[282] A different inscription on the same gate reads that another

[272] Cic. *Fam.*, VII.23 (61 BC).

[273] Annaeus Lucan, Seneca, Petronius Arbiter, Pliny, Statius, and Martial, all speak of citrus wood explicitly.

[274] Neither Juvenal, Lucian, nor Clement of Alexandria specify the type of tabletop wood, while Cassius Dio refers to citrus wood tables in Seneca's time. The last, speaking of maple tabletops, is Athenaeus of Naucratis.

[275] *Periplus* 49.

[276] Shastri 1998: 133–74; Cribb 2000: 39–45; Thapar 2004: 217-25.

[277] Ray 1986: 33–56; Thapar 2004: 225–29; Nakanishi and v. Hinüber 2014: 22–5.

[278] *Periplus* 48; cf. 41, Minnagara (not that of #38) to the north or west was also an inland metropolis. Ptol. *Geog.*, VII.1: 'Ozene-Regia Tiastani,' that is, 'Ujjain, capital of Chastana' of the Western Kshatrapas.

[279] On the *Dakshinapatha*, see: Chandra 1977: 78; Neelis 2011: 205–16.

[280] Dehejia 1992: 36ff.

[281] Bühler 1894: 378, no. 200; Lüders 1912: no. 345. The ivory workers, *dantakara*, are given in the instrumental plural, *da<m=n>takarehi*, rendering translation as 'carving (done) by,' not simply 'of' as in the genitive of a donation.

[282] In *c.* 110 BC, Vidisha was important enough to warrant a visit (and inscription) by the Vishnu-devotee Heliodoros, son of Dion, from Taxila, a Greek ambassador from king Antialkidas of one of the Indo-Greek kingdoms in the Northwest; cf. Salomon 1998: 265–67. Dated to the last decade before 100 BC by Narain 1957: 119.

panel was a gift of the foreman of the artisans of the Satavahana king, Satakarni II, who ruled *c.* 50–25 BC,[283] at a time when both Ujjain, Sanchi, and Vidisha were under Satavahana control.[284]

Neither of these inscriptions were, significantly, intended for public display as such: they were both minute and inscribed at such heights on the monumental gate (respectively some two and six meters above ground level) that they would have been difficult to spot and impossible to read for a casual passer-by. They were, in other words, pious and private, not public, dedications.[285] Even more so, they inform us that not only royal but also urban collectives of skilled craftsmen had group identities with strong inherent religious obligations and communal funds to expend in pursuit of them. And the carving and erection of the Southern Gateway at Sanchi certainly required exactly such groups of highly skilled craftsmen, with substantial financial means at their disposal, as these communal donations confirm were in existence by the later 1st century BC.

Although neither of the two groups in question designate themselves as such, there is ample evidence for Indian associations (*shrenis*) of craftsmen similar to the already introduced professional *collegia* of the Roman world, a topic to be treated extensively in chapter eight. For instance, a Satavahana *shreni* of corn-dealers single-handedly sponsored the excavation of an entire seven-celled monastery cave (*vihara*) at Junnar sometime in the later 1st–2nd century AD,[286] while the earliest Satavahana *shreni* is attested by an inscription near their later royal city of Paithan,[287] possibly dating as far back as the 2nd century BC,[288] and hence providing evidence for the existence of this kind of organisation well before the ivory carvers of Vidisha in the later 1st century BC. In addition, there is circumstantial evidence of an even earlier vocational clustering and specialisation of ivory workers in the Buddhist corpus of folk-tales known as the *Jatakas*, two stories of which mention what amounts to an ivory workers' bazaar in Benares, where all kinds of ivory objects were produced.[289]

Accordingly, by the mid-1st century AD, shipments of beautiful Indian ivory furniture decorations, carved by the members of prominent associations of ivory craftsmen established for at least a century in the larger Satavahana commercial centres, travelled west in merchants' ships, arriving eventually by way of the Persian Gulf or Red Sea and overland caravans in one of the great ports of the Eastern Mediterranean. The Muziris Papyrus, for instance, details the purchase and transport of goods (among other things almost four tonnes of unprocessed ivory) by one Roman entrepreneur in person all the way from South Indian Muziris to Roman Alexandria,[290] but, as we shall see in chapter seven, there is now substantial evidence to indicate that expensive Indian trade goods could equally well have been carried by Indian traders all the way to the shores of the Mediterranean. Indeed, Dio Chrysostom mentions Indians present in Alexandria in the later 1st century AD,[291] which, as we shall see, might not be so far-fetched after all.

Although we cannot state with certainty how large this specific part of the Indian Ocean trade was in terms of quantity, circumstantial evidence quickly piles up: the Roman literary references to the adoption of legs of Indian ivory, specifically, for citrus wood tables in the mid-1st-later 1st century AD; Pliny, the Muziris Papyrus and the *Periplus* on the busy and large-scale (raw) ivory trade by sea with India via Egypt; the find of the Indian statuette in Pompeii 8000 kilometres away from its origin in Western India, where two exact counterparts have been found; the highly similar figurines and carved ivory animal legs from the commercial crossroads of Begram, some 1,700 kilometres to the northwest, from where ivories

283 Lüders 1912; no. 346. The dating is according to Ray 1986: 212, Appendix. II.
284 A recently published inscription from the south of the Satavahana kingdom, the stupa at Kanaganahalli, reveals that Ujjain was formally handed over by the Satavahana king Pulumāvi (r. 85–125 AD) to Chastana of the Western Kshatrapas, cf. Nakanishi and v. Hinüber 2014: 33, I.9.
285 Schopen 2004a: 387–8.
286 Burgess and Indraji 1881: 54, Junnar no. 31. Dating according to Dehejia 1972: 179–81.
287 Paithan was the 'Betana regia' of Ptol. *Geog*, VII.1.
288 Deshpande 1959: 77.
289 Cf. *Silavanaga Jataka*, no. 72, and *Kasava Jataka*, no. 221. Although they are traditionally dated in their oral form to *c.* 400 BC (cf. Thaplyal 1996: 6), they are not surely attested as a genre until the 2nd century BC (as reliefs at Bharhut, e.g., Appleton 2010: 53). Dwivedi 1976: 11–12, 16–27, gives a list of other epigraphic and literary sources for ivory and ivory carvers in India from Harappan until Medieval times, but the epigraphic sources are few, and the more numerous literary references are highly ambiguous.
290 See chapter six.
291 Dio Chrys. *Or.*, XXXII.40.

could equally well reach the Roman Mediterranean, seeing as even fragile Roman imports had made the journey in the other direction; and, finally, the identification of the Satavahana and Begram figurines as a category of well-defined Indian ivory furniture decorations, as well as a survey of contemporary Roman ornate table leg fashion and use of ivory for furniture. All of this, when taken together, cannot but imply that this trade in carved Indian ivory pieces for later, post-export fitting with local high-fashion furniture might, in fact, have been conducted on a surprisingly large geographical scale.

Following the flows of people and products, fashion and furniture

As regards the qualitative aspects of this specific trade, is the simultaneous occurrence of Indian ivory furniture fittings in Roman Italy and the very first literary references to a new development in the fashion for citrus wood tables, now suddenly with ivory legs (some specifically Indian, some explicitly solid), purely coincidental, or, as it seems, an indication of truly long-distance interaction? Favouring the latter answer, this interpretation implies that the literary, epigraphic and archaeological evidence, when put together, attests to the products of Indian ivory carvers, known at this time to have been organised into associations, being integrated into the economic fabric of urban Italy by Roman associations of craftsmen and traders specialised in citrus wood and ivory. And even if the import of Indian ivory legs was only kept up for a comparatively short period of time, the style and fashion of these Satavahana and Begram furniture legs evidently spearheaded a change of fashion among the Roman elite in the early 60s AD, which would plausibly, in turn, have led to the development of a parallel production of cheaper pieces produced by Roman craftsmen from African ivory.[292]

Indeed, this might serve as an explanation of why ivory table legs to Martial could be both Indian and African, as well as providing an answer to the gradual drop-off through the 2nd century AD of references to Indian ivory. In fact, such a process compares nicely with an empirically well-founded model of Roman consumption of luxury imports described by A. Wallace-Hadrill: an initial stage of importation to Italian centres is succeeded by establishment of local workshops mastering the relevant line of production, possibly starting out with the employment of foreign craftsmen, and in the process adapting the product to Roman tastes. Subsequently, in the third stage, consumption and production of the commodity is diffused to the provinces, in which it acquires further local characteristics.[293]

Thus, the initial stage would have been one of rare finished imports of citrus wood tables from Mauretania and hypothetical ivory-adorned furniture from India (from the early 1st century BC onwards), succeeded by nascent Italian manufacture of composite furniture consisting of citrus wood tabletops and carved Indian ivory furnishings, as related by Statius, Martial and Juvenal (circa mid-1st–later 1st century AD)—assembly being conducted by craftsmen such as the *politores* and *fabri eborarii* of Rome and the *citriarii Neapolitani*, while trade was handled by *negotiatores eborarii et citriarii*, organised in a *collegium* no later than the time of Hadrian. The third stage, then, with a more diversified provincial production, is represented by the later literary references (2nd century AD), from which it appears that while ivory legs remained in vogue, the tabletops became more nondescript, the latest reference even being to a more generally available component, namely, maple wood.[294] Moreover, Juvenal is the last to mention an Indian provenance of the ivory legs, so from around 130 AD the predominant source of carved ivories might well have been Africa. Thus, the last attested tables were likely a far cry from their predecessors made of Mauretanian citrus wood and carved Indian ivory imported from afar, although eminently better suited for provincial production and more widespread distribution.

Remarkably, though, but, on second thought, not so surprising after all, it appears that just like Indian carved ivories affected Roman table fashion, so Roman table fashion appears to have impacted Indian table legs. Thus, carved and curved animal-shaped legs in the guise of a lion's lower leg and clawed paw are attested as supports for chairs, footstools, tables, and low stools or tripods, in the South of

[292] Karttunen 1997: 560.
[293] Wallace-Hadrill 2008: 360–1, 435–7.
[294] For the use of maple for furniture, see Richter 1966: 123; Croom 2007: 21; Ulrich 2007: 243.

the Subcontinent in the early centuries of the Common Era—not just in Gandhara to the North, which obviously had previous experience with Greek furniture.[295] Indeed, although traditional Indian furniture leg fashion was quite different, these curved lions' legs cropping up in the sculptural record match so surprisingly well with contemporary Roman table fashion that it can hardly be a coincidence, especially seeing as a recently published relief from a Satavahana *stupa* discovered at Kanaganahalli, dating to the 1st century AD, provides new evidence of Roman-style tables in an Indian context.[296] The depiction in question is of a table supported by curved legs in all likelihood resting on feline paws (the relief breaks off, unfortunately), in turn supporting a base half-way up the height of the table, on which rests three rampant lions holding up the tabletop with their heads,[297] providing a tangible link with one of the foremost Indian polities, the Satavahana kingdom, involved in the seagoing trade with the Roman West.

On the topic of Roman furniture travelling eastwards, moreover, it is worth remarking that the rich finds at Begram also contain a miniature bronze tripod with lion feet, as well as one leg from a similar tripod with the upper part in the shape of a swan, the lower part terminating in a lion's paw; both types of tripods being imports from the Roman Empire, having been unearthed at, for instance, Pompeii.[298] Likewise, Roman folding tables might just have inspired a later Indian fashion for a similar design through overseas export by Roman traders.[299] Thus, Roman and Indian furniture appears to have been in sustained and reciprocal interaction, with artistic flows surging back and forth between the Mediterranean and Indian Ocean, stirred up by consumers, craftsmen and traders, making up interlocking chains of import and export converging from East and West to bridge the immense geographical gap in-between.

In closing, the *collegium* of *negotiatores eborarii et citriarii* and the Indian ivory statuette from Pompeii can be interpreted as rare diagnostic evidence of the trade between Rome and India in the 1st–2nd century AD. As we have seen, the carved ivory products of organisations of specialised Indian craftsmen came to be in demand at Rome, shaping both the city's furniture and its organisations to produce and purvey it in the process. The cultural biography of the Indian ivory statuette from Pompeii, then, when fully elaborated upon, provides important new insights into not only the workings of trade between the Ancient Mediterranean and Indian Ocean,[300] but also very long-distance flows of people and products, fashion and furniture.[301] Moreover, such an active Indian agency in all aspects of this particular strand of the long-distance trade may even be said to finally turn the tables on the old historiographical notion of 'Indo-Roman trade,' Indian craftsmen, traders and shippers, as well as their level of institutional organisation, taking their rightful place besides their Roman counterparts.

[295] Murthy 1982: chairs: 37 i), figs. IX.1–2 (Amaravati), 38 i), figs. IX.3–4 (Nagarjunakonda); footstools: 23 c), fig. VI.29 (Ajanta), 71, fig. XVII.6 (Gandhara); low stools or tripods: 51 iv), fig. XIII.28 (Amaravati), 54 c), fig. XIV.35 (Gandhara); table: 64, fig. XVI.10 (Ajanta). To these can be added one more tripod stand in Dhavalikar 1973: 101, fig. XXVI, 6.

[296] As argued by Zin 2015: 182, photo on p. 183 (Abb. 1).

[297] This part of the table design, the three lions carrying the table on their heads, can be compared with well-preserved three-legged marble tables from Pompeii, where lion protomes support a tabletop, e.g. Moss 1988: C66–7.

[298] Hackin 1954: 277, 281, nos. 26, 88, figs. 340, 459–62. Hiebert and Cambon 2008: 203, no. 219. Pompeian *comparandum* published in Museo Nazionale di Napoli 1989: 180, no. 64.

[299] Roman examples: Richter 1966: 111; Croom 2007: 87–8, fig. 36; Indian *ditto*: Dhavalikar 1973: 99, fig. XXVI.3; Murthy 1982: 63, fig. XVI.6.

[300] As Kopytoff 1986: 67–8, 88–9, remarks, transfers between different systems of exchange, and the entailing changes made to objects and their status, is particularly apt to bring out the divergent ways in which societies classify and construct things.

[301] Augmenting the conclusions of Appadurai 1996, whose historical framework, pp. 27–8, as well as notion of global flows through, *inter alia*, 'ethnoscapes' and 'technoscapes,' pp. 33–4, can be tentatively compared with an ancient scenario such as this. See similarly Ahuja 2016 for an object analysis which disentangles the distinct 'cultural multiplicities' of a Gandharan statuette and argues that these were constructed deliberately by an audience borne out of transculturalism, not syncretism.

Chapter 4

The invisible hand of Roman organisations

Horace, the famous Roman poet of the late 1st century BC, rounds off one of his longer pieces with the scornful remark that he himself would dread if a friend wrote a hyperbolic poem in his praise, so that afterwards, passing down the 'street where frankincense, fragrances and pepper is sold,' he would have to witness vendors wrapping up their wares in scraps torn from copies of this pulp poetry.[302] In addition to informing us that the poetic publications of the untalented amateurs were subsequently, perhaps almost immediately, sold off for their 'scrap paper' value, there is the all too brief reference to some of those who put bad poetry to good use in their shops and stalls: the dealers in spices.

Thus, we learn that there was a specific street (*vicus*) associated with their business, and that the retail sale of traditionally rare and exotic commodities such as incense (*tus*), perfumes (*odores*) and pepper (*piper*), had become a familiar sight in the market streets of Rome already by the later 1st century BC. If the message behind these particular lines had been the magnificence of Rome's mercantile resources, then this might have been mere aggrandisement, but seeing as the street here serves rather the purpose of a backdrop bringing out a self-implicating ironic modesty, we might consider it a sound reference to a scene from daily life in the capital.[303]

In fact, this was only the beginning. By the mid-2nd century AD, according to Aelius Aristides' panegyrical poem in praise of Rome, ships arrived in the imperial capital with all sorts of goods from every people of the earth, every hour, every day, the arrivals and departures of ships in and out of port never ceasing. So that in Rome everything came together: 'trade, seafaring, farming, the scourings of the mines, all the crafts that exist or have existed, all that is produced and grown.'[304] Moreover, Aristides emphasises how this incessant flow of foreign commerce into the city rendered it 'like a workshop common to the whole earth'[305] with such an amount of cargoes arriving from India and Arabia that he imagined these places left bare and destitute, their inhabitants having to travel to Rome to obtain the commodities of their very own countries.

What are we to make of these statements? Surely, they are to some extent exaggerated, boasting the glory of Rome and its role as the 'Great Attractor' of the known world[306]—but underneath there must have been some element of truth to all of this. How organised was this long-distance trade with the Near and Far East, manufacture of every raw material in existence, and daily proximity with spices and foreigners aplenty? And how much of it can we reconstruct on a wider empirical basis, as a history of those who actually processed and traded the long-distance imports, thus, trying to avoid the pitfalls of rhetorical praise and ideological posturing inherent to the literary sources? Quite a bit, in fact, and certainly enough to grow significantly wiser about the organisational aspects of the trade.[307]

This chapter aims to expand on the insights gained from the previous case-study by asking how the western termini of the wider Indian Ocean trade were anchored in Rome. In the process, various types of sources will be employed in an attempt to give a bottom-up answer to the question of who the involved retailers and merchants were, how they organised themselves, and what this implies about demand for items which, by virtue of their far-off origin, could only hail from either India or other areas integrated

[302] Hor. *Epist*., II.1.269–70: —*deferar in vicum vendentem tus et odores et piper / et quidquid chartis amicitur ineptis*; transl. by the author.

[303] The point being that Horace's praise of Augustus is not as lofty or fanciful as the works of some other poets, and that this kind of exaggerated praise embarrassed both author and recipient alike.

[304] Aristid. *Or*., XXVI.11, 13; mid- to later 2nd AD, transl: Behr 1981.

[305] Aristid. *Or*., XXVI.11–12.

[306] Cf. discussion in Bang 2011: 290–1. However, as is argued throughout this study, redistributive processes of tribute exaction cannot be posited to account for the majority of the exchange between the Mediterranean and the Indian Ocean, which was facilitated by merchants, not tributary flows; this view compares more favourably with Bang 2009b: 119–20.

[307] Recent scholarship has forcefully established the role of work and trade in the ancient economy, e.g. Tran 2013, Flohr and Wilson 2016.

into the Indian Ocean exchange circuit. In the following, we shall thus enquire into the retailing of semiprecious stones and gems, pearls, frankincense, myrrh, spices and silk. In order to launch ourselves into such a study, however, a brief consideration of the nature and limitations of source material for networks and *collegia* in Rome involved in the long-distance trade is necessary.

First of all, most of the sources are inscriptions, making it vital to consider the implications of the so-called Roman 'epigraphic habit' for our interpretation of the epigraphs in question.[308] Specifically, most Roman inscriptions were set up from Augustan times onwards, peaking in the mid-second century AD and declining markedly from the third century[309] Accordingly, it is no coincidence that all of the inscriptions attesting *collegia* to be treated below date from the 1st and 2nd century AD, whereas if such organisations existed before (as did the *collegium aromatariorum*, if we are to make any sense of its own time-reckoning) or after (which is more than likely, at least for the 3rd century AD), we simply do not have any surviving comparable evidence to inform us about it. Secondly, if there were any similar organisations involved in the long-distance trade which did not choose to participate in the epigraphic habit, or whose inscriptions have simply been lost during the passage of time, we will never know about them (such as a plausible *collegium sericariorum*).[310] Moreover, it is necessary to keep in mind both that the purpose and popularity of Roman *collegia* changed somewhat in Late Antiquity,[311] and that the epigraphic habit was on the wane, resulting in the disappearance of *collegia* from the epigraphic record from the later fourth century AD onwards,[312] leaving us with preciously little knowledge about the urban organisation of trade in long-distance imports in the 4th–6th century AD.

In addition, other factors must be taken into consideration regarding the inscriptions of *collegia*, craftsmen and traders, namely, that some 3/4 of all inscriptions in Rome and Ostia generally were put up by freedmen,[313] and that 'occupational inscriptions' as a distinct category of their own exhibit some noteworthy characteristics, although numbering only some 1200 inscriptions out of more than 200,000 from Late Republican and Early Imperial Rome.[314] In particular, occupational title appears to have been of little importance in the funerary epitaphs of freeborn citizens, whereas this was quite common among freedmen and slaves, to whom occupation was an important part of their identity. This means that an epigraphic study of occupations in ancient Rome is likely to show a preponderance of freedmen and slaves, but this simply means that they were more likely to mention their professions in inscriptions, not necessarily that freeborn citizens did not work in the same trades, simply that the latter were not in the epigraphic habit of recording it on stone.[315]

As regards those ninety-one individuals who mention their occupation in relation to a Roman *collegium*, though,[316] it is highly significant, then, that they appear to have been predominantly freeborn citizens, only freedmen to a lesser degree, and it is highly conspicuous that most of them have to be categorised as such on other criteria than formal indication of free or freedman status.[317] Indeed, it seems to be the case that formal affiliation with a *collegium* took pride of place over the traditional legal status of citizens, membership or office in the association being more important in the eyes of the deceased and his fellow-member peers, implying that the select community of members had attained priority over the wider community of citizens.[318] Obviously, such a state of affairs fits rather well as a general description with the characteristics of networks treated previously, and with the special case of networks formally consolidated as associations, in particular.

[308] MacMullen 1982.
[309] Updated analysis by Beltrán Lloris 2014: 139–40.
[310] Liu 2013: 357–8.
[311] Sirks 1993; Liu 2009: 279–94; Venticinque 2016: 199–237.
[312] Liu 2013: 367.
[313] Beltrán Lloris 2014: 145.
[314] For these updated numbers, see Hawkins 2016: 204; the main work, however, is Joshel 1992.
[315] Joshel 1992: 47–9 (also 76–91, more generally, on slaves' and freedmen's claim to a position in life through occupation).
[316] Joshel 1992: 113.
[317] Joshel 1992: 100.
[318] Joshel 1992: 117–21. On the 'work status' of professionals organised in *collegia*, see in particular Tran 2006: 89–110.

The collegium of goldsmiths and clusters of craftsmen in the jewellery trade

From various ports along its rim, the Indian Ocean was a major supplier of expensive raw materials for the Roman jewellery business, these items, just like ivory table legs, being quintessential high-value, low-weight, long-distance trade commodities. Arriving in imperial Rome from South Asia via such Mediterranean ports as the chief production centres of jewellery since Hellenistic times, Antioch and Alexandria,319 these precious objects became part of the world of Roman jewellers and goldsmiths, craftsmen and traders.320 Accordingly, just as there was an association of citriarii and negotiatores eborarii et citriarii, so there were associations for those fashioning jewellery from imported gems and pearls, whether these originated in the Mediterranean or farther afield.

Take, for instance, the generically named *collegium aurificum*, that is, association of goldsmiths, of whose existence we learn from an inscription dated to the Augustan period or later in the 1st century AD. From this epigraph's laconic contents, we know that the *collegium* was headed by a president, the *magister quinquennalis*, who in this case was a freedman of apparent Eastern extraction, his personal name being Seleucus.[321] Dating back even earlier, to Republican times, is another inscription revealing the existence of a related association, a *collegium anulariorum*, these ring-makers (who would also have set and perhaps even dressed the ring stones) being headed by *duomviri*, a two-man executive board.[322] The members of such organisations of goldsmiths and ring-makers would inevitably have been bound up with the long-distance trade, as participants in a market for South Asian ring stones, other precious and semiprecious stones, as well as pearls.

Significantly, a complex of stalls attested epigraphically and archaeologically on the Via Sacra itself, just east of the *Forum Romanum*, represents a commercial hotspot which can probably best be described as a market for precious jewellery and similarly expensive items, many of these necessarily of Indian provenance.[323] Here were gathered, *inter alia*, seven pearl traders, *margaritarii*,[324] as well as four goldsmiths, seven gem-cutters, three engravers and bas-relief carvers, a gold-embroiderer, a maker of crowns, and one self-styled trader who was out of the same family as one of the goldsmiths,[325] moving in to Neronian porticoes after the fire of Rome in AD 64, later rebuilt into the *horrea piperataria* by Domitian.[326] Considering the fact that gemstones were widely held to have magical and medicinal properties for their wearers, a location for this cluster adjacent to the major temples and religious sites of Rome was quite fitting.[327]

In addition to the Via Sacra, there were a dozen other *margaritarii* working throughout the city (one styling himself *negotiator margaritarius*),[328] and from topographical lists of the early 4th century AD it appears that a building called the *porticus margaritaria* later served as the designated centre of this line of trade,[329] while clusters of goldsmiths, gilders[330] and ring-makers have been identified in at least seven other localities[331]—the latter occupying the *Scalae Anulariae* leading from the *Forum* up the Palatine.[332] We even learn from Martial and Juvenal that Rome at the turn of the 1st century AD boasted a 'shopping-

---

319 Higgins 1980: 175; Sartre 2005: 244.

320 The best general introduction to the use of precious- and semi-precious stones in Antiquity is now Lapatin 2015: 107–26 with pl. 81–145.

321 *CIL* VI, 9202; Augustan date claimed by Loane 1938: 88. While this is reasonable, albeit early, we can only on onomastic grounds point to the use of the *tria nomina* for a freedmen as providing a *post quem* of the 80s BC and an *ante quem* of the later 2nd century AD, cf. Cooley 2012: 410, 412. However, according to Royden 1988: 137, the use of *co<n=l>legium* for *collegium* indicates 1st century AD usage.

322 *CIL* VI, 9144; cf. dating by Loane 1938: 90; and Waltzing 1895–99, III: 1, no. 7.

323 On the archaeological history of shops in the area from Sulla to Nero, cf. van Deman 1923: 396–402. Holleran 2012: 55–6, 246.

324 *Margaritarii de Sacra Via*: *CIL* VI, 9545–49, 33,872, and *CIL* X, 6492; dated by Loane 1938: 134, n79, to the first century AD, before 64; Tassini 1994: 690f.

325 List of inscriptions: *aurifices* (*CIL* VI, 9207; *Eph.Epigr.* IX, 757), *auri acceptor* (*CIL* VI, 9212), *vascularius* (*CIL* VI, 37824); *gemmari* (*CIL* VI, 9434–5); *caelator* (*CIL* VI, 9221), *cabatores* (*CIL* VI, 9239); *aurivestrix* (*CIL* VI, 9214); *coronarius* (*CIL* VI, 9283); *negotiator* (*CIL* VI, 9662) related to *aurifex* (*CIL* VI, 9207). Cf. Loane 1938: 133–4, n76; Tassini 1994: 689.

326 Van Deman 1923: 388, 415–24.

327 Lapatin 2009: 43–4; 2015: 109.

328 List of inscriptions: *negotiator margaritarius* deceased in Aquileia (Venetia) *ab Roma*: *I.Aquil.* I, 718; *margaritarii* generally: *CIL* VI, 641, 1925, 3051, 3981, 5199, 5972, 9544, 30,973, 37,804; *ICUR* IX, 24,854.1.

329 Its location is disputed, though, cf. Ashby and Platner 2002: *s.v.* 'Porticus Margaritaria'; Richardson 1992: *s.v.* 'Porticus Margaritaria;' *LTUR s.v.* 'Porticus Margaritaria.' On the dating of the topographical lists: Truesdell Merrill 1906.

330 These workers in gold-leaf also had a *collegium* of their own: *CIL* VI, 95.

331 Loane 1938: 88, 90, 135–36.

332 Suet. *Aug.*, LXXII.1; Holleran 2012: 56.

district' north of the *Forum*, centred on the *Porticus Argonautarum* (or *Agrippinia*) in the *Saepta Julia* and the surrounding buildings on the *Campus Martius*, where expensive crafted objects of foreign origin could be purchased: citrus and ivory tables, tortoise-shell dinner couches, Greek bronzes, crystal and agate vases, myrrhine cups, ancient bowls, fine goblets, emeralds encased in wrought gold, pearl earrings, sardonyxes, jaspers and diamond rings—choice young slaves being the non-craft exception. Later, by the mid-5th century AD, the market for silk, jewellery and precious gold-work apparently moved back towards the *Forum*, to the slope of the Capitol.[333]

Although the work status of these *aurifices*, *anularii*, *gemmarii*, and *margaritarii*, to name but the major groups, can sometimes be difficult to ascertain, it appears that many small-timers doubled in the roles of both craftsmen and traders, that is, both buying and selling, boring, trimming, dressing, working in gold or silver, and encasing, but there may also have been some division of labour, reflecting specialised processes within each craft. While some would have been slaves in the households of the rich, most seem to have been freedmen and their freeborn descendants, undoubtedly receiving part of their business from former patrons, as well as from trusted peers and partners in related trades. As regards the expensive material requirements of their craft, legal and epigraphic sources attest that artisans were either owners themselves, had them furnished by their patrons, or, most commonly, received them directly from their customers for the desired task in hand.[334] Excavations at two houses in Pompeii (II.9.2 and III.4b), evidently belonging to gem-cutters, reveal that a single *gemmarius* on his own could hold more than a hundred semiprecious stones in stock, carved and uncarved, of popular varieties such as carnelian, chalcedony, jasper, agate, etc.[335] Some jewellers certainly became quite wealthy through their work, no matter their humble social backgrounds, such as a *gemmarius* who financed a temple on his own,[336] or pearl traders, to be treated below, who donated buildings and money to their *collegium* of choice.[337]

Accordingly, the wares sold by these craftsmen of the Via Sacra and their numerous colleagues would not simply have been pearls, gems or semi-precious stones by themselves, rather, these would have been fitted into rings, necklaces, earrings, etc.[338] For instance, a late 4th century AD epigram evokes a context of imported gems and jewellery by pitting a vessel for drinking wine against an amethyst, believed to have the power to ward of intoxication, both of these objects stated to be of Indian origin.[339] Moreover, larger stones were carved into both sunk relief intaglios, to serve as signet rings, as well as ornate raised relief cameos. Thus, it was Roman craftsmen specialised in jewellery who processed these imports into their final forms, playing a similar role to the traders who marketed Indian ivory transformed into Roman furniture. Physical proximity must have fostered personal relations between the occupants of stalls and likely also a certain amount of cooperation between different crafts, rendering some degree of specialisation possible.[340] Indeed, this seems to be borne out by a Pompeian graffito in which Priscus the engraver 'sends his best wishes' to Campanus the gem-cutter.[341]

Ties of patronage in Rome can also be traced both between individual pearl dealers and jewellers, such as the interesting case of freedmen and -women of different *gentes* working together in a unit as *gemmarii* of the Via Sacra, as well as to powerful senators like Cn. Pompeius.[342] Moreover, there is evidence of two *margaritarii* of Syrian ancestry, a freedman and his freeborn son, out of the Campanian *Calpurnii*, which could, on the one hand, indicate import of Persian Gulf pearls. On the other hand, though, a slave of

[333] Mart. *Epigr.*, IX.59, Juv. VI.153-55, Sid. Apoll. *Epist.*, I.7.8; Loane 1938: 136–7; Holleran 2012: 249–51.

[334] Loane 1938: 86–90, 134–5. Holleran 2012: 26–30. On identified carvers, see Lapatin 2015: 121–22.

[335] Lapatin 2009: 40.

[336] *CIL* VI, 9433.

[337] See also Joshel 1992: 84–5, on the economic circumstances and status of the freed *margaritarius de Sacra Via* commemorated in *CIL* VI, 9545. While he claimed in his funerary epitaph to be poor, this was evidently out of a sense of modesty, seeing as he had the means to erect a tomb and include some of his own freedmen in it.

[338] For the variety of products, see Higgins 1980: 176–85.

[339] Parker 2008: 155, n16. For the magical properties of amethysts, see Pliny *NH*, XXXVII.40. In addition, Claudian's description of the emperor Honorius' attire in 398 AD contains an interesting description of the role of Indian gemstones in elite Roman fashion, cf. both Hildebrandt 2016 and forthcoming.

[340] Holleran 2012: 59–60; Hawkins 2016: 91–2.

[341] *CIL* IV, 8505.

[342] Respectively: Loane 1938: 89, on the *gemmarii* (*CIL* VI, 9435); and Tassini 1994: 689, on the *aurifex* Cn. Pompeius Iucundus (*CIL* VI, 37,781).

apparent Arab extraction serving another member of this *gens* left a graffito in Egypt, on the road to Berenike, where remnants of the transit trade in Indian pearls have been found.[343] Indeed, a number of earrings made from clusters of pearls have been found in the Naples area, as we shall see shortly

As regards the geographical provenance of the exotic stones thus made part of the conspicuous consumption at Rome, Pliny informs us that India was the single greatest producer of gemstones,[344] and while he is of little use as regards the geographical distribution of specific varieties, his treatment of Indian diamonds, sardonyx, turquoise, onyx, rock crystal and amethyst, can be combined with other sources to locate more specific origins.[345] In particular, the *Periplus* informs us that turquoise and lapis lazuli were exported from Barbaricon[346] in the estuary of the Indus, that the Ariake region in modern Gujarat produced onyx and agate, that the Malabar Coast and in particular the *emporia* of Muziris and Nelcynda exported diamonds, transparent stones of all kinds (quartz, Pliny's rock crystal) and sapphires, while, finally, Sri Lanka was known to yield transparent stones.[347] Ptolemy being able to add in the mid-2nd century AD that inland from the river on which was Muziris of the *Periplus* lay a region of the Cheran kingdom rich in in beryls.[348] Indeed, excavations at a few key sites in South India have corroborated the extensive involvement of Tamils in the gem trade, as we shall return to in chapter eight, perhaps even with engravers at work carving Greco-Roman motifs in the Indian ports.

When it comes to pearls, Pliny informs us, with a reference back to the *mensarum insania* above, that just as the affluent men of his day were mad for citrus tables, their wives were equally driven by a desire for pearls,[349] the latter being obtained chiefly from Sri Lanka (ancient *Taprobane*), the greatest producer of pearls, and the Persian Gulf, which produced the best quality.[350] Pearls of an inferior quality were also available in limited quantity within the confines of the Roman Empire: from Britannia, Mauretania, Acarnania (in western-central Greece), Thrace and the Red Sea—but the best quality specimens were imported from the Indian Ocean.[351] Thus, Statius in his poetic summary of exotic revenue of the imperial *fiscus* includes pearls of the Eastern Sea (*pelagus Eous*),[352] while the author of the *Periplus* states that the pearls of the Persian Gulf were inferior to those of India, contradicting Pliny, and adds that not only Sri Lanka exported pearls, but also the Tamil kingdom of the Pandians, as well as the Ganges estuary.[353]

In addition, the trade in both pearls and precious stones attracted fiscal attention and is therefore attested in a register of customs duties on Eastern imports, drawn up under Marcianus, a jurist of the early 3rd century AD, and later included in the *Digest* of Justinian.[354] Seeing as these taxes, *vectigalia*, were most likely exacted at Alexandria, the list is often referred to as the 'Alexandrian Tariff,' and it levies a fee on 'all precious stones,' among others the specific varieties from Barbaricon, Barygaza, Muziris, and Sri Lanka, just discussed, such as pearls, sardonyx, diamonds, lapis lazuli, turquoise and beryls.

Indeed, excavations at the Egyptian Red Sea port of Berenike have yielded two South Asian sapphires (South India and Sri Lanka being the only source of this gemstone in Antiquity[355]), one of them from a late 4th–early 6th century AD satellite village, and a number of mainly onyx but also sardonyx cameo

[343] Father (*CIL*, VI 33,872) and son (*CIL*, VI 9546) both bearing Eastern *cognomina* and the *gentilicum* of the *Calpurnii*, one of the latter governing the province of Syria in 4–1 BC; cf. Tassini 1994: 691; also, Loane 1938: 134–35; for the Puteolian *Calpurnii* and a Greek-speaking *Kalpornios* in Egypt's Eastern Desert, see chapter six. For the finds of pearls at Berenike, see below.

[344] Pliny *NH*, XXXVII.76: *Gemmiferi amnes sunt Acesinus* (the Chenab) *et Ganges, terrarum autem omnium maxime India*. However, while he is right about India as a whole, the rivers Chenab and Ganges are not particularly rich on gemstones, cf. Francis 2004: 503.

[345] Respectively, Pliny *NH*, XXXVII.15, 23, 33, 24, 8, 25. See also Higgins 1980: 36–9.

[346] Possibly to be identified with the site of Banbhore, cf. Khan 1963; and Manassero and Fiorani 2014.

[347] *Periplus* 39, 48–9, 51, 56, 61. On the trade in precious and semi-precious stones as revealed in the *Periplus*, see now Seland 2017.

[348] Ptol. *Geog.*, VII.2.

[349] Pliny *NH*, XIII.29.

[350] Pliny *NH*, primarily IX.54, supplementary VI.24, 28.

[351] Tassini 1994: 690. On the Red Sea pearl production in particular, see Schörle 2015: 46–9. On pearls in Antiquity more generally, see Lapatin 2015: 182–4; Donkin 1998: 80–104.

[352] Stat. *Silv.*, III.3.92: *quodque legit mersus pelagi scrutator Eoi.*

[353] *Periplus* 35, 36, 56, 59, 61, 63.

[354] *Dig.* XXXIX.4.16.7; Jones 1974: 140; Young 2001: 209; Cherry 2007: 740; Parker 2008: 149–50.

[355] Wendrich *et al.* 2003: 62; Lapatin 2009: 45; 2015: 110. Also in Byzantine times, 5th–7th century, cf. Drauschke 2010: 52.

blanks,[356] thus, perhaps mined in Gujarat and exported from Barygaza, as attested by the *Periplus* and archaeology,[357] or from South Indian sites such as Pattanam or Arikamedu, to be detailed in chapter eight, where a number of such cameo blanks have been found. In addition, diagnostic gemstone finds from Berenike include amethyst (either from local Egyptian sources or Indian), lapis lazuli (from the Kokscha Valley of north-eastern Afghanistan), carnelian and sard (most likely from India), and rock crystal, aquamarine beryl and garnet (all from South India or Sri Lanka).[358]

Significantly, these finds can be correlated with five graves excavated in the greater Roman area from the later 2nd century AD, and two graves from Lugdunum (Lyon) in Gaul dating from the early and later third century AD, where jewellery incorporating a diamond and sapphires, both types of which could only have come from India,[359] as well as pieces studded with amethyst, sardonyx, garnet, carnelian, rock crystal and onyx have come to light.[360] What is more, an isotopic study of an emerald from an earring found in Roman Gaul has established that it must have been mined in the Swat Valley of Northern Pakistan,[361] highlighting the possibility that other Roman emeralds did not come from *Mons Smaragdus* in Egypt either, but arrived from down the Indus River with the Indian Ocean trade.[362] Finally, it has been pointed out that Roman jewellers seem to have been aware of the great advantage of using diamonds for drills and cutting in other gemstones, meaning that they must have imported diamond fragments from South Indian ports, where this technique was already well-known.[363]

As regards pearls, two finds have been made at Berenike, one being a gold-wire earring sporting five small pearls of a fashion known from mummy-portraits of the 2nd–3rd century AD, the other a loose specimen.[364] Hence, seeing as The Persian Gulf and the Red Sea constituted largely complementary east-west transport corridors at the time,[365] with very little evidence of direct sea-trade between them,[366] we should expect these pearls found at Berenike to be of either local, Red Sea, or South Asian extraction. Pearl earrings have been excavated at a number of sites in the Empire, e.g. the Naples area,[367] Rome[368] and Lugdunum in Gaul.[369]

Moving back to the personnel of the trade, a sidelight is thrown on the social life, status and business acumen of two *margaritarii* in Rome who have come down to us not as members of the *collegium aurificum*, which they were likely to have been anyway, but as high-ranking presidents of another group, namely, the popular and widespread (being the third most attested of all) *collegium* of *dendrophores*, or, literally, 'tree-bearers.'[370] While it is a contested issue whether the *dendrophores* where merely united by their devotion to *Magna Mater*, and designated as 'tree-bearers' for a conspicuous part of their cultic activities,[371] or because they were indeed devotees of *Magna Mater* but primarily defined as a professional association of

[356] Sidebotham 2011: 237–38, 276. Harrell 1998: 144.
[357] On the latter, see Francis 2004: 503.
[358] Wendrich *et al.* 2003: 54–62; Tomber 2008: 85. Byzantine red garnet from the 5th–early 7th century has been traced to India through chemical analysis; Drauschke 2010: 51f.
[359] On the South Asian origin of diamonds, see Thoresen 2017: 191.
[360] Bedini 1995: the diamond is no. 20 (on which see also Bedini *et al.* 2012; on the rare finds of diamonds, see Thoresen 2017: 168 w. figs. 4–5 and n63); sapphires are nos. 9, 13–14, 18–19, 21, 50, 95; amethysts are nos. 15, 34, 97; sardonyx is no. 16; garnets are nos. 17, 63, 91, 96, 100–1, 109; carnelian is no. 36; rock crystals are nos. 81–83, 93; and onyx is no. 110. In addition, the region around Aquileia has yielded a stupendous number of carved gemstones from Roman times, cf. Sena Chiesa 1966, of varieties including carnelian, quartz, amethyst, onyx, sardonyx and lapis lazzuli.
[361] Giuliani *et al.* 2000.
[362] Bedini 1995 contains a great number of emerald pieces: nos. 11, 22–3, 33, 60, 64, 98–103, 106, 108–9. Those numbering from '98' and upwards are all from Lyon in Gaul, rendering their possible origin in South Asia the more likely.
[363] Gorelick and Gwinnett 1988.
[364] Sidebotham and Wendrich 2002: 30–1, fig. 11. Sidebotham 2011: 237.
[365] Salles 1993.
[366] There is a little archaeological evidence, though, from the Roman Red Sea ports, cf. Tomber 2008: 79; and the *Alexandrian Tariff* (chapter six) lists 'Babylonian' and 'Parthian' skins, which may have been shipped up the Red Sea.
[367] Museo Napoli 1989b: 213, nos. 52–3, p. 216, no. 68, p. 218, no. 90; Schörle 2015: 43, n1. Higgins 1980: 178.
[368] Bedini 1995: no. 39, pearls set in gold earrings (later 2nd century AD).
[369] Bedini 1995: no. 101, garnet, emerald and pearl set in gold earrings (no earlier than 193 AD); and no. 109, garnet, emerald and pearl earring (no earlier than 258 AD).
[370] Van Haeperen 2012: 47–49.
[371] Van Haeperen 2012: 56.

lumberjacks,[372] *margaritarii* would no doubt simply have joined their ranks for the platform of organised support it gave them and for the communal cult.

Be that as it may, Manius Publicius Hilarus, *margaritarius*, became an honorary president of the *dendrophores* of Rome in the mid-2nd century AD, and was honoured by the *collegium dendrophorum* with the erection of a statue in the *basilica Hilariana*, constructed by and named after himself, their patron, which was used as a gathering place for the association, just as with the *schola* of the *negotiatores eborarii et citriarii*. Slightly later, by the end of the 2nd century AD, another affluent pearl trader, Tuticius Hylas, was also honoured by appointment as *quinquennalis perpetuus*, and decided to set up an endowment of 10,000 sesterces with the *collegium dendrophorum* itself, of which the accruing interest was to be expended on an annual commemoration in his honour. In case the *dendrophores* defaulted on the agreement, a clause in the inscription stipulated that the *collegium* would then owe an equal sum to the public treasury—a common enforcement measure to assure compliance of the beneficiary party after the decease of the testator.[373]

Accordingly, we gain a valuable insight into the interaction between wealthy traders in Eastern goods and *collegia*, the former acting as patrons providing meeting-places and money, their host associations meanwhile proving themselves worthy and capable of handling large amounts of communal funds, loaning them out, retrieving the interest and honouring the commemorative requirements attached to their endowments. In each their own way, these two cases involving *margaritarii* reflect the main aspects of the patronage exercised by Julius Aelianus over the *negotiatores eborarii et citriarii*: namely, paying for a 'club house' and providing one-off donations to finance perpetual group activities, necessitating the development of internal financial institutions to yield a profit which could cover the aggregate annual upkeep.

Such inscriptions, providing evidence of how the non-elite strata of Roman commercial society habitually institutionalised communal finance in an honorific context, render us aware of the potential for economic interaction within these *collegia* of craftsmen and traders which provided a formal relationship, norms and measures for internal ordering to colleagues within various occupations united by joint membership. Thus, the professions co-inhabiting the Via Sacra and constituting a jewellery market would not only have had reasons to cooperate due to physical proximity, but some would even have found further incentives deriving from membership of the same associations, impinging on not only social (cult, processions, feasts, funerary activities) and economic aspects (membership fees, endowment-funds to lend out, annual distributions) of the lives of their members, but also, as we have seen with the *collegium* of *negotiatores eborarii et citriarii*, strengthening bonds between select vocations.[374]

Indeed, a Pompeian graffito bears this out eminently well by revealing how 'all of the goldsmiths together,' *aurifices universi*, encouraged passers-by to vote for their profession's favourite candidate for the municipal office of *aedile*. Evidently, vocational bonds easily spilled over into the political dimension of ancient life, no doubt circumscribed by overarching patronage networks.[375] Moreover, organisation into a *collegium aurificum* of craftsmen and retailers may have constituted one important way to keep track of fellow members' dealings and doings, making it possible to monitor, punish, or expel from the formal association of peers, like the *ordo* of the *negotiatores eborarii et citriarii*, anyone who dealt in fake pearls or precious stones. Thus, honest *aurifices* and *margaritarii* needed to avoid purchasing forged pearls from suppliers and to penalise *margaritarii* who concocted fake pearls themselves for onward retail sale, as Egyptian papyri listing formulas for such forgeries reveal were a widespread practice.[376]

[372] Wilson 2012: 140.
[373] Respectively, *CIL* VI, 641, 30,973; and 1925; dated by Loane 1938: 135; and van Haeperen 2012: 57.
[374] Compare Holleran 2012: 63–4.
[375] *CIL* IV, 710.
[376] Schörle 2015: 53, n59.

The collegium of frankincense and perfume traders

There is, in fact, more evidence to adduce for associations being shaped to create highly intentional institutional spaces for select craftsmen and traders who stood to benefit as a whole by strengthening social ties between groups. Consider, for instance, the case of the *collegium thurariorum et unguentariorum* which put up a dedication in the early 2nd century AD for the well-being of the Imperial Household, the task being entrusted to and carried out by Novius Successus, its *quaestor*.[377] Here, the use of the term *cura agente* implies that Novius, as the administrative and executive officer of the group, was merely performing a task that had been decided on collectively by an assembly of the members.[378]

This membership consisted of *thurarii*, who were dealers in frankincense, *tus*, and *unguentarii*, who were perfumers or dealers in unguents, sometimes also known as a *seplasiarii*, named after the *Seplasia*, a famous market for perfume in Capua.[379] Accordingly, *unguentarius* is the Latin rendering of the Greek *muropôlês*, which means the same thing, but better brings out the fact that myrrh was an important component in many of their products (along with a number of other aromatics and fragrant spices of diverse origins). Generally speaking, some practitioners of these crafts were slaves, working as agents (*institores*) of their masters, while most were freedmen and their descendants, and although many will not have been very affluent, some did rise to prominence as *seviri Augustales*, and some left funerary monuments demonstrating their wealth.[380]

No matter their social standing, though, the members of this association were at the receiving end of trade routes which, *inter alia*, started in Hadramawt of present-day Eastern Yemen and Western Oman, as regards the frankincense, and in Qataban of Central Yemen as regards the myrrh,[381] although the sources also speak of imports of some frankincense and a little myrrh from the Horn of Africa.[382] Moreover, it is significant that the attestation of the *collegium thurariorum et unguentariorum* dates to the early 2nd century AD, whereas privately controlled freedmen-networks of aristocratic families are known from the Republican Era and early 1st century AD, perhaps suggesting the development in Rome of a new kind of long-distance retail market, consisting of more minor but independent dealers.[383]

That there should be a close relationship between dealers in frankincense and myrrh at the receiving end begs an explanation: the retail sale of processed frankincense and the production and sale of perfumes and medicinal ointments are not the same line of work. Emphatically, this coupling of incense dealers and perfume vendors was not unique to this one *collegium*, for we also find a joint dedication in Rome from the close of the 1st century BC by an *unguentarius* and a *thurarius* in unison, who had a freedwoman in common.[384] However, someone specialised in either trade would not necessarily fare well in the other without additional training, and individuals seem to have been either one or the other, such as the nine freedmen of the *Trebonii* who were all *thurarii*, or the unique case of the freedmen of the *L. Faenii*, of whom one was actually a far-off *unguentarius* in Gaul while the other five where Italian *thurarii*, and who were likely clients of the prominent Neronian equestrian L. Faenius Rufus.[385] Accordingly, we must seek an alternative explanation for the coupling of frankincense dealers and perfumers in one *collegium*, as well as in individual inscriptions.

---

[377] *CIL* VI, 36819. Dated *c.* 101–30 AD by *Epigraphic Database Roma* (EDR072477). A 2nd century date would fit with the lack of a stated *praenomen*, cf. Cooley 2012: 412.

[378] Raepsaet-Charlier and Allé 2008: 291.

[379] Brun 2000: 290, 299, 302, who also provides a highly useful list of inscriptions attesting these people, pp. 302–6.

[380] Bonsangue and Tran 2008: 259–60. Holleran 2012: 128–9

[381] Singer 2007: 7–9.

[382] Pliny *NH*, XII.33; *Periplus* 8–12.

[383] Salmeri 1997: 531; compare Bonsangue and Tran 2008: 260, on the role of the *collegium*.

[384] *CIL* VI, 5638; dated 25–1 BC on archaeological, linguistic and palaeographic grounds by *Epigraphic Database Roma* (EDR129007). One of the two, Lucius Lutatius Paccius, elsewhere boasts to have belonged *de familia rege Mitredatis*, presumably either Mithridates II or III of Commagene; *CIL* VI, 5639. Cf. Raepsaet-Charlier and Allé 2008: 291.

[385] For the *Trebonii*, *CIL* VI, 9933, 9934, of Republican date, cf. Tassini 1994: 693. Regarding the *Faenii*, one was an *unguentarius*, *CIL* VI 9998 (Gallia Lugdunensis), while the other were *thurarii* in Rome and Italia: *CIL* VI, 5680, 9932 (Rome); *AE* 1979, 124 (Marino); X, 1962 (Puteoli), 6802 (Ischia); dated to the early 1st century AD by Tassini 1994: 692f. The link to L. Faenius Rufus was suggested by D'Arms 1981: 167-8. Cf. Salmeri 1997: 531–2. Other examples in Rome are the three *unguentarii* of the *Popillii* (*CIL* VI, 845, 10,001, 10,003), and the two *thurarii* of the *Cornelii* (*CIL* VI, 9930, 9931)

Although shared areas of origin of the two commodities might at first glance appear to be the most obvious common denominator, this is only partially true, for while frankincense and myrrh were produced in adjacent regions of present-day Yemen, Oman and Somalia, the products of *unguentarii* contained numerous other scented ingredients in combination with myrrh, while some were not based on myrrh at all. Thus, there were both mundane (roses) and more expensive (saffron) ingredients available within the Roman Empire, as well as a large amount of expensive and exotic aromatic components arriving from as far east as India.[386] Consequently, parallel routes of import, processing and sale might be a plausible explanation, attracting our attention to the intertwining of trade routes, not least at the major junction of Alexandria, where both frankincense and perfume ingredients were imported, processed and re-exported to other parts of the Mediterranean.[387]

Closer to Rome, in Campania adjoining the Bay of Naples, Capua was the second most famous Roman manufacturing centre for perfumes after Alexandria,[388] with production also attested archaeologically at nearby Pompeii and Paestum,[389] while the port of Puteoli had strong commercial links with both Alexandria, Gaza and the rest of the Levant,[390] securing a steady supply of frankincense, myrrh, nard, etc.[391] Early evidence for this traffic dating back to 73–71 BC is embedded in Cicero's speeches against Gaius Verres for maladministration during his proconsulship of Sicily: ships made landfall in Sicilian Syracuse *en route* to Puteoli, hailing from Asia, Syria, Tyre and Alexandria, bringing Tyrian purple, frankincense, perfumes, linen robes, jewels and pearls, etc.[392] In Puteoli, there was even a specific street associated with *thurarii* and glass-makers, the most plausible connection being that the latter produced the containers, *unguentaria*, that is, flasks and phials, for the perfumes and unguents of associated *unguentarii* and *seplasiarii* not mentioned explicitly alongside the *thurarii*.[393]

In Pompeii, moreover, *unguentarii* had a sales-branch, an *officina*, in the middle of the forum, and, although not formally established as a *collegium*,[394] were certainly organised and acted like one in 'pushing' their candidates for civic administrative offices in electoral *graffiti* on the walls of nearby houses.[395] Accordingly, we know that they identified themselves in these communal exhortations as *unguentarii*, enlisted the mass support of the city's poor (*pauperes*), and that they attempted to influence the election of *aediles*,[396] whose office entailed supervision of market quality, standards, and measurements. All of this reminding us of Quintus Tullius Cicero's remark, in his 'Handbook of Electioneering,' that gaining the support of *collegia* was vital in running for office.[397]

In fact, a remarkable passage in Pliny indicates that the *unguentarii* of Capua in particular, but perhaps including the other perfume production centres in Campania and their retailers in Rome, could set in motion concerted legal action at the highest level, if they felt their interests to be threatened. Thus, Pliny mentions in an aside that '—some dealer dominating the market may whip up the selling price; we have not forgotten that, under the emperor Nero, Demetrius was prosecuted before the Consuls by the entire Seplasia.'[398] Although we cannot make out the exact causes and details of this trial, it appears at the conclusion of Pliny's 33rd book which is rounded off with a discussion of price fluctuations in specific product markets. Accordingly, it appears that Demetrius was a speculator who had managed to corner the market for perfume ingredients or finished products in such a way that the *tota Seplasia*

[386] Pliny *NH*, XIII.2 (the ingredients of unguents). Miller 1969: 8, 21–23, summarises what Pliny and Dioscorides have to say on the subject, and on pp. 65–109 deals with the spices of India, Arabia, Persia and East Africa. See Ricotti 1994a: 110–13, on Indian products in Roman perfume recipes.

[387] Pliny *NH*, XII.32 (incense-dressing workshops), XIII.6 (perfume production); and Strabo XVII.1.13 (re-exports).

[388] Pliny XIII.6. Frederiksen 1959: 110f.

[389] For Pompeii, see Mattingly 1990; for Paestum, see Brun 2000.

[390] To be explored in greater detail in chapters six and seven.

[391] An updated list of the numerous *unguentarii* and *thurarii* attested epigraphically in the Campanian area is now available in Camodeca 2016.

[392] Cic. *Verr.*, II.5.145–6, II.5.154.

[393] *ILS* 1224b. The inscription mentions a *clivus vitriarius sive vicus turarius*.

[394] Liu 2008b argues convincingly that the occupational groups acting collectively in Pompeian *graffiti* were not formally organised as *collegia*.

[395] Giordano and Casale 2007: 25–6.

[396] *CIL* IV, 609 (p. 38 w. 195), 9932a. Other mercantile groups would not be associated with the poor, *CIL* IV, 9839b.

[397] Cicero *Comment. Pet.*, 8.30: *habeto rationem urbis totius, collegiorum omnium, pagorum, vicinitatum.*

[398] Pliny *NH*, XXXIII.57: *—aliquis praevalens manceps annonam flagellet, non obliti Demetrium a tota Seplasia Neronis principatu accusatum apud consules...*

came up in arms against him.[399] Evidently, this was literally a noteworthy occurrence, making it into the pages of Pliny's writings, and emphasises the potential communal resources accruing from professional organisation, whether it be formal, as in a *collegium*,[400] or informal.[401]

Moving on to Rome, the retailing of frankincense and perfumes appears to have taken place in the same quarter of the city, namely, on and around the *vicus Tuscus* connecting the *Forum Romanum* with the *Forum Boarium* on the southern bank of the Tiber and the *Circus Maximus*. Indeed, it was on this very street that Horace reported that incense, perfumes, and pepper was sold,[402] to which can be added, as we shall see below, silk and other expensive garments. While this street may later have been dubbed the *vicus Thurarius* for the prominence of its trade in frankincense[403]—unless it is simply a late antique misnomer[404]—there certainly was a *vicus Unguentarius*, which seems to have been conveniently situated as a side street branching off the bustling *vicus Tuscus* westwards along the edge of the Forum.[405] Accordingly, these adjoining *vici* made up a specialised market for frankincense, perfumes, spices and fine textiles, just around the corner from the hub of jewellers and goldsmiths on the eastern part of the Via Sacra,[406] attested above, where at least one prominent *unguentarius* also had a shop.[407] Indeed, a cargo consignment lead-tag from Rome dated to the 1st century AD most likely records a shipment of six pounds and one-third of nard-scented oil or perfume, nard being an aromatic component derived from an Indian plant, but more on this in the next chapter.[408]

These commercial intertwinings, then, are likely to constitute the basis of the otherwise mysterious vocational affiliation between *thurarii* and *unguentarii*—the provenance, processing and properties of the goods themselves shaped the organisations dealing with them. The more so as frankincense and perfumes were both mainly marketed for their olfactory properties, whereas spices, which could and did play persistently important roles in perfumes as well as medicines because of their aromatic characteristics, also had culinary uses.[409] This fact evidently set them apart as the domain of yet another organisation bringing retailers of Eastern wares together, namely, the *collegium aromatariorum*.

The collegium of spice traders and the Pepper Warehouses

The *collegium aromatariorum* is known from an inscription traditionally dated to the reign of Augustus, in which a dedication is made to Jupiter Optimus Maximus by its *magister quinquennalis*, Titus Annius[410] Philippus, son of Titus, of the voting-tribe Collina—no other occurrence of *aromatarii* being attested epigraphically.[411] Based on the *cognomen* he might have been of freedman origin, Philippus pointing towards the Greek-speaking East. The dedication is recorded as having been made in the 28th *lustrum* since the founding of the *collegium*, *lustra* being five-year periods adopted by the *collegia* from the length of office of the *censores* of the Republic.[412] Remarkably, having reached its 28th *lustrum* implies that the *collegium aromatariorum* was an impressive 140 years old. Still, this is plausible enough, seeing as we know that the *collegia fabrum tignariorum*, that is, builders, of Ostia and Rome reached at least their 36th (in AD

[399] Following Brun 2000: 301, n102; *contra* Loane 1938: 143, and D'Arms 1981: 167.
[400] For *collegia* defending their interests with the aid of powerful patrons or obtaining desired privileges see, e.g., Tran 2007b (with Flohr 2013: 336); Tran 2011: 199–214; Liu 2013: 364.
[401] Compare with the likewise noteworthy trial of Vestorius the businessman against the senator Sempronius Rufus, chapter six.
[402] Hor. *Epist.*, II.1.269–70; identified as the *vicus Turarius* specifically by Porphyrion, *Comm. Hor.*, II.1.269f.
[403] So thinks Ashby and Platner 2002: *s.v.* 'vicus Tuscus;' *LTUR s.v.* 'vicus Tuscus;' and Holleran 2012: 57. In addition to the note above, the street is also so named in Porphyrion, *Comm. Hor.*, I.20.1; and Pseudo-Asconius, *Cic. Verr.* II.1.154. Cf. Salmeri 1997: 531 w. n9.
[404] The opinion of Richardson 1992: *s.v.* 'vicus Thurarius.'
[405] Rodriguez-Almeida 1987; Richardson 1992: *s.v.* 'vicus Unguentarius;' *LTUR s.v.* 'vicus Unguentarius;' Holleran 2012: 57, 128f.
[406] On the economic significance of such 'clustering' see Goodman 2016, especially pp. 320–2.
[407] For this *unguentarius de Sacra Via*: *CIL* VI, 1974. Moreover, a slave working as *unguentarius de Sacra Via* is attested as far away as Ithaca in AD 35; *AE* 1932: no. 22.
[408] Weiss 1991: 215–18 (=*AE* 1991, 332).
[409] Cf. Miller 1969: 2–5, *condimentum* (preservatives and ingredients in food or drink).
[410] For a plausible connection with the Puteolian Annii, see chapter six.
[411] *CIL* VI, 384; dated on the sole basis of Loane 1938: 142, whose criteria are unknown. Royden 1988: 139, 188, abstains from dating it.
[412] Royden 1988: 25; Cooley 2012: 402f.

235–39) and 48th *lustrum* (in AD 229–33), respectively, the former having been founded in AD 60, the latter in 7 BC.[413]

Significantly, though, if the *collegium aromatariorum* dates from the time of Augustus, as is traditionally assumed, this would push back the date of its foundation to the 120s BC at the very latest, making this one of the earliest attested *collegia* in the epigraphic record, only preceded with certainty by a Faliscan *collegium coquorum* on Sardinia of the early 2nd century BC.[414] Nevertheless, considering the numerous references to the culinary and fragrant uses of spices in the plays of Plautus (d. 184 BC),[415] the existence of an association of cooks even outside Rome itself as early as the time of the playwright's death, as well as early 2nd century BC evidence of Ptolemaic commercial consortia sailing down the Red Sea to market *arõma* from the Horn of Africa in Alexandria,[416] the establishment of a Roman *collegium aromatariorum* in the later 2nd century BC is not impossible.[417] However, on purely onomastic grounds an early imperial date of the 1st century AD is also possible,[418] rendering the year of foundation less extravagantly ancient, albeit in no way detracting from the fact that this association of spice traders was of impressively long standing and therefore among the oldest attested *collegia* of Rome.

As related above, in discussing the ingredients of perfumed unguents, a large number of plant products which can be subsumed under the general heading of 'spices' were imported into the Roman Empire from East Africa, Arabia, Persia and India (in Late Antiquity, arguably also from Southeast Asia and China),[419] having both aromatic, medicinal, religious and culinary—even magical—uses. Thus, these exotic spices were used variously as burnt offerings to the gods, on funeral pyres, in medicinal and magical potions, and, of course, in food.[420] How was the great demand of the city of Rome for such commodities in sufficient quantities to go around met, though? In other words, how was the available supply managed by those in charge, merchants as well as public authorities?

Arguably, the most popular spice of all was pepper, which, according to Horace, was sold in Rome on the *vicus Tuscus*, alongside perfumes concocted from other spices and exotic commodities such as sumptuous garments. Branching off from this street was the *vicus Unguentarius*, being even more of a specialised bazaar in scents and ointments, while the *vicus Tuscus* itself emanated from the Forum and the Via Sacra, which hosted goldsmiths, jewellers, pearl traders and at least one other *unguentarius*. As if all of this did not take up enough space at the very heart of Rome's commercial and religious topography, Domitian decided to alter the northern of the two porticoes along the Via Sacra erected by Nero after the fire of AD 64, as a replacement for the old shops of the *aurifices* of the Via Sacra, into a commercial space known later, in the mid-4th century AD, as the *horrea piperataria* of Domitian.[421] By the latter time, these 'Pepper Warehouses' had themselves been replaced by the Basilica of Constantine.

However, we know from Cassius Dio, writing in the early 3rd century AD, that a fire preceded the death of Commodus (d. 192 AD) and leapt from the *Templum Pacis*—whose surrounding square, the *Forum Vespasiani* (or *Forum Pacis*), adjoined the north-western corner of the *horrea piperataria*—and set fire to the 'warehouses of Egyptian and Arabian wares,' which must necessarily have been the same as the *horrea piperataria*, and destroyed the state archives on the Palatine.[422] Accordingly, the Pepper Warehouses,

[413] Royden 1988: 25–27, 134–36. The reckoning in *lustra* might also point back to an earlier re-establishment of even older organisations.

[414] Known from an inscription in their native Etruria, *CIL* VI, 3078. Cf. Harcum 1914: 16–17; Tran 2006: 1–2.

[415] Miller 1969: 9.

[416] *SB* III, 7169; treated extensively in chapter six. More generally, see Davies 2015: 305–8, on Greek trade in and consumption of eastern incense and aromatics from Classical into Hellenistic times.

[417] Indeed, equally far away from the areas of production mid-2nd century BC Aï Khanoum in northern Afghanistan has yielded two containers marked 'incense' and two alabaster bottles marked 'cinnamon;' Rougemont 2012: nos. 99–100, 146–7.

[418] That is to say, in including filiation and tribe the inscription fits with a general epigraphic pattern restricted to the early empire; cf. Cooley 2012: 410.

[419] Miller 1969: 34–64. An interesting light on imports is thrown by the archaeobotanical finds from the Roman Red Sea ports of Myos Hormos, treated in v. der Veen 2011, and Berenike, treated in Cappers 2006.

[420] As examples can be mentioned: burnt offerings: Sidebotham 2011: 226–7; funeral pyres: Mart. *Epigr.*, XI.54; medicine: Dioscorides, *Materia Medica*, espec. I.1–28, and Ricotti 1994b: 88–97; magic: Pollard 2013; food: Warmington 1928: 182; Ricotti 1994c: 101–8, and Miller 1969: 10–11, on Apicius' *De Re Coquinaria*. Insightful cases-studies in Cobb 2013: 139–48.

[421] Mommsen 1892, I: 146. For the Republican and Augustan shops, replaced by Neronian porticoes, cf. van Deman 1923.

[422] Cass. Dio LXXII.24. For the sources on the fire, see Tucci 2008: 134–6.

constructed sometime in 81–96 AD, housed not only the eponymous pepper, but also other spices and Eastern commodities, of which the Arabian goods might obviously have included frankincense and myrrh.

Remains of this rather grand warehouse complex are preserved below the Basilica of Constantine, whose extent and architectural layout is determined by the ground plan of the older warehouse buildings, on which its foundations have been superimposed. Thus, the two structures share more or less exactly the same ground plan, with the *horrea* having extended west-to-east along the *Via Sacra* up the slope of the Velian Hill, which forced the complex to be divided into three consecutive buildings with rooms around central courtyards, each one on a platform raised above the preceding one, rising in three steps towards the east. Afterwards, the builders of the heavy Basilica had to erect foundations for the pillars of the nave at the bottom of each step, well away from its edge, thus, preserving the original layout of the *horrea piperataria* in the position of its columns and three series of bays.[423]

Each of these *horrea* appears to have been centred on a series of rooms leading off a central courtyard, at least one of which (the westernmost) was fitted with an inner water tank, and which in the course of renovation work in the 2nd century AD had additional water basins installed against its doorjambs. Likely, this is to be interpreted as a means to dampen the atmosphere of the storehouses, which could easily have grown intolerable due to microscopic spice dust hanging in the air, potentially choking the inhabitants (ground pepper and cinnamon being particularly suffocating).[424]

Moreover, there is evidence from other *horrea* owned by the emperors, as the *horrea piperataria* of Domitian must have been, hence, their name,[425] that the actual people making up their staff ordinarily consisted of imperial slaves and freedmen, which is hardly surprising.[426] However, a small group of inscriptions whose testimony cannot be ignored attests the presence inside imperial *horrea* of people such as textile traders, marble merchants, shawl-sellers and a fishwife,[427] who were, accordingly, not merely renting space for a year, but advertising their line of trade and presence over the long-term inside specific warehouses. One even describes himself as 'foremost of the stone-merchants, possessing a *statiōn* in the *horrea Petroniana*.'[428] None of these individuals, it must be emphasised, state anything in their inscriptions which should cause us to believe that they were not simply independent craftsmen and traders working there in a private capacity.[429] In addition, there are inscriptions attesting *collegia* whose mercantile activities were associated with specific *horrea*, rendering it more than likely that their members also used rented premises not merely for temporary storage, but as offices for the sale of their goods.[430]

So much for the general picture. As it happens, though, we are fortunate enough to be significantly wiser about the workings of the *horrea piperataria*. First of all, an inscription from Rome has come to light, dated to the 2nd–3rd century AD, which mentions three *Publii Veracii* of which two, but most likely all three, belonged to the *coh • pip (centuria) Firmi*.[431] In light of the fact that organisation into *cohortes* in a pseudo-militaristic manner is well attested in similar inscriptions for contemporary *horrea*,[432] and that this would fit well with subdivision into *centuriae*, as is known from *collegia*,[433] these people must have been part of the organisation of some warehouse in Rome. The three relevant letters unequivocally read

[423] Minoprio 1932: 23–25, and pl. I. Summary on scholarship available in *LTUR s.v.* 'horrea piperataria,' including a note on the latest, unpublished, excavation conducted in 1989, and the latest ground plan of the westernmost of the three *horrea*.
[424] Rickman 1971: 104–6.
[425] Up until the 1st century AD, public *horrea* could be either private or state-owned, but after this time most were built or taken over by the emperor, especially from the time of Hadrian, cf. Rickman 1971: 170–3, 182–3. On the organisation of warehouses, pp. 194–209.
[426] Rickman 1971: 176–80.
[427] *CIL* VI 9972 (*vestiarius*), VI 33,886 (*negotiator marmorarius*), 33,906 (*sagarius*), 9801 (*piscatrix*).
[428] *IGUR* II, 413.
[429] This much is clear, at least, although the evidence for the internal workings of the *horrea* is ambiguous, cf. Rickman 1971: 174–76.
[430] Cf. Broekaert 2013: 34 (*AE* 1915, 97; AD 100–25: association of *negotiantes*) and 45 (*CIL* VI, 8826; AD 102: *collegium Liberi Patris et Mercuri negotiantum cellarum vinariarum*).
[431] Zappata 1994 on *AE* 1994, 297.
[432] Rickman 1971: 177.
[433] Zappata 1994: 734, n1. Liu 2013: 358.

PIP, being finely carved and preserved, and, seeing as this root is rare in Latin, it can only meaningfully be interpreted as a conventional epigraphical abbreviation for *pip(erariorum)* or *pip(eratariorum)*.[434]

Consequently, this epitaph provides evidence of free Roman citizens enrolled in the apparently single cohort, subdivided into centuries, making up the staff of the *horrea piperataria*. In fact, this is quite surprising, because, as already mentioned, inscriptions from similar imperial warehouses were all left by imperial slaves and freedmen, and while it is clear that some members of *cohortes horreariorum* in general were not ordinary workers involved in the daily running of the warehouse, they still played some role in its organisation. Although an ambiguous piece of information, the fact that the only known members of staff at the imperial *horrea piperataria* were free citizens certainly provides ample warning against assuming that this was a full-blown state monopoly in spices, housing state-run shops.[435]

Furthermore, it has been noted that Galen (d. AD 199), the famous physician, actually provides a first-hand account of a warehouse on this stretch of the Via Sacra. In a storeroom (*apothêkê*, being a standard unit in *horrea*) which was destroyed in the fire that devastated the *Templum Pacis* and libraries on the Palatine, he kept his books, five or six kinds of cinnamon (*kinnamōmon*) 'in such a quantity that it would be impossible to find as much among all the traders combined,' 80 pounds of concocted medicine (*theriac*), as well as 'numerous other rare products all of which filled my storeroom.' Obviously, Galen is referring to the same fire as Cassius Dio, above, which broke out in early AD 192 and ravaged the 'warehouses of Egyptian and Arabian wares' as well as other buildings.[436] However, seeing as the *horrea piperataria* on the northern side of the Via Sacra lay right across from the *horrea Vespasiani* on the southern side of the road,[437] either warehouse could strictly speaking have housed Galen's storeroom, only identified as being 'on the Via Sacra,' although an *apotheca* to let in *horrea* on that very road, where one could safely store rare and expensive spices, would have made the specially equipped *horrea piperataria* a logical choice over the ordinary *horrea Vespasiani*.[438]

Extraordinarily, a recently rediscovered manuscript of Galen's adds some surprising new information to our knowledge about what we assume to be the Pepper Warehouses, namely that:

> In fact, trusting the warehouses located along the Via Sacra, that they believed would never be touched by a fire, people deposited there their most precious treasures, and they were confident <so they said> because there was no wood, except for the doors, and they were not close to a private house, and furthermore because they were watched over by a military guard (*stratiōtikê froura*), since the archives of four procurators (*epitropoi*) of Caesar were kept in that place (*apokeisthai ... grammata*). And for this reason, we paid a considerable rent if we hired those storerooms located in the warehouses, and it was with confidence that we deposited our precious belongings there.
>
> (*On the avoidance of grief*, 8–9)[439]

First of all, this passage leaves no doubt that the *horrea piperataria* were put to private as well as public uses. However, we know that the stores of the imperial palace were not kept in this place, for Galen records concocting medicine (*theriac*) containing cinnamon dating back to Hadrian and Trajan for the emperor Septimius Severus, that is, necessarily after the death of Commodus in 192 and the devastating fire that preceded it.[440] Secondly, it is surprising to learn that the presence of a military contingent was occasioned by the fact that no less than four imperial *procuratores* kept their records in these warehouses specifically. Apparently, the documents were well worth keeping under armed guard, and seeing as they

434 Zappata 1994: 733.
435 In accordance with the view of Rickman 1971: 176; *contra* Loane 1944, and McLaughlin 2014: 193–4. While it is an intriguing hypothesis that a couple of lead-tags labelled *fisc(us) Alex(andrinus)* found in Rome reveal imports of taxes in kind on eastern goods from Egypt, this is contrary to the most recent research on the nature of this and similar provincial taxes, cf. Alpers 1995: 283–307.
436 Houston 2003: 45, 47; Tucci 2008: 133–4, 141, 146, 149; transl. by the latter.
437 Counted among the public works of Domitian, though, cf. Mommsen 1892, I: 146. On their history, see *LTUR s.v.* 'horrea Vespasiani.'
438 Tucci 2008: 136–9, providing a minor *corrigendum* to Houston 2003: 48–9.
439 Quoted from the English translation in Tucci 2008: 138, 140; based on Boudon-Millot 2007: 88.
440 Tucci 2008: 139.

were stored in the *horrea piperataria* of all places, they most likely had some connection to the trade in spices and incense, rather than matters relating to civic administration in Rome itself.[441] We shall return to these procuratorial archives later on.

In summary, the Pepper Warehouses established by Domitian provided prime storage space for private individuals, often being used as retail venues in contemporary *horrea* generally, and we even know that they were not run as a state franchise staffed by imperial servants in the normal sense. In this way, direct state involvement was limited to facilitating the storage of Indian, Arabian and Egyptian wares for the capital by providing the physical room, or infrastructure, for rented private outlets, which by virtue of the location automatically became embedded in the vibrant commercial and religious context of the Via Sacra, immediately east of the *Forum Romanum*. A location, it must be emphasised, which further underlines that these were not merely 'luxury goods' intended for conspicuous consumption, but also for essential religious, funerary, and medicinal purposes.

Unsurprisingly, taking into consideration the meagre evidence for such organisations, the *collegium aromatariorum* is not explicitly attested in relation to the *horrea piperataria*, but, then, neither are the other potential users of 'Egyptian and Arabian wares' from the *collegium thurariorum et unguentariorum*. Indeed, a comparison with the workings of the *annona* in Ostia with its numerous *horrea* where *collegia* handled the receipt, transhipment, measurement, temporary storage and river transport up to Rome of Egyptian grain for the capital,[442] suggests the potential role as official retailers working out of the *horrea piperataria* of one or both of the above-mentioned *collegia* specialised in exactly these wares. As already remarked upon, the antiquity of the *collegium aromatariorum* in particular emphasises its importance and utility, its known life-span even being comparable to that of the *collegium* of builders of Ostia, who rendered that city special service as fire brigade.[443]

Under all circumstances, we know that from the late 1st century BC representatives of all three groups, being the *aromatarii*, *thurarii* and *unguentarii*, plied their trades on the nearby *vicus Tuscus* and *vicus Unguentarius*, not 300 meters distant, and they, whether members of the respective *collegia* of their professions or not, must have been the people to have rented space at these warehouses from the late 1st century AD onwards. Small-timers could have rented merely chests or lockers, while successful retailers, such as Cosmus or Niceros, *unguentarii*, whose expensive perfumes were indispensable to the finer women of Rome at this very time, according to Martial,[444] could have rented entire private storerooms for their spices and ingredients, just like Galen did. Furthermore, seeing as we know that the general populace purchased exotic goods in the nearby retail streets, it is worth considering if the *horrea piperataria* might not plausibly have housed mainly wholesale transactions inside, while retail business, at least of the more upmarket kind, was conducted in more sumptuous shops and stalls in the nearby *vici*.

Some would even have it, though, that there was also a centre for trade in pepper and spices on the upper street of the Market of Trajan, allegedly named the *via Piperatica*, from the 2nd century AD onwards.[445] However, the extant street name is, in fact, *via Biberatica*, and it is not attested before AD 1003. Thus, it is more plausible that it acquired this form from *bibere*, referring to the numerous *tabernae* lining this street, or from *viper*, a viper, derived centuries earlier from a statue of the nearby Serapis temple on the Quirinal Hill which conferred this name on adjacent buildings.[446]

441 Tucci 2008: 138 n11.
442 Meiggs 1973: 278–82, 293–98, 311–32; Rohde 2012: 92–113, 123–64, 181–84; Tran 2008.
443 Rohde 2012: 164–80.
444 Mart. *Epigr.*, for Cosmus: I.87, III.55, IV.53 (cf. Rodriguez-Almeida 1987: 115), IX.26, XI.8, 15, 18, XII.55, 65, XIV.59, 110, 146; for Niceros: X.38, XII.65; also VI.55 (Nicerotius).
445 Händel 1985: 34.
446 *LTUR* s.v. 'Mercati di Traiano,' pt. 4.

The organisation of silk-weavers and traders

Finally, let us consider what evidence there is for the sale of silk, the Eastern luxury par excellence, in Rome. Thanks to a reference in Martial, we know that by the later 1st century AD the finest silk was to be found in the *vicus Tuscus* of all places,[447] where—as we know quite well by now—pepper, frankincense and perfumes were also sold, the trade in expensive textiles being further corroborated by inscriptions attesting *vestiarii tenuarii*, a *vestiarius* and a *purpurarius de vico Tusco.*[448] Concerning co-habitation with these related trades, it is significant that textile fragments from Palmyra reveal a strong connection between the import of silks from the East and a Mediterranean production of delicate half-silk garments (mixing silk with other fabrics in a composite weave) as well as purple-dyeing, as we shall see shortly. Conspicuously, then, silk was traded along with other long-distance imports from Arabia and India in the *de facto* Eastern goods and expensive textiles market centred on the *vicus Tuscus*.

Based on the talk about town and moral commotion alone, there can be little doubt that fine Chinese silks, *serica* (as different from the coarser wild silks, *bombycina*, likely from India and known from Hellenistic times), first began to be properly available in Rome from the later 1st century BC,[449] the annexation of Egypt in 30 BC probably leading to this sudden, or at least hitherto unprecedented, inflow. As with the other professions involved in marketing long-distance imports from the East dealt with above, epigraphic evidence for participants in the silk trade, dating from the early 1st century AD onwards, has a pronounced tendency to cluster in the vicinity of Rome.[450] Moreover, again, as with the other specialist professions already treated, the main distinction seems to have been between those who mainly processed the objects, sometimes selling the products of their own workshops as well, and those who were full-time traders of the finished goods.[451]

Thus, we find one Late Antique 'silk-maker' explicitly, *sirikopoiôs*, of Puteoli but hailing from Antioch,[452] while those specifically identified as silk traders are attested as, respectively, *negotiator* and *negotians sericarius* (to be dealt with below), as well as *(h)olosiricoprates*,[453] the latter evidently dealing in pure silks only. As regards those individuals simply identified in inscriptions as *sericarius* (sometimes misspelt *siri-*) or *sericaria*, one group appears to have served as specialised (slave) maids or servants in charge of their mistress' or master's wardrobe of silks (one servant possibly possessing the skills to weave silk as well),[454] while the remainder to all appearances seem to have been actual weavers of silk,[455] or at least craftsmen capable of adorning finished silk textiles or dyeing them.[456]

In support of this interpretation, highly technical analyses of more than a hundred fragments of silk garments recovered from seven Palmyrene tower tombs, dated 9 BC–mid-2nd century AD,[457] reveal that

[447] Mart. *Epigr.*, XI.27.

[448] Respectively, *CIL* VI, 37,826, 33,923, 9976; XIV, 2433 (*purpurarius de vico Tusco*, more on this below); and possibly two more *purpurarii* in VI, 9848. On trade in expensive textiles in the *vicus Tuscus*, see also Holleran 2012: 57, 84, 246. On expensive Roman textiles generally, see the brief overview in Lapatin 2015: 186–90.

[449] Hildebrandt 2012a: 13–16; 2017: 34–37. However, these articles will in due time be superseded by Hildebrandt's monumental habilitation on all aspects of silk in Greco-Roman Antituity, as yet unpublished, which I am highly grateful to its author for having shared with me. On Indian silk production, see chapter eight.

[450] On the small corpus of available inscriptions, the best and most thorough published treatment is now Hildebrandt 2017: 40–45; on the dating of the earliest inscriptions mentioning *sericarii*, p. 40. In Hildebrandt (unpublished): 130 n671, one more *sericarius* is recorded, to be found in Fittschen 2015.

[451] Keeping in mind that *eborarii* could be *politores, fabri* or *negotiatores*, *citriarii* could be *fabri* or *negotiatores*, and that *margaritarii* could be craftsmen like the *aurifices* or *anularii*, as different from a *negotiator margaritarius*, as set out above. Compare Hildebrandt 2017: 40.

[452] *IG* XIV, 785; dated early 1st century AD by Kádár 1967: 91, based on loose assumption about the historical context, but 4th–5th century AD on more substantial palaeographic grounds in the recent publication (1990–5) of *I.Napoli* II, 122.

[453] *CIL* VI, 9893; the Latin rendering of a Greek occupational title indicates Eastern origins, as does the man's Jewish name, Paulus.

[454] *CIL* VI, 9891 (later 1st–2nd century AD), 9892 (early 1st century AD); *ICUR* III, 7583 (4th century AD); *IG* II^2 13445 (Attica, 4th century AD); cf. Hildebrandt 2017: 40–41, 44.

[455] *CIL* XIV, 3711–2 (2nd century AD), cf. Hildebrandt 2017: 41, 42; and a Jewish *sirêkarios* of later 2nd–early 3rd century AD Berytus, cf. Jones Hall 2004: 324–6, and Hildebrandt 2017: 44. Presumably also *CIL* VI, 9890, to be dealt with below.

[456] In addition to the above-mentioned occupational roles, another highly specialised group (not attested epigraphically) appears to have been professionals, *sêrikodiastai*, who mounted the silk warp threads on looms, the warps regularly numbering some 1600–2500 threads; Hildebrandt 2017: 42.

[457] Good 2012: 18–9, discusses the technical feasibility of thread identification. For the dating and archaeological context: Schmidt-Colinet 2000a: 1–4.

silks were not only imported ready-made from the East but also processed in the Mediterranean area.[458] First of all, unlike the majority of silks retrieved (some 80 per cent) which were entirely produced in China,[459] a small group of silks were clearly woven in China but refashioned by the addition of embroidery done somewhere in Syria, Mesopotamia, Parthia or Central Asia, likely to increase their local market appeal and potential sales price.[460] Second, a group of nine mixed-weave textiles made from silk in combination with local varieties of thread, as well as four whole-silk textiles, were produced in Palmyra itself or the surrounding region, the whole-silks using an evidently adopted Chinese style of weaving (dominated by the (longitudinal) warp, not the (latitudinal) weft as was traditional in the West).[461] As regards the latter, one of these locally woven silk garments incorporated a pattern made using Chinese silk thread dyed with Phoenician purple (from *Murex* snails), revealing how Chinese silk was imported on the reel for local textile manufacture, that is, dyeing and subsequent weaving.[462]

On present evidence, then, we can therefore suggest that the *sericarii* in Rome, like their Near Eastern counterparts, would have woven new garments from scratch out of imported silk threads or in other substantial ways reworked finished silks imported from the East[463] to suit Roman tastes,[464] doing needlework to change their looks and dyeing them with suitable colours, such as *Murex* purple.[465] Even when an independent Western sericulture was established in the sixth century AD,[466] making domestic production from cocoons to finished woven silk textiles possible, the Chinese silk production was still superior to its Byzantine counterpart in quality,[467] so some Western import of Chinese silk thread on the reel might well have continued for high-end products.[468]

Although the inscriptions left by participants in the silk trade at Rome are not overly informative as a whole, one brief inscription merits the inclusion of a section about *sericarii* in this study.[469] Namely, the laconic inscription *sericari(i) d(ederunt) d(edicaverunt)* on the shaft of a column found in a garden on the Quirinal Hill, that is, some way north of the *vicus Tuscus* on the southern side of the Forum, but immediately east of the fancy shopping district in the *Saepta Julia* on the *Campus Martius*.[470] Of course, we can never tell what the silk workers of Rome dedicated in unison, to whom or why, but the essential point is that this simple plural, *sericarii*, is attested in a public context of explicit cooperation, perhaps even association, because we know that similar groups working with and dealing in long-distance imports

---

[458] Compare the following analysis with Sartre 2005: 243; and Zuchowska 2013a: 143–7.

[459] That is, these textiles were made from *Bombyx mori* silk using traditional Chinese weaving techniques; Stauffer 2000: 12–13, 26–8. The catalogue numbers below and in the ensuing notes all refer to Schmidt-Colinet 2000b. Particularly characteristic specimens are the three complex warp-faced compound tabbies, the decorations of two of which sport Chinese characters, cat. nos. 223, 240 (w. decorative frieze arguably intended for a Western audience), 521. In addition, decorations with contemporary parallels found in Xinjiang are preserved on nos. 449, 450. On the production of silk in Han China, see Zuchowska 2013a: 135–7.

[460] Catalogue nos.: 218, 221, 317, 447, 451–2, 518–9. Schmidt-Colinet 2000c: 47.

[461] Catalogue nos. for mixed-weaves, all with one exception made with Chinese *Bombyx mori* silk: 224 (w. cotton), 254 (wild (Indian?) silk w. cotton), 320–21 (w. wool), 454 (w. wool), 455 (w. flax), 489–91 (w. wool). The whole-silks are nos.: 219, 319, 429, 453 (perhaps also no. 431). Significantly, *Diocletian's Edict* of 301 AD distinguishes between weavers specialised in production of either whole- or half-silks (*holo-* and *subserica*, respectively), cf. on this latter point Hildebrandt 2017: 39.

[462] Schmidt-Colinet and Stauffer 2000: 53–55; cat. no. 429. Raw purple-dyed silk thread being by far the most expensive type of textile listed in *Diocletian's Edict* at 150.000 *denarii* per Roman pound, cf. Hildebrandt 2017: 38. Remarkably, a passage in Heliodorus' 3rd–4th century AD novel *Aethiopica* has emissaries from the *Seres*, that is, 'silk people,' presenting the king of Ethiopia with silk coloured with Phoenician purple, see Hildebrandt (unpublished): 71. Although Heliodorus' Ethiopia was the Meroitic kingdom, not Axum, this bit of fiction is highly interesting in light of the latter kingdom's prominent role in the long-distance trade between the Mediterranean and Indian ports in Late Antiquity, more on which in chapter seven.

[463] 'East' is deliberately vague, seeing as silk arriving in the Mediterranean area could originate in either China (domesticated *Bombyx mori* silk) or India (so-called wild silk). Six silk fragments uncovered at Palmyra were not made from the Chinese variety, but, rather, from wild, that is, presumably Indian, silk, cat. nos.: 254, 305, 308, 312 (originally identified as specifically Indian wild silk), 313, 314. For more on this issue and on an Indian production of silk, see chapter eight.

[464] Silk floss, thread, and cloths being widely available in the ports of India, in particular, as well as Scythia (*Periplus* 39, 49, 56, 64), and therefore also available within the Mediterranean for shipment to Rome as imports via the Red Sea, cf., e.g., the 'Alexandrian Tariff,' *Digest*. XXXIX.4.16.7, treated in chapter six.

[465] An example from the literary record is to be found in Luc. *Pharsalia*, X.123 (1st century AD), for the Tyrian purple of expensive textiles in a context of Eastern imports; X.141, for the reshaping in Alexandria of a 'Seric' silk garment named after it being woven or dyed, or both, at Sidon; cf. the new and more sensible interpretation of the latter passage presented by Hildebrandt 2012b.

[466] Proc., *History of the Wars*, VIII.17.1–8.

[467] Good 2012: 17.

[468] There is, however, little archaeological evidence of it, cf. Hansen 2012: 20 w. n41, but there may be one textual reference from the later 6th century AD, cf. Mango 1996: 145.

[469] *CIL* VI, 9890; the description given of its archaeological context by the editors is merely 'in scapo columnae hortorum Quirinalium.'

[470] Mentioned above.

from the East were formally organised: the *collegium negotiatorum eborariorum et citriariorum*, *collegium aurificum*, *collegium thurariorum et unguentariorum* and *collegium aromatariorum*. Moreover, as we have seen, *graffiti* from Pompeii advertise the communal political allegiance of *aurifices* and *unguentarii*, further emphasising that the *sericarii* of Rome can have constituted a comparable body, either formally regulated as a *collegium* or as a professional group and network with a public profile.

As regards *negotiatores sericarii*, however, there is evidence of both modest success in the epitaph of Marcus Aurelius Flavius,[471] as well as an inscription testifying to the wealth and success of one Aulus Plutius Epaphroditus, most likely a freedman.[472] Specifically, the latter is known to have lived at Gabii[473] in the vicinity of Rome, and to have single-handedly sponsored the construction of a local temple for Venus in AD 168, including furniture and decorations, as well as bequeathed an endowment of 10,000 sesterces to the municipality for the annual celebration of his daughter's birthday. In case of failure to fulfil the stated goals of his endowment, however, Epaphroditus stipulated that the funds and entailing obligation should be transferred to neighbouring Tusculum. Further highlighting his status in local society, Epaphroditus held the office of *accensus velatus*, investing him with an auxiliary role in municipal administration and religion at Gabii.[474]

Fortunately, it is possible to sketch a tentative outline of this *negotiator sericarius*' commercial network. First of all, his business must evidently have taken him to Rome regularly, for a gravestone was erected in the capital itself for a Telesphorianus by his father, Aulus Plutius Epaphroditus, who, on the balance of probabilities, is likely to have been none other than the very same silk merchant.[475] Second, a group of freedmen were grateful enough to Epaphroditus, and had enough money between them as a group, to commemorate him as their patron with a statue and inscribed base, thus, they may have been craftsmen or agents assisting their former master in his métier as silk merchant, such as has already been revealed for patron-client networks in the ivory, jewellery, incense and perfume trades of Rome.[476] Indeed, the plausibility of Epaphroditus possessing commercial ties extending to lower-tier agents is further borne out by one-off handouts of money (to mark the inauguration of his temple) to *inter alia* the 'shopkeepers conducting business inside the city walls,' receiving one *denarius* each, thus, revealing his overarching patronage of the rank and file of Gabii's mercantile milieu.[477]

Finally, he may very well himself, as a successful freedman, have been part of patronage networks linking numerous *Auli* and *Lucii Plutii* of freedmen status, predominantly from Gabii and Tusculum (which latter was also Epaphroditus' second choice as trustee of his endowment).[478] Significantly, two of these freedmen *Plutii* are also attested as being involved in the textile trade at Rome, one working as *plumarius*, a tapestry weaver, the other being the very *purpurarius de vico Tusco* mentioned at the beginning of this subchapter,[479] once again bearing out the organisational similarity to the networks previously attested in Rome, which were often controlled by equestrian or senatorial families. Moreover, this *purpurarius* was commemorated in an inscription at Marino, five kilometres from neighbouring Tusculum to the northeast, which itself neighboured Gabii ten kilometres to the north-north-east, these three suburban towns describing a short arc to the east-south-east of Rome at a radius of twenty kilometres, arguably rendering it the more likely that Epaphroditus also conducted business in Rome, like the *purpurarius* of Marino did.[480]

---

471 *CIL* VI, 9678 (first half of 3rd century AD); cf. Hildebrandt 2017: 44.
472 *CIL* XIV, 2793; receiving thorough treatments in Amiri 2012 and Hildebrandt 2017: 42–3.
473 On Gabii, see Amiri 2012: 127 n10.
474 On this office, see Amiri 2012: 128–9.
475 *CIL* VI, 24356.
476 *CIL* XIV, 2812.
477 *CIL* XIV, 2793, ll. 5–6: *tabernarii intra murum negotiantes*; which may possibly have been the designation for a specific group at Gabii, such as a *collegium* or formal collective, cf. Amiri 2012: 134–5.
478 Amiri 2012: 130–1, 137–9, w. table pp. 141–3.
479 *CIL* VI, 9814 (*Lucius Plutius Agatho, plumarius*; for the nature of this profession, cf. Hildebrandt 2017: 43); XIV, 2433 (*Lucius Plutius Eros, libertus* and *purpurarius*, attested in an inscription at Marino by a fellow freedwoman of the *Plutii*).
480 Or, for that matter, the *negotiator eborarius* who died at Capena, cf. chapter three, or the *margaritarius ab Roma* attested at Aquileia, above.

As it happens, just such networks of silk merchants are described in greater detail by Jewish and Christian writers of the Roman East, providing the contextual substance of moral and theological analogies, thus shedding a rare light on this particular trade. Specifically, a Talmudic commentary details the workings of what can best be described as an extended Jewish trust network:

> Abba ben Abba was a dealer in silk. Once Rabbi Judah ben Beteirah ordered some silk from him and Abba laid it aside in his name. But Rabbi Judah found no opportunity to come for the merchandise for a long time. When he finally arrived, Rabbi Abba gave him the very silk he had ordered. Rabbi Judah said: 'Why has thou kept it for me though I did not send thee a deposit?' Rabbi Abba replied: 'Thy word is stronger in my eyes than money.'[481]

According to the commentary, Abba ben Abba, who was also a distinguished religious figure, was granted a son shortly afterwards as a divine reward for his trustful nature, this event fixing the alleged episode to around AD 165.[482] Less is known about the Judah ben Beteirah in question (the third of his name), but he was a namesake and descendant, possibly the great-grandson, of the Jewish rabbi who founded a famous Jewish school at Nisibis in Adiabene.[483] At the time, Abba ben Abba was living in Nehardea on the middle Euphrates, noted for its weavers,[484] while Judah ben Beteirah was a resident of Nisibis, renowned later for its border trade with Persia,[485] these two cities hosting communities of Jews having fled there from Parthian Ktesiphon,[486] being the Mesopotamian terminus for routes across the Iranian plateau to Central Asia and beyond.[487]

Thus, the facts come together nicely to verify the details of this anecdote about the requisition from afar of consignments of silk, deposits as standard practice and extension of long-term, long-distance credit for trusted partners, clients or co-religionists. The more so, seeing as this set of practices is echoed by the later church father, John Chrysostomos (*c.* 349–407 AD), who lived most of his life at Antioch.[488] In consequence, his experience of silk traders most likely pertains to the 'Northern Mesopotamian route'[489] via Nisibis, providing a rare *comparandum* for the Talmudic passage:

> wealth consists in possessing what is your own. He that is in possession of the goods of others, never can be a wealthy man; since at that rate even your very silk vendors, who receive their goods as a consignment from others, would be the wealthiest and the richest of men. Though for the time, indeed, it is theirs, still we do not call them wealthy. And why forsooth? Because they are in possession of what belongs to others. For though the piece itself happens to be theirs, still the money it is worth is not theirs. Nay, and even if the money is in their hands, still this is not wealth.[490]

Accordingly, individual silk merchants, lacking the fortune necessary for them to have been the actual owners of their own stock, were instead acting as retail agents of wealthier entrepreneurs or patrons, whose wares they marketed in return for a share in the profit, or a commission.[491] A very sensible system, being to the benefit of both *negotiatores sericarii* of more moderate means, such as Marcus Aurelius Flavius, as well as prosperous silk merchants with very affluent customers, like Aulus Plutius Epaphroditus, or major financiers operating out of key port cities such as Puteoli, Alexandria and Antioch, as we shall see

481 *Midrash Samuel* X, in Newman 1945: 204.
482 Hoffmann 1873: 8–9.
483 Jastrow and Krauss 1902: *s.v.* 'Bathyra.'
484 Rajak 1998: 317.
485 *FHG* 4, Petrus Patricius, frag. 14 (*c.* 298 AD); *Expositio* 22 (mid-4th century AD).
486 Rajak 1998: 315. According to Pliny *NH*, VI.30, the Parthians wanted to populate their new foundation of Ktesiphon with inhabitants from adjoining Seleucia, which had, in turn, for centuries been drawing off the population of Babylon, and, hence, the Jews migrating to Nehardea and Nisibis represented the ancient Jewish diaspora of Mesopotamia.
487 Strabo XVI.1.16 w. XVI.1.27; Isidor *Parthian Stations*, 1; Ptol. *Geog.*, I.12. Palmyra, where a hundred silk fragments of primarily Chinese origin have been found, had early 1st century AD commercial links with the older cities of the region: Seleucia, *Inv.* IX 6A and 6B, and Babylon, *Inv.* IX 11.
488 Ritter 2012: 37–8. As mentioned above, we know of one 'silk-maker' from Antioch who died at Puteoli, and a Jewish silk-weaver was from nearby Berytus.
489 Young 2001: 187-200.
490 John Chrysostomos, *Homily on the Ephesians*, II.13.58; transl. in Schaff 1889, XIII.
491 Cf. Broekaert 2013: 38, who erroneously attributes the words to Dio Chrysostom (of Prusa).

in subsequent chapters. In this light, some kind of formal coordination, cooperation or association is more than likely in the case of the *sericarii* of Rome as well.

Organising the world of consumption

Remarkably, the existence of not only individual traders and craftsmen dealing in citrus wood, ivory, precious and semi-precious stones, pearls, frankincense, exotic perfumes, spices, pepper and silk, but even of geographical clusters of such people in specialised market-streets, as well as private networks, formal *collegia* and state-maintained warehouses, reveals a thriving market for long-distance imports in imperial Rome. As we have seen, moreover, a closer look at the import, processing and retail trade in long-distance commodities from the Indian Ocean in Rome, reveals the at first glance invisible hand of a number of professional *collegia* and similar occupational collectives in strengthening network ties between traders and craftsmen, thus aiding them in managing the worst fluctuations of the market. Although the inscriptions attesting these *collegia* are laconic, we are fortunate enough to have the fragmentarily preserved charter of the *collegium* of *negotiatores eborarii et citriarii*, who were also involved in the trade with Eastern goods, to inform our understanding of the organisation and workings of these associations, which combined collective occupational identity with social and religious activities as well as public standing and profile. In so far as none of these professions were new to Late Republican and Early Imperial Rome (with the likely exception of the *sericarii*), we must assume that it was not the establishment of *collegia* which made occupational networks come into being, but, rather, the other way around—members of existing networks of professional craftsmen or traders could choose to unite in *collegia*, those who wished to remain apart having the choice to continue their work without becoming members.

Emphatically, then, the economic benefits to members of a *collegium* were derived from the fact that relations between members represented relatively strong ties in their individual networks, seeing as activities internal to the association were governed by rules and regulations, provided opportunities to share information, and increased interaction generally and thereby the likelihood of transactions between members. In addition, membership provided access to colleagues themselves and possibly, in case of collaboration, to their networks, increasing the potential advantage of weak ties, as well as the collective ability to obtain aid from patrons. All of these factors, in turn, facilitated the making of relational contracts with relevant partners or agents, particularly with people inside the association, but also with people outside it whom one gained access to via another member. While none of these things were unique to *collegia*, ordinary networks having the same potential to foster social capital which could be turned to economic advantage, it is obvious that the multifaceted relations generated by associations helped create new or strengthen existing network ties.

However, it would be wrong to overstate the ability of Roman *collegia* in particular to exercise strong private ordering enforcing the transactions between members by naming, shaming and excluding those who would cheat or treat their peers unfairly in business external to the running of the *collegium* itself.[492] Rather, this kind of professional exclusion had to rely on the wider occupational network, which could single out individuals for social and economic punishment as it saw fit, abiding by no established rules as *collegia* did (and none of whose rules, as far as we know, related to the private economic interests of members in their dealings with one another). On the same note, it would be wrong to assume that *collegia* possessed sufficient closure to create economic cartels, running non-member competitors out of business and manipulating market prices to obtain greater profits.[493] Indeed, this kind of guild-like

[492] Cf. Gabrielsen 2016b: 96 and throughout. Thus, while the above conclusion agrees with much in Hawkins 2012 and 2016: 68–129, it does not agree with the idea of the *collegium* as a 'governance structure' in itself for transactions between members, a hypothesis which is quite difficult to support on the basis of the extant evidence, cf. Hawkins 2016: 121, 'Although no explicit evidence demonstrates that misbehavior in economic transactions in particular might elicit dishonor and sanctions of this sort within a professional *collegium*...,' going on to cite Pliny the Younger's letter to Trajan about Christian congregations (Plin. *Ep.* 10.96–7) in analogy instead.

[493] Although this study is in overall agreement with a number of points in Bang 2011: 239–89, this is a markedly different interpretation than Bang 2011: 287, who equates personal and communal networks as tools of exclusion. However, only the former, not the latter, could *attempt* to ostracize individuals or keep out newcomers (at least as regards communal networks in the guise of formal associations—diasporas as such were another matter, see the beginning of chapter six).

behaviour cannot be demonstrated for any *collegia*, not even those of Roman Egypt which were part of a different economic system, anyway, as we shall see towards the end of chapter six.[494]

Instead, the vital contribution of Roman *collegia* was their general propensity to foster relational contracts through the whole range of activities embedded in their institutional setup, thus, they were able to foster some degree of economic collaboration on market terms by virtue of the intensified interaction with peers which they offered, but this does not mean that they could wield collective clout over either insiders or outsiders in matters not pertaining narrowly to the administration of the association itself, nor that they could single-handedly dominate, and thus dictate, the market. In short, *collegia* might have advertised both 'carrot and stick' as their policy of obtaining professional order and cohesion, but it was the carrot, not the stick, which was their main asset to existing and would be-members, who could sorely need the reinforced institutional setting of a formal organisation for creating *ad hoc* partnerships based on relational contracts in order to stay in the lucrative but volatile market for long-distance goods, collaborating with some of their peers, competing with others, in durable or shifting constellations as circumstances required.

[494] *Contra* Hawkins 2016: 73, 78.

Chapter 5

Demand and supply in Rome and the provinces

In the following, it will be argued that even the common—if not exactly poor—man on the streets of Rome, Trier or in the *vicus* of Vindolanda, would sometimes find it within the means of his shrunken purse to spice up his daily stew with a dash of pepper. Indeed, he might also be able to suppress both the fact that it might have been a couple of days since he last visited the local baths, and that the open gutters in the streets of his neighbourhood gave off a stench to knock out a donkey, by daubing himself with some exotically scented unguents and burning some frankincense for the *Lares* of his family hearth. The middling classes, moreover, could mix and match the things they desired according to their varying economic capabilities, and, crucially, consumption of these commodities extended well beyond the geographical limits of Rome itself, the economic and political centre of the Empire.

Due to the very nature of the commodities under study here, aromatics and spices which only grow in South Arabia, East Africa and India, it should be plain that their availability far inside the western provinces of the Roman Empire at prices putting them within the reach of private consumption cannot be due to local supply. Rather, an empire-wide demand for commodities which had previously been the prerogative of the aristocracy at Rome and in the major port cities of the Mediterranean during the Republic, came to stimulate an utterly impressive long-distance supply of aromatic nard from the Ganges plain of North India, black pepper from South India, and myrrh from South Arabia, as will be substantiated below. Furthermore, it is evident that this supply operation was not carried out at the behest of the Roman state, direct tax-funded redistribution in other words, but was the consequence of private commerce on a very large scale, that is, the institution of the market, demand acting as the engine of supply. Indian and Arabian producers simply responded to the business opportunities offered by Roman, Arabian and Indian sea-going traders who knew that aggregate demand in the West for these goods was more than strong enough to secure them stable, good prices for their wares, no matter that some of their goods ended up covering distances in excess of 10,000 km.

Luxurious spices at everyday prices?

A few statements by the ancients themselves shed a valuable light on the scale of the long-distance trade with the East which, to some of them, at least, appeared to be on a ludicrously grand scale. Most famous are Pliny's statements that 'in no year does India drain our empire of less than fifty million sesterces, giving back her own wares in exchange, which are sold among us at fully one hundred times their prime cost,' and that 'at the very lowest computation, India, the Seres and the Arabian Peninsula, withdraw from our empire one hundred millions of sesterces every year—so dearly do we pay for our luxury and our women.'[495] The final remark is important, seeing as it reveals that Pliny's primary concern, here as in numerous other passages of the *Historia Naturalis*, is really the consequences of the new *luxuria* for the traditional Roman virtues, *mos maiorum*, not for the imperial finances as such.[496] In support of such an allegedly ruinous Eastern trade,[497] two passages from Strabo are often cited, stating that under the Ptolemies only some 20 ships ventured down the Red Sea and hardly beyond it, whereas after the Roman annexation of Egypt large fleets set out annually for the far shores of Africa and the ports of India, 120 ships sailing out of Myos Hormos alone.[498]

This all sounds very impressive. The exact numbers assigned to the drain of bullion and to the merchant fleets give off an alluring ring of mathematics, but, sadly, we are here rather confronted with the 'mathemagics' of 50 growing to twice 50 million sesterces, and 20 increased by 100 ships, meaning simply

[495] Pliny *NH*, VI.26, XII.41.
[496] E.g. Pliny *NH*, XII.1.
[497] A literary genre receiving further support from notables such as Tac. *Ann.*, III.53, and Dio Chrys. *Or.*, LXXIX.5–6.
[498] Strabo II.5.12, XVII.1.13.

'a lot more' in both cases. Neither Strabo nor Pliny can have had access to non-existent 1st century AD central government archives providing an empirical basis for their calculations and statistics. Although the utmost care was taken for fiscal purposes to register every Eastern cargo entering the Roman Empire for payment of the *tetarte*, or 'quarter-tax,' and proceeding across internal toll barriers,[499] the local records kept by individual tax-farmers at multiple points of entry spread across Egypt, Nabataea, Syria and Commagene were with almost absolute certainty never collated.[500] Moreover, records of the quarter-tax can hardly have provided the basis for a computation of the Roman trade deficit vis-à-vis India measured as *export of bullion*, being a customs fee levied on *imports estimated at Roman prices*. So, to do a calculation like that for Pliny's alleged trade balance, one would have needed records of all *denarii* and *aurei* shipped eastwards for use as bullion in trade,[501] compiled by officials exacting the various customs fees for wares exiting Egypt. The nature of such an Eastern export tax is not known, whether it be 25 per cent as on imports[502] or much lower like *portoria* in other parts of the empire to encourage export,[503] but excavations at Berenike have yielded a number of *ostraca* revealing that export fees were paid in Koptos, receipts being carried to the customs gate of Berenike to allow easy clearing upon arrival.[504]

A complete set of such records from all points of departure for the East, caravan cities and ports, held up against an equally complete set of *tetarte* records, could, in theory, have made the calculation of a balance of trade possible. However, unlike the relatively more numerous literary and epigraphic references to the *tetarte*, yielding a stupendous income and therefore being of great contemporary interest, the export tax and its collection seems to have been a more low-key, locally handled affair. Thus, it is highly unlikely to have been documented meticulously, records being shipped to Rome from all along the Eastern frontier, and collated for budgetary purposes of the *fiscus*. Theoretically, such archives might have been available from at least the reign of Commodus, for we now know from Galen that the records of four senior imperial administrators were kept in a warehouse on the Via Sacra, most likely the *horrea piperataria*, as discussed above—but on the balance of probability this is highly unlikely. However, the important point is that neither Strabo nor Pliny, who provide the only numbers we have, lived in times for which sources supporting the existence of collated records of an imperial balance of trade with the East can be adduced. Indeed, although a rather large number of Roman *denarii* and *aurei* have been unearthed in Early Historic India, there seems, on the whole, to be little reason to believe in Pliny's 'coin haemorrhage,' when taking into account both the production of Roman mines and state income from the quarter-tax on Eastern imports.[505]

Nonetheless, having disqualified the only general numbers available, and accused Pliny in particular of being a stuck-up moralist, this does not mean that we should discard early imperial testimonies about the trade with the East being on a grand scale.[506] Rather on the contrary, for while we cannot trust in details such as the numbers, we must certainly acknowledge the substance of what Strabo, Pliny, Dio Chrysostom and Tacitus, among others, were saying.[507] Namely, that the trade had increased significantly in their own lifetimes, that the objects of the trade were conspicuously visible in the greater urban centres, and, in consequence, that the ever-growing availability of these once rare 'luxury goods' was challenging old social hierarchies by creating new avenues of conspicuous consumption.[508]

Returning to Pliny, he does leave a hint as to the source of his knowledge regarding the alleged 'drain of 100 million sesterces:' in the very same passage, he cites 'experts in these matters' for the fact that Nero

499 E.g. the valuation for payment of the *tetarte* on the *verso* of *SB* XVIII, 13,167, see chapter six; and the Egyptian ship register of *P.Bingen* 77 recording cargoes and ports of origin.
500 Raschke 1978: 336. On the *tetarte* in Egypt, see the next chapter.
501 E.g. *O.Petr.* 290.
502 So thinks Sijpesteijn 1987: 4–5.
503 So Laet 1949: 310–11; and Rathbone 2002: 184.
504 See below.
505 Romanis 2006: 55–9; Tchernia 2011: 301–14; Cobb 2015a recasts the issue somewhat.
506 Compare Millar 1998: 123; and Parker 2008: 183–89.
507 Cf. nn495–98.
508 On the moral commotion caused by the increased availability of wares accordingly labelled 'eastern luxuries,' see especially Parker 2008: 165–8, and the masterful analysis by Cobb 2013, while on the ancient notion of 'luxury' more widely, Gorman and Gorman 2014, and Lapatin 2015: 1–16. Silk constitutes a particularly illuminating case: Edwards 1993: 68–9, 77, and Hildebrandt 2012a: 32–5.

burnt more incense on the pyre of Poppaea, his mistress, than Arabia produces in a year.[509] These experts, then, are most likely also the source of his price data, and must have been the merchants and investors associated with the market for Eastern goods in Rome,[510] that is, the *vici Tuscus et Unguentarius* in Pliny's time, augmented later in the 1st century AD by the addition of the *horrea piperataria*, and the exclusive shops in and around the *Saepta Julia*. In other words, when Pliny speaks at length about the availability, origins and prices of citrus wood, African and Indian ivory, precious stones, frankincense, myrrh, nard, pepper, silk, etc., his information most likely stems from the collective sharing of information and experience within both informal as well formal occupational networks, such as the *collegia* of *negotiatores eborarii et citriarii, aurifices, thurarii et unguentarii, aromatarii*, and, as argued previously, the *sericarii*.

Accordingly, the relevant chapters in Pliny's encyclopaedic *Historia Naturalis* leave us on firmer ground, for whereas it is highly doubtful that the capital's 'experts' on trade in incense, spices, perfumes, etc., could know much about the imperial balance of trade vis-à-vis Arabia, India and China, they were eminently well placed, within the largest market of the Empire with its associated organisations of professional craftsmen and traders, to know everything about the prices of exotic commodities in Rome.[511] Indeed, later in his monumental treatise, Pliny himself reflects on the relative usefulness of price data: '—I have found it necessary to state the prices usual at Rome (*quae plerumque erant Romae*), in order to give an idea of a standard value of commodities (*ut exprimeretur auctoritas rerum*).'[512]

Simply put, unavoidable fluctuations in prices will have been the norm, and what is listed by Pliny as the average price will, in fact, sometimes have represented the retail cost, sometimes the wholesale, and sometimes neither, as prices soared and dived, and will obviously always have depended on the quality of the commodity in question. A notorious example is oil of malabathrum (cinnamon-scented leaves from the Himalayan foothills) which oscillated between a freakish 1 to 400 *denarii* per Roman pound of 323 grams—in such cases speaking of an average wholesale vs. retail price makes no sense, rather, such values represent an approximate price-range.[513] However, the important point is that to Pliny, as an ancient observer of the market in Rome for long-distance imports, it made sense to speak of 'the common' or 'real price' of a ware, acknowledging market volatility as a recurrent phenomenon but not, crucially, the norm.

Keeping these circumstances in mind, let us have a closer look at the general affordability of widely in demand Eastern imports such as pepper (for spicing), frankincense (for burning), and myrrh (for perfume). Significantly, all three commodities were subdivided into three price categories each, based on quality and demand, so that there was something for purses of every size: for the wealthy, the middling and the common man.

Accordingly, pepper was divided into 'long pepper' at 15 *denarii*, 'white pepper' at seven *denarii*, and 'black pepper' at four *denarii* per pound.[514] Likewise, first grade frankincense was available at six *denarii* per pound, second grade at five *denarii*, and the lower third grade stuff at three *denarii*.[515] Finally, myrrh was divided into the 'Trogodytic' variety at 16.5 *denarii* per pound, 'Erythraean' at 16 *denarii*, and the less expensive 'perfumier's' grade at 12 *denarii*.[516] Now, working on the basic assumption that most people would very rarely, if ever, need to buy an entire pound of either commodity at any one time, but, rather, prefer to buy smaller amounts, such as the packages of *tus et odores et piper* wrapped in scrap paper on the *vicus Tuscus*, a calculation can be made for one quarter pound (*c.* 80 grams) of the lowest quality, putting the price of a small sachet of pepper at one *denarius*, frankincense at three quarters of a *denarius*, and myrrh at three *denarii*.

509 Pliny *NH*, XII.41: *periti rerum*.
510 Rathbone 2000: 47.
511 For lists of relevant price data, cf. the tables in Miller 1969: 26–8; and Young 2001: 222.
512 Pliny *NH*, XXXIII.57; quoted previously in chapter two.
513 Rathbone 2000: 47–8; Pliny XII.59.
514 Pliny *NH*, XII.28.
515 Pliny *NH*, XII.32.
516 Pliny *NH*, XII.35.

Obviously, price has to be considered relative to income, and although this is a vexed question as regards the majority of the inhabitants of Rome, who were not part of the equestrian or senatorial classes, some headway can be made. Specifically, one approach is to gauge the value of the free grain distribution to the inhabitants of Rome, which represented the bare subsistence level, exclusive of other costs, for families living in the capital. Accordingly, it has been calculated for the 1st century AD that a poor family had to survive on grain valued at some 10–12½ *denarii* per month.[517] Another approach is to compare with the salaries of the military rank and file: the basic payment for a legionary *c.* 31 BC– AD 85 was 18¾ *den.*/month, 25 *den.*/month from *c.* 85–200 AD, rising to about 40 *den.*/month in the 3rd century AD.[518] Seeing as the wages of legionaries represented a good, but in no way extravagant, salary, we arrive at rough measure of some 10–20 *denarii* per month as the income of the poor and common strata of Rome throughout the 1st century AD.

While those closer to the lower end of this income range would only rarely have had extra money left over at the end of the month, the self-indulgence inherent to purchasing a small amount of pepper or frankincense at ¾–one *denarius* (or less) might occasionally have been possible. However, those with an income closer to 20 *denarii* could, if willing, be more frequent consumers of the cheaper kinds of spices and incense in modest quantities, while the middling and wealthy citizens could buy bigger and better amounts. Accordingly, it should be apparent that pepper and frankincense for everyday household use was certainly not prohibitively expensive. The more so if these commodities were used sparingly, 'sprinkling sacred pepper light as dew on the pan,'[519] and only burning a few grains of frankincense at the time, so that even modest purchases would last for as long as possible.[520]

As regards the various unguents in which myrrh, cinnamon, malabathrum, nard, etc., were commonly used as ingredients, it is quite difficult to assess their cost, but Pliny leaves no doubt that prices ranged from a few *denarii* to several hundred for the most expensive products: the natural extract of myrrh, *stacte*, cost 3–50 *denarii* per pound, with myrrh of the lowest grades employed for perfumes, *quae odoraria vocant*, costing 12 *denarii* per pound—both necessarily making for many pounds of perfumes in which they were but one aromatic ingredient.[521] Cinnamon perfume, although starting at a reasonably humble 35 *denarii*, could cost up to 300 *denarii*.[522] Malabathrum oil went for as much as 400 *denarii* and as little as one *denarius*, depending on quality and supply, its leaves going for around 60 *denarii*.[523] Raw nard plant components went for between 40–100 *denarii* depending on their grade,[524] while one pound of finished perfume appears to have cost 300 *denarii*.[525] Finally, prices for unadulterated balsam oil started at 300 *denarii* per pint (i.e., a *sextarius* of 546 ml).[526] Martial, in some of his epigrams, jokes about the highly fashionable unguents of Cosmus and Niceros, which were, *inter alia*, balsam-, cinnamon- and nard-scented, costing eight to ten *aurei* per pound, that is, 200–250 *denarii*.[527]

More concretely, it has been calculated that the best quality of 'Italian rose' (*rodinon italikon*) perfume from Campania was sold for around three *denarii* per pound in the Egyptian Fayyum in the 1st century AD. A more common retail measure, such as a quarter-litre container, would therefore have cost two *denarii*, making it worth four days' wages for an Egyptian farmhand of the 2nd century AD (for which income

517 Young 2001: 222–3, based on Duncan-Jones 1974: 145–7.
518 Duncan-Jones 1974: 10, 12. This is exclusive of both special distributions as well as mandatory payments docked for equipment, etc.
519 Pers. VI.21, of a miser: *ipse sacrum inrorans patinae piper* (mid-1st century AD); Miller 1969: 24.
520 Conclusion in accordance with Salmeri 1997: 535–7.
521 Pliny *NH*, XII.35–36.
522 Pliny *NH*, XIII.2.
523 Pliny *NH*, XII.59.
524 Pliny *NH*, XII.26. Note that Pliny does *not* give a price for nard unguent here, although the price for spikes is often quoted in the literature as that of 'spikenard oil.' However, in a context of prices given for different parts of the nard plant, 'pretium spicae in libras (denarii) C' must be taken as referring to the price of the actual spike (*spica*) of the plant, not as a sort of shorthand for an augmented *spica* (*oleum*).
525 Mark XIV, 3–5; John XII, 3–5. The price of 300 *denarii* quoted in the Gospels fits with Pliny stating in subsequent sentences within the same passage (*NH* XIII.2) that cinnamon oil cost up to 300 *denarii*, followed *en passant* in the next sentence by a description of nard oil, implicitly on a par with the preceding item's listed cost.
526 Pliny *NH*, XII.54. Pliny states that one *sextarius* of pure balsam purchased at 300 *denarii* was resold for as much as 1,000 *denarii*. However, it is unclear whether this passage implies that due to adulteration the quantity was increased, making it possible to sell more at the same price per measure, or that the demand in places like Rome was great enough for the middlemen to be able to hike up the price by 700 *denarii*.
527 Mart. *Epigr.*, for ingredients: VI.55, XI.8, XIV.146; for price: XII.55, 65.

data is available).[528] Although a comparison with the Roman market for perfumes based on this Egyptian example must clearly remain inadequate in many ways, it might serve to indicate that the cheaper unguents made in Campania from ingredients imported via Egypt might have cost something within the same order of magnitude as Campanian imports in the Egyptian Fayyum, and certainly nothing like the hundreds of *denarii* expended on perfumes by the wealthier citizens of Rome.[529] Consequently, perfumes scented with exotic Eastern aromatics would probably also have been available among a wider Roman audience of consumers, not just the elite, even though the price data is less solid than for spices and incense.

In fact, as we shall see below, there is additional evidence for provincial trade in both pepper and exotic perfumes, both of which were certainly not meant for the super-rich at Rome, but must be taken to reflect, on the one hand, provincial demand for these commodities, and, on the other hand, a sufficiently large supply of these goods at Alexandria and Rome to branch out through distribution networks to places in rural Venetia and inland Gaul, even as far as the northern frontier of *Britannia*.

Pepper trade in the provinces

Until now, the discussion about price and availability has been limited to Rome, the 'great commercial attractor' of the Mediterranean, holding a unique position within the empire as the epicentre of elite consumption—but what about the rest of the Roman West? As regards inscriptional evidence, *thurarii* and the frankincense they were selling are attested in the province of Italia from the bay of Naples to Altinum in the northeast and Torino in the northwest, while we find two *thurarii* in southern and eastern Gaul (and an additional *unguentarius* in the latter who was related to *thurarii* in Rome and Italia[530]), and, finally, an inhabitant of inland Africa Proconsularis who dealt in frankincense as well as pepper.[531]

On the subject of pepper, in addition to the African trader just mentioned, an approach encompassing different types of evidence (silver tableware, papyri, iconography, archaeobotany, lead-tags and writing-tablets) can provide a more comprehensive picture, indicating a trade reaching far beyond the elite circles of Rome, extending *ad ultimos fines imperii*. Starting out with silver pepper pots (*piperatoria*/*piperantes*),[532] 3rd–4th century AD specimens have been unearthed as far apart as Britannia (Hoxne), Gaul (Viennes and Chaourse), Thrace (Nicolaevo) and Syria (Sidon),[533] as well as being mentioned in Egyptian papyri (one from Oxyrhynchus).[534] To complete this picture of pepper consumption by the provincial elite can be added a mosaic from a Sicilian villa, which depicts a deified female India, surrounded by an elephant, a tiger, an ivory tusk and a a phoenix, holding in her arms yet another tusk and a small tree (possibly representing *cinnamomum*), whilst, crucially, the background sports a fruit-laden plant which has recently been interpreted as an attempt to depict the pepper vine with berries at different stages of ripeness.[535]

More concretely, actual archaeobotanical finds of black pepper have been made not only at and near the ports of entry in Egypt, namely, Berenike (3,617 peppercorns as loose finds and one uncounted cache of a staggering 7.5 kg; 1st–2nd century AD, 4th–early 6th century) and its satellite village of Shenshef

[528] Brun 2000: 299–300.

[529] Extravagant expenditure on perfumes generally being criticised by Pliny *NH*, XIII.4.

[530] Cf. n385.

[531] Italia: *CIL* X, 1962; *ILS* 1224b (Puteoli); *CIL* X, 6802 (Ischia); *ILS* 7614 (Torino); *CIL* V, 2184 (Altinum). Gaul: *CIL* XII, 4518; XIII, 5356. Africa Proconsularis: *CIL* VIII, 16,878 (Madauros).

[532] Warmington 1974: 183f n8, contains an outdated and to a large extent unverifiable list of pepper dishes, pots and pantry jars. Two early Pompeian silver specimens have now been convincingly reinterpreted as wine-testers, cf. Johns 2010: 77, while a small Pompeian amphora inscribed '*pip(er)*' (*CIL* IV, 5763), as well as a vase similarly labelled '*piperi*' from Tarraco in Hispania (*CIL* II, 4970, no. 392; unknown to Warmington), must rather be understood in light of the attested use of *Piper* as a rare name, and, thus, a potter's mark in Gaul (one of them, or possibly the one and only maker of all the pots, bearing the praenomen *L(ucius)*), cf. *CAG* vols.: III, p. 156; XXI-03, p. 378; XXVI, p. 343; LXIII-01, pp. 190, 252; LXXX-01, p. 125 (*L. Piper*); LXXXIX-01, p. 432.

[533] Johns 2010: Hoxne, nos. 33–36, pp. 78–92, 219–20; the other specimens all treated on p. 77. The Sidonian *piperatorium* is illustrated in Kondoleon 2000: no. 49. The role of pepper pots as an essential part of aristocratic silver tableware is further borne out by Paulus *Sent.*, III.6.86 (2nd-3rd century AD).

[534] *P.Corn.* 33, *P.Oxy.* VI.921. Note that pepper appearing as a commodity in Egyptian papyri generally is not treated here, being a rather more common occurrence; see chapters six and seven.

[535] New hypothesis by R. Hobbs related in Johns 2010: 75; best photographic reproduction of mosaic to be found in Carandini *et al.* 1982: plate XXXI.

(16 peppercorns, late 4th–early 6th century), as well as at Myos Hormos (71 peppercorns; early 1st–3rd century AD), and at the inland sites of Mons Claudianus (two peppercorns, 1st–mid 3rd century AD) and Qasr Ibrim near the Nubian frontier (one single peppercorn), but also all along the Germanic *limes* from Straubing in Raetia (52 peppercorns, late 1st–early 2nd century AD), past Hanau (12 peppercorns, 2nd century AD) and Biesheim (one peppercorn; 2nd half of 1st century AD) in Germania Superior, to Oberaden across the Rhine from Germania Inferior (eight peppercorns; 11–8/7 BC).[536] A reported find from Bath in *Britannia* has now been discredited.[537] Recent reports from Pattanam in Kerala, moreover, likely the great South Indian port of Muziris, provide the first archaeobotanical finds of pepper in the subcontinent at the place of export.[538]

In addition, a lead-tag uncovered in the area of the Römerbrücke across the Mosel in Trier, northern Gaul, attests eight Roman pounds of pepper in a single load, dated palaeographically to the 2nd century AD.[539] The pepper was designated as 'fresh,' which, according to Isidore of Seville in the early 7th century AD, signified a better quality and higher price than for 'old' pepper.[540] The *verso* of the lead-tag, moreover, lists a fragmentary price which must have been in the range of 20–39 *sesterces*. Hence, the entire load of high-quality pepper was either valued at no more than a paltry maximum of one and one quarter *denarii* per pound, or the price stated was not the aggregate value but per measure, making for some five to ten *denarii* per pound—more in line with Pliny's 70s AD price of four *denarii* per pound of black pepper. However, a different possibility is that the two lines on the lead-tag are rather to be read as '*Novelli piperinum*,' that is, as a pepper-based compound product belonging to Novellus, not as pure fresh pepper, and therefore also valued at less.[541]

Fortunately, there is yet another piece of important written evidence for provincial trade in pepper. On the utmost frontier of the Empire we find pepper being sold by an anonymous trader in AD 120–28 at the fort of Vindolanda, just south of Hadrian's Wall (being constructed in those very years). On a writing-tablet is listed the sale of pepper worth two *denarii* to Gambax, son of Tappo, out of the *centuria* of Ucenus.[542] Unfortunately, the measure of the pepper sold is not registered, but other purchases made by Gambax' colleagues and recorded on the same tablet were, *inter alia*, towels, thongs and tallow, all costing around two *denarii*. In fact, out of the transactions in the entire corpus of Vindolanda Tablets with surviving prices or valuations attached, the most commonly attested figure is two-and-a-half *denarii* (that is, the median of the price series in technical terms).[543]

In other words, Gambax' purchase of pepper was in no way extravagantly expensive, rather, it cost him less than what the inhabitants of Vindolanda normally paid for goods from near or far, at a time when the monthly salary of an auxiliary soldier was just short of 21 *denarii* per month. Although mandatory payments for equipment and food were to be deducted from the latter, there is ample evidence that soldiers in the Western Empire were not necessarily strapped for cash. In various documents we find them transferring money among themselves, lending at interest (100 *denarii*), and getting as much as 75 *denarii* paid out to them in one of several annual pay-check instalments.[544] Accordingly, two *denarii* was not a large sum of money for Gambax, who may, moreover, have been pooling resources with his messmates to spice up their communal meals.[545]

Hence, considering that Pliny listed the price of one pound of black pepper in Rome some 50 years earlier as four *denarii*, and that the roughly contemporary lead-tag from Trier may give a price of some

[536] For all of these finds generally, cf. Cappers 2006: 117–9, fig. 4.59; for Myos Hormos, cf. v. d. Veen 2011: 41, table 2.1; for Oberaden, Kučan 1992: 243, 245–6; for Straubing, Hanau, and Biesheim, see further below.

[537] Find referred by Cappers 2006: 119, but debunked by Johns 2010: 75, n52.

[538] See chapter eight.

[539] Schwinden 1985: 123–9. Nr. 1 reads: (front) *novel(l)u[m]* / *piper*[... | (back) *p(ondo)* VIII / *ṇ(?ummum) sẹ(?stertium)*XX[...

[540] Isidore *Origines*, XVII.8.8.

[541] However, this alternative interpretation is based on second-hand readings and should therefore be treated with due caution; Weiss 1991: 218.

[542] *Tab.Vindol.* 184, i, l. 4–5.

[543] Evers 2011: 21, data listed in Appendix; the price-data of *Tab.Vindol.* 861, published subsequently, conforms well.

[544] *Tab.Vindol.* 650; Tomlin 1998: no. 29; also from Carlisle, Tomlin 1992: 147; Speidel 1996: nos. 2, 3.

[545] E.g. *Tab.Vindol.* 590 is an inventory of a unit's cooking ware deposited with its members by the cook (*magirus*).

five to ten *denarii*, a comparison with the sale recorded in the tablet from Vindolanda gives an absolute maximum measure of 160 grams, i.e., half a pound, of pepper at the most, and some 60 grams at the very least. Ultimately, however, the unknown quantity is less important than the concrete fact that pepper as a commodity was traded alongside with, and no more expensive than, something as mundane as tallow and towels, approximately 10,000 km by sea and land from the spice's area of origin in South India.

Nor can this be explained away by the workings of a huge imperial supply apparatus attentively addressing the every need of its border forces, from the Germanic *limes* to Vindolanda, that is, by redistributive forces moving pepper around as opposed to market-induced supply and demand. Although it is true that every *archaeobotanical* find of peppercorns in Europe has been made in contexts related to military garrisons on the imperial border, the peppercorns at Straubing were found in the river port,[546] those of Hanau in the well of the *vicus*,[547] thus, alerting us to the fact that demand created by the presence and spending power of the army was not supplied by army or state personnel.[548]

Indeed, the list recording sale of pepper at Vindolanda was almost certainly drawn up by a civilian entrepreneur and supply-contractor, as were other similar lists, the author of one of which was also in charge of a substantial part of the camp's grain supply and identified himself as a *homo tra<n>smarinus* with trade goods, *merx*, and Roman citizen status which (should have) protected him from physical punishment.[549] Another example of civilians supplying the army with their goods and services is that of Vitalis from Vindolanda and Albanus from Carlisle (40 km further west), both *seplasiarii*, here likely to be rendered as pharmacists rather than perfumers.[550] We know from a Vindolandan strength report of the 90s AD that out of 31 soldiers unfit for duty due to various illnesses, one third were suffering from eye inflammation, and these would have been treated with *collyria*, eye-salves, one common ingredient of which was peppercorns, as we know from recipes of Roman Egypt.[551] So, seeing as pepper was being traded freely, we should be able to assume that the pharmacists also had a medicinal stock of peppercorns at hand for their salves.

Moreover, the same argument must be propounded for the context of the 8 pounds of pepper at Trier attested by the load's surviving lead-tag. There is no reason to assume anything else than a civilian merchant owner, whose activities in Trier of all places were, of course, to a large extent fuelled by the demand created by the Roman army and state in the region.[552] Thus, even at the military establishments we must—in accordance with the extant evidence written evidence—interpret the trade in pepper as civilian, supplied by merchants acting in response to the demand exerted by concentrations of soldiers and officers paid with tax-money raised throughout the provinces.[553] Crucially, then, the archaeobotanical evidence must be supplemented with that of pepper pots distributed across the rest of the Empire, from Britannia via Gaul to Thrace, Syria and Egypt, and coupled with the writing-tablet from Vindolanda, lead-tag from Trier, mosaic from Sicily, and inscription from Africa Proconsularis, which complete the picture: far outside the confines of Rome, pepper was also an object of consumption among even the western provincials, and not merely restricted to those living in military centres and *vici*, or at the confluence of trade routes with the East.[554]

---

[546] Küster 1995: 137–8, 196.

[547] Kreuz 1995: 66–70.

[548] Likewise, the pepper find from Biesheim in France was either made in pits of a *vicus* immediately west of the fort or in a great storage or latrine pit just in front of the western rampart, hence, like the other finds it was made *outside* the military area itself; Jacomet and Schibler 2001: 64–6.

[549] In addition to *Tab.Vindol.* 184, nos. 181, 182, and 861 (all from the preceding period 4, AD 105–20) constitute similar lists of sales, *Tab.Vindol.* 181 belonging to the same hand as *Tab.Vindol.* 180 (distribution of grain) and *Tab.Vindol* 344 (complaint about physical abuse and loss of goods). For market exchange and civilian traders at Vindolanda, see Evers 2011: chapter three, and for a case-study of the *homo transmarinus* in particular, pp. 18–19, 27–9.

[550] For Vitalis, see *Tab.Vindol.* 586, 877; for Albanus, see Frere and Tomlin 1991: 299f, no. 24.

[551] Strength report: *Tab.Vindol.* 154; for *collyria* recipes, e.g. *P.Oxy* LXXX, 5243, col. iii, l. 3f, l. 16f, being two 2nd–3rd century AD recipes for different kinds of eye-salve, both requiring 50 peppercorns; on the use of pepper in *collyria*, see Nielsen 1973: 20–21, 48–49.

[552] Interestingly, a 'Sabinus from Trier' figures as purchaser of unknown goods worth 38 *denarii*, 10 *asses*, on a list of sales (*Tab.Vindol.* 182, l. 4) at Vindolanda from one decade before the 'pepper tablet' (*Tab.Vindol.* 184), revealing networks of exchange along the supply route to *Britannia* through Gaul.

[553] A phenomenon well attested by the Vindolanda Tablets, cf. discussion in Evers 2011: 42–5.

[554] Thus, a negative evaluation of the possibility of civilian consumption of pepper in the provinces based on the sparse archaebotanical finds

Perfume trade in the provinces

Significantly, this point is borne out further by evidence for a significant provincial trade in perfumed oil of South Arabian myrrh and North Indian nard from Iulia Concordia in eastern Venetia, north-eastern *Italia*. Although not a regional centre in itself, Concordia had access by river to the sea, some 20 km away, and was situated on the *Via Annia* connecting Patavium and Altinum (where a *thurarius* is attested[555]) on the Venetian Lagoon to the west with Aquileia to the east (where a *negotiator margaritarius ab Roma* was buried[556] and which was a great centre for gemstone carving and trade[557]), thus making it a node on a major imperial route branching out eventually to Noricum, Pannonia and Dalmatia. The lead-tags in question were brought to light during excavations of quayside structures along a canal acting as the city's *decumanus*, which was likely connected to a riverine port outside the city walls, providing a commercial context for the long-lost wares in question.[558]

All six of the lead-tags listing cargoes record bales of wool (*vel(lera)*) as one half of the specific consignments, ranging from 2–48 bales, the average being 21.[559] However, while three tags list mundane items as the second half of the loads (brooms, fish-sauce and animal glue), the other three attest additional consignments of myrrh (*myrrinus* (*oleum* or *unguens*)) and nard perfume (*nardinus* (*oleum* or *unguens*)).[560] Seeing as the lead-tags are dated palaeographically to the 1st–2nd century AD, we can compare with the 70s AD prices of these wares listed in Pliny: for myrrh perfume we have to make do with the price of *stacte*, 3–50 *denarii*, being used for pure myrrh unguents in which even the use of oil was avoided,[561] while a pound of nard perfume fetched as much as 300 *denarii*, with the lowest quality likely valued at around 35 *denarii*, as with the parallel case of cinnamon oil.[562] Regarding the wool, one single lead-tag gives both a quantity and a price, namely, 2 bales worth 5 *denarii*, and while the value would likely depend on the specific quality and exact quantity, a price around 2½ *denarii* can serve as a broad indicator of the price.[563]

Thus, one Aebutius, whose *nomen* is attested in Aquileia and Altinum as well as throughout Gallia Cisalpina, is attested as the owner of a cargo shipped via river and canal through Iulia Concordia in the early imperial period, consisting of 48 bales of wool, worth approximately 120 *denarii*, and 25¾ pounds of oil of myrrh, that is, 8.21 kg, worth between 77¼ and 1287½ *denarii*, depending on the quality.[564] Likewise, the freedwoman Cincia Tyche, whose *gens* is known from inscriptions in Concordia and Altinum, was owner of a similar but smaller cargo, consisting of 9 bales of wool, worth some 22½ *denarii* and 4 pounds of myrrh oil, about 1¼ kg, worth 12–200 *denarii*.[565] Finally, a member of the *gens* Hostilius, well-attested throughout Venetia, with the *cognomen* Asiaticus, plausibly related to his trade in Eastern commodities, also shipped the apparently conventional half-cargo of wool, 40 bales, worth 100 *denarii*, the other half consisting of 27 pounds of nard oil, some 8.86 kg, worth between 945 and 8100 *denarii*, depending on the

alone, as Bakels and Jacomet 2003: 553, is misleading.

555 *CIL* V, 2184.

556 *I.Aquil.* I, 718.

557 Sena Chiesa 1966.

558 Marrone and Pettenò 2009–10: 81–82.

559 Marrone and Pettenò 2009–10: nos. 1–6. Henceforth to be abbreviated as *LC*.

560 Weiss 1991: 215 nn13, 15, has argued that the goods in question, as well as the cargo of nard recorded in a lead-tag from Rome (mentioned in chapter four), had to be myrrh- and nard-infused wine. However, a number of objections to this interpretation can be raised: a) wine was a standard freight commodity transported in amphorae of standardised measure marked with *dipinti*, not containers with individual amounts designated by lead-tags; b) wine was traditionally measured in *modii*, not *pondera*; c) such exotically scented-wine would most likely have been mixed in households for private use, not shipped as commercial goods; d) although in all likelihood more expensive than ordinary brands of wine, the quantities transported here (from less than one-sixth to about one standard wine amphora) would not have added up to much in terms of value; and, finally, e) the assumption that oil of nard and myrrh would be too expensive entirely only takes the maximum prices of Pliny into consideration, whereas the consignments in question could be valuable without being excessively costly.

561 For this use of *stacte* cf. Pliny *NH*, XIII.2. Of course, the retail price of a pure myrrh perfume produced from *stacte* might have been considerably higher than 50 *denarii*, matching the prices of perfumes based on cinnamon, malabathrum, nard and balsam of Judaea, all topping around 300–400 *denarii* per pound, but the lower grade of perfumier's myrrh was, in fact, also comparatively cheaper at 12 *denarii* than a pound of malabathrum leaves (60 *denarii*), nard plant (40–100 *denarii*) or cinnamon (as much as 300 *denarii*, although dirt-cheap stuff likely unsuitable for perfume production could be had for 10 *denarii*).

562 For these prices, see treatment above.

563 *LC* 3.

564 *LC* 1.

565 *LC* 2

quality.[566] While the upper price ranges of these estimates are surely unrealistic in this context, we can use the value of the associated bales of wool as a vague indicator of the potential minimum value of the perfume consignments, easily being worth a hundred *denarii* or more.

To put it bluntly, these aptly named *Laminae Concordienses* reveal a surprisingly large volume of provincial trade in perfumes processed from raw plant materials necessarily imported from Arabia and India, whereas the similar lead-tag from Rome recording the transport of some six pounds of nard perfume is nothing more than we would expect. Although Iulia Concordia was not exactly on the road to nowhere, it was, after all, merely a somewhat ordinary municipality in the Venetia and Histria region. Ships carrying costly supplies for the main markets of the region would have headed directly for the estuaries and ports of Patavium, Altinum, Aquileia or Pola, while those wishing to export foreign goods to Noricum, Pannonia or Dalmatia, via the Adriatic Sea, would have made use of Aquileia or Tergeste as main staging posts. Thus, it is, in fact, most likely that the myrrh and nard perfume attested in the canal and warehouse zone of Concordia had already been transhipped from original, larger cargo shipments of Eastern goods carried to the major nearby ports, such as Altinum and Aquileia (sporting epigraphical evidence of trade in frankincense, and pearls and gemstones, respectively, as we have seen), where they had been broken up.[567]

Nonetheless, Iulia Concordia's role as an ancient way-station on the overland trade route in woollen textiles between Patavium in Venetia and Magdalensberg in Alpine Noricum is well attested,[568] as are the trade connections of merchant families of Iulia Concordia itself, keeping up a presence in Iulium Carnicum (the last city in Venetia before entering Noricum) as well as in Magdalensberg.[569] Ultimately, the pepper in Straubing, Raetia, could have arrived there via Iuvavum in Noricum by way of either Iulium Carnicum or Virunum (the Roman settlement succeeding Magdalensberg) from even a small city such as Iulia Concordia, although Aquileia would be more likely.

Accordingly, the breaking up of shiploads in the greater regional ports would explain how expensive perfumes ended up mixed with local goods such as wool and brooms in the possession of traders native to Venetia and its cities, as we can tell from their names that Aebutius, Cincia Tyche and Hostilius Asiaticus were[570] (unlike the *negotiator margaritarius* who died in Aquileia, but was operating out of Rome). The perfumes must then have been marketed in Iulia Concordia itself, or been transhipped once more to even smaller river craft and carried further up the river to Concordia's remote hinterland or farther afield, to Noricum. Interestingly, it has even been suggested by the latest editors of the lead-tags that the coupling of bales of wool and fragile containers of precious perfumes in one cargo, could have been an expedient means of creating wool-padded, shock-absorbing consignments for long-distance transport.[571] However, while this would also make sense for wool-bales coupled with animal glue and fish-sauce, which must also have been conveyed in containers (although sturdy transport amphorae could have been used for the fish-sauce), brooms and wool make up another joint cargo of a lead-tag, which can hardly have been for reasons of protective packaging.[572]

Further light is shed on the vivacity of local commerce in Concordia by two unusual lead-tags which do not designate consignments, but record transactions defined by dates two-and-a-half and three months apart, hence, likely loans or forwarded payments.[573] Presumably, the possessors of the lead-tags were the creditors, for there is no other mention of such, while the relevant years were designated with reference to eponymous magistrates out of leading families of the town,[574] perhaps of a prominent local *collegium*,

---

566 *LC* 4.
567 Marrone and Pettenò 2009–10: 81f.
568 On the Patavium-Magdalensberg trade: Bonetto 2001: 155–61, with Bizzarini 2006; and on Iulia Concordia's role as an old regional node: di Filippo Balestrazzi 1999: 111–5.
569 Marrone 2001: 121–22, and Zaccaria 2001: 145–9.
570 Marrone and Pettenò 2009–10: 67 n67, 68 n70, 71 n77, respectively.
571 Marrone and Pettenò 2009–10: 81.
572 *LC* 3.
573 *LC* 7–8.
574 Marrone and Pettenò 2009–10: 77 n97, 79f n100.

as is known from Ostia and Rome.[575] For instance, we have already seen in chapter four how the *collegium aromatariorum* kept its own time reckoning in terms of five-year *lustra*. One of these two 'accountancy-tags' (no. 7) records an outstanding transaction of 55 *denarii* with a silversmith (*argentificus*) and one of 15 *denarii* with a goldsmith (*aurificus*), both unnamed, while the other tag (no. 8) records a transaction of 3 *denarii* with a named individual.[576] Particularly the loans to a silversmith and a goldsmith in the context of the trade attested in the other lead-tags hint at commercial loans taken out by local craftsmen.

Finally, a surprisingly similar lead-tag unearthed at ancient Pausulae in Picenum, more than 300 km south along the Italian coast of the Adriatic Sea from Iulia Concordia and 200 km north of Rome across the Apennines, prove that the *Laminae Concordienses* are not exceptional in attesting a substantial provincial trade in Eastern goods. When compared with the readings of the Concordia *corpus*, this tag appears to record a cargo of 30 bales of wool and 13 pounds of *nar(dinus)* (*oleum* or *unguens*), that is, 4¼ kg of nard, worth some 455–3900 *denarii*.[577] Significantly, the owner belonged to the *gens* Cascel(l)ia, a member of which was active in the province of Asia in 59 BC.[578] Another lead-tag found on the same site also seems to record an actual perfume or ingredients for such, namely, cedar oil or resin.[579]

No doubt, then, this small city, being 20 km up a river from the Adriatic, was part of an overall commercial circuit which brought cargoes of Eastern wares to the major ports of both Venetia and Picenum, where they were broken up, and from where the exotic perfumes found their way in smaller mixed consignments to places like Concordia and Pausulae. Levantine ships plying this route could have had their origin in any of the ports of Asia Minor,[580] Syria, Judaea or Egypt, Alexandria always being a likely contender—especially in light of the fact that the Muziris Papyrus mentions the import of no less than 80 boxes of Gangetic nard (worth 4,500 *denarii* each) to Alexandria as part of one return cargo from Muziris.[581] Notably, there is further evidence for such voyages in the *Digest*, quoting a 2nd century AD maritime contract for a voyage bringing goods from Syrian Berytus to Apulian Brundisium,[582] from where imports could have been transhipped to supply the major markets of the entire Adriatic seaboard, all the way to northernmost Aquileia.[583] Local families could also have been directly involved in the import all the way from the Egyptian Red Sea ports, as we know that the family of the *Peticii* were, based some 140 km further south along the Adriatic coast in inland Sulmo, likely even exporting their own production of wine.[584]

Indeed, finds of Eastern Terra Sigillata in Concordia provide additional archaeological confirmation of Levantine cargoes (likely also containing perfumes and spices) arriving from western Asia Minor, Cilicia and Syria, mainly during the 1st–2nd century AD. In fact, Eastern ceramics are even attested, albeit sparsely, as far inland along the trade routes as Magdalensberg in Noricum.[585] Nonetheless, the myrrh and nard perfumes in question might, in fact, also have arrived with outbound cargoes from Ostia, where one of the most prominent and well-established associations of shippers was the *corpus naviculariorum maris Hadriatici*, whose main line of work seems to have been the transport of wine from Adriatic ports to Rome.[586]

Thus, the evidence of lead-tags from Venetia and Picenum reveal sub-networks of inconspicuous local traders, men and women, supplying provincial demand for exotic perfumes in quite impressive

[575] Marrone and Pettenò 2009–10: 77, referring to Royden 1988.
[576] Marrone and Pettenò 2009–10: 80 n101.
[577] Marengo 1989: 44–7, no. 4. The corpus of ten lead-tags is tentatively dated early imperial to 3rd century AD, p. 54.
[578] Cic. *QFr.*, I.2.5.
[579] Marengo 1989: 42–4, no. 3: *ced(rium?)*.
[580] Note that the owner of nard from Concordia bore the cognomen Asiaticus, and that an ancestor of the family trading nard in Pausulae was active in inner Lydia at the time of Cicero.
[581] *SB* XVIII, 13167, *verso*, col. ii, l. 1. See chapter six.
[582] *Dig.* XLV.1.122.
[583] A Syrian from Antioch was buried at Concordia in Late Antiquity; indeed, Syrian merchants settled in steadily growing numbers in Northern Italy from the 1st century BC–5th centuryAD, cf. de Giorgi 2015: 181.
[584] Gianfrotta 1989, enlarged upon by Tchernia 1997; to be detailed in chapter six.
[585] Cf. Cipriano and Sandrini 2003, for the former, and Zabehlicky-Scheffenegger and Schneider 1998: 437, for the latter.
[586] Rohde 2012: 114–5.

quantities, as much as some 25 and 27 pounds of myrrh and nard unguents, respectively. Significantly, we can even tell that these consignments must represent local distribution at the stage after the breaking up of ships' cargoes arriving from Eastern Mediterranean ports. Although perfumes made from more local ingredients, such as those produced in Campania, must have been more readily available (and, presumably cheaper), the provincials of the Italian countryside evidently demanded the same foreign scents as their peers in Rome, revealing the end point of networks of demand and supply extending all the way to the myrrh groves of Qataban in South Arabia and the Himalayan foothills of North India in which spikenard grows.[587]

The long reach of interlocking markets

Summing up, prices in Rome with its great warehouses as low as three to four *denarii* per entire pound of frankincense or pepper imported from ancient South Arabia, Somalia and South India some 5000–8000 km away, implies a very substantial import to keep the major Mediterranean cities as well as even the more outlying provinces in good supply. Indeed, that the latter were not exempt from an apparently almost empire-wide market in Eastern commodities such as frankincense, myrrh- and nard-based perfumes, and, as the *primus inter pares*, pepper, has been substantiated by a survey of the different categories of available evidence. Considering the distances and geographical as well as cultural and fiscal barriers involved, only a consistent and widespread Roman demand for these commodities can have engendered a supply carried West by sea-going merchants of the Indian Ocean, camels and Nile barges in Egypt and Mediterranean exchange circuits, which could keep prices as comparatively low as attested in the above.

In fact, such a distribution of and trade in long-distance goods is supported by what limited and disparate source material there is for the scale of imports and exports between the Mediterranean and Indian Ocean in the early centuries AD. For instance, although Berenike in Egypt was merely a port of transit for the pepper trade, and we should only expect peppercorns to have been deposited there due to losses during its handling for transhipment by caravan, and, significantly, for votive uses (burnt offerings) and religious donations (like the 7.5 kg stored at one temple), more than 3600 stray finds were made—twice the number of lentils, which is considered to have been a main staple of the inhabitants. In light of the fact that only a small part of the entire archaeological site has been excavated, this implies that the volume of pepper passing through the port area must have been truly enormous, with potential future finds from further excavations having to be counted in tens of thousands of peppercorns.[588] Perhaps Zosimus was not too far off the mark, then, when he stated that part of Alaric the Visigoth's ransom for sparing Rome in 408 AD was an incredible 3000 pounds of pepper, to be collected from the more prominent inhabitants of the capital.[589]

However, this is a volume of trade which fits eminently well with the only surviving commercial document attesting Eastern trade in Roman times, the 'Muziris Papyrus,' to be treated extensively in chapter six, which records a cargo belonging to one single merchant returning to Alexandria from South India in the mid-2nd century AD, amounting to no less than some 150–180 tonnes and a total value before the quarter-tax of 2.3 million *denarii*. Now, with sums of money of this magnitude involved, it is perhaps not so surprising that Pliny and his contemporaries would balk at the scale of imports. Roman demand internal to the Mediterranean theatre had by Pliny's time already seen the readily available supplies of Mauretanian citrus wood and Libyan ivory used up, as chapter three showed, revealing an unsustainable rate of consumption. Naturally, the demand was subsequently met by supply from India, the Muziris Papyrus attesting import by one merchant alone of 3.85 tonnes of ivory from South India in the mid-2nd century AD. Indeed, that aggregate Roman imports of ivory were on a great scale is substantiated by old excavations at the monumental warehouse complex of the *horrea Galbana* in Rome. In one single storage

[587] There is also evidence from oculists' stamps (Voinot 1999) and literary sources (Nielsen 1973: 7–53) that Roman eye-medicine contained eastern aromatics, although the evidence is ambiguous with some archaeological samples containing exotic components (such as cinnamon, vanilla and myrrh), while modern testing cannot identify the labelled ingredients in others (Jackson 1996: 2242-3; Boyer *et al.* 1990). For a brief general overview of the subject, see Jackson 1996.

[588] Following Cappers 2006: 114.

[589] Zos., *Historia Nova*, V.41.4.

room was found 'huge tusks of ivory, forming a total volume of 675 cubic feet,' calculated to amount to some 2,500 tusks, a trove which must date from the abandonment of the complex in the 4th century AD.[590]

The concrete consequences of early imperial Roman demand can also be traced over longer distances, though. Thus, the Qatabanic and Hadramawtic kingdoms of South Arabia had traditionally only harvested their myrrh and frankincense groves once a year, in summer in tune with the natural cycle, but in Pliny's time producers had instituted a second annual harvest in spring in response to the much-increased demand from the Romans to their northwest. Significantly, the products of the new spring harvests were known to be of markedly lower quality than the summer crops, and therefore less profitable, but the market demand for myrrh and frankincense of both fine and lower grades was consistent enough to make the additional harvest work, collection, processing and transport worth everybody's efforts, anyway.[591]

The Hadramawtic king even expanded production further east (into the Dhofar region of modern Oman) where there were frankincense producing areas of the highest quality. The greater importance of this region is reflected in the mid-1st century AD re-founding as a city proper of a 3rd century BC settlement on the coast, Sumhuram (modern Khor Rori), and the corresponding growth of the main Hadramawtic harbour of Qana, to which the incense harvests from Sumhuram were shipped. In addition, the off-shore possession of Socotra, known to the Greeks as Dioscourides (to which we shall return in chapter seven), was also brought under sufficient control to be able to profit from its plentiful frankincense groves.[592] Thus, Roman demand set in motion concerted activities in Hadramawt to increase supply accordingly, a demand even made physically visible by the large numbers of basalt rocks scattered across the beaches of Myos Hormos and Berenike in Egypt, having been carried from Qana (and Aden) as ship's ballast because of the high price but low weight of incense cargoes.[593]

Remarkably, the same kind of reciprocal relationship between spiralling Western consumption and demand, on the one hand, and efforts in the East to increase production and supply, can now be identified in regard to the trade in pepper between the Roman Empire and South India. Thus, although the pepper trade considered in isolation might have been *the* most lucrative strand of the long-distance trade, Roman demand and the huge amounts of imports taken into consideration, the production of pepper in Early Historic India has until recently been very poorly attested. Presently, however, it is becoming increasingly clear that what little South Indian archaeobotanical data can be brought to bear on the subject, provides tentative evidence of both upland forest destruction and the beginning of permanent settlements in the newly cleared spaces from the 1st century AD. Seeing as this was the ecozone where pepper grew naturally and could therefore be cultivated for increased production, such a development appears to have been a reaction to increased Roman demand.[594]

However, when it comes to coral, the forces of supply and demand were able to facilitate long-distance trade in the other direction, too: from the Western Mediterranean to *Taprobane*, ancient Sri Lanka. According to Pliny, the best quality of coral was to be found in the waters off Gaul and Sicily, and this particular kind was held in as high esteem by Indians as pearls of the Indian Ocean were by Romans. Indeed, it appears that whereas this Western Mediterranean coral had previously been used by Gaulish warriors to adorn their panoply, they were now bereft of it,[595] as were the Romans themselves,[596] all the available coral that could be fished out of the sea now being exported eastwards, bringing in higher profits.

[590] Reported in Lanciani 1888: 250; calculation by Loane 1938: 50. On the *horrea Galbana* generally, cf. Rickman 1971: 97–104, and for their dating p. 165.
[591] Pliny *NH*, XII.32, 35.
[592] Singer 2007: 22f. For developments at Qana, se especially, Sedov 1992: 125–6; 2007: 76–9. For the re-founding of Sumhuram, cf. the new interpretation by Avanzini 2002–7, vols. 1–2; and Avanzini and Sedov 2005.
[593] Peacock, Williams and James 2007: at Berenike, all the basalt boulders were from Qana, whereas at Myos Hormos 70 per cent of the boulders where from Qana and 30 per cent from Aden, port of the myrrh-producing kingdom of Qataban.
[594] Morrison 2002: 110–11; Morrison and Lycett 2013: 137.
[595] Pliny *NH*, XXXII.11.
[596] The use of coral also had a long tradition among the Greeks and Romans, cf. Lapatin 2015: 184–6.

This state of affairs is corroborated by the *Periplus*, which informs us that coral was imported by Qana in South Arabia, Barbaricon at the mouth of the Indus, Barygaza in Western India, and by the ports of Limyrike in south-western India.[597] Great unworked quantities of the lower quality Red Sea coral has, moreover, been found at Berenike, and even five beads of the prized Western variety, and although it is impossible to tell with certainty whether they were meant for export or local use, the former is perhaps the more likely considering the price they could fetch with Indian buyers.[598] There is even later Sri Lankan written sources which allege that a beautiful coral net made on royal orders and donated to an important Buddhist monastery, in the 1st century AD, was crafted from corals acquired via Roman traders.[599] Accordingly, this case constitutes the opposite scenario to that of Rome consuming the produce of far-away lands, here with South Asia acting as the Great Attractor and Gauls and Romans alike being cornered out of the market for their own local coral.

Another kind of Indian demand being met by an accommodating Western supply can be identified by analysis of the Roman coin finds in India.[600] Specifically, there is a pronounced tendency for coins in hoards to be either early *denarii*, mainly Julio-Claudian, but also some Republican, predating the Neronian debasement of the silver bullion value, or 2nd century AD *aurei*, particularly of Antoninus Pius and Septimius Severus. In other words, this picture in no way resembles a random or natural distribution. Rather, the known hoards suggest careful selection of particular *denarii* issues with good silver bullion value and later preference for gold by Indian merchants, especially seeing as the majority of the Republican and Julio-Claudian *denarii* did most likely not arrive in the Subcontinent until the later 1st-early 2nd century AD.[601] Hence, Indian demand for precious metals, first silver and later gold, prompted meticulous screening and collection by Roman merchants of specific coins of good bullion value to be shipped East and used in exchange for desired imports. In fact, the *Periplus* does name coins as a Roman export and well-known item of import at the South Indian ports, including Muziris, and at the important harbour of Barygaza in Western India.[602]

The same pattern of selective Roman exports informed by Indian tastes has now been documented by a corpus of *ostraca* unearthed at the customs station (*pylê*) of Berenike on the Red Sea, where they functioned as receipts proving that customs fees on merchandise for export had been paid at Koptos by the owner, dating from the first years of the 1st century AD until the final years of Trajan.[603] As regards the cargoes ordered to clear customs at Berenike, the most frequently attested commodity, which also appears in the largest quantities, is wine, while the second runner-up, albeit much less frequent, is oil. Crucially, moreover, the wines dominating the Berenike *ostraca* are Italian and Laodicean, being the specific varieties in demand at Adulis (*Periplus* 6), the port of Axum, and Barygaza (#49) in Western India.[604] Moreover, wine generally, specific vintage not stipulated, found a market at South Arabian Muza (#24) and Qana (#28), Avalites (#7) in East Africa, Barbarikon (#39) at the mouth of the Indus, and in the major ports of the Malabar Coast, especially Muziris (#56).[605] This is in marked contrast to the only other local archive of *ostraca* providing information about transport of goods to the Red Sea ports, which has been argued to reflect only the transport of wine for local supply and consumption at the Roman ports themselves.[606]

In order to account for these reciprocal relationships between demand and supply, consumption and production, exerted alternately by the Roman Mediterranean and the Indian Ocean, some kind of

597 *Periplus* 28, 39, 49, 56.
598 Sidebotham 2011: 238–9.
599 Romanis 1997a: 188–91.
600 Compare the more extensive treatment in Cobb 2015a: 187–92.
601 Turner 1989, augmented by review of Berghaus 1992, and 1998 article, Berghaus' main argument being based on MacDowall 1991 and subsequent 1996. A very important point, because it is often argued that the numerous Julio-Claudian *denarii* reflect an early and short peak in the long-distance trade with India. See, however, the objection raised in Tomber 2008: 36.
602 *Periplus* 49, 56.
603 Bagnall *et al.* 2000: 7–11; 2005: 4–5. Further discussion in Nappo and Zerbini 2011: 61–8, 76–7.
604 Bagnall *et al.* 2000: 14–21.
605 On Roman export of wine to India more generally, see now Cobb 2015a: 193–6.
606 Ruffing 1993: 17–25.

long-distance market integration must have existed. Otherwise, the production, collection and export of specific in-demand wares via Egypt, as regards Roman exports,[607] and, vice versa, from ports in the kingdoms of South Arabia and Southern India, as regards Arabian frankincense and myrrh, and Indian ivory, gemstones, pearls, aromatics, spices and silk, would simply not have happened on the scale attested in the preceding chapters. Obviously, this is not to say, either, that there was a unified Mediterranean and Indian Ocean market economy, exhibiting full integration of prices between East and West.[608]

However, it is, in fact, to say that the accumulated evidence for the long-distance trade supports the existence in the early centuries of the Common Era of what we might call 'interlocking markets:' local, provincial and imperial exchange conducted within the Roman Empire as, mainly, market trade, but driven in part by redistribution in the guise of state expenditure of taxes and provision of protection, as well as conspicuous consumption by the elites fuelled by reciprocal status obligations, interacted with a similar hierarchical setup of local, intra-state and foreign exchange conducted by the kingdoms of the Indian Ocean, likewise based on market trade, state redistribution and reciprocity.[609] In succession, and with considerable delay, information about supply and demand, as well as the actual commodities of the trade, would travel back and forth between the extremities of East and West, from market to adjacent market, being channelled towards centres of consumption at either end of the geographical spectrum, as well as to important nodes along the way.

This explains how Rome and Alexandria, in particular, but also Vindolanda, Trier and Concordia, ended up receiving coveted commodities from Arabia and India, and, as we shall see in the subsequent chapters, how ports of the Western Indian Ocean and, particularly, Western and South India received Roman trade goods. Indeed, this sort of long-distance percolation through intervening markets, in certain periods arguably increasing to more of a surge, explains how Chinese silk arrived in Rome, as we have seen, via the ports of South Asia, and, conversely, how a wine amphora from the Campanian estate of Marcus Livius Caustrus ended up in landlocked Mathura in Northwest India in the Augustan period,[610] as well as how Roman glasswares ended up not only in Begram in Afghanistan and Pattanam in South India (on the latter, see chapter eight), but even in China itself.[611]

To some extent, the surprising efficacy of such a system of interlocking markets can be explained by the relatively small amount of foreign goods traded over long-distances (as compared to regional trade in grain or ceramics), because the essential in-demand nature of these goods meant that whatever a merchant could manage to bring to market would always be sold, the aggregate demand of the elite and middling classes inevitably outstripping supply, even in hard times. This fact is reflected in a 1st century AD passage from Persius' *Satires*, in which a lazy trader is berated to be among the first to purchase goods such as ivory, frankincense and pepper upon their arrival from afar, whilst still literally 'fresh off the camel.' In consequence, although these wares were non-essential commodities compared to food staples, demand was permanent, that is, structural, not elastic.[612]

In turn, this meant that information about supply and demand did not have to travel quickly in order to connect distant markets, which was always an impossibility. Rather, the merchants of the long-distance routes were more concerned about the reliability of information than its speed of dissemination. Slow, but trustworthy, information on far-away market conditions would certainly not be able to bring about a system of integrated markets in any kind of modern sense, but it would, on the other hand, provide for that *primum mobile* quality which would attract sellers and buyers, and thus, in turn, set in motion import and export. Accordingly, while nodes in the network of shipping lanes like Rome, Puteoli and Alexandria were integrated into a somewhat fluid system of information-exchange based on a higher

607 Brilliantly argued by Cobb 2015a: 199–200, based on a thorough analysis of the available archaeological data for Roman exports.
608 Seland 2008a argues that the Indian Ocean trade was if not 'globalised,' then at least 'oikoumenised.'
609 This is an expanded version of the model outlined in Evers 2011: 43–6.
610 Lyding Will 1991: fig. 9.4, p. 154, and n11, p. 156; augmented by Tchernia 1997: n2, p. 248. For more on this M. Livius Caustrus and the *Livii*, see Los 2000: 256.
611 Laing 1991; Kinoshita 2009; Hoppal 2016.
612 Pers. V.132-137; compare Hildebrandt (unpublished): 233, on silk.

speed of communication, even places as far distant as Berenike, Adulis, Qana, Barbaricon, Barygaza and Muziris found a place in this network by virtue of the dissemination of slow and reliable information.

While slow information rules out making a profit from a short-term discrepancy in the market, like a temporary grain shortage, it was, however, eminently capable of conveying information about permanent, that is, structural, market opportunities, such as the potential level of demand for ivory, pearls, frankincense, silk, coral, precious metal, wine, etc. in major Roman and Indian ports. Accordingly, the fact that these market opportunities were based on different geographical and cultural potentials for production and consumption at different sites of the Indian Ocean, made for a system of exchange based on interlocking markets which thrived quite well on the dissemination of reliable information—in fact, exactly the kind of information which we find in the *Periplus*, whose account of supply and demand in different localities we have already consulted innumerable times.[613] The following chapters will substantiate this proposed model of interlocking markets operated by networks of various kinds (personal, diasporas and associations) acting on reliable information.

In closing, this chapter has surveyed prices of Eastern products, provincial trade in pepper and perfumes concocted from Eastern aromatics, and other evidence for the workings of very long-distance demand and supply coming together to move traders and goods back and forth between East and West. Moreover, the case-studies of provincial trade in pepper and perfumes, in particular, revealed that this trade was not confined to the largest urban centres, such as Rome in its role as the 'Great Attractor' of the Mediterranean, but percolated into the furthest, that is, Western, regions of the Empire, being traded at prices and by people which do not warrant that consumption of these goods was merely confined to the elite. Indeed, although Rome constituted the most important market for expensive imports, this and the preceding chapter has endeavoured to show that merchants involved in the Eastern trade must have split their time between the capital and rural homes or trade circuits among the provincial aristocracy. There can be no doubt that demand was also the great mover in the provincial areas, supply being a very long-distance effort only feasible in light of strong and inflexible consumer demand.[614]

[613] On the *Periplus* as a synthesis of information compiled from various sources about ports, regions and their trade, see the innovative approach of Seland 2016b. On the feasibility of information-sharing by shippers and merchants of the Greco-Roman world more widely, see especially Terpstra 2017.

[614] Indeed, this demand even appears to have been consistent over the very long run, as attested by the continued trade in gemstones (Thoresen 2017: 168–70) and spices (Mrozek 1982, Corbier 1985: especially, p. 101; McCabe 2009) into and beyond Late Antiquity (on Byzantine imports, 4th–7th century AD, from the East, see Mango 1996: 145–8), as well as by Early Medieval European consumption of spices, drugs, incense, myrrh and silk (McCormick 2001: 708–24), and by the Byzantine organisation of trade in perfumes, spices and silk into associations, traditionally called 'guilds', around AD 900 (*Book of the Eparch*, edition Dujcev 1970: IV (pp. 26–28), VI–VIII (pp. 31–38), X (pp. 41–3); Maniatis 2009). A fitting illustration of this long history of long-distance trade is that at the death of St. Bede in AD 735, at Jarrow on the river Tyne in Northern England, he wanted some pepper and frankincense in his personal possession shared among his fellow monks (Colgrave and Mynors 1969: 585), whereas some 600 years earlier, Gambax, son of Tappo, had purchased two *denarii* worth of pepper at Vindolanda, only sixty kilometres to the west, as related above.

Chapter 6

The *modus operandi* of Roman long-distance trade

In the preceding chapters, the main focus has been on urban networks of craftsmen and traders in Rome and the Western provinces, handling the import, processing and retail sale of goods originating in South Arabia or India. Some of these networks, furthermore, were formalised in the guise of official associations uniting fellow artisans or merchants in the institution of a *collegium*, complete with formal membership and internal rules. Consequently, these groups were characterised by being more or less stationary and grounded in their local communities, having specialised in making a living from a specific urban market in their own wares or services.

However, when it comes to the actual supply of Eastern goods to any city, be it Rome or Concordia, different kinds of organisations loom prominently in the sources, namely, those of trans-local personal networks or diasporas, of which some of the latter could also be organised as *collegia* or similar associations, though.[615] Accordingly, it is important to distinguish between local and trans-local (or intra-community and inter-community) networks, diasporas and associations, seeing as these faced different challenges in the conduct of their daily business.[616] Competing for local buyers against peers in a specific urban market is not the same as striving as a group to obtain a profit from managing the import from outside the Empire of Indian Ocean commodities, which subsequently had to be shipped onwards to trusted partners in Mediterranean ports with access to wholesale merchants or retail traders in major urban markets.

In order to make such long-distance networks function in the Roman world, recent studies have highlighted the ability of diasporas in particular to forge strong personalised links based on shared geographical origin, which could maintain trust and trade between members through private ordering and enforcement.[617] Indeed, as set out previously, diasporas are a prime example of potentially very potent networks, that is, often exhibiting a marked degree of closure, thus, providing a range of weak and strong ties between members grounded in common ethnicity, religion, profession, kinship, etc.—being a fertile breeding ground for relational contracts, in other words. However, the potential for any such group to raise prices by obtaining a near-monopoly on long-distance supply seems to have been offset by the existence of numerous such trans-local personal networks or diasporas at any given time, each obtaining its goods through different channels intertwining back along the supply chain to Alexandria or the old Phoenician ports, or even beyond to entrepôts in the lower Red Sea and Gulf of Aden and perhaps onwards to the original ports of export in South Asia. In this chapter, we shall investigate the workings of personal networks and diasporas involved in the import of Indian Ocean goods as they operated within the confines of the Empire[618]—the more far-flung operations of Palmyrene and Nabataean networks will be dealt with in the next chapter.

All routes lead to Rome—and India!

Straddling the comparatively narrow land mass adjoining the continent of Africa with that of Asia, Egypt occupies a geographical junction through which goods to be exchanged between Mediterranean and Indian Ocean maritime circuits had to pass. Indeed, the find of peppercorns (*piper nigrum* from South India) in the embalming of Ramses II's mummy, reveals that very early trade circuits extended from India across the Arabian Sea to Pharaonic Egypt as early as the 13th century BC.[619] Intriguingly, though, the first navigator of the Arabian Sea whom we know by name was a Greek mercenary from Western Asia Minor,

---

615 See especially Verboven 2011b.
616 Following Terpstra 2013: 54, 116–17.
617 Terpstra 2013; and case-study in 2015. Also Bang 2011: 241–89, although, as pointed out by Terpstra in the note above, he has a tendency to conflate the workings of local associations and trans-local diasporas.
618 See also the concise analysis of organisational delegation of agency in Ruffing 2013.
619 Cappers 2006: 119.

Scylax of Caryanda, who on the orders of the Achaemenid ruler Darius I sailed down the Indus river and managed to make his way around the Arabian Peninsula to Persian ruled Egypt, sometime around 500 BC.[620] Subsequently, the Ptolemaic rulers of Egypt from the 3rd century BC onwards established routes with simple way-stations and some degree of water supply in the Eastern Desert, as well as the ports which continued into Roman times, most notably Myos Hormos and Berenike.[621] A contract for a commercial venture from Egypt to the Spice-bearing Land, that is, East Africa, survives from the early 2nd century BC, revealing regularised Greek navigation in and out of the Red Sea,[622] while Strabo relates that the find of a half-dead Indian sailor in Ptolemaic waters set in motion an expedition which sailed to and returned from India, led by Eudoxus of Cyzicus, also from Western Asia Minor, in the later 2nd century BC.[623] Indeed, an epitaph from the necropolis of Hellenistic Rhodes states that one Amphilochos 'sailed both the streams of the Nile and on farthest Indus,' seemingly supporting regularised Indian Ocean traffic by traders and adventurers from the Hellenistic Mediterranean more generally, not only Ptolemaic Egypt.[624]

With the annexation of Egypt in 30 BC by the later Augustus, however, the source material for trade and traders involved in commerce between the Mediterranean and South India increases notably. In the words of Strabo, the seagoing commerce expanded drastically in the very first decade of Roman rule, exceeding the long-distance trade of the late Ptolemies by an order of magnitude.[625] This expansion of the Eastern trade was very much driven by Roman demand, the ensuing supply generated by sea-going merchants and captains of the Indian Ocean being channelled through Alexandria. Significantly, this particular consequence of long-distance demand was remarked on already by Strabo, who noticed that Alexandria received the majority of its commodities from up the Nile, its imports by sea being exceeded by its exports: 'This any person may ascertain, either at Alexandria or Dicæarchia [Puteoli], by watching the arrival and departure of the merchant vessels, and observing how much heavier or lighter their cargoes are when they depart or when they return.'[626]

Accordingly, Puteoli had been developed over the years to serve as the original deep-sea port of Rome,[627] again according to Strabo: 'This city has become a place of extensive commerce, having artificially constructed harbours... [Its inhabitants having constructed] moles in the sea, thus forming bays along the open coast, in which the largest transport ships may safely ride.'[628] Indeed, the importance of trade during the Early Empire between Puteoli and Alexandria in particular, but also other ports of the Eastern Mediterranean, is attested by an inscription from Puteoli revealing the presence of merchants collectively identifying themselves as those 'who conduct trade with Alexandria, (and the provinces of) Asia and Syria.'[629]

In addition to the ordinary trade carried on by private entrepreneurs, the largest merchant fleet of the ancient Mediterranean also happened to ply its way back and forth between the ports of Alexandria and Puteoli (later also Portus by the mouth of the river Tiber), in order to ensure the vital supply of Egyptian grain to the imperial capital, delivering some 250 shipments *per annum,*[630] as many as a dozen grain ships[631] sailing out of the port of Alexandria every week during the summer sailing season.[632] From assumed

620 Hdt. IV.44; sometime between Darius' conquest of the Indus Valley in 515 BC and death in 486 BC.
621 Strabo XVII.1.45; Pliny *NH*, VI.33. Sidebotham 2011: 28–58.
622 To be dealt with below.
623 Strabo II.3.4; the death of Euergetes II in 116 BC being an *ante quem*. See Habicht 2013: 201–2, 205–6, who convincingly sums up studies on the story of Hippalus, 'discoverer' of the monsoon and allegedly the first to use it to sail straight from Egypt to India and back (according to the *Periplus* 57), concluding that it was an ancient myth.
624 *IG* XII,1 144; I thank Christian A. Thomsen for this reference. Interestingly, some of the earliest amphorae excavated at Arikamedu were late Rhodian, dated 1st century BC, cf. Lyding Will 1996: 318, cat. nos. 28–39.
625 Strabo XVII.1.13, II.5.12.
626 Strabo XVII.1.7.
627 See generally Zevi 1993 and particularly the chapter of Romanis 1993.
628 Strabo V.4.6.
629 *CIL* X, 1797; dealt with in greater detail below.
630 Rohde 2012: 94.
631 Hass 1997: 42, scaling down the traffic of the Late Empire in accordance with the numbers available for the High Empire.
632 On the sailing seasons generally, see Casson 1971: 270–3; the sea was 'open' April–October (although only 'safe' from May until September)) and 'closed' November–March. In the winter season, some ships would still take to sea, though (e.g., Pliny *NH*, II.47), and grain freighters could try to cram in one more passage—sometimes with dire consequences, as in *Acts* 27.6–44 in which the ship is wrecked on the shores of Malta.

humble beginnings under Augustus, probably in the guise of chartered experienced grain shippers of Alexandria formerly in Ptolemaic service,[633] there is a string of imperial rulings from Claudius to Marcus Aurelius conferring fiscal privileges on private transport contractors willing to serve the *annona.*[634] Various sources inform us about the routes,[635] work routines,[636] and even sizes of these ships.[637]

By the mid-2nd century AD, two inscriptions from Portus reveal that towards the end of that century, the 'Alexandrian grain fleet' had attained sufficient organisational complexity to be formally headed by a common *epimelêtês* and make joint dedications,[638] while shippers and merchants trading out of Alexandria possessed an office in Ostia's *Piazzale delle Corporazioni.*[639] Although the raison d'être of the *Piazzale delle Corporazioni* in Ostia was intimately connected with the *annona*, six *stationes* reveal that trade in other commodities was also concentrated there: skins, wood, (African) ivory, wild animals for circus games, and amphorae containing dates or wine. Accordingly, this mainly post-Hadrianic square and its many small 'offices,' prominently placed at the heart of Ostia, constituted a space where well-defined and permanent groups of specialised traders and shippers could, on the one hand, assemble for internal organisational purposes, and, on the other hand, proudly advertise their services in the supply of the capital as well as offer imports from their home cities and arrange for return exports.[640] Such a setup with groups from afar setting up representations in ports serving lucrative markets was not a new development of the Imperial period, though, being even more well attested as concerns trade between Rome and Egypt in the preceding centuries.

Dating back to Hellenistic times, organisations of Romans involved in trade with Alexandria as well as Alexandrians involved in long-distance trade with the rest of the Mediterranean, including *Italia*,[641] are both to be found on Delos. Thus, a Roman community of merchants and shippers evidently firmly established at Alexandria issued joint honorary decrees in the later 2nd and early 1st century BC,[642] being a successor to groups present in Alexandria in the early 3rd century BC and described in a papyrus as 'the foreigners arriving by sea, the merchants, the warehouse-owners, and others.'[643] One such member of the Roman business community at Alexandria is attested in a mid-2nd century BC papyrus, where he acts as middleman financier for a small consortium of Greeks sailing down the Red Sea to purchase spices in East Africa,[644] and Roman middlemen in and around Alexandria can, as it happens, be traced right down to Augustan times.[645] Likewise, several Alexandrian organisations were active at the commercial hotspot of Delos in the later 2nd century BC,[646] one having to designate itself as 'the elder,' implicitly to distinguish it from 'the younger,' association of warehouse-owners on the isle,[647] while yet another group kept in close communication with affiliated branches in other ports of the Levant.[648] Even more specifically, a link between Puteoli and Alexandria can be dated back beyond 105 BC, when restoration work was

[633] Casson 1991: 208.

[634] Erdkamp 2005: 244–49. Also Rohde 2012: 93, 116 n223. Both emphasising the private, not public, nature of the ships making up this 'fleet.' On the grain fleet generally, cf. Casson 1991: 206–12.

[635] Casson 1950: 43–51, on Lucian's *Navigium*. Casson 1971: 297.

[636] *BGU* 27 (2nd–3rd century AD), the letter of a crew member of a grain ship docked in Puteoli or Portus.

[637] E.g., Casson 1971: 172 n25, 184–8; and *P.Bingen* 77, ll. 9–10, on the latter text see Drexhage and Ruffing 2008.

[638] *IG* XIV, 917, 918. A comparable group known from the *Piazzale delle Corporazioni* is the *navicularii Africani*, cf. *AE* 1955, 183.

[639] *CIL* XIV, 4549, no. 40: *Ale*]*xandrin*(*orum*). This could imply either *navicularii* or *negotiatores Alexandrini*, both occupations being attested in nearby mosaics, cf. discussion in Rohde 2012: 107 n175.

[640] Noy 2002: 160–64; Rohde 2012: 108–113; Terpstra 2013: 107–16. Concrete examples of traders operating out of Alexandria who might have made use of such *stationes* in Italian ports include: I) Ptolemy of Alexandria who had a Pompeian banker auction his stock of linen in Campania (later 50s AD), *CIL* IV, 3340.100; cf. Andreau 1974: 218, 284, 289, 293. II) Trypho of Alexandria who had to appear in court at Puteoli to settle a debt of 3,000 sesterces (mid-1st century AD), *TPSulp* 13. III) the *nauklêros* Menelaos of Keramos who appears to have been a regular freight contractor on the Alexandria–Puteoli route, providing a Puteolian associate as guarantor for a transport deal (AD 38), *TPSulp* 78; cf. Tchernia 2011: 340–2.

[641] According to Fraser 1972: 159, Alexandrian (artistic) influences are evident at Pompeii from the later 2nd century BC, being transmitted through the trade route: Alexandria-Delos-Puteoli.

[642] *ID* 1526 (*nauklêroi kai emporoi*), 1699 (*Alexandreae Italicei*).

[643] *P.Cairo.Zen.* 59021, ll. 9–11 (*hoi xenoi hoi eispleontes kai hoi emporoi kai hoi egdocheis kai alloi*); 258 BC. The meaning of the term *egdocheis* is ambiguous: Rostovtzeff 1941, II: 1268, translated it as 'warehouse-owners.'

[644] See below.

[645] Bowman 2000.

[646] On the Delian commercial milieu and the organisation of mercantile personnel in associations, see Rauh 1993.

[647] *ID* 1528 (*he synodos tõn en Alexandreiai presbyterõn egdocheõn*).

[648] *ID* 1521 (*synodos* communicating with *koinon*).

undertaken on the former port's oldest Serapeum by worshippers with Italian names, likely Romans who had been converted during extended stays at commercial hotspots such as Delos or Alexandria.[649]

Moreover, jumping forward again to the mid-2nd century AD, a 'House of the Alexandrians' is known from Tomis on the Black Sea[650] at a time when a local *oikos tõn nauklêrõn* was also prominent in this city,[651] and when such *oikoi* were formal entities approved of by the emperor himself and adhering to their own sets of ratified rules (*nomoi*).[652] Nearby, the 'Alexandrians conducting business' were a recognised civic subgroup in Perinthos on Propontis.[653] Therefore, we need not hesitate in imputing to the *navicularii* or *negotiantes Alexandrini* of the contemporary *Piazzale delle Corporazioni* in Ostia a substantial organisational setup, as with the *collegia* already attested in Rome itself or the maritime organisations just mentioned, and as developed over time by the Alexandrian grain fleet.

In consequence, expensive long-distance imports were shipped to Rome from the Eastern entrepôt of Alexandria either on the well-built, reliable transport ships serving the *annona*, as a supplement to their primary cargoes of grain and in the same manner that they carried paying passengers,[654] or on similarly highly dependable merchantmen plying the route independently, some (or most) necessarily organised within the framework of the Ostian *statio* of the *Alexandrini*. Indeed, it can be argued that Egyptian grain, *annona* ships and Eastern goods were inextricably linked. The grain supply was of vital concern for Rome and the emperors residing there, and anything that made transport service in the *annona* more attractive (profitable) to shippers, such as the option of carrying additional low-weight, high-value cargo consignments of foreign imports, was therefore also perceived of as being in the common best interest.[655]

However, one important consequence for the import of Eastern commodities to the Western Mediterranean of being shipped from Alexandria and other ports of the Levant, was that goods could only arrive in the West from early May until late September or early October at the latest, in accordance with the rhythm of the Mediterranean sailing season. Indeed, if these precious goods had been loaded on *annona* freighters, only one or two runs per ship, depending on whether they had wintered in Puteoli or Alexandria, respectively, could safely be made within the navigational year.[656] Significantly, this would have caused market demand to soar just prior to the arrival of the first ships in early May (when stocks from the closing of the last sailing season had become almost entirely depleted) and supply to peak towards late September (when all the annual products of the Alexandrian warehouses had arrived)—a phenomenon which is mirrored by the well-documented speculation in hoarding privately purchased Egyptian grain in the dockside warehouses of Puteoli until late April.[657] In consequence, the interplay between the Mediterranean navigational year and the climatic circumstances (flooding of the Nile, monsoon winds cycle, etc.) determining the speed with which Indian Ocean imports could reach Mediterranean ports, was of vital importance for both those who had lent out money, as well as the borrowers, who were waiting to recoup their expenses and make a profit by marketing their imports at major markets such as Alexandria or Rome.[658]

Although there is no doubt that the Alexandria–Puteoli/Portus route constituted the major maritime conduit for Eastern imports, there is, nonetheless, also evidence in the major ports of *Italia* of diasporas, indicating regularised trading with their cities of origin on the seaboard of the Eastern Mediterranean.

---

649 *CIL* X, 1781 = Tran Tam Tinh 1972: IS. 12; on worshippers of Isis and Serapis in Campania more generally, see the latter, pp. 1–49.

650 *IGR* I, 604 (*oikos tõn Alexandreõn*).

651 *IScM* II, 60, 132.

652 Ehrhardt and Günther 2013: an *oikos nauklêrõn* obtaining permission to be established in Miletus by Hadrian, who also reaffirmed their charter of rules.

653 *IGR* I, 800 (*Alexandreis hoi pragmateuomenoi*).

654 On passengers, see especially Casson 1968.

655 Wallace-Hadrill 2008: 331–2.

656 For the length of the passages, cf. the estimates given by Casson 1950: 51; 1971: 297–9; 1991: 207–8. On the sailing season, see above.

657 Cf. the transactions involved in the two cases constituted by *TPSulp* 46, 53, 79 (40 AD), and *TPSulp* 45, 50, 51, 67, 68 (37 AD), elucidated by Jones 2006: 92–102.

658 Cooper 2011, Seland 2011, Beresford 2012: 213–35, Cobb 2014. For instance, Seland 2011 shows that goods imported from the Indian Ocean via the Nile would reach Alexandria around the end of the sailing season, whereas goods imported via the Persian Gulf to, for instance, Antioch, would reach Mediterranean ports by the very beginning of the sailing season.

Significantly, for the purposes of this study, one particularly profitable strand of this commerce will have consisted in the re-export further westward, either immediately or after processing to enhance the value, of wares obtained from the Indian Ocean maritime exchange circuit, mainly via the Persian Gulf,[659] but secondarily from the Red Sea (coming up the Gulf of Aqaba),[660] and perhaps even goods from Central Asia and the Far East via the ancient Eurasian overland routes traversing the Iranian Plateau.[661]

Specifically, Antioch, at the head of the great caravan routes,[662] can be linked to *Italia* by the presence in Rome of Syrian worshippers of Jupiter Dolichenus, a cult originating in northern Syria (now across the border in modern Turkey),[663] providing a tentative link between the imperial capital and the foremost city of Syria when correlated with the presence in Rome of Antiochenes, a Syrian inhabitant of Nisibis on the northern trade route through Mesopotamia, and a citizen from Seleucia Pieria, the port of Antioch, as attested in epigraphy.[664] In Late Antiquity, when numerous *Syrii* can be found at Rome, the ethnicon 'Syrus' even became synonymous with merchants and moneylenders, being associated with trade in luxury goods, as well as slaves, in particular.[665]

We are on much firmer ground, though, when it comes to the active presence in *Italia* of Phoenician diasporas hailing from the great old trading centres of Berytus and Tyre.[666] Conspicuously less visible in Roman than Hellenistic times, though, is the presence of Sidonians,[667] especially famous in that period for their high quality glassmaking (an industry easily combined with the production of *unguentaria* for perfumes), but also for silk production.[668] In contrast, the city of Tyre was famously active in Roman commerce, being fabled throughout the Mediterranean for its purple-dyeing industry (some of which was used to dye Chinese silk found at Palmyra, cf. chapter four), while both Tyre and Berytus were renowned for their production and export not only of linen textiles far and wide, but especially of silk garments.[669] The point being, of course, that such silks of Roman Phoenicia would, until the transfer to the West of sericulture around the mid-6th century AD,[670] have been imported as finished textiles, or dyed, woven and embroidered like the actual fragments of silk found in Palmyrene funeral towers, using either domesticated silk imported from China or Indian wild silk, by way of Central Asian overland routes or the Indian Ocean.[671] Accordingly, it is highly significant that communities of Tyrians and Berytians can be traced to Puteoli and Rome in the Imperial period.

[659] See chapter seven on Palmyrene long-distance trade via the Persian Gulf.
[660] Likewise, see chapter seven on Nabataean long-distance trade via the Red Sea.
[661] For these so-called 'Silk Routes,' which are not included in the present study, see, e.g., Millar 1998: 126–30; Young 2001: 188–97; and Andrade in the note below
[662] Liebeschuetz 1972: 76–78; Kondoleon 2000: 16, cat.nos. 49, 84. An Antiochene city-councillor and collector of the *tetarte* exacted on Eastern imports was honoured by Palmyrenes in AD 161, *Inv.* 10.29, suggesting that the city might have acted as entrepôt for Palmyrene imports; an embassy from the South Indian kingdom of the Pandians reached the Mediterranean by way of Antioch, cf. Strabo XV.1.4, 73; Isidore of Charax' itinerary through the Middle East takes Antioch as its starting point, *Parthian Stations* 1; and both Ptolemy's account of merchants travelling all the way to *Sera* from Heliopolis (*Geogr.* 1.11–12, transl. in Berggren and Jones 2000: 72–3; on which route see now Andrade 2015), as well as Strabo's account of merchants travelling from Zeugma to Seleucia (XVI.1.27), arguably take Antioch as their implicit point of departure; the *Expositio* XXXIII, 4–5, states that Antioch received numerous peoples from all over and enjoyed an abundance of all worldly goods; and, finally, John Chrysostom informs us about the organisation of Antiochene silk traders, and one late Antique silk-maker who died at Puteoli hailed from Antioch, cf. chapter four.
[663] Noy 2002: 244; Terpstra 2013:161–2. On the Syrian cults of Jupiter Dolichenus in Campania, see Tran Tam Tinh 1972: 134–5.
[664] Antiochenes: *CIL* VI, 17356, 26883; *IGUR* II, 306, 749, 1027; *SEG* XXX, 1224. Nisibis: *CIL* VI, 700. Seleucia Pieria: *IG* XIV, 934.
[665] Noy 2002: 236, and the Appendix, pp. 319–20. Cf. also the Antiochene link to Iulia Concordia with its earlier trade in South Arabian- and Indian-scented perfumes, mentioned in chapter five.
[666] Sartre 2005: 258, nn165–7.
[667] Millar 1993: 285. Although Sidonian involvement in maritime trade is revealed by sources such as *TPSulp* 106 (Puteoli, AD 57) in which legal claims are made against a docked Sidonian ship, to be redeemed either by auctioning of the ship itself or its cargo, cf. Terpstra 2013: 64; and *P.Bingen* 77, ll. 19–25, revealing the arrival in 2nd century AD Alexandria over two days of two ships from Sidon and a third with a Sidonian cargo.
[668] Glass: Strabo XVI.2.25; Pliny *NH*, V.17. Silk: Luc. *Pharsalia*, X.141. On the importance of the city more generally in Roman times and in commerce: Strabo XVI.2.22, 24. Moreover, see Kondoleon 2000: cat.nos. 73 (*piperatorium*, early 3rd century AD, reportedly from Sidon), 84 (later, 6th–8th century AD, example of glass *unguentarium* shaped like caravan dromedary).
[669] Strabo XVI.2.22–3 (greatness of Tyre, Tyrian dye); Luc. *Pharsalia*, X.107ff (Tyrian dye); Pliny *NH*, V.17, IX.60–5 (Tyrian dye); *Expositio* XXIV (Tyrian commerce), XXXI, ll. 6–8 (wealth and linen exports of Berytus and Tyre); Jerome on the mercantile nature of Syrians in general and Tyrians in particular (trading in textiles, among others silk), in Jones Hall 2004: 27, n36; and Proc., *Secret History*, XXV.14 (longstanding silk trade of Berytus and Tyre).
[670] See chapter four.
[671] On this often overlooked silk production of the Levant, particularly in Late Antiquity, see Jones Hall 2004: 25, 225–6.

Particularly informative is an inscription put up in Puteoli to commemorate how, in the year AD 174, the Tyrian settlers in that port beseeched their mother city of Tyre about financial support, amounting to 250 *denarii* per year, for the upkeep of the Tyrian *statio*, at the same time managing through shrewd diplomacy to secure the status and independence of their community vis-à-vis a similar establishment of their countrymen in Rome.[672] From the account in the inscription it appears that this *statio* was a physical building of some size and decoration, housing both the cult of the gods of their homeland and organising the local Tyrian community's role in and expenses for municipal events such as religious festivals. According to the *stationarii* in Puteoli their community had been dwindling for years, and therefore they were now in need of some financial support every year to keep the *statio* running, for unlike the *stationarii* in Rome, they, for unknown reasons, no longer accrued any income from merchants and shippers.[673] In fact, there even appears to have been a 'Tyrian district,' *pagus Tyrianus*, somewhere in Puteoli, perhaps associated with their *statio*,[674] and a Tyrian deity was transhipped from Sarepta, north of Tyre, to Puteoli in AD 79 under the supervision of a native religious magistrate.[675]

Likewise, a dedication from AD 116 was put up by the 'worshippers (*cultores*) of Jupiter Heliopolitanus, Berytians living in Puteoli,' which group is most likely to be associated with an undated inscription by a *corpus Heliopolitanorum*, the latter according to the inscription owning property in town (among other things shops, *tabernae*), as well as advertising a communal code of conduct, *lex et conventio*.[676] In addition, a small group of inscriptions reveal the existence in town of a temple to Jupiter Heliopolitanus, later renovated, with religious personnel divided into three groups: the first named in Latin, *sacerdotes*, the second by a Greek loanword, *lucophori*, and the third by an ambiguous Semitic word rendered into Latin as *geremellenses*.[677]

Furthermore, just as the Tyrians had *stationes* with strong religious and communal obligations in Puteoli and Rome (the latter explicitly raking in money from merchants and shippers), so the Berytian worshippers of Jupiter Heliopolitanus had a dominant presence in Rome at the sanctuary of the Syrian gods, possibly dating back to the later 1st century AD but better attested from the later 2nd century AD, on the Janiculum Hill above bustling and mercantile Trastevere. The most prominent patron of the Heliopolitan temple was an immigrant, likely Syrian, bearing the Semitic cognomen *Gaionas*, and one of the six inscriptions attributable to him was set up in Portus, dedicated to the co-emperors Marcus Aurelius and Commodus, AD 176–180, revealing a highly interesting connection between what is most likely to have been an affluent member of the Berytian diaspora at Rome and trade by sea.[678]

Shifting our gaze from the other ports of the Eastern Mediterranean involved in the long-distance trade with the Indian Ocean back to Alexandria in isolation, we shall now enquire into the role of this city as *the* great hub of the Eastern trade. Thus, Strabo and Dio Chrysostom, writing about a century apart, in the early 1st and early 2nd century AD, both emphasise how Alexandria was a city situated at the cross-roads of the world, enjoying an advantage so great, we are told, that it almost amounted to a monopoly on the import of goods from the Indian Ocean and their subsequent re-export to Mediterranean ports, Rome included.[679] Accordingly, although grain was Alexandria's most important export, the city was not only famous for its production of and trade in papyrus, glass (found as far away as Begram, as we saw in

[672] *CIG* 5853; brilliantly treated in Sosin 1999.
[673] *TPSulp* 4 attests a Tyrian freedman at Puteoli in AD 52, who could have been either a *stationarius* or a visiting trader liable to pay a fee towards the upkeep of the *statio*; he was summoned to appear in court at Puteoli to settle a debt of 1200 *sesterces* with a local banker (of the *Sulpicii*). Cf. Terpstra 2015: 89.
[674] Unpublished inscription, dated to the end of the 1st or 2nd century AD: Camodeca 2000: 283; Terpstra 2013: 77 n97.
[675] *IGR* I, 420 = Tran Tam Tinh 1972: S. 18, w. p. 137; and Torrey 1949; a third inscription about this divine translocation is mentioned in Sartre 2005: 503, n165.
[676] *CIL* X, 1634, 1579, respectively = Tran Tam Tinh 1972: S. 12–13; Terpstra 2013: 84–5.
[677] *CIL* X, 1578, w. Tran Tam Tinh 1972: S. 9–11.
[678] Noy 2002: 240–2; Sartre 2005: 503f, n167; Terpstra 2013: 162–4. The Portus inscription is *CIL* XIV, 24, while Gaionas' Eastern ancestry is further emphasised by an epitaph in Greek, preceded and succeeded by standard Latin funerary phrases, *CIL* VI, 32316 = *IGUR* 1157.
[679] Strabo XVII.1.7, 13; and Dio Chrys. *Or.*, XXXII.36. Note that the Muziris Papyrus, treated below, supports these claims in detailing how 150–180 tonnes of merchandise purchased in South India were transported under seal all the way to Alexandria before being released for sale on the market.

chapter three), and linen (also exported to Indian Ocean ports[680]), but likewise for its dominant part in the long-distance trade in spices, perfumes, exotic candies, medicines, rare quarried stone and gems.[681]

A description by Pliny of the Alexandrian workshops dressing frankincense for retail trade is particularly evocative in bringing out the economic potential of the import, processing and onward sale of products from the East. Here, Pliny is discussing the lack of security against theft required by the South Arabian growers of frankincense in their groves, put in perspective by the strict security measures applied in Roman Egypt:

> At Alexandria, on the other hand, where the frankincense is prepared for sale (*ubi tura interpolantur*), good heavens! no vigilance is sufficient to guard the workshops (*officinae*). A seal is put upon the workmen's aprons, they have to wear a mask or a net with a close mesh on their heads, and before they are allowed to leave the premises, they have to take off all their clothes...[682]

In fact, just such a well-organised and closely supervised production of similar commodities arriving from outside the Eastern boundaries of the Empire is attested about 250 years later, in the *Liber Pontificalis*, for estates having come into the possession of the emperor Constantine. Out of five estates mentioned, one was explicitly situated in the suburbs of Alexandria, two perhaps in Hermonthis just south of Thebes and Koptos, and in unison they produced an annual yield, in addition to rents in excess of 2300 golden *solidi*, of *inter alia*: 800 pounds of nard oil, 250 pounds of cassia, 150 pounds of spices, and around 750 pounds of pepper.[683] Produce from such imperial estates can also explain two Egyptian seals reading 'spice of the emperor(s),' dating from the mid-2nd century AD.[684]

Indeed, the great variety of exotic goods flowing into Alexandria from afar is illustrated by the passage in the *Digest* previously referred to as the 'Alexandrian Tariff,' having been formulated in the early 3rd century AD and evidently still being of relevance to the jurists of the 6th century AD. A select list of the 'goods subject to toll (*vectigal*)' having either certainly or at least plausibly arrived from beyond the Eastern frontier (most of the original list, in fact), appears thus:

> cinnamon (*cinnamomum*), long and white pepper (*piper longum* and *-album*), putchuk (*costum* and *costamomum*), spikenard (*nardi stachys*), Tyrian cassia (*cassia turiana*), cassia bark (*xylocassia*), myrrh (*smurna*), *amomum*, ginger (*zingiberi*), cinnamon leaf (*malabathrum*), Indian spice (*aroma Indicum*), asafoetida (*laser*), aloe-wood (*aloe*), (*berberis*) *lycium*, astragalus (*sarcocolla*), Arabian onyx (*onyx arabicus*), cardamom (*cardamomum*), cinnamon bark (*xylocinnamomum*), Babylonian furs (*pelles babylonicae*), Parthian furs (*pelles parthicae*), ivory (*ebur*), Indian iron (*ferrum Indicum*), pearls (*margarita*), *sardonyx*, bloodstones (*ceraunium*), aquamarine or sapphire (*hyacinthus*), diamonds (*adamas*), lapis lazuli (*saffirinus*), turquoise (*callainus*), beryls (*berylus*), Indian drugs (*opia indica*), raw silk (*metaxa*), garments entirely or partly made from silk (*vestis serica vel subserica*), silk yarn (*nema sericum*), Indian eunuchs (*spadones Indici*), and Indian hair (*capilli Indici*).[685]

Puzzling omissions from this list are the 'mainstream' products black pepper (*piper nigrum*) and frankincense (*thus*). However, a later, 4th century AD, official document from the Thebaid nome adds further to our knowledge of the trade in exotic products by accounting for taxes collected for Alexandria. Pepper is listed twice, along with entries for cinnamon leaf, cassia, spikenard, aloe, myrrh, and putchuk, so there is no reason to believe that either pepper or frankincense enjoyed some special fiscal exemption.[686]

---

680 See the list of textiles traded from Egypt to Eastern ports in Casson 1989: 39–40; in particular, though, *Periplus* 39, 56, mention 'multicoloured textiles' (*polymita*) for which Alexandria was famous, cf. Pliny *NH*, VIII.74; while *Periplus* 6 mentions 'wraps' (*stolai*) from Arsinoë in the Fayyum.

681 Hass 1997: 35–6, 43–4.

682 Pliny *NH*, XII.32.

683 *Liber Pontificalis* XXXIV.19–21; following Seland 2012; see also Tacoma 2006: 83.

684 *IGR* I,5 1375 (Antoninus Pius), 1376 (Marcus Aurelius and Verus); further details in De Ricci 1903: nos. 63–4, p. 443.

685 *Dig.* XXXIX.4.16.7; see Miller 1969: 279–80, Appendix, which is also the paramount work for identifying the numerous plant products mentioned; also Parker 2008: 149–50.

686 *PSI* XII, 1264.

On this note, of the flow of Eastern commodities from the Thebaid down the Nile to Alexandria, one of the most interesting facts about the Egyptian trade with the Indian Ocean is, arguably, how intimately it was connected with Alexandria on the Mediterranean, even though some 1,000 km of river and desert passage separated that city from the Red Sea.[687] Thus, Strabo speaks of the ships of Alexandrian merchants sailing up the Nile and through the Arabian Gulf to India, and, conversely, of the major part of imports from Ethiopia, Arabia and India arriving at Myos Hormos, being carried by camels along a route with stations and water to Koptos in 6–7 days, and from there freighted down the Nile to Alexandria.[688] Similarly, Pliny states that the voyage up the Nile from Alexandria to Koptos was made in twelve days, from whence a journey conducted by night to Berenike through the desert on camels, following a route interspersed with stations supplied with water, took another 12 days.[689] Remarkably, the Alexandria–Red Sea route was not only known to great scholars such as Strabo, Pliny and Seneca the Younger,[690] but also, it appears, to the reading public of the Empire and the theatre-goers of Oxyrhynchus.

That is, Xenophon of Ephesos assumes a certain knowledge on behalf of his readers in the 2nd century AD, when he makes the plot of his *Ephesian Tale* revolve around the routes of the long-distance trade in Egypt's Eastern Desert. The Ephesian heroine, Anthia, is sold as a slave by pirates in Alexandria to an Indian king, who happens to be in town to do some shopping, later attempting to return home to India via heavily laden caravan from Koptos across the desert, when he is slain by robbers preying upon the merchants passing through on their way down to the sea.[691]

Echoing this story is a fragment of a play from Oxyrhynchus, dated 1st–2nd century AD, in which the Greek heroine, Charition, has ended up in the possession of an Indian king (who happens to speak Greek[692]) in a land on the shores of the Indian Ocean. In all likelihood, she had been enslaved by pirates like Anthia was. Fortunately for Charition, though, her brother arrives from across the sea with a rescuing party and manages to affect her escape by getting the Indians drunk on wine. Interestingly, nearly all the lines of the Indian characters are given as 'gibberish language,' being a Greek rendition of Indian speech,[693] and some scholars would have it that this language could, in fact, reflect an ancient version of Kannada, the language spoken in the South Indian state of Karnataka.[694]

In summary, the novel and the play reveal both a wider interest in, as well as popular knowledge of, trade and interaction with Indians in the ports and on the sea lanes of the Indian Ocean. As it happens, one prospective viewer, 'Gaion, also known as Diodorus,' listed as a tax-payer in the Oxyrhynchite metropolis of Arsinoe in AD 72–73, spent that year away 'in India.'[695] Consequently, to Gaion, upon his eventual return, the antics of Charition and the Indians of Malpe, as well as the later exploits of Anthia, might not have seemed so very outlandish after all.

Finally, we even have a few descriptions of the foreign elements of Alexandria's population. An oration by Dio Chrysostom held at Alexandria in the early 2nd century AD and addressed to its inhabitants

[687] That is, 800 km by water craft up the Nile, and then, from Koptos, either 180 km to Myos Hormos or 380 km to Berenike; for the latter distances, Sidebotham 2011: 128. In addition to the early examples in the following notes, the mid-4th century AD *Expositio* XXXV states that Alexandria was in abundant supply of spices and the products of barbarian peoples, because the race of the Indians lay beyond the Thebaid nome.

[688] Strabo II.5.12, XVI.4.24; drawing on XVII.1.45 for details about the route from Myos Hormos to Koptos—Berenike is also mentioned but as a place of less importance. An *ostracon* from the fort of Krokodilo has made it possible to calculate that a caravan (*poreia*) could travel from Koptos to Myos Hormos in as little as five days, see *O.Krok.* 4, calculation by Bülow-Jakobsen 2003: 406–7.

[689] Pliny *NH*, VI.26. A Byzantine period graffito from the desert route between Berenike and Koptos shows that a traveller covered the distance in 15-6 days by foot; Romanis 1996a: 215, no. 17; Cuvigny *et al.* 1999: no. 52, calculation of remaining distance in the latter, p. 161.

[690] Who had lived in Alexandria for a while during his youth, writing a lost work on India (Pliny *NH*, VI.21), and who refers to the 'road for Indian Ocean commerce' passing from the Nile through the desert to the sea, in *Nat.Quaest.* II.4.

[691] Xen. Ephes. *Anthia and Habrocomes*, III.11, IV.3; the Indian king, Psammis, carries an old Egyptian name, though. Parker 2008: 80–2, cites references to India in two more of the Greek novels.

[692] *P.Oxy.* 413, *recto*, col. iii, l. 88ff; note that Zōskalês, the king of Axum, is reported to have been well-versed in Greek, cf. *Periplous* 5.

[693] The 'Indian language' even being spoken or imitated in the play by the Greek character 'B,' the buffoon, on the *recto*, col. iii, ll. 75, 79–80.

[694] See discussion and bibliography in Salomon 1991: 733–4; w. additional bibliograpy in Salomon 1993: 593, no. 2. In fact, inscribed sherds from the Egyptian Red Sea ports reveal the presence of South Indian and Tamil visitors, cf. chapter seven. Moreover, the word *malpiniak* occuring on the *recto*, col. iii, l. 81, might be further testimony of popular knowledge about Early Historic Indian ports, cf. Gupta and Aruni 2005: 49–53; Gupta 2007b.

[695] *Stud.Pal.* IV, pp. 58-78, ll. 549, 579; Raschke 1975: 241.

enumerates the peoples observed by the speaker amongst his audience at the theatre: Greeks and Italians (obviously), people from Syria, Libya, and Cilicia (not surprising), as well as Ethiopians and Arabs (as we would expect), 'and even Bactrians and Scythians and Persians and a few Indians.'[696] Likewise, the considerably more unreliable *Historia Augusta* relates that Aurelian in his triumph after defeating the second revolt of Palmyra and of Firmus[697] in Alexandria, in 273 AD, paraded not only prominent Palmyrene and Egyptian prisoners through the streets of Rome, but also visiting Blemmyes (bordering South Egypt and expanding in to the Eastern Desert, as we shall see in chapter seven), Axumites, Arabs, Indians, Bactrians, etc.[698]

Naturally, literary claims about finding Indians, Bactrians and Scythians in Alexandria arouse suspicion that this might be mere hyperbole, intended to emphasise the truly cosmopolitan nature of the city. However, as it happens, a number of new and old sources which we shall go through in the next chapter seem to provide corroborating evidence. Accordingly, we should not dismiss offhand Dio Chrysostom's testimony about Indians, Bactrians, and Scythians dotting the theatre of Alexandria in the early 2nd century AD.

Networks at work: from Campania to the Red Sea coast and beyond

According to Suetonius, Vespasian was once reprimanded by his son, the later emperor Titus, for having introduced a tax on the distribution of urine from public toilets to tanneries. In reply, the emperor made Titus smell a coin from the first crop of the tax, forcing him to acknowledge that money made from urine smells no different from any other kind of income.[699] Whether or not this anecdote contains any truth in itself, it certainly reflects normative contemporary sentiments of the senatorial aristocracy: the proper source of wealth was land, whereas commerce and crafts, urine included, were considered indecent sources of income.[700]

This may be so, and is under all circumstances difficult to disprove taking in to account the elite bias of our literary sources, but it can nonetheless be shown that influential Campanian families, just like powerful Egyptian families to be treated below, were so involved in the Eastern trade that we find their agents as far afield as Egypt's Eastern desert, or, in a single case, beyond, sailing around the Indian Ocean.[701] The money they earned out of the long-distance trade did not smell too much, it appears, and if it did, it will have carried not only the sweet smell of profit, but also of spices, incense, myrrh and other exotic odours of the East. Moreover, the trade was, of course, carried out through numerous affiliated intermediaries of the families in question, these groups constituting personalised commercial networks in their own right, albeit continuously interacting with other actors involved in the trade.[702] Accordingly, case-studies of *inter alia* the *Annii*, *Calpurnii* and *Vestorii* can act as concrete examples of how the long-distance trade was anchored in Roman commerce and society more generally, providing some degree of evidence for links to relevant *collegia*, networks of merchants, craftsmen and retailers, as well as elite financiers and government organisations taxing the trade.

Starting out with the *gens Annii* of Puteoli,[703] we find early members occupying influential magistracies in nearby Capua around the end of the 2nd century BC,[704] as well as what we may assume to be individuals conducting trade abroad: one in late 2nd–early 1st century BC Athens, another on mid-2nd century BC

696 Dio Chrys. *Or.*, XXXII.40.
697 *SHA*, *Firmus*, 3–5: allegedly from Antioch's port of Seleucia Pieria, but grown wealthy and powerful at Alexandria, often sending ships to trade with India.
698 *SHA*, *Aurelian*, 33.
699 Suet. *Vesp.*, 23.3.
700 Finley 1999: especially pp. 57–61.
701 The best general treatments of the topic being: Romanis 1996a: 241–59; and Tchernia 2011: 62–9; while Schörle 2015: 49–52, deals with a few of the families.
702 The seminal work on this matter being D'Arms 1981, but see also the recent analysis of Broekaert 2016 on the role of freedmen and patrons in the economy.
703 Camodeca 1979.
704 Frederiksen 1959: 127–8, Appendix, nos. 10, 11, 15.

Delos, and a third listed in 133 BC as a *paroikos* in Pergamum.[705] More concretely, Marcus Annius, an *eques Romanus*, is referred to repeatedly as a pillar of society in Cicero's second speech against Verres in 70 BC,[706] providing testimony of the latter's criminal activities against merchants returning from Asia Minor, Syria, Tyre and Alexandria, by way of Syracuse, carrying precious cargoes of Tyrian purple, frankincense, perfumes, linen robes, jewels, pearls and Asiatic slaves.[707] According to the rhetorics of Cicero, 'all of Puteoli' had turned up at the trial, being 'wealthy and honest merchants' like Marcus Annius' Puteolian peer, Publius Granius,[708] having had their ships and cargoes confiscated, and partners and freedmen imprisoned or murdered by Verres and his henchmen.[709]

Accordingly, it is highly significant that Lysas, slave of Publius Annius Plocamus, left two graffiti, one in Greek and one in Latin, in a cave shelter, the *paneion* of wadi Minayh, on the desert route between Koptos on the Nile and the Red Sea port of Berenike in July of AD 6,[710] being the month of the year when ships set out for East Africa, Scythia and India.[711] Furthermore, we learn from Pliny, narrating about an embassy from the king of Sri Lanka to the emperor Claudius, that an Annius Plocamus had previously farmed the taxes of the Red Sea (*maris rubri vectigal a fisco redemerat*, i.e., the *tetarte*),[712] and, unrelated to this, that a freedman of his had been sailing around Arabia when he got caught up in a northern gale over by the coast of Parthian Carmania, sending his ship skipping before the wind till it made landfall in Sri Lanka.[713] On the balance of probabilities, this Annius Plocamus, who had been a tax-farmer no later than the reign of Claudius, was likely a direct descendant, son or grandson, of the one already active in the long-distance trade in AD 6, and his freedman must have been on a commercial expedition, either on behalf of or financially supported by his master. The original destination of the venture is difficult to tell, though, for the description does not fit contemporary direct routes from the Gulf of Aden across the high seas to either Barygaza or Muziris,[714] but Ommana outside the mouth of the Persian Gulf was in good supply of Gulf pearls as well as slaves, and further East along the coast lay the important port of trade, Barbaricon, being the likely primary destination.[715]

From Bauli, just West of Puteoli, another freedman of Publius Annius Plocamus is attested, named Eros, while one Aulus Annius Plocamus is known from a 1st century AD ownership-declaration on a water piper in Rome, and two contemporary tile stamps from Rome also read *An]ni Plocami*.[716] In the very same years, moreover, a freedman named Publius Annius Seleucus was in charge of the Barbatian warehouses, owned by the emperor Claudius' mother-in-law, at Puteoli, where Alexandrian wheat was stored.[717] During the reign of Claudius, we find a freedman named Lucius Annius Felix appointed as Augustalis in Ostia, being the likely ancestor of the owner of an Ostian warehouse with the auspicious pun *omnia felicia Anni(i)* inscribed, accompanied by a carved brick depicting a ship under sail loaded with oil jars and another brick with a man selling them.[718] Meanwhile, in Puteoli a suburban neighbourhood might have been officially known as the *vicus Annianus*,[719] and we know from the better epigraphically attested 2nd century AD that *Annii* reached high civic positions and were voted public honours, fittingly enough within the space of

705 Hatzfeld 1912: 14 (Delos); 1919: 42 n1 (Athens), 48 n2 (Pergamon).

706 Cic. *Verr.*, II.1.14, 5.74, 5.156.

707 Cic. *Verr.*, II.5.145–6.

708 The *Granii* were one of the most prominent families of Puteoli, D'Arms 1974: 108 *et passim*; active on 2nd century BC Delos, Hatzfeld 1912: 40–1; and in Athens, Hatzfeld 1919: 42 n7.

709 Cic. *Verr.*, II.5.154.

710 Meredith 1953; Romanis 1996a: 211f, no. 5a-b; Cuvigny *et al.* 1999: nos. 2–3. The fact that there is an interval of three days between the calendar dates given in the graffiti is explained as the consequence of a miscalculation made in employing the unfamiliar Latin calendar in a Greek *milieu*.

711 *Periplus* 14, 39; Pliny *NH*, VI.26.

712 Burkhalter 1999: 51f, no. 4.

713 Pliny *NH*, VI.24.

714 *Periplus* 57; Pliny *NH*, 6.26.

715 *Periplus* 36, 38–9. The port of Oraea in between could have been visited en route, *Periplus* 37, this coast being rich in bdellium trees (an aromatic gum resin).

716 Rathbhone 1983: 88; *CIL* X, 2389; XV, 7391, 798.1–2. On Eros, see also D'Arms 1981: 166.

717 *TPSulp* 46 of March 13th, AD 40; prior in sequence and related is *TPSulp* 53 of the same day, where the freedman Publius Annius Felix acts as witness. *Annii* are also mentioned in *TPSulp* 57 (freedman scribe), 121 (witness, fragmentary).

718 Meiggs 1973: 275; w. *CIL* XIV, 4617. Cf. Gianfrotta 2007: 75 n78, and D'Arms 1981: 176, Appendix, no. 6.

719 *AE* 1977: 201, ll. 8–9: *inquilini [v]ici | [Anni?]ani*. Camodeca 1979: 30f; 2000: 281, 283.

the *basilica Augusti Annianae* provided by the family for the meetings of the city council of Puteoli, thus, further emphasising its local standing.[720]

Accordingly, we should probably refrain from disregarding it as mere coincidence that the five-year president of the *collegium aromatariorum* in Rome, attested as celebrating its 140th year in the later 1st century BC–1st century AD, bore the family name Annius.[721] Now, seeing as the *nomen gentilicum* Annius was not rare in the Empire, this *magister quinquennalis* could strictly speaking have been out of an entirely different branch of *Annii*.[722] However, that he should carry this name, of all the statistically possible *nomina* of a Roman citizen in early imperial times, seems highly noteworthy in light of the demonstrated involvement from Late Republican through Augustan to Claudian times of the Puteolian *Annii* in the long-distance trade with the East. The more so, seeing as the case of Annius Plocamus, the tax-farmer, shows that the *Annii* were sufficiently well-established in the Eastern trade to be partners of the state in a contract worth millions of *denarii* (a value revealed by the Muziris Papyrus, see below), running a large organisation of customs inspectors (*arabarchai*) and associated warehouses, from the Red Sea ports via Koptos to Alexandria. Such a family might well, during those very same years, have had affiliated members, like Titus Annius Philippus, installed in prominent positions such as senior official of the *collegium aromatariorum*.

Another high-ranking Puteolian family, that of the *Calpurnii*, was also involved in the long-distance trade, both at home and further afield.[723] Like with the *Annii*, an early Calpurnius almost certainly related to the Puteolian family is known from bustling late 2nd century BC Delos.[724] In Puteoli itself, the family sponsored the construction of a temple to Augustus, whereas by the time of Domitian a neighbourhood in Puteoli had been named *vicus Calpurnianus* after them, and in AD 187 a member served as city councillor.[725]

Remarkably, however, there is an undated dedication to two *Calpurnii* jointly by 'the merchants who conduct trade with Alexandria, Asia Minor and Syria,' revealing the family's patronage of merchants trading with the ports of the Eastern Mediterranean, expensive long-distance goods from further East being a mainstay of this trade, as mentioned by Cicero in his speech against Verres, paraphrased above in dealing with the *Annii*. Furthermore, the merchants sailing out of Puteoli to busy ports of the Levant like Ephesos, Antioch, Tyre, Berytus and Alexandria, the latter receiving pride of place in the inscription and standing instead of the name of the province (as for *Asia* and *Syria*), had enough communal spirit to set up an honorary dedication as a group characterised not only by profession, *mercator*, but as a specialised subgroup of these dealing with the East.[726]

Indeed, this does not necessarily imply too much in the way of formal organisation, beyond being a network advertising its collective profession publicly, but this puts it right alongside related groups such as the *sericarii* of Rome, the politically active *aurifices universi* and *unguentarii* of Pompeii, and most likely also the eponymous *vitriarii* and *thurarii* of a neighbourhood of Puteoli itself named after their professions.[727] What is more, such selective elite patronage of the mercantile personnel involved in a sector of the economy from which the patron's family derived a substantial income might very well have been behind Julius Aelianus' patronage and economic support of the *collegium* of *negotiatores eborarii et citriarii* in Rome, although this hypothesis is unlikely ever to be proven.

[720] D'Arms 1974: 107–9; espec. *CIL* X, 1782, 1784, while 1783 preserves the name of the building in full. In addition, Camodeca 1979: 20, reports an unpublished inscription mentioning an Annius being *duumvir*.
[721] See chapter four.
[722] Such as the 'imperial ones,' cf. D'Arms 1974: 108 n35.
[723] The family is mentioned briefly in D'Arms 1974: 113.
[724] Hatzfeld 1912: 23.
[725] *CIL* X, 1613 (temple), 1631 (*vicus*), 1784 (decurion).
[726] *CIL* X, 1797: (...) *mercatores qui Alexandr(iai) Asiai Syriai negotiantur*. Dated 20 BC–AD 20 by the *Epigraphic Database Roma* (EDR129292) on prosopographic, palaeographic, and linguistic grounds. One of the honorands might possibly be the sponsor of the Augustan temple mentioned in *CIL* X, 1613.
[727] Cf. chapter four.

The involvement of the *Calpurnii* in the long-distance trade via Egypt is documented by a graffito left in the same cave shelter, at wadi Minayh on the Koptos–Berenike route in Egypt, as that recording a visit by an agent of the *Annii*.[728] The present graffito is dated to the end of October 4 BC, making it the earliest known at the site, and was written by Laudanes, slave of Calpurnius Moschas. Of some significance for our understanding of the networks involved in the Eastern trade, both the name of the slave himself, as well as the *cognomen* of his master, can be traced back to Semitic roots. Thus, the name Laudanes is attested twice in southern Syria, one of the times in Bostra, making it likely that this was a Safaïtic or Nabataean name, while Moschas could likewise be the Greek transliteration of an Arab name.[729] As we shall see in chapter seven, both Nabataeans and South Arabians are well attested in the Eastern Desert, making such an interpretation of the origins of this Calpurnian agent and his slave the more likely.

In fact, this Egyptian connection of the *Calpurnii* is further borne out by an early 2nd century AD funerary inscription from the cemetery of Portus, put up by Calpurnia Ptolomais for herself and her husband, supplemented by two bricks carved with reliefs of ships. 'Ptolomaios,' i.e., Ptolemy, was, of course, a common name in Roman Egypt, so a woman involved in shipping and settled in the port of Rome at the time of its Trajanic expansion, carrying a family name that would make her a dependant of the Puteolian *Calpurnii*, and with ties to Egypt with which this family traded and where they had previously had agents employed, fits well with the overall picture.[730]

Indeed, in Rome itself, as it might be remembered from the above analysis of the Eastern trade's retail organisation in Rome in chapter four, the *Calpurnii* seem, like the *Annii*, to have had their own people centrally placed: one Calpurnian freedman of Syrian ancestry was a *margaritarius* of the Via Sacra in the early 1st century AD, and his freeborn son succeeded him to become an affluent *margaritarius* himself in that fashionable retail street prior to the fire of AD 64.[731] In other words, affiliates of the *Calpurnii* had been set up as *margaritarii* among the cluster of goldsmiths and jewellers on that prominent street, whose occupants will have been among the members of the *collegia anulariorum* and *aurificum*. Consequently, it can not only be shown that members of the *Calpurnii* family were important and long-standing municipal notables of Puteoli, but also that they were involved in Indian Ocean commerce via Berenike, a specialised area of economic activities which must have been aided by their conveniently fashioned links to merchants trading with the Eastern Mediterranean, especially Alexandria, and groups and organisations of specialised craftsmen in Rome.

However, it is possible to get an even better impression of Campanian based distribution networks by taking a closer look at the *Vestorii* of Puteoli. According to Vitruvius in his work on architecture, one Vestorius transplanted the manufacture of blue dye from Alexandria, where the process was invented, to Puteoli. For this reason, the colour was by Pliny's time known as 'Vestorian *caeruleum*,' valued at a thumping 11 *denarii* per pound.[732] Seeing as Vitruvius wrote his treatise under Augustus, the Vestorius in question could well be the Gaius Vestorius who is mentioned as a friend in several of Cicero's letters to Atticus, two of which were written during stays at Vestorius' house in Puteoli. Moreover, the latter is described as a 'practical mathematician,' i.e., businessman, who seems not to have been overly interested in literature and philosophy, but instead acted as a sometime business partner of Cicero and Atticus.[733]

In consequence, having introduced the production of a new kind of fancy blue dye to Campania from Alexandria, it should come as no surprise to find that the family's network of dependants and agents include Egyptian connections. However, not only do we find a Titus Vestorius Arpocra Minor conducting business in AD 38 Puteoli, his *cognomen* evidently being a Latinisation for the Ptolemaic deity

[728] Romanis 1996a: 211, no. 2; Cuvigny *et al.* 1999: no. 1.
[729] Lacerenza 1995: 191–3.
[730] Gianfrotta 2007: 75 n77.
[731] Cf. Gianfrotta 2007: 74f n76.
[732] Vitr. *De Arch.*, VII.11.1; Pliny *NH*, XXXIII.57.
[733] Cic. *Att.*, espec. XIII, 46; XIV, 9–12, 21; XV, 4.

Harpocrates,[734] and a Titus Vestorius mentioned in a 2nd century AD papyrus from the Fayyum,[735] but a graffito on a rock outside the *paneion* of wadi Minayh also mentions a Titus Vestorius Ialysos, dated AD 21/22.[736] Accordingly, it would seem that the Puteolian *Vestorii* were not only into the manufacturing of blue dye, but also exploited their commercial ties with Alexandria to participate in the Eastern trade.

Several individual *Vestorii* are known from Puteoli, albeit not from later times, and the family was prominent enough during the early Empire to have a part of town known as the *regio vicus Vestorianus* no later than Domitian, same as the *Calpurnii* and *Annii* did.[737] However, in combination a study of Ciceronian letters mentioning Vestorius and the excavation of a shipwreck have revealed some highly interesting details about the commercial partnerships of a man like Gaius Vestorius, which might well reflect similar trade circuits of subsequent *Vestorii* involved in Indian Ocean trade.

Specifically, we know that the senator Sempronius Rufus spent the early summer of 51 BC at Puteoli, where he had a villa, dodging a confrontation with an angry Vestorius who was trying to track him down. In fact, Rufus was so keen on avoiding Vestorius that he slighted his former patron Cicero by not visiting him, he being a close friend of Vestorius', and by keeping busy when Cicero passed him in the market of Puteoli. In the autumn, however, the quarrel developed into a full-blown court case at Rome, which pitted Sempronius against Vestorius and an affiliate whose identity can be reconstructed as Marcus Tuccius Galeo, a producer of oil or wine (and perhaps the amphorae containing it, too). The verdict, when it came, was a sound defeat for the senatorial Rufus, enhancing the status and influence of Vestorius among his peers.[738]

Now, add to this tale, based on the letters of Cicero, the discovery in 1968 of amphorae bearing the stamp of this Galeo together with colourful dyes including Vestorian blue in a Late Republican wreck off Marseille.[739] Although we only know for sure that Vestorius produced *caeruleum*, there is no good reason why he should not himself have been into the profits accruable from its shipping, as well, in competition with wholesale merchants at Puteoli and other copycat producers. Indeed, we know from Cicero's letters that he was highly entrepreneurial and, in addition to his production of blue dye, also made big money from fixing up and renting out real estate.[740] Accordingly, there is good reason to think that Vestorius and Galeo formed a business partnership marketing their respective wares in Mediterranean ports like Massalia,[741] and that their dispute with Sempronius Rufus, who apparently was something of a permanent fixture on the Puteolian market,[742] related to this partnership. He could well have financed part of their joint commercial venture, contributed wares from his own estates for shipping, or possessed or part-owned the ship(s) carrying the cargo.

Therefore, this case may serve as an informative example of how one family's involvement in large-scale production and trade fitted into the larger picture of Late Republican society. First of all, Vestorius was a wealthy and entrepreneurial Puteolian who had transplanted the manufacture of an expensive Alexandrian product to Puteoli, implying an intimate knowledge of upper-end commerce and crafts at Alexandria. In fact, this is a prime example of a process of initial importation from the Eastern Mediterranean, followed by the establishment of Roman production in an Italian city, and subsequently branching out to supply the provinces, which fits well with Wallace-Hadrill's model, introduced in chapter three, where it was applied to the production of ivory-legged citrus wood tables.[743] Entrepreneurs like Vestorius would have been the brains behind the development of the latter fashion during the reign of Nero.

---

[734] *TPSulp* 43; see Romanis 1996b: 736 n38.

[735] *SB* VI, 9254, l. 12.

[736] Romanis 1996b: 734f; Cuvigny *et al.* 1999: no. 71.

[737] *CIL* X, 1631; D'Arms 1974: 113 n80. On attestations of *Vestorii* in town, and elsewhere in *Italia*, see Romanis 1996b: 737 nn40, 42.

[738] Based on D'Arms 1981: 49–55. See also Broekaert 2012: 224–5.

[739] Tchernia 1968–70: 59–69.

[740] Cic. *Att.*, XIV.9–11.

[741] Arguably indicative of the way Eastern commodities which bypassed Rome were marketed in ports of the Western provinces, just like we have seen for the supply of perfumes in the Adriatic Sea.

[742] D'Arms 1981: 50 n7, 54.

[743] Wallace-Hadrill 2008: 360.

Second, the original transfers of technological know-how necessary for there to be a *clivus vitriarius sive vicus thurarius* in Puteoli, most likely specialised in the production of perfumes containing South Arabian ingredients, and the *collegium thurariorum et unguentariorum* of Rome, can probably be compared with Vestorius' introduction of *caeruleum* production in Puteoli. Third, Vestorius' involvement in large-scale commerce and production in first Alexandria and subsequently Puteoli must be correlated with his friendships and occasional partnerships with senators like Cicero and Sempronius Rufus, as well as eminent equestrians like Atticus, and not least the fact that Vestorius was able to defeat a former senatorial business partner in a court of law. This was an economic entrepreneur whom even the political elite could not afford to double-cross. Finally, Vestorius' involvement in business at Alexandria and Puteoli taken into consideration, it comes as no surprise that we find a later generation of *Vestorii* having branched into the Eastern trade, as well.

Returning to the *paneion* of wadi Minayh, two more Campanian families can plausibly be identified from the remaining graffiti. The first is that of the *gens Numidii* which is attested in three graffiti from early spring of 2 BC.[744] Discounting an African provenance of these *Numidii*, on the basis of the attested links to Campania revealed in the analyses of the previous graffiti of wadi Minayh, the only other option is the much better fitting Capua.[745] Significantly, the author of two of these graffiti, Gaius Numidius Eros, was seemingly of freedman origin, as indicated by his *cognomen*, and he explicitly stated in both of his graffiti that he was 'returning from India,' *ex India rediens*, so we need not necessarily assume that the Campanian agents attested on the Berenike road were only going down to the port to trade or liaise with returning ships. Moreover, the fact that Eros wrote two almost verbatim messages in Latin at a *paneion* covered by predominantly Greek graffiti could imply that he was not familiar with Greek and must therefore have arrived in Egypt from the West.[746] The third graffito of this group was left by Thaliarchus, slave of Gaius Numidius (either Eros or a third person), whose Greek name is rare enough in Egypt to warrant an origin elsewhere in the Mediterranean,[747] revealing a hierarchy of agents employed by the *Numidii* consisting of both freedmen and slaves.[748]

The last of the Campanian connections to be identified at the *paneion* is a graffito of the *Munatii*,[749] whose *nomen gentilium* is documented at Herculaneum, Capua, Puteoli and Pompeii.[750] In this graffito, dated to the Julio-Claudian period, Gaius Munatius (*cognomen* unknown) made an 'act of worship,' a *proskynema*, in accordance with Greco-Egyptian practice, revealing an acute awareness on his behalf of local religious mores. A funerary monument from Pompeii dated slightly later, to Neronian times, likewise preserves the memory of a Gaius Munatius, plausibly a relative, who bore the *cognomen* Felix and was an *Augustalis*, thus, certainly a freedman. Significantly, one side of his monument was decorated with a merchant ship where a large figure at the stern appears to be ordering some seamen to furl sail. In consequence, a profession related to maritime trade emphasises the possible relation between Munatius Felix of Pompeii and Gaius Munatius travelling on the Berenike road, especially when we recall that the House of the Indian Statuette was decorated with graffiti of ships and navigational instruments,[751] making the *Gaii Munatii* representative examples of the unknown family owning the house and statuette.[752]

Finally, these Campanian case-studies of higher- and lower-ranking families from the Bay of Naples whose involvement in the transit trade of Indian Ocean goods via Egypt to Rome is attested by graffiti on the desert road from Koptos on the Nile to Berenike on the Red Sea, can be supplemented with a similar case from the inland area of ancient Samnium, east of Rome. By collecting widely scattered attestations of the mercantile activities of the *Peticii* family, an outline can be sketched of the workings of four generations

[744] Romanis 1996: 211, nos. 3a–b, 4; Cuvigny *et al.* 1999: nos. 4–6.
[745] Romanis 1996: 244 n13.
[746] Romanis 1996: 243.
[747] Cuvigny *et al.* 1999: 141, commentary at no. 6.
[748] Romanis 1996: 245–6.
[749] Romanis 1996: 214, no. 2; Cuvigny *et al.* 1999: no. 10.
[750] Romanis 1996: 254 nn52–55.
[751] Cf. chapter three.
[752] *CIL* X, 1030; Romanis 1996: 254–6.

of merchants over a century:[753] the first was a Roman merchant shipper, Peticius, attested in 48 BC off the Eastern coast of Greece;[754] the second was a wine trader, Caius Peticius, whose amphorae have been found at Carthage, deposited around 20 BC;[755] the third was also named Caius Peticius and left graffiti recording his name in both Latin and Greek in the first decades of the 1st century AD at the *paneion of* wadi Hammamat, on the road between Koptos and Myos Hormos on the Red Sea;[756] and the fourth and last was Peticius Marsus, a wine merchant whose wine containers have been found in a wreck off the Ligurian coast dated to the mid-1st century AD, and who is also attested as dedicant of a bronze statuette at Sulmo in Abruzzo, a region where the family name, Peticius, is attested in various localities.[757]

From this area, moreover, dating to the last quarter of the 1st century BC, has been found a funerary monument showing a dromedary carrying wine amphorae and led by a man, a row of men and a woman shown below, the original find-spot of the relief being, unfortunately, unknown. The point is, of course, that this is plausibly a family grave monument of the very *Peticii* who were wine merchants and conducted trade via Myos Hormos on the Red Sea. The dating would fit the early years of the Caius Peticius attested in Egypt's Eastern Desert. If not, it simply adds to our picture of this kind of commercial operation, for in that case there must have been yet another family of wine merchants from inland Samnium conducting trade with the East.[758] Accordingly, the case of the *Peticii*, whom we find participating in the long-distance trade yet operating out of inland Samnium, is an important supplement to the more plentiful evidence from Campania. Begging the question, in fact, whether similar families were not suppliers of the trade in nard- and myrrh-oil perfumes documented by lead-tags at Pausulae in neighbouring *regio Picenum* and at Iulia Concordia further north in *regio Venetia*.[759]

Before moving on, though, there is evidence of a different kind for a final connection to be made between Puteoli and the long-distance trade through the Eastern Desert of Egypt. Namely, an inscription narrating the career of Marcus Artorius Priscillus, hailing from Puteoli, who after military service in Germania Inferior, Moesia and Pannonia, became *praefectus montis Berenicidis*, that is, military governor of the area in which lay Koptos, Myos Hormos and Berenike,[760] no later than AD 109. Afterwards, he travelled to Puteoli to become a high priest and patron in that city, only to return to Egypt again sometime in AD 113–17 as *epistrategos* of the Thebaid nome, in which lay the area of his old prefecture, eventually going back home to have his *cursus honorum* inscribed at Puteoli.[761] Obviously, Artorius' return to his old stomping grounds in the Eastern Desert after an intermezzo as municipal notable at Puteoli is very interesting, considering the commercial links between Campanian families and the Red Sea ports.[762] Indeed, other individuals who served as *epistrategoi* of the Thebaid are also attested as receivers of the *tetarte*, that is, the office of *Arabarch*, and as active participants in the long-distance trade via the Indian Ocean, as we shall shortly see below.

Eastern commerce, Western contracts: from Alexandria to Muziris

Extraordinarily, the widespread use of papyri in Ancient Egypt combined with this country's super arid climate means that unique documents pertaining to the actual financing, purchase, transport, taxation and final dissolution of long-distance commercial expeditions, have survived from Ptolemaic and Roman Egypt. A number of references have already been made to one of these contracts, the Muziris Papyrus (*SB* XVIII, 13,167), concerning a mid-2nd century AD voyage from Egypt to Muziris in the South Indian kingdom of the Cheras, particularly to its *verso*, which provides us with the only extant example of a

[753] Gianfrotta 1989; also Tchernia 1997: 239–43.
[754] Plut. *Vit. Pomp.*, 73.3.
[755] *CIL* VIII, 22640.65.
[756] Bernand 1972a: nos. 120–1.
[757] Gianfrotta 1989: pl. 81–2.
[758] Tchernia 1997: 243–7, relief displayed on pl. 4, p. 246.
[759] Cf. chapter five.
[760] For this office, see Cuvigny 2003, II: 295–301.
[761] *CIL* VI, 32929. Pflaum 1960–61: I, no. 88, pp. 185–6; Cuvigny 2003, II: 303–4, providing an updated list of relevant sources (papyri and *ostraca*).
[762] Especially when compared to his near contemporary L. Bovius Celer, who was a fellow-Puteolian rising to equestrian office in Egypt (head of the gladiator school at Alexandria), but whose career shows no similar bent to indicate commercial interests: Pflaum 1960–61: I, no. 55, pp. 126–8.

cargo inventory from the Eastern trade. Thus, we get a concrete idea of how the *Annii*, *Calpurnii*, *Vestorii*, etc., and their Alexandrian counterparts, actually organised the long-distance trade with India via Alexandria, Koptos and the Red Sea ports. In the following, these immensely helpful documents will be subjected to a thorough analysis.

Starting out with the oldest contract, this source has come down to us as a fragmentary papyrus from the first half of the 2nd century BC, most likely originating in Ptolemaic Alexandria, and was first published in 1925.[763] Although its many *lacunae* leave us in the dark regarding specific details, the basic structure of the agreement can be ascertained.[764] One Archippos, son of Eudemos, lent an unknown sum through a certain Gnaius to five borrowers, of which one was from Sparta and another from far-away Massilia, apparently all Greeks, being designated as 'the five sailing in company to the Spice-bearing Land' (East Africa).[765] The loan was for one year, and the contract stipulated that if they did not repay it before the ordained time, or within 50–90 days of returning to Egypt, a penalty of two per cent interest per month, i.e., 24 per cent per year, would come into effect.[766] However, the original loan does not appear to have been interest-bearing, indeed, the overdue-interest by itself was simply the maximum allowed by law under the Ptolemies,[767] so instead it appears that a set lump sum or share of the profit was agreed upon as repayment on top of the principal—probably to circumvent the maximum lawful interest, the risk inherent to a venture like this prompting a financier to expect more than a quarter in return.[768]

Five people are listed as providing security for the loan on behalf of the lender, one being from Thessalonike in Greece, another from Elea in South Italia, and one more person from Massilia. Four of the guarantors were apparently part of the Ptolemaic army, while the fifth was a Hellenised Carthaginian merchant 'of those sailing the sea.'[769] Indeed, these guarantors were vital to the validity of the agreement, for as is evident from the wording of the contract, lender and borrowers did not know beforehand what Egyptian Red Sea port the five-man party would be returning to (or, for that matter, what specific ports they would visit).[770]

Seeing as *arõmata* was a Ptolemaic royal monopoly, that is, a commodity that could only be sold at a fixed price by importers to the state, which could then retail it at an elevated rate and pocket the difference, the motley consortium of Greeks constituted by lender, borrowers and guarantors, must still have considered a profitable journey a feasible undertaking subject to such circumstances.[771] Moreover, taking into consideration the financial clout needed and wide-flung origins of some of the characters involved, such a picture fits well with the contract having been written at Alexandria (as deducted by Wilcken from its provenance as mummy cartonnage), where most maritime loans must have been agreed upon, but from where hardly any papyri have survived.[772]

In fact, Alexandria would be a highly fitting base of operations for Gnaius, who, although only mentioned in passing, played a crucial role in the setup.[773] Specifically, he was the one through whom the loan was made by Archippos to the five borrowers, but the wording does not imply that he was a professional banker, the relevant passage merely reading *dia Gnaiou*, 'through Gnaius.' Furthermore, the name indicates that this financial middleman was an Italian, thus, in all probability a member of the diaspora of Roman businessmen, *negotiatores*, settled at Alexandria (mentioned above).[774] Accordingly, it was

[763] Wilcken 1925: 89–92; *P.Berl.* 5883 + 5853 = *SB* III, 7169.
[764] Following Bogaert 1994: 210–16; and Ste. Croix 1974: 53–4.
[765] *SB* III, 7169, ll. 6–12.
[766] *SB* III, 7169, ll. 13–16. In l. 15, the period of grace from return to Roman port until repayment can only be read as]*êkonta*, making 50, 60, 70, 80, or 90 days the possible alternatives; *hexêkonta* most likely being too short, though.
[767] Bogaert 1994: 211 n31.
[768] *SB* III, 7169, ll. 23–6. Wilcken would, moreover, read *ato*]*ka* at the beginning of l. 13, but this must remain mere hypothesis.
[769] *SB* III, 7169, ll. 16–22.
[770] *SB* III, 7169, ll. 14, 15, 24, 25; Bogaert 1994: 213.
[771] Wilcken 1925: 101–2; Bogaert 1994: 212 n34. In comparison, *P.Tebt.* I, 35, is a Ptolemaic circular from 267 BC fixing the price of myrrh. For the workings of Ptolemaic and Roman monopolies in the perfuming industry and trade, see below.
[772] Wilcken 1925: 92; Ste. Croix 1974: 54.
[773] *SB* III, 7169, l. 12.
[774] Bogaert 1994: 214–6.

probably thanks to people like Gnaius and other *Alexandreae Italicei* that the Republican Rome of Plautus was well-acquainted with Eastern commodities like frankincense, *amomum*, myrrh, cinnamon, saffron, cassia, etc.[775] In effect, this made Gnaius an early precursor of the Campanian families and Puteolian notables involving themselves in the Eastern trade through Egypt after its annexation by Rome, some two centuries later.

Now, the odd thing about this contract for a commercial endeavour down the Red Sea to the Horn of Africa is that it is reminiscent of so-called maritime loans known from the forensic speeches of Classical Athens, one exemplar being embedded in a speech by Demosthenes.[776] However, if we are not to believe that all the identifiable hallmarks of a maritime contract have, by a peculiar twist of fate, been lost in the *lacunae* of the document, then this loan agreement simply does not contain any of the standard technical terminology, neither does it demand ship and cargo as hypothecated security (this is the role played by guarantors instead), nor does it mention, which is the defining characteristic of a maritime loan, that the principal is at the risk of the lenders if ship and goods perish *en route*.[777] Accordingly, this contract does not constitute a traditional maritime loan of the period, but rather a special adaption of this form of commercial finance to suit the exigencies of both the Ptolemaic economic system and the risks inherent to early Greek Red Sea sailing, being potentially very profitable but also high-risk ventures.[778]

So much for the *modus operandi* of the Ptolemaic period. Extraordinarily, an even more well-preserved (although by no means complete) papyrus dating from the mid-2nd century AD sheds light on the financing, logistics, and imports of the subsequent Roman Red Sea trade with India. This document was first published in 1985,[779] the *recto* containing a written agreement concerning the arrival back in Egypt of an individual who had obtained a loan to purchase goods at South Indian Muziris, the *verso* being an inventory of goods, among other things Gangetic nard, ivory and ivory fragments, listed with a series of calculations. Most likely, the *recto* and the *verso* relate to one another, so that the former is a description of the practical arrangements, while the latter details the merchandise actually purchased in India. An English translation of a compiled version incorporating the most recent readings is appended below, for the convenience of the reader:

The Muziris Papyrus (*SB* XVIII, 13167)

Recto, column ii[780] (column one being lost)

1 - - -] your other administrators or managers, and on agreement(?)
2 I will give(?)] to your trustworthy camel-driver [- - -] (?) for the conduct*
3 of the journey up] to Koptos; and I will convey (the goods) through the desert under guard and protection
4 up to the] public tax-receiving warehouses at Koptos, and
5 I will] place them under the [authority] and seal of yourself, or of your administrators or whichever
6 one of them is present, until their loading at the river; and I will load them
7 at the requi]red time onto a safe ship on the river; and I will convey them down
8 to the warehouse for receiving the quarter-tax [at Alex]andria, and
9 likewise] will place them under the authority and seal of yourself or your men.
10 All the payments out of my own pocket from now to collection of the quarter-tax, and of(?) the*
11 desert tran[sport] and the carrying-charges of the river-workers and the other incidental(?)
12 exp[ens]es [- - -] on occurence of the date for repayment specified in
13 the contracts of lo[an] for (the trip to) Muziris, if I do not
14 then] duly discharge the aforesaid loan in my name, that then

[775] Miller 1969: 9–10.
[776] Dem. XXXV; on the institution of maritime loans in Classical Athens, see Ste. Croix 1974: 41–52.
[777] Bogaert 1994: 212–14; Ste. Croix 1974: 53f.
[778] Compare Bogaert 1994: 214.
[779] Harrauer and Sijpestein 1986: 128–33. *P. Vindob. G* 40822 = *SB* XVIII, 13167.
[780] Translation by Rathbone 2000: 40; with amendments (*) by Morelli 2011: in l. 2, cf. pp. 200–1, and l. 10, cf. pp. 201–6.

15 you] and your administrators or managers are to have the option and
16 com[plete] authority, if you so choose, to carry out execution without
17 notifica]tion or summons to judgement, to possess and own the
18 afore[said] security and pay the quarter-tax, to convey the
19 three] parts which will be left where you choose and to sell or use them as security
20 and] to transfer them to another person, if you so choose, and to deal with the
21 items of the security in whatsoever way you choose, and to buy them for yourself at the
22 price current at the time, and to subtract and reckon in what falls due
23 on account of the aforesai]d loan, on terms that the responsibility for what falls due
24 lies] with you and your administrators or managers and we are free from
25 accus[at]ion in every respect, and that the surplus or shortfall from the capital
26 goes] to me the borrower and giver of sec[urity - - -

Verso, column i[781] (only the right hand side is preserved)

1	talents	] minas 59
2	talents	] minas 14¾
3	talents	] minas 58
4	Gangetic nard, 80 boxes, the share of the quarter-tax, bo]xes 20	
5	Sound ivory, in tu]sks(?) 167, 105 talents-weight, 13 minas	
6		] 26 talents, 30 minas
7		]... of the quarter-tax
8		like]wise 11¾ minas-weight
9		] 26 talents 18¼ minas
10	Of fragments?	] 17 talents-weight, 33 minas
11		] 4 talents, 46 minas
12		]... commerce(?)
13		] 4 talents, 23¼ minas
14		] 30 talents, 41½ minas
15		]...21
16		]8
17	w]eight[	]23¼ minas
18	]1200[(+?)	] 4 minas
19		silver?] talents 220[(+?) drachmas
20	Of pepper?	]3308 talents-weight [minas
21		talents-weight] 3215, 3 minas
22		]... of which ...[
23		...
24		...
25		]771 talents silver
26		] 4632 drachmas
27		talents?] 44¼ minas
28...		

Verso, column II[782]

29(1) Gangetic nard: 60 boxes, of which likewise
30(2) the price is reckoned with the box at 4500 drachmas of silv-
31(3) er, 45 talents.

781 Based on Morelli 2011, Greek text and Italian translation, pp. 207–9, and commentary, pp. 210–12.

782 Translation by Rathbone 2000: 44; with amendments (*) by Morelli 2011, in ll. 38(10), 41(13), 43(15), 44(16), 54(26), 57(29), cf. his Greek text and Italian translation, pp. 208–10, and commentary, pp. 212–14. Plain line numbers are according to Morelli's consecutive numbering from column one to column two, numbers in parenthesis refer to Rathbone's original numbering in accordance with the *editio princeps*.

32(4) Ivory: first, sound, 78 talents-weight, 54¾ minas,
33(5) of which likewise the price is reckoned, 78 talents-weight, 43 minas
34(6) which become by the standards of the quarter-tax, the
35(7) talent being reckoned at 95 pounds, 7478 pounds
36(8) from which the equivalent is, reckoning pounds to the talent
37(9) on the ratio which is normally reckoned among merchants,
38(10) 76 talents-weight 41 minas, with the mina at 100 drachmas, total 76 talents, 4100 drachmas*
39(11) Then, the remaining tusks, taken at the higher (weight) by the arabarchs for
40(12) the collection of the quarter-tax in the sum of tusks,
41(13) besides that put aside of whole tusks of two cubits, 11¾ minas*
42(14) with the mina at the same 100 drachmas, 1175 drachmas.
43(15) Makes total 76 talents, 5275 drachmas*
44(16) Then, fragments ..., 13 talents-weight, 9¾ minas*
45(17) of which likewise the price is reckoned, 12 talents-weight, 47 minas,
46(18) which, as above, become by the weights of the quarter-tax
47(19) 1214 pounds, [[and]] according to how among the merchants it is reckon-
48(20) ed, 12 talents-weight, 27 minas, with the mina at 70 drachmas,
49(21) 8 talents, 4290 drachmas of silver.
50(22) Then, the remaining, taken at the higher (weight) for collection of the quarter-tax,
51(23) as above, 22¾ minas, with the mina at the
52(24) same 70 drachmas, 1592½ of silver.
53(25) Total for fragments: 8 talents, 5882½ drachmas of silver
54(26) Total price of ivory [85 talents 5157½] of silver*
55(27) Makes the price of the 3 parts of the cargoes shipped out
56(28) in the ship *Hermapollon*
57(29) 1151 talents, 5852 drachmas of silver.*

However, the exact interpretation of the *recto* and *verso* of the Muziris Papyrus continues to spark scholarly debate.[783] The original editors, H. Harrauer and P. Sijpesteijn, in 1985 took the *recto* to constitute a freight agreement between a shipowner and a merchant at Muziris for the trip back to Alexandria, as well as a maritime loan obtained from this merchant by the captain, who pledged his ship and a quarter of the cargo as security. The *verso*, meanwhile, was interpreted as the captain's account of customs dues paid in Alexandria.[784] One year later, in 1986, L. Casson suggested that the *recto* was rather a normal loan contract drawn up at a Red Sea port, as a supplement to a non-extant maritime loan (believed to be mentioned in *recto ii*, ll. 12–3) agreed between merchants at Muziris.[785] In 1987, in response to the original article of 1985, G. Thür likewise argued that the *recto* was a contractual supplement to a maritime loan, although of an otherwise unknown type of document dealing with the security for such a loan, both written at Alexandria. The *verso* he took to be a copy of the customs declaration produced by fiscal officers upon return.[786] Having become acquainted with each other's articles in the meantime, Thür in 1988[787] and Casson in 1990[788] each re-argued their own case against that of the other. Adding further distance to Thür, moreover, Casson now also included the *verso* in his study, considering it just as likely to be a private draft of the customs declaration written up before arrival.[789]

Ten years later,[790] D. Rathbone in 2000 provided a new and improved reading of both sides of the document. Rathbone followed Thür and Casson in interpreting the *recto* as a supplement to a maritime loan, but

[783] Brief accounts of the historiography of this document can be found in Rathbone 2000: 39; and Romanis 2014: 78–9, 81–2.
[784] Harrauer and Sijpestein 1986: 145–6, 150.
[785] Casson 1986a: 76–8.
[786] Thür 1987: 240–5.
[787] Thür 1988: 230–33.
[788] Casson 1990: 220–6; especially the disagreement about 'in-' or 'for Muziris,' being dependant on the proper interpretation of *kata Mouzeirin* in *recto ii*, l. 12, of the *editio princeps*.
[789] Casson 1990: 198 n6.
[790] Not including here Romanis 1996a: 183–200, nor Romanis 1998, which are now superseded by Romanis 2012 and 2014, both of the latter to be dealt with below.

believed that both were drawn up at Alexandria for a trip to Muziris, the description of the outward journey being lost as only the second column, about the Muziris to Alexandria leg, is preserved on the *recto*. However, in contrast to Thür's unique 'loan security' document and Casson's quayside supplement drawn up upon arrival in a Roman port, Rathbone interpreted the unspecific character (no names, dates, or numbers) of the *recto* as deriving from it being a generic master contract used by a financier often engaging in such overseas endeavours. Thus, such a document would supplement a concise specific contract containing all the relevant data, the latter referring in everything to the master contract for standard operational procedures.[791] Regarding the *verso*, a new reading made Rathbone realise that this was an account of the value of goods after the deduction of the *tetarte* (*verso ii*, l. 55(27)), amounting to just short of seven million *drachmai*, weighing more than 150 tonnes before taxes, and consisting in part of boxes of Gangetic nard, sound ivory and ivory fragments. In this light, so Rathbone argued, the assignment of wholesale prices to each category of goods makes better sense if we keep in mind a clause on the *recto* stipulating that the merchant could sell the entire cargo to his creditor (*recto ii*, ll. 21–2), not only if he did not make the deadline for repayment, but also voluntarily, because it was a simple method of clearing his debts and obtaining a quick profit. The *verso*, then, concerns the purchase by the financier of the cargo at current prices in Alexandria from the borrower.[792]

After yet another decade,[793] F. Morelli published an article with new readings based on close inspection of the original document with a microscope, as well as a reconfiguration of a fragment of the *verso*. In addition to slight emendations of the Greek text of the *recto*, Morelli interpreted this part of the document as a second loan contract written upon arrival at a Red Sea port, superseding an original loan contract agreed upon at Alexandria.[794] Regarding the interpretation of the *verso*, Morelli was better able to make out the barely visible numbers than previous scholars, believing that a consignment of goods in the fragmentary first column weighing 3215 talents (*verso i*, l. 21) was valued at 771 talents (*verso i*, l. 25), which he argued to be pepper after taxes (see below), out of a total value after fiscal deductions of 1151 talents and 5852 *drachmai* (*verso ii*, l. 57(29)), weighing in excess of 180 tonnes (before taxes).[795] Unrelated to these calculations, he argued that the *verso* was written on board a Nile vessel either at Koptos before departure or *en route* down the Nile to Alexandria, loaded with imports which had been registered and sealed by fiscal officials at Koptos, being a valuation of the cargo remaining after *tetarte*, drawn up for the creditor at Alexandria by either the borrower or a supercargo agent of the creditor.[796]

Finally, in a recent article F. de Romanis has challenged the view that the *recto* constitutes a supplement or second document, arguing that the reference to 'the date for repayment specified in the contracts of loan for Muziris' (*recto ii*, ll. 12–13) is not to another specific document (in which case the use of plural, 'contracts,' is confusing), but to the established traditional practice of commercial sea-voyages from Roman Egypt to Muziris, in accordance with the annual cycle of the monsoon winds. Indeed, Pliny informs us that already by his time (at least half a century before the earliest possible date of the *recto*) the conventional date for latest departure from Muziris was the Ides of January, being the 13th of that month, while the ships would have set out for India in July.[797] Accordingly, this fits the precedence of the Ptolemaic contract running for one year for a voyage to East Africa, during which time the borrower could travel from Alexandria to Muziris and back again.[798] Romanis' interpretation therefore has the admirable advantage of doing away with the postulated non-extant document required for the *recto* to be a supplement or second contract, as imagined by Casson, Thür, Rathbone, and Morelli.

791 Rathbone 2000: 41.
792 Rathbone 2000: 45–6.
793 Not considering Pérez López 2007 (*non vide*) on which see Romanis 2014: 79, 81f, 82 n39.
794 Morelli 2011: 200–7.
795 Morelli 2011, for the sum value, p. 214, commentary on l. 57; for the total weight, pp. 227–8.
796 Morelli 2011: 229–33.
797 Pliny *NH*, VI.26; July as the time for setting out also being mentioned in the *Periplus* 14, 56.
798 Romanis 2014: 80–3.

Regarding the *verso*, Romanis also takes this document as a valuation of the cargo after deduction of *tetarte*.[799] However, building on his own new readings combined with those of Morelli (a number of which he disagrees on, though), Romanis goes through a series of calculations which allows him to assign exact shares of the total value to the extant consignments of Gangetic nard, ivory and ivory fragments (like Rathbone, which is uncontroversial), as well as to what is presumed to be pepper (as did Morelli, based on presumption and calculation), and even to malabathrum and tortoise shell, which he believes to have made up the remaining parts of the cargo (adding two additional layers of speculation and calculation). What is more, these calculations lead Romanis to claim a total cargo weight of approximately 20,500 talents before taxes, that is a thumping 625 tonnes.[800]

Now, as concerns the interpretation of the right-hand fragments of lines surviving from the first column of the *verso*, different scholars obviously reach quite different conclusions, which should alert us to exert due caution in evaluating their work. Indeed, even as regards the conversions conducted by the ancient scribe in the fully preserved second column, there is room for disagreement about their nature and purpose.[801] To serve as an example, both Morelli and Romanis venture to presume that the article in the first column of the *verso* valued at 771 talents worth of silver (*verso i*, l. 25) must be pepper, the former by reaching a reasonable price per measure estimate compared to Pliny's,[802] the latter based on Muziris, mentioned as destination on the *recto*, being a major supplier of pepper as well as the only non-Ganges based supplier of Gangetic nard, mentioned in the second column of the *verso*.[803]

However, while Morelli simply connects the value of 771 talents with figures to be read in the lines above (*verso i*, ll. 20–1), thus estimating a pre-tax weight of 4410 talents (139 tonnes),[804] Romanis calculates backwards from the value of 771 talents to figure out the weight of the alleged pepper. Next, he explains away a seemingly obvious fit with the number in *verso i*, l. 21 (3215 talents), because he presumes the illegible *verso i*, ll. 22–4 to contain recalculations by heavier weight standards parallel to those done for ivory and ivory fragments, but not boxes of Gangetic nard, in column two of the *verso*. Based on hypothetical recalculations, Romanis then argues that the real weight after taxes must have been 13,223 talents and 2 minas, proceeding to reread this number from *verso i*, l. 21 by postulating a lost *m(yriados) a'* (10,000) in the *lacuna* just in front of the extant number and arguing for a different interpretation of the letter-shapes so as to make out 1]3,223 talents and 2 minas, explaining away the palaeographic oddities originating from his new reading in a footnote. Consequently, after a few more calculations, Romanis ends up with a final pre-tax weight figure for the pepper of no less than 17,744 talents and 59 minas (544 tonnes), that is, four times as much as estimated by Morelli.[805]

Furthermore, while Morelli goes as far as identifying another consignment of unknown goods weighing 1200 talents before taxes in *verso i*, l. 18,[806] Romanis proceeds to identify this and yet another consignment by inference from the information about exports from Muziris given in the *Periplus*.[807] One of the articles, he presumes, must be malabathrum, and the other is taken to be tortoise shell. Accordingly, based on a different reading than Morelli's in *verso i*, l. 18 for the weight of malabathrum, and conducting calculations similar to those he made for pepper, Romanis is able to inform us about the weights and values of these two commodities, being worth 223.5 talents after taxes as regards the malabathrum and 24.5 talents as regards the tortoise shell.[808]

So, in summary, Rathbone identified goods weighing in excess of 150 tonnes, including nard, sound ivory and ivory fragments. Subsequently, Morelli identified goods totalling more than 180 tonnes, arguing that

---

799 Romanis 2012: 77 w. n19.
800 Romanis 2012: 78–89.
801 Rathbone 2000: 45–46; Morelli 2011: 218–20; Romanis 2012: nn27, 38.
802 Cf. chapter five.
803 On the exports of Muziris: *Periplus* 56.
804 Morelli 2011: 222–5.
805 Romanis 2012: 79–85.
806 Morelli 2011: 225–6.
807 See n803.
808 Romanis 2012: 85–8.

in addition to the extant commodities of column two, 139 tonnes of pepper could be identified in column one. Finally, Romanis has argued that the cargo was as large as 625 tonnes, of which 544 tonnes were pepper, further including malabathrum and tortoise shell in the ensemble.

Only twelve years separate these three articles, but the real divide is twofold: on the one hand, it is due to closer studies of the *verso* by Morelli and Romanis, individually; on the other, it is due to their willingness to fill out certain gaps in the text of the document with imputed numbers and specific objects of trade inferred from other sources. Obviously, Romanis has taken this approach to the greatest lengths. What, then, might we conclude from the Muziris Papyrus, seeing as so many details about the setup and scale of the venture are contested? Quite a lot, fortunately, even if we have to tread a methodologically strict path and forbear judgement on some interesting issues.

Starting out with the account of the *recto*, it is evident that if column one in any way resembled column two, the more than two dozen lines of the lost column will have dealt in minute detail with the purchase of a cargo at Muziris and its return across the sea to a Roman port (which might not have been specified, as in the Ptolemaic contract). This is only logical, seeing as the cargo acted as the hypothecated security of the financier, being his one and only chance of retrieving the principal and pocketing some kind of profit falling due from the loan, either interests or a lump sum, although the former was the same as the latter when interests were calculated per voyage, and not *per annum*.[809]

Regarding the loan obtained, it is referred to explicitly a number of times: first, in connection with the 'contracts of loan for the trip to Muziris,' *hai kata Mouzeirin tou da[neiou s]yngrafai* (*recto ii*, ll. 12–3); twice simply as 'the loan,' *to daneion* (*recto ii*, ll.14, 23); and, finally, in connection with the borrower styling himself *egō to dedaneismenon kai hypotethei[*, that is, 'I, the borrower and giver of security' (*recto ii*, l.26). Accordingly, there is no mention of the standard terminology of maritime loans or contracts, *daneion nautikon* and *nautikê syngrafê*, as is otherwise attested in a contemporary document (AD 149) issued by a banker in Theadelphia in the Fayyum on behalf of two clients, one of which was resident in the same city, to four borrowers from Ascalon, on security of their small merchant vessel and its last cargo.[810] Neither is there any extant hint at the defining clause of a maritime loan, as mentioned above, namely, that in case of a *force majeure* loss of part or the entire principal, the borrower is to be held free of debt, the creditor accepting the entire risk. Of course, such a basic stipulation might, along with a lot of other relevant data, have been contained in the lost first column of the *recto*. However, add to this the lack of maritime loan terminology, instead finding references to a normal loan, and the implication is that we should not consider this venture a maritime loan proper.

The hypothecation of cargo as security (*recto ii*, ll. 17–21), to be purchased for the money borrowed, does not make it a maritime loan either, and whereas other hazards (such as jettison and protection money paid out to extorters) were traditionally at the risk of the lender, here we only learn that the borrower had to pay for the desert and river passages as well as any other expenses (*recto ii*, ll. 10–12). However, there was some minimal measure of protection of the borrower included, in that if he managed to get the cargo to Egypt but could not repay in time, the creditor, although allowed to seize, sell or buy the entire shipment, had to hand over any surplus made after deduction for the principal and interests (or lump sum agreed) to the borrower—who would, conversely, though, also be held financially responsible for a deficit (*recto ii*, ll. 22–6).

Significantly, the *recto* corroborates the picture drawn by the literary sources for a direct Alexandria–Indian Ocean link: from the moment of arrival on the Red Sea coast, the entire cargo was on its way to Alexandria, being impounded in warehouses of the tax authorities at Koptos *en route*, all the while being under bonds until the payment of the *tetarte* at Alexandria (*recto ii*, ll. 4, 8, 17–9). In this way, it would be difficult for creditor and borrower not only to cheat the *fiscus* out of its due 25 per cent, but also for

809 Ste. Croix 1974: 46, 55–6.

810 Originally published in Casson 1956, later republished in Casson 1986b. *P. Vindob. G* 19792 = *SB* VI, 9571.

either party to attempt to appropriate any part of the cargo for themselves by hiding it away, seeing as the entire cargo must have been registered by arabarchs (e.g., mentioned in *verso ii*, ll. 39(11)–40(12)) in the service of the provincial government when it was first unloaded in port. In this way, nothing could 'disappear' before the wares were impounded at Koptos and subsequently at Alexandria for the actual levying of the *tetarte*. A tax which according to the actual wording of the Muziris Papyrus was collected in kind, leaving three parts as the security of the creditor after payment of the *tetarte* (*verso ii*, l. 55(27) w. *recto ii*, l. 19).[811] Or, rather, three parts less some 2.6 per cent of the cargo, which the arabarchs kept by converting the goods released back to the merchants into Roman pounds at 95 pounds per talent, rather than the 97.5 pounds per talent which was current on the market (*verso ii*, ll. 33(5)–38(10), 45(17)–49(21)). Small amounts of the whole tusks as well as fragmentary ivory avoided this biased conversion upon return (*verso ii*, ll. 39(11)–41(13), 50(22)–51(23)), presumably for logistical reasons to do with the actual weighing of the goods.[812]

Evidently, the financier had administrators (*epitropoi*) and managers (*frontistai*) who could oversee the arrival of the merchant and his cargo all the way from the ports themselves via Koptos to Alexandria (*recto ii*, ll. 1, 5–6, 9), in which cities his own presence was even possible (if not merely his seal entrusted to a reliable servant). Apparently, these men were in addition to one or more supercargoes, on the grounds that the financier's men in the ports are referred to as 'your other' agents, *sos eteros* (*recto ii*, l. 1), implying that the merchant was already, or had been (for instance, in Muziris), in contact with a supercargo or agent abroad before this point in narrated time. Moreover, for the transport across the desert, the cargo was to be handed over to 'your trustworthy camel-driver,' *sos kamêlitês axiochreōs* (*recto ii*, l. 2), which must mean that the financier either made use of a regular Nile-based transport service, similar to the camels of 'Nikanor and Sons' in Koptos (but with more animals, see below), or had his own men and sufficiently large herd of camels to do the job.

However, the overland leg must have been an incredible logistical burden, for aside from obtaining 'guard and protection,' *parafylakê kai asfaleia* (*recto ii*, l. 3), which must have been a military escort to protect the caravan against desert nomads in particular, the formation of a camel caravan large enough to carry just a part of the cargo attested required very substantial means. Seeing as one camel could carry six talents of 31.5 kg, each animal could transport a maximum of 189 kg, of course depending on the size of the beast itself, the bulkiness of the cargo and the required speed of travel.[813] To transport the amount of goods attested on the *verso*, then, it would take at the very least(!) some 800 camel trips for a cargo of around 150 tonnes (Rathbone), 950 camel trips if it was 180 tonnes (Morelli), and an army of 3300 camels for a cargo of 625 tonnes (Romanis).[814]

Now, things might have looked different if the cargo had been transported by donkey-led wagon train, as we know operated on the Myos Hormos road,[815] and one large-scale operator of which is known from Thebes just south of Koptos,[816] or by barge on Trajan's Canal (if that was ever feasible, see chapter seven), but the *recto* speaks explicitly of a *kamêlitês*. Regarding the feasibility of large-scale camel transport in Roman Egypt, it is first and foremost evident that if the authorities wanted something moved, it would be moved—no matter its weight and bulkiness or the distance and terrain. The transport of gigantic single-piece columns, weighing as much as 200 tonnes apiece, from the imperial quarry at Mons Claudianus through 160 km of desert to Kainepolis on the Nile, reflects this capacity eminently well.[817] Significantly, the miners and garrison of this quarry in the desert (some 900 people) needed a minimum of 150 camel loads per month to keep them supplied with food alone,[818] while it is estimated that Late Roman Berenike, being smaller than the Early Roman port, housed approximately 500–1000 people, varying with the

811 As argued by Rathbone 2000: 43, 45, referring to the 'three parts of the goods remaining,' to be moved or sold, after payment of the *tetarte*.
812 Following Rathbone 2000: 45–6. Note that Romanis 2012 interprets the conversions differently, cf. his nn27, 38.
813 Adams 2007: 230f.
814 Compare estimates in Rathbone 2002: 192.
815 *O.Krok.* 4, and K596 quoted in Bülow-Jacobsen 2003: 409.
816 *O.Wilcken*. 392, 395 (AD 44–7).
817 Adams 2007: 199f.
818 Adams 2007: 208–10.

season, entailing a similar need for 80–160 camel loads per month of victuals alone, transported the 380 km from Koptos.[819]

Indeed, we know that the state requisitioned camels for transport service on the Berenike route,[820] and at that port one fragmentary 'caravan register' has been uncovered containing at least 50 camels, sub-divided into smaller groups headed by individual cameleers, one of these being designated as the leader (*dekanos*).[821] Furthermore, the largest privately owned herd of camels attested in a single papyrus consisted of 26 camels, and the well-attested Koptos-based transport company of Nikanor seems to have had as much as 36 camels at its disposal for single trips.[822] Finally, as a slightly anachronistic comparison, Early Islamic caravans in western Arabia appears to have regularly numbered 1000–2500 camels.[823]

As should be apparent, then, a cargo weighing 180 tonnes, that is, 950 camel loads, to go by Morelli's figure, could be carried back to Koptos as a return cargo by the Berenike supply caravan of 150 animals alone in a little more than six return trips. However, we know that the borrower had to make use of the financier's 'trustworthy cameleer,' which implies that in addition the financier had his own men and enough animals working on the transport of the goods back to Koptos, so as to ensure that the goods could cross the desert as speedily as possible. Otherwise, the borrower would be a very long time indeed about bringing all the goods to Alexandria, paying taxes, and repaying his loan before its due date—a contingency of which the otherwise highly detailed *recto* makes no mention. On this note, it is worth mentioning that the cost of camel transport of alum in the Western Desert of mid-2nd century AD Egypt appears to have been approximately 45 *drachmai* per fully loaded beast,[824] making the 950 camel trips of the present example cost a hefty 7 talents, 750 *drachmai* worth of silver. Something for which the borrower had to pay out of his own pocket, that is, out of the loan already obtained, according to the explicit wording of the contract (*recto ii*, ll. 10–11).

On top of the desert transport and its related expenses, the borrower also had to arrange a 'safe ship,' *asfales ploion*, and pay the freight-charges of the river-men (*recto ii*, ll. 6–7, 11). Significantly, the loading of 150–180 tonnes of goods into a Nile River vessel would have posed no problems in comparison with the desert passage: counted in grain alone, the Nile carried as much as 150,000 tonnes annually down to Alexandria,[825] the largest regular barges in Roman times being of 150 tonnes burden, while the biggest vessels in the Ptolemaic era had exceeded 500 tonnes. So, even paying extra for a good ship handled by an experienced crew, this final part of the journey would likely not have cost anywhere near the money already spent on camels in the desert, being business as usual on the Nile.[826] As regards the total amount of work, estimated as man/days and animal loads, of the entire operation, that is, unloading returning ships at the ports, putting cargoes in temporary storage, loading beasts of burden, transport across the desert, temporary storage at tax-receiving warehouses in Koptos, and, finally, loading Nile vessels for the last leg down to Alexandria, this must have represented a significant but seasonally fluctuating demand for local labour in the Thebaid nome. Thus, work will have been concentrated when ships returned in spring and when ships where being prepared for departure in mid-summer, making the Eastern trade a vital part of the region's economy, especially at Koptos and the ports, providing part-time work for several thousand people during the busy times of year.[827]

Considering the amount of money involved in a venture like this, the financier's potential presence in Alexandria (and Koptos) as mentioned on the *recto*, the cargo's direct route to Alexandria where it was

[819] Using population size and distance from Sidebotham 2011: 68, 128. Disregarding the now outdated calculation in Ruffing 1993: 5–7.
[820] Adams 2007: 234, on *P.Lond.* II, 328 (AD 163), see also p. 202.
[821] *O.Ber.* II, 212. In addition: A cameleer is designated as part of a hierarchy implying transport agents and their patron-cum-employer, see *O.Ber.* I, 87, cf. Bagnall *et al.* 2000: 62 nn2–3. A cameleer may also be mentioned in *O.Ber.* II, 189, l. 5. Two *ostraca* mention *dekanoi* who may have been caravan chiefs: *O.Ber.* II, 205–6; and a person mentioned in *O.Ber.* I, 26, is also mentioned in an *ostracon* found at the *praesidium* of Didymoi as *dekanos*, cf. Bagnall *et al.* 2000: 7, 11.
[822] Adams 2007: 222–3.
[823] Maraqten 1996: 215–6.
[824] Adams 2007: 231.
[825] Khalil 2012: 41.
[826] Rathbone 2007b: 711.
[827] Rathbone 2002: 192.

finally released by the office of the *tetarte* to be further disposed of, the role of Alexandria as entrepôt of the Eastern trade, and even the old Ptolemaic contract which also seemed to have Alexandria as its base, we must assume that in the present case creditor and borrower no doubt both operated out of this very city. Accordingly, this author would argue that the contract constituted by the *recto* was drawn up at Alexandria between a wealthy financier, conducting this sort of operation regularly, with numerous agents in the Eastern Desert (perhaps also supercargoes on the ships or in Muziris) as well as a great many camels at his disposal, and an experienced merchant operating the long-distance trade route from Alexandria to Muziris via the Red Sea ports. In light of the missing first column, there is no need to postulate a lost first contract for the sea-going part and a second contract for the Red Sea port to Alexandria leg; the whole itinerary would have been contained in this one document. Probably, the borrower did not possess a ship himself, but merely rented cargo space or chartered an entire vessel.

Thus, Romanis (2014) would appear to be right in assuming that this is the one and only contract for a loan, not a supplement to one. The reference to the 'date for repayment specified in the contracts of loan for Muziris' (*recto ii*, ll. 12–13) is not to multiple contracts for the same loan held by the borrower, but to the traditionally established timeframe of a year from having the loan paid out prior to departure in July, until having to repay it after returning to Alexandria with the cargo sometime in early or late Spring, having started the voyage back from India in December–January. In other words, following the natural rhythm of monsoon seafaring, now enshrined in contract. Nonetheless, Rathbone's hypothesis that the second column of the *recto* has the appearance of a generic master contract without names, dates or numbers, still deserves consideration. In particular, it would make good sense for a wealthy Alexandrian who financed such ventures regularly to have a standard contract, with relevant data easily filled in at the beginning, describing the standard *modus operandi* which the signatories thereby agreed to abide by. In the present case, then, we must understand the *recto* as the contract proper, the missing initial lines having contained the lost names of lender and borrower, the sum lent, and interests or lump sum to be repaid, while the rest of the first column stipulated the planned purchase at Muziris of goods as hypothecated security and the return to Egypt, where the second column takes over upon arrival in port.

Regarding the *verso*, the less hypothetical reading of Morelli, being akin to Rathbone's earlier tentative reading, seems preferable to Romanis' (2012) approach, the resulting huge cargo of which might, strictly speaking, be possible, but most certainly does not seem plausible. Neither does this author agree with Morelli in taking the 3215 talents-weight (*verso i, l.* 21) worth 771 talents silver (*verso i, l.* 25) after taxes as pepper, just as it does no not seem wise of Romanis to think that he can identify additional calculated consignments as malabathrum and tortoise shell by inference. Any argument for connecting the weight and value of an unknown commodity in the highly fragmentary first column of the *verso* with a commodity exported from Muziris, based on the simple list of exports in the *Periplus*, amounts to nothing more than modern guesswork, leading Morelli and Romanis to results that differ by as much as 400 per cent, both as regards the weight of pepper and its price per measure. In order to strengthen the credibility of his very high figure for Roman pepper trade, Romanis draws on parallels with the tonnage and imports of Portuguese ships from the Malabar Coast in the 16th century AD.[828] However, such an approach would seem to understate the technological developments of European seafaring (which made it possible for Portuguese shippers to sail south around Africa, saving them from employing armies of camels in crossing Egypt's Eastern Desert) and overstate the productive potential of the Early Historic kingdoms of Tamilakam, particularly the Cheras.[829]

When exactly the contents of the *verso* were written up, by whom, and for what purpose, is more difficult to tell. While there is no doubt that it was written after assessment of the cargo by arabarchs, which might well have happened in a superficial manner at the ports and with due care no later than Koptos, we cannot tell whether the cargo was still *en route* to Alexandria (Morelli), stored in the Alexandrian

[828] Romanis 2014: 76–7; Romanis 2015.

[829] See also Lo Cascio on the danger of such a comparison becoming a circular argument, 2015: 165–6.

warehouses for receiving the *tetarte*, or just released after levying of the *tetarte* and in the process of being sold to one party, most likely the financier (Rathbone).

On a sound methodological basis, though, we can still claim to know the total value of the cargo after taxes, being 1151 talents, 5852 *drachmai* of silver, amounting to 6,911,852 *drachmai*, and that the merchant in question as part of his cargo, weighing at least 150–180 tonnes before taxes, was shipping back 3.3 tonnes of sound ivory (perhaps 167 tusks (*verso i*, l. 5)), 553 kg of ivory fragments, and 80 boxes of Gangetic nard. Remarkably, this was but *one* cargo involving *one* financier and *one* borrower. Yet, the above value accruing to the contracting parties, as well as the fourth part falling to the *fiscus*, being a thumping 2,303,951 *drachmai*, is by no means insignificant in itself.[830] To put the figure in perspective, the merchant's share of seven million *drachmai* amounts to the value of one per cent of Egypt's annual grain harvest;[831] or one per cent of the total cost of the Roman army;[832] or the price of the entire aqueduct of Alexandria Troas sponsored by Herodes Atticus (four million) and Hadrian (three million) in unison;[833] whereas the whole consignment of more than nine million *drachmai* constitutes almost one quarter of the tax raised from the *Tres Galliae* after Caesar's conquest.[834] To put it differently, a successful merchant bagging anything remotely like this kind of profit would rocket past the property threshold of Roman knights, corresponding to 400,000 *drachmai*, and qualify for the senatorial fortune requirement of 1,000,000 *drachmai* (worth of property) almost seven times over.

This is the more remarkable, seeing as even though the cargo listed in the Muziris Papyrus represented a huge value at Alexandria, and, accordingly, even more at Rome which exerted a greater demand and was farther away from the supply lines of the Indian Ocean, the goods in question would probably not have filled up an India merchantman's entire cargo hold. Although the average size of ships plying the Red Sea to India sea lanes is not known with certainty, they were likely to have been large enough to cope with the hardships of prolonged blue water sailing, carrying enough provisions for long sea legs, and being built sturdy enough to endure strong winds and potentially rough seas. Thus, these Indian Ocean ships would have had to meet much the same basic requirements as the grain freighters on the Alexandria to Rome *annona* route, the preferred size of which was around 340 tonnes cargo capacity.[835]

While some Roman ships of the Red Sea ports would obviously have been smaller, or even bigger (Mediterranean freighters of 500 tonnes capacity not being uncommon, a few even exceeding 1,000 tonnes), an average tonnage of some 300 tonnes is certainly plausible,[836] not least in light of the fact that the Muziris Papyrus implies a capacity of at the very least some 200 tonnes minimum, including the weight of necessary victuals and stores of equipment, if it was the only cargo of a ship. Significantly, one harbour berth at the Red Sea port of Berenike could take ships 19–22 meters wide and 36–61 meters long, that is, of the very largest kind.[837] However, while a few Roman wrecks have been identified in the Indian Ocean and superficially examined, we still lack concrete data on ship sizes.[838]

In this respect, the great weight and value recorded in the Muziris Papyrus poses a methodological conundrum: on the one hand, it would be unwise to assume on the basis of this one document that all ships carried such valuable cargoes,[839] and, on the other hand, it is equally problematic to postulate that

[830] Especially not seeing as a comparative analysis of price development in Roman Egypt, based on wheat, only shows a 25 per cent increase for the entire 2nd century AD compared to the 1st century AD, hence, the prices and values of the Muziris Papyrus cannot be considered grossly inflated; Duncan-Jones 1974: 365, Appendix. 16.

[831] Rathbone 2000: 49; although his older reading of the final sum is slightly different from the one employed here (Morelli's), the difference of 15,000 *drachmai* is so small compared to 7 million *drachmai* that it makes no difference to Rathbone's calculation and argument.

[832] Wilson 2015: 23 n41.

[833] Casson 1990: 205 n29.

[834] Wilson 2015: 30f.

[835] Casson 1989: 34–5, 284–5, 291 n2; 1990: 205 n29. Cf. also *P.Bingen* 77, ll. 9–10: a ship from Ostia of 600+ tonnes grain-carrying capacity arriving in an Egyptian port, 2nd century AD.

[836] Casson 1971: 171–3, 183–90.

[837] Sidebotham 2011: 195.

[838] Strauss 2006: cat. nos. 500–2; Pedersen 2008; Blue, Hill and Thomas 2012. For the recent discovery of a South Indian wreck and its cargo, see Bopearachchi *et al.* 2016.

[839] As, for instance, does McLaughlin 2014: 94.

the only extant contract represents a rare and uniquely successful venture. Instead, we must acknowledge that the potential profits accruing from some of these long-distance trading endeavours were immense, while other agents and independent traders engaging in the trip down the Red Sea barely managed to return without losing their money or their lives. In the following subchapter, we shall *inter alia* consider the only other piece of surviving documentary evidence from the Indian Ocean trade routes, constituting a case of the latter venture, rather than the former.

Taxes, the Alexandrian elite, and how it takes a fox to catch a fox

By now, we have already touched upon the subject of the tax on imports from across the frontier several times, so a brief account of what we actually know about it is overdue, but makes better sense at this point, because the most important relevant source material has by now been presented in detail. The *tetarte*, or 'quarter-tax,' of 25 per cent *ad valorem*, was only one, albeit by far the highest, of a multiplicity of customs dues, *portoria*, imposed at both internal as well as external boundaries of the Roman Empire. While the empire-wide customs system was not very consistent, the most common toll overall for carrying goods between provinces was the *quadragesima*, or 'fortieth-part,' amounting to 2.5 per cent.[840] As regards the *tetarte*, we know that it was collected all along the Eastern frontier from Northern Mesopotamia to Egypt.[841]

A tradition for hefty customs dues on imports to Egypt goes back to the Ptolemies, who already had special officials levying tolls on Arabian, African and Indian products, in Gaza by the mid-3rd century BC,[842] as well as elsewhere in Egypt.[843] Thus, a stele was put up in the later 2nd century BC, most likely at Koptos, by the officer in charge of overseeing the security of the Eastern Desert as regards mines, ships and those coming down from the Eastern Desert plateau to Koptos with cargoes of frankincense and other foreign goods.[844] From 74/73 BC it appears that the local *strategos* at Koptos was also in charge of the Red and Indian Seas,[845] while three inscriptions from the Southern temple of Philae reveal that one Kallimachos remained *epistrategos* of the Thebaid nome and *strategos* in charge of the Red and Indian Seas from at least 62 BC until the end of the 50s BC.[846]

The Roman institution for collecting the *tetarte* and related dues was called the *arabarchia*, the chief official of which was an *arabarchês*, being the wealthy tax-farmer who won the concession to collect these taxes from the Roman government. A number of the individual *arabarchai* who appear in papyri and *ostraca*, though, are to be understood as lower functionaries in the employ of the tax-farmer who was *the Arabarchês*.[847] While the epithet dates back at least to the time of Cicero (who uses it in jest of Pompey in 59 BC), likely making the office and title a Ptolemaic innovation,[848] the first known tax-farmer as holder of the official Roman title is Ptolemy the Arabarch, whose son, Apollonious, in AD 2 left an inscription mentioning his father beyond the furthest extremes of Egypt proper, at the Temple of Dakka in Nubia. The son, Apollonios, was, at the time, *strategos* of the southern Ombite nome and region around Elephantine and Philae, as well as, significantly, receiver of dues from the Red Sea, but subsequently Apollonius, so we can tell from a supplement to his inscription added by his own son, being the grandson of Ptolemy, also attained the title of arabarch.[849] The last arabarch known by name is one Anastasios of the 6th–7th century AD, also an office-holder of the Egyptian Church,[850] while the longevity of the office of the *arabarchia* is documented by 6th century AD sources such as the *Codex Justinianus* and a papyrus from

840 Duncan-Jones 2006: 4–6.

841 Laet 1949: 306–11, 333–8. Raschke 1978: 635–6, 670. Jördens 2009: 355–67. On customs duties in Egypt generally, including the *tetarte*, see now the succinct introduction in Vandorpe 2015, whereas for Egyptian customs in relation to the Eastern trade specifically, see the brief overview in Young 2001: 66–69.

842 *PSI* 6.628, ll. 3–4, *c.* 259 BC (belongs with *P.Cair.Zen.* 59009 and *P. Cair.Zen.* 4, *add. et corrig.*, p. 285 (59009)); see Durand 1997: 143–9, nos. 19–21.

843 E.g. *SB* III.7176; VI.9416.

844 *Pan du desert* 86. Preaux 1939: 364; Fraser 1972: 180.

845 *Portes du desert* 49.

846 *I.Philae* 52, 53, 56.

847 Burkhalter 1999: 44–5, 48–50. Rathbone 2002: 183.

848 Cic. *Att.*, II.17(3). Burkhalter 1999: 50.

849 *Tempel v. Dakke* III 47a–b; see Burkhalter 1999: 50–1, nos. 1–2.

850 Burkhalter 1999: 53, no. 9.

Antinoopolis.[851] In later times, though, specifically from sometime between AD 174 (latest attestation of *tetarte* at Palmyra, see below) and the 220s AD (a law by the jurist Severus Alexander), the tax collected might have been halved to 12.5 per cent, known as the *octava*, but it is not sure whether the latter in fact replaced the *tetarte* or was a new tax on trade generally.[852]

Remarkably, an epitaph from the suburbs of Rome, dated epigraphically to Hadrianic times, mentions a secretary, Bassus, to the procuratorial office of the arabarchy in Pelusium.[853] This implies that the office of tax-collector in Egypt's Eastern Desert for collecting the *tetarte* had been turned into a position in the imperial civil service by the time of Hadrian,[854] whereas in AD 90 the arabarchy was still being leased out, as we know from the 'Koptos tariff:' a toll charter establishing the prices to be paid for Eastward passage through the desert (that is, for an *apostolion*, 'travel permit') to the tax-farmers of the Arabarch in Koptos, imposed by the prefect of Egypt, inscribed and set up by the prefect of Berenike.[855]

Back in the 1st century AD, however, private tax-farmers paid the *fiscus* up front for the expected revenue to be collected over a year, as we know that Annius Plocamus did for Egypt,[856] and just like tax-farmers continued to do at least until the 170s AD in Antioch and Palmyra.[857] However, we now know that by the mid-2nd century AD, the *tetarte* in Egypt was collected in kind at Alexandria (with *arabarchai* registering arriving cargoes at the Red Sea ports and storing them at Koptos, as described in the Muziris Papyrus) as one literal fourth from every cargo arriving from the East.[858]

Such an arrangement is, however, difficult to reconcile with private individuals of the 1st century AD bidding at public auction to farm the taxes, as payment in kind would have forced tax-farmers to convert the tax products collected into cash by putting them up for sale on the market—a laborious and expensive procedure which would have lowered their bids for the tax-farming contract. Thus, it might be that while private individuals farmed the right to collect Egyptian taxes in the 1st century AD, these were collected in cash, whereas later, when state officials took over at some point between AD 90 and before the death of Hadrian in AD 138, taxes began to be collected in kind. Nonetheless, the leap in value which a commodity underwent as a result of its transhipment across the ancient Indian Ocean, being purchased abroad where it was in good supply and carried home to a market where it was in great demand,[859] might well have meant that an ordinary merchant would find it exceedingly difficult to put down 25 per cent of his cargo's value in cash upon return (having spent a lot of his available money on a return cargo and its transport, still needing money to pay for transport in Egypt from the Red Sea to Alexandria). In consequence, payment in kind could have been the only practically feasible way from the very outset of Roman rule in Egypt of levying a 25 per cent import toll on Eastern goods arriving by sea, individual merchants' consignments running up a duty, as we know from the Muziris Papyrus, of more than half a million *denarii*.[860]

Procuratores in charge of the *arabarchia* levying *tetarte* in Egypt from at least Hadrianic times onwards will, in consequence, have amassed at Alexandria as imperial taxes in kind one quarter (later perhaps one eighth) of all Indian Ocean products imported annually to the Empire via Egypt. This hugely valuable stock of goods must have mainly been converted into money on the market of Alexandria, perhaps to

[851] Burkhalter 1999: 45 n20.

[852] Duncan-Jones 2006: 5; Wilson 2015: 27–8.

[853] *AE* 1999, no. 418: *Bassus (...) adiutor procuratio a<l=r>abarchia Pelusium*. See comments in Jördens 2009: 359 n15.

[854] Jördens 2009: 369–70.

[855] *I.Portes* 67. See mainly Cuvigny 2003, II: 374–5; but also Young 2001: 48–50.

[856] Pliny *NH*, VI.24: *Annius Plocamus, qui Maris Rubri vectigal a fisco redemerat...*

[857] *Inv.* X.29 (AD 161, an Antiochene *bouleutês* and *tetartõnês*), X.113 (AD 174, a *mancipes IIII mercaturae* with an *actor*, in the Greek a *tetartõnês* with a *pragmateutês*). Roman *Publicani* are attested in Palmyra as early as the reign of Nero: Gawlikowski 1998 and *Inv.* 8.57; while Palmyrene customs collectors are known from as early as AD 10/11, Gawlikowski and As'ad 1993.

[858] Van Minnen 2008: 237, doubts that the quarter of the cargo belonging to the state was actually paid in kind, though, preferring to assume that the individual merchants transferred the value of 25 per cent to the state in another document. While misgivings about the state's abilities as a seller on the market are understandable, I find this assumption flying in the face of concrete evidence somewhat questionable on methodological grounds. Some choice products may in addition have been exacted as a sort of tribute: Stat. *Silv.*, III.3.85–97; discussion in Raschke 1978: 650 n996.

[859] Compare Romanis 2006: 58.

[860] Wilson 2015: 24.

a lesser extent been shipped back to Rome for the private consumption of the imperial household. On the grounds that the transport expenses for importing foreign goods to Rome could easily be passed on to individual shippers, merchants, and their financiers, by selling the tax-products in Alexandria, it is unlikely that the state itself would have shipped products to the capital for retail sale to the public—just like it did not take possession of its rightful quarter until merchants had paid for its transport all the way down to Alexandria.[861] Thus, import to Rome was most profitably left to private operators, not least because the goods would then be subject to a further 2.5 per cent export toll at Alexandria, as remarked upon as early as Strabo.[862] However, both options entail a need for central records to have been kept in order to ensure that money and commodities were disposed of in a responsible manner, ending up as coin in the *fiscus* or stock at the imperial palace, respectively, and not in the pockets of far-away imperial agents and middlemen, which might in part explain one or more of the procuratorial archives in the *horrea piperataria* at Rome from no later than 192 AD onwards, as set out in chapter four.[863]

Consequently, it should be apparent that the Roman state profited in a significant way from the customs dues of 25 per cent levied on expensive foreign imports,[864] on top of which must be added, moreover, the more modest income from tolls on the movement of goods for export through Egypt to the Red Sea ports[865] and the duty on their final export from the province (each being one to three per cent *ad valorem*),[866] as well as the money paid for travel permits (*apostolia*) through the Eastern Desert by the personnel of the Indian Ocean trade, just mentioned. Now, working with the only figures that we have for a consignment of goods which in all likelihood did not make up one entire ship's cargo, from South India to mid-2nd century AD Roman Egypt, the share of the *fiscus* was 2,303,951 *drachmai*. To put the latter number in perspective, the *tetarte* thus collected in a single transaction is almost six times that of the 400,000 *sesterces* accruing annually from the port revenues of Lycia under Nero.[867] Clearly, it would not take too many ships carrying cargo holds full of such valuable goods to make a substantial contribution through the *tetarte* to even the overall imperial budget, and thus the role of long-distance trade in an ancient economy a la Finley needs to be reconsidered.

Furthermore, just as we saw above that prominent Campanian families were involved in the Eastern trade, so can top-tier members of the elite of Roman Alexandria be shown to have been not only deeply involved in the Eastern trade, but also to have acted as the senior and indispensable partners of the state's fiscal organisation in the province. Specifically, a known farmer of the Egyptian *tetarte* on imports from the East, and contemporary of Annius Plocamus, was Gaius Julius Alexander, also simply known as 'Alexander the Arabarch,' out of one of the leading Jewish families of Alexandria, his brother being Philo, the famous philosopher. Alexander was immensely wealthy and he not only embellished the gates of the Temple of Jerusalem with silver and gold, but also, significantly, in AD 36 agreed to lend to the later king Herod Agrippa of Judaea a sum of 200,000 *drachmai*, 30,000 being handed over at Alexandria where the loan was agreed, the remaining 170,000 *drachmai* to be paid out at Puteoli.[868]

Accordingly, this bank transfer of Alexander the Arabarch bears out his financial connections to the port city of Puteoli, with its strong maritime and commercial links to Alexandria—Puteolians even rising to high equestrian offices in Egypt.[869] Moreover, we know that Alexander and Philo had a third brother, Julius Lysimachus, who was an important merchant at Alexandria, and that while Alexander's oldest son had been *epistrategos* of the Thebaid nome (encompassing the Eastern Desert) in AD 42, and became equestrian prefect of the province of Egypt in AD 66–9, the younger son, Marcus Julius Alexander (who

[861] Wilson 2015: 24–5.

[862] Strabo XVII.1.13; see comment in Rathbone 2002: 184 n22.

[863] For the setting up of procuratorial positions in Egypt by the emperor in the 2nd century AD, see Jördens 2012: 57.

[864] Sidebotham 1986: 110–12, 175–81; Rathbone 2000: 49; Young 2001: 210–11; Duncan-Jones 2006: 12; Romanis 2006: 57–9; Wilson 2015: 22–4, 30–31.

[865] Laet 1949: 312–30; Sijpesteijn 1987: 16–26; Duncan-Jones 2006: 4–5.

[866] Best attested in the customs declaration *ostraca* from Berenike: Bagnall *et al.* 2000: 8–11; 2005: 5. The issue of the *quintana* tax levied by a *quintanensis* will not be raised here, but see Bagnall *et al.* 2000: 12; 2005: 5–7, for this additional fee on transport through the Eastern Desert.

[867] Wilson 2015: 30f.

[868] Joseph. *AJ*, XVIII.6.3.

[869] Cf. nn761–2.

was married to a Jewish princess and died in AD 44), is known to have had supplies carried from Koptos on the Nile to agents of his at both Myos Hormos and Berenike in AD 37–43/44.[870] In consequence, the activities of these Jewish *Julii* of Alexandria imply that the family had a permanent presence at the Red Sea ports, either for buying from returning ships or to outfit their own vessels, at the same time as one of them was the official magistrate in charge of the region, and either meanwhile or after the father had been the customs official tasked with exacting 25 per cent tolls on imports. Finally, a later descendant of Julius Alexander is attested at Rome, in the first half of the 2nd century AD, as the owner of a large-scale brick-making workshop, further enhancing the family's links to not only Puteoli but even the capital itself.[871]

Another interesting case-study of Alexandrian elite involvement to equal that of the *Julii* is constituted by the documented activities of Gaius Norbanus Ptolemaios, who is known to have been a landowner and shipped legumes on the Nile, as well as to have served simultaneously as both provincial procurator in charge of jurisdiction (*iuridicus*) and procurator in charge of special revenues (*idios logos*) in AD 63.[872] In addition, though, two *ostraca* dated *c.* 36–41 AD reveal that one Isidora, acting as agent, received shipments of grain and medical supplies (or drugs, *pharmaka*) at Myos Hormos for the account of Gaius Norbanus Ptolemaios, most likely indicating outfitting of ships for distant destinations.[873] He might even have been shipping the products of his own Egyptian vineyards, for at Koptos three amphora stoppers have been identified with his name stamped on them.[874] Enjoying this kind of career, especially the procuratorial part of it, there is no doubt that Ptolemaios must have spent a substantial amount of his time in Alexandria, there being even two minor hints at an Italian connection. Namely, that the first Gaius Norbanus Ptolemaios might have been a freedman of Italian *Norbanii* rising to prominence in the 1st century AD, and that it was a highly unusual occurrence for the equestrian offices of *iuridicus* and *idios logos* to be held by the same person, even more so by someone from the province itself, implying that he was personally approved of by Nero's court at Rome.[875]

Like Annius Plocamus, in other words, the *Julii* and Norbanus Ptolemaios were not only deeply involved in the Eastern trade as private individuals but also eminently well placed as fiscal officials (and as holders of other government offices) to profit from it. Fortunately, a recently published papyrus sheds further light on the manner in which businessmen based in Egypt could, in addition to more traditional activities such as agriculture or textile manufacture, be participating in Indian Ocean trade on the side— being the only other documentary papyrus surviving from the Indian Ocean trade itself in addition to the Muziris Papyrus. This is a letter from an agent (perhaps a freedman or a slave), dated 5th June AD 97, reporting to his master, *despota*, apparently based at Oxyrhyncha in the Fayyum, that he had made it back to Berenike. Significantly, the writer's ship had been part of a group of such returning together, *ta ploia*, likely from East Africa as he refers to wares (perhaps dye for textiles) left over by or for *barbaroi*, and he complains to his master that although he had requested items from Oxyrhyncha in several letters, *inter alia* blankets, he had received nothing.[876] On the note of dyes and textiles, the village of Oxyrhyncha in the Fayyum is known to have hosted a thumping 314 women producing textiles from wool in Ptolemaic times,[877] and the *Periplus* mentions wraps and cloaks from the Fayyum as exports to Adulis (the port of Axum) and Avalitês in modern Eritrea, and blankets as imports at Muza, the main port of the Himyarites.[878] Accordingly, the *modus operandi* in this setup is different from the 'free' borrower and *de facto* junior partner of the Muziris Papyrus, the agent in the present letter being employed and supplied directly by his master.

---

870 *O.Petr.Mus.* 130–1, 135, 173, 194; shipments of grain, cordage, wooden (writing?) equipment, and goatskin sacks.
871 Burkhalter 1999: 41–4, and 51, no. 3; Fuks 1951: 214–6.
872 For these offices generally, se Jördens 2012: 57, 62.
873 *O.Petr.Mus.* 122, 125.
874 Cuvigny 1998; providing pictures of the stoppers and a handy list of relevant *papyri*.
875 Rathbone 1983: 89.
876 Peppard 2009.
877 Clarysse 2008: 65.
878 *Periplus* 6, 8, 24; cf. Peppard 2009: 198 n15.

Furthermore, if the above-mentioned combination of trade and tax-farming is anything to go by, additional participation in the Eastern trade by elite holders of the arabarchy based at Alexandria can be assumed in certain cases. Even more so, because it is evident that some arabarchs were directly involved in the production of wine for supply at the Red Sea ports or overseas trade, stamped amphora stoppers reading *arabarx* having been found at mid-1st–2nd century AD Myos Hormos and early 1st century AD Koptos.[879] Accordingly, the first plausible candidate is one Demetrios, who like the *Julii* was an Alexandrian Jew of the foremost lineage and wealth, being likewise married to one of the daughters of the Jewish king Agrippa, and held the office of *arabarch* sometime around AD 53. Another is Claudius Gemius who served as both *arabarch* and *epistrategos* of the Thebaid, being a potentially highly profitable combination, going on to become *idios logos* in AD 89–91/92. And a third possibility is M. Aurelius Mindius Matidianus Pollio who is known from inscriptions put up at Ephesos and Halicarnassos, during the reign of Commodus, to have served as both *arabarch* and *dioiketes*, that is, head of the finances of the province, whilst also being—among a string of other highly prominent appointments—head of the 2.5 per cent-tax of the province of Asia for no less than 30 years.[880]

The crucial point concerning all of these tax-farmers of the *tetarte* is that they supplied the state with services rooted not only in their private wealth, but also in their extensive knowledge of the 'rules of the trade,' that is, its basic conditions, possibilities for profit and potential pitfalls. In particular, it would have been pertinent for an efficient tax-farmer to close all the possible economic loopholes of his peers, being financiers and their merchant agents, to avoid them dodging taxes. With holders of the arabarchy pulled from the very ranks of the wealthy and well-connected Alexandrians engaged in large-scale Indian Ocean commerce, the state obtained the supplementary services of the individual merchant-cum-arabarch's already established expert network of itinerant agents and local managers who knew the business from the inside—it takes a fox to catch a fox. Consequently, although the state put warehouses at Koptos and Alexandria at the disposal of the arabarchy (cf. the *recto* of the Muziris Papyrus), it was reliant on the organised commercial networks of the merchant community itself to aid it in its collection of the highly valuable quarter-tax. As we shall see in chapter seven, the outsourcing by states of difficult but precious fiscal obligations to self-organising merchant groups is exactly one of the hallmarks of ancient Indian Ocean trade.

The not-so-invisible hand of Egyptian organisations

Speaking of self-organising mercantile groups, the relative abundance of Egyptian papyri makes it possible to reconstruct, to a considerable extent, the organisation of retail trade in exotic perfumes in Egypt, to compare with the analyses of such trade in Rome and Campania, as detailed in chapter four. Thus, we find in Alexandria, dating from approximately Augustan times, the base of a statue dedicated by one Ammonios, *myropôlês*, that is, perfumer, to an association, *synodos*, of which he was formerly president.[881] Although we know of professional associations in Alexandria,[882] there is no telling whether that of which Ammonios was president identified itself as such, like that of the *collegium thurariorum et unguentariorum* in Rome, but as we shall see below, Egyptian *myropôlai* certainly did organise themselves. Another well-off *myropôlês* was Kasios (perhaps a local rendering of 'Cassius'), son of Origen, whose elaborate metrical epitaph, discovered at Memphis, has come down to us from the High Empire. Judging from the self-laudatory content of the inscription, Kasios must have been a major producer and retailer of perfumes, having been crowned many times, implying either municipal honours or those awarded by an association in recognition of his prominent civic standing.[883]

---

879 Thomas 2011: 25, 27.

880 Burkhalter 1999: 52–3, nos. 5–7; for Mindius, see also the more expansive treatment in Pflaum 1960–61, vol. I, 523–31, no. 193.

881 *I.Alex.* 96.

882 E.g. *I.Alex.* 99: the weavers of Tarsican linens, being Romans of Alexandria (3rd century AD). Likely also *IGR* I, 1314: *to kollegion* (1st century AD), which might well have been an established group of Roman merchants, *Romaioi*, as in *Nysa* 2, ll. 35–8. Note that although there was intermittent government resistance to associations in Alexandria, there was never any general ban; see specifically Arnaoutoglou 2005.

883 Bernand 1969: no. 27.

There is even a laconic graffito in Demotic by Pakhes, son of Paneboursphy, who styles himself a 'perfumer' in that language at the rock-shelter (*paneion*) of Al-Buwayb, on the desert road from Koptos to Berenike. While this graffito is impossible to date on its own, dates occurring in the surrounding 45 *graffiti* from the site place the corpus in the years of Augustus and Tiberius.[884] Although the work status of Egyptian Pakhes is unknown, seeing as he could have been a retailer or in the employ of a native temple making use of his skills for religious rituals and embalming, it is significant to find a craftsman whose work requires supplies of myrrh, frankincense and spices, on the road to one of the two major ports receiving these goods in large quantities.[885]

Remarkably, we learn from two papyri written more than 200 years apart that under the Ptolemies and the Romans the trade in perfumes was organised in the same manner. The state would lease out for a set period of time the right to conduct business in a given area to one or more main contractors, who would then proceed to sublet smaller concessions within their area to sub-contractors, all being documented by written contracts. Thus, in the first half of the 1st century BC, the holders of the perfume monopoly for the Arsinoite nome granted Seos, a *myropōlēs* at Philadelphia, the concession to (literally) boil and make perfumes in that city.[886] Likewise, in AD 161 in the same nome, one Sarapion obtained from the main contractor Castor, an Alexandrian to judge from his titulation by tribe and deme, a fourth part of the half share belonging to the latter in Theadelphia, not including the right to sell on market days and festivals, for the second year of Castor's lease only (telling us that it ran for more than one year), at a total rent of 45 *drachmai* to be paid in monthly instalments.[887] Accordingly, it is evident that *myropōlai* organised their line of business throughout the centuries of Ptolemaic and Roman rule by contracting and sub-contracting, either by contract between a financial entrepreneur having won the bid for the monopoly and individual *myropōlai*, or between greater and lesser *myropōlai*.

Indeed, such a habit of economic self-ordering, in the service of the province's continued fiscal policy of auctioning the perfume monopoly in parcels, aids us in understanding an archive of papyri from Oxyrhynchus in the early 300s AD. Here, groups of craftsmen each make an oath through representatives to the local *logistes*, or *curator* in Latin, that they will all abide by set prices for dealing wholesale in the raw materials of their respective trades for the month,[888] these professional groups being, for instance, the fish-merchants, fullers, potters and, of particular interest, the perfume-sellers, *myropōlai*. In four surviving papyri we can therefore follow the products and prices of the *koinon tōn myropōlōn* of Oxyrhynchus in AD 310/11, 312, 327 and 329, of which quite a number of articles were imports from the East: pepper, frankincense, cinnamon leaf, styrax (tall and short), putchuk, *amomum*, bdellium, cassia, cassamum, myrrh and ginger.[889]

While it might thus seem that we have here a formal association of Oxyrhynchite perfumers, like that of the earlier *collegium thurariorum et unguentariorum* in Rome, as well as the politically active *unguentarii* of Pompeii, certain differences have to be noted.[890] First of all, the term *koinon* can imply not only the existence of an association with rules and well-defined membership, but also the 'joint-,' 'collective-' or 'combined group' of people, in this case those following a certain profession. A better documented example is that of the salt merchants of nearby Tebtynis, who back in AD 47 lodged a document with their village scribe, in which they detailed how their mutual business, in the area for which they had acquired the concession together, was to be arranged for the following year. This included electing a supervisor to collect their mutual payment to the authorities for the local concession to deal in salt, delegating specific rights to individual members to sell salt (and gypsum) at pre-ordained prices in different localities, as

---

884 Bernand 1972a: nos. 141, 143–5.
885 Colin 2003: 102–3, no. 1.
886 *P. Lond.* 2859A; cf. Skeat 1966.
887 *P.Fay* 93; cf. Johnson 1936: no. 238.
888 Coles *et al.* 1987: 239 n2, see also 232–3, Appendix III. Because of the inflation of the period and the attempt at government intervention constituted by the Price Edict of Diocletian (AD 301), these early 4th century AD prices are difficult to compare with earlier price figures.
889 *P.Oxy.* LIV, 3731, 3733, 3765 (ll. 32–40), 3766 (col. V, ll. 77–113). A much earlier example of Ptolemaic fixing of prices on myrrh is *P.Tebt.* I, 35, from 111 BC.
890 On Egyptian associations defined by vocation, see most recently: Venticinque 2010; 2013; 2016; Gibbs 2011, 2015.

well as agreeing on fines for transgression of the mutual agreement and the setting of a date for monthly meetings. They even authorised the supervisor to arrest members who owed the group money for their share in the monopoly.[891]

As should be apparent, then, such local Egyptian *koina* as those of the perfume-sellers of Oxyrhynchus and the salt merchants of Tebtynis seem to have established formal business arrangements rather than associations, as such, for reasons to do with their joint leasing (or sub-leasing) of trade monopolies,[892] and, as a practical consequence, for the collection of taxes to be paid on these government concessions.[893] Consequently, a number of Egyptian *koina*, particularly those of perfumers and salt merchants dealt with here, are not to be understood as traditional associations as such, and certainly not as examples of how business was administered in associations elsewhere in the Mediterranean. Rather, they should be interpreted as *ad hoc* contractual partnerships to be renewed annually, operating within a well-known traditional framework for Egyptian associations, the institutional blueprint of these institutions thus being exploited both by the groups themselves and the government because of their economic utility.[894]

Having now examined how professional networks in Roman Egypt organised their business in accordance with the unique economic administration of that particular province within the Empire, accordingly also relating to the organisation of trade in Indian Ocean commodities, the rich Egyptian evidence does also reveal other details about the internal working of actual associations. Thus, an additional non-administrative benefit to members of formal associations of Roman Egypt was the possibility to borrow money from the common coffers for private purposes, or collectively on security of communal assets. Although these loans must not be mistaken for commercial credit, they would have helped tide members over if they experienced a sudden cash flow crisis, household and workshop economies never being segregated.[895] Whether such practices can also be applied to the *collegia* of the Western Mediterranean is an open question, though.

Big fish and small fry: well off merchants and small-time traders

In addition to all of the above networks involved in the trade between East and West, and in particular the two best-documented cases of the mid-2nd century AD merchant returning from Muziris with a valuable cargo to repay his Alexandrian financier and the late 1st century AD agent of a master in the Fayyum returning from trade in East African ports, there is a source from Byzantine Egypt providing ambiguous testimony about the actual traders travelling the long-distance routes.

This is a text by an anonymous Nestorian Christian, traditionally named as Cosmas *Indicopleustes* ('who sailed to India'), which expounds his idiosyncratic religious topography of the world, therefore called the *Christian Topography*, and apparently written around the mid-6th century AD in Alexandria.[896] Throughout the text, though, the anonymous author continually refers to his previous exploits during the first half of the 6th century, as a merchant having sailed both the Mediterranean, Red Sea and Persian Gulf.[897] He explicitly mentions having visited the ancient Ethiopian kingdom of Axum's Red Sea port of Adulis,[898] as well as travelling further down the Gulf of Aden, bypassing the island of Socotra on a trip towards India,[899]

[891] *P.Mich.* V, 245; cf. Boak 1937.
[892] Gibbs 2011: 298–99.
[893] On the collection of taxes by professional associations in Tebtynis, see Langelotti 2016; in Roman Egypt more generally, van Minnen 1987: 48–9, and Venticinque 2016: 44–45.
[894] See especially Gabrielsen 2016b: 92–95, but also Liu 2009: 15, Gibbs 2011: 296, and Langelotti 2016: 121.
[895] For loans of professional associations in Roman Egypt, see van Minnen 1987: 65–6, and Venticinque 2016: 42–3, 82–3, 92. In *BGU* IV, 1137, the priest of an association (an unspecified *synodos*) receives money to clear the debt of a member to a third party, crediting the advanced amount against his own debts to the association (Alexandria, 6 BC). Compare the hypothecated loan of an Alexandrian association of spice- or condiment-dealers, *P.Ross.Georg.* II, 30 (2nd cen AD). Ptolemaic era loans extended by associations are also attested: Martinez 1997, and Martinez and Williams 1997. For *eranos*-loans in Alexandria, 19–10 BC: *BGU* IV, 1133–6, 1165; on this type of loan and associations of *eranistai* from Classical times into the Roman period, see now Thomsen 2015.
[896] Wolska-Conus 1968, I: 15–19; this edition of the *Christian Topography* abbreviated below as *Chr.Top.*
[897] On his identification as a merchant: *Chr.Top.* II.54, 56, and on having sailed the 'three gulfs' for commerce: II.29.
[898] *Chr.Top.* II.54–64.
[899] *Chr.Top.* III.65.

but, unfortunately, never made it further than the Horn of Africa on this occasion due to a storm.[900] In addition, he possesses a wealth of information about Sri Lanka, in particular, but also, it appears, about the entire network of trade routes extended between East Africa, the Persian Gulf, Southern India, Sri Lanka and China, the latter being of particular interest as the origin of high-quality silk.[901]

However, whether or not the author of the *Christian Topography* ever travelled in person to South India or Sri Lanka or instead obtained his information from other merchants who may have gone there, or, at least, thought or claimed that they did, is an open question.[902] Nonetheless, there can be no doubt that the author himself provides an illuminating picture of an independent, and surprisingly erudite, Alexandrian merchant whose personal exploits included having sailed at least the Red Sea and Gulf of Aden (perhaps also the Persian Gulf and the waters off South India and Sri Lanka) and whose mercantile activities regularly brought him into contact with other more or less well-informed Eastern travellers. As such, this sea-going merchant turned Christian topographer may add a third facet to our concrete knowledge of traders travelling down the Red Sea, representing a traveller who appears to have been more free and independent than the agent returning from East Africa, but less resourceful and experienced than the successful merchant returning from Muziris.

In summary, then, the *modus operandi* of the Roman long-distance trade with the Indian Ocean over the centuries involved Italian families sending out slaves, freedmen and freeborn members themselves to the Red Sea ports of Egypt, Alexandrian merchants and financiers possessing far-flung networks of agents operating a route stretching all the way to South India and back, as well as members of the economical and political elite of Egypt participating both as backers of the trade and collectors of the tax on it. While all of these examples have been comparatively early, dating mainly to the 1st and 2nd century AD, we have now touched briefly upon later evidence for involvement in the trade, too, in the guise of merchants of Byzantine Alexandria, being a later development which will be corroborated further in the following chapter.

900 *Chr.Top.* II.30.
901 On the network of trade routes revealed in the *Chr.Top.* see especially Mango 1996: 153–62, on II.45-46, 49-57, 64; III.65; XI.13-19, 21-24.3
902 Cf. the cautious and well informed discussion in Faller 2011.

Chapter 7

Towards a wider world of trade in the ancient Indian Ocean

Building on the findings of the last chapter on the role of private networks, diasporas and associations within the Empire in the supply of Indian Ocean goods to Roman ports and cities, this chapter will simply move the focus beyond the borders of the Roman Empire. In consequence, various kinds of mercantile organisations originating elsewhere in the Near East and along the littoral of the Indian Ocean will be subjected to further study, particularly as regards their active presence in the margins of the states involved, being the Roman Empire as well as East African, South Arabian and Indian kingdoms. In this way, the chapter will criss-cross back and forth between East and West, highlighting trade routes and seeking out concrete evidence of the traders operating them. Thus, the ground will be prepared for the next chapter, which will provide an overview of both the role of Indian organisations in producing and exporting desired goods to the Roman Mediterranean, as well as of some important Roman commodities being exported to India in reply to a similarly consistent kind and level of demand. The people trading and moving these goods between East and West, as well as their ways of organising themselves, are the subject of the present chapter.

Egyptian ports of the desert, gateways of the sea

The city of Koptos played a crucial role as the linchpin of Roman infrastructure in the Eastern Desert. Situated on the banks of the Nile, Koptos was both an important religious and administrative centre, as well as a commercial hub due to its riverine port and position at the head of the desert routes to Myos Hormos and Berenike.[903] Thus, Koptos was not only 'the market next to the Nile for Indian and Arabian trade goods,'[904] but also the seat of the 'prefect of the desert of Berenike,' being the military commander in charge of infrastructure and security in the Eastern Desert, especially as concerns the vital roads with forts and wells, the imperial quarries and mines, and, of course, the Red Sea ports.[905] The role of the city in the long-distance trade is attested by papyri which show how the silver price in Koptos was known to fluctuate on a daily basis in the early 2nd century AD,[906] silver being a vital export for use as a means of exchange in the trade with India,[907] and how great loans were taken out in town, likely to help finance endeavours seeking to profit from the long-distance trade.[908]

This mixed role of the city is brought out in exemplary fashion by the already mentioned 'Koptos tariff' of AD 90, listing a number of groups regularly using the established roads to traverse the Eastern Desert, but keeping in mind that some groups might have been exempt from payment (like merchants, transporters and soldiers, otherwise attested in *ostraca*), and that some professions might simply have been lumped into the closest comparable category 'by proxy.' The professions at the top of the list are clearly related to the technical aspects of Red Sea maritime trade, being: Red Sea helmsman (eight *drachmai*), officer in charge of the bow of the ship (ten *dr.*), guard? (ten *dr.*—the reading of this word is uncertain, though), sailor (five *dr.*), shipwright (five *dr.*), and artisan (eight *dr.*). Next come different categories of women: for prostitution (108 *dr.*), leaving by sea (20 *dr.*), and women of the soldiers (20 *dr.*—that is, partners outside of marriage). Then, for a pass-ticket (*pittakion*) in itself, the presumably mandatory seal of which cost extra

---

903 Rathbone 2002; Cuvigny 2000 and Ballet 2000.

904 Pliny *NH*, V.11. Also Strabo XVII.1.45: 'all the Indian, Arabian, and such Ethiopian merchandise as is imported by the Arabian Gulf is carried to Koptos, which is the market for such commodities.'

905 *Praefectus Montis Berenicidis*, 'mons' here referring to the high plateau of the Eastern Desert, not to a mountain as such; the corresponding title in Greek was *eparchos orous Berenikês*. Often used in an abbreviated form, 'prefect of Berenike,' which will henceforth be employed here. See Cuvigny 2003, II: 295–305.

906 *P. Giss.* I, 47 (AD 117). Johnson 1936: 444–45, no. 277.

907 *O.Petr.* 290, recording the delivery at Myos Hormos in AD 62 of three talents of silver (worth 4500 *denarii*) and one basketful of tetradrachms (since Tiberius of the same metal value as Roman *denarii*). Johnson 1936: 382, no. 230.

908 *P.Lond.* II, 196 (AD 117/8), cf. Rathbone 2002: 189. Here, one soldier borrowed more than 23,000 *dr.* from another soldier on security of an estate in the Fayyum, which can be compared with the activities of Ptolemaic soldiers vouching as guarantors for a trip down the Red Sea to East Africa, see chapter six.

(two *obols*): for camels (one *ob.*), for each outward journey ticket of a man going up into the desert (one *dr.*), for all women going up (four *dr.*), for a donkey (two *ob.*), for a covered wagon (four *dr.*), for a mast (20 *dr.*), and for a sail yard (four *dr.*). Finally, burial parties passing up and down the road also had to pay (one *dr.*, three ob.).[909] In consequence, through this inscription documenting control over traffic through the desert and the imposition of 'road pricing,' we obtain an interesting 'cross section'-view of those travelling on the roads, as well as of the intertwining of commercial logistics and local administration.

Previously, under the Ptolemies, Berenike had been reached from the Nile city of Apollinopolis Magna further south, and Myos Hormos from Koptos.[910] The earliest Roman building programme opening up the Koptos–Berenike route, by constructing cisterns (*lacci*) in two places (as well as at Berenike and Myos Hormos), appears to date back to 30–4 BC,[911] still requiring travellers to spend some of their nights sleeping in unfortified shelters (*mansiones*, such as at the *paneion* of Wadi Minayh, attested by dated graffiti to have been in use from 4 BC–AD 46), as described later in a 12-day itinerary by Pliny, who also names three wells (*hydreumata*, from the Greek) added in the meantime.[912] Subsequently, two of the central stations on the route were expanded to comprise fortlets (*praesidia*), wells and cisterns, in AD 76/7, and a third such station was added just outside Berenike, by order of the prefect of Egypt, the work being carried out by the prefect of Berenike.[913] Meanwhile, the route to Myos Hormos saw a similar development with the construction of well-watered fortlets, particularly during the Flavian period.[914] Likewise, Koptos under Domitian saw not only the erection of the 'road tariff,' but also the construction in AD 90 of a bridge near that city.[915] During the reign of Trajan, the string of stations providing water and protection on the route to Myos Hormos reached its greatest extent with intervals of only some 25 km in between.[916]

Particularly in light of the later conflicts erupting in the region, it should be apparent that most travellers might, in fact, have been quite happy to pay a fare for their passage in return for the services of the prefect of Berenike in policing an otherwise inhospitable territory and garrisoning fortified roadside stations, in light of the danger posed by plundering nomads. A danger vividly attested by *ostraca* unearthed at *praesidia* on the routes, as well as at the imperial quarry of Mons Claudianus to the north of them.[917] For instance, a message was sent in great haste from the southern frontier of the Eastern Desert to the *praesidia* on the Myos Hormos route, warning them to be on the alert in light of a sustained attack by 60 Bedouins (*barbaroi*) on a *praesidium* in the South. The defenders managed to repel the marauders after at least two days of sustained fighting, 13th–14th March AD 118, losing one infantryman and a child on the first day, as well as a woman and two children abducted, probably losing a cavalryman on the second day and having at least one more soldier wounded—the remaining lines of the account are, unfortunately, illegible.[918] In AD 186/7, we even hear of two Roman soldiers deserting their comrades in the face of 'weak and unarmed' Bedouins, leading to the surrender of the remaining Roman soldiers of the unit, as far north as Mons Claudianus, 80 km north of the Koptos–Myos Hormos route.[919]

These dangers aside, we have a pretty good idea about the use of these roads in the long-distance trade in the 1st and 2nd century AD, because three different groups of sources shed light on it: first, the so-called Nikanor Archive, covering the entire Julio-Claudian period, reveals how consecutive generations of a family of cameleers transported victuals and goods to the ports, deducting the costs from their customers' accounts, *logoi*, kept at the main office in Koptos.[920] Second, the already mentioned corpus of *ostraca* unearthed at the customs station (*pylê*) of Berenike, dating from the beginning of the 1st century

[909] *I.Portes* 67 = *OGIS* 674 = *IGGR* 1183. See mainly Cuvigny 2003, II: 374–5; but also Young 2001: 48–50.
[910] Brun 2003: 188–191; Sidebotham 2011: 28–31.
[911] *I.Portes* 56. Romanis 1996a: 219–24. However, others would date it differently, cf. Rathbone 2002: 182 n14.
[912] Pliny *NH*, VI.26.
[913] Bagnall *et al.* 2001: 325–9 (*I.Pan* 68 and two recently found inscriptions).
[914] Brun 2003: 196–8.
[915] *I.Portes* 68.
[916] Brun 2003: 198.
[917] For a list of *ostraca* attesting skirmishes with 'desert barbarians,' see Cuvigny 2003, II: 351–2. Note that the raiding of caravans between Koptos and the Red Sea had even become a literary trope, cf. the *Ephesian Tale* mentioned above, chapter six.
[918] *O.Krok.* 87.
[919] Bülow-Jacobsen 2013.
[920] Seminal article by Fuks 1951, followed by Ruffing 1993. Now, the best treatment available is Funghi *et al.* 2012: 143–64.

AD to the early 2nd century AD, documents customs fees on export goods for the outfitting of ships, paid at Koptos by merchants and their agents involved in the long-distance trade.[921] And third, as we have seen above, the *recto* of the Muziris Papyrus informs us about movement in the opposite direction, that is, from the ports to Koptos, in the mid-2nd century AD.[922] Finally, *ostraca* uncovered at the forts reveal very little about the long-distance trade, merely mentioning the occasional passage of a merchant or helmsman, as well as attesting the use of frankincense and pepper by the inhabitants (military and civilian) of the forts themselves.[923]

In addition, two other 'direct' routes from the Nile to the Red Sea were established in the early 2nd century AD, namely, Trajan's Canal and the *Via Nova Hadriana*. The former was a canal created by dredging up an old arm of the Nile branching far enough eastwards to connect that river with the Gulf of Suez. There is no scholarly agreement, however, about whether the canal was mainly used for irrigation, or also served as an important route (perhaps only during the annual inundation of the Nile) for barge traffic between its riverine outlet at Babylon on the Nile (near modern Cairo) and the Red Sea port called variously Arsinoë, Cleopatris or Clysma.[924] In fact, the same thing can be said about Hadrian's 'new road' (established in AD 137) from Antinoopolis on the Nile, straight across the desert to the sea, following the coast south through every port all the way to Berenike. Although this route went through safe and level places, being equipped with wells, way-stations and small forts, according to the inscription, there is hardly any actual evidence for its use in the Eastern trade.[925] The scarcity of sources attesting use of these two monumental initiatives of the emperors, who also seem to have had military and administrative purposes in mind, seems to indicate that they could not compete with the long-established routes of the Eastern Desert. Remarkably, these two cases may, in other words, attest top-down imperial policies being rejected by the established commercial networks.

By the end of the 2nd and beginning of the 3rd century AD, though, the *praesidia* of the Myos Hormos route gradually ceased to function and were never systematically reoccupied,[926] this port being abandoned around that time. However, although Koptos became embroiled in several conflicts from around AD 270 until the very end of the century, being captured by both Blemmyes and rebels and sacked by Roman generals a couple of times, the city evidently flourished in Late Antiquity (also being a Christian religious centre).[927] The route to Berenike continued to operate, in spite of a later Blemmye takeover of at least the lower part of the Eastern Desert, until that port's final demise in the mid-6th century AD.[928] By that time, the ports of Clysma (former Arsinoë/Cleopatris) in the Gulf of Suez and Aila in the Gulf of Aqaba had risen to prominence in the Indian Ocean trade, growing in importance from the 4th–7th century AD.[929]

After many years of debate, Myos Hormos has now been firmly identified as the present site of Quseir-al Qadim,[930] possibly dating back as far as the 3rd century BC, although no substantial Ptolemaic finds have been made dating back earlier than 50 BC. The harbour was expanded in a major way by the Romans in the late 1st century BC and early 1st century AD, with maintenance being evident for the late 1st and early 2nd century, while silting becomes severe from the late 2nd century, ultimately leading to the obstruction of the harbour and its consequent abandonment around the mid-3rd century.[931] The settlement seems to have grown haphazardly with no proper street grid, the busiest seasons (July and

[921] Treated both in chapter five and six; Bagnall *et al.* 2000–5, vols. I–II.
[922] Chapter six.
[923] *O.Krok.* 41, l. 58 (*emporoi*); *O.Didym.* 84, l. 7 (*emporos*); 125 (*emporos* and camels/cameleer); 248 (*emporos*); 319, l. 15 (frankincense); 323, l. 10 (frankincense); 327, l. 3 (pepper); 328, l. 4 (pepper); 364, l. 9 (pepper); 399, between ll. 1–3 (pepper); 466 (ship drawing, and *archikybernis*?~master helmsman?). From the old Apollinopolis Magna–Berenike route, a shipper is also attested in Roman times (*c.* 200 AD?): *I.El-Kanaïs* 57 (*nauklêros*).
[924] Young 2001: 75–7; Romanis 2002; Adams 2007: 33–5; Cooper 2009; Jördens 2009: 417–23; Sidebotham 2011: 179–8; Wilson 2015: 21 n31; Aubert 2015.
[925] *Pan du désert* 80. Young 2001: 78–9; Adams 2007: 41–2; Sidebotham 2011: 127–30, 138–9, 144.
[926] Brun 2003: 201–2.
[927] Rathbone 2002: 194–6; Brun 2003: 203–4; Fournet 2000.
[928] Sidebotham 2011: 133–5, list, and chapter 13. Power 2012: 33–46.
[929] Tomber 2008: 66, 69; Parker 2009: 82–3; Ward 2007: 161–71; Mayerson 1996; Power 2012: 28–32. On the distribution at Indian Ocean sites of the characteristic 'Aila/Aqaba amphora,' see Damgaard *et al.* 2013.
[930] Bülow-Jacobsen *et al.* 1994; and Cuvigny 2003, I: 26–7.
[931] Peacock and Blue 2006: 174–176.

January) perhaps seeing the small resident population rising to a thousand people.[932] Imports from South or Southeast Asia of black pepper, rice, coconut and mung bean, have been identified at the site, dated to the 1st–early 3rd century AD.[933]

Further south, the early 3rd century BC port of Berenike peaked in size and apparent activity in the 1st century AD, experiencing a long period of stagnation in the 3rd century, but then went on to see an increased trade with India and Sri Lanka from the mid-4th century until sometime in the 5th century, before being finally abandoned around AD 550.[934] The settlement appears to have been of a similar size to, or even slightly larger than, Myos Hormos, at least in the early Roman period (1000+), and was also better planned and laid out, building materials generally being of a higher quality. For instance, Late Roman Berenike, which has been more thoroughly excavated, had a commercial quarter with multiple-storey buildings, one or more warehouses next to the harbour, a potential lighthouse, and a large church-like complex.[935] Archaeobotanical finds at Berenike from South and Southeast Asia include coconut, Job's tears, rice, emblic, black pepper and mung bean.[936]

Contrary to the apparent early 1st–2nd century AD peak in the Indian Ocean trade and subsequent slow demise which might be surmised from the state of the roads and ports, though, a survey of the papyrological evidence reveals that Indian spices are non-existent in 1st century AD papyri (as in Ptolemaic), and rare in those of the 2nd century, while the great majority appear in papyri and *ostraca* from the 3rd–4th century.[937] A case in point is a rather well-preserved letter from the 2nd half of the 3rd century, measuring a number of Indian, Arabian and East African spices and aromatics in 'pounds of Koptos.'[938] Thus, we should beware of taking the condition of the military roads through the desert, or the demise of Myos Hormos and struggle of Berenike in the 3rd century AD, as directly indicative of the level of trade with the Indian Ocean.

One very good reason for this being that while the equipment of the routes reflects the active involvement of the Roman imperial authorities in the province,[939] the actual trade through the desert was kept up by merchants from near and far, not the state, and they would continue to keep the trade going as long as it was profitable (and possible) for them. Remarkably, it did not much matter to them whether they conducted their business under the aegis of Romans, Arabs, Blemmyes, Axumites or any of the Indian kingdoms involved in the Indian Ocean trade. Accordingly, the weakening of Roman rule and influence along the western coast of the Red Sea was merely offset by the rise of Blemmyes in the lower part of the Eastern Desert,[940] now being entitled to taxes instead, and by the commercial and regional ascendancy of the kingdom of Axum in the southern Red Sea,[941] as well as an increased importance of Indian trading networks in the West, as we shall see shortly.[942]

So, who were the people who kept up trade between the Mediterranean and the Indian Ocean via Egypt from the 1st–6th century AD, in addition to those we have already encountered in the previous chapter? First of all, Koptos itself yields further evidence of the upper echelons of society in Roman Egypt engaging in the long-distance trade. First, a later 2nd–early 3rd century AD inscription from just south of Koptos, at the important temple of Medamud, informs us that two women of curatorial or equestrian status, being free to conduct business without a guardian (*matrōnai stolatai*), were 'merchants and shippers of the Red Sea,' employing a man also named in the inscription as either their manager of affairs in the

[932] Peacock and Blue 2011: 345, 347.
[933] v. d. Veen 2011: 40–53; also the less well-known myrobalan.
[934] Sidebotham 2011: 221, 261, 279–80.
[935] Sidebotham 2011: 55–65, 68, 268–75.
[936] Cappers 2006: 49–135, catalogue.
[937] Raschke 1975: 244.
[938] *PSI* XV, 1558; Cuvigny 2000: 172, w. cat. 138, p. 173.
[939] On Roman policy and actual state involvement in the region see now, in addition to Sidebotham 1986, the chapter by Nappo 2015.
[940] Sidebotham 2011: 267, 280. On the question of who or what the Blemmyes actually were, see also Barnard 2005.
[941] Phillips 1997: 449–56; Phillipson 2012: 195–207; Tomber 2008: 88–93; detailed representative case-study illustrating this development by Manzo 2005.
[942] Compare the interpretation of apparent decline in Roman trade with India in Cobb 2015b, especially p. 191: 'it may be that the evidence does not reflect simply a downturn but rather shifting patterns of trade.'

trade or as the captain of their ships, depending on the specific restoration of a lacuna in the text.[943] While these aristocratic and entrepreneurial woman could have been either from Alexandria or Koptos, the dedicant of an inscription dated *c.* 260 AD was certainly a local city councillor of Koptos, *bouleutês*, and either merchant or shipper of the Red Sea, seeing as the qualifying adjective *E]rythraïkos* is securely preserved, but the noun before has been lost.[944] Thus, the local local elite was also involved in the long-distance trade.

This fact is borne out further by the attested involvement of a prominent Egyptian family of magnates resident at Koptos. According to the Greek inscriptions of this family's epigraphic dossier, a peristyle was dedicated in AD 21/22 to the gods Isis (the main deity of Koptos), Harpocrates (her son), and Pan (Egyptian Min) by 'Paminis, son of Parthenios, and Parthenios, the son.' This was followed ten years later, in AD 32, by a dedication to Kronos (father of Isis), by 'Parthenios, son of Paminis, *prostatês* of Isis.' Two similar dedications by this son and *prostatês* of Isis, meaning that he was in charge of the finances of the main temple of Koptos, can probably be dated to the later years of Tiberius, and he is also mentioned in this function in an inscription from the reign of Claudius.[945] The Greek inscriptions are a minority in the corpus, though, and by the latest count the total number of documents including hieroglyphic and Demotic texts exceed twenty, dating from Tiberius to Nero. In other words, the Paminis family played a crucial role in the religious life of Koptos for decades.[946] However, Paminis, the father, and two of his other sons were also involved over many years in the supply of wheat to the ports and settlements of Myos Hormos and Berenike, employing at least seven different agents at the ports, from at least AD 26–38/9.[947] Most likely, these agents of the Paminis family forwarded consignments of goods back to their masters in Koptos, having obtained them either dockside in Myos Hormos and Berenike or by venturing out to sea themselves.

Other Greco-Romans and Egyptians active in the trade between Koptos and the Red Sea ports are merely attested by their names, occurring in *ostraca* and papyri excavated at Berenike.[948] Moreover, in previous chapters we have already encountered a number of people involved in the long-distance trade: the *Annii*, *Calpurnii*, *Vestorii*, *Numidii*, and *Munatii* of Campania, who had agents on the route to Berenike, the *Peticii* of Samnium with agents on the route to Myos Hormos, likewise Alexandrian families, such as the *Julii* and the *Norbanii*, whose *modus operandi* is documented in detail by the Muziris Papyrus, as well as landed families of the Fayyum as attested in the letter from an agent returning to Berenike. Finally, trade in the later period, 4th–mid-6th century AD, is attested by Byzantine travellers leaving graffiti at wadi Minayh (which appears to have been out of use from the mid-1st–early 4th century AD[949]), two of these even recording the names of the ships they had seen off at Berenike, *Eirene* and *Theoktistos*, another recording that it had taken him 13 days to walk back from that port.[950]

Presently, we come to the role of Nikanor and his sons (referred to previously), as transporters on the desert route from Koptos to Myos Hormos and Berenike, whose activities yield valuable information about transport, commodities and the identities of people involved in the long-distance trade, as well as their agents. A corpus of 95 *ostraca*, spanning the years from 18 BC–AD 69,[951] reveal how this family firm based at Koptos transported commodities for people holding accounts with them, called *logoi*, to either Myos Hormos or Berenike, delivering the goods to agents (a few being women[952]) of the owners against a written *ostracon* receipt, the latter being carried back to Koptos and eventually discarded. These receipts for goods being carried to the ports can in turn be compared to the 'let pass'-*ostraca* from the

[943] *SEG* 8:103; Jouguet 1931. For other female shippers from the Roman period, see Broekaert 2013: nos. 417 (Siracusa), 419 (Constanta).
[944] *IGR* I,5 1181. For this and the previous inscription, see Tacoma 2006: 84–5.
[945] *Pan du Desert* 78. *Portes du Desert* 58–61.
[946] Reinach and Weill 1912; Denecker and Vandorpe 2007: 123, nn104–7.
[947] Funghi *et al.* 2012: 159–60, nos. 3–6, 9, 16–7, 19, 21.
[948] Cf. the considerable lists of names derived from the Berenike *ostraca* and papyri: Bagnall *et al.* 2000: 24–30; 2005: 9–14.
[949] During which period, at least up until the early or mid-3rd century AD, the nearby forts of Didymoi (to the north-west) and Aphrodito (to the east) will have provided shelter instead. The present *post quem* for the abandonment of Didymoi being AD 235/6, cf. Brun 2003: 201. Sidebotham 2011: 135, believes that it continued to function into the 4th century AD.
[950] Cuvigny *et al.* 1999: nos. 48, 50, 52; there are at least fourteen Byzantine graffiti.
[951] An up-to-date list of *ostraca* and their timeframe is available in Funghi *et al.* 2012: 143. See also Ruffing 1993: 1–2.
[952] Such as Isidora, daughter of Menodoros, agent of Gaius Norbanus Ptolemaios, treated above, in *O.Petr.Mus.* 122, 125—for other possible business relations of hers, see Funghi *et al.* 2012: 157.

customs station at Berenike, which document the arrival of goods in port on which the relevant taxes had duly been paid in Koptos. Only two *ostraca* from the Nikanor archive document deliveries to other destinations, namely, to the *praesidium* of *Persou* on the route to Myos Hormos, and to *Apollonos Hydreuma*, on the route to Berenike,[953] that is, to military recipients.

In addition to Nikanor himself, both his sons and grandsons appear in the *corpus* as active in the family business,[954] the exact nature of their profession being apparent from an *ostracon* in which Nikanor is referred to as a *kamêlitês*, that is, 'cameleer' or 'transporter by camel caravan.'[955] The largest attested amount of goods carried by them on a single outbound trip required at the very least a caravan of 36 camels (carrying 6.5 tonnes of wheat), but the family could have owned or been able to hire more, if necessary.[956] Recipients were military personnel of various ranks, imperial slaves, and, of course, private individuals, while the goods carried were mainly grain (almost half of all cargoes), barley, bread, wine (one quarter of all cargoes, Egyptian as well as Mediterranean), and, finally, the enigmatic *pharmaka*, weighed by liquid measure, being either some kind of medicinal drug, dye or chemical reagent.[957] A few other kinds of items were also transported, albeit only infrequently and in small numbers.[958]

Significantly, a comprehensive analysis by K. Ruffing comparing the goods transported, and at what times of year, with the products listed as exports in the *Periplus*, reveals that Nikanor and Sons' activities must have predominantly pertained to the supply of people at the ports, the departure dates of ships for East Africa, South Arabia and South Asia being July–September, while the most active months in the Nikanor archive are May–June. In particular, when the goods transported are broken down into commodity groups, it becomes apparent that the most important commodity, grain, was transported in connection with the Egyptian harvest (May), not ship departures, and that the second most transported good, wine, arrived mainly in October–January, that is, when ships started their return to Egypt from abroad.[959] Some grain and wine could, of course, have been stockpiled throughout the year for use in supplying the ships before their late summer departures. However, it is certain that Myos Hormos and Berenike were reliant on large imports of foodstuffs, especially preceding departures in late summer and upon returns in late winter or early spring, when the population peaked.

In summary, though, the people attested as holders of accounts, *logoi*, with Nikanor should not merely be seen as engaged in the business of supplying the ports generally, but as financiers and merchants of the long-distance trade with dependants at the ports (the agents, administrators and managers of the Muziris papyrus), whose consignments were used to sustain their own people and stockpile supplies for outbound ships, any surplus supplies likely finding eager buyers in the rather tenuously connected market of the port settlements.[960] Regular state-supervised supply of food to the ports (which does not mean that it was free, only that the state considered it of vital interest), as different from the private supplies of individual merchants, is, on the other hand, the explicit subject in half a dozen *ostraca* concerning the transport of 'monthly provisions' (*epimênia*) to the ports, in an *ostracon* from a fort on the route to Myos Hormos referring to 'those who carry the food supply to Myos Hormos,' and in an *ostracon* indicating that Nikanor was under contract to supply a *praesidium* on the route to Berenike with grain on a monthly basis.[961]

At this point it also becomes relevant to survey the *ostraca* unearthed at the customs station of Berenike more widely. Significantly, a lot of the goods mentioned in these *ostraca* were expressly destined for the 'outfitting' or 'equipping,' *exartismos*, of ships, the name of one of the ships so mentioned, the

953 *O.Petr.Mus.* 112, 149; both of grain.
954 Also, a partner is briefly attested, see Ruffing 1993: 3; Funghi *et al.* 2012: 147f.
955 Funghi *et al.* 2012: 148–9; *O.Petr.Mus.* 192, l. 2.
956 Adams 2007: 222–3.
957 Funghi *et al.* 2012: 151–64; note that *purpur* is no longer read by the editors on *O.Petr.Mus.* 172, l. 4, removing this product from the list of commodities carried by Nikanor, p. 164. An older list is provided by Ruffing 1993: 8–10, 26.
958 For a list, see Ruffing 1993: 14.
959 Ruffing 1993: 17–25.
960 Compare Ruffing 1993: 24, and Adams 2007: 224–5.
961 See Adams 2007: 222, 225 n19; *O.Petr.* 227, 246; *O.Ber.* I, 4, 20, 43, 78; Bülow-Jacobsen *et al.* 1994: *O.Max.* 4, ll. 12–13 (2nd century AD).

Gymnasiarchis, being included and preserved on one *ostracon*.[962] The *corpus* as a whole dates from the very first years of the 1st century AD until the final years of Trajan, and is therefore to a large extent contemporaneous with the Nikanor Archive.[963] In addition to a minor group of miscellaneous *ostraca*, the majority of the available *corpus* is made up by dossiers of 'let pass'-chits issued by seven named individuals,[964] whose exact official titles and capacities remain unclear, though, and they might well have held different positions within the military and fiscal administration of the Eastern Desert.[965] Moreover, their names attest both Egyptians, Greeks and Romans, mixed affiliations being common.[966]

As regards the cargoes ordered to clear customs at Berenike, the most frequently attested commodity, which also appears in the largest quantities, is wine, while the second runner-up, albeit much less frequent, is oil (not wheat and wine, respectively, as in the Nikanor Archive). Most individual cargoes are, however, comparatively small, as were the majority of cargoes carried by Nikanor, but in the Berenike *corpus* many consignments are explicitly for the outfitting of ships, *eis exartismos*, and we must therefore assume that most merchants had their assembled exports broken down into smaller lots to be carried across the desert in several consecutive caravans, being reassembled over time in warehouses at the ports prior to loading aboard a ship for departure.[967] One such involved merchant is even attested in an *ostracon* clearing his goods through customs on his own authority, implying a certain rank and influence at the port.[968] Moreover, not all consignments were small scale, as the dossier of Sarapion, son of Kasios, reveals: although the size of his cargoes of wine was not out of the ordinary, he also shipped 1286 bags (contents unknown) to Berenike in 12 different caravans, the largest single shipment running into 235 bags, the second-largest shipments being three of 160 bags each.[969]

Of special interest, moreover, is the dossier of twelve *ostraca* issued by an official abbreviating his own name as *Herak()*, all pertaining to consignments cleared through customs for a certain Varus. All twelve 'let pass'-chits specify that the goods, among which Laodicean wine figures prominently, are intended for outfitting. However, while the majority of these texts read 'release for outfitting of those (people) of Varus,' *apolyson tōn Ouraou exartismon*, two instead mention the clearing of goods 'for the outfitting of the (ships) of Varus,' *eis exartismon tōn Ouarou*, implying that Varus might have been an important businessman with a number of people stationed at Berenike outfitting several ships for him at the same time, either vessels he owned or had chartered.[970] However, the differing formulations might also simply be down to a scribal lack of care, in which case Varus was only in the process of outfitting one ship after all.

Finally, a combination of the information contained in the Archive of Nikanor and the Berenike customs *corpus*, supplemented by evidence from stamped amphora stoppers, allows us to glean something about indirect imperial involvement in the long-distance trade via Koptos and the Red Sea ports.[971] First of all, seven slaves of the consecutive emperors Tiberius, Caligula, Claudius and Nero, possibly even Vespasian, are attested on *ostraca* in the Red Sea port of Berenike, receiving food supplies as well as wine.[972] Second, *ostraca* reveal at least six freedmen of the emperors Augustus, Claudius and Nero, involved in the shipment of supplies (including wine for the outfitting of ships) to Myos Hormos and Berenike. [973] Third, the names of about a dozen freedmen, mainly of Claudius and Nero but also with at least one representative each for Augustus and the Flavians, have been read on the plaster plugs of Egyptian wine amphora stoppers

[962] Bagnall *et al.* 2000: 8–11; 2005: 5. The ship *Gymnasiarchis* is mentioned in *O.Ber.* I, 86, l. 5.
[963] Bagnall *et al.* 2000: 7; 2005: 4–5.
[964] Bagnall *et al.* 2000: 4–7; 2005: 3.
[965] At least one was a tax-farmer, *telonarios*, mentioned in *O.Ber.* I, 89, l. 3, and *O.Ber.* II, 219, l. 2, might similarly contain a *misthwtês*.
[966] Bagnall *et al.* 2000: 28–30.
[967] Bagnall *et al.* 2000: 14–6.
[968] *O.Ber.* I, 94.
[969] Bagnall *et al.* 2005: 63–4.
[970] Bagnall *et al.* 2000: 13–14, *O.Ber.* I, 68–79; Rathbone 2002: 189 n34.
[971] On slaves and freedmen handling imperial property in Egypt generally, see Parassoglou 1978: 21, 52; on the involvement of the imperial *familia* in the Red Sea trade specifically, see the cautions remarks by Bowman 2010: 106.
[972] Funghi *et al.* 2012: 153–4. *O.Petr.Mus*, 161, 163–4, 166–7, 181–2, 171, 186. *O.Ber.* I, 106; II. 184–88.
[973] Funghi *et al.* 2012: 155. *O.Petr.Mus*, 137–8, 145, 147, 179, 204. *O.Ber.* I, 51–66, 80–5; II, 147–8.

found in Myos Hormos, Berenike and Koptos, dated 1st–early 2nd century AD, revealing a connection to imperial estates producing wine for use in the Eastern trade (as supplies or exports).[974]

So much for the Roman side of things in Egypt's Eastern Desert. In the following, we shall delve into the roles of foreign groups who did not sit idly in their home ports waiting for visits by Roman traders, but frequented not only the Egyptian Red Sea ports, but even Koptos across the desert, some of them perhaps making it as far as Alexandria.

Arabs, Axumites, and Indians in the desert

Remarkably, it appears that even Koptos itself was a city of outlandish people, being 'common to both Egyptians and Arabs,' according to Strabo,[975] and having a quarter of town called 'of the Arabs' after its original inhabitants.[976] Therefore, the Arabarch is likely to have been so named from Ptolemaic times onwards for the power he had to wield over 'Arabs,' understood simply as people living in the desert, that is, both local inhabitants from the Eastern Desert as well as foreign visitors from Arabia proper.[977]

Indeed, South Arabian inscriptions from the 5th–2nd century BC mention that the ancient kingdom of Maīn conducted long-distance trade with Egypt.[978] One Minaean was explicitly attached to a temple of the Egyptian goods as importer of myrrh and calamus, and was buried in that country.[979] Furthermore, men from Maīn are known to have taken (and duly paid for) wives from Egypt, generally, and Gaza, specifically, the latter of course being the Ptolemaic terminus of the 'Incense Trail,' on which see below.[980] A Minaean is even attested in Ptolemaic times by his graffito near wadi Minayh, which would later become a popular halt for Roman traders in the early 1st century AD, on the route between Koptos and Berenike.[981]

The long history of trade between South Arabia and Egypt as well as the Arab roots of Koptos taken into consideration, it should thus come as no surprise to find one *Hermerōs*, son of *Athêniōn*, being a citizen of Aden, *Adaneitês*, and Red Sea merchant, *emporos Erythraios*, erecting a dedication in AD 70 at Koptos to Isis and Hera.[982] Aden was otherwise known to the Romans as *Eudaemon Arabia*, being an important South Arabian port, albeit possibly experiencing a decline in the 1st century AD, followed by a revival in the 2nd century.[983] Remarkably, Hermeros of Aden is documented by an *ostracon*-receipt as dispatching Egyptian wine to Berenike already in AD 57, thus, revealing his long-standing establishment as Red Sea merchant at Koptos, at the very least 13 years, evidently being a regular credit-worthy customer of Nikanor's transport firm.[984]

A slightly earlier inscription from Koptos might likewise have been erected by a merchant from Aden, but here the reading of the toponym is, sadly, uncertain.[985] However, another very well integrated 'Arab' was Rhobaos, bearing a Semitic name, who ordered goods for the outfitting of ships to clear the customs station at Berenike in the later 1st century AD.[986] Indeed, two graffiti on the route to Berenike combine the Greek theophoric name 'Kronios' (Egyptian Geb, being associated with Koptos), apparently as a patronymic, with Semitic names, indicating 'Greco-Arab' family ties.[987] Testifying to a movement in the opposite direction during those same years, a Greek woman named Hikane wrote a letter from Berenike to a son of hers, a harbour-man, imploring him to help one of his brothers who, along with several other

974 Thomas 2011: 24–5, 27. One of the slaves crops up again here as freedman and *arabarch* with his name on amphora plugs; three of the freedmen attested on *ostraca* also reappear in this category.
975 Strabo XVII.1.44.
976 Rathbone 2002: 194 n53.
977 Compare Rathbone 2002: 183 n19. For the early history of the office see chapter six.
978 *Iscrizioni sudarabiche* 1974, vol. I: no. 247; Bron 1998, vol. III : nos. 7, 10.
979 *Iscrizioni sudarabiche* 1974: no. 338.
980 Bron 1998: nos. 93A–D, 95, 97.
981 *Répertoire d'épigraphie sémitique* 1900–68: no. 3571. See Cuvigny *et al.* 1999: 165.
982 *Portes du désert* 65. Wagner 1976.
983 *Periplus* 26 (1st century AD decline); Ptol. *Geog.*, VI.7 (2nd century AD revival); Sedov 2007: 98; Tomber 2008: 101–2.
984 *O.Petr.Mus.* 184.
985 *Portes du désert* 62.
986 Bagnall *et al.* 2000: 5, 27, nos. 36–49.
987 Cuvigny *et al.* 1999: nos. 61–2.

members of the family, was away in Arabia.[988] Thus, these cases serve to prove that not only traders but entire families were moving around, crossing borders, settling down, having children and setting themselves up in business abroad, some perhaps rising to office in the local administration of taxes and trade, as Rhobaos did.

More loosely attributable to the first centuries of the Common Era are a number of itinerant South Arabians, known from graffiti in the desert between the Nile and the ports. On the route to Myos Hormos have been found, *inter alia*, one graffito with a toponym from the frankincense producing kingdom of Hadramawt, one referring to a god of the myrrh producing kingdom of Qataban, and a third naming a tribe of Maīn.[989] Likewise, on the route to Berenike, a Himyarite royal monogram and a Minaean name are attested.[990] Specifically, trade between Myos Hormos and Berenike, on the one hand, and Aden, the port of Qataban, as well as Qana, the port of Hadramawt, on the other, is indicated by the large amount of basalt beach boulders identified at the Egyptian ports, mentioned in chapter five, taken on board at the Arabian ports to compensate for expensive but lightweight cargoes of frankincense and myrrh, later to be dumped on the Red Sea shore after arrival.[991]

Finally, storage jars from Hadramawt and cooking pots from Aden have been found at the early Roman ports, the more plentifully attested Hadramawtic specimens continuing into at least the fourth century AD at Berenike.[992] Among the finds at Myos Hormos were two storage jars with ancient South Arabian lettering, as well as one Hadramawtic jar with a post-firing Greek graffito, to which can be added an Indian pot with a South Arabian monogram, indicating circulation among different ethnic groups of pots from other material cultures.[993] Something we might well expect on the basis of the evidence surveyed for Arabs mingling with Greeks in the Eastern Desert.

Another group of people which can just about be made out at the ports is Ethiopians, being inhabitants of the kingdom of Axum, sailing out of their harbour of Adulis in present-day Eritrea.[994] As previously mentioned, Dio Chrysostom referred to 'Arabs and Ethiopians' in the theatre of Alexandria in the early 2nd century AD, and the *Historia Augusta* also included 'Axumites and Arabs' amongst the prisoners in Aurelian's triumph after his defeat of the rebellion in Egypt in 273 AD.[995] In fact, an Ethiopian graffito invoking the Christian god, dated 4th–6th century AD, has been found at wadi Minayh, revealing movement from Berenike to Koptos on the Nile,[996] while an *ostracon* from the late 4th–early 5th century AD at Berenike may contain Axumite writing.[997]

Somewhat enigmatically, these two instances of writing by visitors from Axum can be supplemented with an *ostracon* reading 'trogodite' from late 2nd–early 3rd century AD Myos Hormos, being the conventional term for an inhabitant of East Africa, albeit here more plausible referring to a person from neighbouring Axum.[998] Significantly, a Ptolemaic 'interpreter of Trogodytes' is known from 134 BC, which might imply that an 'interpreter and secretary' known from an AD 113–7 inscription at Berenike could likewise have been a Greek–East African mediator of sorts.[999] Of only two foreign coins found at Berenike, moreover, one was a late 3rd–early 4th century AD bronze coin from Axum.[1000] More substantial traces of Axumites present in Egypt is provided, though, by coarse wares found at both Myos Hormos and Berenike from the

[988] *O.Ber.* II, 129; Foubert 2015.
[989] Colin 1988; Cuvigny 2003, II: 276. Bülow-Jacobsen *et al.* 1995: 6 A, C, E. Meyer 1995: 200, no. 8; on the Semitic origin of the name, see Cuvigny 2003, II: 284.
[990] Cuvigny *et al.* 1999: nos. 68–70.
[991] See n593.
[992] Tomber 2008: 78.
[993] Peacock and Blue 2011: 5–9, cat. 3, 4, 5, 8.
[994] Described in *Periplus* 4–6; for archaeological reports from excavations at the site, see Peacock and Blue 2007, Zazzaro and Manzo 2012, Zazzaro 2013.
[995] See chapter six.
[996] Cuvigny *et al.* 1999: no. 53.
[997] Gragg 1996.
[998] Tomber 2005a: 41, 47f.
[999] *UPZ* II, 227 (Thebes); *O.Ber.* II, 121; for both, see Mairs 2012b: 10.
[1000] Sidebotham 2011: 248; and Sidebotham and Wendrich 2002: 30, fig. 9.

1st century AD, extending into the 5th/early 6th century AD at the latter, while a pottery assemblage at Myos Hormos even indicates that a smithy area was associated with East Africans.[1001]

Another group implicated by their pottery as users of the same smithy area at Myos Hormos was Indians, who are likewise mentioned at Alexandria and in Aurelian's procession at Rome, by Dio Chrysostom and the *Historia Augusta*—the only other foreign coin found at Berenike also being, as it happens, a silver specimen from the later 4th century AD by a Western Kshatrapa king in western India.[1002] Although evidence of what was recently thought to be a perfectly Hellenised Indian trader of the Ptolemaic period is rather based on a misinterpretation,[1003] there is by now, nonetheless, quite a considerable amount of evidence indicating the active role of people from West and South India in the long-distance trade via Roman Egypt.

First and foremost, what amounts to some twenty specimens of Indian fine wares, especially the so-called Rouletted Ware which was produced in the Ganges estuary and distributed all over India's eastern seaboard,[1004] has been found at Myos Hormos and Berenike, dated 1st century BC–1st century AD, three sherds of Rouletted Ware even cropping up at Koptos. Likewise, both ports have yielded finds of 'Arikamedu Type 10,' seemingly produced in the region of ancient Arikamedu, modern Pondicherry in Tamil Nadu, and found as far East as Bali.[1005] Indian coarse wares (one type securely sourced to Kerala on the Malabar Coast, where lay Muziris), moreover, are very common at the ports in Early Roman contexts, for instance, constituting nine per cent of one ceramic assemblage at Berenike, while two finds from Myos Hormos are of much older coarse wares suggesting contact during Ptolemaic times. In later years at Berenike, though, Indian ceramics appear to be less common. Whereas the Indian pottery at Myos Hormos is concentrated in certain areas, perhaps indicating separate living quarters for Indians (like the smithy area), the distribution at Berenike is even, although South Indian basketry has been shown to cluster in dumps at this port. Finally, the 7.5 kg of pepper found in a 1st century AD context at the Serapis temple of Berenike where, fittingly enough, stored in a large jar of Indian making, sunk into the floor of the complex.[1006]

Remarkably, the ceramic evidence can be supplemented by four finds of Indian writing and graffiti at Myos Hormos, as well as one graffito from Berenike, which are similar to finds made at Sumhuram in south-eastern Hadramawt, and at Kodumanal and Arikamedu in South India.[1007] The most substantial piece of written evidence is a unique Indian *ostracon* proper, found at Myos Hormos, written in a southern variety of Brahmi, reflecting 'an upper south Indian connection' such as the lower Krishna river, dated palaeographically to the 2nd–3rd century AD. The first two lines of this Prakrit text indicate that it constitutes an inventory of goods held in common by three named Indians, *Hālaka*, *Vinhudata* and *Nākada*, enumerating quantities of oil, meat and wine, hence, likely stores for them to live off either in port or during their eventual voyage home.[1008] In addition, Myos Hormos has now yielded three inscribed sherds, two in Tamil and the Tamil-Brahmi script dated palaeographically to the 2nd century AD, reading *Kanan* and *Cātan*,[1009] likely owner's names, and another Tamil-Brahmi graffito (twice repeated on the pot) dated from the letters to the 1st century BC, either reading 'pot (suspended) in a rope net' or *Panai Ori*, as a more conventional name.[1010] Furthermore, an inscribed Tamil-Brahmi sherd from a Dressel 2–4 amphora has been uncovered at Berenike, dated 1st century AD, reading '*Korra*[*n*] the chieftain.'[1011]

[1001] Tomber 2008: 61, 77–8.

[1002] Sidebotham 2011: 248; and Sidebotham and Wendrich 2002: 30, fig. 10.

[1003] *I.El-Kanaïs* 38, interpreted and translated by Salomon 1991: no. 3, as 'Sophon, the Indian.' However 'mahout/elephant driver' was a military rank, *indos*, in Ptolemaic Egypt (La'da 2002: 105, E872–3), as already pointed out by the editor of *I.El-Kanaïs* (Bernand 1972b: 100) and this inscription is from the Apollinopolis Magna–Berenike route, along which the Ptolemaic kings imported elephants via the Red Sea from Ethiopia (Sidebotham 2011: 39–53). In fact, *I.El-Kanaïs* 9bis mentions such an elephant-hunting expedition (with elephant drawing, pl. 54). Neither were the *arabotoxotai*, or 'Arab archers,' Arabs, rather, they were named after their Arab bows in accordance with the Ptolemaic system of military ethnics, see Hennig 2004: 275–6. The case of 'Sophon' is now exhaustively debunked by Mairs 2006: 201–5.

[1004] Schenk 2006; 2015.

[1005] Shoebridge and Coningham 2009-10.

[1006] Tomber 2008: 74–7. On the pepper jar, see also Cappers 2006: 114 and fig. 4.58, p. 116; and Sidebotham 2011: 60.

[1007] For a more exhaustive catalogue of finds in South Asia, see Mahadevan 1996a: 287–91.

[1008] Salomon 1991: no. 1, fig. 1.

[1009] Originally published in Whitcomb and Johnson 1979: pl. 27:j; and Whitcomb and Johnson 1982: pl. 61:o. See also Salomon 1991: no. 2; and Mahadevan 1996a: 291, no. 3.

[1010] Tomber 2011: 8, no. 7.

[1011] Mahadevan 1996b; 1996a: 291, no. 4.

Significantly, the *ostracon* from Myos Hormos and the inscribed Roman amphora sherd from Berenike, in particular, strongly indicate that Indian traders were resident at the ports. The *ostracon* because it concerns supplies that were available and necessary at the desert port, thus, likely being drafted there, and the find from Berenike because there must have been an agent of the Tamil chieftain present in that port to mark his locally purchased amphora with an owner's graffito. Obviously, though, any seagoing Indian merchants travelling West to trade at the Roman ports will have been forced to stay in harbour until the change of the monsoon, making for visits of several months at least. To these observations must be added, moreover, that the presence of rice in particular, but also coconuts, which were used as long-distance rations and for their useful coir fibres,[1012] at both ports is a further sign of the more long-term presence of Indian shippers and merchants. Relatively sparse finds of rice, both husked spikelets and de-husked naked grains, at Myos Hormos (22 specimens, mainly early 1st century AD) are accompanied by empty husks, thus, attesting actual de-husking in port prior to consumption.[1013] More substantial finds of rice were made at Berenike, spanning almost the entire 600 years of Roman occupation.[1014]

Interestingly, the ancient Tamil port site, settlement and production centre of Arikamedu, just south of modern Pondicherry, where Roman amphorae, terra sigillata, ceramic lamps, bulbous unguentaria and seal stones with Greco-Roman iconography have been found,[1015] has yielded not only numerous sherds with similar Tamil graffiti inscribed, mainly dated 1st–2nd century AD, but also three interesting *comparanda*. First of all, one rare 1st century AD sherd appears to give the title of 'accountant,' and lists three numbers, thus, providing an, admittedly more laconic, parallel to the Myos Hormos *ostracon*, which is otherwise considered unique.[1016] An 'accountant, chief of scribes,' is known from contemporary Madurai, capital of the Pandians.[1017] Second, the name 'Kanan' also occurs on a sherd at Arikamedu,[1018] as does, lastly, an inscribed pottery fragment dated roughly 50 BC–25 AD mentioning a 'Catan the Younger.'[1019]

In addition, a Tamil-Brahmi inscribed sherd dated 1st century AD has quite recently been unearthed at Sumhuram, the eastern port of Hadramawt, mentioned earlier, comparing remarkably well with the Tamil finds from the Roman Red Sea ports. This sherd reads *{n}antai Kiran*, that is, the personal name Kiran and an honorific title to be translated as 'elder,' 'venerable' or 'honourable,' marking the person out as of high and important standing, in this case seemingly a senior merchant.[1020] From Madurai, yet another comparable example is a Tamil-Brahmi inscription where the dedicator is also titled *antai*, being head of a local merchants' association and supervisor of the royal Pandian pearl fisheries—we shall return to this epigraph later.[1021] And like with the graffito by Korran the Chieftain from Berenike, the ownership mark by the Honourable Kiran at Sumhuram was made on a fragment of Roman amphora, here re-used as a lid,[1022] once more documenting activities by overseas Tamil agents.

The long arm of organised commerce: Petra and Palmyra

Another significant group of Arabs present in the Eastern Desert was the Nabataeans of Petra, famous for their role as middlemen on the last leg of the 'Incense Trail' before it reached the Mediterranean at Gaza:[1023]

> The incense, after being collected, is carried on camels' backs to Shabwa [capital of Hadramawt], at which place a single gate is left open for its admission. To deviate from the high road while conveying it, the laws have made a capital offence. At this place, the priests take by measure, and not by weight,

[1012] On coconuts, see Sidebotham 2011: 228–9.
[1013] v. d. Veen 2011: 46–7.
[1014] Cappers 2006: 104–5 (1st–2nd and 4th–5th century AD, even a few finds from the 5th–6th century AD).
[1015] Treated in chapter eight.
[1016] Mahadevan 1996a: 301, no. 5; *contra* Salomon 1991: 733 n11.
[1017] Mahadevan 2003: no. 40 (from Alagarmalai, but donors were likely from the nearby capital, like at Mangulam).
[1018] Mahadevan 1996a: 309, no. 22.
[1019] Mahadevan 1996a: 311, no. 26.
[1020] Subramanian 2012.
[1021] Mahadevan 2003: no. 3; treated in chapter eight.
[1022] Pavan 2015: 124 n19.
[1023] Diod. Sic. III.42, XIX.94; Strabo XVI.4.4, 18.

> a tenth part in honour of their god, whom they call Sabis; indeed, it is not allowable to dispose of it before this has been done: out of this tenth the public expenses are defrayed, for the divinity generously entertains all those strangers who have made a certain number of days' journey in coming thither. The incense can only be exported through the country of the Gebanitæ [the people of the kingdom of Qataban], and for this reason it is that a certain tax is paid to their king as well. Thimna, which is their capital, is distant from Gaza, a city of Judæa, on the shores of our sea, 4436 miles [*c.* 2,500 km on a modern map], the distance being divided into 65 days' journey by camel. There are certain portions also of the frankincense which are given to the priests and the king's secretaries: and in addition to these, the keepers of it, as well as the soldiers who guard it, the gate-keepers, and various other employees, have their share as well. And then besides, all along the route, there is at one place water to pay for, at another fodder, lodging at the stations, and various taxes and imposts besides; the consequence of which is, that the expense for each camel before it arrives at the shores of our sea is 688 *denarii*; after all this, too, there are certain payments still to be made to the farmers of the revenue of our empire.[1024]

Accordingly, re-export of South Arabian aromatics might explain the establishment by Nabataeans of stations and temples in the Eastern Nile Delta as early as the 1st century BC, as focal points of a merchant diaspora or caravan network trading with Egypt.[1025] Remarkably, though, an official tax-collector of the *tetarte* was stationed in the Nabataean port of Leuke Kome on the Red Sea around AD 70, when the Nabataean kingdom was still an independent vassal-state of the empire.[1026] Likewise, Roman *publicanii* were present in the Judaean port of Gaza at the time of Pliny, being part of the empire proper and the main Mediterranean outlet of the Nabataeans. In consequence, merchants could not exploit Nabataean territory as a geographical gap in the customs barrier of the Empire even prior to its annexation in AD 107,[1027] although merchandise solely destined for Nabataean consumption might have been exempt.

All of this taken into consideration, it comes as no surprise that Nabataean graffiti appears at strategic points in the Eastern Desert from the 1st–3rd century AD: on the route from Arsinoë at the head of the Gulf of Suez down to its mouth (some specifically by 'cameleers'[1028]), on the route from the northernmost Red Sea passing close by the imperial quarries to Koptos,[1029] in a major way along the route from Myos Hormos to Koptos (apparently of later, 2nd–3rd century AD date, mainly after the abandonment of the forts), and in and around wadi Minayh on the route to Berenike.[1030] Seeing as the Nabataean port of Leuke Kome, somewhere on the eastern side of the upper Red Sea, was itself an entrepôt of the Indian Ocean trade, especially receiving small craft from South Arabia,[1031] the Nabataeans active in the Eastern Desert might not all have arrived overland, as the graffiti indicate that some certainly did. Commercial connections with their own exchange networks in Western Arabia can well have been kept up through boat traffic back and forth between Myos Hormos and Leuke Kome.[1032]

Incidentally, letters between a Roman army staff officer hailing from Egypt to family members back in that province[1033] shed an interesting light on Nabataean participation in long-distance trade with lucrative goods other than simply South Arabian aromatics. During a posting in the recently annexed Nabataean kingdom, in March AD 107, the officer reports that merchants sailing out of Alexandria arrived every day at inland Bostra, at this time only second to the former capital of Petra in importance, from

[1024] Pliny *NH*, XII.32. Here Pliny leaves out mention of the kingdom of *Maīn*, 'through whose country is the sole transit for the frankincense, along a single narrow road' (XII.30), that is, from Qataban the Minaeans transported frankincense and myrrh the long trek north (some 1,400 km) to the southernmost outpost of the Nabataean kingdom, where merchants from the latter took over and carried the cargoes down to Gaza. Singer 2007: 11–18. Groom 1981: 165–213.
[1025] Strugnell 1959; Jones *et al.* 1988; see now Hackl *et al.* 2003: S.001.01–2.
[1026] *Periplous* 19.
[1027] Cass. Dio LXVIII.14.5.
[1028] Littmann and Meredith 1953: nos. 34=37, 46a; see now Hackl *et al.* 2003: S.003.01.
[1029] Plausibly due to Nabataean import and processing of amethyst from the mine at Safaga, cf. Johnson 1987: 71–8.
[1030] Durand 2012.
[1031] Strabo XVI.4.23–4; *Periplus* 19.
[1032] Attestations of Nabataean activity in the East (outside their own realm) is listed in Roche 1996: nos. 1–14, while Schmid 2004 adds ceramic evidence (nos. 1–15) and a few more coin finds (nos. 16–17).
[1033] On the archive of Gaius Iulius Apollinarius, see Claytor and Feucht 2013.

the Mediterranean port of Pelusium,[1034] and that Tyrian wares (presumably purple-dyed textiles), fine garments, ivory, pearls and unguents (*myra*), were available in plenty.[1035]

Likewise, Palmyrenes could also have been considered desert dwelling 'Arabs,' not least because the evidence from the Eastern Desert reveals them in the roles of merchants conducting caravans and archers patrolling the route from Koptos to Berenike. Thus, a fragmentary bilingual Greco-Palmyrene inscription from Denderah, the site of an important temple just north of Koptos on the Nile,[1036] mentions merchants, apparently having travelled together in a caravan.[1037] From Koptos itself, two Palmyrene inscriptions in Greek have survived. One is by a member of a unit of Palmyrene archers, dated AD 216.[1038] The other inscription is a dedication by Palmyrene merchants in honour of a member of the 'Red Sea shippers of Palmyra,' who had taken it upon himself to erect a gateway, three colonnades and the attached chambers, out of his own means, evidently part of a building complex belonging to Palmyrene merchants and shippers. In all likelihood, these two professional groups were united in some kind of formal association, as we shall see that other groups of professionals were at Palmyra itself.[1039]

Significantly, moreover, Palmyrene soldiers are attested epigraphically at Berenike. One inscription is in Greek, set up by a Palmyrene member of a unit of archers in September AD 215,[1040] while the other is a Greco-Palmyrene bilingual dedication for the 'good fortune of Palmyra,' honouring a prefect of Berenike and leader of a cavalry unit, known to have been garrisoned at Koptos from AD 180/85, along with one of its officers. Apparently, the inscription was commissioned by their Palmyrene subordinates collectively, and the stone was worked by a Palmyrene sculptor, most likely sometime in AD 180/85–212.[1041] Thus, we can infer that Palmyrene troops (archers and mounted soldiers) were deployed by the Roman authorities in the Eastern Desert on the long route between Koptos and Berenike from the later 2nd century AD. Moreover, Berenike has yielded *ostraca* with a female version of a Palmyrene name, Hierabole,[1042] as well as pen writings in cursive Aramaic hybrids in-between Palmyrene and Nabataean,[1043] whereas excavations at Myos Hormos have produced one vessel of a Palmyrene amphora type with an owner's graffito or content *dipinto* written with ink in a Palmyrene Aramaic cursive.[1044] Evidently, then, not only Palmyrene soldiers, but also merchants and even commodities from Palmyra were to be found at the Red Sea ports in the early centuries AD.

To a remarkable degree, both Nabataeans and Palmyrenes were highly adept at founding mercantile diasporas abroad, in the process taking control of key positions on the long-distance transport routes linking their home cities to markets of import and export (including Rome, as we shall see below). The Nabataeans occupied key nodes on the caravan routes of northern Arabia, namely, Hegra (Medain Saleh)[1045] on the Incense Trail proper, and Dumata (Jawf),[1046] the latter on the one hand connecting Petra with the Arabian Gulf coast and on the other hand connecting Bostra with Arabia via the wadi Sirhan. In fact, a passage in Pliny informs us that there was even a Nabataean 'colony of cave-dwellers,' that is, settlers, in East Africa who dispatched gums and aloe-wood to the coast from further inland for shipping back home.[1047] Nabataean fine ware has, moreover, been found along the main sea lanes of the Red Sea

[1034] *P.Mich.* VIII, 466.
[1035] *P.Mich.* VIII, 465.
[1036] Strabo XVII.1.44.
[1037] *Portes du Desert* 39; Clermont-Ganneau 1903. Dated later 2nd–early 3rd century AD.
[1038] *Portes du désert* 85.
[1039] *Portes du Desert* 103 (dated 3rd century AD, the fall of Palmyra in AD 272 being an *ante quem*). The excavated meeting place of an Egyptian funeral society at Koptos was once erroneously interpreted as the 'club house of the Palmyrenes:' e.g. Reinach 1913: 46–51, 63, debunked in Seyrig 1972: 120–5. See now on this matter Galliano 2000: 134–7.
[1040] Verhoogt 1998: 193–6, with photo and drawing on pp. 31, 33.
[1041] Dijkstra and Verhoogt 1999: 207–18.
[1042] *O.Ber.* I, p. 27; the male name 'Hierabolos' is attested in Koptos in *Portes du désert* 85.
[1043] *O.Ber.* II, 254–5.
[1044] Tomber *et al.* 2011: 7–8, no. 6 (dated late 1st–early 2nd century AD).
[1045] Bowersock 1983: 48, 57, 60, 95; Bowsher 1986; Johnson 1987: 103–8; Young 2001: 104–5, 115, 121–22.
[1046] Bowersock 1983: 58, 98–99, 154–58; Johnson 1987: 115–17; Young 2001: 92–4, 110–11, 115.
[1047] Pliny *NH*, XII.44: *per nabataeos trogodytas, qui consedere ex nabataeis*. See Hackl *et al.* 2003: 575; Johnson 1987: 118–19.

and Gulf of Aden, from Myos Hormos and Berenike via the Farrasan Islands in the southern Red Sea to the ports of Qana and Sumhuram in South Arabia.[1048]

Likewise, Palmyrene merchants built temples and rose to high office in key commercial centres in the periphery of Parthia, such as Vologesias on the lower Euphrates and Spasinou Charax and Phorath at the head of the Persian Gulf[1049]—even on the island of Tylos, modern Bahrain. Two inscriptions from Palmyra inform us further that Palmyrenes owned ships at the Gulf harbours, likely at Spasinou Charax,[1050] on which they sailed to Scythia, being the area around the estuary of the Indus where lay Barbaricon, to trade. In addition, Palmyrene troops of different kinds (some auxiliaries of the Roman army, others highly irregular) are known from the Syrian frontier city of Dura-Europos and the islands of 'Ana and Bijan on the Euphrates, as well as defending caravans on the return track through the desert.[1051]

Consequently, this is the context within which the Nabataean and Palmyrene activities in the Eastern Desert need to be understood. That is, as a branching out of their original commercial networks in the Persian Gulf (Palmyra) and South Arabia (Petra), being extended to tap into the lucrative trade route between the Mediterranean and the Indian Ocean via Egypt, which, although having existed in a quiet way for centuries under the Ptolemies, developed into the most lucrative of long-distance trade routes under the Romans—this much is eminently clear from the size and value of the imported cargo in the Muziris Papyrus. In the Palmyrene case, military and mercantile networks even converged at Koptos and Berenike, likely to the economic benefit and general advantage of both groups.

Remarkably, it is possible to outline the same process of organisation of the long-distance trade, as has been shown for Roman *collegia* and professional groups of craftsmen, for the Nabataeans and Palmyrenes. Thus, we have already encountered the formal organisation of 'Palmyrene merchants and Red Sea shippers' with communal property at Koptos, whose activities must be viewed in the light of the Denderah inscription attesting Palmyrene caravan ventures in the Eastern Desert, the latter perhaps carrying specifically Palmyrene products into Egypt, like the amphora found at Myos Hormos. In addition, a Palmyrene visitor, either a sailor or an ambassador of sorts, is now known from later 3rd century AD Dioscourides, modern Socotra, on the main sea lane from Roman Egypt to all of the ports of South Asia (see below), rendering it even more plausible that the Palmyrene Red Sea shippers, merchants and caravan traders of Egypt were organised to profit as active participants in the Indian Ocean trade via Egypt.

As just mentioned, though, the main commercial thrust of Palmyra was from the Syrian desert via the Euphrates to the trade centres of Lower Mesopotamia and harbours at the head of the Gulf, that is, in vassal states of Parthia, some entrepreneurial individuals even travelling by sea to overseas markets in South Asia. Thanks to the prominent epigraphic habit at Palmyra, we can tell that this long-distance trade was highly organised.[1052] Thus, Palmyrene commercial expeditions to Mesopotamia could either be organised by formal collectives of merchants, *emporoi*,[1053] or as communal caravans proper, *synodia* (Palmyrene Aramaic *šyrt'*),[1054] headed by designated leaders termed *synodiarchai* in the 1st–2nd century AD[1055] and *archemporoi* in the 3rd century,[1056] who were entrusted with the passage and safety of the caravan and in the conduct of which they often had to draw on a number of resources. Moreover, in addition to these concrete members of any given caravan, financial support and investment was needed from both merchants at home and in the diaspora abroad (both inside and outside the confines of the Roman

1048 Schmid 2004: nos. 6, 8, 9, 10, 11.

1049 Especially *PAT* 1062 (AD 145?) for the existence of temples at Vologesias (one of them to Augustus), somewhere on the lower Euphrates, and at Spasinou Charax, at the head of the Persian Gulf (both in Parthia). On which, see now Speidel 2016: 110–14.

1050 On these ports, see Yon 2016.

1051 Cf. Gawlikowski 1996, in which the relevant inscriptions are all listed, now made available in a convenient digital corpus by Fox and Lieu 2011. The main work on Palmyrene trade is now Seland 2016c. On the 'caravan police' in particular, see especially Young 2001: 157–66, 229–30. The inscriptions revealing Palmyrene sea-going trade with Scythia are *PAT* 1403 and 2763, on which Delplace 2003.

1052 See Seland 2016c: 63–74; but also the influential article by Yon 1998, and the work of Sommer 2005: 202–13.

1053 The earliest of which appears to be *PAT* 270–271 (AD 19).

1054 The first epigraphic mention being *PAT* 1397 (AD 135).

1055 The earliest attestation being *PAT* 262 (AD 142).

1056 Only recorded in AD 257/8, *PAT* 282, and AD 267, *PAT* 288.

Empire), logistical support was needed from the nomadic population of the desert steppes, and economic, political and (para-)military support was required from the Palmyrene elite all along the way.[1057] As is evident, the Greek versions of Palmyrene Aramaic inscriptions erected by *emporoi* and *synodia* in honour of the Palmyrene gods, caravan leaders, elite patrons and other powerful and influential helpers, borrow the technical terms from Greek associations of merchants, who were often united in *synodoi* or similar private organisations, and headed by leaders such as *archemporoi* or bearing other titles.[1058]

Fortunately, we know of one specific Palmyrene occupational organisation which was vital to Palmyra's role as a hub in the trade between the Mediterranean and the Indian Ocean, and another which was evidently profiting from the situation.[1059] The first is that of the highly specialised *asconautopoioi*, or waterskin-raft makers, who erected a dedication in AD 257/8 in unison, as a *symposion*, with their close colleagues from the more general profession of leather-workers, *skyteis*.[1060] These waterskin-rafts were vital in facilitating easy outbound transport to Lower Mesopotamia, embarking at Hit on the Euphrates, being the point where easy downstream navigation by rafts becomes feasible.[1061] We know from the Palmyrene tax-law that the leather-workers were organised and based in urban workshops, and the same must have applied to the waterskin-raft makers.[1062]

Another professional group that will have profited from Palmyra's involvement in the long-distance trade is that of the 'joint crafts association,' *syntechnia*, of gold- and silversmiths, in the Palmyrene Aramaic described with the Greek loanword *tagma*, designating a professional status group, rank or order.[1063] Significantly, an *ordo* was the authoritative assembly at the core of many Roman *collegia*, as with the *collegium* of *negotiatores eborarii et citriarii* whose *ordo* could evict members and officials alike.[1064] Furthermore, Palmyrene sculptural portraits of women in particular are rich in details attesting the products of the Palmyrene gold- and silversmiths in the form of elaborate jewellery.[1065] Some of these ornaments seem to have been adorned with pearls,[1066] the Persian Gulf being one of the greatest production centres of pearls in the ancient world,[1067] while other adornments will have reflected Palmyrene imports of precious stones via the Persian Gulf, for instance, turquoise and lapis lazuli from the export market of Barbaricon in Scythia or other South Asian gemstones.[1068] Significantly, excavations at two Palmyrene tomb towers have, in fact, revealed jewellery incorporating objects with an Eastern provenance, namely, pearls, agate, carnelian and ivory, the latter in the shape of two hair pins.[1069]

Similarly, there is evidence at Petra of not only the economic importance of the transit trade of frankincense and myrrh from South Arabia, but also the development of means, that is, skilled craftsmen, investors, technology, additional ingredients and workshops, to process the long-distance imports and thereby increase their value before further export or active retailing. Thus, literary and archaeological evidence from Petra document how a Nabataean production of aromatic unguents developed and thrived from the late 1st century BC–mid-3rd century AD, entailing the local cultivation of fragrant plants to add to the myrrh (and incense) perfume bases, and large-scale production of characteristic containers, the so-called piriform *unguentaria*.[1070] There is even evidence from smaller sites near Petra of olive oil

---

1057 Following Seland 2014b.
1058 Poland 1909: 107, 114, 115, 225, 360, 368.
1059 Bounni 1990: 80–1.
1060 *I.Palmyra* 59. For the identification of the *asconautopoioi* with makers of waterskin-rafts, see Seyrig 1963: 159–66. Neo-Assyrian commercial expeditions in the 7th century BC also routinely made use of waterskin-rafts in combination with donkeys for the different legs of the journey, see Radner 1999: 119.
1061 Seland 2016c: 48–9.
1062 Matthews 1984: 177, l. 80.
1063 *I.Palmyra* 56 = *CIS* 3945. On *tgm'* see Kaizer 2002a: 151 n7.
1064 See chapter three.
1065 Chehade 1987: particularly illustrations 4, 5, 7, 8.
1066 Schörle 2015: 46.
1067 See discussion in chapter four.
1068 *Periplus* 39.
1069 Witecka 1994: nos. 1–2 (earrings with pearls), 9 (ring w. banded agate), 11 (carnelian intaglio); Higuchi and Saito 2001: nos. 2–3 (ivory pins), 25–6 (agates encased in gold), 73–4 (large cylindrical agate beads). See Zuchowska 2013b: 383.
1070 Johnson 1987: 36–71; Fiema 2003: 41, 49. Cf. the mention of availability of *myra* at Bostra in AD 107, mentioned above.

cultivation and production, no doubt for use as the main solvent in perfumes like those produced in the big city.[1071]

Whereas the Nabataeans had previously, from at least the later 4th century BC, been vital in the import of frankincense and myrrh to the Mediterranean, they evidently set about organising a specialised production of unguents in addition to their caravan trade, being firmly established by the early 1st century AD. This phenomenon obviously coincides with enlarged demand exerted in the wake of the Roman annexation of Egypt, as well as the consequent competition facing Nabataean caravans from Roman traders sailing directly to Aden and Qana via Egypt's Red Sea ports.[1072] Unfortunately, we do not know any details about how Nabataean unguent production, export and retail was organised, but we might assume that the basic structure was similar to that attested at Palmyra—especially seeing as we know that Nabataeans and Palmyrenes shared one West Semitic cultic institution, namely, the *marzeah*, which at Palmyra was also translated as a *symposion*, which we have already seen could be constituted by professions.[1073] Thus, we have encountered the *symposion* of waterskin-raft makers and leather-workers, based in urban workshops, as well as the similar *syntechnia*, or *tagma*, of gold- and silversmiths, and we can therefore hypothesise the existence of a specifically Nabataean kind of association uniting the heads of workshops and retail outlets in something like a formal organisation of '*unguentarii*.'

The more so, because Nabataean evidence from Puteoli provides further support to the idea of formal Nabataean organisations being the backbone of the trade. At Puteoli, a dedication in Aramaic attesting the construction in the mid-1st century BC and restoration in AD 5 by Nabataeans of a temple to their supreme god, Dushares, have come to light,[1074] along with an increasing number of architectural elements from this building with the Latin *Dusari sacrum* inscribed.[1075] This is significant in itself, because a well-established Nabataean presence at the maritime commercial hub of Puteoli must be related to Nabataean re-export of frankincense, myrrh and (subsequently) unguents, from Petra via Gaza. What is more, though, the Semitic word used to denote the temple allegedly also carries the connotation of a meeting place or club house, a *schola*, like that of the *negotiatores eborarii et citriarii*.[1076] Moreover, as mentioned in chapter six, we know of the existence at Puteoli of both a later *statio* of Tyrians, affiliated with another *statio* at Rome and previously accruing money from *emporoi kai nauklêroi*, as well as a *corpus* of Berytians with communal property and cult. Accordingly, it is the more likely that the Nabataean temple was part of a similar organisation linking traders at Puteoli with organised caravan import and perfume production at home. An interesting epitaph provides an example of one of the members of the Nabataean community in Puteoli by attesting the death in that port of Tholomaios, also known as 'Maximus,' age 33, from Petra—having obtained a local Latin nickname, he must have been one of the long-time regulars of the city.[1077]

Likewise, three inscriptions involving Nabataeans are to be found at Rome. All three are bilingual, two in Nabataean Aramaic and Latin, one in Latin and Greek. Two were found on the Capitol, one being a highly fragmentary dedication to a god, plausibly Dushares, tentatively dated mid-1st century BC–mid-1st century AD,[1078] the other being a commemoration by two emissaries on an embassy from a Nabataean king to Rome, either in 8/7 BC or AD 37[1079]—in fact, two such embassies are mentioned in the ancient literature.[1080] The third is more interesting, being an epitaph raised by a relative over Abgarus, a 30-year old man from Petra, with a likely *post quem* of AD 70, indicating the presence in Rome of what is likely

1071 Erickson-Gini and Israel 2013: 48–9, 50–1.
1072 Johnson 1987: 20–34; Fiema 1996: 191–2.
1073 McLaughlin 2001: 45–61. Kaizer 2002b: 229-34. Maciá 2007: 168–82. The Palmyrene inscriptions with parallel texts giving '*marzeah* leader' as *symposiarch* are *PAT* 316, 1357.
1074 Tran Tam Tinh 1972: S. 1; Roche 1996: no. 15; Hackl *et al.* 2003: A.002.01; Terpstra 2015: no. 2.
1075 Tran Tam Tinh 1972: S. 3–6; Roche 1996: no. 17; Hackl *et al.* 2003: A.002.03; Terpstra 2015: nos. 3–10.
1076 Tran Tam Tinh 1972: 128, 142. For the *schola* of the *eborarii et citriarii*, see chapter three.
1077 *IG* XIV, 842a; Terpstra 2015: 81, no. 12. In addition, two 'camels' were dedicated at the Nabataean temple in AD 11: Tran Tam Tinh 1972: S. 2; Roche 1996: no. 16; Hackl *et al.* 2003: A.002.02; Terpstra 2015: no. 1.
1078 Roche 1996: no. 18; Hackl *et al.* 2003: A.001.03; Terpstra 2015: no. 15.
1079 Roche 1996: no. 19; Hackl *et al.* 2003: A.001.02; Terpstra 2015: no. 14.
1080 Roche 1996: nos. 20–1.

to have been settled representatives of the Nabataean commercial network which extended from their royal capital via Gaza to Puteoli and Rome.[1081]

Neither can there be any doubt that Rome housed a long-lived and well-established community of Palmyrenes, as attested by the gravestone of a 32-year old *Palmyrenus* buried along the Via Appia,[1082] and apparently centred on a succession of temples in Trastevere.[1083] The first structures at this site can be tentatively dated to the later 1st century AD, but the earliest inscriptions were put up by people with Roman names in honour of Sol, the deified Sun. While this might possibly, then, constitute an early connection with the Palmyrene pantheon, such a development is in no way certain.[1084] Fortunately, though, subsequent bilingual inscriptions (Greek/Latin and Palmyrene Aramaic) leave no doubt that from no later than AD 116, a shrine to the deities of Palmyra was established at the site, paid for by worshippers manifestly stressing their Palmyrene origin.[1085] A dedication of unknown provenance might indicate that the temple was still in position in AD 236, seeing that this marble relief of Palmyrene gods also mentions the erection of a silver statue with accompanying paraphernalia, likely to have been housed in a cultic building just like it.[1086]

Finally, there is the highly ambiguous case of an altar dated roughly later 1st-early 2nd century AD, perhaps from the same area, portraying the deified Sun on its front and left side, Saturn on the right, and a cypress tree with a youth on its back.[1087] Crucially, the front bears a dedication in Latin to the most sacred Sun by Tiberius Claudius Felix, his wife Claudia Helpis, and their son, Alypus, in fulfilment of a vow, being *Calbienses de coh(orte) III*, while the left hand side bears an appended (that is, not in an engraved field, but simply incised below the frieze on the stone's smooth surface) dedication in Palmyrene Aramaic by 'Tiberius Claudius Felix and the Palmyrenes' to Malakbêl and the gods of Palmyra.[1088] Obviously, the two inscriptions are connected, the common denominator being Claudius Felix, who must have paid for this elaborately decorated altar, on top of which comes the two depictions of a deified Sun on the front and left sides of the monument. Nonetheless, the fact that some elements are related does not entail that the Latin and Palmyrene inscriptions are verbatim translations of one another—their contents differ, so they are evidently not the same,[1089] and they were not accorded the same prominence on the stone, the Palmyrene inscription evidently being a later addition.

Accordingly, Claudia Helpis and Alypus were not necessarily counted implicitly among the 'Palmyrenes' in the subsequent Aramaic inscription,[1090] nor can a direct link be established between Palmyrenes and the *horrea Galbana*. Claudius Felix, on the other hand, does appear to have been associated with the running of the Galban warehouses (if that is indeed the meaning of *Calbienses* in this context[1091]), just like the *Publii Veracii* encountered in chapter four who were members of a *centuria* of the *cohors* administering the *horrea piperataria*. However, Claudius Felix was explicitly not subsumed under the collective heading 'Palmyrenes' in the right-hand side inscription, although he did pay obeisance to Malakbêl, as the Palmyrene version of *Sol sanctissimus*, and the gods of Palmyra, but this just makes him a syncretistic worshipper of Eastern cults of the Sun, not a Palmyrene as such.[1092]

[1081] Roche 1996: no. 22; Hackl *et al.* 2003: A.001.01; Terpstra 2015: no. 13.
[1082] *CIL* VI, 19134.
[1083] Noy 2002: 242–4.
[1084] Schneider 1987: 69–70; Terpstra 2013: 152–55.
[1085] *IGUR* I, 117–8, 120, especially, but likely also *IGUR* I, 121–3, cf. Terpstra 2013: 155–6.
[1086] *IGUR* I, 119, in accordance with Schneider 1987: 82, incl. fig. 13; and Terpstra 2013: 158–9.
[1087] Schneider 1987: 73f–76, incl. figs. 3–6; however, the captions of figs. 4–5 mix up the left- and right-hand sides.
[1088] *CIL* VI, 710 and *CIS* II.3, 3903.
[1089] Houston 1990.
[1090] *Contra* Noy 2002: 243.
[1091] On the interpretation of *Calbienses*, see Schneider 1987: 76–7; and Houston 1990: 190–1.
[1092] Compare Smith 2013: 170; differing from Terpstra 2013: 157–8, 160. Note, moreover that the tentative dating of this altar corresponds with the apparent change in religious focus at the site, mentioned above, from worship of the deified Sun by believers with Latin names, to worship of the Palmyrene pantheon by believers with explicitly Palmyrene names and origins.

A woman named *Claudia Palmyris* is known from an unrelated inscription, though, revealing one attested connection between freedmen *Claudii* and Palmyra,[1093] rendering it possible that one of their number, such as Felix here, was the Romanised descendant (1st, 2nd or 3rd generation, depending upon the age of the altar) of a Palmyrene slave freed under Claudius or Nero.[1094] A direct link between Palmyrenes settled in Rome and sea-borne commerce coming up the Tiber to the Galban Warehouses thus eludes us, the altar merely providing evidence of Palmyrenes in Rome associated with a freedman of an imperial warehouse complex, whose primary choice of emic identification was explicitly Latin-Roman (unlike most Palmyrenes who preferred Aramaic and in some contexts Greek), secondarily expressing worship of the Palmyrene Pantheon. Nonetheless, as reviewed above, inscriptions from Palmyra itself, as well as one from Egyptian Koptos, provide ample testimony that branches of the Palmyrene mercantile diaspora established temples to their native gods (and the Emperors) in cities where they settled to trade.[1095]

Allegory of the cave. An inside out view of maritime trade

Returning to the ocean-going trade between Roman Egypt and South Asia, particularly West and South India, Pliny and the *Periplus* provide unequivocal testimonies to the feasibility of ancient blue-water navigation. According to both sources, Roman shippers would leave the coastline behind them in the Gulf of Aden and head directly across the Arabian Sea, steering either towards the north-eastern ports of Scythia and Ariake, mainly Barbaricon and Barygaza, or more or less due east to Limyrike, where lay Muziris. The ships would have set out from the ports of Roman Egypt with the onset of the southwest monsoon in July, when winds in the Red Sea were northerly, arriving in some 30 days in the Gulf of Aden (1500–700 km) and likely re-supplying in a South Arabian port, from which the straight leg to India could be made in another 40 days (2700–3000 km). The return trip from South Asia could be made from December, and no later than mid-January, employing the winds of the northeast monsoon and catching the southerly winds of the Red Sea prevailing until April. We even know from casual references in the *Periplus* that Indian ships would be heading west as well, to the ports of the Gulf of Aden.[1096]

In the same passage, Pliny enjoins that ships needed to carry archers on board to ward off pirates, and the *Periplus* implies that the inhabitants of the West Arabian coastline would conduct piratical raids on ships if they strayed too near.[1097] For this reason, the Roman provincial government appears to have had at least a few ships stationed in the northern and southern Red Sea, at least in the 1st–2nd century AD, to exercise some kind of maritime control.[1098] In addition, there are indications that Roman vessels banded together in groups or 'small fleets,' both local transport or fishing craft as well as ships returning from trade with East Africa[1099]—perhaps they would sometimes have been guarded by a solitary navy escort.

As it happens, though, recent findings from the Gulf of Aden provide fresh insights into commercial activity in the Arabian Sea from the 2nd–5th century AD, so in the following we shall proceed to conduct a case-study of this new corpus of evidence, and relate it to the overall organisation of trade between the Mediterranean and the Indian Ocean.[1100] The new source material in question is constituted by travellers' graffiti from the island of Socotra in the Gulf of Aden, thus, representing an obvious Indian Ocean

[1093] Barbieri 1982: I, no. 55. Only one other woman with the *cognomen* 'Palmyris' is known, in *CIL* XIV, 2864 (from Praeneste). Cf. Schneider 1987: 83 n79–80.

[1094] Schneider 1987: 77 n41, 82.

[1095] Terpstra 2016 argues from circumstantial evidence that the Palmyrene community in Rome was an active commercial diaspora.

[1096] Pliny *NH*, VI.26 and *Periplus* 57 (also 14, 31). For winds of the Red Sea, see Whitewright 2007: 79–81. Peppard 2009, treated in chapter six, provides an account of ships struggling up the Red Sea against contrary winds and making it into Berenike in early June, evidently having returned too late to catch the last of the southerlies.

[1097] *Periplus* 20.

[1098] *O.Petr.Mus.* 142 records a 'liburnian,' being a warship smaller than the trireme (Casson 1971: 141), at Myos Hormos in AD 52; *P.* 004, in van Rengan 2011, records a *tesseraria*, 'messenger ship' or 'dispatch vessel,' with soldiers on board, at Myos Hormos in AD 93; *O.Krok.* 59 appears to be a message from a member of the *classis Alexandrina* to the Prefect of Berenike, revealing traffic to Myos Hormos of navy personnel (one other fragmentary *ostracon* also refers to the navy, cf. Cuvigny 2003, II: 338; finally, two inscriptions from the Farrasan Islands now attest the existence in AD 144 of a 'port' under the leadership of a prefect with a legionary detachment, auxiliary troops, and 'people of the camp' at his disposal, thus, likely a naval station of sorts, cf. Phillips *et al.* 2004, and Villeneuve 2005-6.

[1099] Bülow-Jacobsen *et al.* 1994: 29–31, no. 1 (2nd century AD); and Peppard 2009 (AD 97).

[1100] The rest of this subchapter builds extensively on Evers 2014–5, parts of which are reproduced here with the kind permission of the editor. This article also contains maps and relevant photographs of the cave and select graffiti.

comparandum to the graffiti from wadi Minayh in Egypt, which has been treated in the above chapters to great effect, providing a wealth of information about participants in the trade crossing through Egypt's Eastern Desert.

Fortunately, both the mid-1st century AD *Periplus* and early-6th century anonymous author of the *Christian Topography* yield information about Socotra, known in Greek as Dioscourides. Thus, it appears that in the 1st century AD the island was inhabited by a mixed maritime trading diaspora of Arabs, Indians and some Greeks, the latter apparently numbering less than the other two groups. At the time, moreover, the island belonged to the territory of the South Arabian kingdom of Hadramawt, who had recently farmed it out (*ekmisthoō*) to an unknown consortium and was therefore keeping it under official guard, so as to be off limits to outsiders. Up until this disruption of ancient Socotra's position in the maritime trade routes, merchants had previously anchored from both Muza of the Himyarite Kingdom of Western Yemen, from Barygaza of the Western Kshatrapas in Western India, and from the Malabar Coast of South India, although only for stopovers *en route* to more important ports.[1101] Some 450 years later, according to the author of the *Christian Topography*, who had only passed by the island while riding off a storm, the inhabitants of Socotra still spoke Greek, some were evidently Christians seeing as (Nestorian) clerics were sent there from Persia, and some kept up overseas trade with Axumite Adulis in the Red Sea, for it was in this port that the anonymous author met visitors from the island.[1102]

As regards the intervening centuries, archaeological excavations at the northern site of Hajrya and western site of Kosh on Socotra have unearthed, respectively, a single Roman amphora handle, a little Mediterranean red glazed ware, and some fragments of apparently indeterminable Arab Gulf[1103] or Indian[1104] provenance, as well as, unsurprisingly, ceramics in the Hadramawt style, at Hajrya, and what appears to be more substantial South Asian than Roman ceramic finds at Kosh.[1105] Consequently, these sparse archaeological finds fit the testimonies of the *Periplus* and *Christian Topography* neatly enough, but without further evidence we would not be much wiser about Indian Ocean trade in the period.

Thus, the discovery of more than 200 ancient graffiti distributed all along the walls of the almost 2,000 meters deep Cave Hoq on the north-eastern shoulder of Socotra seems fortuitous in the extreme.[1106] Palaeographic analyses of the graffiti as a corpus reveal that the majority dates approximately from the 2nd–early 5th century AD, with a subset of about a dozen slightly earlier South Arabian graffiti dating from the 2nd century BC–2nd century AD.[1107] Significantly, not a single graffito can be identified as left behind by a permanent inhabitant on the isle (being under Hadramawtic sovereignty throughout, albeit with two shorter spells of Axumite control, *c.* 175/200–270 AD and 500–75 AD,[1108] but less than one in ten graffiti being attributable to these groups), whereas drawings of ships indicate visitors to the cave from overseas [2:16, 5:11, 6:13], as do their languages of choice in making graffiti as well as explicitly stated professions and places of origin.[1109] In short, it appears that the Cave Hoq instead acted as a place of pilgrimage for visitors already stuck on Socotra during the summer months, when the monsoon winds made it impossible to leave the island—during their forced stay ashore they might as well visit the cave to pray for a safe voyage onwards.[1110]

Obviously, though, we should be cautious about generalising from the distribution of Hoq graffiti in terms of the composition of visitors to the cave with various provenances to the composition of all visitors to Socotra in the same period, for we cannot know how many people would have chosen to spend time visiting the cave and leaving a graffito behind, as compared with those who would have chosen to spend

1101 *Periplus* 30–31.
1102 *Chr.Top.* III.65.
1103 Sedov 2007: 100.
1104 Naumkin and Sedov 1993: 605.
1105 Strauch 2012a: 379.
1106 De Geest 2012. In the following "[x:y]" in the main text refers to site no. x, graffito no. y, in Strauch 2012c, 'Catalogue.'
1107 Cf. table in Strauch 2012c: 30. Only one Brahmi graffito [10:2, likely AD 232] and a Palmyrene writing-tablet [4:6, AD 258] provide fixed dates.
1108 Robin 2012: 440.
1109 Strauch 2012a: 405.
1110 Strauch 2012b: 542–4.

their idle time differently. However, we can, nonetheless, on a secure methodological footing use the Hoq graffiti as a relative diagnostic indicator of the movements of merchants and shippers, especially, in the Indian Ocean of the 2nd–5th century AD. In other words, the Cave Hoq can provide us with a unique inside out view of maritime trade, if only we are able to read and interpret its long-forgotten contents in a meaningful way, to some extent similar to how Plato's 'allegory of the cave' provided a key to his overall metaphysical model.[1111]

Starting out with the Roman evidence, it is remarkable in itself that only three graffiti out of more than 200 were written in Greek, two of them (if not all three) apparently left by visitors from Roman Egypt. One of these latter graffiti mentions Septimius Paniskos, a *nauklêros*, whose name would indicate an early 3rd century AD date [11:26], whereas the second graffito contains the names Alexandros and Petros, the latter perhaps as a misspelt patronymic [11:28]. In light of the obvious Christian connotations of the name 'Petros,' this traveller might be associated with the Byzantine (some explicitly Christian) graffiti at wadi Minayh mentioning ships setting out from Berenike,[1112] thus, likely datable to the 4th–5th century AD, taking the fatal decline of Berenike in the mid-6th century AD into consideration.[1113] Significantly, such a Christian traveller may well have benefitted from his faith in the mercantile world of the Indian Ocean in Late Antiquity, seeing as a specifically Christian diaspora (albeit possibly divided by schisms, particularly between Byzantine Orthodox adherents and Nestorians of Persia) was established in ports of the Red Sea, South Arabia and on Socotra, as well as along the Konkan and Malabar coasts of Western India, and on Sri Lanka.[1114] Thus, these two graffiti attest visitors to Socotra after the traditional interpretation of the 1st and 2nd centuries AD as a high point in Roman trade with the Indian Ocean.

However, the apparent lack of Greek-speaking visitors to the cave may also be due to meteorological phenomena, rather than simply the 'downturn of the third century,' namely, the fact that Roman ships set out for Indian Ocean ports in summer, when the southwest monsoon made landing on the inhabited northern shore of Socotra impossible,[1115] as it had been for the author of the *Christian Topography*, whereas Roman ships upon return from India starting in December would also have found the island buffeted by strong winds in December and January. Indian ships, on the other hand, arriving on the same northeast monsoon, would have had better time to enjoy a safe anchorage along the northern coast of Socotra from February onwards before returning home with the southwest monsoon sometime in May.[1116]

The third Greek graffito, [16:15], simply reads 'Aukar' and is therefore presumably a Greek rendition of the Aramaic name Abgar, which must refer to the same person of that name who left a dedication in Palmyrene Aramaic on a wooden tablet elsewhere in the cave, [4:6], being dated to AD 258. Indeed, we have already encountered Palmyrene bilingualism both in the inscriptions of Palmyra itself and as near to Socotra as Roman Berenike on the Red Sea, so this kind of ambiguous Greek-Palmyrene self-expression is unsurprising—there is even an *ostracon* from Berenike inscribed in a Semitic language which mentions the name of one 'Abgar.'[1117] Whether this Palmyrene visitor would have been out of the Persian Gulf or coming down the Red Sea is an open question, though, we have seen that Palmyrene shippers plied both trade routes, but, in fact, he might also have come overland: Palmyrene emissaries are attested in royal inscriptions from mainland Shabwa, the capital of Hadramawt.[1118]

On this note of cultural multiplicity, it is remarkable that the very bottom of the Cave Hoq also contains a laconic graffito in Prakrit commemorating the visit of a so-called *Yavana*, [14:17], being a Sanskrit ethnicon derived from Prakrit *Yona* but originally borrowed from Achaemenid Persian for a 'Ionian,' meaning

[1111] Pl. *Resp.* VII, 514a–520a.
[1112] See the beginning of this chapter.
[1113] Compare Bukharin 2012: 497–8.
[1114] Overview in Seland 2013: 384–88.
[1115] Strauch 2012a: 381; 2012b: 543.
[1116] For the annual monsoonal wind patterns of the island, cf. Doe 1992: 11.
[1117] *O.Ber.* II, 256 (3rd quarter of 1st century AD).
[1118] Bron 1986, Robin 2012: 488–91. On diplomatic missions between Arabian kingdoms and Palmyra (and Rome), see now also Schiettecatte and Arbach 2016.

anyone Greek to the latter.[1119] However, as we shall see in the next chapter, these names acquired highly specific meanings in an Indian context, so that whereas *Yona* would often be applied to 'Indo-Greeks' of the old successor kingdoms of Alexander's conquests,[1120] *Yavana* came to denote in Southern India people arriving from the West, such as seagoing merchants, no matter their actual origin.[1121] In consequence, it is quite telling that this so-called 'Westerner' chose to identify himself as such by the use of a Sanskrit ethnicon written in the Prakrit language and the Brahmi script, seeing as he was on an island where at least some of the inhabitants spoke Greek from the writing of the *Periplus* in the 1st century AD to the *Christian Topography* in the 6th century. In addition, he would have had to pass close by the two graffiti by Greeks from Roman Egypt, had they been made at the time of his visit, in order to write his own graffito at very bottom of the cave.[1122]

What is more, the author of this graffito chose to render his name as '(the) *Yavana* of Cadrabhutimukha'—*yavano* being in the nominative singular, whereas the name given, *Cadrabhutimukha*, is in the genitive singular of Prakrit: *Cadrabhutimukhasa*.[1123] In so doing, this visitor to the Cave Hoq on ancient Socotra chose to replicate a grammatical oddity which eight out of the only nine known epigraphical attestations of *Yavanas* also exhibit, namely, giving their ethnicon in the singular followed by a name in the genitive.[1124] What has often been called the 'irregular syntax' of these inscriptions, and the conventional straightened out translations which is therefore often forced upon them erroneously, was pointed out by the eminent Indologist Otto Stein already in the 1930s with reference to the nine recorded inscriptions of Maharashtra, but is now forcibly re-emphasised by the graffito from Socotra. We will return to this matter in the next chapter, but for now it appears that this *Yavana* was not very Greek at all, only a 'Westerner' by (Indian) name, and he, and the other *Yavanas* known from inscriptions, may very well have been part of larger social organisations or networks, if we are to refrain from consistently correcting their allegedly wrong use of the genitive case.

However, leaving aside these few graffiti which attest, or, in the last case, does not seem to attest after all, visitors from the Roman West, there is no doubt that the real eye-opener provided by the *corpus* of graffiti from the Cave Hoq is that nearly all of them were made by visitors to the island of Western Indian origin, to judge from their scripts and language.[1125] Although most of their graffiti are, in the nature of things, laconic, giving only a name, a few visitors added supplementary details of great value. Thus, a brief survey of what can be ascertained about the Indian visitors reveals that these were merchants [2:1, *vanij*], captains [6:1, 10:4=11:1, 14:15, *navika*; 11:12, *niryamaka*], Buddhist monastic attendants [7:4, 11:30; *aramika*] and monks [11:32, 14:16; *shramana*], hailing from ports and cities like Hastakampra [2:23], Barygaza [11:11, 11:12 , 11:17, 11:25, 17:1] and perhaps Vidisha [17:2], being Shakas [6:7, 14:16] and Kshatrapas [12:2, 15:5], as well as a multitude of individuals with Buddhist, Vaishnavite and Shaivite names.[1126]

Although it was already known from the *Periplus* that Indian merchants from Barygaza would sail to Socotra (#31) and the Horn of Africa (#14), there has otherwise been preciously little evidence available for Western Indian traders in the Red Sea and Gulf of Aden. Moreover, it is intriguing that out of the half dozen inscribed sherds found so far in Myos Hormos and Berenike of Roman Egypt, as well as at Sumhuram in Hadramawt, five have been written in Tamil-Brahmi, while the final ostracon was inscribed in a South Indian variety of Brahmi, as we have already seen. Yet, among the nearly 200 graffiti from the Cave Hoq, not one can be attributed to a Tamil visitor, even though the *Periplus* also alleges that traders came to Socotra from Limyrike (#31), corresponding roughly to the Malabar Coast, which, according to a recent study,[1127] probably extended beyond Cape Comorin to Korkai on the eastern side of the peninsula's

[1119] Narain 1957: 165–9; Ray 1988: 312; Sancisi-Weerdenburg 2001.
[1120] Tarn 1966; Narain 1957; Mairs 2014.
[1121] Zvelebil 1956; 1973: 35 w. n1.
[1122] See Strauch 2012c: 123, fig. 2.
[1123] Differing from the interpretation of Strauch 2012c: 183.
[1124] Stein 1935. See historiographical note in Brancaccio 2005: n6.
[1125] Strauch 2012a: 341–2.
[1126] For the theophoric names, cf. table in Strauch 2012a: 356–57.
[1127] Romanis 2011.

tip in Antiquity. Perhaps Indian merchants sailing out of ports in Western and South India, respectively, headed for different ports, being integrated into different long-distance trading networks, so that Tamils would mainly head directly for Roman ports in the Red Sea, whereas traders from Barygaza would anchor in South Arabian ports acting as entrepôts for goods from Roman Egypt and elsewhere.

Moreover, the epigraphic record has previously had little to offer on the subject of Indian captains of merchant ships, that is, the profession of *navika*. Some individuals are known, though: e.g. two inscriptions from the commercially vibrant Krishna estuary in Andhra Pradesh, both attesting the title *mahanavika* and implying captains of ocean-going ships crossing the Bay of Bengal to the Malay Peninsula,[1128] where a third inscription attesting a *mahanavika* has been found in Malaysian Kedah, the latter according to his inscription hailing from a port town in the Ganges estuary.[1129] Significantly, the ships of these captains might have carried Chinese silk back to India, where it entered the Subcontinent's ports as well as the accounts of the *Periplus* and the *Christian Topography*. In addition, a Tamil *navika* is attested in an inscription near the ancient Sri Lankan capital of Anuradhapura, while two Sinhalese *navikas* are known from other inscriptions on that island.[1130] Now, however, the title of *navika* crops up four times (attesting three individuals) in the graffiti from Socotra [6:1, 10:4=11:1, 14:15], one of these captains explicitly hailing from Barygaza, with the highly interesting addition of one *niryamaka* also sailing out of that port [11:12]. The terms *navika* and *niryamaka* seem to have meant more or less the same, both implying a senior member of the crew, being either the helmsman, navigator or captain, the boundaries between these positions being blurred anyway.[1131]

In this light, it is striking that the *Supparaka Jataka*, part of the *corpus* of Buddhist folk tales conceived in the last centuries BC,[1132] relates a story about a leader of the shippers' community in Barygaza, in the Pali titled *niyyamakajetthaka*; '*jetthaka*' being a traditional epithet for the presidents of associations of craftsmen.[1133] This 'master mariner,' as his title is traditionally translated,[1134] later steps down from his office and agrees to act as ordinary captain, *niyyamaka*, of a ship full of merchants, *vanija*. Now, with the graffito from Socotra [11:12], the literary tradition of the *Jatakas* on the terminology for merchant captains sailing out of Barygaza is reaffirmed epigraphically.

Other ports and cities involved in Indian Ocean trade are also mentioned in the *corpus* of graffiti. Thus, there seems to be a reference in one graffito to Vidisha [17:2], the ancient inland political and commercial centre which we have already encountered due to its renowned ivory carvers who made a collective contribution to the adornment of one of the monumental gateways at the Sanchi stupa in the late 1st century BC. Ivory, much in demand at Rome, was, significantly, one of the major Indian exports via coastal outlets such as Barygaza and the ports of the Konkan Coast (*Periplus* 49).[1135] Another graffito states that a visitor hailed from Hastakavapra [2:23], modern Hathab, known to the Greeks as Astakampra (*Periplus* 41, 43), where excavations have revealed the existence of a port site with a warehouse complex yielding numerous sealings of the 3rd–4th century AD.[1136]

Moving on from the majority of Western Indian graffiti, there is a simple graffito [16:13] in the Kharoshthi script giving the name *Upali* or *Upala* in Gandhari, the former being a typical Buddhist name.[1137] Thus, although the information contained in the graffito is minimal, the fact that we have a Kharoshthi graffito on an island at the entrance to the Gulf of Aden, some 3000 kilometres as the crow flies from the heartland of Gandhara, is of great interest. Specifically, this case brings to mind the cache of beautiful Roman glass vessels produced in Egypt but found in Kushan Begram, mentioned in chapter three, alongside

---

1128 Sarma 1978; Ghosh 2005.
1129 Ray 1989: 53.
1130 Paranavitana 1970, vol. I: xc, and no. 94; 1983, II.1: nos. 11, 45.
1131 Strauch 2012a: 346–48.
1132 *Jataka* no. 463; Fausbøll 1963, IV: 136–43. See n289.
1133 Thaplyal 1996: 42.
1134 E.g. Rouse 1901, IV: 86f.
1135 All dealt with in chapter three.
1136 Pramanik 2004; 2005; 2008.
1137 Strauch 2012c: 206.

other wares from the Mediterranean, India, and China—the glass most likely having travelled East by sea, continuing as far up the Indus as possible before the final overland trek.[1138] However, in light of the absolute predominance of Western Indian places of origin in the Hoq graffiti, it is not so likely that this Gandharan traveller had come to Socotra direct from a port in the Indus estuary, such as Barbaricon, rather, it is more likely that he would have arrived on a ship from the Gulf of Khambhat.[1139]

Finally, as concerns exotic individuals, there is the interesting case of a visitor who left one graffito [14:13] in Prakrit, using Brahmi script, reading simply 'of Humiyaka,' then further inside the cave writing two lines on a broken-off piece of stalactite, [16:8], the first line being 'ΟΜΟΙΑΓΟ' in Greco-Bactrian script and the Bactrian language, translating into (H)umeyag, the second line being simply a reiteration of his earlier Brahmi graffito. Accordingly, this visitor could have been from as far away as Bactria proper, or, at the very least, from a Kushan stronghold in the Northwest of India where Bactrian was used alongside Kharoshthi or Brahmi, such as Mathura.[1140] (H)umeyag's graffiti are prime examples of bilingualism, and the exhibited language proficiencies, employing the Bactrian and Brahmi scripts, are surprising. However, from the same site where (H)umeyag left a Brahmi graffito with his prakritised name, we find another graffito, [14:15], within a couple of feet mentioning the same name, this one in Sanskrit, the Brahmi reading *nāvika-humiyaka-pu*[*tra*], thus renderable in translation as either 'the son of the captain Humiyaka' or 'the captain, son of Humiyaka.'[1141] The name Humiyaka being highly unusual in an Indian context,[1142] it would be quite a coincidence, indeed, if this graffito does not refer to the same person.

Thus, either the father himself or his son was a captain, most likely based in a port like Barygaza, from which two of four captains [10:4=11:1=11:11, 11:12] attested in the graffiti came, together with three others [11:17, 11:25, 17:1] who did not designate their profession. This would certainly go a long way towards explaining how a father hailing from an area where Bactrian was in use, whether Bactria, Gandhara or Kushan Mathura, would have been proficient in Prakrit as well, and felt the need to express himself in terms of both languages, while having sired a son who chose to make use of Sanskrit. Significantly, other examples of Bactro-Brahmi bilingualism are quite rare, one example being a bilingual sealing with elements of Buddhist iconography from Gandhara.[1143] Another is four Brahmi-Bactrian inscribed *ostraca*, dated 1st–5th century AD, written by three hands (one of them a monk, another possibly a caravan leader—*sarthavaha*), from a major Buddhist monastery at Termez in Uzbekistan.[1144] This was one of the most important crossings of the Oxus river, with routes leading north to either Sogdian Samarkand or the Tarim kingdom of Kashgar.

Taking a step back from analyses of specific graffiti, a general survey of the corpus also yields important insights. Accordingly, although less exotic and more to be expected, the graffiti support an early presence on the island of Arabs and later Axumites, sovereignty in the Gulf of Aden passing gradually from the former to the latter as Axum rose to ascendancy in the region from the early 3rd century AD onwards.[1145] However, while the *Periplus* mentions Arab traders from Muza, and the presence on the island of 'locals' from Hadramawt is unsurprising [e.g., 6:3], one Arab graffito [2:33] appears to give a Minaean clan name, once again providing evidence of the far-flung activities of this tribe as middlemen in South Arabian trade.[1146]

Furthermore, while three Axumite graffiti of the 4th century AD or later provide early evidence of Christianity on Socotra [2:25, 2:27, 2:34],[1147] this small group of some eight graffiti in total, dated 3rd–6th century AD, is perhaps most important as a reminder of the often-forgotten seafaring activities and

[1138] Mairs 2012a.
[1139] Strauch 2012a: 405.
[1140] E.g. Konow 1931–32.
[1141] Strauch 2012c: 181.
[1142] Strauch 2012c: 202–3, Sims-Williams' commentary.
[1143] Rahman and Falk 2011: 162f, 15.06.02.
[1144] Fussman 2011: nos. 19, 22, 186, 209.
[1145] Robin 2012: 440.
[1146] Strauch 2012c: 61, with Robin's commentary.
[1147] Robin 2012: 440.

involvement in the wider Indian Ocean trade of the Axumites via their port of Adulis (also the ocean gateway for kingdoms even further inland, such as Kushite Meroe[1148]). At present, evidence of Axumite trade has been reported from a number of commercial hotspots along the Ocean rim, in addition to the Egyptian Red Sea ports, as we have already seen: near to the old route between Axum and Adulis has been found a hoard dated to the early 3rd century AD consisting of a hundred Kushan gold coins,[1149] but discovered in a convent not established before the 6th century AD;[1150] in Yemen, an Axumite coin hoard has been uncovered at Aden, as well as three coins and ceramic wares from 4th–5th century AD levels at Qana;[1151] in India, finds amount to one Axumite handle fragment dated late 4th–5th century AD from Kamrej, a mixed hoard with Axumite coins from Mangalore in Kerala, a potential coin from Pandian Madurai, and two imitations from Cheran Karur, the coins being dated to the 4th–5th century AD;[1152] and, lastly, one Axumite coin and one imitation have come to light at Tissamaharama in Sri Lanka.[1153] The fact by itself that imitations of Axumite coins circulated widely, not only in South Asia but also in the Eastern Roman Empire, further underlines that Axum played a major role in the later Eastern trade.[1154]

This discussion aside, another valuable feature of the recent evidence from Socotra is that it augments the empirical basis for a new perspective on the later trade between India and the Roman Empire. That is to say, it supplements a growing body of archaeological evidence which does not fit with the traditional picture of 'Indo-Roman trade' as set out in the works of the last century, which would see the trade go into a marked decline from no later than the 3rd century AD onwards.[1155] An idea to a large part based on a too short-sighted interpretation of the development and abandonment of Roman army facilities in Egypt's Eastern Desert. Instead, the numerous presence on Socotra of shippers and merchants from Western India throughout the 2nd–early 5th century AD must now be correlated with the archaeological data for sustained long-distance trade between Late Roman Berenike and India.

While Roman ships and crews would have been used to beating against the prevailing northerlies of the upper Red Sea, where lay Clysma and Aila, this would not necessarily have been the case with ships out of the Indian Ocean,[1156] the captains of which would therefore have preferred the more southern ports of Berenike and Myos Hormos, having no other choice except the former after the latter fell out of use. Both ports have, significantly, yielded 1st–2nd century AD evidence of Indian-made cotton sails,[1157] likely indicating the re-fitting in port of Indian ships. Berenike has, moreover, produced numerous finds from the 4th–5th century AD attesting continued trade with India and Sri Lanka, especially pepper, but also sapphires, cotton textiles and beads, even Indian domestic items and staples.[1158] Accordingly, Late Roman Berenike might have owed much of its trade to visits by Indian ships from Barygaza, proving true the hypothesis of Berenike's excavators that its strong, late involvement in the Indian Ocean trade was not due to Roman initiative as such, but rather reflected the port's inclusion in expanding Indian Ocean trade networks.[1159]

However, while the finds at late Berenike of pepper, sapphires and beads from South India and Sri Lanka cannot easily be correlated with the Socotran graffiti, the fragments of 4th–5th century AD cotton textiles can now, due to their style of weave and dyeing, be sourced to India,[1160] Western India being a particular hotspot for textile production in the early Common Era. Thus, the *Periplus* mentions the export of all kinds of cloth, especially cotton,[1161] from the areas inland from Barygaza and the cities of the

1148 Cf. Haaland 2014.
1149 Mordini 1967: 23–4.
1150 Finneran 2007: 204.
1151 Tomber 2008: 102, 103ff.
1152 Tomber 2005b: 99–100.
1153 Sidebotham 2011: 249.
1154 Sidebotham 2011: 277.
1155 Cf. chapter one.
1156 Whitewright 2007.
1157 Myos Hormos: Blue *et al.* 2011: 196–7; Berenike: Sidebotham 2011: 243.
1158 Sidebotham 2011: chapter 12–13. And see above, this chapter.
1159 Sidebotham 2011: 261.
1160 Wild and Wild 2000: 271–3; 2005; 2014: 101–2.
1161 For a recent overview of sources from Roman Egypt attesting this textile trade, see Droß-Krüpe 2013: 150–1; on the specific textiles mentioned

Satavahanas on the Deccan-plateau (#48, 49, 51); moreover, as we shall see in the next chapter, there were prominent organisations of weavers in the Western Deccan; and, finally, the Berenike cotton fragments with their resist-dyed decorations match 5th century AD paintings from Ajanta in Maharashtra.[1162] They even appear to be similar in weave as well as dyeing to 3rd century AD cotton fragments found at equally far-away Karadong in the Tarim Basin, where they must have been imported by way of Gandhara across the Karakorum Mountains,[1163] providing a parallel example of long-distance trade in textiles to rival that of Berenike.

There is, in other words, good cause to believe that the Western Indian traders attested on Socotra kept up trade with the Roman Red Sea during and after the traditional slowdown of commerce in the 3rd century AD. Moreover, the two Greek Hoq graffiti dated 3rd–4th century AD, the earlier of which was explicitly made by a *nauklêros*, constitute further proof against assuming that trade between the Roman Mediterranean and Indian Ocean had largely died out by the 3rd century AD. As mentioned, Socotra did not fit into the traditional monsoon circuits of Roman merchant ships, so perhaps the presence of these two Greeks on the island at this time indicates that they were tapping into a Western Indian trade circuit, meeting up with Indian merchants on Socotra rather than having to travel all the way to India. There is, nonetheless, additional late evidence for Roman merchantmen sailing out of Berenike and all the way to India, namely, finds throughout Berenike town of South Asian teak beams recycled from scrapped Roman-fashion ships, indicating repairs made to Roman vessels in South Asian.[1164]

Summing up on the Socotran graffiti, though, it is important to emphasise that the testimonies of the *Periplus* and the Hoq graffiti on specifically Indian and Roman trade with Socotra are not contemporaneous, but, rather, supplementary: the former addresses the situation in the mid-1st century AD through the eyes of a Greco-Roman trader, while the latter constitutes diagnostic evidence of some of the visitors to the island in the 2nd–early 5th century AD. In order to properly understand what was going on at Socotra from the 1st–early 5th century AD, then, the gradual creation of the more than 200 Hoq graffiti must be interpreted in the context of wider developments in the Gulf of Aden from the turn of the Common Era to the Muslim Expansion, that is, from the later 1st century BC–7th century AD. Specifically, excavations at Qana, the main port of Hadramawt, have revealed three different phases of activity during these centuries, throughout which 75 per cent of the ceramic assemblage at the site was made up of imported pottery from the entire circumference of the Indian Ocean Rim. The so-called Lower Period is dated roughly 50 BC–later 1st century AD and is dominated by Roman amphorae (making up more than half of the entire assemblage), coarse wares and fine wares, with a few diagnostic Indian finds, and some eight per cent of all sherds being Mesopotamian glazed ware.[1165] This is the time of the *Periplus*' description of Qana (#27–8) as a Hadramawtic port receiving small craft from along the coast, with incense to be stored and shipped inland to the capital of Shabwa, as well as trading with East Africa, Barygaza, Scythia, Ommana at the mouth of the Persian Gulf and the adjacent coast of Parthia.

The Middle Period is dated 2nd–5th century AD, and the characteristic feature of this phase is the marked increase of Indian and Mesopotamian wares, thus, although Mediterranean wares continue to be present at Qana they decrease proportionally. From the 4th century AD, however, a Greek inscription and an *ostracon* have come to light, both Christian. In comparison, neighbouring Sumhuram further east along the coast has allegedly yielded South Indian pottery of the 3rd–2nd century BC, and Western Indian ceramics of the early centuries of the Common Era. Rare finds there are an Indian bronze figurine of around the 3rd century AD, as well as a coin of Kanishka from a layer dated early 4th century AD. Mesopotamian Glazed ware, likewise from the centuries before and after the Common Era, has also been identified. Moreover, Indian cooking pots being the most numerous of all coarse wares at both Qana and

in the *Periplus*, Wild and Wild 2014: 91–101.

[1162] Sidebotham 2011: 243.

[1163] Desrosiers *et al.* 2001.

[1164] Sidebotham 2011: 203–5, 239.

[1165] Sedov 1992: 116–24; 2007: 76–78f, 101; Tomber 2008: 104.

Sumhuram, this must indicate the presence of a sizeable Indian diaspora.[1166] Remarkably, the *Periplus* (32) mentions that already in the mid-1st century AD, Indian ships which were too late in departing back home for Barygaza or Limyrike would winter at Sumhuram.[1167]

Finally, the Late Period at Qana, dated 6th–7th century AD, saw a drastic reduction of Indian ceramics at the port, whereas the dominant pottery had by now become Axumite (beginning to occur already from late Middle levels) and Byzantine period Aila amphorae, while Mesopotamian glazed ware, perhaps also torpedo jars, reveal continued trade with the Persian Gulf. Consequently, the transition from the Lower to the Middle Period at Qana has been interpreted by its excavators as a change from the port serving the local commercial interests of Hadramawt and acting as a place of transit in the collection of frankincense, to a situation where Qana became an active entrepôt for not only Hadramawtic and Roman merchants and shippers, but also traders from India, Mesopotamia (so, perhaps the Palmyrene visitor to Socotra arrived from there, after all, not Egypt) and Axum. Subsequently, in the last two centuries before the port's gradual decline and abandonment, Indian traders are markedly absent in light of the prospering connections with Aila and Axum.[1168]

Thus, the archeological horizon of the Hadramawtic ports provide a neat fit with the numerical and chronological distribution of graffiti in the Hoq Cave, and we must therefore take the abundant evidence for Indian merchants and shippers on Socotra from the 2nd–early 5th century AD as a reflection of Indian overseas trade with the ports of Qana and Sumhuram, probably the former in particular. Judging from the amounts of Indian coarse wares, moreover, Indians must have been at least temporarily settled at Qana and Sumhuram, perhaps waiting for a shift of monsoon, whereas Socotra already had a part-Indian settled diaspora by the mid-1st century AD. Consequently, the much more abundant archaeological evidence from mainland Hadramawt and the Hoq graffiti complement each other nicely and provide quite a detailed picture of maritime trade in the early Indian Ocean.

Note, in closing, moreover, that the above analysis leaves out the role of Mesopotamian merchants sailing out of the Persian Gulf,[1169] this subject sadly being beyond the scope of the present study. However, recent research has established that many 'amphorae' found in India are rather to be properly identified as Mesopotamian torpedo jars which, in combination with finds of Mesopotamian turquoise glazed ware, reveals the importance of a Sasanian maritime trade route to India, both directly from the Gulf and via common entrepôts like Qana and Sumhuram in South Arabia.[1170] Remarkably, there is even evidence of a similar organisation of craftsmanship and trade in Late Antique Southern Mesopotamia to rival the charters of Roman professional *collegia*, some of these formal associations, which were headed by chiefs of the merchants, goldsmiths, silversmiths and highly specialised weavers, no doubt also being involved in the import, export and processing of long-distance trade goods travelling up and down the Gulf.[1171]

Taxes, trade, and contracting corporations of merchants

On the basis of the Hoq graffiti and archaeology of the ports of Hadramawt, however, we are no wiser about the identity of the organisation which leased Dioscourides in the mid-1st century AD according to the *Periplus*, nor can the *corpus* tell us anything about the purpose of such a setup.[1172] In all likelihood, though, the purpose was to ensure the Hadramawtic king an easy and assured annual income from a logistically far-off piece of territory, by farming out to lessees the taxes to be collected on the island's

[1166] Sedov 1992: 136–7; 2007: 79–86, 92, 104; Tomber 2008: 104, 106–7; Pavan 2015.
[1167] Seland 2008b.
[1168] Sedov 2007: 86–9, 104–5; Tomber 2008: 104–5.
[1169] Whitehouse and Williamson 1973.
[1170] Tomber 2007; Tomber 2008: 39ff, 51; 2009: 50–51.
[1171] See, on the one hand, Chabot 1902: 331f, no. 18; on which Wiesehöfer 1996: 192–4, and to be supplemented by Braun 1915: 58–75, together with Wiessner 1968; on the other hand, Brock 2009, with further evidence for assemblies/associations in Seleucia, in Harrak 2005: 43–9, nos. 19–22.
[1172] *Contra* Bukharin 2012: 497, 514–17.

natural produce, which the *Periplus* reports to have been cinnabar and tortoiseshell, but which must also have included frankincense and myrrh, thriving abundantly on the island into recent times.[1173]

Obviously, these lessees could have been prominent members of the island's mixed diaspora of Arabs, Indians and Greeks, having contracted for the island's annual produce as tax-farmers.[1174] However, they could also have been wealthy Arab merchants from mainland Hadramawt. Putting the island under guard would simply have been a way of securing the rights of the tax-farming consortium to all the produce, making it impossible for outsiders to sail in and buy cargoes at the source. This would not necessarily have interfered with the island's mercantile diaspora, who could still sail out to trade, just not exporting frankincense and myrrh unless it was cleared with the contractors.

Indeed, contemporary Roman Egypt employed the same system, to a large extent, with influential families of Alexandria (and Campania at least once, as proven by the case of the *Annii*), who were themselves deeply involved in the Eastern trade, contracting for the right to exact the quarter-tax on imports, from the later 1st century BC–early 2nd century AD. A customs process, it should be noted, which was intimately intertwined with the Roman state and its fiscal infrastructure, therefore no doubt backed up at the last resort by relevant magistrates and their enforcers, comparable to the Hadramawtic king putting Socotra under guard. As a related example, the local *strategos* of Koptos complained to the prefect of Egypt in AD 139 that private tax-contractors were misbehaving and upsetting the public order, disobeying their local superiors (himself included), to which the prefect answered that the regional *epistrategos* should compel them, potentially by force (*epanagkazô*).[1175]

Such a setup on mid-1st century AD Dioscourides is significant in itself, but obviously even more so in conjunction with evidence for similar mercantile organisations contracting to farm state taxes on long-distance trade or operate commercial concessions in logistically inconvenient places. Just some 300 km south-west from Dioscourides, the north-facing shore of the Horn of Africa was called *ta peran*, the 'Far-side' or 'Other Side,'[1176] where high-quality *trogodytic* myrrh, cinnamon, etc., were to be had.[1177] Nonetheless, there was no central authority in the area, only chiefs of each individual market town.[1178] In the above, we have already encountered the so-called 'Nabataean trogodytes' having settled in East Africa to forward precious inland produce out to partners on the coast,[1179] where also Sabaeans ventured from across the Gulf to buy *trogodytic* myrrh at the source.[1180] In addition, Pliny narrates how local inhabitants on the shore, *Troglodytes*, who were intermarried with Ethiopians (from Axum), bought up cinnamon from their neighbours and freighted it across the sea on rafts to the king of Qataban at Ocelis, who due to some unknown political influence had the sole right to market the cinnamon. A story was even circulating at the time about the *Barbaroi* setting fire to the forests producing the cinnamon as a way of getting back at those in power.[1181] *Ta peran* might, then, in light of these Nabataean, Sabaean and Qatabanian influences have to be interpreted more like we do with the so-called 'Rhodian *peraia*,' where the adjective *peraios* is understood not merely as the 'Other Side,' but as signifying a Rhodian possession on the opposite coast,[1182] here the 'Other (Arab) Side.'

In fact, this interpretation is supported by a similar sort of setup even further afield, also reminiscent of the contracting for the Egyptian arabarchy and the leasing out of Dioscourides, namely the management of the Azanian market town of Rhapta, being rich in ivory and tortoise-shell. Due to some 'ancient right' this port and town was under the sovereignty of the Sabaeans, who were at the time themselves subject

1173 Casson 1989: 169f; Doe 1992: 39–40; Singer 2007: 7f, 22f, 24; Sedov 2007: 100; Seland 2010: 44–5.

1174 Perhaps comparable, or functionally equivalent at least, to contemporary Roman economic partnerships, *societates*, cf. Broekaert 2012 for a recent overview, or, more plausibly, tax-farming companies (*publicani*) of the Republic, Badian 1983, and early Empire, Corbier 2008: 216–23.

1175 *BGU* III, 747; Rathbone 2002: 194; Johnson *et al.* 1961: 209, no. 254.

1176 *Periplus* 7.

1177 On the precious plant products of the Far-Side: *Periplus* 7–13; and the below notes on Pliny.

1178 *Periplus* 14.

1179 Pliny *NH*, XII.44.

1180 Pliny *NH*, XII.33.

1181 Pliny *NH*, XII.42.

1182 E.g. Gabrielsen 2000.

to the neighbouring inland kingdom of the Himyarites, and the taxes of the place had been farmed out to merchants of the joint kingdoms' major commercial port, Muza.[1183] These contractors kept in touch with their royal concession by sending out vessels staffed with Arab shippers and crewmen, and had become acquainted with the area and its language by mingling with the natives and intermarrying with them.[1184]

Significantly, the Roman fiscal policy on long-distance trade with India settled on a similar organisational solution in Late Antiquity.[1185] Thus, the still unidentified island of Iotabê in the northern Red Sea had by the later 5th century AD become the main customs station for the Eastern trade, presumably situated somewhere near the mouths of the Gulfs of Suez and Aqaba, where taxes on incoming cargoes would be exacted, and goods transhipped from ocean-going ships to smaller vessels better able to manage the capricious winds and dangerous reefs of the gulfs. The first thing we hear about the subject is that in AD 473 a Saracen occupied the island and evicted its Roman tax collectors, afterwards growing wealthy from the taxes himself. Subsequently, a Roman general retook Iotabê sometime around AD 498, on the grounds that it had previously accrued a not inconsiderable revenue for the emperor. Therefore, he installed on the island a group of Roman merchants, *pragmateutai*, perhaps Jewish according to a later source, who were to re-export or forward, *ekporeuõ*, Indian imports and keep up the collection of taxes on them. Significantly, these merchants were settled 'under their own laws,' *autonomõs*, the customs station being outside the ordinary provincial administration.[1186] In AD 534 Iotabê was recaptured once more and trustworthy tax collectors installed, the island evidently having been lost again in the meantime.[1187]

In consequence, we seem to have a Late Roman parallel to the outsourcing by the state of an important fiscal responsibility, accruing enough revenues to warrant continuous military expeditions to recapture the island, to self-organising merchant groups able to facilitate trade, transhipment and dependable customs collection, even beyond the actual boundaries of the state. During those very same years, after Western Indian graffiti in the Hoq Cave had ceased and Indian pottery more or less disappeared from Qana, both during the 5th century AD, merchants and shippers kept up a brisk trade along the route from Aila, Clysma, and Iotabê in the Red Sea to Elephanta Island—also known as Puri or Gharapuri Island—in the bay of Mumbai Harbour. This island having already previously been involved in maritime trade, as attested by a rectangular brick wharf on its south side and associated ceramics, dated 2nd–5th century AD.[1188]

However, the beaches of Mora Bander on the north-eastern side of Elephanta are strewn with not only Indian fine and coarse wares, but also what may be the greatest assemblage of amphorae sherds in India (Late Roman types and Aila amphorae, but also Mesopotamian torpedo jars), datable to the 6th century AD, perhaps extending into the 7th century. During this period, a local dynasty known as the Konkan Mauryas are known to have controlled Elephanta, patronised the construction of the famous Hindu cave temples, and minted and circulated a lead coinage restricted to this island alone. They were so successful, in fact, in creating a maritime commercial entrepôt that they attracted the attention of the Chalukyas, who launched a successful invasion of the island in AD 634.[1189] A poem celebrating the victorious king describes his conquered prize as '—the fortune of the western sea, with hundreds of ships in appearance like arrays of rutting elephants.'[1190]

What is of special interest here is that no other Indian Ocean site contains the diversity of Late Roman amphorae attested at Elephanta, one of these types having only otherwise been found in the Red Sea at Adulis, and that while coins from earlier neighbouring dynasties occur on Elephanta, none of the lead coins from Elephanta have yet been identified on the mainland. In combination, these factors indicate

[1183] *Periplus* 21–4, on Muza, the Sabaeans and the Himyarites.
[1184] *Periplus* 16-17.
[1185] On Roman policy generally in the Red Sea in this period, see Nappo 2009.
[1186] de Boor 1963: 141, ll. 12–7.
[1187] Mayerson 1992; 1996: 123. Wilson 2015: 29–30.
[1188] Ray 1986: 63.
[1189] Tripathi 2004; Tomber 2008: 128, 165–6; Mangalam 1992; 1993.
[1190] Kielhorn 1900: 10, vv. 20–21.

that the rocky island, with no other resources available than the commerce of its port facilities, managed to make itself an important centre for long-distance trade with Aila and Clysma via Adulis in the Axumite kingdom, but nonetheless operated a closed monetary system of comparatively worthless lead coins. Accordingly, one might suspect a setup similar to contemporary Iotabê at the other end of the trade route, with the Konkan Mauryas managing to focus at Elephanta alone the long-distance trading activities between the Red Sea and the ports of the Konkan coast under their dominion.

This would have facilitated centralised collection of customs dues on import and export, followed by re-export of the goods to the rest of the coast from the wharfs of Elephanta. The coinage could, hypothetically, then be explained by analogy with Ptolemaic Egypt, in which Greek and Roman traders arriving with gold and silver currencies from their home polities in Alexandria had to hand in their foreign coins for re-minting (likely at a fee) at the royal mint, receiving back the substantially more debased Ptolemaic currency, while the king accrued the difference in bullion weight. We even know from a mid-3rd century BC papyrus that the arriving traders were eager to do so, the potential profits from trade exceeding their financial loss from being short-changed by the Alexandrian mint. Moreover, one characteristic consequence of the over-valued Ptolemaic coinage is that it is not found in significant quantities outside Egypt, seeing as it was only of nominal value in its country of origin, being at a clear and well-known bullion value disadvantage everywhere else.[1191]

A similar closed currency system short-changing arriving traders to provide gold and silver for the Konkan Mauryas controlling the long-distance entrepôt of Elephanta may perhaps explain the ubiquitous local lead coinage of the island. None of the visiting merchants would have had any interest in bringing these coins with them outside that port, where their bullion value would have been close to nothing. We know from the Early Roman Empire that trading partners in the Indian kingdoms could be exceedingly picky about the kinds of coins they received in exchange,[1192] so the Ptolemaic comparison might well serve as a plausible hypothesis in this particular case. Furthermore, a later Chalukyan inscription, this one from Porigere on the mainland, dated *c.* 725 AD, reveals how the collection of taxes and conversion of currencies might also have been handled earlier at Elephanta: in the city of Porigere in Karnataka, the collection of taxes from the townspeople was entrusted to local associations of craftsmen, *shrenis*, including those of braziers and oil-men, respectively, but further details are lost due to the fragmentary state of the following lines.[1193] In other words, the phenomenon of leasing out fiscal obligations by states on the Indian Ocean Rim to organisations of merchants is paralleled slightly later in India by tax collection being entrusted to local professional associations. The merchants of 6th–7th century AD Elephanta, then, being the actual importers of Late Roman and Aila amphorae via Axumite middlemen, might well have served the otherwise inconspicuous Konkan Mauryas in a similar capacity to the contemporary *pragmateutai* of Iotabê, comparable to earlier lessees of Dioscourides and Rhapta, rendering Elephanta Island *the* hotspot of Late Antique Indian Ocean commerce.

Merchants making money at the margins

Summing up on the evidence surveyed and cases presented in this chapter up until now, it should be apparent that Indian Ocean trade from the 1st–6th century AD was very much the result of the combined commercial efforts of Romans, Nabataeans, Palmyrenes, Arabs of Southern Arabia, Axumites and Indians from the West and South of the Subcontinent. In particular, it has been shown that no single group or empire dominated the trade, all taking part in overseas trading ventures according to their geographical position and commercial interests, and that there is no natural 'end' to the long-distance trade between the Mediterranean and the Indian Ocean, for although routes and the roles played by individual polities did change, the trade continued on different hands through the centuries. Thus, prominent developments sketched in the above (being only part of the overall picture) include the 'rise and fall' of direct Roman state involvement in Egypt's Eastern Desert from the late 1st century BC–early 3rd century AD, the major

[1191] Howgego 1995: 52–4, 113, 131–2; Austin 2013: 535, no. 299; *P.Cairo Zen.* 59.021; on this document, see now Bresson 2015.
[1192] Cf. chapter five.
[1193] Barnett 1917–8; referred to as *senige* in the Kanarese. Majumdar 1920: 78; Thaplyal 1996: 124.

growth and subsequent waning of West Indian mercantile involvement in the Gulf of Aden in the 2nd–early 5th century AD, as well as the slow rise and ensuing commercial importance of Axumite shippers and merchants from the 4th century AD onwards, culminating in the subsequent centuries.[1194]

In the process, it has been demonstrated that the ports and boundary zones of the involved states and regions were full of foreign traders, seeking out markets across the sea and travelling there in ships of their own, some, at least, staying for prolonged periods of time, if only to wait for a change of monsoon. Moreover, we find organisations of merchants taking over the collection of important taxes from state authorities in marginal areas, be it the personalised merchant networks of Arabarchs in the Roman Red Sea ports, the autonomous community of traders, tax collectors and transhippers on Iotabê, the Socotran lessees of the king of Hadramawt, the merchants of Muza upholding the Sabaean dynasty's traditional sovereignty in Azanian Rhapta, or some of the less clear-cut cases nonetheless attesting unambiguous commercial organisation or concentration of the long-distance trade, such as export from the 'Far-Side' or import to Elephanta. What looms large in all of these examples is the importance of private merchant networks and modes of organisation with their inherent propensity for the forging of relational contracts, less so the active role or participation of states, who, it appears, rather preferred to be passive recipients of fiscal revenues, only projecting just enough power (if that) into the boundary zones to protect these fiscal interests in the guise of those who traded and those who taxed.[1195]

Such commercial spaces where people of widely different cultural origins met and conducted business have been described in various ways over the years, e.g., as 'ports of trade,'[1196] 'cross-cultural trade diasporas,'[1197] 'middle grounds,'[1198] and 'emporia.'[1199] To differing degrees these concepts emphasise the vital role of religion, state administration, protection, equal force deterrence, common legal framework, consensual convention, ethnicity, symbolic exchange, isolated markets, economic reciprocity, etc.—some of these factors being, obviously, mutually exclusive. However, a view from the 'bottom up' of the commerce and people passing through Indian Ocean ports in the 1st–6th century AD does not provide unanimous empirical grounding for either of these concepts.

For instance, the Roman Red Sea ports of Myos Hormos and Berenike were not merely state-regulated and primitive 'ports of trade,' nor were they developed urban settings with established 'cross-cultural trade diasporas,' or 'middle grounds' based on negotiated consensus and equal force, or even politically or economically separate 'emporia.' Rather, they were port settlements with state representation (offering minimal protection and collecting taxes), hosting a population of Roman citizens involved in trade as well as visiting foreign merchants and shippers (the number of both groups fluctuating with the monsoon), there being no ambiguity about the ultimate cultural or political affiliation of these two sites. In short, they were commercial ports open to whomever wanted to conduct business and pay taxes, long-distance supply and demand bringing people and commodities together in ports near and far from the sources of production. However, traders operating in Far-Side territory or administering Rhapta might well have experienced these places as 'middle grounds,' and the long-standing diaspora of Dioscourides was, obviously, just that, likely accompanied by shorter-lived Indian diasporas in Qana and Sumhuram during the 2nd–early 5th century AD.

On the contrary, if a common institutional framework needs to be invoked, it should be that of the 'merchant organisation,' organised merchants being the active partners of the respective states in the fiscal administration of the significant commerce created by the merchants themselves, in and through areas beyond the effective reach of the Indian Ocean states, Rome included. Such merchant organisations could be formal or informal, ethnic or professional, private or public, these three pairs of opposites

[1194] Compare Seland 2008a: 76–8.

[1195] Cf. Das and Poole 2004: 3–30, on the dynamic processes which arise in the margins of states, sometimes gaining such economic importance that the marginal character of the area in question has to be protected to ensure the continuation of this income.

[1196] Polanyi 1965: 263.

[1197] Curtin 1984.

[1198] White 1991; Malkin 2011; Woolf 2011.

[1199] Demetriou 2012.

merely representing supplementary spectra by which we can seek to classify individual instances of organisation: whether they be personalised elite networks involved in public tax-farming and private trade (e.g. the *Julii* and *Norbanii*), informal ethno-religious and professional organisations (e.g. South Arabian and Nabataean Far-Side involvement, caravan- and trading-stations, Nabataean representation at Puteoli, Indian shippers and merchants out of Barygaza, etc.), formal professional associations (e.g. Palmyrene merchants and shippers, waterskin-raft makers, gold- and silversmiths), or traders organised for public contracting (e.g. merchants of Muza, lessees of Dioscourides, *pragmateutai* of Iotabê), etc.

Emphatically, though, this is not to say that states did not play a role of their own in facilitating long-distance trade across the Indian Ocean in the early centuries of the Common Era, nor to say that they did not exert themselves to try and increase, channel and control the possible taxes accruing from this mercantile activity. However, while this point has been made in a sound way for states,[1200] the supplementary counterpoint, namely, that non-state actors in the guise of private networks and merchant organisations also played an important role, particularly in the margins of the states where centralised power was difficult, or too expensive, to wield, has received little attention and only a predominantly negative assessment.[1201] Nonetheless, a wider view of the role of trading networks, diasporas and associations in Roman Egypt and the Indian Ocean reveals their vital value as agents of their respective states in areas otherwise considered beyond efficient fiscal control.

[1200] See especially Seland 2007b, 2010.

[1201] E.g. Seland 2010: 79–80.

Chapter 8

The invisible hand of Indian organisations

This chapter is a direct counterpart to chapter four on *collegia* in Rome and the long-distance trade. In the former chapter, though, the organisations satisfying actual demand at Rome were under study, whereas here, the Indian organisations creating the necessary supply will be investigated. These organisations are in no way 'invisible' in Indian studies of production and trade in the Indian Ocean in the Early Historic period,[1202] however, the majority of studies taking Roman consumption, that is, imports, as the point of departure, mostly fail to move beyond the ports and coastline of the Subcontinent, assuming a more or less ready-made inland supply of goods for the sea-going 'Indo-Roman trade.'[1203] Remarkably, though, a closer study of the modes of organisation involved in the creation of an Indian supply of commodities widely in demand elsewhere along the Indian Ocean rim reveals striking institutional parallels with related organisations in contemporary Rome, such as the *collegium* of *negotiatores eborarii et citriarii*, *collegium thurariorum et unguentariorum*, *collegium aromatariorum* and groupings of *aurifices* and *sericarii*. Thus, although demand and supply was channelled through organisations which were in many ways worlds apart, these organisations were, in fact, interacting economically from the extreme opposite ends of trade routes operated by the multiple economic actors outlined in the last two chapters—the demand represented by the organisations at Rome was met by organisations harnessing supply in India.

At long last, then, we turn to the evidence for associations in Early Historical India, a large array of sources being available for the study of organisation of crafts and commerce from the width and breath of the Subcontinent. However, there is a clear divide in the nature of the epigraphic and literary source material, almost all of the inscriptions relating to Indian associations being concerned with the setting up and running of endowments (which is also the case with some Roman inscriptions featuring *collegia*, but nowhere near the majority, as related at the beginning of chapter three),[1204] whereas the literary sources consistently concern themselves with formalistic matters only, especially the relationship between groups and the state, and, in consequence, which rules and regulations ought to govern associations. Accordingly, the inscribed and written sources complement each other nicely.[1205]

As with the Roman tradition for occupational *collegia*, the Indian literary tradition alleges that the inception and early development of associations can be traced as far back as the early 5th century BC, or earlier,[1206] but none of these sources were put down in writing until sometime in or after the 3rd century BC.[1207] However, the earliest epigraphical evidence attesting early Indian professional associations supports their existence from at least the later 2nd century BC, examples being recorded both in the Western, Eastern and Southern Deccan.[1208] In consequence, the earliest Roman and Indian associations seem to have emerged at around the same time, the 2nd century BC, if we are to date this development by epigraphy alone.

Nonetheless, we need to turn to a literary work like the *Arthashastra*, a treatise on statesmanship, if we are to become any wiser about the internal workings of these associations.[1209] While this work is traditionally attributed to *c*. 300 BC, an important study has argued that whereas parts of it may be older, the main text

1202 Majumdar 1920; Ray 1986; Thaplyal 1996; Thapar 2004: 248–53.
1203 As set out in chapter one on historiography.
1204 A few monumental dedications can be mentioned, though: e.g. Deva 1937–38 (*shreni* of stonemasons erecting stone seats at bathing ghat); Burgess and Indraji 1881: 54, no. 31(*shreni* of corn-dealers establishing seven-celled *vihara*); arguably also the relief by the ivory carvers of Vidisha, dealt with in chapter three; in this chapter, the 'charter-like' inscription of the silk-weavers of Mandasore will also be dealt with in detail below.
1205 Thaplyal 1996: 2–6.
1206 Majumdar 1920: 9–13; Thaplyal 1996: 20–6.
1207 Compare the extant fragments of Buddhist texts appearing in Ashokan edicts, cf. Thapar 1995: 81f, 85.
1208 Epigraphical evidence from the (later) 2nd century BC: Mahadevan 2003: nos. 3, 6 (Mangulam, S. Deccan); Lüders 1912: no. 1335 (Bhattiprolu, E. Deccan); Deshpande 1959: 77 (Pitalkhora, W. Deccan).
1209 Kangle 1965–72.

appears to have been composed in the early centuries of the Common Era, perhaps even as late as the 3rd century AD.[1210] However, what is arguably the oldest part of the work, book two,[1211] refers to associations as both *sangha*, traditionally translated as 'corporation,'[1212] and *shreni*, translated as 'guild.'[1213]

Significantly, the *Arthashastra* suggests that municipal magistrates charged with supervising the economic life of their city should enter 'the laws, transactions, customs and fixed rules' of corporations, as well as other groups, in public registers.[1214] Indeed, other sources for early Indian law advise similarly, stating that professional groups should formally establish their own rules in accordance with religious doctrine, and afterwards get the king to ratify and respect these official charters.[1215] After having been set down in a document and agreed upon, all members and officers had to abide by these codified rules, or risk being prosecuted by the assembly if they did not, and new members therefore also had to sign the charter to gain entry into the association.[1216] Not only did the rules concern relations between members generally, though, the rules of an association in regard to its members having the force of public laws,[1217] they also vested power to contest the decisions of elected leaders with the member assembly, in which case the dispute was to be settled by a royal court.[1218]

Moreover, there is early evidence in the *Arthashastra* on the collective responsibilities of corporations of artisans regarding fulfilment of agreements entered into as a group and the internal division of earnings between members, these rules being enforced by fines or exclusion.[1219] Indeed, this potential for communal action and economic activity is further borne out by slightly later Indian lawmakers, who inform us that the member assembly of an association could authorise one of their own number to represent and contract on behalf of the association as a whole,[1220] while transactions relating to both individual members and the group should be settled in accordance with 'whatever be the customary law of the corporation.'[1221]

Finally, a number of inscriptions scattered all over the Subcontinent reveal that Indian associations also acted as recipients and managers of endowments (*akshayanivi*), concrete examples of which we shall encounter below, the collective responsibility of associations for guaranteeing the materials entrusted with their craftsmen members, as recorded in the *Arthashastra*, shedding a sidelight from the literary sources on this economic capability of professional organisations.[1222] Indeed, the highly institutionalised nature of endowments serves well to broaden the analysis of Indian associations into the intertwined spheres of the social, religious and economic. For while the actual setting up of perpetual endowments was in itself a highly economic procedure, their purposes were exclusively pious (either charitable or commemorative), creating circumstances conducive to the fostering of strong social and religious ties between both the enactor of an endowment, its managers and the recipients.[1223]

As such, endowments are uniquely attested examples of an 'embedded' sector of the economy: on the one hand, the money had to be lent out at interest to finance the stipulated purpose of the endowment, on the other hand, the money was protected against the ordinary risks inherent to putting money to work on a financial market by being entrusted with a group accepting full economic responsibility for

1210 Trautmann 1971. See, however, the critique of the former in Mital 2004.
1211 Thapar 2004: 184f.
1212 *Arthas.* II.7(2), but also, e.g. III.14(12). Attempt at terminological clarification in Thaplyal 1996: 164.
1213 *Arthas.* II.4(16), but also e.g. IV.1(2). Cf. Thaplyal 1996: 7–8.
1214 *Arthas.* II.7(2); Thaplyal 1996: 73.
1215 Thaplyal 1996: 25 (*Gautama Dharmasutra*), 34 n117 (*Manusmriti*).
1216 Thaplyal 1996: 37–39, 74 (drawing on the *Brihaspatismriti* and *Katyanasmriti*).
1217 Thaplyal 1996: 96–106.
1218 Thaplyal 1996: 53–4 (*Brihaspatismriti*).
1219 *Arthas.* III.14(12–18). This is remarkably similar to a mid-5th century AD Roman inscription, constituting a formal agreement between a builders' association and the local magistrate of Sardis in Asia Minor: *Sardis* VII.1.18. Treated in detail in Garnsey 1998, especially p. 79.
1220 Thaplyal 1996: 41–2 (*Brihaspatismriti*).
1221 While *Arthas.* III.7(40) concerns inheritance specifically, Kangle notes that the *Manusmriti* (8.41) states that all matters regarding corporations were to be handled in accordance with their customary laws.
1222 *Arthas.* IV.1(2–3).
1223 On the topic of endowments entrusted with Indian associations generally, see Thaplyal 1996: 85–96.

the preservation of the principal sum.[1224] In other words, profit creation on market terms being subjected to overriding socio-religious concerns embodied in the ties between managers of an endowment, the donator and the pious purposes stipulated by the latter.[1225]

Remarkably, the Western Deccan in which the habit of Indian endowments first bloomed from the 1st century AD, in both Buddhist and Brahmanic contexts, monastic and ascetic, was also the region which reaped the greatest profits from long-distance trade with the West, particularly, but not exclusively, derived from Romans merchants arriving with gold and silver to exchange for goods available at the ports of the Gulf of Khambhat and along the Konkan Coast. Thus, it has recently been argued that the sudden increase in 'depositable wealth' in the form of silver and gold sparked the institutional invention of the endowment in an Indian context,[1226] spreading rapidly to Gandhara which also enjoyed considerable profits from its location at a major Eurasian crossroads where routes intersected from Central Asia, India and the Western Regions of China in the Tarim Basin.[1227] Thus, Roman and Indian endowments as institutional *comparanda* may, fascinatingly, even be related phenomena, in so far as interaction in the form of profits from the long-distance trade between Rome and India made for fortunes at the former city, some of which were used to set up endowments with *collegia*, and private fortunes and royal revenues in India, some of which were used to set up endowments with associations paying interests to the benefit of entitled religious communities.

Whether this specific hypothesis is true or not, we have already observed in the above how such a combination of collective economic, social and religious interests and purposes as revealed here for Early Historical Indian associations, was also the very essence of the association phenomenon in the ancient Mediterranean. Thus, we have seen how the *collegium* of *negotiatores eborarii et citriarii* was strictly organised around an annual round of communal banquets (New Year's Day being religious, others relating to the cult of the emperor) and the distribution of money entrusted with the association both by its members and its patron; how the *collegium thurariorum et unguentariorum* expressed itself as a community making an offering for the well-being of the imperial household; how the *collegium aromatariorum* represented by its president made a public dedication to Jupiter Optimus Maximus; and, finally, how what little we know indicates that the *sericarii* also made a communal religious dedication. Significantly, moreover, individuals belonging to these professions acted in a like manner on their own: a *gemmarius* and a *negotiator sericarius* both constructed temples, a *margaritarius* erected a basilica as a meeting-place for the *collegium* over which he presided as president, and another *margaritarius* and the same *negotiator sericarius* just mentioned set up commemorative endowments.

In addition, we know that Nabataeans involved in the supply of incense and unguents for Rome established a temple at Puteoli to their own supreme god, as did Tyrians and Berytians to their deities of choice, and that the Palmyrene Red Sea shippers and merchants of Koptos possessed a monumental complex in that city, which must have housed both social, religious and professional activities, to name but a few examples from the preceding chapters. As we shall see in the following, though, there is equally substantive evidence attesting the important social and religious dimensions of Indian associations. Thus, professional associations and merchant organisations of the Subcontinent were not merely passive recipients of endowments benefitting ascetics, but also active donors to temples, monasteries and their personnel, these communal acts of religious piety (financed by the crafts and trade of the members) evidently being of the utmost importance, seeing as they not only created a feeling of community internal to the group, but also advertised this constructed communality outwards to the surrounding society.

Remarkably, then, both the historical and institutional developments of Roman and Indian professional associations mirror one another to quite an extent. As regards their basic rules and regulations, these seem to have been surprisingly similar, but what is even more striking is their mutual intertwining

1224 Cf. the 'chains of credit' constituted by Greek associations participating in such financial activities; Gabrielsen 2005: 146.
1225 Compare more generally Parry and Bloch 1989: 23–28, and more spercifically Parry 1989: 66–77.
1226 Falk 2008: 145.
1227 On the sudden booming of wealth, property and endowments in Gandharan monasticism, see Schopen 1994, 2004b, 2007.

of social, religious and economic activities within a common institutional framework, namely, that of their respective traditions for 'associating,' offering members ample opportunities to find partners for relational contracts. Nonetheless, it is clear that these traditions developed separately far apart, each phenomenon being firmly rooted in the wider historical trajectory of its own region, the Mediterranean and South Asia, respectively, with the possible exception of endowments.[1228] In consequence, the underlying explanation of some of their functional similarities in activities related to economic matters, in the widest sense of the word, should rather be sought in analogous institutional solutions to similar circumstances, here created by the challenges and opportunities of the market in the role of Eurasian societies generally,[1229] as well as the growing importance of long-distance trade in connecting markets near and far across the width and breadth of Eurasia.[1230]

In summary, the complex societies involved in Indian Ocean trade at the turn of the Common Era hosted self-organising groups facilitating production, long-distance trade and retail, managing themselves through formal rules, shared social norms and conventions, as well as by religious worship and cultic activities. To a surprising degree, moreover, these comparable groups from near and far even happened to exhibit institutional similarities derived from a shared experience of trade on market terms, a process of alignment which was further reinforced by their subsequent long-distance trade with one another.[1231] These claims will be substantiated in the following.

Ivory carvers, weavers, and sea-going merchants in Western India

In chapter three, the West Indian kingdoms of the Western Kshatrapas and the Satavahanas were briefly introduced, the former based in present-day Gujarat, ancient Ariake, the latter in Maharashtra (extending into Andra Pradesh), ancient Dachinabades, locked in a struggle for supremacy over the northern Konkan Coast. The present study will not delve further into the intricacies of the political history of this period, instead focusing narrowly on the evidence for economic organisation, production and long-distance trade in the Western Deccan in, mainly, the 1st–6th century AD. In fact, we have already encountered the ivory carvers of Vidisha (chapter three), as well as merchants and shippers sailing out of Barygaza (chapter seven), the former being representatives of organised Indian producers of ivory goods in demand in the Roman west, the latter being concrete examples of exporters of such commodities to the Gulf of Aden and Red Sea, while Greco-Roman merchants are also known to have travelled directly to Barygaza to purchase wares closer to the source, as we know from the *Periplus*.[1232]

While the ivory carvers of Vidisha are only known from a laconic inscription, nonetheless indicating that they advertised themselves as a formal community, more informative evidence is available from Nashik in the Thalgat Pass, on the northernmost of three routes heading inland through the Sahyadri Mountains from the ports of Sopara and Kalyan on the Konkan coast, both mentioned in the *Periplus*.[1233] Beyond the Sahyadris lay the central regions of the Satavahana kingdom, in particular their main city of Paithan, as well as the important commercial and production centres of Ter and Bhokardan, mentioned previously for their role in the production of carved ivories.[1234] Significantly, though, these Satavahana cities and ports of the Dachinabades country were known to the author of the *Periplus* for entirely different exports:

> Paithan, twenty days' travel to the south from Barygaza; and, from Paithan, about ten days to the east, another very large city, Ter. From these there is brought to Barygaza, by conveyance in wagons over

1228 For a more thorough analysis of the formal aspects of not only ancient Roman and Indian but also early Medieval Chinese associations, see Evers: forthcoming.

1229 Compare the argument of Graeber 2011 about the societal upheavals caused by the development of market trade in Eurasia, building on the concept of an 'Axial Age' introduced by Jaspers 1949.

1230 Cf. the similar argument about the impetus of long-distance trade to state formation in the Indian Ocean, in Seland 2010: 85–86.

1231 Indeed, such interaction and commercial alignment has recently been shown to exist already between Harappan and Egyptian (gold) weights, and between 1st millennium BC Indian and Mesopotamian weighing measures, cf. Falk 2015: 112.

1232 *Periplus* 41–9, 64. A wreck off Bet Dwarka some 400 km west of the Gulf Khambhat may have been a Roman ship—it was certainly carrying Roman amphorae; Gaur *et al.* 2006.

1233 *Periplus* 50–2.

1234 Ray 1986: 67–70, 83–5, 131–3.

> very great roadless stretches, from Paithan large quantities of onyx, and from Ter large quantities of cloth of ordinary quality, all kinds of cotton garments, garments of *molochinon* [unidentified], and certain other merchandise...[1235]

These Satavahana trade goods were shipped overland to Barygaza[1236] at the time of the writing of the *Periplus*, for the simple reason that the Western Kshatrapas were occupying and blocking the former Satavahana ports (and mountain passes leading down to them) for a number of years during the mid-1st century AD.[1237] As mentioned in chapter four, onyx was an important material of Roman goldsmiths and jewellers, specimens lost *en route* having been unearthed at Berenike. However, what is even more interesting is the mention of inland Satavahana production of 'all kinds of cotton garments,' which was subsequently re-exported from Barygaza, there described as 'cotton cloth of all kinds.'[1238] Fragments of Indian cotton textiles have, as we have already seen, been discovered at Berenike, and inscriptions from Nashik[1239] provide vital details about the organisation of Satavahana textile production—some of which might have been in the service of the king, who is known from a tax-sealing dated *c.* 18 AD to have levied regional taxes in cotton, which would subsequently have had to be processed into textiles.[1240]

Specifically, a later 1st century AD inscription by the son-in-law, Ushavadata, of an important Western Kshatrapa king, specifies how he made a perpetual endowment (an *akshayanivi*) with two different weavers' associations (*shrenis*) in the neighbouring town of Govardhana, the major principal, 2000 *kahapanas* (for *karshapanas*), at 12 per cent interest per year to be spent on clothes for the Buddhist monks at Nashik, the minor principal, 1000 *kahapanas*, at nine per cent interest per year for monks' food during the rainy season, this endowment to be announced and registered, significantly, with the *nigama* assembly of Govardhana [**Figure 17**].[1241] Specifically, individual traders or merchants are signified by Sanskrit *naigama* (Prakrit: *negama*), being the inhabitants of a *nigama* (same spelling and meaning in Prakrit), meaning a 'market town' or 'city of merchants.'[1242] Accordingly, the crafts associations of weavers, *shrenis*, based at Govardhana, were subject to that market town's merchant assembly, constituting a corporate and authoritative body—somewhat like a contemporary Roman *ordo* with authority over its own members.

What is more, another inscription of Ushavadata's at Nashik commemorates how he had equipped the route from Barygaza (*Bharukachha*) to Govardhana with rest-houses, wells and free ferries, no doubt intended to facilitate the arrival of merchants and their goods from the Satavahana kingdom as mentioned in the *Periplus*.[1243] This is the more remarkable, because Ushavadāta's inscription detailing the perpetual endowment to Buddhist monks has an appendage concerning a much larger cash grant to the Brahman ascetics of Nashik. One year before the endowment to the Buddhist monks, Ushavadāta had pledged a donation of a thumping 70.000 *karshapanas*, which at the time of this inscription, being four years later, he finally honoured in the form of 2.000 *suvarnas*, that is, Sanskrit for gold coins, the exchange value being specified in writing as 1:35. Seeing as grants had formerly been made in the Western Deccan in *karshapanas*, the traditional silver currency, and that the *Periplus* informs us that Roman gold and silver money was overvalued at Barygaza, we might well believe F. de Romanis who has recently argued that Ushavadata's 2.000 *suvarnas* were Roman gold *aurei*.[1244]

1235 *Periplus* 51, transl. Casson 1989: 83. This was the southernmost leg of the trunk road, *Dakshinapatha*, to North India, see n279.

1236 Long-distance overland trade routes are further attested by the *nigama* (see definition below) of Karad inscribing a dedication at the Bharhut *stupa*, more than 1000 km away in North India, and by individual dedications of three of its inhabitants (Lüders 1912: nos. 705, 767, 809, 891), as well as by affluent travellers from Vidisha (no. 712), Bhokardan (no. 797) and Nashik (no. 799). Furthermore, new epigraphic evidence of Satavahana inland trade is provided by inscriptions at the *stupa* of Kanaganahalli, cf. Nakanishi and v. Hinüber 2014: especially, I.10, p. 34, a caravan leader from the North; II.1.1, p. 41, a financier from Dhanyakataka; II.4.1.1, p. 60, a banker-merchant from Bhokardan.

1237 *Periplus* 52, cf. Casson 1989: 215, commentary 52:17.19–21; and Seland 2010: 55. Also Cribb 2000: 45.

1238 *Periplus* 49.

1239 Ray 1986: 71–2, 83.

1240 Falk 2009a: 198–200.

1241 Senart 1905–6: 82–5, no. 12; for the *nigama sahhā* (assembly), see Majumdar 1920: 135; Thaplyal 1996: 11, 90. For the currency, see Sircar 1965: 428.

1242 Sanskrit: *s.v. nigama* in Monier-Williams 1979; *s.v. naigama* in Apte 1957–59. Prakrit: *s.v. nigama* and *negama* in Rhys Davids and Stede 1921–5. See discussion in Thaplyal 1996: 6–12; 1972: 227–9; and Ray 1986: 111.

1243 Senart 1905–6: 78–81, no. 10.

1244 *Periplus* 49. Romanis 2006: 69–73; Falk 2008: 143–4. Also Sircar 1965: 428.

Figure 17
Outside view of the *vihara* at Nashik whose verandah is inscribed with Ushavadata's endowment along its upper walls, Maharashtra. Photograph by the author.

By established convention, these were valued at 1:25 in relation to the silver *denarius* in the West, which would indeed have made exchange of *aurei* with Indian traders at Barygaza at 1:35 a profitable business. Thus, the inscriptions of Ushavadata not only refer to the trade route between Barygaza and Govardhana, but also attest the actual investment at such inland production centres of gold coins acquired by this Kshatrapa royal via the thriving commerce between local Indian merchants and visiting Romans at Barygaza.[1245] Consequently, the Indian cotton fragments found at Berenike can be connected with the export of cotton textiles from Barygaza, arriving from the Satavahana kingdom being a large producer of cotton garments, some of the royal proceeds from this trade between Rome and India finding its way back inland to the very production centres creating the necessary supply of goods for export.

This is certainly the case with the 3000 silver '*kahapanas*' deposited with the two associations of weavers at Govardhana, who accordingly had to put the money to work accruing interests no smaller than nine and 12 per cent, respectively, while part, or all, of the 2.000 *suvarnas* were likely invested in the same way, seeing as this donation was also 'registered' at Govardhana. The more likely because perpetual endowments, *akshayanivi*, are subsequently known from the entire Subcontinent, in both Buddhist and Brahmanic contexts.[1246] Finally, a 3rd century AD inscription at Nashik informs us that perpetual endowments continued to be a viable financial construction, by recording the intent of providing medicine for sick monks through investment of thousands of *karshapanas* at interest with at least four different associations, *shrenis*, of craftsmen, likely also in Govardhana.[1247] Similarly, a perpetual endowment was set up in AD 333 at Nagarjunakonda in the Eastern Deccan, also former Satavahana heartland, so-called *dinari* (likely *aurei* or their imitations[1248]) being divided among four different *shrenis*, the interest to be used for

[1245] This is the case upon which Falk 2008 bases his hypothesis about profits from the long-distance trade providing the impetus for the development of Indian endowments, as mentioned above.
[1246] See generally, Schopen 1994; and more specifically, Konow 1931–2: 55–61, no. 10 (Mathura); Falk 2008: 145–7 (Gandhara); Sankaranarayanan 1977 (Alluru).
[1247] Senart 1905–6: 88–9, no. 15.
[1248] Romanis 2006: 77–82. See also Sircar 1965: 428.

the embellishment of a temple, and the local *nigama* being charged with supervising their conduct and enforcing the payment of interests.[1249]

As in Rome, then, where affluent *margaritarii* endowed large sums of money with *collegia* contemporary with the *shrenis* of weavers, these Indian professional groups must have been stable, sufficiently well-organised economically, and involved in business profitable enough for them to manage and sustain 'perpetual' foundations. A state of affairs, which, as we have seen, receives support from Indian legal literature on the possession of communal funds and financial corporativity.

Likewise, the economic importance of *shrenis* is manifest at Junnar in the second pass over the Sahyadris, the middle one through the Nanaghat, where rock temples were carved and established from the mid-1st–2nd century AD.[1250] A Shaka (that is, Kshatrapa) member of a local *shreni*, an affiliation meriting mention in his commemorative inscription, was wealthy enough to endow two pieces of productive land to the ascetic community,[1251] while another inscription is parallel to the foundations at Nashik in recording the dual endowment of money with the *shreni* of bamboo-workers, at 21 per cent per year, and with that of the braziers, their stipulated rate of interest being lost.[1252] Significantly, moreover, a third inscription by the *shreni* of corn-dealers itself reveals that associations were not merely recipients of other people's charitable wealth, but could also possess means of their own and expend it on similar purposes (like the ivory carvers of Vidisha): they sponsored a seven-celled *vihara* and an accompanying cistern on their own.[1253]

Remarkably, a unique inscription sheds further light on the internal life and workings of not just an ancient Indian *shreni*, but, of particular interest to this study, one of silk-weavers, dating from the 5th century AD:[1254] (stanzas central to the below analysis are marked in **bold**).

(May this poem be) successful.

1. Worshipped by the hosts of gods that they may live, by *siddhas* [demigods] for their success, by *yogis*, only intent on meditation, their senses under control, seeking salvation, and by sages with devotion, their only wealth their intense austerities, able to curse and bless, cause of the sinking and rising of the world—May the maker of Light protect you.
2. Even the divine sages, wise in the knowledge of the truth, do not know him fully, however hard they try; him who with his rays far reaching feeds the whole three worlds, praised as he rises by *gandharvas* [demigods], gods, *siddhas*, *kinnaras* [demigods] and men together, bestowing their desires upon his worshippers—hail to that Savitr [here, another name for *Surya*, the Sun].
3. Shining forth day by day, the net of his beams pouring from the wide and lofty summit of the mountain of dawn, his beams as ruddy as the flushed cheek of a tipsy woman. May *Vivasvan* [epithet of the Sun-god], adorned with a garland of rays, protect you.
4. Men famed throughout the world for their craft came from the region of Lata, where the hills are covered with forests lovely with lofty trees bowing low with the burden of blossoms, and with fine temples, halls and monasteries.
5. Drawn by the virtues of the kings of this country, caring nothing for the real and manifold hardships of the journey, filled with respect, first with their minds and then bodily, they came to Dashapura, bringing their children and kinsfolk.
6. In course of time the city became the crest-jewel of the land, the land adorned with a thousand hills whose rocks are damp with the drops that fall from the cheeks of rutting elephants, the land whose lovely ornaments are trees bowed low with flowers;

[1249] Sircar 1963–64: 4–7.
[1250] Ray 1986: 72–3, 83, 131; Shinde *et al.* 2007. Dating according to Dehejia 1972: 180–1.
[1251] Burgess and Indraji 1881: 45–6, no. 13.
[1252] Burgess and Indraji 1881: 47–8, no. 16.
[1253] Burgess and Indraji 1881: 54, no. 31.
[1254] Editions and translations in Fleet 1888, III: 84-88, no. 18; and Basham 1983, the latter being reproduced here with some notes; see also discussion in Thaplyal 1996: 180–94.

7. where lakes are alive with wild-fowl, their waters glittering by the banks, all bright with many petals fallen from the flowering trees on the shore, adorned with full-blown lotuses;
8. where on the pools the wild geese seem shut in golden cages, formed by scattered yellow pollen from lotuses swayed by tremulous ripples, pools radiant with many water lilies which bend with the weight of their stamens;
9. where the trees are bowed with the burden of blossom, and hum with bold tribes of bees made drunk with their nectar, and where the women of the town, forever singing, make beautiful the groves;
10. where the tall houses seem like pale peaks of cloud bright with flashes of lightning, so very high, so very white, with fluttering banners and women.
11. Other houses, high as the peak of Kailasa, radiant with tall turrets and pavilions, are loud with the sound of music, their frescoed walls lovely amid the groves of swaying banana trees.
12. The houses, wearing roof-pavilions like garlands, rise as though they have torn through the earth, like a chain of heavenly palaces bright as the rays of the full moon.
13. The city shines, embraced by the dancing ripples of two fair rivers, like the body of Smara by large-breasted Priti and Rati [all gods, the latter two of affection and sexual pleasure, respectively].
14. With Brahmanas adorned with truthfulness, forbearance, restraint, peace, firmness in keeping vows, purity, resolution, learning, good conduct, modesty, strength of purpose, and intellect, paragons of wisdom and penance, never losing their nerve the city is resplendent, like the sky with a host of shining planets.
15. **So, all together, through constant association their friendship expanding from day to day, honoured by the kings like their own sons, they [the weavers] dwelt happily, rejoicing in the city.**
16. **Some became pastmasters in archery, pleasant to the ear (from the twang of the bowstring); others became knowers [i.e., tellers] of varied tales, about hundreds of good deeds; while others, unassumingly virtuous, fully devoted to discoursing on righteousness (*dharma*), were skilled in speaking that which is useful, pleasantly, not harshly.**
17. **Some remained excellent in their (ancestral) craft, and others, knowers of the self, mastered astrology; others, even today, reckless in battle, strive to wreak harm upon their foes.**
18. **Wise, having charming wives, of famed and widespread family, adorned with conduct worthy of their stock, true to their vows, ready to help their friends, others are firm and trustworthy in their friendships.**
19. **The guild (*shreni*) is even more glorius from other such men, their attachment to the senses conquered, their conduct righteous, gentle, with virtue predominant, like gods on an earthly journey, noble and free from passion, the crest-jewels of their families.**
20. **Though she be endowed with youth and beauty, though she be adorned with golden necklaces and garlands of flowers, a woman will not go to meet her lover in secret until she has put on two silken garments.**
21. **And these men, who have adorned their whole earth in robes of silk, pleasant to the touch, lovely to the eye, with varied stripes of different colours,**
22. remembered that the whole world was very fickle, unstable, blown by the wind like the flower in the ear of a fairy, as was all that is human, and all wealth, however large, and so they made an auspicious and firm resolve.
23. When Kumara Gupta was ruler of the earth, whose undulous girdle is made of the four oceans, whose large breasts are Sumeru and Kailasa [mythical mountains], whose laughter is the full-blown flowers wafted from the woods' edges;
24. there was (ruling in Dashapura) the governor, king Vishvavarman. His mind was as keen as Shukra's or Brihaspati's [legendary lawmakers]; most eminent of kings throughout the world, his deeds in battle equalled Arjuna's [an epic hero].
25. Full of compassion for the poor, fulfilling his word to the wretched and distressed, very merciful, lord of the lordless, a wishing-tree to those who loved him, a giver of protection to those in fear, he was the friend of all the land.

26. His son, endowed with firmness and good judgement, dear to his kinsmen, as if his subject's kinsman, removing the sorrows of his kinsmen, King Bandhuvarman, was extremely skilful in destroying the ranks of his proud enemies.
27. Handsome and young, expert in battle, endowed with modesty, who, though a king, was never carried away by infatuation, surprise, or similar (undesirable emotions), the embodiment of erotic sentiment, though unadorned, he shines in beauty, like a second god of love.
28. Remembering him, even today, the large-eyed enemy beauties, broken by the fierce affliction of widowhood, shiver in fear, and their firm breasts are weary and pained (from their constant trembling).
29. **When Bandhuvarman, the noble, the bull among kings, the strong-shouldered, was well protecting this flourishing Dashapura, the silk-weavers, who had formed a guild, skilled in their craft, with hoarded wealth had this incomparably noble temple made for the god with burning rays.**
30. Its broad-based pointed tower is like a mountain, white as the mass of the pure rays of the risen moon, it shines, lovely to the eye, like a glorious crest-jewel set in (the turban) of the City of the West [i.e., Dashapura].
31. At the time when women are united with their lords, pleasant from the slight warmth of the (once-) fiery rays of the sun, when the fish lie low in the water, when no one watches the rays of the moon or the terraces of palaces, or uses sandal paste or fans or garlands, when the cold destroys the lotus,
32. in the season lovely with humming of bees, drunk with the nectar of full-blown flowers of *rodhra* and *priyangu*, and of jasmine, when the solitary branches of *nagana* trees dance with the force of a cold wind, harsh with drops of dew;
33. when the fall of the dew is scorned by young men in the grip of passion, closely embracing the full and swelling thighs and breasts of women they love;
34. **when four hundreds of years had passed, and ninety-three more from the establishment of the clan of the Malavas, when (men) look forward to the thunder of the clouds;**
35. **in the bright half of the month Sahasya, on the auspicious thirteenth day, with a ceremony of benediction this temple was established.**
36. **Then, under other kings, when much time had passed, part of this temple fell into disrepair, so now**
37. **this house of the sun has been again repaired, for the increase of their fame, and made altogether most noble, by the noble guild.**
38. **It is very high and white, as though touching the sky with its lovely pinnacles, a resting place for the first clear rays of the rising moon and sun.**
39. **When five hundred years, and twenty more, and nine had passed, on the second (day) of the bright half of the month Tapasya;**
40. When he [Kamadeva, god of love] whose body was destroyed by Hara [epithet of Shiva] has (an) increased (supply of) arrows, thanks to the fresh bursting forth of flowers of pendulous *atimukta* vines and of wild jasmines;
41. when every separate branch of the *nagana* bush resounds with the clans of bees, gay with drinking honey, in the season when the *rodhra* tree is lovely with luxuriant blossom;
42. as the clear heaven (is adorned) by the moon, as the breast of Vishnu by the *kaustubha* jewel, this wholly noble city is adorned by the best of temples.
43. As long as the Lord [Shiva] bears a mass of tawny matted hair from which the pure new moon arises, as long as Vishnu wears on his shoulders a wreath of full-blown lotuses, so long may this temple endure. May it last forever.
44. **The temple of the sun has been built with devotion (*bhakti*) on the orders of the guild, and the above has been painstakingly composed by Vatsabhatti.**

What is expounded in this long poem by a local Brahman poet on the behalf of a professional association, or *shreni*, of silk-weavers[1255] is a highly selective account of this group's recent history and accomplishments. First of all, we learn that they had migrated from the region of Lata, being east of Barygaza and just north of the old Satavaha kingdom, to the small kingdom of Dashapura approximately 250 km further north, whose ruler was tributary to the Guptas.[1256] Although some of their number took up new occupations upon arrival in Dashapura, the core of the group evidently remained 'excellent in their craft' as silk-weavers, being trustworthy and helpful to one another, as a group conducting themselves in such a manner as to be the most noble and pious of all.[1257] While such self-praise may seem overly excessive, the genre of associations lauding themselves for their exceptionally high moral and religious standards is also well-known from Greek[1258] and Roman[1259] associations, too.

However, all the poetical detours aside, the actual purpose of the inscription was to commemorate how the silk-weavers had paid for and built a temple to the divine Sun in AD 436,[1260] this being done on the occasion of the temple's subsequent restoration in AD 473, evidently having suffered some damage in the intervening period.[1261] In addition, we can infer from the flowery descriptions that a *shreni* like that of the silk-weavers constituted a network with a high degree of closure, ties being grounded not merely in shared occupation, but also encased in kinship, religion and cooperation (the latter defined by trustworthiness and friendship[1262]). Significantly, however, they kept defining themselves by profession, this apparently being the most important common denominator. Furthermore, an association like this could not only possess the substantial means to build a temple on its own, but was also an institution imbued with such longevity and stability that it could travel between places offering different prospects of work, and maintain communal assets, such as the temple, for decades. Obviously, such a group easily signalled enough institutional and corporate reliability to be considered a secure recipient of perpetual endowments, being able to pay out the annual interest for charitable purposes by making the money work at greater interest for themselves, the association acting as guarantor against potential risks involved in sub-lending.

As regards the provenance of the silk woven by this association, one must distinguish between, on the one hand, processed (i.e., de-gummed) Chinese silk obtained from domesticated silk moths (*Bombyx mori*), and, on the other hand, raw silk collected from indigenous wild silk moths. Different species of the latter can be found along the entire expanse of the west coast of India (*Antheraea mylitta*), as well as in Assam to the northeast (*Antheraea assamensis*),[1263] and there is now substantial evidence of *wild* silk products in Harappa and Chanhudaro of the Indus Valley Civilisation, *c.* 2450–1900 BC,[1264] as well as from Nevasa in Western India, *c.* 1500 BC.[1265] From further afield, wild Indian silk finds are reported from Bactria (Sapalli Tepe, Uzbekistan), mid-2nd millennium BC, and from 4th century BC *tumuli* in the Altai Mountains between Mongolia and Kazakhstan.[1266]

Indeed, in addition to the prehistorical finds of Indian wild silk, early Indian literary sources make it clear that such products were produced on a significant scale in the centuries well before and after the turn of

---

1255 The nature of their association and its profession is spelled out in stanzas 19–21.
1256 Basham 1983: 95, cf. stanzas 4–5.
1257 Basham 1983: 97–8, stanzas 15–19.
1258 Gabrielsen 2007: 195; 2016b: 100–3.
1259 Verboven 2007.
1260 Basham 1983: 101, stanza 29; dating: 103, stanzas 34–5, 44.
1261 Basham 1983: 103–4, stanzas 36–9.
1262 Cf. stanzas 15 and 18, in particular.
1263 Good 2012: 17 w. figs. 2 and 3. The more complicated version is that Chinese products could also be made from wild silk, *Antheraea pernyi* (Good 2012: 21), and that processing (degumming) of wild silk is now known to have been practiced in India as early as *c.* 2000 BC (Kenoyer 2017: 19), see below.
1264 Good *et al.* 2009; Kenoyer 2017: 18–20. From Harappa, one sample is identified as *Antheraea assamensis* and two as *Antheraea mylitta*, while the sample from Chanhudaro may be *Antheraea assamensis*. Remarkably, one of the Harappan fragments is woven silk (not simply a string or tassel from spun threads), while the Chanhudaro fragment is partly degummed and had been reeled—none of these techniques have previously been identified outside China at such an early date. In comparison, the earliest archaeological finds of silk in China have been made in the lower Yangze Valley, dating to 2850–2570 BC, cf. Good *et al.* 2009: 458; and Hansen 2012: 19.
1265 Gulati 1961.
1266 Mierse 2013: 213.

the Common Era.[1267] Correlating prehistorical find-spots of Indian wild silk with information about Early Historic outlets of silk, it is noteworthy that the sites of Harappa and Chanhudaro are upstream on the Indus of the later port of export, Barbaricon, while the area around Nevasa supplied textiles to Barygaza which was also an exporter of silk.[1268] Significantly, moreover, a fragment of silk unearthed at Dura-Europos on the Upper Euphrates is made from wild silk (mid-3rd century AD), as is another from Abu Simbel in Upper Egypt on the Nubian frontier (4th century AD),[1269] and at 1st–2nd century AD Palmyra five recovered textile fragments were woven completely and a sixth specimen partially, from wild silk.[1270]

To clarify, silks produced in India could have been made from either wild silk of the indigenous moths of the Western Deccan or Assam, or from imported Chinese silk thread available already by the mid-1st century AD at the ports of Barbaricon and Barygaza, along the Ganges, and on the Malabar Coast[1271]—as we have already seen that specifically Chinese silk thread was employed at Palmyra. We do not know which variety the Indian association of silk-weavers at Dashapura used, perhaps Chinese silk thread for more expensive work and cheaper local wild silk for more affordable products, both varieties being readily available in the Western Deccan. Accordingly, some of the silk textiles available at Barygaza and other South Asian ports although labelled 'Chinese silk,' *sêrikon*, in the *Periplus*, might have been of local Indian craftsmanship, as might some of the thread, *nêma*, for all we know.[1272] Either way, this organisation, and the eloquent inscription attesting it, is a fascinating *comparandum* to both the early *sericarii* of Imperial Rome, as well as the silk-weaving centres of the Roman East, treated above.

Returning to the southernmost of the three routes between the Konkan Coast and the Satavahana kingdom further inland, the Bhorghat Pass is the site of the Karla *chaitya*, being the single largest rock temple complex in India, excavated around the third quarter of the 1st century AD **[Figure 18]**.[1273] Significantly, six of the 30-odd monumental pillars supporting the vaulted roof of the main nave of the *chaitya* were explicitly donated by *Yavanas*, a category of people we have previously encountered and briefly dealt with during the survey of graffiti in the Hoq Cave (chapter seven). On Socotra, this visitor commemorated himself as '(the) *Yavana* of Cadrabhutimukha' in Prakrit, arriving sometime in the 2nd–early 5th century AD, alongside numerous other visitors sailing out of the Gulf of Khambhat and Barygaza in particular.[1274]

This being quite an unusual epithet, it is highly remarkable that his earlier namesakes from Karla exhibit the same 'onomastic habit:'[1275] '**The gift of a pillar by** [standard epigraphic formula which will not be repeated] the *Yavana* of the Sihadhayas from Dhenukakata,' '—the *Yavana* of the Dhamadayas from Dhenukakata,' '—the *Yavana* of the Culayakhas from Dhenukakata,' and 'the *Yavana* of the Yasovardhanas from Dhenukakata;' special cases being '—the *Yavana* Cita of the Gatas from Umehakakata' and '—Dhamma-*Yavana* from Dhenukakata.'[1276] To these six epigraphs, moreover, can be added another three from more or less contemporary Junnar, just treated: 'the meritorious gift of two cisterns by the *Yavana* Irila of the Gatas,' 'the meritorious gift of the facade of a hall by the *Yavana* of the Candras,' and 'the meritorious gift of a refectory by the *Yavana* Cita of the Gatas.'[1277] Finally, an inscription from Nashik records the excavation and dedication of a cave by '—Idragnidata, son of the Northerner from Datamiti, the *Yonaka* Dhammadeva.'[1278]

A number of observations are immediately apparent. First of all, 'Greeks' or descendants of such, from the old Indo-Greek successor kingdoms of Alexander's conquests in the Northwest, were designated by the

[1267] Gopal 1961: 61–69; Mierse 2013: 213–14; Zuchowska 2013a: 143.
[1268] *Periplus* 38–39 (Barbaricon and its inland supply route), 51 (Nevasa lay next to Paithan which supplied Barygaza by wagon trains).
[1269] Mierse 2013: 210.
[1270] Schmidt-Colinet 2000b: cat.nos. 254 (w. cotton), 305, 308, 312, 313, 314. No. 312, especially, singled out as of definite Indian origin, but the same may as well apply to the rest. See also Stauffer 2000: 13.
[1271] According to the *Periplus* 39, 49, 56, 64.
[1272] Compare Mierse 2013: 221; Hildebrandt 2017: 38; and Zuchowska 2016: 36.
[1273] Dehejia 1972: 177–8.
[1274] Graffito 14:17.
[1275] The following translations are all in accordance with Stein 1935, correcting the *editio princeps* translations listed in the footnotes below.
[1276] Burgess and Indraji 1881: Karla, nos. 7, 10; Vats 1925–26: nos. 1, 4, 6, 10.
[1277] Burgess and Indraji 1881: Junnar, nos. 5, 7, 33.
[1278] Senart 1905–6: no. 18.

Figure 18
Inside view of the Karla *chaitya* hall, Maharashtra. Photograph by the author.

Prakrit ethnicon *Yona*, as attested by a pillar at Vidisha, dated to the last years of the 2nd century BC. The inscription records the visit of the Greek ambassador Heliodoros, son of Dion, to the court of an Indian king—significantly, this *Yona* was either a Vaishnavite devotee or accustomed to equating Indian and Greek deities in a syncretistic framework.[1279] The nearby *stupa* at Sanchi from around the third quarter of the 1st century BC also mentions a *Yona*, this being '(the) *Yona* from Setapatha,' his ethnicon being applied as a proper name, evidently a Buddhist worshipper.[1280] Similarly, the inscription from Nashik mentions that Dhammadeva, the *Yona*, father of the dedicant, had arrived from the North, his name implying Buddhist faith too.[1281] Accordingly, we may tentatively identify *Yona* as designating a 'Greek' out of the old Indo-Greek kingdoms of the North, albeit commemorating themselves in an Indian language and flagging Indian faiths.

Second, the nine *Yavanas* (a Sanskrit word) of Karla (six) and Junnar (three), in contrast, appear to have been local to the area. That is, five of those attested at Karla are identified as coming from Dhenukakata, the site of which has never been identified securely, but which we know from other inscriptions at Karla to have been the home of perfumers, carpenters, traders and farmers, as well. Moreover, a pillar at Karla was donated by this '*vanija-gama*' of Dhenukakata, that is, the 'community of traders' or 'merchant community' (but smaller than a *nigama*).[1282] Consequently, it seems that Dhenukakata must have been a prosperous nearby settlement, the traders of which benefited from its location in the pass through which inland commerce had to travel. Furthermore, one *Yavana*, Cita of the Gatas, appears both at Karla and Junnar, in his inscription at the former place mentioning that he hailed from the likewise unknown Umehakakata, which must have been relatively local, though, seeing as he acted as a major Buddhist patron at both Karla and Junnar, only some 70 km apart.

Third, picking up on the *Yavana* on Socotra who took part in the sea trade with the Gulf of Aden via Barygaza, we find that seven out of eight individual *Yavanas* known from Karla and Junnar are described as belonging to larger groups, described by the use of plural genitives. Five of them, furthermore, are designated by the use of their ethnicon as a personal name alone, simply being known as '(the) *Yavana* of X,' the unique identifier of the person therefore being his group affiliation, e.g. 'of the Dhamadayas.' Three have personal names, though, namely, 'Cita,' 'Irila,' and 'Dhamma,' the two former being further defined as 'of the Gatas,' whereas 'Dhamma,' a Buddhist to judge from his name, was simply 'from Dhenukakata.' Hence, *Yavanas* could also be identified by name, either in addition to overall group affiliation or just by their name alone—like with the *Yonas* treated above.

Evidently, though, the affiliation weighed more for six out of a total of nine attested individuals (incl. the Socotran graffito) than a personal name, only one out of nine leaving it out entirely in favour of personal name plus ethnicon alone. Although evidence of organised groups is comparatively rare, there is the case of the *Sagarapaloganas* who sponsored a cave at the monastic complex of Kanheri, between the main Konkan ports of Sopara and Kalyan, their name meaning something like 'group or company of sea traders.'[1283] Likewise, a well was donated in AD 188/288 by the *Saviras* in Gandhara,[1284] being a genitive plural in Kharoshthi designating an association similar to the more numerous Gandharan *sahaya* groups, meaning 'companions' or 'business partners,'[1285] who are all identified by adding a name, e.g. '(this) well was caused to be dug as the gift of the Travasakura companions/business partners in the Khudacha *vihara*.'[1286]

1279 Mairs 2014: 117–33. Another prime example being Falk 2009b: 26–9, no. 1, a bilingual Greek-Kharoshthi dedication to the god 'Chaos' in the Greek, 'Boas' in Kharoshthi.

1280 Lüders 1912: no. 547; here translated in accordance with Stein 1935.

1281 Stein 1935: 351.

1282 Vats 1925-26: no. 3.

1283 The inscribed word (*sagarapaloganam*) being interpreted as a name in the genitive plural ('gift of the *S.*'): Burgess 1883: Kanheri no. 23; Stein 1935: 345. Dated *c.* 200 AD by Gokhale 1991: 17, 152, no. 56, who surprisingly takes the word as an accusative singular, denoting the name of the cave—however, this leaves the dedication text without a donor, which is both highly unusual compared with the large *corpus* of contemporary Buddhist dedicatory inscriptions with which it can be compared (especially seeing as this was an entire cave), and would make it the only known named cave at Kanheri out of more than a hundred. Accordingly, Burgess and Stein's earlier interpretations are preferred here.

1284 Konow 1929: 170-71, no. 87; Falk 2009c: 31, no. 3.6; *CKI* 160.

1285 Baums 2012: 201, uses 'brotherhood;' whereas 'business associates' is preferred in Falk 2009c.

1286 *CKI* 45, 47, 51, 58, 61 (quoted here; dated AD 84), 116, 156, 160, 829 (dated 17 BC- AD 275); all except nos. 45 and 116 treated in Falk 2009c. Also

Accordingly, with the added emphasis of the corroborating graffito from Socotra, there is now no reason not to take the actual wording of the *Yavana* inscriptions seriously, laying to rest the idea that the *Yavanas* misspelt their own inscriptions,[1287] and instead start interpreting these affluent sponsors of Buddhism as members of larger social structures, such as kinship groups or merchant organisations embedded in local settlements, like the *vanija-gama* of Dhenukakata. The more so, because the supplementary evidence we have is, on the one hand, from Kanheri, where merchants and financiers making money in the ports of Kalyan and Sopara loom large in the *corpus* of dedications (see below), and, on the other hand, from what appears to be Gandharan associations of merchants venting their success in the form of pious donations of wells. In addition, the fact itself that we only find epigraphs by *Yavanas* on the maritime trade stop-over of Socotra and in the busy passes between the ports and inland Satavahana production centres, testifies to the commercial interests of these evidently successful (to judge from their donations) individuals and the families or organisations of which they were part and proudly boasted their membership.

Indeed, the *Yavanas* of the Western Deccan may have grown so influential in the mid-1st century AD, even outright powerful, that they became a threat: an inscription at Nashik from the early years of the 2nd century AD commemorates how the Satavahana king Gotamiputta Sātakaṇṇi, who reigned from roughly 60–90 AD,[1288] 'destroyed the Shakas, Yavanas and Pahlavas,' that is, the Western Kshatrapas, *Yavanas* and so-called Indo-Parthians.[1289] From the Tamil South, a contemporary poem in the praise of a Cheran king describes a victory over *Yavanas*, appropriating their goods.[1290] Whether or not these tales of conflict and royal Indian victory are real or mere aggrandisement, *Yavanas* were evidently considered a force to be reckoned with in their own right, which supports the idea that they were parts of networks possessing wealth, group coordination and means of protection in case of hostility, a scenario not too unlikely in light of last chapter's survey of similar organisations operating in the margins of states along the Indian Ocean Rim.

As regards the question of the identity of the *Yavanas*, whether they be more or less Roman, the epigraphs provide no clue beyond the obvious ethnicon to support an interpretation of them as anything but Buddhists speaking Indian vernacular, writing in Prakrit, belonging to Indian social structures, settled in local trading centres, and engaged in commerce with the West. The more so, seeing as the *Yavana* visitor to Socotra could have chosen to identify himself in another way in the neutral religious space of the Hoq Cave, and is certain to have written the simple Prakrit graffito there himself (no local stone-cutter acting as mediator). Thus, although these people were mainly defined by their ethnicon, probably because they were originally so categorised by their host society and subsequently appropriated the ethnicon as a voluntary marker of identity themselves, we cannot ascribe any specifically 'Roman' or merely 'Western' characteristics to them. Indeed, the only three names revealing additional information are Indian (Cita and Irila) and Buddhist (Dhamma).

In addition, '*Yavana* of Cadrabhutimukha' seems to imply dependency, like the Roman slaves and freedmen acting as itinerant business agents for their masters, e.g. the *Annii*, *Calpurnii* and *Vestorii*, while the affluent *Yavana* patrons of Buddhism at Junnar and Karla could also fit such a model, being agents who had risen to a greater standing (and wealth enough to act as sponsors) in the service of Indian masters involved in the Indian Ocean trade with the West. Remarkably, such a setup might have a much later historical parallel, namely, the *dubashes* of the 18th–early 19th century AD Coromandel Coast in the Indian South. *Dubash* means 'man of two languages,' and this group of people from the rural and religious upper classes of the Tamil countryside rose to power and influence as the confidential interpreters, stewards, agents and bankers, of European families in English Madras, French Pondicherry, Danish Tranquebar, etc. In fact,

a seal in Rahman and Falk 2011: 15.07.10.

1287 All the original editors reconstructed the 'bad grammar:' Burgess and Indraji 1881: 31; Senart 1902–3: 53f; Lüders 1912; Vats 1925–26: 326. A strange misconception, though, because the epigraphs would have been made by a trained stone-cutter and cannot have avoided being 'proofread' by indigenous co-religionists before being incised in prominent positions in, arguably, the most monumental single Buddhist temple of Early Historic India.

1288 Dating according to Nakanishi and v. Hinüber 2014: 23.

1289 Senart 1905–6: Nashik, no. 2.

1290 Zvelebil 1956: 404, quoting *Patirruppattu*, II. *patikam*, v. 4–10. Zvelebil 1973: 52.

the *dubashes* were so successful as advisers and economic mediators (often expanding into tax-farming) that they ended up being viewed with suspicion by the colonial authorities. In consequence, the East India Company in Madras took active steps to curb their influence by the end of the 18th century,[1291] as did king Gotamiputta Sātakaṇṇi of the Satavahanas in relation to the *Yavanas* of his day.

Thus, the *dubash* institution can serve as an informative later example with the roles reversed, for in Early Historic India the central mediators in the sea-going trade would have been *Yavanas* in the employ of Indian families or mercantile organisations participating in the long-distance trade through exactly such agents and dependants. This could explain why the *Yavanas* were simply known as such, the ethnicon implying their role as *dubash*-style mediators, their close affiliation with Indians explaining their emphatically Indian self-representations, for although 'men of two languages' their social milieu was thoroughly Indian. While their original origins may have been mixed families of Indian ports where the monsoonal trade pattern dictated prolonged periods of waiting for the crews and embarked traders of Roman ships, or Roman slaves sold into servitude with Indian masters, gradually rising to freedom or greater authority through their work, the only concrete link between these *Yavanas* and the Westerners arriving across the sea seems to have been the commerce in which both were involved, the former likely as local mediators or brokers in trade with the latter.[1292]

Corroborating evidence for the role of Roman trade with the Satavahana kingdom comes not only in the form of early Roman amphorae finds from Satavahana sites near the coast, such as the port of Chaul and Nashik in the mountains, for further inland finds have also been made at the major centre of Paithan, while Nevasa on the route to the latter has yielded more than 60 sherds datable to 1st–3rd century AD.[1293] In addition, moulded clay amulet pendants (called *bullae*), dated 1st–2nd century AD, have been unearthed at Ter, Paithan and Nevasa, impressed with imitations of classical Western bust images in profile, clearly copied from Roman coins,[1294] these three cities also having yielded a few finds each of what appears to be fragments of Roman glass vessels.[1295] Finally, a small carved alabaster piece found at Junnar depicts Eros cradled inside an egg.[1296]

While the site of Barygaza has never been properly identified and excavated, lying below modern Bharuch,[1297] we have already surveyed the role of ports in the Gulf of Khambhat in the sea-going trade from the perspective of visitors to the Hoq Cave on Socotra. The region has produced both early and late Roman amphorae,[1298] as well as a Roman quartz cameo[1299] and a bronze jug handle adorned with an Eros riding an amphora.[1300] While the Hoq Cave graffiti provide concrete evidence of *navikas*, a *niryāmaka* and at least one *vanij*, that is, shippers and merchants sailing out of Barygaza, we can combine this information with the *Jataka* story about merchants sailing out of that very town under the leadership of a former *niyyāmakajetthaka*, a head or leader of the shippers (already mentioned in chapter seven), to sketch a picture of maritime organisation.

Thus, the basic setup resembles the situation in the better empirically attested contemporary Mediterranean, where the vocational interdependence between sea-going merchants and shippers was commonly expressed in the combinations *emporoi kai nauklêroi* or *navicularii et negotiantes*, who would often organise themselves in associations either by individual or combined professions (cf. the Palmyrene inscription at Koptos, as well as the maritime associations working out of Alexandria). At Barygaza it appears that the commercial personnel organised themselves in a similar manner: the

[1291] Neild-Basu 1984; Brimnes 1999: 92–4; Sebro 2014: 294–9.
[1292] Augmenting the conclusions of Stein 1935: 356; Ray 1988: 316-17, 322; Karttunen 1994: 332; and Fauconnier 2012: 98–101.
[1293] Tomber 2008: 132, distribution map p. 127, registry p. 176; Gupta *et al.* 2001.
[1294] Brancaccio 2005; for *bullae* in India generally, Ghosh 1990: 177f, 6.4; Deo 1991: 40; for the *bullae* from Nevasa (in terracotta, lead and gold), Sankalia 1960: 200f.
[1295] Stern 1991: 115.
[1296] Cimino 1994b.
[1297] Tomber 2008: 125.
[1298] Tomber 2008: 127, 176.
[1299] Deo 1991: 41, fig. 3.5; Tomber 2008: 128; from Karvan.
[1300] De Puma 1991: 101, fig. 5.34–5; from Akota.

professions of *navika* and *vanij* came together in maritime commerce, shippers evidently being organised in associations headed by an elected and expert member. Later evidence from the Kathiawar Peninsula, forming the western coast of the Gulf of Khambhat, in the form of a charter, dated AD 592, establishing the rules, taxes, and privileges of the *vanij-gama* of Lohata, shows how well-organised and regulated such a community of traders (*vanij*) could be, different *shrenis* being allocated different markets in town, rights of foreign and local merchants vis-à-vis each other being defined, etc.[1301]

The earlier *vanij-gama* of Dhenukakata, where at least five *Yavanas* were settled, might well have been similarly ordered, especially seeing as we know from contemporary Nashik that *nigamas* at that time also exercised authority over local *shrenis*, and that the *Arthashastra* contains rules similar to those of the later charter of Lohata about tax-exemptions for shippers and merchants conducting long-distance trade, about legal privileges of foreign merchants who were not part of local partnerships or organisations, and the allocation of separate markets to mercantile associations.[1302] Furthermore, the corporativity of *vanij-gamas* and their involvement in long-distance trade is documented by a *c.* 503 AD copper plate grant from nearby Sanjeli in Gujarat, recording an endowment in the form of a cess imposed on trade in certain commodities for the benefit of a temple. This endowment was registered on a copper plate by a *vanij-gama* of 'foreign businessmen coming from all the four quarters (of the earth), local inhabitants and travelling traders,' some of the signatories being from Mathura, Kanauj and Ujjain, revealing links to commercial centres of the Gangetic plain and the great inland trade routes connecting North and South India.[1303]

Moreover, the Buddhist site of Kanheri, previously mentioned, provides a rare view of the urban mercantile communities importing, exporting and financing the overseas trade in the 2nd century AD.[1304] Dedicatory inscriptions at the site reveal a network of people, professions and localities, linking inland centres with the main ports of the coast, some of those inscribing their professions being goldsmiths (*heranika, suvarnakara*),[1305] jewellers (*manikara*),[1306] traders (*vanij*),[1307] merchants (*negama*),[1308] and financiers (*sethi*),[1309] most patrons living at the thriving nearby port of Kalyan, five at the equally nearby harbour of Sopara, and two at Chaul further south on the coast.[1310] In addition, two donors at Kanheri from Nashik and Dhenukakata (which must have been close to Karla), as well as one from Paithan, indicate the lines of supply feeding commerce on the coast,[1311] while movement in the other direction is indicated by two goldsmiths (*heranika*) from Kalyan acting as monastic sponsors at Junnar, at which site patrons from Barygaza are also attested.[1312]

The economic potential of these mercantile networks only documented by inscriptions in the form of pious donations is, fortunately, preserved in the form of 2nd century AD perpetual endowments (*akshayanivi*) of the very same type and purpose as those already treated at Nashik and Junnar. One very wealthy Buddhist patron enlarged monastic complexes at Kanheri, Sopara, Kalyan and Paithan, at the latter establishing a new monastery as well and endowing it with a perpetual grant to secure its daily running.[1313] Less extravagantly, three individual endowments set up by merchants (*negama*) from Kalyan reveal that such financial constructs could consist of cash, property, productive fields or a combination, the interest (perhaps from depositing money with associations), rent and revenue to be derived from

1301 Sircar 1953–54, especially p. 171, no. 12, which seems to correspond with *Arthas.* II.1(32), II.4(16).
1302 *Arthas.* II.4(16) (II.1(32) has a similar purpose), II.16(11–13).
1303 Mehta and Thakkar 1978; Chakravarti 2008; Neelis 2011: 165–6.
1304 Ray 1994a: 38–41. Gokhale 1991: 15–6; datings of Kanheri inscriptions below are according to their entries in Gokhale's catalogue.
1305 Gokhale 1991: 3, 15, 18 and 20.
1306 Gokhale 1991: no. 46 (*c.* 200 AD).
1307 Gokhale 1991: no. 5.
1308 See n1314.
1309 Gokhale 1991: no. 32, 45 (latter *c.* 200 AD).
1310 Gokhale 1991, nos.: Kalyan, 3, 4, 6, 25, 28–9, 40, 43, 55; Sopara, 6, 17, 24, 32, 46; Chaul, 20, 50.
1311 Gokhale 1991, nos.: Nashik, 2; Dhenukakata, 38; Paithan, 6.
1312 Burgess and Indraji, 1881: Junnar, no. 20, 28, 30.
1313 Gokhale 1991: no. 6 = Lüders 1912: no. 988 = Burgess 1883: Kanheri, no. 5.

these sources being explicitly allocated as shares or cash distributions to clothes and food for the monks, as well as for repair of their caves and halls.[1314]

In other words, the financial sophistication and institutions of Indian merchants and craftsmen, individually as well as collectively in associations or similar organisations, were remarkably similar to those of their contemporary counterparts in Rome, where traders grown rich from business and *collegia* in search of sponsoring patrons institutionalised the granting and receipt of endowments at interest for stipulated purposes. Concrete examples treated in the above are the two *margaritarii* setting up their own endowments with the *collegium dendrophorum*, the money entrusted with and managed by the *collegium* of *negotiatores eborarii et citriarii* for their annual celebrations, and the endowment nested with the municipality of Tusculum by a rich *negotiator sericarius*. These are just the examples directly related to Roman long-distance trade with the East, though, many other cases of endowments nested with *collegia* of the Western Empire being known, even more if we count other recipients as well.[1315]

A Roman *emporos*, like the author of the *Periplus* or the lender in the Muziris Papyrus, arriving in Barygaza, would, in other words, not have found the Indian world of commerce facing him too foreign to comprehend. Trade conducted in an institutionalised milieu constituted by the economic activities of Indian merchants, shippers, financiers and associations with comparable formal and informal rules and pious ideals, and the management and liabilities of money with social and religious strings attached put to work at interest, should, in fact, have been recognisably familiar to him. Although remote from each other in many ways, Roman and Indian merchants traversing the staggering distances to conduct trade in each other's ports were consequently well equipped to interact with local economic institutions resembling those of their home markets—business as usual in worlds apart trading together, in other words.

Producing pearls, precious stones, and pepper in South India

As already touched upon, South India was an important supplier of long-distance commodities for Roman consumption. Thus, pearls from the shallow waters between India and Sri Lanka, as well as precious and semi-precious stones from inland mining centres (for the *margaritarii*, *gemmarii*, etc., of the *collegium aurificum*), and pepper from the tropical forests of the South Deccan (for the *collegium aromatariorum* and *horrea piperataria*), were farmed, mined and gathered, by inhabitants of the ancient kingdoms of the South. Not only Pliny, the *Periplus* and the Muziris Papyrus (which in addition to the just mentioned products firmly documents export from the region of ivory and re-export of nard from North India) bear testimony to this trade, but also Roman coins, amphorae, the archaeology of key port sites and ancient local epics, known as *Sangam* poetry.

More than 4,000 *denarii* and 700 *aurei* have been unearthed as part of hoards in South India, representing more than 70 per cent and 90 per cent of the respective Roman coin finds in the Subcontinent, a distribution pattern mirrored by copper coins. While the majority of *denarii* are Julio-Claudian, *aurei* are mostly either later Julio-Claudian, 2nd century AD, or of the 4th–5th century, extending as far as the 6th–early 7th century AD, while bronze coins are rare in the early centuries of the Common Era, but quite common in the 4th–5th century AD.[1316] As regards amphorae, seven sites in South India and one in south Sri Lanka, Tissamaharama, have yielded early Roman specimens, the distribution being clustered mainly on the east coast, although by far the largest assembly (now dwarfing all other finds in India put together) is from the single west coast site of Pattanam, presumably ancient Muziris. In addition, late Roman amphorae have been uncovered at one inland site (the Cheran capital of Karur), one east coast site (Arikamedu), and again from Sri Lankan Tissamaharama.[1317]

[1314] Gokhale 1991: no. 25 = Lüders 1912: no. 1024 = Burgess 1883: Kanheri, no. 15; Gokhale 1991: no. 28 = Lüders 1912: no. 998 = Burgess 1883: Kanheri, no. 16; Gokhale 1991: no. 40 = Lüders 1912: no. 1000 = Burgess 1883: Kanheri, no. 18.
[1315] As set out at the beginning of chapter four.
[1316] On Roman coin finds in India, see chapter five, and recent overview in Tomber 2008: 30–7.
[1317] Tomber 2008: 136–8, 142, 147, and map p. 127.

Taking a closer look at what used to be (considered) the best excavated archaeological site in Early Historic India containing material remains attesting trade with the Roman Empire, Arikamedu outside modern Pondicherry on the Coromandel Coast, there is highly interesting evidence of sustained long-distance trade.[1318] First of all, the 530-odd amphorae sherds from Arikamedu which have been subjected to closer study appear to date mainly from the 1st century BC–1st century AD, while at least three sherds date from different times in the 3rd–6th century AD, some 60 per cent of all having acted as wine containers, a few per cent having held olive oil (mainly Istrian) and fish-sauce, *garum*. Although Greek amphorae make up the majority of the wine containers, Campanian and Egyptian, and even a few Gallic (one-and-a-half per cent), amphorae have also been identified, with a few sherds of Spanish olive oil and fish-sauce containers constituting the westernmost origins.[1319] Second, amphorae appear more frequently in the so-called North Sector of Arikamedu than the South Sector, which may imply either different economic functions of these areas, or inhabitants with a different pattern of consumption.[1320] Third, Roman fine wares in the guise of some 50 sherds of Italian *terra sigillata* with different makers' stamps, dated 10 BC–AD 50, and a couple of sherds each of Eastern Sigillata A (south-western Asia Minor) and B (the Levant), as well as Egyptian faience, re-emphasise the widespread Mediterranean origins of the wares uncovered at Arikamedu.[1321]

Consequently, while wine may well have been imported for Indian as well as Roman consumers,[1322] the attested import of fish-sauce, in particular, but also olive oil, as well as *terra sigillata*, may well indicate the presence in Podukê of the *Periplus* of Roman visitors, just like we know that South Indian visitors spent time at Berenike and Myos Hormos, leaving Tamil-Brahmi incised sherds, Rouletted Ware, and rice behind for posterity to find. However, the archaeological site as a whole is thoroughly South Indian, the imported ceramics making up less than one per cent of the total pottery assemblage.[1323] Moreover, a Tamil cultural context is further borne out by the 31 inscribed sherds excavated at the site, the majority being in Tamil-Brahmi, two containing names referring to regional clan chieftains who were the traditional rulers of ancient Tamil society.[1324] Such inscribed sherds also having been found, as the reader will recall, at Myos Hormos and Berenike of Roman Egypt, as well as in Sumhuram of ancient Hadramawt, revealing active Tamil participation in the long-distance maritime trade.

In addition, the site of Pattanam is now widely recognised as a likely contender for the ancient port of Muziris,[1325] or at least to have made up a small part of the area constituted by that ancient riverside port, which we used to know mainly from Pliny, the *Periplus* and, of course, the fittingly named Muziris Papyrus. While Pliny talks disparagingly of Muziris, probably due to a period of strife between the Cheran and Pandian kings while he was writing,[1326] the *Periplus* mentions that there was a market in the ports of the Malabar Coast for wheat for 'those involved in shipping,'[1327] hence, Westerners consuming grain like Indians did rice in the ports of Roman Egypt. In fact, five Roman gaming counters have recently come to light at the site,[1328] indicating how some Roman travellers might have tried to pass the time while waiting for a change of monsoon.[1329] Moreover, there is a highly enigmatic depiction of a temple labelled *templum Augusti* in the *c.* 300 AD *Tabula Peutingeriana*, likely compiled from earlier maps,[1330] but without further corroborating evidence this detail probably belongs in the *hic sunt dracones*-genre.[1331]

1318 On the chronology of the site, see Begley 2004: 1–14, and more pessimisticly Ravitchandirane 2007.
1319 Lyding Will 1991; 1996, 2004; Slane 1991: 204; Tomber 2008: 136–7.
1320 Sidebotham 2004: 192; Begley 2004: 135. Tomber 2008: 137.
1321 Slane 1996; Tomber 2008: 136.
1322 On the question of who consumed the wine contained in the amphoras, see the concise remarks by Tomber 2015: 388–89.
1323 Begley 1996: 23.
1324 Mahadevan 1996a: 296; Champakalakshmi 1996: 135.
1325 Selvakumar, Shajan, and Tomber 2009.
1326 Pliny *NH*, VI.26. Romanis 1997b: 107–8.
1327 *Periplus* 56.
1328 Until now the excavations have only been published as *Interim Reports of the Pattanam Excavations/Explorations 2007-12*, henceforth referred to as *IRPEX-[**year**]*, followed by object identification number internal to the relevant report. The preliminary nature of the published data must be taken into consideration.
1329 *IRPEX-2012*: p. 24, 25, incl. figs. 10, 67 and 83.
1330 Segment 11. Talbert 2010: 133–57.
1331 See, however, Speidel 2016: 103–10.

The recent archaeological excavations, however, have furnished much more concrete evidence: more than 6000 amphorae sherds,[1332] mainly dating from the later 1st century BC–1st century AD, with some sherds continuing into the 2nd–3rd century AD, and at least one late Roman type, the Aila/Aqaba amphora, which was either imported in the 5th–6th century AD or arrived later, in Islamic times. The majority of sherds belong to Dressel 2–4 wine amphorae from Southern Italy, most notably Campania, while a few others were produced in Baetica and Hispania Tarraconensis in Spain, Cilicia in Asia Minor and Mareotis just outside Alexandria in Egypt. Other wine amphorae hail from Gaul, Rhodes, and Cilicia and Egypt once more, whereas sherds of olive oil and *garum* containers can be traced to Spain and the Adriatic coast of Italy.[1333] In addition, some 120 sherds[1334] of *terra sigillata* are made up of a majority from Italy, dating from the late 1st century BC– AD 10, with a few sherds of *sigillata* from south-western Asia Minor (ESB) and northern Syria (ESA), the latter datable to the 2nd century BC–AD 10.[1335]

Whereas at least some of the amphorae, particularly the oil and fish-sauce containers, and the relatively humble amounts of *terra sigillata* might have been meant for use and consumption by a Roman diaspora at the port, as at Arikamedu, the finds of some 1600 fragments of Roman pillared glass,[1336] on the other hand, indicates in-demand exports for a foreign market. However, while raw glass, *hyelos argê*, is listed in the *Periplus* (56) as an import to the ports of the Malabar Coast, and ingots of raw glass have, in fact, been found at the northern Red Sea port of Clysma,[1337] apparently awaiting further export, glasswares as such are not mentioned as a commodity at Muziris. However, might we, in light of the huge local production of glass beads at the port site, as revealed by the numerous presence of wasters,[1338] as well as the attested (and highly surprising) activity of gemstone carvers producing archetypical Greco-Roman motifs, to be dealt with below, speculate about the potential production of these Roman pillared glass bowls on site, made from imported blocks and ingots of raw glass? In this way, an otherwise fragile type of export would not be in danger of breaking in the cargo holds of subsequent ships, barges and smaller vessels before arrival.[1339] Either way, that is, with or without the presence of Roman artisans proficient at producing them, these pillared Roman bowls in different hues (*inter alia* varieties of dark green and dark blue) appear to have been an important object of trade in South India, previously only attested by a few specimens unearthed at Arikamedu.[1340]

Significantly, moreover, substantial amounts of Mesopotamian torpedo jar fragments and of turquoise glazed ware indicate connections (not necessarily direct, though) with the Persian Gulf of Sasanian times,[1341] while ubiquitous archaeobotanical finds of frankincense in all trenches attest trade with ancient South Arabia,[1342] and the abundant presence of Rouletted Ware sherds attests strong connections with

[1332] *IRPEX-2012*: p. 22, gives the total as 6782 sherds.

[1333] Tomber 2015: 383–7.

[1334] *IRPEX-2012*: p. 22, gives the total as 137 sherds.

[1335] Tomber 2015: 389–91.

[1336] The only published total is Cherian 2011, table 1, index no. 10, which gives the number collected throughout 2007–2011 as 1338 fragments, but note that Cherian 2013 listed the updated total for 2007–12 as 1657 fragments. A number of these finds can be identified in the reports as pillared bowl glass fragments specifically, e.g. *IRPEX-**2008***: 526, 1457, 2580; ***2010***: 236, 2863, 3510, 4672; ***2011***: 20725, 21399, 21434, 23042, 23043, 23178, 23187, 23240, 23336, 23348, 23350, 23438, 23473, 23503, 23563, 23580, 23860, 23881, 24037, 24229, 24326, 24424, 24438, 24439, 24459, 24469, 24547, 24560, 24593, 24599, 24613, 24642, 24687, 24696, 24722, 24739, 24743, 24778, 24815, 24852, 24947, 24956, 24978, 24997, 25034, 25043.

[1337] Wilson *et al.* 2012b: 377. On Roman shipping of raw glass generally and long-distance trade in glass with the East, more specifically, see Stern 1999: 475–8.

[1338] For instance, the excavation season of 2012 alone produced 38 glass wasters, cf. *IRPEX-2012*: p. 23.

[1339] Especially seeing as ribbed/pillared bowls were not a prominent product of Egypt and are therefore more likely to have been produced at a site along the Syro-Palestinian coast (e.g., Sidon, see chapter six), if shipped as finished glass vessels; cf. Stern 1991: 117.

[1340] Stern 1991: 117, reports the secure identification of one amber-coloured fragment of a ribbed bowl, whereas fragments from four or five ribbed bowls recorded by Wheeler could not be accounted for. Other ribbed bowls have been found at Dharanikota in the Eastern Deccan and at Taxila in the Northwest. In addition, she identified at Arikamedu one fragment from a light-blue glass dish and other fragments from a blue glass bowl with horizontal ridges. Finds of painted (also called 'mosaic') and decorated glass fragments at Pattanam may also attest the presence of other kinds of glass vessels, comparing with the dish and bowl from Arikamedu and painted glass from Begram, e.g. painted fragments: *IRPEX-**2011***: 24694, 24850, 24896; other decorations: *IRPEX-**2010***: 3603 (double spiral design); ***2011***: 23399 (green with white decoration), 23400 (blue with white decoration) 23443 (white with green and black design on rim), 24990 (feather-like decoration); and vessel-types with handles: *IRPEX-**2011***: 23693 (broken handle of small cup), 24470 (green handle).

[1341] *IRPEX-2012*: p. 22, gives the total number of sherds unearthed as 1720 of turquoise glazed ware and 3384 of torpedo jars. On the role of the Persian Gulf in trade with India, see chapter seven.

[1342] More than a hundred entries in the reports record finds of one or more lumps of frankincense, e.g. *IRPEX-**2008***: 3022; ***2009***: 1376; ***2010***: 4283; to list but a few.

Figure 19
View of the drip ledge and cave shelter on Mangulam Hill sponsored by the president of the merchants of nearby Vellarai. His inscription can be traced (faintly) along the side of the chiselled cliff face. Tamil Nadu. Photograph by the author.

the east coast of India.[1343] Nonetheless, as at Arikamedu, imported ceramics make up a minuscule part of the total ceramic assemblage.[1344] Furthermore, the most important archaeobotanical discovery at the site consists of substantial finds of black pepper, which, although unsurprising, provides concrete evidence for the maritime export of inland pepper to the Roman West, such as has been found in considerable quantities at Berenike.[1345] In consequence, taking the combined evidence from Arikamedu and Pattanam/ Muziris into consideration, there is very good archaeological evidence for the existence on a large scale of long-distance maritime trade between ancient South India and Roman ports in particular.

From an even earlier date, though, there is epigraphic evidence to support the existence in the Tamil South of organised merchants' communities involved in long-distance trade in the Indian Ocean, just like the *vanij-gamas* and *nigamas* appearing in the Western Deccan from the 1st century AD, just treated. Thus, the hill of Mangulam lying within the geographical confines of the ancient kingdom of the Pandians, mentioned along with the neighbouring kingdoms of the Cheras to the west and the Cholas to the east as early as the 2nd and 13th Rock Edicts of Ashoka in the mid-3rd century BC,[1346] provides rare epigraphical information about the organisation of commerce in the Pandian kingdom. Jain monks had settled on the hill, being, in actual fact, a small mountain ridge in itself, and wealthy patrons from nearby Madurai, capital city of the Pandians, equipped the chosen hermitage of the monks with drip ledges for their open caves (more like shelters, really), preventing water from seeping down in to them, and carved stone beds, providing the ascetics with somewhat level places in which to sleep [**Figure 19**].[1347] Fortunately, six Tamil-Brahmi inscriptions, two of which were inscribed by members of the Pandian royal court, provide interesting details about the donors, being dated palaeographically to the 2nd century BC.[1348]

Accordingly, two inscriptions record how the stone beds of one cave and the drip ledge of another were carved, respectively, through the sponsorship of the 'members of the *nigama* of Vellarai,' and 'the honourable (*antai*) Assutan, the superintendent of pearls and official (*kaviti*) of the *nigama* of Vellarai.'[1349] The Tamil word employed for *nigama* is *nikamat(t)u*, and the word for members of a such is *nikamator* (nom. pl.), corresponding to Sanskrit *naigama*, therefore providing a close fit with the terminology attested for

[1343] *IRPEX-2012*: p. 22, gives the number of Rouletted Ware sherds as 9537; on the distribution of rouletted ware, see n1382.
[1344] Cf. *IRPEX-2012*: p. 22–23, table L).
[1345] The only proper record of finding pepper appears to be *IRPEX-2008*: p. 18, which also mentions the exciting find of cardamom (both of which are repeated in Cherian 2011), repeated in Cherian and Menon 2014: 3, 21, 86–87, 121.
[1346] On these three ancient kingdoms, see Champakalakshmi 1996: 92–129, and the more theoretically informed *corrigendum* in Anna Abraham 2003.
[1347] Mahadevan 2003: 25 (on the physical characteristics of the caves), 90ff (on the chronology of the Tamil-Brahmi cave inscriptions), 127ff (on Jainism in the South)
[1348] Mahadevan 2003: Mangulam, no. 1–6; 1 and 2 referring to the Pandian king.
[1349] Mahadevan 2003: Mangulam, nos. 3, 6.

similar organisations in the Western Deccan.[1350] Evidently, this very early Tamil merchants' organisation was closely intertwined with the Pandian court, sponsoring cave improvements on the same rocky ridge, and involved in religious matters, the beneficiaries being Jain ascetics.

Moreover, we can distinguish between the general membership, who donated carved beds, and what appears to be the leader or head of the organisation, *antai* Assutan, who carried the royally bestowed title of *kaviti*, often conferred on ministers of the court, and was superintendent of pearls. The latter detail is particularly significant, seeing as we know from both Pliny and the *Periplus* that the coast of South India was famous for its pearl production, which, accordingly to the latter, was also carried out under royal supervision in the mid-1st century AD: 'Beyond Komar [Cape Comorin] the region extends as far as Korkai, where diving for pearls goes on; it is carried out by convicts. The region is under King Pandion.'[1351] Such royal involvement could very well have been handled by appointed superintendents of pearls, who were selected on the basis of their standing in the mercantile community, making it easier for them to arrange buyers and good prices for the precious output of the pearl fisheries, in consequence assuring a steady income for the Pandian king.[1352]

We should therefore expect the *nigamas* prominent as early as the 2nd century BC in the organisation of Pandian trade generally, and the pearl production in particular, to have remained at the heart of economic matters in the region in the ensuing centuries, as they did further north. One fragmentary inscription even evokes the financial setup of perpetual endowments in the Western Deccan by appearing to refer to the endowment of the produce of specified rice fields to the Jain community of a cave.[1353] The more so, seeing as we find the exact same system in place across the water in the likewise pearl producing northern Sri Lankan kingdom based at Anuradhapura.[1354] In the fourth century AD, the son of a royal minister made a perpetual endowment of large quantities of rice, pulses and beans, with the assembly of the *nigama* (Sinhalese: *niyama*) at Kalahumana in the northern quarter of Anuradhapura, to be lent out at high interest as seed grain, the interest to be used for sponsoring a religious festival of a specific Buddhist community in the countryside.[1355] Perhaps a little later, in the fifth century, another minister's son endowed a hundred *kahapanas*, that is, coin, with the *nigama* of Mahatabaka in the eastern quarter of Anuradhapura, the interest here also to be used for paying for the religious festival of a specific monastery—another fragmentary inscription at the same site recording an endowment of twenty *kahapanas* with the same monastery.[1356]

Evidently, then, Sri Lankan *nigamas* of merchants acted as deposit banks for endowments and were categorised by having been allotted positions in different quarters of the city, just like we know from Indian sources like the *Arthashastra*, Western Deccan inscriptions recording endowments nested with *shrenis*, and the charters of the *vanij-gamas* of Lohata and Sanjeli. In other words, the *margaritarii* of the Via Sacra, whether they be members of the *collegium aurificum* in particular or the *collegium dendrophorum*, were the organised representatives of market demand at the other end of a trade route originating in South Asian production and long-distance trade, supervised by senior leaders of wealthy merchants' organisations, enjoying royal patronage, possessing group cohesion and the tools for communal finance, and exhibiting religious piety.

Remarkably, there is corroborating evidence for a similar organisation from the major semi-precious stone bead-production site of Kodumanal in the ancient Cheran kingdom. Kodumanal was occupied and active as a manufacturing centre from approximately the 3rd century BC–4th century AD, and while there is also evidence of sustained shell bangle, ceramic, metal and textile production, it is the rich finds of unfinished and part-finished beads which is most remarkable: beryl, sapphire, quartz, amethyst, agate,

1350 Mahadevan 2003: commentary 3.4, 6.2, and p. 141, 4.16.1.
1351 *Periplus* 59; transl. Casson 1989 (plus 56 for their export as 'good supplies of fine-quality pearls' from the Malabar ports). Rajan 2008: 534.
1352 Mahadevan 2003: 123, 4.6.6.
1353 Mahadevan 2003: no. 16, Varichiyur 2 (*c.* 2nd century BC).
1354 Perera 2001: 174–76.
1355 Paranavitana 1928–33a: 172–88.
1356 Paranavitana 1928–33b: 247–53.

carnelian, lapis lazuli, jasper and onyx, to mention but some of the varieties, only the three first varieties (and possible the fourth) being mined locally. Waste from stone bead production is found all over the site, the almost complete lack of finished products indicating production for trade, with some evidence that different stages were carried out in different areas, and from a technological perspective the diverse styles of craftsmanship applied not only indicates a high degree of social complexity but possibly also different cultural groups at work.[1357]

Significantly, though, a plausible explanation is offered by one of the 200 Tamil-Brahmi inscribed sherds unearthed at Kodumanal, which carries the word *nikama*. Indeed, one or more of these highly organised merchants' organisations being involved in trade at Kodumanal would do very well to explain how this complex long-lived and long-distance manufacturing and commercial centre functioned.[1358] Cave inscriptions commemorating carved seats and drip ledges for Jain ascetics even furnish us with specific information about an affluent gold merchant of nearby Karur, capital of the Cheras, and a goldsmith from Madurai, capital of the Pandians, being examples of the individuals who will have profited from the trade in jewellery originating in South Indian production centres.[1359] Accordingly, the highly organised activities of craftsmen, merchants and *nigamas* at Kodumanal present us with the beginning of the trade route terminating at Rome with the *collegium aurificum* and the *gemmarii*, *aurifices*, etc., of the Via Sacra.

Indeed, this trade is well attested at the major ports of the region. Thus, the archaeological site of Pattanam/Muziris in Kerala has yielded no less than 53 cameo blanks,[1360] mostly of carnelian followed by chalcedony and a few banded agates,[1361] as well as 29 so-called 'ring stones' or 'inlays'[1362] of carnelian, onyx, agate, amethyst, malachite, chalcedony and quartz,[1363] at least two of the carnelian ring stones being already finely carved with intaglios of, respectively, Tyche/Fortuna and a leaping lion.[1364] Moreover, the finds of more than 700 semi-precious stone beads,[1365] including evidence of their production on site in the form of debitage,[1366] reveal lapidary workshops dealing in agate, amethyst, beryl, carnelian, chalcedony, garnet, quartz/crystal, topaz and onyx. Likewise, Arikamedu was also a centre for the manufacture of rock-crystal, amethyst and almandine garnets, while almost a hundred onyx cameo blanks have been uncovered during excavations.[1367] In addition, the site has yielded an unfinished quartz intaglio depicting a winged Cupid with a bird, and reportedly a carnelian intaglio portraying Augustus (both surface-finds, the latter since lost).[1368]

The untrimmed yet engraved state of the quartz Cupid intaglio begs the question whether engravers with knowledge of Greco-Roman iconography were present in Podukê,[1369] and the hypothesis was formerly that native craftsmen might have been inspired by imported Western models or that some Western craftsmen were present in the settlement.[1370] However, a by now substantial corpus of seals with Classical motifs from not only Gandhara and Taxila but also North Indian Varanasi, dating to the early centuries AD,[1371] implies

1357 Champakalakshmi 1996: 136–7, 182; Rajan 2008: 535–6; Francis 2004: 480–81; Kelly 2009.

1358 On the Tamil-Brahmi inscribed sherds at the site generally: Mahadevan 2003: 44; Rajan 2008: 44–5; Rajan 2009: 74. On the specific inscribed sherd from Kodumanal: Rajan 1996: 103–4, fig. 7.b.

1359 Mahadevan 2003: no. 36, Alagarmalai 1 (*c.* 1st century BC); no. 69, Pugalur 9 (*c.* 3rd century AD).

1360 *IRPEX-2012*: p. 24.

1361 Those which can be securely identified in the reports are, carnelian: *IRPEX-**2008***: 159, 1034, 1035, 2489; ***2009***: 6923; ***2010***: 246, 440, 3174, 3912, 4883, 5166, 5175; ***2011***: 21657, 23246, 23494, 24026, 24261, 24402, 24581, 24601, 24627, 24836, 24836, 24884, 25019; chalcedony: *IRPEX-**2008***: 2776; ***2009***: 3670, 5168, 8136; ***2010***: 1234, 3987; ***2011***: 23211, 23228, 23243, 23245, 23419, 23793, 24103, 24718, 24719, 25013; and agate: *IRPEX-**2008***: 317; ***2011***: 23128, 23822, 24386.

1362 *IRPEX-2012*: p. 24.

1363 Those which can be securely identified in the reports are, carnelian: *IRPEX-**2010***: 805 (the 'lion intaglio'), 3391, 3553, 4625, 4852; ***2011***: 22491; onyx: *IRPEX-**2010***: 4565(?); ***2011***: 23615, 23796, 24096; agate: *IRPEX-**2010***: 2324, 3108(?); ***2011***: 24959; amethyst: *IRPEX-**2010***: 6043; ***2011***: 22401; malachite: *IRPEX-**2010***: 2109 (or beryl); ***2011***: 20782; chalcedony: *IRPEX-**2011***: 20676; and quartz: *IRPEX-**2011***: 20832

1364 Published in Cherian and Menon 2014: 82–85. The lion intaglio can be identified with *IRPEX-**2010***: 805.

1365 *IRPEX-2012*: p. 24, gives the exact number as 735.

1366 The season of 2012 alone yielded 275 pieces of semi-precious stone debitage, on top of which came some 55 pieces of bead blanks, rough-outs and raw material chunks, cf. *IRPEX-2012*: p. 24.

1367 Francis 2004: 504.

1368 Jouveau-Dubreuil 1940: 449; Wheeler 1946: 21, 101, pl. XXIIIB, 11–12; Begley 1996: 3, 29.

1369 Wheeler 1946: 101.

1370 Begley 1996: 29f.

1371 Thaplyal 1972: 243–7, notice especially pl. XXXV, no. 13: a winged Nike; for Gandharan seals, cf. Rahman and Falk 2011: 68–94, 180–96, especially the dated seals from Taxila, TM 06.02.01–06.14.01, remarking that TM 06.07.02 is both roughly contemporary and surprisingly similar

that a capable South Asian engraver could equally well have arrived by way of ship from the Ganges estuary, which kept up a brisk coastal trade with the Coromandel ports, Podukê included.[1372] Nonetheless, now that the securely identified quartz intaglio and alleged carnelian intaglio from Arikamedu can be considered in light of the two carved carnelian intaglios from Pattanam, where a Roman diaspora is more than likely, as argued above, it feels even more safe to assume that professional engravers, whether Roman, Indian or *Yavana*(!), were posted to the two ports with the explicit purpose of adding extra value to at least some of the semiprecious stones destined for export by processing them into easily marketable intaglios.[1373] Other ring stones, as well as cameo blanks, are likely to have remained unworked, however, so as to be engraved according to the wishes of their ultimate buyers in Mediterranean ports and cities.

Furthermore, it is worth emphasising that such evidence for organisation of production in Early Historic South India fits with other kinds of evidence, as well, like the enormous amounts of glass beads produced at sites such as Arikamedu (7000 finds) and Porunthal (2000), but exported from ports like Pattanam (56,000),[1374] and found all the way from Berenike in Roman Egypt to Yaoi Japan.[1375] To produce such enormous quantities, but only limited types of great uniformity, entails considerable standardisation which can perhaps best be explained by the involvement of *nigamas* of merchants in charge of export and *shreni-type* associations of specialised craftsmen in charge of production—as, indeed, influential families and craftsmen's guilds are known from ethnological studies of bead production sites at Cambay (Gujarat) and Papanaidupet (Andra Pradesh) in India.[1376]

Finally, the archaeobotanical finds of, and written evidence for trade in, pepper in the Roman Empire, is now supplemented by substantial finds of pepper at Pattanam, as well as by the earliest Tamil literary sources, the so-called *Sangam* epic poetry created from the 1st century BC to the 3rd century AD,[1377] which contain references to *Yavanas* arriving in ships from the West to Muziris with wine and gold to purchase pepper brought down to the port from the mountains further inland.[1378] In addition, as mentioned in chapter five, there is also tentative evidence from South India indicating the clearance and settlement of upland slopes, beginning in the 1st century AD, evidently a reaction to increased Roman demand for forestry products, foremost of which would have been pepper.

The people involved will have been specialised foragers trading their Ghat forest produce on the market for necessary products such as food, textiles and metal tools, thus creating regional trade networks exchanging upland pepper and other spices (such as cardamom) for items of the lowland cities. While it is not known exactly how pepper was grown in Early Historic India, later times saw a combination of foraging and cultivated swidden field plots, and under all circumstances the Ghat peoples must have expended a very great amount of labour for the gathering of pepper, monitoring and tending of wild plants, drying and processing of the spices required prior to transport, and onward sale, all of these activities constituting value-adding labour.[1379]

Thus, if it had not been for the skills and work of the actual producers of pepper on the upland slopes of the Ghats, the Cheran and Pandian merchants of the Malabar ports would have had nothing to trade with, rendering it necessary to rehabilitate the role of the former in relation to the latter to obtain a better understanding of the organisation of the production and long-distance trade in South Indian pepper in the early centuries of the Common Era. Keeping the *collegium aromatariorum* at Rome supplied, the *horrea piperataria* stacked, and pepper moving all the way to the northern- and westernmost frontiers of the

to the 'Cupid with bird' ring stone from Arikamedu (assuming a circa 1st century AD date).

[1372] *Periplus* 60. On the trade between the Ganges delta and South India, see also n1382.

[1373] In addition, *IRPEX-2011:* 22401 is recorded as an amethyst inlay set in a gold ring, which might be further evidence of goldsmiths and engravers enhancing the value of semi-precious stones for overseas markets.

[1374] Anna Abraham 2013, the number of glass beads from Pattanam having been updated with reference to *IRPEX-2012*: p. 23, which lists a total of 56440.

[1375] Katsuhiko and Gupta 2000; Sidebotham 2011: 238.

[1376] Francis 1991; 2004: 467–8.

[1377] Zvelebil 1992: chapter 4, especially 128—on the dating of *Yavanas*, 117–8.

[1378] Particularly *Puram* 56; 343; and *Akam* 149, quoted in Zvelebil 1956. See also Zvelebil 1973: 35, n1.

[1379] Morrison and Lycett 2013.

Roman Empire, in response to a demand exerted across more than 8000 km and via several commercial circuits, was certainly no mean feat.

Organising the world of production

As should hopefully be plain by now, the case-study conducted in chapter three, revealing how Roman associations of citrus workers and ivory and citrus merchants were at the receiving end of a trade route starting in the Western Deccan with associations of Indian ivory carvers, can be augmented with smaller similar case-studies. Thus, we have seen how Roman *collegia* can be compared with Indian *shrenis* and *nigamas*, not just as regards the actual products they handled at the demand and supply end, respectively, but, remarkably, also as concerns their internal rules and regulations, social functions and religious involvement.

The ivory carvers of Vidisha contributed to the magnificent adornment of the Sanchi *stupa*, while *shrenis*, *nigamas* and *vanij-gamas* of Nashik, Junnar and Karla were involved in commerce between the Satavahanas, Western Kshatrapas and Roman Egypt, lending endowment principals at interest, and religious sponsorship of nearby Buddhist establishments, from the later 1st century BC–2nd century AD. *Yavanas* appear as participants in commerce and religion, as well, but as members of Indian kinship groups or corporations which we cannot securely identify, although they might well have been similar to contemporary associations known in one instance from Kanheri and in several versions from Gandhara.

Indeed, the highly regulated nature and potential for communal action, both economic and religious, of *shrenis* and *vanij-gamas* in particular is borne out by 5th–6th century AD evidence of the *shreni* of silk-weavers and the *vanij-gamas* of Lohata and Sanjeli. Finally, the Western Deccan—in combination with the Hoq Cave—also furnishes 2nd–early 5th century AD evidence for the vocational interdependence and cooperation of Indian shippers and merchants sailing out of Barygaza, the former being organised with leaders of the shippers' community (the latter presumably in a *vanij-gama* or *nigama*), and of the merchants (*vanij*, *negama*) and financiers (*sethi*) of the ports and hinterland, as represented by their 2nd century AD pious inscriptions and endowments at Kanheri, testifying to their financial acumen. All of these activities and modes of organisation compare surprisingly well with contemporary Roman and Greek forms of organisation among merchants, shippers and craftsmen, and as regards associative life in general.

As we have just seen, moreover, these similarities extend to South India, where the available evidence, although more sparse, speaks strongly of the role of the *nigama* as an important organiser of large-scale supply of pearls and semi-precious stones, but likely also beads and pepper. In fact, the stupendous amount of glass beads produced and distributed to sites more than 12,000 km apart, as well as the prominence of pepper in Roman society from the last years of the 1st century BC onwards, should force us to reconsider whether Tamil production and export was not a lot more sophisticated than the one-eyed heroic focus of *Sangam* poetry might lead us to think, the plentiful Roman artefacts found in the South being an indicator not of Western dominance in the trade, but of a huge Roman demand. Furthermore, we know for certain that in a Tamil and Sinhalese context, too, *nigamas* were not only concerned with business, but also closely connected to the ruling circles of society, involved in religious sponsorship, and active in financial transactions, as documented by their role in administering endowments.

Emphatically, though, it needs to be stated that the mirror held up here to the organisation of Roman demand forcing us to consider the parallel organisation of Western Deccan and South Indian supply, could also, had it fallen within the scope of this study, have shed more light on the commercial roles of Sri Lanka, the Eastern Deccan, North India and even Southeast Asia beyond. For instance, we know from the *Periplus* (49, 56) and the Muziris Papyrus (*verso*, col. ii) that boxes containing Gangetic nard from the Himalayan foothills of North India were available in good supply (80 boxes for one buyer) at ports like Muziris and Barygaza. Who organised the collection, processing, packaging and transport from the North to ports of India's western littoral?

Based on analogy with the evidence from the Western Deccan and South India, this complex supply operation might well have been organised by groups such as the perfumers' (*gandhikas*) association of Kausambi, which became prominent enough to issue its own coins around the 2nd century BC, in cooperation with the merchants of important *nigamas* employing their own corporate seals, dated from later Mauryan to Guptan times from sites such as Bhita and Varanasi. Perhaps the most vivid example is the more than 270 seals found at Guptan Vaishali, which all contain different versions, some longer, some shorter, of the compound: *sreshthi-sarthavaha-kulika-nigama*, that is, a seal bearing the authority of the chief merchant, caravan leader and head craftsman of the *nigama* in unison.[1380] Contemporary copper plate administrative documents show how these specific officials also worked together in local municipal administration.[1381] Moreover, recent analyses of the distribution of Rouletted Ware clearly show how a busy trade circuit extended from the Ganges delta along the east coast down to the South, by which way the nard would have passed in ships[1382]—organised business as usual, in other words.

As regards the furthest reach of the interlocking markets outlined in the previous chapters, we have already touched upon the arrival in Indian ports via Southeast Asia (supplemented by a route via Central Asia to Western India[1383]) of supplies of Chinese silk, and the corresponding percolation further East to China of Roman glasswares and of South Asian glass beads as far as Japan. While Roman knowledge of Southeast and East Asia was scant,[1384] and Chinese historical accounts of encounters with Roman travellers arriving by sea are highly dubious,[1385] there is, nonetheless, sound evidence for early Indian contacts with and trade around the Malay Peninsula (above we have already encountered some of the *mahanavikas* who would have sailed there from ports of Eastern India, cf. chapter seven),[1386] with Indian Rouletted Ware and the so-called Arikamedu Type 10 cropping up as far afield as Java, Bali and Indonesia,[1387] and Buddhist monks providing evidence of regularised sea-travel between the Ganges estuary, Sri Lanka and China via ports on the north-east coast of Sumatra from no later than the early 5th century AD.[1388] However, in this regard the scope of ancient long-distance trade between Rome and India in Antiquity even exceeds the limits of this, arguably, otherwise fairly wide-ranging study.

1380 All listed in Thaplyal 1996: Appendix 4, 170, 5.A–C, 172–74. 1972: 224–37.

1381 Basak 1919–20: 129–32 (Damodarpur).

1382 See map in Schenk 2006: 130, revealing a distribution spanning from the lower Ganges in the North to Korkai and Sri Lanka in the South, from as early as the 3rd century BC. Now also 2015: 153–60.

1383 *Periplus* 64; *Chr.Top.* II.45–46, for the latter cf. Faller 2011: 215–16.

1384 E.g. *Periplus* 63–66, Ptol. *Geog.*, I.13–14 (in Berggren and Jones 2000), VII.3, and the reference to China in the *Christian Topography* in the note above.

1385 The overly optimistic interpretations of Leslie and Gardiner 1996: 148–50, 153–62, are all rejected (with one possible exception, p. 78) in the expert review by Pulleyblank 1999 (p. 72: 'They are babes in the woods when it comes to Chinese historical phonology').

1386 Ray 1994b: 91–111. Jacq-Hergoualc'h 2002: 30–64 (on the feasibility of crossing the peninsula versus circumnavigating it), 89–105. To complement the evidence for Indian shippers in the Peninsula, we now have the touchstone of a Tamil master goldsmith, dated 3rd–4th century AD; cf. Karashima and Subbarayalu 2009: 283, no. 10.

1387 For Java, cf. Glover 1989: 4; for Bali, Ray 1994b: 109–10; and for Indonesia, Begley 1996: 24–5.

1388 Hansen 2012: 160–64.

Conclusion

Worlds apart trading together

As should hopefully have become clear in all of the above, the historiography of studies on trade between the Roman Mediterranean and India is now more in need of an update than ever. On the one hand, this is due to an old-fashioned colonial perspective inherent to some of the early and most ambitious treatments of the topic by Rawlinson, Charlesworth, Warmington and Wheeler, whose notions of 'Indo-Roman' trade can, arguably, more fittingly be described as 'Roman trade with India,' being severely biased towards Roman carriers, chronology and sources. Even after post-colonialism made a forceful entry unto the academic stage, the basic framework of this older 'Romano-centric' narrative has lingered in some Western work on the subject, though. On the other hand, our present understanding of the scale and nature of the trade between Rome and India in the early centuries of the Common Era has benefited greatly from recent discoveries: the publication and subsequent re-editions of the Muziris Papyrus, a great amount of archaeological work on the ports and especially ceramic assemblages of the Indian Ocean rim, the discovery of the graffiti in the Hoq Cave, and the identification and gradual excavation of Muziris at modern Pattanam, to name but some of the major advances of the last thirty years. Thus, the main aim of this study has been to integrate these new finds, so that we might become wiser about the organisation of long-distance trade between the Roman Empire and Early Historic India. In doing so, moreover, the particular focus has been on the networks, diasporas and associations making this trade possible.

Throughout, a different methodology engaging with the 'source material on the ground,' that is, created by those who traded and transported the commodities in question back and forth across the Indian Ocean, has provided a strong *corrigendum* to top-down analyses based mainly on literary sources, most often Roman, written by the ancient elites. Consequently, detailed case-studies, like the ones this study is based on, force us to look at the products being exchanged, by whom, how and why—concrete 'bottom-up' questions which we can attempt to answer when combining the available sources from both the Roman West and the Indian East within a synchronic timeframe.

This pragmatic approach is perhaps nowhere better applied than in the case-study of the Indian ivory figurine from Pompeii. Building on a technical analysis of one specific artefact and endeavouring to write its cultural biography, the origin, production and use of an Indian category of long-distance commodities is described, as well as its import to Rome, adaption for a new market and influence on Roman elite consumption. Crucially, though, we can also identify the human component of this trade, revealing the existence of contemporary and interacting Indian and Roman associations of craftsmen (*citriarii* and *dantakaras*) and merchants (*negotiatores eborarii et citriarii*), organising supply in India and demand at Rome, in unison making a complex long-distance trade in ivory furniture components possible, facilitated by sea-going merchants of the Indian Ocean.

Accordingly, it comes as no surprise that we find other examples of demand for specific long-distance goods organised at Rome in the shape of *collegia* and similar groupings, strong demand and stable supply even giving rise to the construction of the *horrea piperataria* at the heart of Rome, providing storage space for *inter alia* the *collegium aromatariorum* just south of the *Forum Romanum* itself. The *collegium aurificum* and various traders and craftsmen of the Via Sacra, especially the *margaritarii*, had South Indian counterparts in the *nigama* of merchants involved in semi-precious stone production at Kodumanal, and the *nigama* of Vellarai whose most senior member also acted as royally appointed supervisor of the Pandian pearl production.

The *collegium thurariorum et unguentariorum* had an Egyptian parallel in the monopoly contractors of the Oxyrhynchite *koinon myropōlōn*, Arabian parallels in the form of Nabataean merchants' propensity for setting up branches abroad, whether in Puteoli, Egypt, along the Incense Trail in Arabia, or as far south as the Horn of Africa, even conducting value-adding processing into unguents at Petra, and in the anonymous consortium leasing Dioscourides to reap the fiscal profits from its harvest of frankincense. A North Indian association of perfumers and *nigamas* potentially involved in the re-export of nard from the commercial centres of the Ganges via South India to Roman Egypt have also been briefly mentioned as constituting an example of organised supply.

Furthermore, the *sericarii* of Rome were if not formally organised into a *collegium* then at least organised enough to act in public as a community defined by profession. While we do not know of any exactly matching Palmyrene group, we do know that silk was both imported as finished textiles, modified by stitch-work and woven entirely from scratch, the Palmyrene epigraphic evidence instead contributing to our understanding of the organisation of import: caravans institutionalised along the lines of contemporary merchants' organisations, and shippers and merchants setting themselves up in far-away entrepôts like Koptos as associations, as did groups in Palmyra either producing the necessities for river transport or creating jewellery from imported stones and pearls.

In the Western Deccan, though, from which both silk thread, silk textiles, and all sorts of clothing made from cotton were imported to the West, there is strong evidence for the organisation of supply in the form of associations. Production was organised in *shrenis* of weavers, some mainly working in cotton, others being silk-weavers, which were well-established, profitable and trustworthy enough to re-invest and keep safe the money from pious perpetual endowments, or build their own temples and maintain them over time. Export was handled by traders, *vanij*, and merchants, *naigama*, inhabiting well-regulated *vanij-gamas* and *nigamas*, the shippers, *navika* or *niryamaka*, carrying the goods being sufficiently well-organised to elect formal leaders, *jetthaka*, of their own professional communities. Accordingly, the organisation of both of these vocations can be compared to Greco-Roman associations of merchants, *emporoi*, shippers, *nauklêroi*, and the two combined, as at Ostia, Puteoli and Alexandria.

In order to circumvent the critique that the long-distance trade under study here was exceptional in merely reflecting elite consumption and spending power at Rome, an attempt has been made at widening the scope of the analysis to the provinces of the Roman Empire, enquiring into the existence of a provincial demand for South Arabian and Indian products, as well as its concomitant supply. Although a notoriously difficult topic to deal with, it is possible to obtain a better appreciation of the aggregate Roman demand and scale of supply across very long distances by comparing price figures from Pliny with archaeological and archaeobotanical finds, as well as documentary evidence in the form of cargo consignment lead-tags and one unique writing-tablet recording a transaction.

The resulting picture is one of comparatively modest prices for the cheaper versions of long-distance aromatics and perfumes, which even the lower strata of society might have been infrequent and sparing consumers of, pepper being traded by civilians all the way to the Germanic and Caledonian *limes*, and exotic perfumes being shipped by small-time traders to remote provincial markets in northern and eastern *Italia*. In consequence, although these findings must be considered tentative, neither demand nor supply were limited to imperial Rome, which informs us that not only the central market of Rome, the Great Attractor, was kept in supply, but also regional markets as far away as Hadrian's Wall. In order to make such an empire-wide market-mediated distribution possible, the total imports of nard from North India, pepper from South India and Arabian myrrh must have been on a grand scale—this long-distance interaction and exchange being facilitated by what has been defined above as the long reach of 'interlocking markets.'

Indeed, Alexandria and India were closely linked in both ancient academic as well as popular perception, being very much the place where Western demand met Eastern supply, in the eyes of the Romans, at least. Nonetheless, other major ports of the Eastern Mediterranean also had important roles to play as entrepôts of Eastern imports. Furthermore, as the analysis of Roman, Arab, Indian and Axumite agents in the trade has shown, demand made itself felt across the Indian Ocean at both the South Arabian and Indian centres of production and supply. On the Roman side, graffiti from Egypt's Eastern Desert reveals active participation in the long-distance trade by both Campanian families from South *Italia*, as well as by wealthy Alexandrian financiers extending loans to merchants who would travel all the way to India in person to purchase as much as 150–80 tonnes of merchandise, to be brought back to Alexandria for taxation, repayment of the loan, and subsequent sale on the market. Remarkably, the value of just a single merchant's cargo could be immense, providing fiscal revenues of great importance to the state, and private fortunes to be made on the markets for long-distance imports at Alexandria and Rome bypassing those of many ordinary Roman senators.

Emphatically, Roman traders were not the only active participants fitting out ships for markets across the sea. In Egypt, we find evidence of very well-integrated Arabs, a substantial number of Indians visiting the ports of Myos Hormos and Berenike, and even some evidence indicating the presence of Axumite merchants. Remarkably, this is a picture which is forcefully corroborated by an analysis of graffiti from the Hoq Cave on Socotra, especially when combined with archaeological results from excavations at Qana, in particular, but also Sumhuram, of the ancient South Arabian kingdom of Hadramawt. While Roman merchants may have been dominant in the trade in the later 1st century BC–later 1st century AD, the role of sea-going Indians from the Western Deccan seems to have been ascendant in the 2nd–5th century, with Axumite traders attaining prominence from no later than the 6th century. As regards the Indian side of things, we can tell that South Indian agents were active on behalf of their Tamil masters in Roman and Arabian ports, and Kanheri in the Western Deccan supplements the picture of maritime trade obtained from the Hoq Cave graffiti by providing a view of port-side traders, merchants and financiers, with connections to inland production centres. Likewise, the *Yavana*s of Socotra, Karla and Junnar are yet another prominent example of the sophisticated and complex commercial networks brought into existence by the East–West trade.

Notably, moreover, these merchant networks of diverse origins criss-crossing the Indian Ocean during the period were well-organised, trustworthy, and financially efficient enough to supplement the various states bordering the Ocean by contracting for the collection of important taxes on remote possessions or the long-distance trade itself. Thus, merchant networks provided a key service in the margins of the states, not only managing to conduct trade over very long distances and through very difficult terrain and climate zones, in the process generating highly substantial fiscal revenues, but parts of the merchant communities were even entrusted with and paid to collect these very same taxes. Obviously, however, no one was better placed with expert knowledge of the workings of the trade routes than the merchants themselves and their rich financiers, therefore supplementing the institutions of the state where these proved out of their depth.

Finally, on this note of the prevalence and efficacy of organisations in the Indian Ocean trade during the 1st–6th century AD, perhaps the most surprising finding of this study has been the close institutional similarity between the two main *comparanda*, namely, Roman and Indian professional associations, chosen for their roles in harnessing demand and supply, respectively. However, while their comparable economic functions are evident, it is the more surprising that tight-knit professional groups from both sides would find it so important to forge social ties between members and enshrine these, alongside the communal relationship with the host society, in shared cult and religious observance. In other words, Greco-Roman associations and their Indian counterparts conspicuously chose to merge their common professional and economic activities with the social and religious spheres of ancient daily life.

Seeing as this amalgamation of otherwise distinctly different institutions, the economic, the social and the religious, is characteristic of both phenomena developed in parallel far apart, we must perceive of this development as in answer to a universal experience or challenge common to both worlds. Namely, the institution of the market with its potentially disruptive effects on social hierarchies and religious norms, in theory abiding by no moral restraints, driven only by the interplay between supply and demand connecting across sometimes very great distances, as the present analysis of trade between the Roman Mediterranean and Indian Ocean in the early centuries of the Common Era has shown.

Accordingly, what we witness in the institutional microcosms on parade here, the Roman and Indian professional associations, is the active process of embedding interpersonal relations, otherwise mainly defined by joint profession and therefore potential economic competition, in two other dimensions of society which could reinforce the voluntary creation of communal relations with strong social and religious ties in the face of opposing interests, that is, strengthening group propensity for the creation of relational contracts. Indeed, as the popularity of nesting endowments with associations shows, conducting business with social and religious strings attached was a perfectly ordinary communal task for these groups. In conclusion, embedding transactions between co-professionals of one specific trade or craft within restraining ties of purposefully constructed community constituted by an imposed social hierarchy encompassing all members and universal religious values constantly reaffirmed collectively, appears to have been the Greek, Roman and Indian method of choice for creating strong and durable professional organisations, in turn facilitating the establishment of personal networks and private partnerships. As a result of their complex and flexible institutional setup, associations in particular were better able to manage the market, supplement the state, and create community.

In closing, it is worthwhile to emphasise that the above analysis of the organisation of Indian Ocean trade in the 1st–6th century AD has not only turned the tables on the historiographically outdated concept of 'Indo-Roman trade,' but also, significantly, on the degree to which an 'Ancient Economy á la Finley' can any longer be considered to have been characterised by the state as the major economic actor, with markets being fragmented, shallow and oppressed by high transaction costs. Finley himself having previously claimed that a long-distance reciprocal economic relationship between the Roman Mediterranean, India and China, was entirely out of the question. Although this may be the view from the top, a view from the ground up focusing on concrete demand, commodities, and traders and their organisations, reveals the role of the institution of the market even in very long-distance exchange as being paramount. Trade and the exigencies of the market were central in defining commercial organisation, that is, the economic structure, not the state in isolation, although the latter obviously did have its own important role to play. Emphatically, this is the more evident because we can study the process in connected Mediterranean and Indian Ocean contexts where merchants and their organisations although worlds apart were trading together.

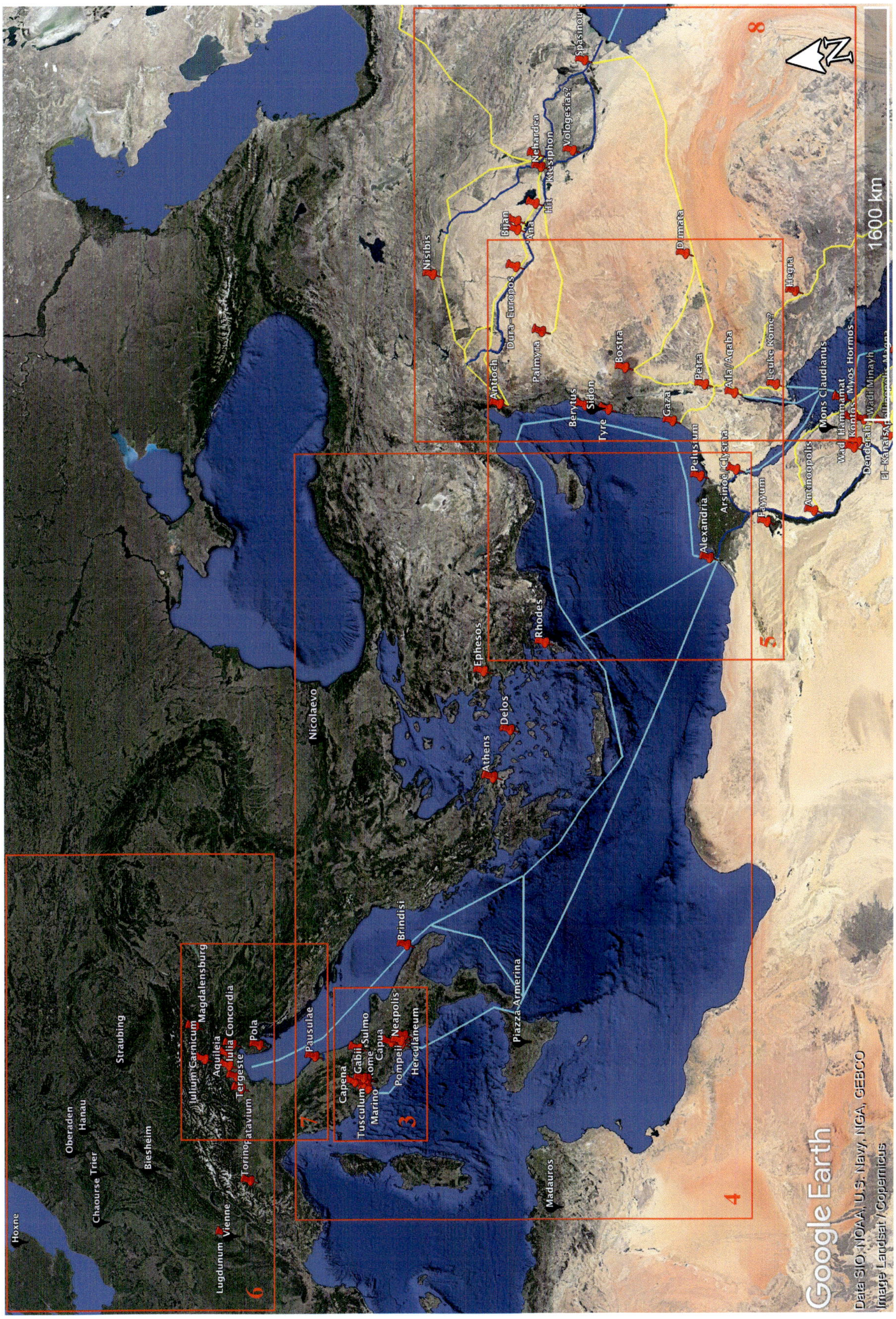

Map 1: Overview of the Mediterranean World

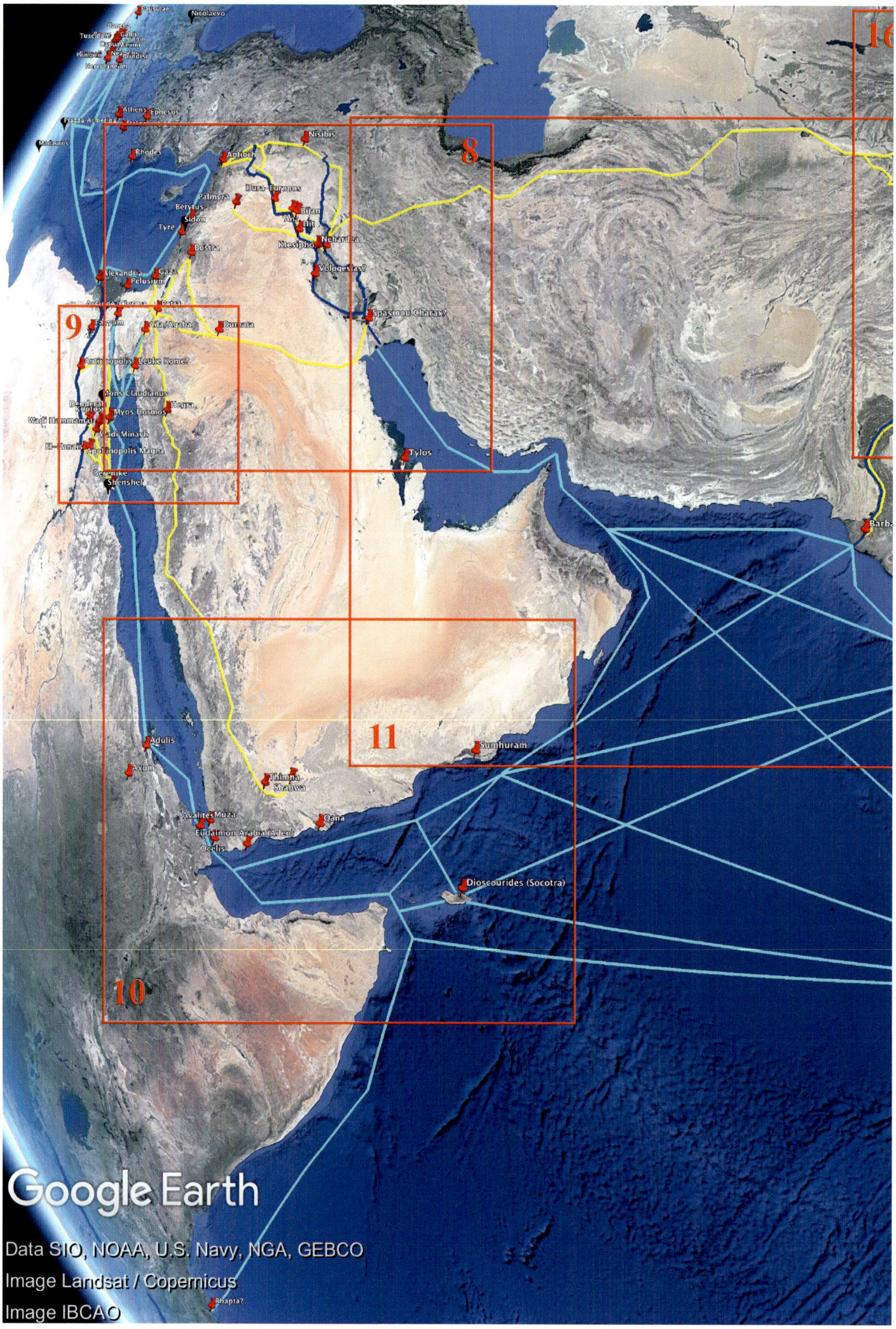

Map 2: Overview of the Indian Ocean

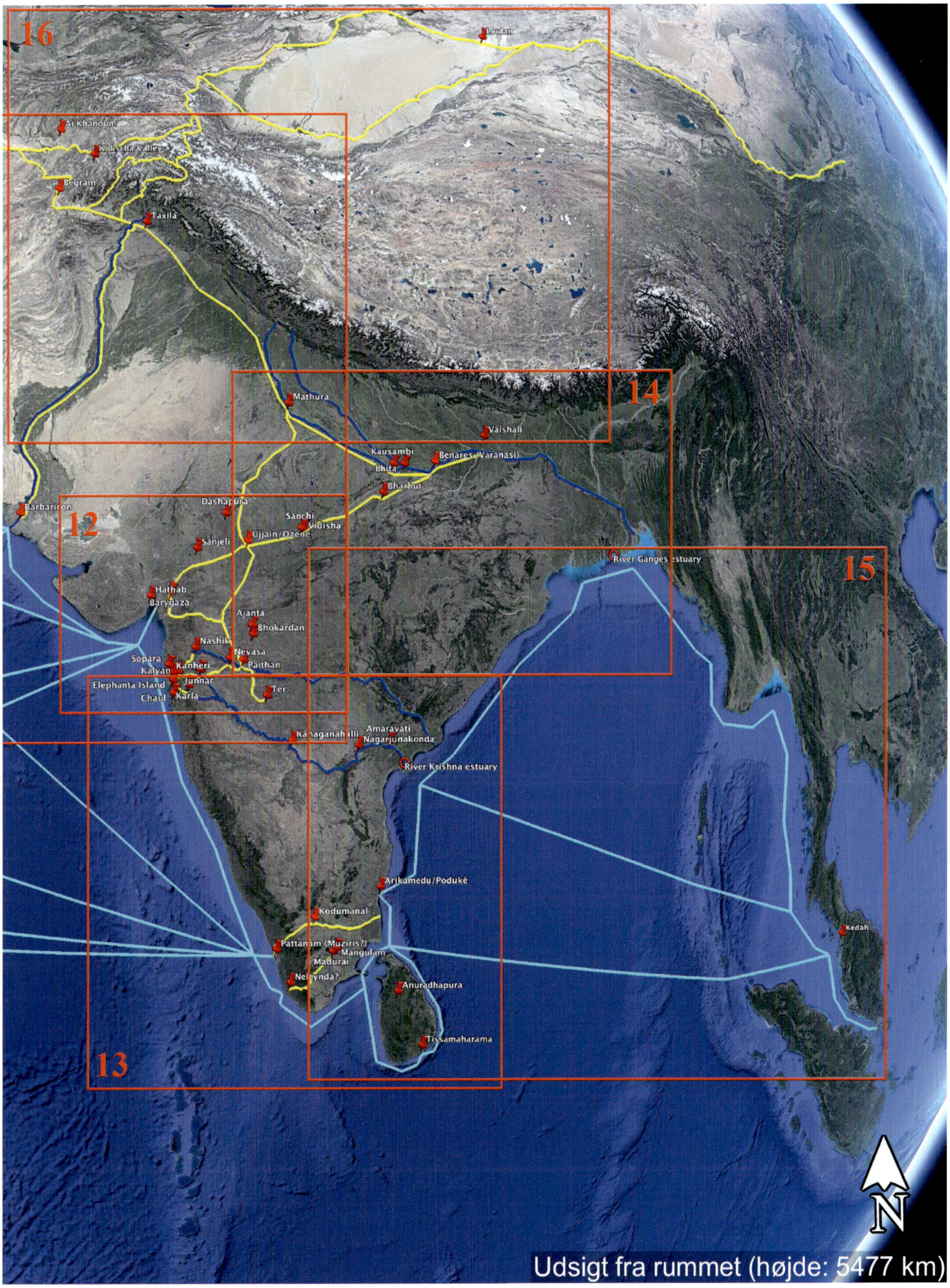
16
Loulan
Ai Khanoum
Kokscha Valley
Begram
Taxila
14
Mathura
Vaishali
Kausambi
Bhita
Benares (Varanasi)
Bharhut
Barbaricon
Dashapura
12
Sanchi
Vidisha
Ujjain/Ozene
Sanjeli
River Ganges estuary
15
Hathab
Barygaza
Ajanta
Bhokardan
Nashik
Nevasa
Sopara
Kalyan
Kanheri
Paithan
Elephanta Island
Junnar
Chaul
Karla
Ter
Kanaganahalli
Amaravati
Nagarjunakonda
River Krishna estuary
Arikamedu/Poduké
Kodumanal
Kedah
Pattanam (Muziris?)
Mangulam
Madurai
Nelcynda?
Anuradhapura
Tissamaharama
13
N
Udsigt fra rummet (højde: 5477 km)

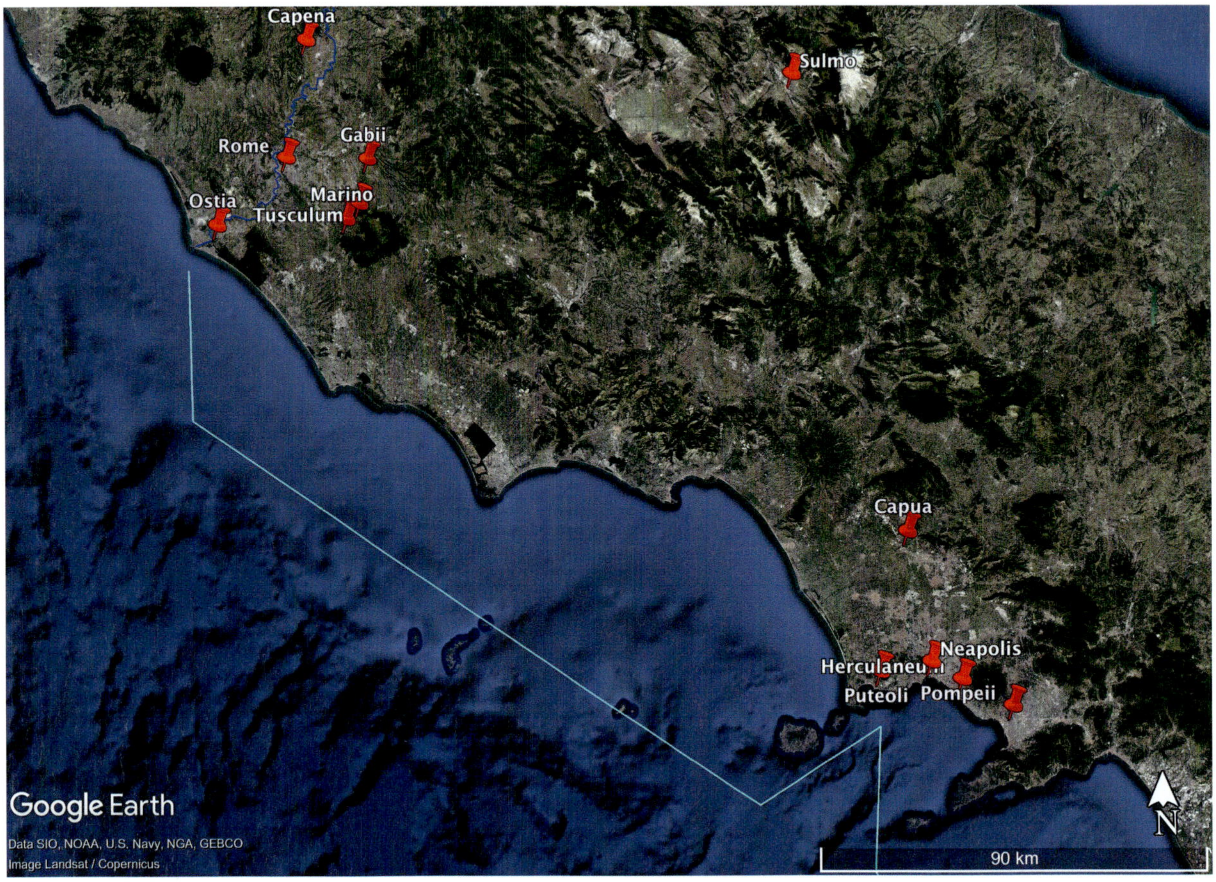

Map 3: Latium and Campania, Italia

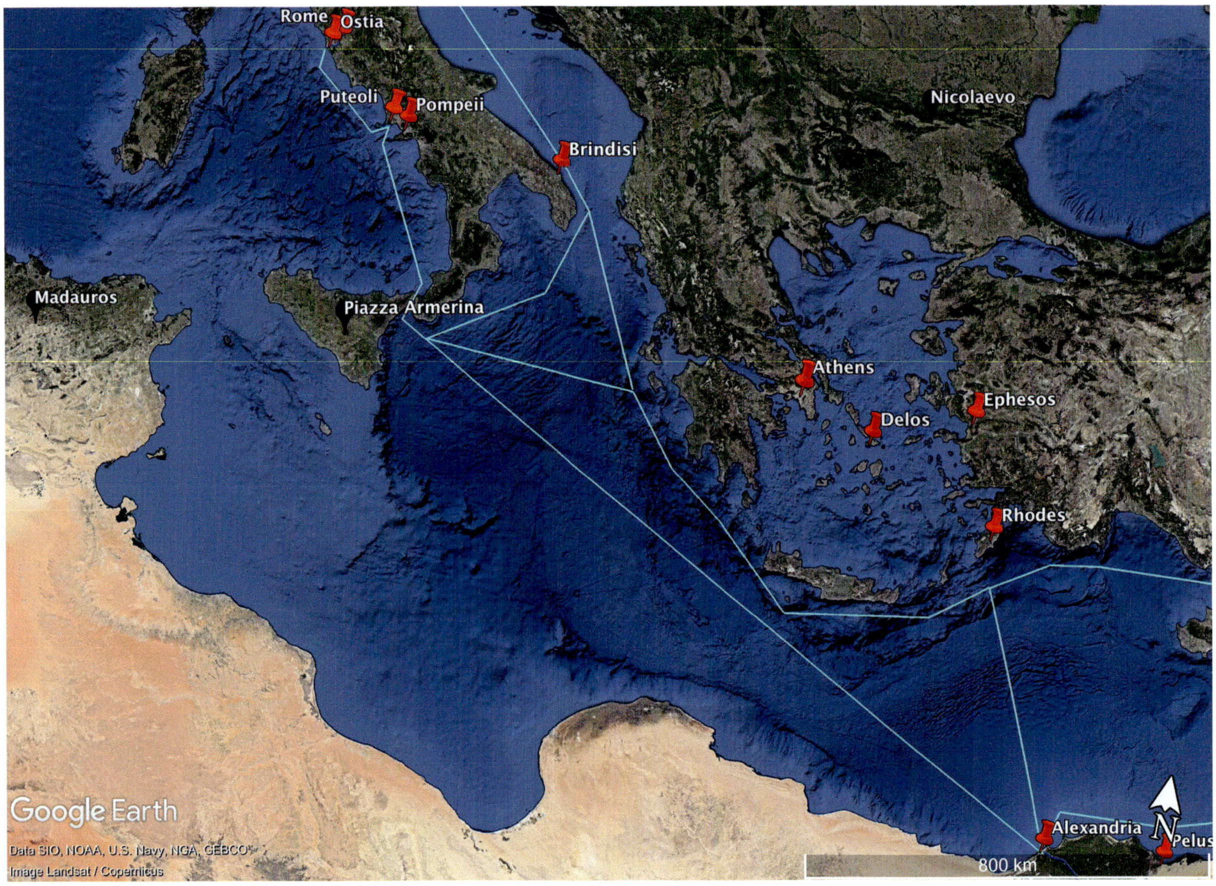

Map 4: Central Mediterranean

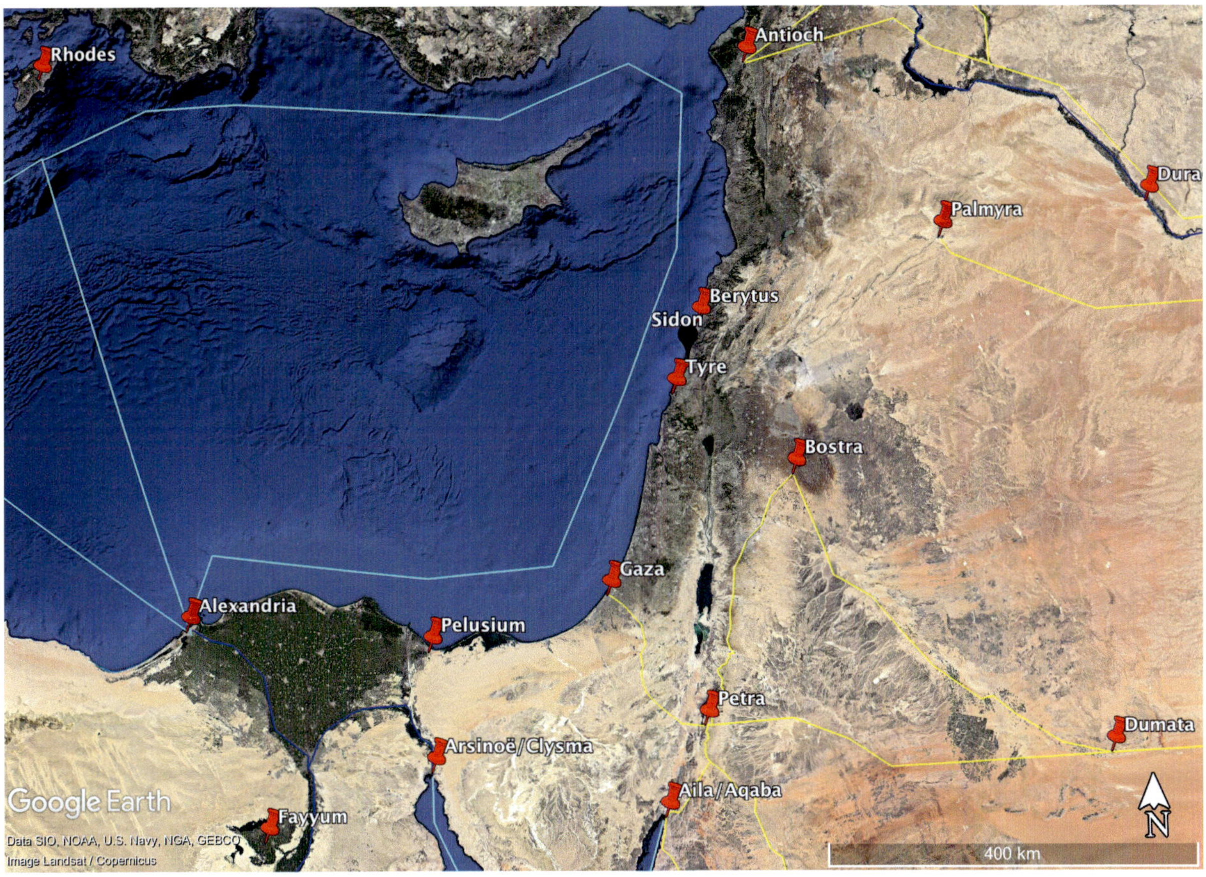

Map 5: Eastern Mediterranean

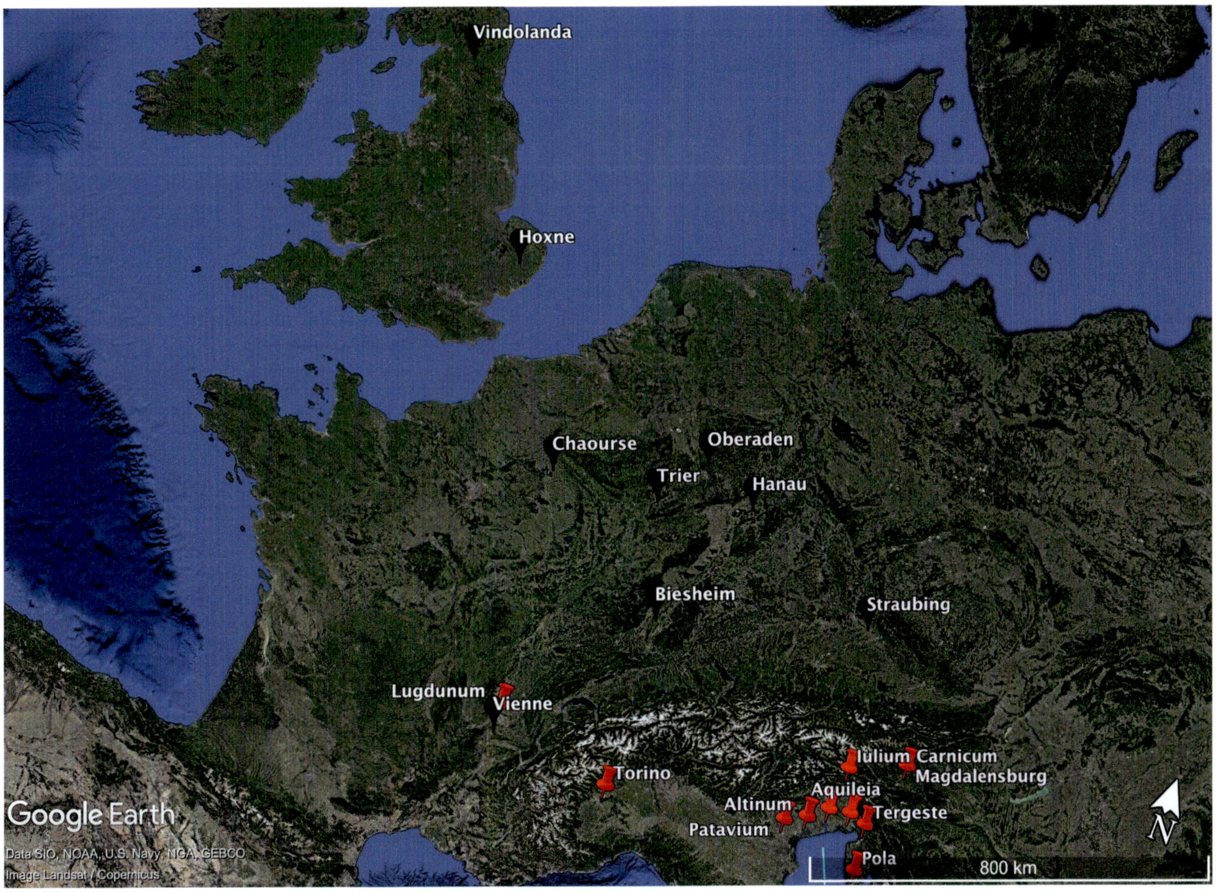

Map 6: Western Provinces

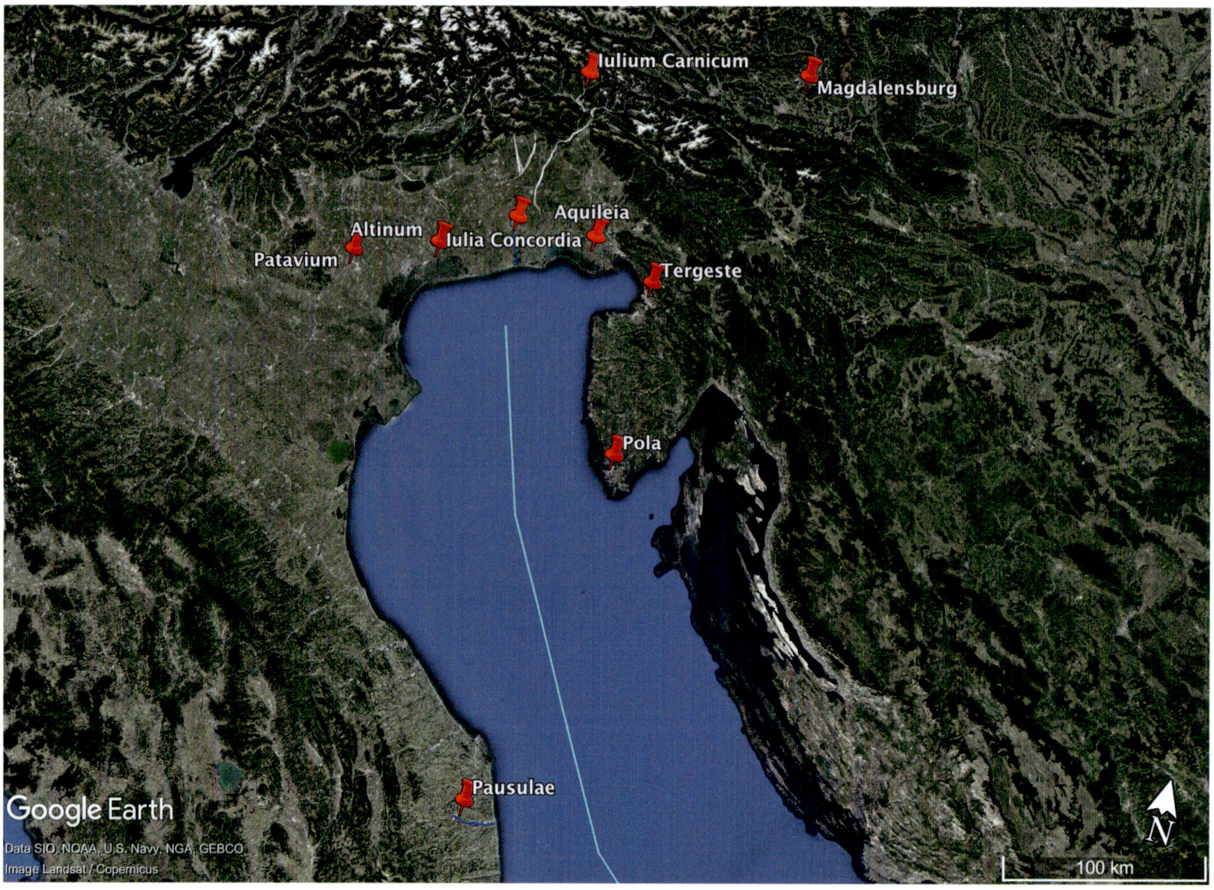

Map 7: Upper Adriatic Sea

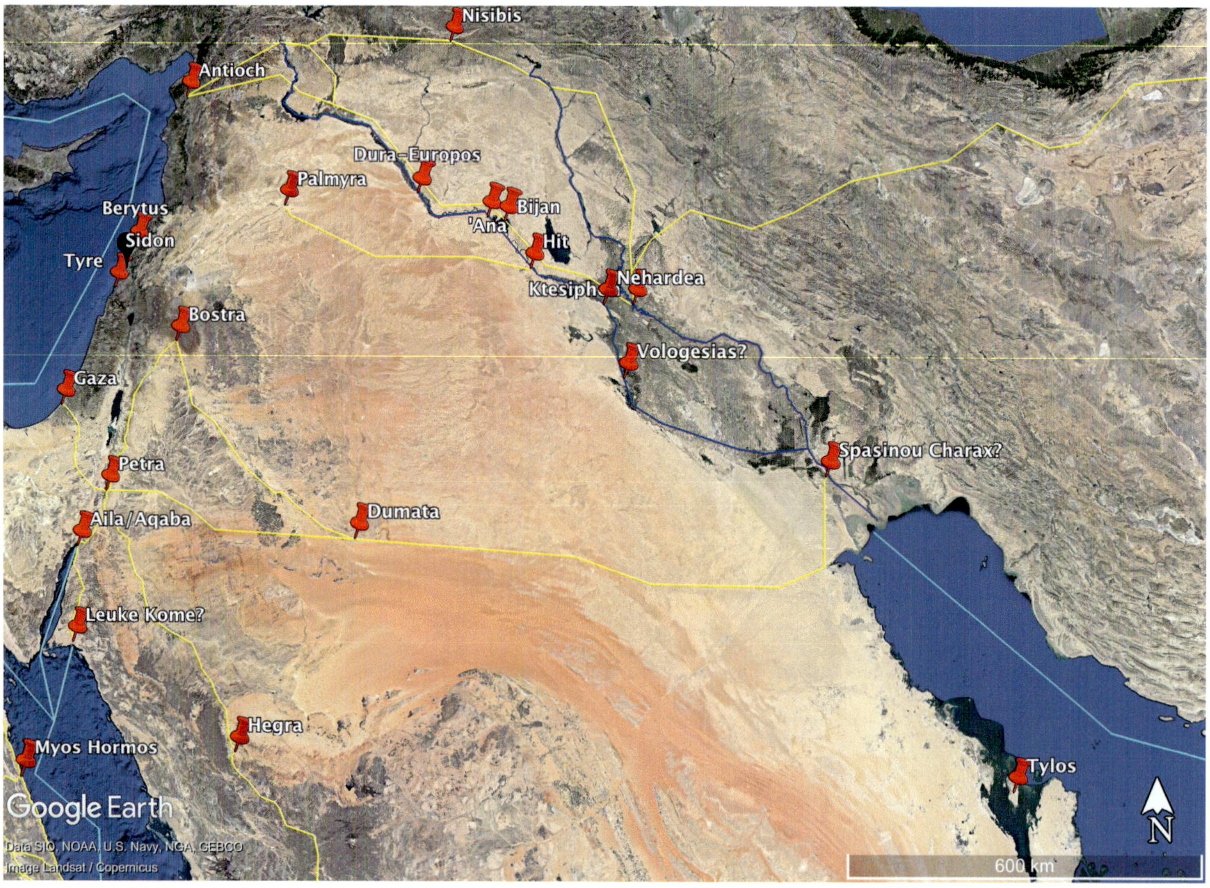

Map 8: Near East

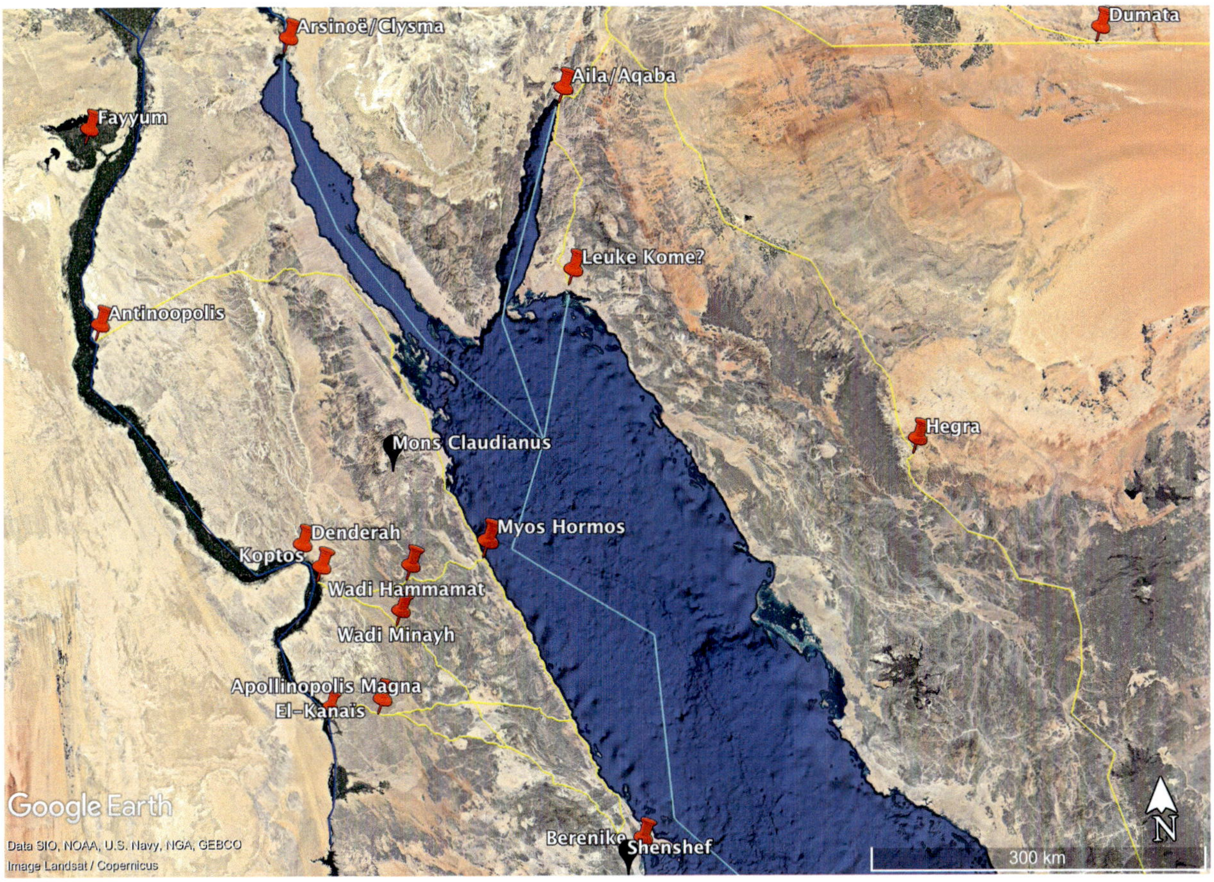

Map 9: Upper Red Sea

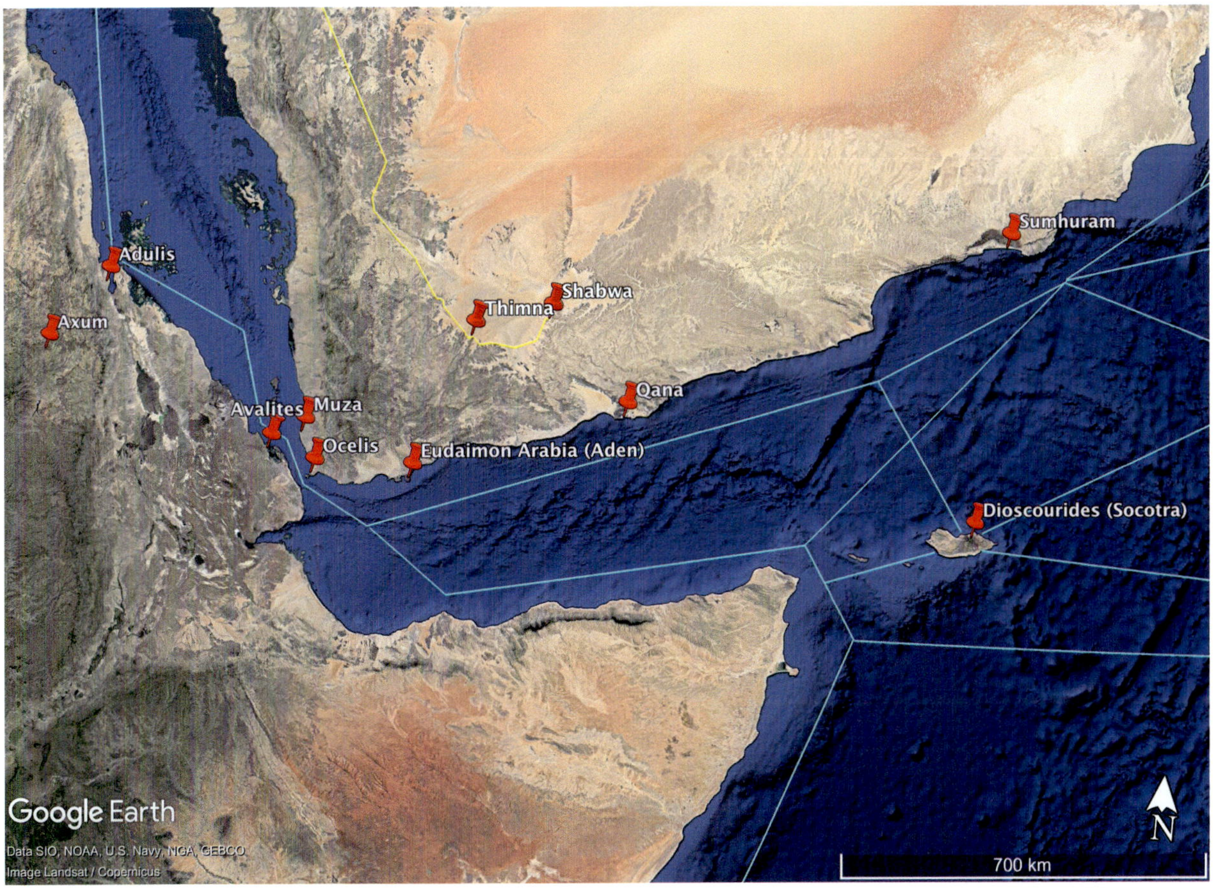

Map 10: Bay of Aden

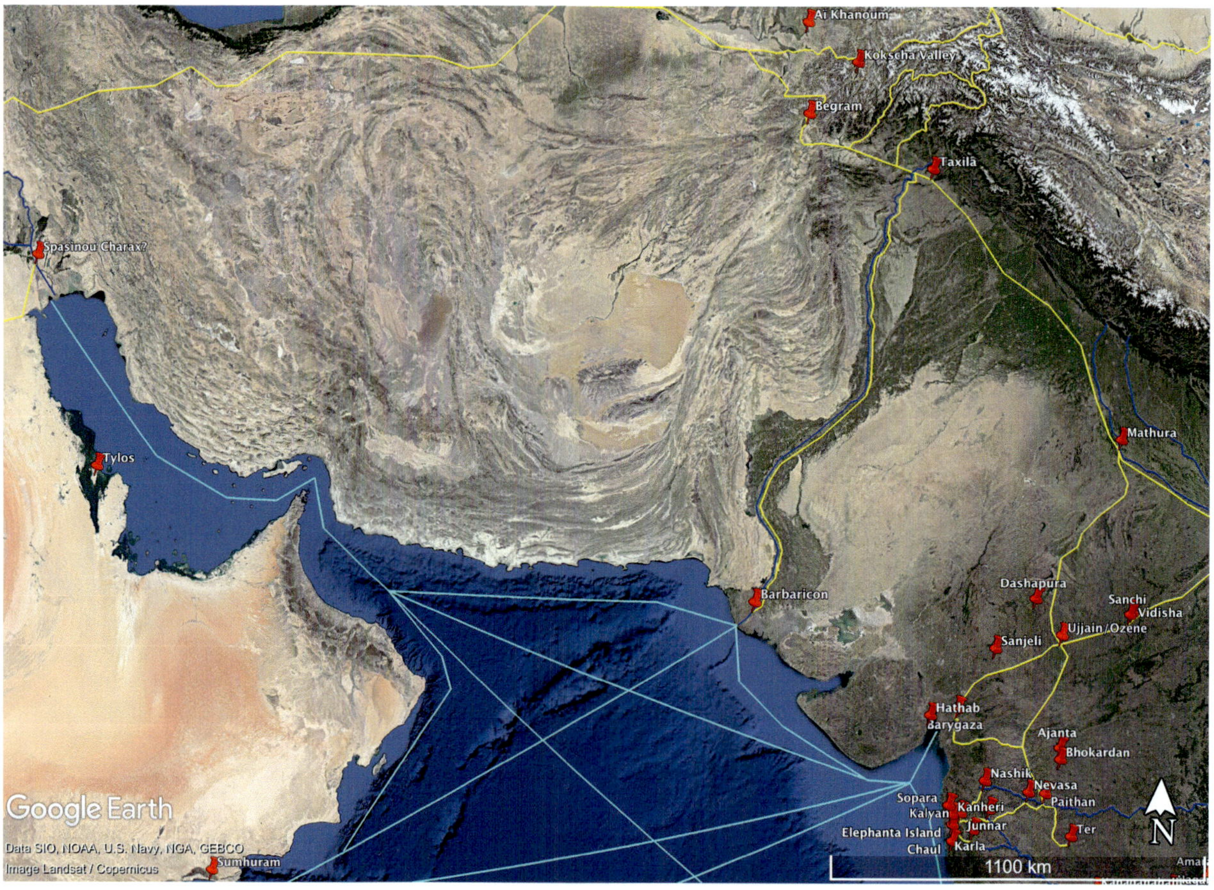

Map 11: Western Indian Ocean

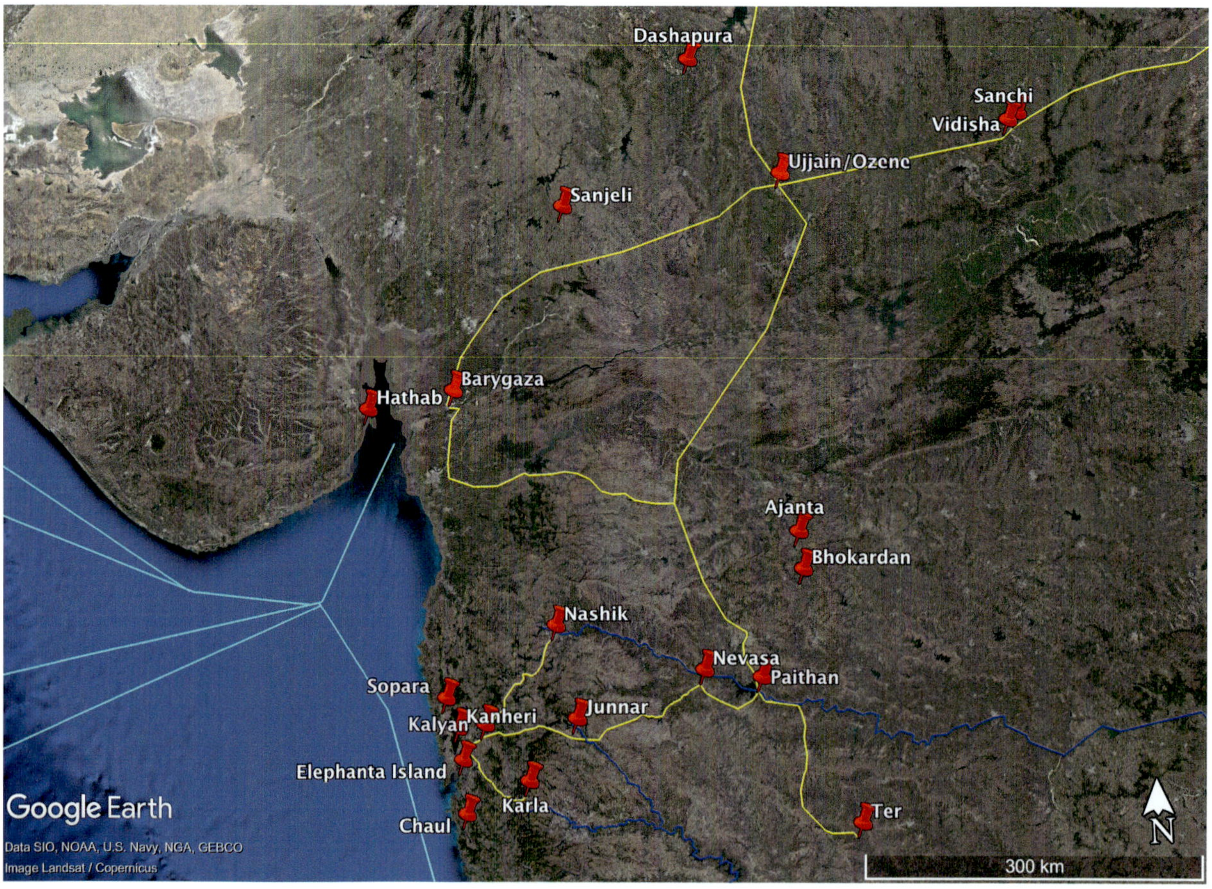

Map 12: Western India

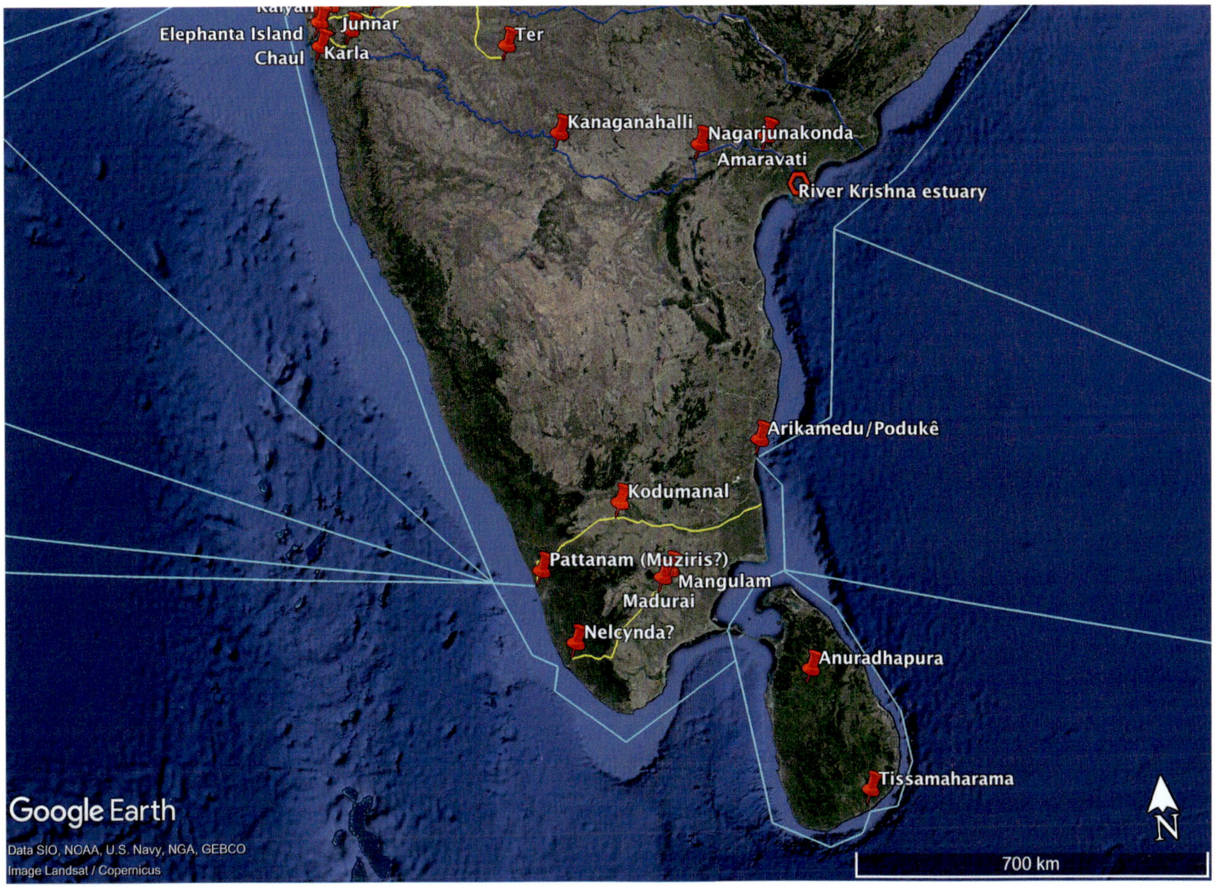

Map 13: South India and Sri Lanka

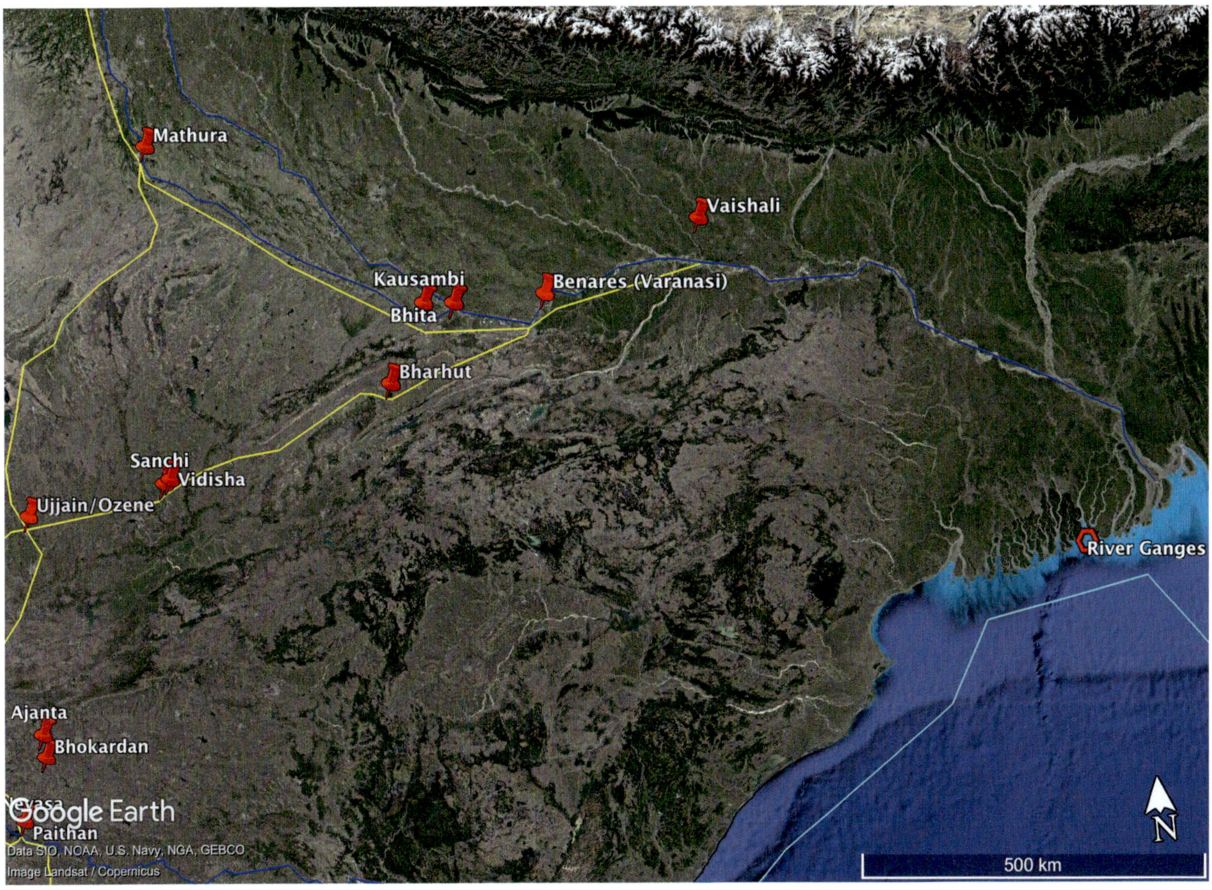

Map 14: North India

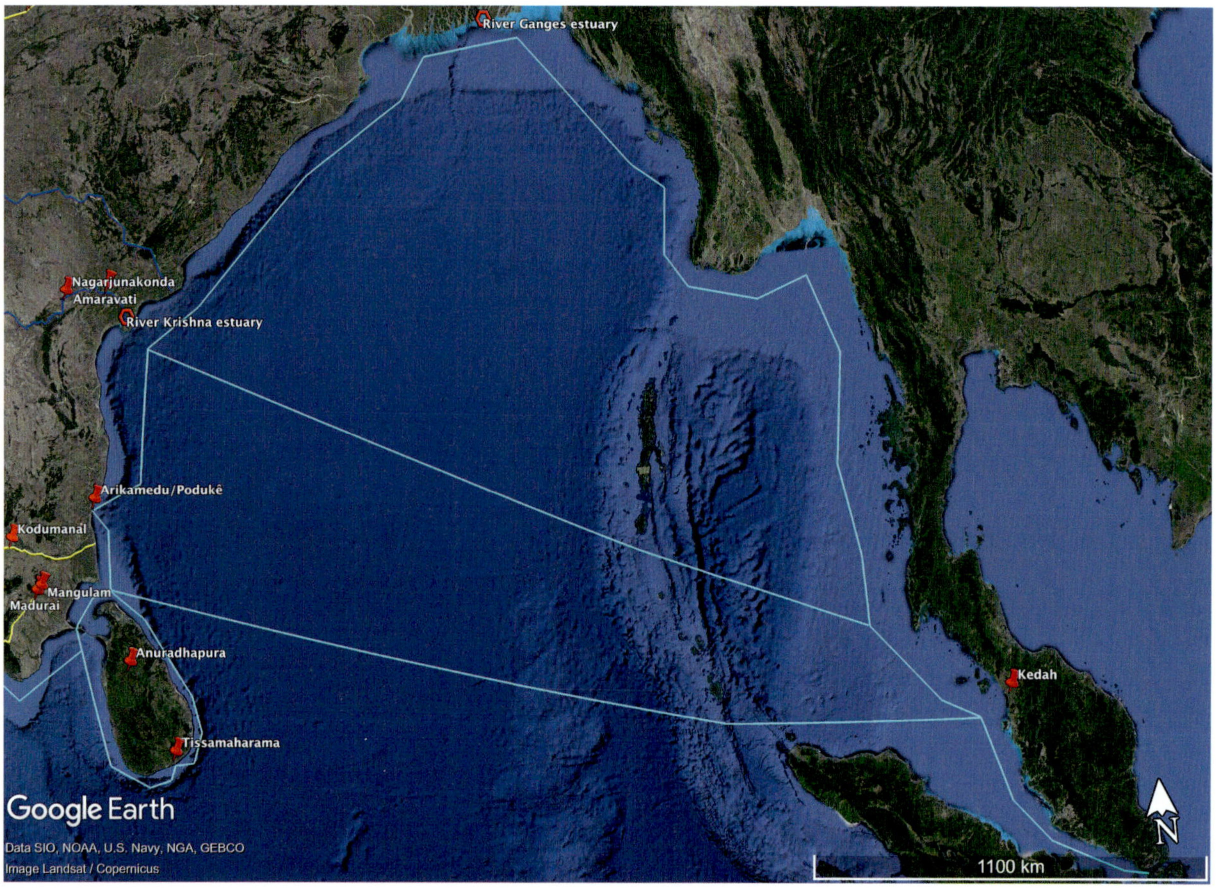

Map 15: Eastern Indian Ocean

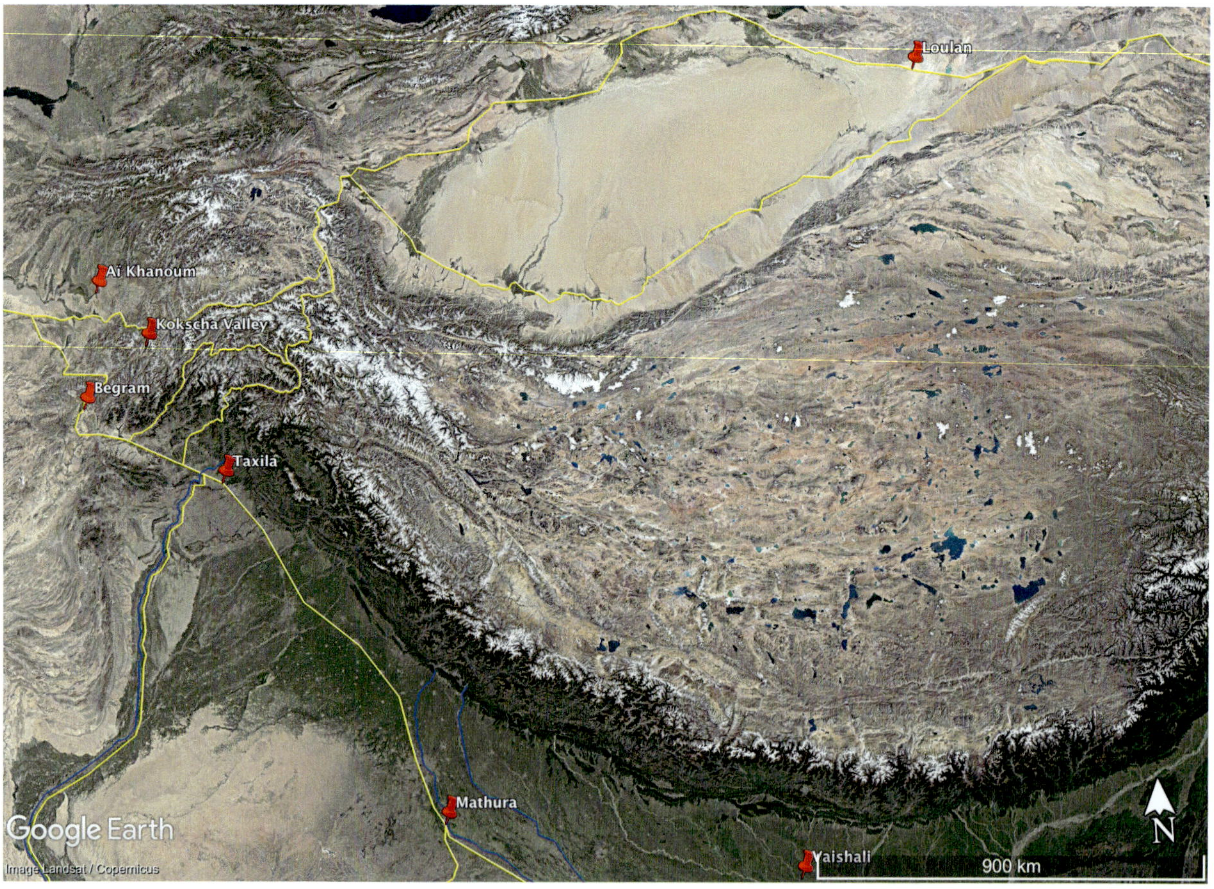

Map 16: Central Asia and Tarim Basin

Bibliography

Adams, C. 2007. *Land Transport in Roman Egypt. A Study of Economics and Administration in a Roman Province.* Oxford and New York.

Ahuja, N. 2016. The British Museum Hariti: Toward Understanding Transculturalism in Gandhara, in S. Alcock, M. Egri and J. Frakes (eds), *Beyond Boundaries. Connecting Visual Cultures in the Provinces of Ancient Rome*: 247–63.

Albenda, P. 1985. Mirrors in the Ancient Near East. *Notes in the History of Art* 4(2/3): 2–9.

Alpers, M. 1995. *Das nachrepublikanische Finanzsystem. Fiscus und Fisci in der frühen Kaiserzeit.* Berlin and New York.

Ambers, J., C. Cartwright, C. Higgitt, D. Hook, E. Passmore, St. J. Simpson, G. Verri, C. Ward and B. Wills (eds) 2014. *Looted, Recovered, Returned: Antiquities from Afghanistan.* Oxford.

Amiri, B. 2012. Negotiator sericarius: sur la route de la promotion sociale. *L'Antiquité Classique* 81: 125–43.

Andrade, N. 2015. The voyage of Maes Titianos and the dynamics of social connectivity between the Roman Levant and Central Asia/West China. *Mediterraneo Antico* 18(1–2): 41–74.

Andreau, J. 1974. *Les affaires de monsieur Jucundus.* Rome.

Andreau, J. 1977. Fondations privées et rapports sociaux en Italie Romaine (Ier–IIIe s. ap. J.-C.). *Ktema* 2: 157–209.

Anna Abraham, S. 2003. Chera, Chola, Pandya: Using Archaeological Evidence to Identify the Tamil Kingdoms of Early Historic South India. *Asian Perspectives* 42(2): 207–33.

Anna Abraham, S. 2013. In Seach of Craft and Society: The Glass Beads of Early Historic Tamil South India, in S. A. Abraham, P. Gullapalli, and T. P. Raczek (eds), *Connections and Complexity: New Approaches to the Archaeology of South Asia*: 239–61. Walnut Creek, C.

Appadurai, A. 1996. *Modernity at Large. Cultural Dimensions of Globalization.* Minneapolis, MN.

Appleton, N. 2010. *Jataka Stories in Theravada Buddhism: Narrating the Bodhisatta Path.* Farnham.

Apte, V. 1957–1959. *Revised and enlarged edition of Prin. V. S. Apte's The practical Sanskrit-English dictionary.* 3 vols. Poona.

Archibald, Z. 2005. Markets and Exchange: The Structure and Scale of Economic Behaviour in the Hellenistic Age, in Z. Archibald, J. Davies and V. Gabrielsen (eds), *Making, Moving and Managing: The New World of Ancient Economies, 323–31 BC*: 1–26. Oxford.

Archibald, Z. and J. Davies 2011. Introduction, in Z. Archibald, J. Davies and V. Gabrielsen (eds), *The Economies of Hellenistic Societies, Third to First Centuries BC*: 1–18. Oxford.

Arnaoutoglou, I. 2002. Roman law and *collegia* in Asia Minor. *Revue Internationale des droits de l'Antiquité* 49: 27–44.

Arnaoutoglou, I. 2003. *Thusias heneka kai sunousias. Private religious associations in Hellenistic Athens.* Athens.

Arnaoutoglou, I. 2005. Collegia in the Province of Egypt in the First Century AD. *Ancient Society* 35: 197–216.

Arnaoutoglou, I. 2011. Craftsmen associations in Roman Lydia—a tale of two cities? *Ancient Society* 41: 257–290.

Ascough, R., P. Harland and J. Kloppenborg 2012. *Associations in the Greco-Roman World. A Sourcebook.* Waco, TX.

Ashby, T. and S. B. Platner, 2002. *A Topographical Dictionary of Ancient Rome.* Rev. edn. Oxford.

Aubert, J.-J. 2015. Trajan's Canal: River Navigation from the Nile to the Red Sea, in F. de Romanis and M. Maiuro (eds), *Across the Ocean: Nine Essays on Indo-Mediterranean Trade*: 33–42. Leiden and Boston.

Ausbüttel, F. 1982. *Untersuchungen zu den Vereinen im Westen des Römischen Reiches.* Kallmünz.

Austin, M. 2013. *The Hellenistic World from Alexander to the Roman Conquest. A Selection of Ancient Sources in Translation.* 2nd edn. Cambridge.

Avanzini, A. 2002–7. *Khor Rori Report.* 2 vols. Pisa and Rome.

Avanzini, A. and A. Sedov 2005. The stratigraphy of Sumhuram: new evidence. *Proceedings of the Seminar for Arabian Studies* 35: 11–17.

Badian, E. 1983. *Publicans and sinners: private enterprise in the service of the Roman Republic; with a critical bibliography.* 2nd edn. Ithaca, NY; and London.

Bagnall, R., C. Helms and A. Verhoogt 2000. *Documents from Berenike. Greek ostraka from the 1996–1998 seasons.* Vol. I. Bruxelles.

Bagnall, R., C. Helms and A. Verhoogt 2005. *Documents from Berenike. Texts from the 1999-2001 seasons.* Vol. II. Bruxelles.

Bagnall, R., A. Bülow-Jacobsen and H. Cuvigny 2001. Security and water on the Eastern Desert roads: the prefect Iulius Ursus and the construction of *praesidia* under Vespasian. *Journal of Roman Archaeology* 14: 325–33.

Bakels, C. and S. Jacomet 2003. Access to luxury foods in Central Europe during the Roman period: the archaeobotanical evidence. *World Archaeology* 34(3): 542–557.

Ball, W. 2000. *Rome in the East. The transformation of an empire.* London and New York.

Ballet, P. 2000. La ville de Coptos à l'époque romaine, in M. Gabolde (edr), *Coptos. L'Egypte antique aux portes du desert*: 176–87. Lyon.

Bang, P. 2009a. The Ancient Economy and New Institutional Economics. *Journal of Roman Studies* 99: 194–206.

Bang, P. 2009b. Commanding and Consuming the World. Empire, Tribute, and Trade in Roman and Chinese History, in W. Scheidel (edr), *Rome and China. Comparative Perspectives on Ancient World Empires*: 100–20. Oxford.

Bang, P. F. 2011[2008]. *The Roman Bazaar. A Comparative Study of Trade and Markets in a Tributary Empire.* Cambridge.

Barbieri, G. (edr) 1982. *Il lapidario Zeri di Mentana.* Roma.

Barnard, H. 2005. Sire, il n'y a pas de Blemmyes: A re-evaluation of historical and archaeological data, in J. Starkey (edr), *People of the Red Sea.* Proceedings of the Red Sea Project II: 23–40. Oxford.

Barnett, L. D. 1917–8. No. 14. Laksmeshwar Pillar Inscription of the Yuvaraja Vikramaditya. *Epigraphia Indica* 14: 188–91.

Barnett, R. D. 1982. *Ancient Ivories in the Middle East.* Jerusalem.

Barrett, D. 1960. *Ter.* Bombay.

Barrow, R. (edr) 1973. *Prefect and Emperor. The Relationes of Symmachus, A.D. 384.* Oxford.

Basak, R. 1919–20. No. 7. The five Damodarpur copper-plate inscriptions of the Gupta period. *Epigraphia Indica* 15: 113–45.

Basham, A. L. 1983. The Mandasor Inscription of the Silk-weavers, in B. Smith (edr), *Essays on Gupta Culture*: 93–105. Delhi.

Basu, C. 2010. The Heavily Ornamented Female Figure from Pompeii, in B. P. Venetucci (edr), *Il fascino dell'Oriente nelle collezioni e nei musei d'Italia*: 59–63. Rome.

Baums, S. 2012. Catalog and Revised Texts and Translations of Gandharan Reliquary Inscriptions, in D. Jongeward, E. Errington, R. Salomon and S. Baums (eds), *Gandharan Buddhist Reliquaries*: 200–51. Seattle and London.

Bäumler, A. 2014. Prestigekohärenz bei römishcen Festen? Vergemeinschaftung und Distinktion bei Festen von römischen Vereinen am Beispiel der *lex collegia eborariorum et citriariorum* (CIL 6, 33885), in B. Backes and C. von Nicolai (eds), *Kulturelle Kohärenz durch Prestige*: 59–82. Munich.

Bedini, A. 1995. *Mistero di una fanciulla. Ori e gioielli della Roma di Marco Aurelio da una nuova scoperta archeologica.* Milan.

Bedini, A., S. Ehrman, S. Cesaro, M. Pasini, I. Rapinesi and D. Sali 2012. The Vallerano Diamond from Ancient Rome: A Scientific Study. *Gems and Gemology* 48(1): 39–41.

Begley, V. (edr) 1996. *The Ancient Port of Arikamedu. New Excavations and Researches 1989-92.* Vol. 1. Pondicherry.

Begley, V. (edr) 2004. *The Ancient Port of Arikamedu. New Excavations and Researches 1989-92.* Vol. 2. Paris.

Begley, V. and R. de Puma 1991. *Rome and India. The Ancient Sea Trade.* Wisconsin.

Behr, C. (transl.) 1981. *P. Aelius Aristides. The Complete Works.* Vol. 2. Leiden.

Beltrán Lloris, F. 2014. The 'Epigraphic Habit' in the Roman World, in C. Bruun and J. Edmonson (eds), *The Oxford Handbook of Roman Epigraphy*: 131–46. Oxford.

Ben-Artzi, Y. 2004. The Idea of a Mediterranean Region in Nineteenth- to Mid-Twentieth-Century German Geography. *Mediterranean Historical Review* 19(2): 2–15.

Bendlin, A. 2011. Associations, Funerals, Sociality, and Roman Law: The *collegium* of Diana and Antinous in Lanuvium (CIL 14.2112) Reconsidered, in M. Öhler (edr), *Aposteldekret und antikes Vereinswesen: Gemeinschaft und ihre Ordnung*: 207–296. Tübingen.

Beresford, J. 2012. *The Ancient Sailing Season.* Leiden.

Berggren, J. and A. Jones 2000. *Ptolemy's Geography. An annotated translation of the theoretical chapters.* Princeton and Oxford.

Berghaus, P. 1992. Zu den römischen Fundmünzen aus Indien. *Schweizerische numismatische Rundschau* 71: 226–47.

Berghaus, P. 1998. Republican and early Roman imperial *denarii* from India, in A. K. Jha and S. Garg (eds), *Ex Moneta. Essays on Numismatics, History and Archaeology in honour of Dr. David W. MacDowall.* Vol. 1: 119–27. New Delhi.

Bernand, E. 1969. *Inscriptions métriques de l'Égypte gréco-romaine.* Paris.

Bernand, A. 1972a. *De Koptos à Kosseir.* Leiden.

Bernand, A. 1972b. *Le paneion d'el-Kanaïs: Les inscriptions grecques.* Leiden.

Bianchi, R. 1985. Reflections of the sky's eyes. *Notes in the History of Art* 4(2/3): 10–18.

Bizzarini, L. 2006. Quattro Laminette Plumbee da Altino. *Annali del Museo Civico di Rovereto* 21 (2005): 121–35.

Blue, L., J. Whitewright and R. Thomas 2011. Ships and Ships' Fittings, in D. Peacock and L. Blue (eds), *Myos Hormos - Quseir al-Qadim. Roman and Islamic Ports on the Red Sea. Finds from the excavations 1999-2003.* Vol. 2: 179–209. Oxford.

Blue, L., J. Hill and R. Thomas 2012. New Light on the Nature of Indo-Roman Trade: Roman Period Shipwrecks in the Northern Red Sea, in D. Agius, J. Cooper, A. Trakadas and C. Zazzaro (eds), *Navigated Spaces, Connected Places.* Proceedings of Red Sea Project V: 91–100.

Boak, A. 1937. An Ordinance of the Salt Merchants. *American journal of philology* 58(2): 210–19.

Bogaert, R. 1994[1965]. Banquiers, courtiers et prêts maritimes à Athènes et à Alexandrie, in R. Bogaert, *Trapezitica Aegyptiaca*: 205–18. Firenze.

Bonetto, J. 2001, Mercanti di lana tra Patavium e il Magdalensberg, in F. Leitner (edr), *Carinthia Romana und die Römische Welt. Festschrift für Gernot Piccottini zum 60. Geburtstag*: 151–61. Klagenfurt.

Bonsangue, M., and N. Tran 2008. Le métier de parfumeur à Rome et dans l'Occident romain, in L. Boudiou and V. Mehl (eds), *Parfums et odeurs dans l'Antiquité*: 253-260. Rennes.

de Boor, C. (edr) 1963. *Theophanis Chronographia.* Hildesheim.

Bopearachchi, O., S. Disanayaka and N. Perera 2016. The Oldest Shipwreck in the Indian Ocean, in M.-Γ. Boussac, J.-F. Salles and J.-B. Yon (eds), *Ports of the Ancient Indian Ocean*: 411–34. New Delhi.

Borsari, L. 1887. Di un importante frammento epigrafico rinvenuto nel Trastevere. *Bullettino della Commissione Archeologica Comunale di Roma* 15: 3–7.

Boudon-Millot, V. 2007. Un traité perdu de Galien miraculeusement retrouvé, le *Sur l'inutilité de se chagriner*: texte grec et traduction francaise, in V. Boudon-Millot, A. Guardasole and C. Magdelaine (eds), *La science médicale antique. Nouveaux regards. Études réunies en l'honneur de Jacques Jouanna*: 73–123. Paris.

Bounni, A. 1990. Métiers et fonctions à Palmyre. *Travaux du centre d'archéologique Méditerranéenne de l'académie Polonaise des sciences* 30(15): 77–86.

Boussac, M.-F. and J.-F. Salles (eds) 1995. *Athens, Aden, Arikamedu. Essays on the interrelations between India, Arabia and the Eastern Mediterranean.* New Delhi.

Boussac, M.-Fr., J.-Fr. Salles and J.-B. Yon (eds) 2012. *Autour du Périple de la mer Érythrée.* Topoi, Supplément 11. Lyon.

Boussac, M.-F., J.-F. Salles and J.-B. Yon (eds) 2016. *Ports of the Ancient Indian Ocean.* New Delhi.

Bowersock, G. 1983. *Roman Arabia.* Cambridge, MA; and London.

Bowman, A. 2000. Some Romans in Augustan Alexandria. *Sociéte d'archéologie d'Alexandrie, bulletin* 46: 13–24.

Bowman, A. 2010. Trade and the Flag - Alexandria, Egypt and the Imperial House, in D. Robinson and A. Wilson (eds), *Alexandria and the North-Western Delta*: 103–9. Oxford.

Bowsher, J. 1986. The Frontier Post of Medain Saleh, in P. Freeman and D. Kennedy (eds), *The Defence of the Roman and Byzantine East*: 23–9. Oxford.

Boyer, R., V. Bel, L. Tranoy, W. Mourey, J.-N. Barrandon, C. Binant, M. Bui-Thi-Mai, M. Girard, B. Gratuze and B. Guineau 1990. Découverte de la tombe d'un oculiste à Lyon (fin du IIe siècle après J.-C.). Instruments et coffret avec collyres. *Gallia* 47: 215–249.

Brancaccio, P. 2005. Perceptions of "Westerners" in Satavahana Times: The Archaeological Evidence, in C. Jarrige and V. Lefèvre (eds), *South Asian Archaeology 2001.* Vol. 2: 401–5. Paris.

Braudel, F. 2002. *The Mediterranean in the Ancient World.* London.

Braun, O. 1915. *Ausgewählte Akten Persischer Märtyrer. Mit einem Anhang ostsyrisches Mönchsleben.* Kempten & Munich.

Bresson, A. 2015. The Cost of Getting Money in Early Ptolemaic Egypt: The Case of *P.Cair.Zen.* 1 59021 (258 B.C.E), in D. Kehoe, D. Ratzan and U. Yiftach (eds), *Law and Transaction Costs in the Ancient Economy*: 118–44. Ann Arbor.

Bresson, A. 2016. *The Making of the Ancient Greek Economy. Institutions, Markets, and Growth in the City-States.* Princeton and Oxford.

Brimnes, N. 1999. *Constructing the Colonial Encounter. Right and Left Hand Castes in Early Colonial South India.* Richmond, Surrey.
Brock, S. 2009. Regulations for an Association of Artisans from the Late Sasanian or Early Arab Period, in P. Rousseau and M. Papoutsakis (eds), *Transformations of Late Antiquity. Essays for Peter Brown*: 51–62. Farnham, UK, and Burlington, USA.
Broekaert, W. 2011. Partners in Business: Roman merchants and the potential advantages of being a *collegiatus*. *Ancient Society* 41: 221–256.
Broekaert, W. 2012. Joining forces: commercial partnerships or *societates* in the early Roman empire. *Historia. Zeitschrift für alte Geschichte* 61(2): 221-253
Broekaert, W. 2013. *Navicularii et Negotiantes. A prosopographical study of Roman merchants and shippers.* Rahden.
Broekaert, W. 2016. Freedmen and Agency in Roman Business, in M. Flohr and A. Wilson (eds), *Urban Craftsmen and Traders in the Roman World*: 222–53. Oxford.
Bron, F. 1986. Palmyréniens et chaldéens en Arabie du sud. *Studi epigrafici e linguistici sul Vicino Oriente antico* 3: 95–98.
Bron, F. (edr) 1998. *Maʿīn. Inventaire des inscriptions sudarabiques.* Vol. 3. Paris and Rome.
Broodbank, C. 2013. *The Making of the Middle Sea. A History of the Mediterranean from the Beginning to the Emergence of the Classical World.* Oxford.
Brousseau, E. 2008. Contracts: From Bilateral Sets of Incentives to the Multi-Level Governance of Relations, in E. Brousseau and J.-M. Glachant (eds), *New Institutional Economics: A Guidebook*: 37–66. Cambridge.
Brughmans, T. and J. Poblome 2016. Roman bazaar or market economy? Explaining tableware distributions through computational modelling. *Antiquity* 90(350): 393–408.
Brun, J.-P. 2000. The Production of Perfumes in Antiquity: The Cases of Delos and Paestum. *American Journal of Archaeology* 104(2): 277–308.
Brun, J.-P. 2003. Chronologie de l'équipement de la route à l'époque gréco-romaine, in H. Cuvigny (edr), *La Route de Myos Hormos. L'armée romaine dans le désert Oriental d'Égypte*. Vol. 1: 187–206. Cairo.
Bukharin, M. 2012. The Mediterranean World and Socotra, in I. Strauch (edr), *Foreign Sailors on Socotra. The inscriptions and drawings from the Cave Hoq*: 494–539. Bremen.
Buonocore, M. and O. Diliberto 2003. L'*album* e la *lex* della *Familia Silvani* di *Trebula Mutuesca*. Nuove considerazioni. *Atti della Pontificia Accademia Romana di Archeologia. Serie III. Rendiconti* 75: 327–93.
Burgess, J. and B. Indraji 1881. *Inscriptions from the Cave-Temples of Western India*. Bombay.
Burgess, J. 1883. *Report on the Elura Cave Temples and the Brahmanical and Jaina Caves in Western India*. London.
Burkhalter, F. 1999. Les fermiers de l'arabarchie: notables et hommes d'affaires à Alexandrie, in J. Leclan (edr), *Alexandrie: une mégapole cosmopolite*: 41–54. Paris.
Bühler, G. 1894. Further votive inscriptions from the Stûpas at Sañchi (II). *Epigraphia Indica* 2: 366–407.
Bülow-Jakobsen, A. 2003. The traffic on the road and the provisioning of the stations, in H. Cuvigny (edr), *La Route de Myos Hormos. L'armée romaine dans le désert Oriental d'Égypte*. Vol. 2: 399–426 Cairo.
Bülow-Jacobsen, A., H. Cuvigny and J.-L. Fournet 1994. 'The Identification of Myos Hormos. New Papyrogical Evidence.' *Bulletin de l'Institut français d'archéologie orientale* 94. 27-42.
Bülow-Jacobsen, A., H. Cuvigny, J.-L. Fournet, M. Gabolde and C. Robin 1995. Les inscriptions d'Al-Muwayh. *Bulletin de l'Institut français d'archéologie orientale* 95: 103–24.
Bülow-Jacobsen, A. 2013. Translation of a letter of the *praefectus Aegypti*, in R. Ast, H. Cuvigny, T. Hickey and J. Lougovaya (eds), *Papyrological Texts in Honor of Roger S. Bagnall*: 47–51. Durham, NC.
Camardo, D. 2001. La villa del Pastore a Stabiae, in D. Camardo and A. Ferrara (eds), *Stabiae dai Borbone alle ultime scoperte*: 93–5. Napoli.
Cambon, P. 2008. Begram: Alexandria of the Caucasus, Capital of the Kushan Empire, in F. Hiebert and P. Cambon (eds), *Afghanistan. Hidden treasures from the National Museum, Kabul*: 145–61. Washington, D.C.
Cambon, P. 2010. The Begram glasses from Afghanistan, in B. Zorn and A. Hilgner (eds), *Glass along the Silk Road from 200 BC to AD 1000*: 81–92. Mainz.
Camodeca, G. 1979. La gens Annia puteolana in eta giulio-claudia: potere politico e interessi commerciali. *Puteoli* 3: 17–34.
Camodeca, G. 2000. Un vicus Tyanianus e i mestieri bancari a Puteoli: rilettura del graffito ercolanense CIL IV 10676. *Ostraka* 9: 281–8.
Camodeca, G. 2016. *Unguentarii* e *turarii* in Campania: Nuovi dati da Puteoli e Cumae, in G. Camodeca and M. Giglio (eds), *Puteoli. Studi di storia e archeologia dei Campi Flegrei*: 23–39. Naples.
Cappers, R. 2006. *Roman Foodprints at Berenike. Archaeobotanical evidence of subsistence and trade in the Eastern Desert of Egypt*. Los Angeles.

Carandini, A., A. Ricci and M. de Vos 1982. *Filosofiana. The villa of Piazza Armerina. The image of a Roman aristocrat at the time of Constantine*. Palermo.

Lo Cascio, E. 2015. Afterword, in F. de Romanis and M. Maiuro (eds), *Across the Ocean: Nine Essays on Indo-Mediterranean Trade*: 165–9. Leiden and Boston.

Casson, L. 1950. The Isis and Her Voyage. *Transactions and Proceedings of the American Philological Association* 81: 43–56.

Casson, L. 1956. New light on maritime loans. *EOS. Commentarii Societatis Philologae Polonorum* 48(2): 89–93.

Casson, L. 1968. Maecius Celer's Ship (Statius, *Silvae* iii. 2.22, 28). *The Classical Review*, New Series, 18(3): 261–2.

Casson, L. 1971. *Ships and seamanship in the Ancient World*. Princeton, NJ.

Casson, L. 1986a. P. Vindob G 40822 and the Shipping of Goods from India. *Bulletin of the American Society of Papyrologists* 23: 73–9.

Casson, L. 1986b. New light on maritime loans: P. Vindob. G 19792 (= *SB* VI 9571), in R. Bagnall and W. V. Harris (eds), *Studies in Roman Law in memory of A. Arthur Schiller*: 11–7. Leiden.

Casson, L. (edr) 1989. *'The Periplus Maris Erythraei.' Text with introduction, translation, and commentary*. Princeton, NJ.

Casson, L. 1990. New Light on Maritime Loans: P. Vindob G 40822. *Zeitschrift für Papyrologie und Epigraphik* 84: 195–206.

Casson, L. 1991. *The Ancient Mariners. Seafarers and sea fighters of the Mediterranean in Ancient Times*. 2nd edn. Princeton, NJ.

Chabot, J.-B. (edr) 1902. *Synodicon Orientale ou Recueil de synodes nestoriens*. Paris.

Chakravarti, R. 2008. Three copper plates of the sixth century AD. Glimpses of socio-economic and cultural life in Western India, in E. Raven (edr), *South Asian Archaeology 1999*: 395–9. Groningen.

Champakalakshmi, R. 1996. *Trade, Ideology and Urbanization. South India 300 BC to AD 1300*. Delhi.

Chandra, M. 1960. An ivory figure from Ter. *Lalit Kala* 8: 7–14.

Chandra, M. 1977. *Trade and Trade Routes in Ancient India*. New Delhi.

Charlesworth, M. 1926[1924]. *Trade-Routes and Commerce of the Roman Empire*. 2nd edn. Chicago.

Charlesworth, M. 1969. Roman trade with India: a resurvey, in P. Coleman-Norton (edr), *Roman Economic and Social History in Honor of Allan Chester Johnson*: 131–43. New York.

Chehade, J. 1987. Zu Scmuckdarstellungen auf palmyrenischen Grabreliefs, in E. Ruprechtsberger (edr), *Palmyra. Geschichte, Kunst und Kultur der syrischen Oasenstadt*: 193–9. Linz.

Cherian, P. 2011. Pattanam archaeological site: The wharf context and the maritime exchanges. Paper given at *The 2011 Asia-Pacific Regional Conference on Underwater Cultural Heritage Proceedings*. The MUA (Museum of Underwater Archaeology) Collection, accessed February 25, 2016, http://www.themua.org/collections/items/show/1204.

Cherian, P. 2013, Archaeological evidence from Pattanam. Paper given at the conference *Maritime Networks and Urbanism in the Early Medieval World*, hosted 11th-12th April 2013 by the Viking Ship Museum, Roskilde, Denmark.

Cherian, P. and J. Menon 2014. *Unearthing Pattanam. Histories, Cultures, Crossings. Catalogue for the 2014 exhibition*. New Delhi and Trivandrum.

Cherry, D. 2007. The frontier zones, in W. Scheidel, R. Saller and I. Morris (eds), *The Cambridge Economic History of the Greco-Roman World*: 720–40. Cambridge.

del Chiaro, M. 1973. *Roman Art in West Coast Collections*. Santa Barbara, C.

Cimino, R. (edr) 1994a. *Ancient Rome and India. Commercial and cultural contacts between the Roman world and India*. New Delhi.

Cimino, R. 1994b. An exceptional find in India: a small sculpture depicting Eros issuing from an egg, in A. Parpola and P. Koskikallio (eds), *South Asian Archaeology 1993*: 171–82. Helsinki.

Cipriano, S. and G. Sandrini 2003. Sigillate orientali a *Iulia Concordia*. Primi dati da un'area campione: lo scavo del Piazzale antistante la Cattedrale di Santo Stefano. *Aquileia nostra* 74: 425–50.

Clarysse, W. 2008. Graeco-Roman Oxyrhyncha, a village in the Arsinoite nome, in S. Lippert and M. Schentuleit (eds), *Graeco-Roman Fayum - Texts and Archaeology*: 55–73. Wiesbaden.

Claytor, W. and B. Feucht 2013. (Gaii) Iulii Sabinus and Apollinarius. Leuven Homepage of Papyrus Collections; accessed February 25, 2016, http://www.trismegistos.org/arch/archives/pdf/116.pdf.

Clermont-Ganneau, C. 1903. Inscription gréco-palmyrénienne d'Égypte. *Recueil d'archéologie orientale* 5: 300–6.

Cobb, M. 2013. The Reception and Consumption of Eastern Goods in Roman Society. *Greece and Rome* 60: 136–152.

Cobb, M. 2014. The Exchange of Goods from Italy to India during the Early Roman Empire: The Range of Travelling Times. *Ancient West and East* 13: 89–116.
Cobb, M. 2015a. Balancing the Trade: Roman Cargo Shipments to India. *Oxford Journal of Archaeology* 34(2): 185–203.
Cobb, M. 2015b. The Chronology of Roman Trade in the Indian Ocean from Augustus to Early Third Century CE. *Journal of the Economic andSocial History of the Orient* 58: 362–418.
Cobb, M. (forthcoming). *Rome and the Indian Ocean Trade: From Augustus to the Early Third Century AD.*
Cohon, R. 1984. Greek and Roman Stone Table Supports with Decorative Reliefs. Unpublished PhD dissertation, New York University.
Coleman, J. 1988. Social Capital in the Creation of Human Capital. *American Journal of Sociology* 94: 95–120.
Coles, R., H. Maehler and P. Parsons (eds) 1987. *The Oxyrhynchus Papyri.* Vol. 54. London.
Colgrave, B. and R. Mynors (eds) 1969. *Bede's Ecclesiastical History of the English People.* Oxford.
Colin, G. 1988. À propos des graffites sud-arabiques du Ouadi Hammamat. *Bulletin de l'Institut français d'archéologie orientale* 88: 33–6.
Colin, F. 2003. Le parfumeur ([pa ant]). *Bulletin de l'Institut français d'archéologie orientale* 103: 73–109.
Congdon, O. 1985. Greek mirrors. *Notes in the History of Art* 4(2/3): 19–25.
Coningham, R. 2006. *Anuradhapura. The British-Sri Lankan Excavations at Anuradhapura Salgaha Watta 2. The Artefacts.* Vol. 2. Oxford.
Cooley, A. 2012. *The Cambridge Manual of Latin Epigraphy.* Cambridge.
Cooper, J. 2009. Egypt's Nile-Red Sea Canals: Chronology, Location, Seasonality and Function, in L. Blue, J. Cooper, R. Thomas and J. Whitewright (eds), *Connected Hinterlands.* Proceedings of Red Sea Project IV: 195–209. Oxford.
Cooper, J. 2011. No easy option: Nile versus Red Sea in ancient and medieval north-south navigation, in W. Harris and K. Iara (eds), *Maritime Technology in the Ancient Economy: Ship Design and Navigation.* Journal of Roman Archaeology Supplementary Series 84: 189–210.
Corbier, M. 1985. Dévaluations et évolution des prix (Ier-IIIe siècles). *Revue numismatique* 27: 69–106.
Corbier, M. 2008. The *Lex Portorii Asiae* and Financial Administration, in M. Cottier, M. Crawford and C. Crowther (eds), *Customs Law of Asia*: 202–27. Oxford.
Cribb, J. 2000. Early Indian History, in M. Willis (edr), *Buddhist Reliquaries from Ancient India*: 39–54. London.
Croom, A. T. 2007. *Roman furniture.* Stroud.
Curtin, P. 1984. *Cross-Cultural Trade in World History.* Cambridge.
Cuvigny, H. 1998. Bouchons cachetés des fouilles d'Adolphe Reinach à Coptos. *Bulletin des musees et monuments lyonnais* 4: 2–7.
Cuvigny, H. 2000. Coptos, plaque tournante du commerce érythréen, et les routes transdésertiques, in M. Gabolde (edr), *Coptos. L'Egypte antique aux portes du desert*: 158–75. Lyon.
Cuvigny, H. (edr) 2003. *La Route de Myos Hormos. L'armée romaine dans le désert Oriental d'Égypte.* 2 vols. Cairo.
Cuvigny, H., A. Bülow-Jacobsen, L. Nehmé and C. Robin 1999. Inscriptions rupestres vues et revues dans le désert de Bérénice. *Bulletin de l'Institut français d'archéologie orientale* 99: 133–93.
Damgaard, K., H. Euler, R. Hoffbauer, M. Raith and P. Yule 2013. The View from Zafar - An Archaeometric Study of the ʿAqaba Pottery Complex and its Distribution in the 1st Millennium CE. *Zeitschrift für Orient-Archäologie* 6: 320–50.
D'Ancona, M. 1950. An Indian Statuette from Pompeii. *Artibus Asiae* 13(3): 166–80.
D'Arms, J. H. 1974. Puteoli in the Second Century of the Roman Empire: A Social and Economic Study. *The Journal of Roman Studies* 64: 104–24.
D'Arms, J. H. 1981. *Commerce and Social Standing in Ancient Rome.* Cambridge, MA; and London.
Das, Veena and D. Poole 2004. State and Its Margins. Comparative Ethnographies, in V. Das and D. Poole (eds), *Anthropology in the Margins of the State*: 3–33. Santa Fe, CA; and Oxford.
Davies, J. K. 2001. Hellenistic Economies in the Post Finley Era, in Z. Archibald, J. Davies, V. Gabrielsen and G.J. Oliver (eds), *Hellenistic Economies*: 11–62. London and New York.
Davies, J. K. 2015. Towards a general model of long-distance trade: aromatics as a case study, in E. Harris, D. Lewis and M. Woolmer (eds), *The Ancient Greek Economy*: 299–315. Cambridge.
Dehejia, V. 1972. *Early Buddhist Rock Temples. A chronological study.* London.
Dehejia, V. 1992. The collective and popular basis of early Buddhist patronage: sacred monuments, 100 BC–AD 250, in B. Miller (edr), *The Powers of Art. Patronage in Indian Culture*: 35–45. Delhi.
Delplace, C. 2003. Palmyre et l'Inde (à propos de l'inscription *Inv.* X, 88), in P. Defosse (edr), *Hommages à Carl Deroux. III - Histoire et épigraphie, Droit*: 159–67. Bruxelles.
van Deman, E. 1923. The Neronian Sacra Via. *American Journal of Archaeology* 27(4): 383–424.

Demetriou, D. 2012. *Negotiating Identity in the Ancient Mediterranean. The Archaic and Classical Greek Multiethnic Emporia*. Cambridge.

Denecker, E. and K. Vandorpe 2007. Sealed amphora stoppers and tradesmen in Greco-Roman Egypt: archaeological, papyrological and inscriptional evidence. *BABESCH Annual Papers on Mediterranean Archaeology* 82: 115–28.

Deo, S. B. 1974. *Excavations at Bhokardan (Bhogavardhana) 1973*. Aurangabad.

Deo, S. B. 1991. Roman Trade: Recent Archaeological Discoveries in Western India, in V. Begley and R. de Puma (eds), *Rome and India. The Ancient Sea Trade*: 39–45. Madison, WI.

Deshpande, M. N. 1959. The Rock-Cut Caves of Pitalkhora in the Deccan. *Ancient India* 15: 63–93.

Deshpande, M. N. 1961. Some observations on the ivory figure from Ter. *Lalit Kala* 10: 55–6.

Desrosiers, S., C. Debaine-Francfort and A. Idriss 2001. Two resist-dyed cottons recently found at Karadong, Xinjiang (third century AD), in P. Rogers, L. Jørgensen and A. Rast-Eicher (eds), *The Roman Textile Industry and its Influence. A birthday tribute to John Peter Wild*: 48–55. Oxford.

Deva, K. 1937–38. Kosam inscription of Bhadramagha's reign: the year 81. *Epigraphia Indica* 24: 253–6.

Dhavalikar, M. 1973. *Ajanta. A cultural study*. Poona.

Dihle, A. 1978. Die entdeckungsgeschichtlichen Voraussetzungen des Indienshandels der römischen Kaiserzeit, in H. Temporini (edr), *Aufstieg und Niedergang der römischen Welt. Principat.* Vol. 9, pt. 2: 546–80. Berlin and New York.

Dijkstra, M. and A. Verhoogt 1999. The Greek-Palmyrene Inscription, in S. Sidebotham and W. Wendrich (eds), *Berenike 1997. Report of the 1997 Exvacations at Berenike and the Survey of the Egyptian Eastern Desert, including Excavations at Shenshef*: 207–18. Leiden.

Diosono, F. 2007. *Collegia. Le associazioni professionali nel mondo romano*. Rome.

Dirven, L. 1996. The nature of the trade between Palmyra and Dura-Europos. *ARAM* 8: 39–54.

Dittmann-Schöne, I. 2001. *Die Berufsvereine in den Städten des kaiserzeitlichen Kleinasiens*. Regensburg.

Doe, B. 1992. *Socotra. Island of Tranquility*. London.

Donkin, R. A. 1998. Beyond Price. *Pearls and Pearl-Fishing: Origins to the Age of Discoveries*. Philadelphia.

Drauschke, J. 2010. Byzantine Jewellery? Amethyst Beads in East and West during the Early Byzantine Period, in C. Entwistle and N. Adams (eds), *Intelligible Beauty. Recent Research on Byzantine Jewellery*: 50–60. London.

Drexhage, H.-J. and K. Ruffing 2008. P. Bingen 77 und der Handel zwischen Asia Minor und Ägypten, in E. Winter (edr), *Vom Euphrat bis zum Bosporus. Kleinasien in der Antike. Festschrift für Elmar Schwertheim zum 65. Geburtstag*: 153–65. Bonn.

Droß-Krüpe, K. 2013. Textiles and their Merchants in Rome's Eastern Trade, in M. Gleba and J. Pásztókai-Szeőke (eds), *Making Textiles in pre-Roman and Roman times. People, places, identities*: 149–60. Oxford.

Dubois-Pelerin, É. 2008. *Luxe privé à Rome et en Italie au Ier siècle après J.-C.* Naples.

Dujcev, I. (edr) 1970. *The Book of the Eparch*. London.

Duncan-Jones, R. 1974. *The Economy of the Roman Empire. Quantitative Studies*. Cambridge.

Duncan-Jones, R. 2006. Roman Customs Dues: a Comparative View. *Latomus* 65(1): 3–16.

Durand, X. 1997. *Des Grecs en Palestine au IIIe siècle avant Jésus-Christ. Le dossier syrien des archives de Zénon de Caunos (261–52)*. Paris.

Durand, C. 2012. Crossing the Red Sea: the Nabataeans in the Egyptian Eastern Desert, in D. Agius, J. Cooper, A. Trakadas and C. Zazzaro (eds), *Navigated Spaces, Connected Places*: 85–90. Proceedings of the Red Sea Project V. Oxford.

During Caspers, E. 1981. The Indian ivory figurine from Pompei – a reconsideration of its functional use, in H. Härtel (edr), *South Asian Archaeology 1979*: 341–53. Berlin.

Dwivedi, V. 1976. *Indian Ivories. A survey of Indian ivory and bone carvings from the earliest times to the modern times*. Delhi.

Edgar, M. 1904. *Greek Bronzes*. Cairo.

Edwards, C. 1993. *The Politics of Immorality in ancient Rome*. Cambridge

Ehrhardt, N. and W. Günther 2013. Hadrian, Milet und die Korporation der milesischen Schiffseigner. Zu einem neu gefundenen kaiserlichen Schreiben. *Chiron* 43: 199–220.

Elisseeff, V. 1954. Les laques chinois de Begram, in J. Hackin (edr), *Nouvelles recherces archéologiques à Begram (1939–40)*: 151–155. Paris.

Erdkamp, P. 2005. *The Grain Market in the Roman Empire. A social, political and economic study*. Cambridge.

Erickson-Gini, T. and Y. Israel 2013. Excavating the Nabataean Incense Road. *Journal of Eastern Mediterranean Archaeology and Heritage Studies* 1(1): 24–53.

Erno, S. 2015. *Lex collegii negotiantum citriariorum et eborariorum*. Ókor-Történet-Írás 4: 297–320.

Evers, K. 2011. *The Vindolanda Tablets and the Ancient Economy*. Oxford.
Evers, K. 2014–5. Cave of Revelations: Indian Ocean trade in light of the Socotran graffiti.' *Journal of Indian Ocean Archaeology* 10–11: 19–37.
Evers, K. (forthcoming). Rules and regulations of associations. The Eurasian comparandum, in V. Gabrielsen and M. Paganini (eds), *A world of well-ordered societies? The rules and regulations of ancient associations*. Cambridge.
Falk, H. 2008. Money can buy me heaven. Religious donations in late and post-Kushan India. *Archäologische Mitteilungen aus Iran und Turan* 40: 137–48.
Falk, H. 2009a. Two Dated Satavahana Epigraphs. *Indo-Iranian Journal* 52: 197–206.
Falk, H. 2009b. Greek style dedications to an Indian god in Gandhara. *Indo-asiatische Zeitschrift* 13: 25–42.
Falk, H. 2009c. The pious donation of wells in Gandhara, in G. Mevissen and A. Banerji (eds), *Prajnadhara: Essays on Asian, History, Epigraphy and Culture in Honour of Gouriswar Bhattacharya*: 23-36. New Delhi.
Falk, H. 2015. Indian gold crossing the Indian Ocean through the millennia, in F. de Romanis and M. Maiuro (eds), *Across the Ocean: Nine Essays on Indo-Mediterranean Trade*: 97–113. Leiden and Boston.
Faller, S. 2011. The World According to Cosmas Indicopleustes - Concepts and Illustrations of an Alexandrian Merchant and Monk. *Transcultural Studies* 1: 193–232.
Fauconnier, B. 2012. Graeco-Roman merchants in the Indian Ocean: Revealing a multicultural trade, in M.-Fr. Boussac, J.-Fr. Salles and J.-B. Yon (eds), *Autour du Périple de la mer Érythrée*. *Topoi*, Supplément 11: 75–109.
Fausbøll, V. 1963. *The Jataka*. Vol. 4. London.
Feinman, G. 2017a. Reframing ancient economies: new models, new questions, in M. Fernandez-Götz and D. Krausse (eds), *Eurasia at the Dawn of History. Urbanization and Social Change*: 139–49. New York.
Feinman, G. 2017b. Roman Economic Practice across Time and Space: An Outside Perspective, in T. de Haas and G. Tol (eds), *The Economic Integration of Roman Italy Rural Communities in a Globalising World*: 417–25. Leiden and Boston.
Ferguson, J. 1978. China and Rome, in H. Temporini (edr), *Aufstieg und Niedergang der römischen Welt. Principat*. Vol. 9, pt. 2: 581–603. Berlin and New York.
Field, J. 2008. *Social Capital*. London and New York.
Fiema, Z. 1996. Nabataean and Palmyrene commerce - the mechanisms of intensification. *Annales archeologiques arabes syriennes* 42: 189–95.
Fiema, Z. 2003. Roman Petra (A.D. 106–363): A Neglected Subject. *Zeitschrift des Deutschen Palästina-Vereins* 119(1): 38–58.
di Filippo Balestrazzi, E. 1999. Concordia, un polismation tra protostoria e romanizzazione, in *Protostoria e storia del 'Venetorum Angulus'*: 91–116. Pisa and Rome.
Finley, M. 1999[1973]. *The Ancient Economy. Updated with a New Foreword by Ian Morris*. Berkeley and Los Angeles.
Finley, M. 1981. *Economy and Society in Ancient Greece*. London.
Finneran, N. 2007. *The Archaeology of Ethiopia*. London and New York.
Fioravanti, M. and R. Caramiello 1999. Il legno e la sua lavorazione, in A. Ciarallo and E. de Carolis (eds), *Homo Faber. Natura, scienza e tecnica nell'antica Pompei*: 85–6. Naples.
Fittschen, K. 2015. Aschenkiste für den Seidenhändler T. Abvidiacus Primus, in *Katalog der Skulpturen der Sammlung Wallmoden*: 114–115. Munich.
Fitzpatrick, M. 2011. Provincializing Rome: The Indian Ocean Trade Network and Roman Imperialism. *Journal of World History* 22(1): 27–54.
Fleet, J. F. 1888. *Corpus Inscriptionum Indicarum: Inscriptions of the Early Guptas*. Vol. 3. Calcutta.
Flohr, M. 2013. *The World of the Fullo: Work, Economy, and Society in Roman Italy*. Oxford.
Flohr, M. 2016. Innovation and Society in the Roman World, in *Oxford Handbooks Online*: DOI: 10.1093/oxfordhb/9780199935390.013.85 Accessed February 25th, 2016.
Flohr, M. and A. Wilson (eds) 2016. *Urban Craftsmen and Traders in the Roman World*. Oxford.
Foubert, L. 2015. Mobile Women in P.Oxy. and the Port Cities of Roman Egypt: Tracing Women's Travel Behaviour in Papyrological Sources, in L. de Ligt and L. Tacoma (eds), *Migration and Mobility in the Early Roman Empire*: 285–304. Leiden.
Fournet, J.-L. 2000. Coptos dans l'Antiquité tardive (fin IIIe–VIIe siècle), in M. Gabolde (edr), *Coptos. L'Egypte antique aux portes du desert*: 196–215. Lyon.
Fox, G. and S. Lieu (eds) 2011. *Inscriptiones palmyrenae selectae ad commercium pertinentes*. Select palmyrene inscriptions on commerce. Macquarie University; accessed February 25th, 2016, https://www.mq.edu.au/_data/assets/pdf_file/0018/24525/106178.pdf.

Francis, P. 1991. Beadmaking at Arikamedu and beyond. *World Archaeology* 23(1): 28–43.
Francis, P. 2004. Beads and selected small finds from the 1989–92 excavations, in V. Begley (edr), *The Ancient Port of Arikamedu. New Excavations and Researches 1989–92*. Vol. 2: 447–604. Paris.
Fraser, P. 1972. *Ptolemaic Alexandria*. 3 vols. Oxford.
Frederiksen, M. 1959. Republican Capua: A Social and Economic Study. *Papers of the British School at Rome* 27: 80–130.
Frere, S. and R. Tomlin 1991. Roman Britain in 1990. *Britannia* 22: 221–311.
Frier, B. and D. Kehoe 2007. Law and Economic Institutions, in W. Scheidel, I. Morris and R. Saller (eds), *The Cambridge Economic History of the Greco-Roman World*: 113–43. Cambridge.
Fuks, A. 1951. Notes on the Archive of Nicanor. *The Journal of Juristic Papyrology* 5: 207–16.
Funghi, M., G. Messeri and C. Römer (eds) 2012. *Ostraca greci e bilingui del Petrie Museum of Egyptian Archaeology*. 3 vols. Firenze.
Fussman, G. 2011. *Monuments Bouddhiques de Termez. Catalogue des inscriptions sur poteries, volume I.1*. Paris.
Gabba, E. 1984. The Collegia of Numa: Problems of Method and Political Ideas. *Journal of Roman Studies* 74: 81–86.
Gabrielsen, V. 2000. The Rhodian Peraia in the Third and Second Centuries BC. *Classica et Mediaevalia*: 129–183.
Gabrielsen, V. 2005. Banking and Credit Operations in Hellenistic times, in Z. Archibald, J. Davies and V. Gabrielsen (eds), *Making, Moving and Managing: the New World of Ancient Economies, 323-31 BC*: 136–164. Oxford.
Gabrielsen, V. 2007. Brotherhoods of Faith and Provident Planning: the Non-public Associations of the Greek World. *Mediterranean Historical Review* 22(2): 183–210.
Gabrielsen, V. 2011. Afterword, in Z. Archibald, J. Davies and V. Gabrielsen (eds), *The Economies of Hellenistic Societies, Third to First Centuries BC*: 441–44. Oxford.
Gabrielsen, V. 2016a. Associations, Modernization and the Return of the Private Network in Athens,' in C. Tiersch (edr), *Die Athenische Demokratie im 4. Jahrhundert Zwischen Modernisierung und Tradition*: 121–62. Stuttgart.
Gabrielsen, V. 2016b. Be Faithful and Prosper: Associations, trust and the economy of security, in K. Droß-Krüpe, S. Föllinger and K. Ruffing (eds), *Antike Wirtschaft und ihre kulturelle Prägung/The Cultural Shaping of the Ancient Economy*: 87–111. Wiesbaden.
Gabrielsen, V. and C. Thomsen (eds) 2015. *Private Associations and the Public Sphere: Proceedings of a Symposium held at the Royal Danish Academy of Sciences and Letters, 9-11 September 2010*. Copenhagen.
Galliano, G. 2000. La maison des Palmyréniens, in M. Gabolde (edr), *Coptos. L'Egypte antique aux portes du desert*: 134–7. Lyon.
Garnsey, P. 1998. *Cities, Peasants, and Food in Classical Antiquity. Essays in Social and Economic History*. Cambridge.
Gatti, G. 1905. Sepolcri e memorie sepolcrali dell'antica via Salaria. *Bullettino della Commissione Archeologica Comunale di Roma* 33: 154–88.
Gaur, A. S. and S. Tripati 2006. Evidence for Indo-Roman Trade from Bet Dwarka Waters, West Coast of India. *The International Journal of Nautical Archaeology* 35: 117–27.
Gawlikowski, M. 1996. Palmyra and its Caravan Trade. *Annales Archéologiques Arabes Syriennes* 42: 139-45.
Gawlikowski, M. 1998. Deux publicains et leur tombeau. *Syria* 75: 145–51.
Gawlikowski, M. and K. As'ad 1993. Le péage à Palmyre en 11 après J.-C. *Semitica* 41–42 (1991–92): 163–72.
De Geest, P. 2012. The cave Hoq and the Socotra Karst Project, in I. Strauch (edr), *Foreign Sailors on Socotra. The inscriptions and drawings from the cave Hoq*: 231–50. Bremen.
Ghosh, A. (edr) 1990. *An Encyclopaedia of Indian archaeology*. 2 vols. Leiden.
Ghosh, S. 2005. A Mahānāvika in an Inscription from Coastal Andhra Pradesh and Related Archaeological Issues, in C. Jarrige and V. Lefèvre (eds), *South Asian Archaeology 2001*. Vol. 2: 491–3. Paris.
Gianfrotta, P. 1989. Eracle, Peticio e il commercio marittimo, in P. Gianfrotta (edr), *Dalla villa di Ovidio al Santuario di Ercole*: 177–83. Sulmona.
Gianfrotta, P. 2007. Il Commercio marittimo in età tardo-republicana: merci, mercanti, infrastrutture, in J. Ballester and G. Pascual (eds), *Comercio, redistribución y fondeaderos. La navegación a vela en el Mediterráneo*: 65–78. Valencia.
Gibbs, M. 2011. Trade Associations in Roman Egypt: their *raison d'être*.' *Ancient Society* 41: 291–315.
Gibbs, M. 2015. The Trade Associations of Ptolemaic Egypt: Definition, Organization and their relationship with the state, in V. Gabrielsen and C. Thomsen (eds), *Private Associations and the Public Sphere: Proceedings of a Symposium held at the Royal Danish Academy of Sciences and Letters, 9-11 September 2010*: 241–269. Copenhagen.

Giordano, C. and A. Casale 2007. *Perfumes, unguents and hairstyles in Pompeii*. 2nd rev. edn. Rome.

de Giorgi, A. 2015. *Ancient Antioch: from the Seleucid Era to the Islamic conquest*. Cambridge and New York.

Giuliani, G., M. Chaussidon, H.-J. Schubnel, D. Piat, C. Rollion-Bard, C. France-Lanord, D. Giard, D. de Narvaez and B. Rondeau 2000. Oxygen Isotopes and Emerald Trade Routes since Antiquity. *Science, New Series* 287(5453): 631–633.

Glover, C. 1989. *Early Trade Between India and South-East Asia*. Hull.

Gokhale, S. 1991. *Kanheri inscriptions*. Poona.

González-Díaz, M. and L. Vázquez 2008. Make-or-Buy Decisions: A New Institutional Economics Approach, in E. Brousseau and J.-M. Glachant (eds), *New Institutional Economics: A Guidebook*: 255–71. Cambridge.

Good, I. 2012[1995]. On the Question of Silk in Pre-Han Eurasia, in V. Hansen (edr), *The Silk Road. Key Papers. Part 1: the Pre-Islamic Period*. Vol. 1: 16–28. Leiden and Boston.

Good, I., J. Kenoyer and R. Meadow 2009. New evidence for early silk in the Indus Civilization. *Archaeometry* 51(3): 457–66.

Goodman, P. 2016. Working Together: Clusters of Artisans in the Roman City, in M. Flohr and A. Wilson (eds), *Urban Craftsmen and Traders in the Roman World*: 301–333. Oxford.

Goody, J. 2012. *The Theft of History*. Cambridge.

Gopal, L. 1961. Textiles in Ancient India. *Journal of the Economic and Social History of the Orient* 4(1): 53–69.

Gorelick, L. and A. Gwinnett 1988. Diamonds from India to Rome and beyond. *American Journal of Archaeology* 92(4): 547–552.

Gorman, R. and V. Gorman 2014. *Corrupting Luxury in Ancient Greek Literature*. Ann Arbor.

Graeber, D. 2011. *Debt. The first 5,000 years*. Brooklyn and New York.

Graeven, H. 1903. *Antike Schnitzereien aus Elfenbein und Knochen in photographischer Nachbildung*. Hannover.

Gragg, G. 1996. "South Arabian/Axumite" depinto, in S. Sidebotham and W. Wendrich (eds), *Preliminary Report of the 1995 Excavations at Berenike (Egyptian Red Sea Coast) and the Survey of the Eastern Desert*: 209–11. Leiden.

Granovetter, M. 1973. The Strength of Weak Ties. *American Journal of Sociology* 78(6): 1360–1380.

Groom, N. 1981. *Frankincense and Myrrh. A study of the Arabian Incense Trade*. London.

de Grummond, N. 1985. The Etruscan mirror. *Notes in the History of Art* 4(2/3): 26–35.

Guidobaldi, M. 2010. Arredi di lusso in legno e avorio da Ercolano: le nuove scoperte della Villa dei Papiri. *LANX. Rivista della Scuola di Specializzazione in Archeologia* 6: 63–99.

Guidobaldi, M. and D. Esposito 2010. New Archaeological Research at the Villa of the Papyri in Herculaneum, in M. Zarmakoupi (edr), *The Villa of the Papyri at Herculaneum. Archaeology, Reception, and Digital Reconstruction*: 21–62. Berlin and New York.

Gulati, A. N. 1961. A note on the early history of silk in India, in J. Clutton-Brock, Vishnu-Mittre, and A. N. Gulati (edr), *Technical Reports on Archaeolocial Remains*: 55–59. Poona.

Gupta, S. 2002 (edr). The Indian Ocean in Antiquity, special issue on. *Man and Environment* 27(1).

Gupta, S. 2005. A Historiographical Survey of Studies on Indo-Roman Sea Trade and Indian Ocean Trade. *Indian Historical Review* 32(1): 140-64.

Gupta, S. 2007a. *Early Sculptural Art in the Indian Coastlands. A study in cutlrual transmission and syncretism (300 BC - AD 500)*. New Delhi.

Gupta, S. 2007b. Piracy and trade on the western coast of India (AD 1–250). *Azania: Archaeological Research in Africa* 42(1): 37–51

Gupta, S., D. Williams and D. Peacock 2001. Dressel 2–4 Amphorae and Roman Trade with India: the evidence from Nevasa. *South Asian Studies* 17(1): 7–18.

Gupta, S. and S. Aruni 2005. Early Historic Kanara: Was it really Ptolemy's Pirate Coast? *Journal of Indian Ocean Archaeology* 2: 42–54.

Gurney, L. and P. Gurney 1998. The *Scriptores Historiae Augustae*: History and Controversy. *Literary and Linguistic Computing* 13(3): 105–9.

Gurukkal, R. 2013. Classical Indo-Roman Trade: A Historiographical Reconsideration. *Indian Historical Review* 40(2): 181–206.

Haaland, R. 2014. The Meroitic Empire: Trade and Cultural Influences in an Indian Ocean Context. *African Archaeological Review* 31: 649-673.

Habicht, C. 2013. Eudoxus of Cyzicus and Ptolemaic exploration of the sea route to India, in K. Buraselis, M. Stefanou and D. J. Thompson (eds), *The Ptolemies, the Sea and the Nile*: 197–206. Cambridge.

Hackin, J. (edr) 1939. *Recherches Archéologiques à Begram*. Paris.

Hackin, J. (edr) 1954. *Nouvelles recherces archéologiques à Begram*. Paris.

Hackl, U., H. Jenni and C. Schneider (eds) 2003. *Quellen zur Geschichte der Nabatäer. Textsammlung mit Übersetzung und Kommentar*. Freiburg/Göttingen.
van Haeperen, F. 2012. Collèges de *dendrophores* et autorités locales et romaines, in M. Dondin-Payre and N. Tran (eds), *Collegia. Le phénomène associatif dans l'Occident romain*: 47–62. Bordeaux.
Hansen, V. 2012. *The Silk Road. A New History*. Oxford.
Harcum, C. 1914. *Roman Cooks*. Baltimare.
Harl-Schaller, F. 1976–7. Figürliche Gerät- und Möbelfüsse. *Jahreshefte des Österreischischen Archäologischen Institutes in Wien* 51: 45–56.
Harrak, A. (edr) 2005. *The Acts of Mar Mari the Apostle*. Atlanta.
Harrauer, H. and P. Sijpestein 1986. Ein neues dokument su Roms Indienhandel. P. Vindob. G 40822. *Anzeiger* 122 (1985): 124–55.
Harrell, J. 1998. Geology, in S. Sidebotham and W. Wendrich (eds), *Berenike 1996. Report of the 1996 Excavations at Berenike (Egyptian Red Sea Coast) and the Survey of the Eastern Desert*: 121–48. Leiden.
Harris, E. and D. Lewis 2015. Introduction. Markets in Classical and Hellenistic Greece, in E. Harris, D. Lewis and M. Woolmer (eds), *The Ancient Greek Economy*: 1–37. Cambridge.
Hass, C. 1997. *Alexandria in Late Antiquity. Topography and Social Conflict*. Baltimore and London.
Hatzfeld, J. 1912. Les Italiens résidant à Délos mentionnés dans les inscriptions de l'île. *Bulletin de correspondance hellénique* 36: 5-218.
Hatzfeld, J. 1919. *Les Trafiquants Italiens dans l'Orient Hellénique*. Paris.
Hawkins, C. 2012. Manufacturing, in W. Scheidel (edr), *The Cambridge Companion to the Roman Economy*: 175–94. Cambridge.
Hawkins, C. 2016. *Roman Artisans and the Urban Economy*. Cambridge.
Händel, A. 1985. Der Handel mit Drogen und Spezereien im Rom der Prinzipatszeit in Auswertung der Inschriften (Salz und Honig, Gewürze, Medikamente, Duftstoffe, Toilettegegenstände, Farben). *Münstersche Beiträge z. antiken Handelsgeschichte* 4(1): 30–48.
den Hengst, D. 2010. The discussion of authorship, in D. Burgersdijk and J. van Waarden (eds), *Emperors and Historiography: Collected Essays on the Literature of the Roman Empire by Daniël den Hengst*: 177–85. Boston.
Hennig, D. 2004. Arabotoxotai und Eremophylakes im römischen Ägypten. *Chiron* 34: 267–84.
Hiebert, F. and P. Cambon (eds) 2008. *Afghanistan. Hidden treasures from the National Museum, Kabul*. Washington, D.C.
Higgins, R. 1980. *Greek and Roman Jewellery*. 2nd edn. London.
Higuchi, T. and K. Saito (eds) 2001. *Tomb F. Tomb of BWLH and BWRP. Southeast Necropolis. Palmyra, Syria*. Nara.
Hildebrandt, B. 2012a. Der Römer neue Kleider. Zur Einführung von Seide im kaiserzeitlichen Rom, in G. Lehmann, D. Engster and A. Nuss (eds), *Von der bronzezeitlichen Geschichte zur modernen Antikenrezeption*: 11–53. Göttingen.
Hildebrandt, B. 2012b. Some thoughts on the unravelling of Chinese silks in the Roman Empire. A reassessment of Lucan, Bellum Civile 10.141–143, in I. Tzachili and E. Zimi (eds), *Textiles and Dress in the Roman East: a technological and social approach, Proceedings of the Symposium held at Kalamata/Greece, 18-19.03.2011*: 107–115. Athens.
Hildebrandt, B. 2016. Das Gewand des Honorius in der Dichtung Claudians, in H. Harich-Schwarzbauer (edr), *Texts and Textiles in the Ancient World. Materiality - Representation - Episteme - Metapoetics*: 67–85. Oxford.
Hildebrandt, B. 2017. Silk production and trade in the Roman Empire, in B. Hildebrandt and C. Gillis (eds), *Silk. Trade and Exchange along the Silk Roads between Rome and China in Antiquity*: 34–50. Oxford.
Hildebrandt, B. (forthcoming). India's contribution to the wardrobes of the Roman elite and the emperors: Precious fabrics and stones, in L. Varadarajan (edr), *Textiles, Collections, Communities, Culture and Trade. Contributions of a seminar held from 9-10.01.2016 at the K.R. Cama Oriental Institute, Mumbai* (submitted and accepted).
Hildebrandt, B. (unpublished). Seide in der Antike. Terminologie - Produktion - Konsumtion - Distribution. Unpublished professoral habilitation, Gottfried Wilhelm Leibniz Universität Hannover.
Hobsbawm, E. 1997. *On History*. London.
Hoffmann, D. 1873. *Mar Samuel. Rektor der jüdischen Akademie zu Nehardea in Babylonien*. Leipzig.
Holleran, C. 2012. *Shopping in Ancient Rome: The Retail Trade in the Late Republic and the Principate*. Oxford.
Hoppal, K. 2016. Contextualising Roman-related glass artefacts in China. An integrated approach to Sino-Roman relations. *Acta Archaeologica Academiae Scientiarum Hungaricae* 67: 99–114.
Horden, P. and N. Purcell 2000. *The Corrupting Sea. A study of Mediterranean History*. Oxford.
Houston, G. 1990. The altar from Rome with inscriptions to Sol and Malakbel. *Syria* 67(1): 189–193.

Houston, G. 2003. Galen, His Books, and the Horrea Piperataria at Rome. *Memoirs of the American Academy in Rome* 48: 45–51.

Howgego, C. 1995. *Ancient History from Coins*. London.

Iscrizioni sudarabiche 1974. *Iscrizioni minee*. Vol. 1. Naples.

Jackson, R. 1996. Eye medicine in the Roman Empire, in H. Temporini and W. Haase (eds), *Aufstieg und Niedergang der römischen Welt. Teil II*. Vol. 37: 2228–51. Berlin.

Jacomet, S. and J. Schibler 2001. Les contributions de l'archéobotanique et de l'archéozoologie à la connaisance de l'agriculture et de l'alimentation du site romain de Biesheim-Kunheim, in S. Plouin, M. Reddé and C. Boutantin (eds), *La frontière romaine sur le Rhin supérieur. À propos des fouilles récentes de Biesheim-Kunheim*: 60–8. Biesheim.

Jacq-Hergoualc'h, M. 2002. *The Malay Peninsula. Crossroads of the Maritime Silk Road (100 BC - 1300 AD)*. Leiden, Boston and Cologne.

Jaffer, A. 2002. *Luxury Goods from India. The art of the Indian cabinet-maker*. London.

Jaspers, K. 1949. *Vom Ursprung und Ziel der Geschichte*. Munich.

Jastrow, M. and S. Krauss 1902. Bathyra. (commonly called Betera, Beterah), in I. Singer (edr), *The Jewish Encyclopedia*: 589a–599a. London and New York.

Johns, C. 2010. *The Hoxne Late Roman Treasure. Gold jewellery and silver plate*. London.

Johnson, A. 1936. *Roman Egypt to the Reign of Diocletian*. An Economic Survey of Ancient Rome. Vol. 2. Baltimore.

Johnson, A., P. Coleman-Norton and F. Bourne 1961. *Ancient Roman Statutes*. Austin.

Johnson, D. 1987. Nabataean trade: intensification and culture change. Unpublished PhD dissertation, University of Utah; Ann Arbor, MI.

Johnson, W. 2009. *A Dictionary of Hinduism*. Oxford.

Jones, A. 1974. Asian trade in Antiquity, in A. Jones, *The Roman Economy. Studies in Ancient Economic and Administrative History*. Edited by P. Brunt: 140–50. Oxford.

Jones, R., P. Hammond, D. Johnson and Z. Fiema 1988. A second Nabataean inscription from Tell esh-Shuqafiya, Egypt. *Bulletin of the American Schools of Oriental Research* 269: 47–57.

Jones, N. 1999. *The Associations of Classical Athens*. Oxford and New York.

Jones, D. 2006. *The Bankers of Puteoli. Finance, trade and industry in the Roman World*. Stroud.

Jones Hall, L. 2004. *Roman Berytus. Beirut in Late Antiquity*. London and New York.

Joshel, S. 1992. *Work, Identity, and Legal Status at Rome. A Study of the Occupational Inscriptions*. Norman and London.

Jouguet, P. 1931. Dédicace grecque de Médamoud. *Bulletin de l'Institut français d'archéologie orientale* 31: 1–29.

Jouveau-Dubreuil, G. 1940. Les ruines romaines de Pondichéry. *Bulletin de l'Ecole française d'Extrême-Orient* 40(2): 448-450.

Jördens, A. 2009. *Statthalterliche Verwaltung in der römischen Kaiserzeit. Studien zum 'praefectus Aegypti.'* Stuttgart.

Jördens, A. 2012. Government, Taxation, and Law, in C. Riggs (edr), *The Oxford Handbook of Roman Egypt*: 57–67. Oxford.

Kádár, Z. 1967. Serica. Le rôle de la soie dans la vie économique et sociale de l'Empire romain, d'après les documents écrits. Les Ier et IIe siècles. *Acta Classica Univ. Scient. Debrecen.* 3: 89–98.

Kaizer, T. 2002a. The Symposium of the Konetoi in an Inscription Set up in Honour of Odaenathus at Palmyra. *Studi epigrafici e linguistici sul Vicino Oriente antico* 19: 149–56.

Kaizer, T. 2002b. *The Religious Life of Palmyra. A Study of the Social Patterns of Worship in the Roman Period*. Stuttgart.

Kangle, R. P. (edr) 1965–72. *The Kautilya Arthasastra*. 3 vols. Bombay.

Karashima, N. and Y. Subbarayalu 2009. Ancient and Medieval Tamil and Sanskrit Inscriptions Relating to Southeast Asia and China, in H. Kulke, K. Kesavapany and V. Sakhuja (eds), *Nagapattinam to Suvarnadwipa. Reflections on the Chola Naval Expeditions to Southeast Asia*: 271–291. Singapore.

Karttunen, K. 1994. Yonas, Yavanas and related matter in Indian epigraphy, in A. Parpola and P. Koskikallio (eds), *South Asian Archaeology 1993*. Vol. 1: 329–336. Helsinki.

Karttunen, K. 1997. Wooden tables with Ivory Legs, in R. Allchin and B. Allchin (eds), *South Asian Archaeology 1995*. Vol. 2: 557–62. New Delhi and Calcutta.

Katsuhiko, O. and S. Gupta 2000. The Far East, Southeast and South Asia: Indo-Pacific Beads from Yaoi Tombs as Indicators of Early Maritime Exchange. *South Asian Studies* 16: 73–88.

Kehoe, D., D. Ratzan and U. Yiftach (eds) 2015. *Law and Transaction Costs in the Ancient Economy*. Ann Arbor.

Kelly, G. 2009. Craft production and technology during the Iron Age to Early Historic transition at Kodumanal, Tamil Nadu. *Tamil Civilization* 23: 1–14.

Kenoyer, J. 2017. Textiles and trade in south Asia during the Proto-Historic and Early Historic Period, in B. Hildebrandt and C. Gillis (eds), *Silk. Trade and Exchange along the Silk Roads between Rome and China in Antiquity*: 7–26. Oxford.

Khalil, E. 2012. The *ploion hellenikon* of Roman Egypt: What was Greek about it? *British Museum Studies in Ancient Egypt and Sudan* 19: 39–50.

Khan, F. A. 1963. *Banbhore. A preliminary report on the recent archaeological excavations at Banbhore*. Karachi.

Kielhorn, F. 1900. Aihole Inscription of Pulikesin II. Saka-samvat 556. *Epigraphia Indica* 6: 1–12.

Kinoshita, H. 2009. Foreign glass excavated in China, from the 4th to 12th centuries, in M. Mango (edr), *Byzantine Trade, 4th to 12th centuries. The archaeology of local, regional and international exchange*: 253–61. Farnham.

Kondoleon, C. 2000. *Antioch. The Lost Ancient City*. Princeton, NJ.

Konow, S. 1929. *Corpus Inscriptionum Indicarum: Kharoshthi inscriptions*. Vol. 2, pt. 1. Calcutta.

Konow, S. 1931–32. Mathura Brahmi Inscription of the year 28. *Epigraphia Indica* 21: 55–61.

Kopytoff, I. 1986. The cultural biography of things: commoditization as process, in A. Appadurai (edr), *The Social Life of Things. Commodities in cultural perspective*: 64–91. Cambridge.

Kreuz, A. 1995. Landwirtschaft und ihre ökologischen Grundlagen in den Jahrhunderten um Christi Geburt: zum Stand der naturwissenschaftlichen Untersuchungen in Hessen. *Berichte der Kommission für Archäologische Landesforschung in Hessen* 3: 59–91.

Kucan, D. 1992. Die Pflanzenfunde aus dem römischen Militärlager Oberaden, in J.-S. Kühlborn (edr), *Das Römerlager in Oberaden III. Die Ausgrabungen im nordwestlichen Lagerbereich und weitere Baustellenuntersuchungen der Jahre 1962-1988*: 237–65. Münster.

Küster, H. 1995. *Postglaziale Vegetationsgeschichte Südbayerns. Geobotanische Studien zur Prähistorischen Landschaftskunde*. Berlin.

Lacerenza, G. 1995. *Laudanes* schiavo di *Calpurnius Moschas*. Nota su un graffito greco dal wadi Manih (Egitto). *Ostraka* 4: 191–93.

La'da, C. 2002. *Foreign Ethnics in Hellenistic Egypt*. Leuven and Paris.

Laet, S. de 1949. *Portorium. Étude sur l'organisation douanère chez les romains, surtout a l'époque du haut-empire*. Brügge.

Laing, E. 1991. A Report on Western Asian Glassware in the Far East. *Bulletin of the Asia Institute, New Series* 5: 109–21.

Lanciani, R. 1888. *Ancient Rome in the light of recent discoveries*. London.

Langelotti, M. 2016. Professional Associationsand the State in Roman Egypt: The Case of First-Century Tebtunis. *Chronique d'Égypte* 91(181): 111–34.

Lapatin, K. 2001. *Chryselephantine Statuary in the Ancient Mediterranean World*. Oxford.

Lapatin, K. 2009. Luxus, in C. Mattusch (edr), *Pompeii and the Roman Villa. Art and Culture around the Bay of Naples*: 31–51. Verona.

Lapatin, K. 2015. *Luxus. The sumptuous arts of Greece and Rome*. Los Angeles.

Laubry, N. and F. Zevi 2010. Une inscription d'Ostie et la législation impériale sur les collèges, in M. Silvestrini (edr), *Le Tribù Romane. Atti della XVIe Rencontre sur l'épigraphie (Bari 8-10 ottobre 2009)*: 457–67. Bari.

Laum, B. 1914. *Stiftungen in der griechischen und römanischen Antike; ein Beitrag zur antiken Kulturgeschichte*. Leipzig.

Leslie, D. and K. Gardiner 1996. *The Roman Empire in Chinese Sources*. Rome.

Liebeshuetz, J. 1972. *Antioch. City and Imperial Administration in the Later Roman Empire*. Oxford.

de Ligt, L. 2000. Governmental attitudes towards markets and *collegia*, in E. Lo Cascio (edr), *Mercati permanenti e mercati periodici nel mondo romano*: 237–52. Bari.

Littmann, E. and D. Meredith 1953. Nabataean inscriptions from Egypt. *Bulletin of the School of Oriental and African Studies* 15(1): 1–28.

Liu, J. 2005. Local Governments and Collegia: A New Appraisal of the Evidence, in J.-J. Aubert and Z. Várhelyi (eds), *A Tall Order: Imperialism, Law, Religion, and Society in the Ancient World (Essays in Honor of William V. Harris)*: 279–310. Munich.

Liu, J. 2008a. The economy of endowments: the case of the Roman *collegia*, in K. Verboven, K. Vandorpe and V. Chankowski (eds), *Pistoi dia tèn technèn. Bankers, Loans and Archives in the Ancient World. Studies in honour of Raymond Bogaert*: 231–56. Leuven.

Liu, J. 2008b. Pompeii and collegia: a new appraisal of the evidence. *The Ancient history bulletin* 22(1–4): 53–69.
Liu, J. 2009. *Collegia Centonariorum: The Guilds of Textile Dealers in the Roman West.* Leiden and Boston.
Liu, J. 2013. Professional associations, in P. Erdkamp (edr), *The Cambridge Companion to Ancient Rome*: 352–368. Cambridge.
Loane, H. J. 1938. *Industry and Commerce of the City of Rome (50 BC - 200 AD).* Baltimore.
Loane, H. J. 1944. Vespasian's Spice Market and Tribute in Kind. *Classical Philology* 39(1): 10–21.
Los, A. 2000. Les affaires 'industrielles' des élites des villes campaniennes sous les Julio-Claudiens et les Flaviens. *Mélanges de l'Ecole française de Rome. Antiquité* 112(1): 243–277.
Luhmann, N. 1969. *Legitimation durch Verfahren.* Frankfurt.
Lüeders, H. 1912. A List of Brahmi Inscriptions. Appendix. *Epigraphia Indica* 10.
Lyding Will, E. 1991. The Mediterranean Shipping Amphoras from Arikamedu, in V. Begley and R. de Puma (eds), *Rome and India. The Ancient Sea Trade*: 151–56. Madison, WI.
Lyding Will, E. 1996. Mediterranean shipping amphoras from the 1941–50 excavations, in V. Begley (edr), *The Ancient Port of Arikamedu. New Excavations and Researches 1989-92.* Vol. 1: 317–49. Pondicherry.
Lyding Will, E. 2004. The Mediterranean shipping amphoras from the 1989–92 excavations, in V. Begley (edr), *The Ancient Port of Arikamedu. New Excavations and Researches 1989-92.* Vol. 2: 325–403. Paris.
MacDowall, D. 1991. Indian imports of Roman silver coins, in A. Jha (edr), *Coinage, Trade and Economy*: 145–53. Bombay.
MacDowall, D. 1996. The evidence of the gazetteer of Roman artefacts in India, in H. P. Ray and J.-F. Salles (eds), *Tradition and Archaeology. Early Maritime Contacts in the Indian Ocean*: 79–95. New Delhi and Lyon.
Maciá, L. 2007. *Marzeah y thiasos. Una institución convival en el Oriente Próximo Antiguo y el Mediterráneo.* Madrid.
MacMullen, R. 1982. The Epigraphic Habit in the Roman Empire. *The American Journal of Philology* 103(3): 233–246.
Mahadevan, I. 1996a. Pottery inscriptions in Brahmi and Tamil-Brahmi, in V. Begley (edr), *The Ancient Port of Arikamedu. New Excavations and Researches 1989-92.* Vol. 1: 287–316. Pondicherry.
Mahadevan, I. 1996b. Tamil-Brahmi graffito, in S. Sidebotham and W. Wendrich (eds), *Preliminary Report of the 1995 Excavations at Berenike (Egyptian Red Sea Coast) and the Survey of the Eastern Desert*: 205–8. Leiden.
Mahadevan, I. 2003. *Early Tamil Epigraphy. From the Earliest Times to the Sixth Century A.D.* Cambridge, MA; and London.
Mairs, R. 2006. Ethnic Identity in the Hellenistic Far East. Unpublished PhD dissertation, University of Cambridge.
Mairs, R. 2012a. Glassware from Roman Egypt at Begram (Afghanistan) and the Red Sea trade. *British Museum Studies in Ancient Egypt and Sudan* 18: 2–14.
Mairs, R. 2012b. 'Interpreting' at Vindolanda: Commercial and Linguistic Mediation in the Roman Army. *Britannia* 43: 17–28.
Mairs, R. 2014. *The Hellenistic Far East. Archaeology, Language, and Identity in Greek Central Asia.* Oakland, CA.
Maiuri, A. 1938–39. Statuetta eburnea di arte indiana a Pompei. *Le Arti* 1: 111–15.
Majumdar, R. C. 1920[1918]. *Corporate Life in Ancient India.* 2nd edn. Calcutta.
Malkin, I. 2011. *A Small Greek World: Networks in the Ancient Mediterranean. Greeks Overseas.* Oxford and New York.
Manassero, N. and V. Fiorani 2014. The site of Banbhore (Sindh - Pakistan): A Joint Pakistani-French-Italian Project. Current Research in Archaeology and History (2010–14). *The Silk Road* 12: 82–8.
Mangalam, S. J. 1992. Ship-type coins from Elephanta. *Journal of the Numismatic Society of India* 54: 103–12.
Mangalam, S. J. 1993. A note on the coins from Elephanta: coins of the Konkan Mauryas? *Bulletin of the Deccan College Research Institute* 53: 237–41.
Mango, M. 1996. Byzantine maritime trade with the East (4th–7th centuries). *ARAM* 8: 139–63.
Maniatis, G. 2009. *Guilds, Price Formation and Market Structures in Byzantium.* Farnham.
Manzo, A. 2005. Aksumite Trade and the Red Sea Exchange Network: A View from Bieta Giyorgis (Aksum), in J. Starkey (edr), *People of the Red Sea.* Proceedings of the Red Sea Project 2: 51–66. Oxford.
Marangou, L. 1976. *Bone Carvings from Egypt.* Tübingen.
Marangou, L. 2002. *Amorgos I. He Minõa.* Athens.
Maraqten, M. 1996. Dangerous trade routes: on the plundering of caravans in the Pre-Islamic Near East. *ARAM* 8: 213–36.
Marcotte, D. 2012. Le *Périple de la mer Érythrée* dans son genre et sa tradition textuelle, in M.-Fr. Boussac, J.-Fr. Salles and J.-B. Yon (eds), *Autour du Périple de la mer Érythrée. Topoi*, Supplément 11: 7–25.

Marengo, S. 1989. Etichette plumbee ed altro *instrumentum* iscritto su metallo da varie localita del Macerate. *Picus* 9: 35–63.
Marrone, G. 2001. Nascita e sviluppo di Concordia *colonia civium romanorum*, in P. Croce da Villa and E. di Filippo Balestrazzi (eds), *'Concordia Sagittaria' tremila anni di storia*: 119–24. Padua.
Marrone, G. and E. Pettenò 2009–10. *Supellex ex plumbo. Laminae Concordiensis.* Le laminette commerciali da Iulia Concordia. *Atti dell'istituto Veneto di scienze, lettere ed Arti* 168. 43–110.
Marshall, J. 1951. *Taxila*. 3 vols. Cambridge.
Marshall, J. 1960. *The Buddhist Art of Gandhara*. Cambridge.
Martinez, D. 1997. *P. Erasm.* I 10: An order for payment from a cult association. *Zeitschrift für Papyrologie und Epigraphik* 118: 263–6.
Martinez, D. and M. Williams 1997. Records of loan receipts from a guild association. *Zeitschrift für Papyrologie und Epigraphik* 118: 259–63.
Mathew, K. (edr) 2015. *Imperial Rome, Indian Ocean Regions and Muziris. New Perspectives on Maritime Trade.* New Delhi.
Matthews, J. 1984. The Tax Law of Palmyra: Evidence for Economic History in a City of the Roman East. *The Journal of Roman Studies* 74: 157–80.
Mattingly, D. 1990. Paintings, presses and perfume production at Pompeii. *Oxford Journal of Archaeology* 9(1): 71–90.
Mayerson, P. 1992. The Island of Iotabê in the Byzantine Sources: A Reprise. *Bulletin of the American Schools of Oriental Research* 287: 1–4.
Mayerson, P. 1993. A confusion of Indias: Asian India and African India in the Byzantine sources. *Journal of the American Oriental Society* 113(2): 169–74.
Mayerson, P. 1996. The Port of Clysma (Suez) in Transition from Roman to Arab Rule. *Journal of Near Eastern Studies* 55(2): 119–26.
McCabe, A. 2009. Imported *materia medica*, 4th–12th centuries, and Byzantine pharmacology, in M. Mango (edr), *Byzantine Trade, 4th to 12th centuries. The archaeology of local, regional and international exchange*: 273–92. Farnham.
McCormick, M. 2001. *Origins of the European Economy. Communications and Commerce, A.D. 300-900.* Cambridge and New York.
McLaughlin, J. 2001. *The Marzeah in the Prophetic Literature. References and Allusions in Light of the Extra-Biblical Evidence.* Leiden, Boston, Köln.
McLaughlin, R. 2010. *Rome and the Distant East. Trade Routes to the Ancient Lands of Arabia, India and China.* London.
McLaughlin, R. 2014. *The Roman Empire and the Indian Ocean*. Barnsley.
Mehendale, S. 1993. The ivory statuette from Bhokardan and its connection to the ivory statuettes from Pompeii and Ter,' in A. Gail and G. Mevissen (eds), *South Asian Archaeology 1991*: 529–38. Stuttgart.
Mehendale, S. 1997. Begram: New Perspectives on the Ivory and Bone Carvings. Unpublished PhD dissertation, University of California, Berkeley. Accessed on February 26, 2016, http://ecai.org/begramweb/docs/table_of_contents.htm.
Mehendale, S. 2001. The Begram ivory and bone carvings: Some observations on provenance and chronology. *Topoi* 11: 485–514.
Mehendale, S. 2008. Begram: at the heart of the Silk Roads, in F. Hiebert and P. Cambon (eds), *Afghanistan. Hidden treasures from the National Museum, Kabul*: 131–44. Washington, D.C.
Mehta, R. and A. Thakkar 1978. *M. S. University Copper Plates of the Time of Toramana.*Vadodara.
Meiggs, R. 1973. *Roman Ostia*. Oxford.
Meiggs, R. 1982. *Trees and Timber in the Ancient Mediterranean World*. Oxford.
Meredith, D. 1953. Annius Plocamus: Two Inscriptions from the Berenice Road. *The Journal of Roman Studies* 43: 38–40.
Meyer, C. 1995. A Byzantine gold-mining town in the eastern desert of Egypt: Bir Umm Fawakhir, 1992–3. *Journal of Roman Archaeology* 8: 192–224.
Mierse, W. 2013. Indian Silk in the Roman marketplace. *Journal of Indian Ocean Archaeology* 9: 210–22.
Millar, F. 1993. *The Roman Near East 31 BC–AD 337*. London and Cambridge, MA.
Millar, F. 1998. Caravan cities: the Roman Near East and long-distance trade by land, in M. Austin, J. Harries and C. Smith (eds), *Modus Operandi. Essays in honour of Geoffrey Rickman*: 119–37. London.
Miller, J. 1969. *The Spice Trade of the Roman Empire, 29 BC to AD 641*. Oxford.
van Minnen, P. 1987. Urban craftsmen in Roman Egypt. *Münstersche Beiträge z. antiken Handelsgeschichte* 6(1): 31–88.

van Minnen, P. 2008. Money and credit in Roman Egypt, in W. V. Harris (edr), *The Monetary Systems of the Greeks and Romans*: 226-241. Oxford.
Minoprio, A. 1932. A Restoration of the Basilica of Constantine, Rome. *Papers of the British School at Rome* 12: 1–25.
Mital, S. 2004. *Kautiliya Arthasastra Revisited*. New Delhi.
Mokyr, J. 1985. Demand vs. Supply in the Industrial Revolution, in J. Mokyr (edr), *The Economics of the Industrial Revolution*: 97–118. London.
Mols, S. 1999. *Wooden furniture in Herculaneum. Form, technique and function*. Amsterdam.
Mommsen, T. 1892. *Chronica Minora, saec. IV–VII. MGH* I. Berlin.
Monier-Williams, M. 1979. *A Sanskrit-English Dictionary*. Oxford.
Mordini, A. 1967. old Kushana coins in the Convent of Dabra Dammo. *Journal of the Numismatic Society of India* 29(2): 19–25.
Morelli, F. 2011. Dal Mar Rosso ad Alessandria. Il *verso* (ma anche il *recto*) del 'papiro di Muziris' (SB XVIII 13167). *Tyche* 26: 199–233.
Morley, N. 2007. *Trade in Classical Antiquity*. Cambridge.
Morris, I. 1999. Foreword, in M. Finley, *The Ancient Economy. Updated with a New Foreword by Ian Morris*: ix–xxxvi. Berkeley and Los Angeles.
Morris, I., R. Saller and W. Scheidel 2007. Introduction, in W. Scheidel, R. Saller and I. Morris (eds), *The Cambridge Economic History of the Greco-Roman World*: 1–12. Cambridge.
Morrison, K. 2002. Pepper in the hills: upland–lowland exchange and the intensification of the spice trade, in K. Morrison and L. Junker (eds), *Forager-Traders in South and Southeast Asia. Long-Term Histories*: 105–28. Cambridge.
Morrison, K. and M. Lycett 2013. Forest products in a wider world: Early Historic connections across Southern India, in S. Abraham, P. Gullapalli, T. Raczek and U. Rizvi (eds), *Connections and Complexity: New Approaces to the Archaeology of South Asia*: 127–42. Walnut Creek, CA.
Moss, C. 1988. Roman marble tables. Unpublished PhD dissertation, Princeton University.
Mrozek, S. 1982. Zum Handel von einigen Gewürzen und Wohlgerüchen in der spätrömischen Zeit. *Münstersche Beiträge z. antiken Handelsgeschichte* 1(2): 15–21.
Mrozek, S. 2000. Le fonctionnement des fondations dans les provinces occidentales et l'economice de credit a l'epoque du Haut-Empire romain. *Latomus* 59: 327–45.
Murthy, K. 1982, *Ancient Indian Furniture*. New Delhi.
Museo Napoli 1989a. *Le Collezioni del Museo Nazionale di Napoli. I mosaici, le pitture, gli oggetti di uso quotidiano, gli argenti, le terrecotte invetriate, i vetri, i cristalli, gli avori*. Rome.
Museo Napoli 1989b. *Le Collezioni del Museo Nazionale di Napoli. La scultura greco-romana, le sculture antiche della collezione Farnese, le collezioni monetali, le oreficerie, la collezione glittica*. Rome.
Museo Napoli 1999. *Museo archeologico nazionale di napoli*. Naples.
Nakanishi, M. and O. v. Hinüber 2014. Kanaganahalli Inscriptions. *Annual Report of The International Research Institute for Advanced Buddhology at Soka University (ARIRIAB)* 17, Supplement.
Nappo, D. 2009. Roman Policy in the Red Sea between Anastasius and Justinian, in L. Blue, J. Cooper, R. Thomas and J. Whitewright (eds), *Connected Hinterlands*. Proceedings of the Red Sea Project IV: 71–77. Oxford.
Nappo, D. 2015. Roman Policy on the Red Sea in the Second Century CE, in F. de Romanis and M. Maiuro (eds), *Across the Ocean: Nine Essays on Indo-Mediterranean Trade*: 55–72. Leiden and Boston.
Nappo, D. and A. Zerbini 2011. On the Fringe: Trade and Taxation in the Egyptian Eastern Desert, in O. Hekster and T. Kaizer (eds), *Frontiers of the Roman World*: 61–78. Leiden and Boston.
Narain, A. K. 1957. *The Indo-Greeks*. Oxford.
Naumkin, V. and A. Sedov 1993. Monuments of Socotra. *Topoi. Orient - Occident* 3(2): 569–623.
Neelis, J. 2011. *Early Buddhist Transmission and Trade Networks. Mobility and Exchange within and beyond the Northwestern Borderlands of South Asia*. Leiden and Boston.
Neild-Basu, S. 1984. The Dubashes of Madras. *Modern Asian Studies* 18(1): 1–31.
Newman, L. 1945. *The Talmudic Anthology*. New York.
Nielsen, H. 1973. *Oldtidens Øjenmedicin*. København.
Nijf, O. van 1997. *The Civic World of Professional Associations in the Roman East*. Amsterdam.
North, D. C. 1990. *Institutions, Institutional Change and Economic Performance*. Cambridge.
Noy, D. 2002. *Foreigners at Rome. Citizens and Strangers*. London.
Nye, J. 2008. Institutions and the Institutional Environment, in E. Brousseau and J.-M. Glachant (eds), *New Institutional Economics: A Guidebook*: 67–80. Cambridge.

Ogilvie, S. 2005. The Use and Abuse of Trust: Social Capital and its Deployment by Early Modern Guilds. *Jahrbuch für Wirtschaftsgeschichte* 46(1): 15–52.

Olshausen, E. 2013. Der Periplus zwischen Seehandbuch und Literatur, in C. Marx (edr), *Periplus 2013. Jahrbuch für aussereuropäische geschichte* 23: 35–57.

Paranavitana, S. 1928–33a. Tonigala rock inscription of the third year of Srimeghavarnna. *Epigraphia Zeylanica* 3: 172–188.

Paranavitana, S. 1928–33b. Two rock-inscriptions from Labuätabändigala. *Epigraphia Zeylanica* 3: 247–53.

Paranavitana, S. 1970–83. *Inscriptions of Ceylon.* Vol. I–II.1. Colombo.

Parassoglou, G. 1978. *Imperial estates in Roman Egypt.* Amsterdam.

Parker, G. 2002. Ex Oriente Luxuria: Indian Commodities and Roman Experience. *Journal of the Economic and Social History of the Orient* 45(1): 40–95.

Parker, G. 2004. Topographies of Taste: Indian Textiles and Mediterranean Contexts. *Ars Orientalis* 34: 19–37.

Parker, G. 2008. *The Making of Roman India.* Cambridge.

Parker, S. 2009. The Roman Port of Aila: Economic Connections with the Red Sea Littoral, in L. Blue, J. Cooper, R. Thomas and J. Whitewright (eds), *Connected Hinterlands.* Proceedings of the Red Sea Project IV: 79–84. Oxford.

Parry, J. and M. Bloch (eds) 1989. *Money and the morality of exchange.* Cambridge.

Parry, J. 1989. On the moral perils of exchange, in J. Parry and M. Bloch (eds), *Money and the morality of exchange*: 64–93. Cambridge.

Pavan, A. 2015. Trade and Commercial Routes Along the Indian Ocean from the Early Centuries BC to the Beginning of the Christian Era. New lights from the Indian pottery discovered at Sumhuram, in I. Gerlach (edr), *South Arabia and its Neighbours: Phenomena of Intercultural Contacts*: 121–32. Wiesbaden.

Peacock, D. and L. Blue (eds) 2006. *Myos Hormos — Quseir al-Qadim. Roman and Islamic ports on the Red Sea. Volume 1: Survey and Excavations 1999-2003.* Oxford.

Peacock, D. and L. Blue (eds) 2007. *The Ancient Red Sea Port of Adulis, Eritrea. Results of the Eritro-British Expedition, 2004-5.* Oxford.

Peacock, D. and L. Blue (eds) 2011. *Myos Hormos — Quseir al-Qadim. Roman and Islamic ports on the Red Sea. Volume 2: Finds from the excavations 1999-2003.* Oxford.

Peacock, D., D. Williams and S. James 2007. Basalt as Ships' Ballast and the Roman Incense Trade, in D. Peacock and D. Williams (eds), *Food for the Gods. New light on the ancient incense trade*: 28–70. Oxord.

Pedersen, R. 2008. The Byzantine-Aksumite period shipwreck at Black Assarca Island, Eritrea. *Azania: Archaeological Research in Africa* 43(1): 77–94.

Pénard, T. 2008. Game Theory and Institutions, in E. Brousseau and J.-M. Glachant (eds), *New Institutional Economics: A Guidebook*: 158–179. Cambridge.

Peppard, M. 2009. A letter concerning boats in Berenike and trade on the Red Sea. *Zeitschrift für Papyrologie und Epigraphik* 171: 193–98.

Perera, L. 2001. *The Institutions of Ancient Ceylon from Insriptions.* Vol. 1. Kandy.

Pérez López, X. 2007. Pap. Vindob. G 40822: préstamo marítimo y prospectiva romanística, in S. Rodriguez and J. Manzano (eds), *El Derecho Comercial. De Roma al Derecho Moderno.* Vol. 2: 635-679. Las Palmas de Gran Canaria.

Pernice, E. 1908. Der dreifuss 'aus dem Isistempel' in Pompeji. *Jahrbuch des kaiserlich deutschen Archäologischen Instituts* 23: 107–11.

Perry, J. 2006. *The Roman Collegia: The Modern Evolution of an Ancient Concept.* Leiden.

Pflaum, H.-G. 1960–61. *Les Carrières Procuratoriennes Équestres sous le Haut-Empire Romain.* 2 vols. Paris.

Phillips, J. 1997. Punt and Aksum: Egypt and the Horn of Africa. *The Journal of African History* 38(3): 423–457.

Phillips, C., F. Villeneuve and W. Facey 2004. A Latin inscription from South Arabia. *Proceedings of the Seminar for Arabian Studies* 34: 239–50.

Phillipson, D. 2012. *Foundations of an African Civilisation. Aksum and the northern Horn 1000 BC - AD 1300.* Croydon.

Pickert, S. 2005. Die römischen Stiftungen der augusteischen Zeit, in M. Borgolte (edr), *Stiftungen in Christentum, Judentum und Islam vor der Moderne*: 23–45. Berlin.

Poland, F. von 1909. *Geschichte des griechischen Vereinswesens.* Lepizig.

Polanyi, K. 1965[1957]. The Economy as Instituted Process, in K. Polanyi, C. Arensberg and H. Pearson (eds), *Trade and Market in the Early Empires*: 243–70. Chicago.

Polanyi, K., C. Arensberg and H. Pearson (eds) 1965[1957]. *Trade and Market in the Early Empires.* Chicago.

Pollard, E. 2013. Indian Spices and Roman 'Magic' in Imperial and Late Antique Indomediterranea. *Journal of World History* 24(1): 1–23.

Power, T. 2012. *The Red Sea from Byzantium to the Caliphate. AD 500–1000.* Cairo and New York.

Pramanik, S. 2004. Hathab: An Early Historic Port on the Gulf of Khambhat. *Journal of Indian Ocean Archaeology* 1: 133–40.

Pramanik, S. 2005. Navigational Sealings of Early Historic Vanij (Merchants) at Hathab, Gujarat. *Journal of Indian Ocean Archaeology* 2: 107–09.

Pramanik, S. 2008. Excavation at Hathab, District Bhavnagar. *Indian Archaeology 2001-02—A Review* 49: 34–48.

Preaux, C. 1939. *L'Économie royale des Lagides.* Bruxelles.

Pulleyblank, E. 1999. The Roman Empire as Known to Han China. *Journal of the American Oriental Society* 119(1): 71–79.

de Puma, R. 1991. The Roman Bronzes from Kolhapur, in V. Begley and R. de Puma (eds), *Rome and India. The Ancient Sea Trade*: 82–112. Madison, WI.

Radner, K. 1999. Traders in the Neo-Assyrian period, in J. Dercksen (edr), *Trade and Finance in Ancient Mesopotamia*: 101–26. Istanbul.

Raepsaet-Charlier, M.-T. and F. Allé 2008. Les métiers du parfum à Rome: le témoignage des sources épigraphiques, in A. Verbanck-Piérard, N. Massar and D. Frère (eds), *Parfums de l'Antiquité. La rose et l'encens en Méditerranée*: 287–94. Morlanwelz-Mariemont.

Rahman, A. U. and H. Falk 2011. *Seals, Sealings and Tokens from Gandhāra.* Wiesbaden.

Rajak, T. 1998. 'The Parthians in Josephus,' in J. Wiesehöfer (edr), *Das Partherreich und seine Zeugnisse.* Stuttgart. 309–324.

Rajan, K. 1996. Early maritime activities of the Tamils, in H. P. Ray and J.-F. Salles (eds), *Tradition and Archaeology. Early Maritime Contacts in the Indian Ocean*: 97–106. New Delhi and Lyon.

Rajan, K. 2008. Emergence of Trade in Early Historic Peninsular India, in G. Sengupta and S. Chakraborty (eds), *Early Historic South Asia*: 529–56. New Delhi.

Rajan, K. 2009. Archaeological Context of Tamil-Brahmi Script - some issues. *International Journal of Dravidian Linguistics* 38: 57–86.

Raschke, M. 1975. Papyrological evidence for Ptolemaic and Roman trade with India. *Proceedings of the XIV International Congress of Papyrologists. Oxford, 24-31 July 1974*: 241–6. London.

Raschke, M. 1978. New Studies in Roman Commerce with the East, in H. Temporini (edr), *Aufstieg und Niedergang der römischen Welt. Principat.* Vol. 9, pt. 2: 604-1361. Berlin and New York.

Ratbhone, D. 1983. Italian Wines in Roman Egypt. *Opus* 2: 81–98

Rathbone, D. 2000. The Muziris papyrus (SB XVIII): financing Roman trade with India. *Alexandrian Studies II in Honour of Mostafa el Abbadi, Bulletin de la Societe d'Archaeologie d'Alexandrie* 46: 39–50.

Rathbone, D. 2002. Koptos the Emporion. Economy and Society, I–III AD. *Topoi. Supplement* 3: 179–98.

Rathbone, D. 2007a. Merchant Networks in the Greek World: The Impact of Rome. *Mediterranean Historical Review* 22(2): 309–320.

Rathbone, D. 2007b. Roman Egypt, in W. Scheidel, R. Saller and I. Morris (eds), *The Cambridge Economic History of the Greco-Roman World*: 698–719. Cambridge.

Rauh, N. 1993. *The Sacred Bonds of Commerce: Religion, Economy and Trade Society at Hellenistic Roman Delos.* Amsterdam.

Ravitchandirane, P. 2007. Stratigraphy and Structural Context of Arikamedu. *East and West* 57(1/4): 205–33.

Rawlinson, H. 1916. *Intercourse between India and the Western World from the Earliest Times to the Fall of Rome.* Cambridge.

Ray, H. 1959. *History of Ceylon. From the Earliest Times to 1505.* Vol. 1. Colombo.

Ray, H. 1986. *Monastery and Guild. Commerce under the Satavahanas.* New Delhi.

Ray, H. 1988. The Yavana Presence in Ancient India. *Journal of the Economic and Social History of the Orient* 31(3): 311–325.

Ray, H. 1989. Early Maritime Contacts between South and Southeast Asia. *Journal of Southeast Asian Studies* 20(1): 42-54.

Ray, H. 1994a. Kanheri: the archaeology of an early Buddhist pilgrimage centre in western India. *World Archaeology* 26(1): 35–46.

Ray, H. 1994b. *The Winds of Change. Buddhism and the Maritime Links of Early South Asia.* Delhi.

Ray, H. 2003. *The Archaeology of Seafaring in Ancient South Asia.* Cambridge.

Ray, H. and J.-F. Salles (eds) 1996. *Tradition and Archaeology. Early Maritime Contacts in the Indian Ocean.* New Delhi.

Reade, J. (edr) 1996. *The Indian Ocean in Antiquity*. London.
Reinach, A. 1913. *Catalogue des Antiquités Égyptiennes recueilles dans les fouilles de Koptos en 1910 et 1911*. Chalon-sur-Saone.
Reinach, A. and R. Weill 1912. Parthénios fils de Paminis, 'prostatès' d'Isis à Koptos. *Annales du service des Antiquités de l'Égypte* 12: 1–24.
van Rengan, W. 2011. The Written Material from the Graeco-Roman period, in D. Peacock and L. Blue (eds) 2011. *Myos Hormos — Quseir al-Qadim. Roman and Islamic ports on the Red Sea. Volume 2: Finds from the excavations 1999-2003*: 335–8. Oxford.
Répertoire d'épigraphie sémitique 1900–68. Paris.
Rhys Davids, T., and W. Stede (eds) 1921–5. *The Pali Text Society's Pali-English dictionary*. 8 vols. Chipstead.
de Ricci, S. 1903. Bulletin épigraphique de l'Egypte romaine, in U. Wilcken (edr), *Archiv für Papyrusforschung* II: 427–52. Leipzig.
Richardson, L. 1992. *A New Topographical Dictionary of Ancient Rome*. Baltimore and London.
Richter, G. 1958. Ancient Plaster Casts of Greek Metalware. *American Journal of Archaeology* 62(4): 369–77.
Richter, G. 1966. *The Furniture of the Greeks, Etruscans and Romans*. London.
Ricketts, M. 2002. *The Economics of Business Enterprise: An Introduction to Economic Organisation and the Theory of the Firm*. Cheltenham.
Rickman, G. 1971. *Roman Granaries and Store Buildings*. Cambridge.
Ricotti, E. 1994a. Indian Products in Roman Cosmetics, in R. Cimino (edr), *Ancient Rome and India. Commercial and cultural contacts between the Roman world and India*: 110–16. New Delhi.
Ricotti, E. 1994b. Indian Plants in Graeco-Roman Medical Art, in R. Cimino (edr), *Ancient Rome and India. Commercial and cultural contacts between the Roman world and India*: 88–98. New Delhi.
Ricotti, E. 1994c. Indian Products in Roman Cuisine, in R. Cimino (edr), *Ancient Rome and India. Commercial and cultural contacts between the Roman world and India*: 101–8. New Delhi.
Ritter, A. 2012. *Studia Chrysostomica. Aufsätze zu Weg, Werk und Wirkung des Johannes Chrysostomos*. Tübingen.
Robertis, F. de 1973. *Storia delle corporazioni e del regime associativo nel mondo romano*. Bari.
Robin, C. 2012. South Arabia, Ethiopia and Socotra, in I. Strauch (edr), *Foreign Sailors on Socotra. The inscriptions and drawings from the Cave Hoq*: 438–46. Bremen.
Roche, M.-J. 1996. Remarques sur les Nabatéens en Méditerranée. *Semitica* 45:73–99.
Rodriguez Adrados, J.-V. 1989. *Genna aera... citrariorum* (CIL, VI, 9258). *Cuadernos de Filología Clásica* 22: 149–60.
Rodríguez-Almeida, E. 1987. Note di topografia romana: Cosmus myropola, il Vicus Unguentarius e i 'penetralia Pallados nostrae' (Mart., IV, 53). *Rivista dell'istituto nazionale d'archeologia e storia dell'arte* 8–9 (1985–6), 3rd series: 111–7.
Rodziewicz, E. 1968. Small Greek ivory heads as furniture decoration. *Études et travaux* 2: 257–66.
Rodziewicz, E. 1971. Greek ivories of the Hellenistic period. *Études et travaux* 5: 72–89.
Rohde, D. 2012. *Zwischen Individuum und Stadtgemeinde. Die Integration von Collegia in Hafenstädten*. Mainz.
Romanis, F. de 1993. Puteoli e l'Oriente, in F. Zevi (edr), *Puteoli*: 61–72. Naples.
Romanis, F. de 1996a. *Cassia, cinnamomo, ossidiana: Uomini e merci tra Oceano Indiano e Mediterraneo*. Rome.
Romanis, F. de 1996b. Graffiti greci da Wadi Menih el-Her. Un Vestorius tra Coptos e Berenice. *Topoi* 6(2): 731–45.
Romanis, F. de 1997a. Romanukharattha and Taprobane: Relations between Rome and Sri Lanka in the First Century AD, in F. de Romanis and A. Tchernia (eds), *Crossings. Early Mediterranean Contacts with India*: 161–237. New Delhi.
Romanis, F. de 1997b. Rome and the *Nótia* of India: Relations between Rome and Southern India from 30 BC to the Flavian Period, in F. de Romanis and A. Tchernia (eds), *Crossings. Early Mediterranean Contacts with India*: 80–160. New Delhi.
Romanis, F. de 1998. Commercio, metrologia, fiscalità. Su P. Vindob. 40 822 verso. *Mélanges de l'Ecole française de Rome. Antiquité* 110(1): 11–60.
Romanis, F. de 2002. *Traïanòs potamós*. Mediterraneo e Mar Rosso da Traiano a Maometto, in R. Villari (edr), *Controllo degli stretti e insediamenti militari nel Mediterraneo*: 21–70. Roma-Bari.
Romanis, F de 2006. Aurei after the trade: Western taxes and Eastern gifts, in F. de Romanis and S. Sorda (eds), *Dal denarius al dinar. L'oriente e la moneta romana*: 55–82. Roma.
Romanis, F. de 2011. On *Dachinabades* and *Limyrike* in the *Periplus Maris Erythraei*, in M.-Fr. Boussac, J.-Fr. Salles and J.-B. Yon (eds), *Autour du Périple de la mer Érythrée*: 329–40. *Topoi*, Supplément 11.
Romanis, F. de 2012. Playing Sudoku on the Verso of the 'Muziris Papyrus:' Pepper, Malabathron and Tortoise Shell in the Cargo of the Hermapollon. *Journal of Indian Ancient History* 27: 75–101.

Romanis, F. de 2014. Time to Repay a maritime loan: a note on *SB* III 7169 and *SB* XVIII 13167 *recto*. *Sileno* 40(1–2): 73–89.
Romanis, F. de 2015. Comparative Perspectives on the Pepper Trade, in F. de Romanis and M. Maiuro (eds), *Across the Ocean: Nine Essays on Indo-Mediterranean Trade*: 127–50. Leiden and Boston.
Romanis, F. de 2016. An Exceptional Survivor and Its Submerged Background: The Periplus Maris Erythraei and the Indian Ocean Travelogue Tradition, in G. Colesanti and L. Lulli (eds), *Submerged Literature in Ancient Greek Culture*: 97–110.
Romanis, F. de and A. Tchernia (eds) 1997. *Crossings. Early Mediterranean Contacts with India*. New Delhi.
Romanis, F. de and M. Maiuro (eds) 2015. *Across the Ocean: Nine Essays on Indo-Mediterranean Trade*. Leiden and Boston.
Rosen Stone, E. 2004. A Buddhist Incense Burner from Gandhara. *Metropolitan Museum Journal* 39: 69–99.
Rosen Stone, E. 2008. Some Begram Ivories and the south Indian narrative tradition: new evidence. *Journal of Inner Asian Art and Archaeology* 3(3): 45–59.
Rostovtzeff, M. 1941. *The Social and Economic History of the Hellenistic World*. 3 vols. Oxford.
Rostovtzeff, M. 1957. *The Social and Economic History of the Roman Empire*. 2 vols. 2nd rev. edn. Oxford.
Rougemont, G. 2012. *Inscriptions grecques d'Iran et d'Asie centrale*. London.
Rouse, W. 1901. *The Jataka*. Vol. 4. Cambridge.
Royden, H. 1988. *The magistrates of the Roman professional collegia in Italy from the first to the third century AD*. Pisa.
Royden, H. 1989. The Tenure of Office of the Quinquennales in the Roman Professional Collegia. *The American Journal of Philology* 110(2): 303–315.
Ruffing, K. 1993. Das Nikanor-Archiv und der römische Süd- und Osthandel. *Münstersche Beiträge z. antiken Handelsgeschichte* 12(2): 1–26.
Ruffing, K. 2013. The trade with India and the problem of agency in the economy of the Roman Empire, in S. Bussi (edr), *Egitto dai faraoni agli arabi*: 199–210. Pisa and Rome.
St. Clair, A. 2003. *Carving as Craft. Palatine East and the Greco-Roman Bone and Ivory Carving Tradition*. Baltimore and London.
Ste. Croix, G. E. M. 1974. Ancient Greek and Roman Maritime Loans, in H. Edey and B. Yamey (eds), *Debits, Credits, Finance and Profits*: 41–59. London.
Salles, J.-F. 1993. The Periplus and the Erythraean Sea and the Arab-Persian Gulf. *Topoi* 3(2): 493–523.
Salmeri, G. 1997. Dell'uso dell'incenso in epoca romana, in A. Avanzini (edr), *Profumi d'Arabia. Atti del convegno*: 529–40. Rome.
Salomon, R. 1991. Epigraphic Remains of Indian Traders in Egypt. *Journal of the American Oriental Society* 111(4): 731–36.
Salomon, R. 1993. Addenda to 'Epigraphic Remains of Indian Traders in Egypt.' *Journal of the American Oriental Society* 113(4): 593.
Salomon, R. 1998. *Indian Epigraphy. A Guide to the Study of Inscriptions in Sanskrit, Prakrit, and the Other Indo-Aryan Languages*. Oxford and New York.
Sancisi-Weerdenburg, H. 2001. Yaunā by the Sea and across the Sea, in I. Malkin (edr) *Ancient Perceptions of Greek Ethnicity*: 323–46. Cambridge, MA; and London.
Sankalia, H. 1960. *From history to pre-history at Nevasa (1954-56)*. Poona.
Sankaranarayanan, S. 1977. A Brahmi inscription from Alluru. *Sri Venkateswara University Oriental Journal* 20(1–2): 75–89.
Sarianidi, V. 1985. *The Golden Hoard of Bactria. From the Tillya-tepe Excavations in Northern Afghanistan*. New York and Leningrad.
Sarma, I. 1978. Epigraphical discoveries at Guntupalli. *Journal of the Epigraphical Society of India* 5: 48–59.
Sartre, M. 2005. *The Middle East under Rome*. Cambridge, MA; and London.
Schaff, P. (edr) 1889. *A select library of the Nicene and Post-Nicene Fathers of the Christian Church*. Vol. 13. Buffalo, NY.
Schenk, H. 2006. The Dating and Historical Value of Rouletted Ware. *Zeitschrift für Archäologie Außereuropäischer Kulturen* 1: 123–152.
Schenk, H. 2015. Role of ceramics in the Indian Ocean maritime trade during the Early Historical Period, in S. Tripati (edr), *Maritime Contacts of the Past. Deciphering Connections Amongst Communities*: 143–81. New Delhi.
Schiettecatte, J. and M. Arbach 2016. The political map of Arabia and the Middle East in the third century AD revealed by a Sabaean inscription. *Arabian archaeology and epigraphy* 27: 176–196.

Schmid, S. 2004. The distribution of Nabatean pottery and the organisation of Nabataean long-distance trade. *Studies in the History and Archaeology of Jordan* 8: 415–26.

Schmidt-Colinet, A. 2000a. Einleitung, in A. Schmidt-Colinet, A. Stauffer and K. al-As'ad (eds), *Die Textilien aus Palmyra. Neue und alte Funde*: 1–7. Mainz.

Schmidt-Colinet 2000b (w. A. Stauffer). Katalog, in A. Schmidt-Colinet, A Stauffer and K. al-As'ad (eds), *Die Textilien aus Palmyra. Neue und alte Funde*: 99–190. Mainz.

Schmidt-Colinet, A. 2000c. Ornamentik, in A. Schmidt-Colinet, A Stauffer and K. al-As'ad (eds), *Die Textilien aus Palmyra. Neue und alte Funde*: 41–8. Mainz.

Schmidt-Colinet, A. and A. Stauffer 2000. Kulturhistorischer kontext, in A. Schmidt-Colinet, A. Stauffer and K. al-As'ad (eds), *Die Textilien aus Palmyra. Neue und alte Funde*: 49–57. Mainz.

Schneider, E. 1987. Il santuario di Bel e delle divinità di Palmira. Comunità e tradizioni religiose dei palmireni a Roma. *Dialoghi di archeologia*, 3rd series, 5(1): 69–85.

Schneider, R. 1986. *Bunte Barbaren. Orientalstatuen aus farbigen Marmor in der römischen Repräsentationskunst.* Worms.

Schneider, R. 1992. Orientalische Tischdiener als römische Tischfüße. *Deutsches Archäologisches Institut. Archäologischer Anzeiger* 2: 295–305.

Schopen, G. 1994. Doing Business for the Lord: Lending on Interest and Written Loan Contracts in the Mulasarvastivada-vinaya. *Journal of the American Oriental Society* 114(4): 527–54.

Schopen, G. 2004a. What's in a Name. The Religious Function of the Early Donative Inscriptions, in G. Schopen (edr), *Buddhist Monks and Business Matters. Still more papers on monastic Buddhism in India*: 382–94. Honolulu.

Schopen, G. 2004b. The Good Monk and His Money in a Buddhist Monasticism of 'the Mahayana Period,' in G. Schopen (edr), *Buddhist Monks and Business Matters. Still more papers on monastic Buddhism in India*: 1–18. Honolulu.

Schopen, G. 2007. Art, Beauty, and the Business of Running a Buddhist Monastery in Early Northwest India, in D. Srinivasan (edr), *On the Cusp of an Era. Art in the Pre-Kushana World*: 287–317. Leiden and Boston.

Schörle, K. 2015. Pearls, Power, and Profit: Mercantile Networks and Economic Considerations of the Pearl Trade in the Roman Empire, in F. de Romanis and M. Maiuro (eds), *Across the Ocean: Nine Essays on Indo-Mediterranean Trade*: 43–54. Leiden and Boston.

Schwinden, L. 1985. Römerzeitliche Bleietiketten aus Trier. Zum Handel mit Pfeffer, Arznei un Kork. *Trierer Zeitschrift für Geschichte und Kunst des Trierer Landes und seiner Nachbargebiete* 48: 121–37.

Sebro, L. 2014. Personal Encounter in a Colonial Space. European seeing and knowing, in E. Fihl and A. Venkatachalapathy (eds), *Beyond Tranquebar. Grappling Across Cultural Borders in South India*: 282–303. New Delhi.

Sedov, A. 1992. New archaeological and epigraphical material from Qana (South Arabia). *Arabian archaeology and epigraphy* 3(1): 110–37.

Sedov, A. 2007. The port of Qana' and the Incense Trade, in D. Peacock and D. Williams (eds), *Food for the Gods. New light on the ancient incense trade*: 71–111. Oxford.

Seland, E. (edr) 2007a. *The Indian Ocean in the Ancient Period. Definite places, translocal exchange.* Oxford.

Seland, E. 2007b. Taxation of Ancient Indian Ocean Trade. *Journal of Indian Ocean Archaeology* 4: 18–30.

Seland, E. 2008a. The Indian Ocean and the Globalisation of the Ancient World. *Ancient West and East* 7: 67–79.

Seland, E. 2008b. The Indian ships at Moscha and the Indo-Arabian trading circuit. *Proceedings of the Seminar for Arabian Studies* 38: 283–288.

Seland, E. 2010. *Ports and Political Power in the Periplus: Complex Societies and Maritime Trade on the Indian Ocean in the First Century AD.* Oxford.

Seland 2011, E. The Persian Gulf or the Red Sea? Two axes in ancient Indian Ocean trade, where to go and why. *World Archaeology* 43(3): 398–409.

Seland, E. 2012. The *Liber Pontificalis* and the Red Sea Trade of the Early to Mid 4th Century AD, in D. Agius, J. Cooper, A. Trakadas and C. Zazzaro (eds), *Navigated Spaces, Connected Places.* Proceedings of the Red Sea Project V: 117–26. Oxford.

Seland, E. 2013. Networks and social cohesion in ancient Indian Ocean trade: geography, ethnicity, religion. *Journal of Global History* 8: 373–390.

Seland, E. 2014a. Archaeology of Trade in the Western Indian Ocean, 300 BC–AD 700. *Journal of Archaeological Research* 22(4): 367–402.

Seland, E. 2014b. The organisation of the Palmyrene caravan trade. *Ancient West and East* 13: 197–211.

Seland, E. 2016a. Trade Diasporas and Merchant Social Cohesion in Early Trade in the Western Indian Ocean, in A. Chowdhury and D. Akenson (eds), *Between Dispersion and Belonging. Global Approaches to Diaspora in Practice*: 108–17. Montreal.

Seland, E. 2016b. The Periplus of the Erythraean Sea: A Network Approach. *Asian Review of World Histories* 4(2): 191–205.

Seland, E. 2016c. *Ships of the Desert and Ships of the Sea. Palmyra in the World Trade of the First Three Centuries CE*. Wiesbaden.

Seland, E. 2017. Gemstones and mineral products in the Red Sea/Indian Ocean trade of the first millennium, in A. Hilgner, S. Greiff and D. Quast (eds), *Gemstones in the First Millennium AD. Mines, trade, workshops and symbolism*: 45–58. Mainz.

Selvakumar, V., K. Shajan and R. Tomber 2009. Archaeological Investigations at Pattanam, Kerala: New Evidence for the Location of Ancient Muziris, in R. Tomber, L. Blue and S. Abraham (eds), *Migration, Trade and Peoples. Part 1: Indian commerce and the archaeology of Western India*: 29–41. London.

Sena Chiesa, G. 1966. *Gemme del Museo Nazionale di Aquileia*. Aquileia.

Senart, E. 1902–3. The inscriptions in the caves at Karle. *Epigraphia Indica* 7: 47–74.

Senart, E. 1905–6. The inscriptions in the caves at Nasik. *Epigraphia Indica* 8: 59–96.

Seyrig, H. 1963. Le fils du roi Odainath. *Annales Archeologiques de Syrie* 13: 159–72.

Seyrig, H. 1972. Antiquités syriennes. *Syria* 49(1/2): 97–125.

Shastri, A. 1998. *The Satavahanas and the Western Kshatrapas*. New Delhi.

Shinde, V., S. Jadhav, A. Dandekar and S. Ganvir 2007. Junnar: An Early Historic Trading Emporium on the Deccan. *Journal of Indian Ocean Archaeology* 4: 31–54.

Shoebridge, J. and R. Coningham 2009–10. Arikamedu Type 10 and the Reconstruction of Indian Ocean Networks of Contact. *Journal of Indian Ocean Archaeology* 6: 125–41.

Sidebotham, S. 1986. *Roman Economic Policy in the Erythra Thalassa 30 B.C–A.D. 217*. Leiden.

Sidebotham, S. 2004. Trenches of the Southern Sector, 1992, in V. Begley (edr), *The Ancient Port of Arikamedu. New Excavations and Researches 1989-92*. Vol. 2: 16–103. Paris.

Sidebotham, S. 2011. *Berenike and the Ancient Maritime Spice Route*. Berkeley, Los Angeles, CA, and London.

Sidebotham, S. and W. Wendrich 2002. Berenike: a Ptolemaic-Roman port on the ancient maritime spice and incense route. *Minerva* 13(3): 28–31.

Sijpesteijn, P. 1987. *Customs Duties in Graeco-Roman Egypt*. Zutphen.

Simpson, St. J. 2014. Introduction: from Archaeological Discovery to Museum Display, in Ambers, J., C. Cartwright, C. Higgitt, D. Hook, E. Passmore, St. J. Simpson, G. Verri, C. Ward and B. Wills (eds), *Looted, Recovered, Returned: Antiquities from Afghanistan*: 1–39. Oxford.

Singer, C. 2007. The Incense Kingdoms of Yemen: an outline History of the South Arabian Incense Trade, in D. Peacock and D. Williams (eds), *Food for the Gods. New light on the ancient incense trade*: 4–27. Oxford.

Sircar, D. C. 1953–4. Charter of Vishnusena, Samvat 649. *Epigraphia Indica* 30: 163–81.

Sircar, D. C. 1963–64. More inscriptions from Nagarjunakonda. *Epigraphia Indica* 35: 1–36.

Sircar, D. C. 1965. *Indian Epigraphy*. New Delhi.

Sirks, A. 1993. Did the Late Roman Government Try to Tie People to Their Profession or Status? *Tyche* 8: 159–75.

Sivaramamurti, C. 1956. *Amaravati sculptures in the Madras Government Museum*. Madras.

Skeat, T. 1966. A fragment on the Ptolemaic Perfume Monopoly (P. Lond. Inv. 2859A). *The Journal of Egyptian Archaeology* 52: 179–80.

Slane, K. 1991. Observations on Mediterranean Amphoras and Tablewares Found in India, in V. Begley and R. de Puma (eds), *Rome and India. The Ancient Sea Trade*: 204–15. Madison, WI.

Slane, K. 1996. Other ancient ceramics imported from the Mediterranean, in V. Begley (edr), *The Ancient Port of Arikamedu. New Excavations and Researches 1989-92*. Vol. 1: 351–68. Pondicherry.

Smith, A. 1761[1759]. *The Theory of Moral Sentiments*. 2nd edn. London.

Smith II, A. 2013. *Roman Palmyra: Identity, Community, and State Formation*. Oxford.

Sommer, M. 2005. *Roms orientalische Steppengrenze. Palmyra - Edessa - Dura-Europos - Hatra. Eine Kulturgeschichte von Pompeius bis Diocletian*. Stuttgart.

Sosin, J. 1999. Tyrian *stationarii* at Puteoli. *Tyche* 14: 275–84.

Sosin, J. 2000. Perpetual endowments in the Hellenistic World: a case-study in economic rationalism. Unpublished PhD dissertation, Duke University.

Speidel, M. 1996. *Die römischen Schreibtafeln von Vindonissa*. Brugg.

Speidel, M. 2016. Augustus-Tempel in Indien und im Partherreich? Zur Tabula Peutingeriana und zum römischen Kaiserkult ausserhalb des Römischen Reiches, in A. Kolb and M. Vitale (eds), *Kaiserkult in den Provinzen des Römischen Reiches. Organisation, Kommunikation und Repräsentation*: 101–21. Berlin and Boston.

Spink, W. 2008. *Handbook of Oriental Studies, Section 2: South Asia Painting, Sculpture, Architecture: Year by Year*. Boston.

Stauffer, A. 2000. Material und Technik, in A. Schmidt-Colinet, A. Stauffer and K. al-As'ad (eds), *Die Textilien aus Palmyra. Neue und alte Funde*: 8–40. Mainz.

Stein, A. 1921. *Serindia. Detailed Report of Explorations in Central Asia and Westernmost China*. Vol. 4 (plates). Oxford.

Stein, O. 1935. Yavanas in Early Indian Inscriptions, in *Indian Culture* 1: 343–57.

Stein, G. 1999. Rethinking World-Systems: Power, Distance, and Diasporas in the Dynamics of Interregional Interactions, in P. Kardulias (edr), *World-Systems Theory in Practice. Leadership, Production, and Exchange*: 153–77. Oxford and New York.

Stern, E. 1991. Early Roman Export Glass in India, in V. Begley and R. de Puma (eds), *Rome and India. The Ancient Sea Trade*: 113–24. Madison, WI.

Stern, E. 1999. Roman Glassblowing in a Cultural Context. *American Journal of Archaeology* 103(3): 441–84.

Stern, W. and D. Thimme 2007. *Kenchreai. Eastern Port of Corinth. VI. Ivory, Bone, and Related Wood Finds*. Leiden and Boston.

Strauch, I. 2012a. India and Socotra, in I. Strauch (edr), *Foreign Sailors on Socotra. The inscriptions and drawings from the Cave Hoq*: 254–406. Bremen.

Strauch, I. 2012b. Concluding remarks: the discoveries in the cave Hoq: a short evalution of their historical meaning, in I. Strauch (edr), *Foreign Sailors on Socotra. The inscriptions and drawings from the Cave Hoq*: 540–44. Bremen.

Strauch, I. 2012c. Catalogue, in I. Strauch (edr), *Foreign Sailors on Socotra. The inscriptions and drawings from the Cave Hoq*: 25–218. Bremen.

Strauss, E. 2006. Roman Cargoes: Underwater evidence from the Eastern Mediterranean. Unpublished PhD dissertation, University of London.

Strugnell, J. 1959. The Nabataean Goddess Al-Kutba' and Her Sanctuaries. *Bulletin of the American Schools of Oriental Research* 156: 29–36.

Subramanian, T. S. 2012. Potsherd with Tamil-Brahmi script found in Oman. *The Hindu*, October 28th 2012. Accessed February 27th, 2016, http://www.thehindu.com/news/national/potsherd-with-tamilbrahmi-script-found-in-oman/article4038866.ece.

Suresh, S. 2004. *Symbols of Trade. Roman and Pseudo-Roman Objects found in India*. New Delhi.

Tacoma, L. 2006. *Fragile Hierarchies. The urban elites of third-century Roman Egypt*. Leiden and Boston.

Takata, O. 1971. *Ajanta. Cave-temples and Murals*. Tokyo.

Talbert, R. 2010. *Rome's World. The Peutinger Map Reconsidered*. Cambridge.

Tarn, W. 1966[1951]. *The Greeks in Bactria and India*. Cambridge.

Tassini, P. 1994. Produzione e vendita di alcune merci di lusso a Roma, in *Epigrafia della produzione e della distribuzione. Actes de la VIIe Rencontre franco-italienne sur l'épigraphie du monde romain (Rome, 5-6 juin 1992)*: 687-695. Rome.

Tchernia, A. 1968–70. Premiers résultats des fouilles de juin 1968, sur l'épave 3 de Planier. *Études classiques* 3: 51–82.

Tchernia, A. 1997. The Dromedary of the Peticii and Trade with the East, in F. de Romanis and A. Tchernia (eds), *Crossings. Early Mediterranean Contacts with India*: 238–249. New Delhi.

Tchernia, A. 2011. *Les romains et le commerce*. Naples 2011.

Temin, P. 2013. *The Roman Market Economy*. Princeton, NJ; and Oxford.

Terpstra, T. 2013. *Trading Communities in the Roman World. A Micro-Economic and Institutional Perspective*. Leiden.

Terpstra, T. 2015. Roman trade with the Far East: Evidence for Nabataean Middlemen in Puteoli, in F. de Romanis and M. Maiuro (eds), *Across the Ocean: Nine Essays on Indo-Mediterranean Trade*: 73–94. Leiden and Boston.

Terpstra, T. 2016. The Palmyrene Temple in Rome and Palmyra's Trade with the West, in J. Meyer, E. Seland and N. Anfinset (eds), *Palmyrena: City, Hinterland and Caravan Trade between Orient and Occident. Proceedings of the Conference held in Athens, December 1-3, 2012*: 39–48. Oxford.

Terpstra, T. 2017. Communication and Roman Long-Distance Trade, in R. Talbert and F. Naiden (eds), *Mercury's Wings: Exploring Modes of Communication in the Ancient World*: 45–61. Oxford.

Thapar, R. 1995. The First Millennium BC in Northern India (Up to the end of the Mauryan period), in R. Thapar (edr), *Recent Perspectives of Early Indian History*: 80–141. Bombay.

Thapar, R. 2004. *Early India. From the origins to AD 1300.* Berkeley and Los Angeles.
Thaplyal, K. 1972. *Studies in Ancient Indian Seals.* Lucknow.
Thaplyal, K. 1996. *Guilds in Ancient India. A study of Guild organization in Northern India and Western Deccan from circa 600 BC to circa 600 AD.* New Delhi.
Thomas, R. 2011. Roman vessel stoppers, in D. Peacock and L. Blue (eds) 2011. *Myos Hormos — Quseir al-Qadim. Roman and Islamic ports on the Red Sea. Volume 2: Finds from the excavations 1999-2003*: 11–34. Oxford.
Thomsen, C. 2015. The *Eranistai* of Classical Athens. *Greek, Roman, and Byzantine Studies* 55: 154–175.
Thoresen, L. 2017. Archaeogemmology and ancient literary sources on gems and their origins, in A. Hilgner, S. Greiff and D. Quast (eds), *Gemstones in the First Millennium AD. Mines, trade, workshops and symbolism*: 155–217. Mainz.
Thür, G. 1987. Hypotheken-Urkunde eines Seedarlehens für eine Reise nach Muziris und Apographe für die Tetarte in Alexandreia (zu P.Vindob.G. 40.822). *Tyche* 2: 229–45.
Thür, G. 1988. Zum Seedarlehen *katà Mouzeirin*. P.Vindob. G 40822. *Tyche* 3: 229–33.
Tod, M. 1932. *Sidelights on Greek History: Three Lectures.* Oxford.
Tod, M. 1934. Greek Inscriptions at Cairness House. *The Journal of Hellenic Studies* 54(2): 140–162.
Tomber, R. 2005a. Troglodites and Trogodites: Exploring Interaction on the Red Sea during the Roman Period, in J. Starkey (edr), *People of the Red Sea.* Proceedings of the Red Sea Project II: 41–9. Oxford.
Tomber, R. 2005b. Aksumite and other Imported Ceramics from Early Historic Kamrej. *Journal of Indian Ocean Archaeology* 2: 99–102.
Tomber, R. 2007. Rome and Mesopotamia - importers into India in the first millennium AD. *Antiquity* 81: 972–988.
Tomber, R. 2008. *Indo-Roman Trade. From pots to pepper*. London.
Tomber, R. 2009. Beyond Western India: the Evidence from Imported Amphorae, in R. Tomber, L. Bluce and S. Abraham (eds), *Migration, Trade and Peoples. Part 1: Indian commerce and the archaeology of Western India*: 42–57. London.
Tomber, R. 2011. Pots with writing, in D. Peacock and L. Blue (eds) 2011. *Myos Hormos — Quseir al-Qadim. Roman and Islamic ports on the Red Sea. Volume 2: Finds from the excavations 1999-2003*: 5–10. Oxford.
Tomber, R. 2015. The Roman Pottery from Pattanam, in K. Mathew (edr), *Imperial Rome, Indian Ocean Regions and Muziris. New Perspectives on Maritime Trade*: 381–394. New Delhi.
Tomlin, R. 1992. The Twentieth Legion at Wroxeter and Carlisle in the First Century: The Epigraphic Evidence. *Britannia* 23: 141–58.
Tomlin, R. 1998. Roman Manuscripts from Carlisle: The Ink-Written Tablets. *Britannia* 29. 31–84.
Torrey, C. 1948–9. The exiled god of Sarepta. *Berytus* 9: 45–9.
Tran, N. 2006. *Les membres des associations romaines. Le rang social des collegiati en Italie et en Gaules, sous le Haut-Empire*. Rome.
Tran, N. 2007a. Les procédures d'exclusion des collèges professionnels et funéraires sous le Haut-Empire: pratiques épigraphiques, norme collective et non-dits, in C. Wolff (edr), *Les Exclus dans l'Antiquité*: 119–38. Paris.
Tran, N. 2007b. Le 'procès des foulons.' L'occupation litigieuse d'un espace vicinal par des artisans romains. *Mélanges de l'École française de Rome. Antiquité* 119(2): 597–611.
Tran, N. 2008. Les collèges d'*horreariiet* de *mensores*, à Rome et à Ostie, sous le Haut-Empire. *Mélanges de l'École française de Rome. Antiquité* 120(2): 295–306.
Tran, N. 2011. Les collèges professionnels romains: 'clubs' ou 'corporations'? *Ancient Society* 41:197–219.
Tran, N. 2013. *Dominus Tabernae. Le statut de travail des artisans et des commercants de l'occident romain (Ier siecle av. J.-C. - IIIe siecle ap. J.-C.)*. Rome.
Tran, N. 2014. C. Veturius Testius Amandus, les cinq corps de lénunculaires d'Ostie et la batellerie tibérine au début du IIIe siècle. *Mélanges de l'École française de Rome. Antiquité* [Online] 126(1). Accessed on 15th July 2017, http://mefra.revues.org/2043.
Tran, V. Tam Tinh 1972. *Le culte des divinités orientales en Campanie en dehors de Pompéi, de Stabies et d'Herculanum*. Leiden.
Trautmann, T. 1971. *Kautilya and the Arthasastra: a statistical investigation of the authorship and evolution of the text*. Leiden.
Tripathi, A. 2004. Onshore and Offshore Exploration in Elephanta Island: Evidence of Indo-Mediterranean Trade. *Journal of Indian Ocean Archaeology* 1: 116–23.
Truesdell Merrill, E. 1906. The Date of Notitia and Curiosum. *Classical Philology* 1(2): 133–44.
Tucci, P. L. 2008. Galen's storeroom, Rome's libraries, and the fire of A.D. 192. *Journal of Roman Archaeology* 21: 133–49.

Turner, P. 1989. *Roman Coins from India*. London.
Ulrich, R. 2007. *Roman woodworking*. New Haven, CT.
Vandorpe, K. 2015. Roman Egypt and the organisation of customs duties, in P. Kritzinger, F. Schleicher and T. Stickler (eds), *Studien zum römischen Zollwesen*: 89–110. Düsseldorf.
Vats, M. S. 1925–26. Unpublished votive inscriptions in the chaitya cave at Karle. *Epigraphia Indica* 18: 325–329.
v. der Veen, M. 2011. *Consumption, Trade and Innovation. Exploring the Botanical Remains from the Roman and Islamic Ports at Quseir al-Qadim, Egypt*. Frankfurt.
Venticinque, P. 2010. Family Affairs: Guild Regulations and Family Relationships in Roman Egypt. *Greek, Roman, and Byzantine Studies* 50: 273–294.
Venticinque, P. 2013. Matters of Trust: Associations and Social Capital in Roman Egypt. *CHS Research Bulletin* 1(2). Accessed February 27th, 2016, http://nrs.harvard.edu/urn-3:hlnc.essay:VenticinqueP.Matters_of_Trust_Associations_and_Social_Capital.2013.
Venticinque, P. 2016. *Honor Among Thieves*. Ann Arbor.
Verboven, K. 2007. The Associative Order. *Athenaeum* 95: 861–93.
Verboven, K. 2011a. Introduction, Professional collegia: guilds or social clubs. *Ancient Society* 41: 187–195.
Verboven, K. 2011b. Resident Aliens and Translocal Merchant Collegia in the Roman Empire, in O. Hekster and T. Kaizer (eds), *Frontiers of the Roman World*: 335–48. Leiden and Boston.
Verboven, K. 2015. The knights who say *NIE*: can neo-institutional economics live up to its expectation in ancient history research?, in K. Verboven and P. Erdkamp (eds), *Structure and performance in the roman economy: models, methods and case studies*: 33–57. Brussels.
Vergantini, G. 1987. No. 32, in S. Panciera (edr), *La collezione epigrafica dei Musei Capitolini*: 92–4. Rome.
Verhoogt, A. 1998. Greek and Latin Textual Material, in S. Sidebotham and W. Wendrich (eds), *Berenike 1996. Report of the 1996 Excavations at Berenike (Egyptian Red Sea Coast) and the Survey of the Eastern Desert*: 193–8. Leiden.
Vermeule, C. 1981. Bench and Table Supports: Roman Egypt and Beyond, in W. Simpson and W. Davis (eds), *Studies in Ancient Egypt, the Aegean, and the Sudan. Essays in honor of Dows Dunham on the occasion of his 90th birthday, June 1, 1980*: 180–92. Boston.
Villeneuve, F. 2005-6. Farasân Latin inscriptions and Bukharin's ideas: no *pontifex Herculis*! and other comments. *Arabia* 3: 289–296.
Vlassopoulos, K. 2007. Beyond and Below the Polis: Networks, Associations, and the Writing of Greek History. *Mediterranean Historical Review* 22(1): 11–22.
Vogel, J.-P. 1940. Introduction. India. Note on an ivory statuette from Pompei. *Annual Bibliography of Indian Archaeology* 13 (1938): 1–5.
Voinot, J. 1999. *Les cachets à collyres dans le monde romain*. Montagnac.
Wagner, G. 1976. Une dédicace à Isis et à Héra, de la part d'un négociant d'Aden. *Bulletin de l'Institut français d'archéologie orientale* 76: 277–81.
Wallace-Hadrill, A. 2008. *Rome's Cultural Revolution*. Cambridge.
Waltzing, J.-P. 1895–1900. *Étude historique sur les corporations professionelles chez le Romains*. 4 vols. Louvain.
Ward, W. 2007. Aila and Clysma: The Rise of Northern Ports in the Red Sea in Late Antiquity, in J. Starkey, P. Starkey and T. Wilkinson (eds), *Natural Resources and Cultural Connections of the Red Sea*. Proceedings of the Red Sea Project III: 161–71. Oxford.
Warmington, E. 1974. *The Commerce Between the Roman Empire and India*. 2nd edn. London and New York.
Weeber, K.-W. 2003. *Luxus im Alten Rom. Die Schwelgerei, das süße Gift...* Darmstadt.
Weiss, P. 1991. Bleietiketten mit Warenangaben aus dem Umfeld von Rom. *Tyche* 6: 211–20.
Wendrich, W., R. Tomber, S. Sidebotham, J. Harrell, R. Cappers and R. Bagnall 2003. Berenike Crossroads: The Integration of Information. *Journal of the Economic and Social History of the Orient* 46(1): 46–87.
Wheeler, M. 1946. Arikamedu: an Indo-Roman trading-station on the east coast of India. *Ancient India* 2: 17–124.
Wheeler, M. 1954. *Rome Beyond the Imperial Frontiers*. London.
Whitcomb, D. and J. Johnson 1979. *Quseir al-Qadim 1978 Preliminary Report*. Cairo and Princeton, NJ:
Whitcomb, D. and J. Johnson1982. *Quseir al-Qadim 1980 Preliminary Report*. Malibu, C.
White, R. 1991. *The middle ground. Indians, empires, and republics in the Great Lakes region, 1650–1815*. Cambridge.
Whitehouse, D. 1989. Begram, the *Periplus* and Gandharan art. *Journal of Roman Archaeology* 2: 93–100.
Whitehouse, D. and A. Williamson 1973. Sasanian Maritime Trade. *Iran* 11: 29–49.

Whitewright, J. 2007. How Fast is Fast? Technology, Trade and Speed under Sail in the Roman Red Sea, in J. Starkey, P. Starkey and T. Wilkinson (eds), *Natural Resources and Cultural Connections of the Red Sea*. Proceedings of the Red Sea Project III: 77–87. Oxford.
Wiesehöfer, J. 1996. *Ancient Persia from 550 BC to 650 AD*. London and New York.
Wiessner, G. 1968. Zum Problem der zeitlichen und örtlichen Festlegung der erhaltenen syro-persischen Märtyrerakten. Das Pusai-Martyrium, in Göttinger Arbeitskreis für Syrische Kirchengeschichte (edr), *Paul de Lagarde und die syrische Kirchengeschichte*: 231–51. Göttingen.
Wilcken, U. 1925. Punt-Fahrten in der Ptolemäerzeit. *Zeitschrift für ägyptische Sprache und Altertumskunde* 60: 86–102.
Wild, J. and F. Wild 2000. Textiles, in S. Sidebotham and W. Wendrich (eds), *Berenike 1998. Report of the 1998 Excavations at Berenike*: 251–74. Leiden.
Wild, J. and F. Wild 2005. Rome and India: early Indian cotton textiles from Berenike, Red Sea coast of Egypt, in R. Barnes (edr), *Textiles in Indian Ocean Societies*: 11–16. London and New York.
Wild, J. and F. Wild 2014. Berenike and Textile Trade on the Indian Ocean, in K. Droß-Krüpe (edr), *Textile Trade and Distribution in Antiquity*: 91–109. Wiesbaden.
Wilson, A. 2012. Raw materials and energy, in W. Scheidel (edr), *The Cambridge Companion to the Roman Economy*: 133–55. Cambridge.
Wilson, A. 2015. Red Sea trade and the state, in F. de Romanis and M. Maiuro (eds), *Across the Ocean: Nine Essays on Indo-Mediterranean Trade*: 13–32. Leiden and Boston.
Wilson, A., M. Silver, P. Bang, P. Erdkamp and N. Morley 2012a. A forum on trade, in W. Scheidel (edr), *The Cambridge Companion to the Roman Economy*: 287–317. Cambridge.
Wilson, A., K. Schörle and C. Rice 2012b. Roman ports and Mediterranean connectivity, in S. Keay (edr), *Rome, Portus and the Mediterranean*: 367–91. Rome.
Williamson, O. 1985. *The Economic Institutions of Capitalism: Firms, Markets, Relational Contracting*. London and New York.
Witecka, A. 1994. Catalogue of jewellery found in the tower-tomb of Atenatan at Palmyra. *Studia Palmyrenskie/Études palmyréniennes* 9: 71–91.
Wolska-Conus, W. (edr) 1968–73. *Cosmas Indicopleustès. Topographie Chrétienne*. 3 vols. Paris.
Woolcock, M. 1998. Social Capital and Economic Development: Toward a Theoretical Synthesis and Policy. *Theory and Society* 27(2): 151–208.
Woolcock M. 2001. The Place of Social Capital in Understanding Social and Economic Outcomes. *ISUMA Canadian Journal of Policy Research* 2(1): 11–17.
Woolf, G. 2011. *Tales of the Barbarians: Ethnography and Empire in the Roman West*. Chichester.
Yon, J.-B. 1998. Remarques sur une famille caravanière à Palmyre. *Syria* 75(1/4): 153–160.
Yon, J.-B. 2016. Ports of the Indian Ocean: The Port of Spasinu Charax, in M.-F. Boussac, J.-F. Salles and J.-B. Yon (eds), *Ports of the Ancient Indian Ocean*: 125–36. New Delhi.
Young, G. 2001. *Rome's Eastern Trade. International commerce and imperial policy, 31 BC–AD 305*. London and New York.
Zabehlicky-Scheffenegger, S. and G. Schneider 1998. Import östlicher Keramik auf den Magdalensberg, in G. Piccottini (edr), *Die Ausgrabungen auf dem Magdalensberg 1980 bis 1986*: 429–51. Klagenfurt.
Zaccaria, C. 2001. *Iulium Carnicum*. Un centro alpino tra Italia e Norico (I sec. A. C. – I sec. D. C.), in G. Bandelli and F. Fontana (eds), *Iulium Carnicum. Centro alpino tra Italia e Norico dalla protostoria all'età imperial*: 139–57. Rome.
Zappata, E. 1994. *Piperarii*, in *Epigrafia della produzione e della distribuzione: actes de la VIIe Rencontre franco-italienne sur l'épigraphie du monde romain*: 733–8. Rome.
Zazzaro, C. and A. Manzo 2012. A preliminary assessment of the pottery assemblage from the port town of Adulis (Eritrea). *British Museum Studies in Ancient Egypt and Sudan* 18: 233–46.
Zazzaro, C. 2013. *The Ancient Red Sea Port of Adulis and the Eritrean Coastal Region. Previous investigations and museum collections*. Oxford.
Zevi, F. (edr) 1993. *Puteoli*. Naples.
Zhang, L. 2011. Chinese lacquerwares from Begram: date and provenance. *International Journal of Asian Studies* 8(1): 1–24.
Zimmermann, C. 2002. *Handwerkervereine im griechischen Osten des Imperium Romanum*. Bonn.
Zin, M. 2003. The usnisha as a Physical Characteristic of the Buddha's Relatives and Successors. *Silk Road Art and Archaeology* 9: 107–29.

Zin, M. 2015. Nur Gandhara? Zu Motiven der klassischen Antike in Andhra (einschließlich Kanaganahalli). *Tribus. Jahrbuch des Linden-Museums* 64: 178–205.
Zuchowska, M. 2013a. From China to Palmyra: the Value of Silk. *Swiatowit* XI(LII)/A: 133–54.
Zuchowska, M. 2013b. Palmyra and the Far Eastern trade. *Studia Palmyreńskie* XII: 381–387.
Zuchowska, M. 2016. Palmyra and the Chinese Silk Trade, in J. Meyer, E. Seland and N. Anfinset (eds), *Palmyrena: City, Hinterland and Caravan Trade between Orient and Occident. Proceedings of the Conference held in Athens, December 1-3, 2012*: 29–38. Oxford.
Zvelebil, K. 1956. The Yavanas in Old Tamil Literature, in F. Tauer, V. Kubickova and I. Hrbek (eds), *Charisteria Orientalia*: 401–9. Prague.
Zvelebil, K. 1973. *Smile of Murugan. On Tamil literature of South India.* Leiden.
Zvelebil, K. 1992. *Companion studies to the history of Tamil literature.* Leiden.